OFFENCE PARALLELING BEHAVIOUR

WILEY SERIES IN
FORENSIC CLINICAL PSYCHOLOGY

Edited by

Mary McMurran
Institute of Mental Health, University of Nottingham, Nottingham, UK

Clive Hollin
New Academic Unit, Department of Health Sciences, The University of Leicester, Leicester General Hospital, Leicester, UK

OFFENCE PARALLELING BEHAVIOUR

A Case Formulation Approach to Offender Assessment and Intervention

Edited by

Michael Daffern

Lawrence Jones

and

John Shine

WILEY-BLACKWELL

A John Wiley & Sons, Ltd, Publication

This edition first published 2010

Wiley-Blackwell is an imprint of John Wiley & Sons, formed by the merger of Wiley's global Scientific, Technical, and Medical business with Blackwell Publishing.

Registered Office
John Wiley & Sons Ltd, The Atrium, Southern Gate, Chichester, West Sussex, PO19 8SQ, UK

Editorial Offices
The Atrium, Southern Gate, Chichester, West Sussex, PO19 8SQ, UK
9600 Garsington Road, Oxford, OX4 2DQ, UK
350 Main Street, Malden, MA 02148-5020, USA

For details of our global editorial offices, for customer services, and for information about how to apply for permission to reuse the copyright material in this book please see our website at www.wiley.com/wiley-blackwell.

Library of Congress Cataloging-in-Publication Data

Offence paralleling behaviour : a case formulation approach to offender assessment and intervention / edited by Michael Daffern, Lawrence Jones and John Shine.
p. cm.
Includes bibliographical references and index.
ISBN 978-0-470-74448-2 (cloth) – ISBN 978-0-470-74447-5 (pbk.) 1. Criminals–Mental health.
2. Prisoners–Mental health. 3. Criminal psychology. 4. Criminals–Rehabilitation. 5. Recidivism.
I. Daffern, Michael. II. Jones, Lawrence (Lawrence F.) III. Shine, John, 1957-
RC451.4.P68O34 2010
364.3–dc22 2010016196

A catalogue record for this book is available from the British Library.

Typeset in 9.5/11.5pt Palatino by Aptara Inc., New Delhi, India.
Printed and bound in Singapore by Ho Printing Singapore Pte Ltd

1 2010

MD: For Harvey and Billy

LJ: To Mo and family for their forbearance

JS: For Keiran and Paddy

CONTENTS

ABOUT THE EDITORS

Michael Daffern is a clinical psychologist by training. He has worked in prisons and in general and forensic mental health services. Currently, he is a Senior Lecturer with the Centre for Forensic Behavioural Science, Monash University, Consultant Principal Psychologist with Forensicare, and Special Lecturer within the Division of Psychiatry at the University of Nottingham. His research interests include behavioural assessment methods, offender rehabilitation, personality disorder and aggression and other problem behaviours within institutions.

Lawrence Jones is a Consultant Clinical and Forensic Psychologist who is Lead Psychologist for the Peaks Unit at Rampton Hospital, Nottinghamshire Healthcare NHS Trust. He works with personality disordered offenders. He has worked with offenders in community, prison and healthcare settings. He is a former Chair of the Division of Forensic Psychology of the British Psychological Society. His interests include interventions using the milieu, personality disorder, sexual offending, offence paralleling behaviour, motivation and engagement, substance misuse, strength-based interventions and case formulation.

John Shine is a Consultant Forensic Psychologist currently working in the East London and the City Mental Health NHS Trust. He has worked as a forensic psychologist for over 20 years in the prison and probation services including HMP Grendon and HM Inspectorate of Probation. He was a member of the NHS Forensic Mental Health R&D Expert Advisory Committee. His research interests are in the assessment and treatment of personality-disordered offenders, particularly those with psychopathic traits.

LIST OF CONTRIBUTORS

Geraldine Akerman

Forensic Psychologist, HMP Grendon, Grendon Underwood, UK.

Zainab Al-Attar

Head of Psychology, Programmes & Sex Offender Clinical Services, HMP Wymott and Sessional Clinical Practitioner G-MAP, Greater Manchester, UK.

David Atkinson

David Atkinson, Throughcare Manager, HMP & YOI Guys Marsh, York, UK.

Natalie Bond

Forensic Psychologist-in-Training, HMP Gartree, Leicestershire, UK.

Roger Bowles

Professor, Centre for Criminal Justice Economics and Psychology, University of York, UK.

Judith Cornick

Senior probation Officer, HMP Acklington, Northumberland, UK.

Michael Daffern

Senior Lecturer, School of Psychology and Psychiatry, Monash University, Principal Consultant Psychologist, Forensicare, Australia and Special Lecturer, Institute of Mental Health, University of Nottingham, UK.

Jason Davies

Intensive support and Intervention Service, Cefn Coed Hospital, Swansea, and School of Medicine, University of Swansea, UK.

David L. Dawson

Medical Director, Mid Yorkshire Hospitals NHS Trust and Lincolnshire Partnership Trust, Lincoln University, Lincoln, UK.

Helen Dowdswell

Prison Officer, HMP Grendon, Grendon Underwood, UK.

Maisie Dyson

Forensic Psychologist and Head of Sex Offender Treatment Programme Unit, HMP Maidstone, UK.

Katarina Fritzon

Associate Professor, Psychology Department, Bond University, Gold Coast, Queensland, Australia.

Audrey Gordon

Psychologist, Regional Psychiatric Centre, and Professional Affiliate, University of Saskatchewan, Saskatoon, Saskatchewan, Canada.

David M. Gresswell

Deputy Course Director, University of Lincoln, Lincoln, UK, and Consultant Clinical Psychologist, Peter Hodgkinson Centre, Lincoln, UK.

Stephen D. Hart

Professor, Department of Psychology, and Member of the Mental Health, Law, and Policy Institute, Simon Fraser University, Canada.

John Hodge

Consultant Clinical and Forensic Psychologist.

Kevin Howells

Professor of Forensic Clinical Psychology, Institute of Mental Health, University of Nottingham, and Peaks Academic and Research Unit, Rampton Hospital, Retford, UK.

Lawrence Jones

Consultant Clinical and Forensic Psychologist, Lead Psychologist, Peaks Unit, Rampton Hospital, Nottinghamshire Healthcare NHS Trust, UK.

Ruth E. Mann

National Offender Management Service, London, UK.

Trish Martin

Director of Nursing Practice, Forensicare, Australia.

Cynthia McDougall

Co-Director of the Centre for Criminal Justice Economics and Psychology and Senior Advisor to the MSc. in Applied Forensic Psychology, University of York, UK.

Sarah Miller

Head of Psychology, HM Prison Shotts, Scotland, UK.

Phil Morgan

Professional Head of Occupational Therapy, Dorset Community Health Services, UK.

Lawrence

Resident, HMP Grendon, UK.

Dominic Pearson

Senior Psychologist, Durham Tees Valley Probation Trust, County Durham, UK.

John Shine

Consultant Forensic Psychologist, the Millfields Unit, Centre for Forensic Mental Health, London, UK.

Corinne Spearing

Occupational Therapist, the Millfields Unit, Centre for Forensic Mental Health, London, UK.

Gail Steptoe-Warren

Senior Lecturer, Coventry University, Warwickshire, UK.

Peter Sturmey

Professor of Clinical Psychology, Department of Psychology and the Graduate Center, City University of New York, New York, USA.

Glen Thomas

Clinical Nurse Specialist, Rampton Hospital, Retford, UK.

David Thornton

Treatment Director, Sand Ridge Secure Treatment Centre, Wisconsin, USA.

Cleo Van Velsen

Consultant Psychiatrist in Forensic Psychotherapy, The Millfields Unit, Centre for Forensic Mental Health, London, UK

Simone Wakama

Trainee Forensic Psychologist, HMP Whatton, UK.

Victoria Wasteney

Head of Occupational Therapy, the Millfields Unit, Centre for Forensic Mental Health, London, UK.

Stephen C.P. Wong

Professor, Personality Disorder Institute, University of Nottingham, Department of Forensic Mental Health Science, Institute of Psychiatry, Kings College, and Department of Psychology, University of Saskatchewan, Saskatoon, Canada.

FOREWORD

STEPHEN D. HART
Department of Psychology, Simon Fraser University, British Columbia, Canada

Welcome to the next big thing in violence risk assessment: formulation!

Over the last 10 years, I have repeatedly expressed my concerns – that is, whinged – about what I perceive as a lack of innovation in the area of violence risk assessment. For example, in an address to the European Association of Psychology and Law in Belgium, I noted that after two decades of important advances, research on violence risk was in a 'conceptual rut' (Hart, 2003, p. 225). My primary concern was dominance of the predictionist approach to studying violence, including the near-exclusive use of quantitative analytic methods:

> [C]orrelational analysis, logistic regression analysis, Receiver Operating Characteristic analysis, event history (survival) analysis – all of these tools, and the predictionist view of the universe they reflect, assume that the outcome is a simple binary or continuous variable that can be evaluated with perfect accuracy. None was designed to deal with an outcome like violence, which is clearly multidimensional and whose measurement is influenced by various forms of bias or error. Also, most of the tools ignore time. They were intended to account contemporaneously for variance in one measure using another, not to make 'predictions' about dynamic organisms living in dynamic environments. And none of the tools was intended to handle problems such as violence risk assessment, in which risk factors and the interactions among them grow, change, or evolve over time; and in which the outcome, violence, may not be a discrete occurrence but rather a transactional process that itself changes or evolves over time. (Hart, 2003, pp. 231–32)

One way to escape the conceptual rut, I argued, was to use a new and different analytic approach, and in particular 'a tool that relies as little as possible on predictions, numbers, and equations; one well suited to the description of complexity, change, and transaction; one that almost anyone can be trained to use' (Hart, 2003, p. 232). Or, as I put it subsequently (and more succinctly), the future of violence risk assessment and management requires a movement 'from formulas to formulation' (Hart, 2008).

While I whinged, others worked. A number of groups around the world have developed or are still developing approaches to case formulation in forensic mental health. For example, in Canada, my colleagues and I applied a decision theory framework in which violence is viewed as a choice, that is, as purposive, goal-directed behaviour intended to achieve one or more goals. According to this perspective, the task of risk assessment is to understand the causal roles played by risk factors with respect to decisions to engage in violence (i.e. motivators, disinhibitors and destabilizers), and the task of risk management is to determine effective strategies to encourage decisions to act prosocially and discourage decisions to act non-violently. We also applied scenario planning as a means of identifying potentially effective strategies and tactics for risk management for achieving desired and avoiding feared *possible futures*. This approach is described in manuals for structured professional judgement instruments such as the *Risk for Sexual Violence Protocol* (Hart et al., 2003) and the *Guidelines for Stalking Assessment and Management* (Kropp et al., 2008).

Meanwhile, in New Zealand, Tony Ward and his colleagues pioneered the application of the Good Lives Model, or GLM, to sexual and violent offenders (e.g. Ward, 2002; Whitehead et al., 2007). The GLM views violence as a problematic means of trying to obtain *primary goods* – that is, 'activities, experiences, or situations that are sought for their own sake and that benefit individuals and increase their sense of fulfillment and happiness' (Whitehead et al., 2007, p. 581). According to this framework, risk assessment is the process of identifying internal or external factors that prevent people from obtaining primary goods, and risk management is the process of building people's strengths and resources so they can obtain primary goods in a prosocial way.

Finally, the Anglo-Australian conglomerate of Lawrence Jones, Michael Daffern, John Shine and colleagues developed the offence paralleling behaviour, or OPB, approach (e.g. Jones, 2002, 2004; Daffern et al., 2007). I will not describe OPB in detail, as that is the goal of the rest of this volume. Briefly, though, OPB emphasizes the psychological functions of violence, and the focus of assessment and treatment within the OPB framework is the search for and modification of behavioural patterns that parallel violence with respect to function.

As a description of OPB, this book is an unqualified success. The chapters define OPD, trace its evolution, evaluate its current status, outline its clinical application and consider its implementation in various settings. Daffern, Jones and Shine are to be congratulated for putting together a book that will serve as an essential reference for forensic mental health professionals who want to study the OPB approach and use it in their practice. But the editors deserve congratulations too for giving us the opportunity to observe them as they refine OPB. Reading the book, I felt at times like I was sitting quietly at the back of the room while the contributors engaged in spirited and lively discussion – a rare treat.

Finally, I congratulate the editors and the other contributors for pursuing the idea of OPB. It takes time and effort – not to mention a bit of courage – to transcend convention. The ultimate success of OPB will not be judged by whether the framework looks the same in five or ten years; it will not, and it should not. Rather, the success of OPB will be judged by the extent to which it helps forensic mental health professionals view violence not as some sort of uncontrollable phenomenon of the physical world, like an eclipse or earthquake or tornado, to be predicted using statistical methods, but instead to understand violence as a human, psychological phenomenon and thus to prevent it.

REFERENCES

Daffern, M., Jones, L., Howells, K., Shine, J., Mikton, C. & Tunbridge, V. (2007). Refining the definition of offence paralleling behaviour. *Criminal Behaviour and Mental Health*, *17*, 265–73.

Hart, S.D. (2003). Violence risk assessment: an anchored narrative approach. In M. Vanderhallen, G. Vervaeke, P.J. Van Koppen & J. Goethals (Eds.), *Much Ado about Crime: Chapters on Psychology and Law* (pp. 209–30). Brussels: Uitgeverij Politeia NV.

Hart, S.D. (2008). *The Future of Violence Risk Assessment and Management: From Prediction to Prevention, from Formula to Formulation.* Keynote address, annual meeting of the International Association of Forensic Mental Health Services, Vienna, Austria.

Hart, S.D., Kropp, P.R., Laws, D.R., Klaver, J., Logan, C. & Watt, K.A. (2003). *The Risk for Sexual Violence Protocol (RSVP): Structured Professional Guidelines for Assessing Risk of Sexual Violence*. Burnaby, British Columbia: Mental Health, Law, and Policy Institute, Simon Fraser University.

Jones. L.F. (2002). An individual case formulation approach to the assessment of motivation. In M. McMurran (Ed.), *Motivating Offenders to Change* (pp. 31–54). Chichester: Wiley.

Jones, L.F. (2004). Offence paralleling behavior (OPB) as a framework for assessment and interventions with offenders. In A. Needs & G.J. Towl (Eds.), *Applying Psychology to Forensic Practice* (pp. 34–63). Oxford: British Psychological Society and Blackwell.

Kropp, P.R., Hart, S.D. & Lyon, D. (2008). *Guidelines for Stalking Assessment and Management (SAM): User Manual.* Vancouver, Canada: ProActive ReSolutions Inc.

Ward, T. (2002). The management of risk and the design of good lives. *Australian Psychologist, 37*, 172–79.

Whitehead, P.R., Ward, T. & Collie, R.M. (2007). Time for a change: applying the Good Lives Model of rehabilitation to a high-risk violent offender. *International Journal of Offender Therapy and Comparative Criminology, 51*, 578–98.

SERIES EDITORS' PREFACE

ABOUT THE SERIES

At the time of writing, it is clear that we live in a time, certainly in the UK and other parts of Europe, if perhaps less so in areas of the world, when there is renewed enthusiasm for constructive approaches to working with offenders to prevent crime. What do we mean by this statement and what basis do we have for making it?

First, by 'constructive approaches to working with offenders' we mean bringing the use of effective methods and techniques of behaviour change into work with offenders. Indeed, this view might pass as a definition of forensic clinical psychology. Thus, our focus is the application of theory and research to develop practice aimed at bringing about a change in the offender's functioning. The word 'constructive' is important and can be set against approaches to behaviour change that seek to operate by destructive means. Such destructive approaches are typically based on the principles of deterrence and punishment, seeking to suppress the offender's actions through fear and intimidation. A constructive approach, on the other hand, seeks to bring about changes in an offender's functioning that will produce, say, enhanced possibilities of employment, greater levels of self-control, better family functioning or increased awareness of the pain of victims.

A constructive approach faces the criticism of being a 'soft' response to the damage caused by offenders, neither inflicting pain and punishment nor delivering retribution. This point raises a serious question for those involved in working with offenders. Should advocates of constructive approaches oppose retribution as a goal of the criminal justice system as a process that is incompatible with treatment and rehabilitation? Alternatively, should constructive work with offenders take place within a system given to retribution? We believe that this issue merits serious informed debate.

However, to return to our starting point, history shows that criminal justice systems are littered with many attempts at constructive work with offenders, not all of which have been successful. In raising the spectre of success, the second part of our opening sentence now merits attention: that is, 'constructive approaches to working with offenders to prevent crime'. In order to achieve the goal of preventing crime, interventions must focus on the right targets for behaviour change. In addressing this crucial point, Andrews and Bonta (1994) have formulated the need principle:

> Many offenders, especially high-risk offenders, have a variety of needs. They need places to live and work and/or they need to stop taking drugs. Some have poor self-esteem, chronic headaches or cavities in their teeth. These are all 'needs'. The need principle draws our attention to the distinction between criminogenic and noncriminogenic needs. Criminogenic

> needs are a subset of an offender's risk level. They are dynamic attributes of an offender that, when changed, are associated with changes in the probability of recidivism. Non-criminogenic needs are also dynamic and changeable, but these changes are not necessarily associated with the probability of recidivism. (Andrews & Bonta, 1994, p. 176)

Thus, successful work with offenders can be judged in terms of bringing about change in non-criminogenic need or in terms of bringing about change in criminogenic need. While the former is important and, indeed, may on occasion be a necessary precursor to offence-focused work, it is changing criminogenic need that, we argue, should be the touchstone in working with offenders.

While, as noted above, the history of work with offenders is not replete with success, the research base developed since the early 1990s, particularly the meta-analyses (e.g. Lösel, 1995), now strongly supports the position that effective work with offenders to prevent further offending is possible. The parameters of such evidence-based practice have become well established and widely disseminated under the banner of 'what works' (McGuire, 1995, 2002).

It is important to state that we are not advocating that there is only one approach to preventing crime. Clearly, there are many approaches, with different theoretical underpinnings, that can be applied to the task. Nonetheless, a tangible momentum has grown in the wake of the 'what works' movement as academics, practitioners and policy-makers seek to capitalize on the possibilities that this research raises for preventing crime. The task that many service agencies grapple with lies in turning the research evidence into effective practice.

Our aim in developing this *Wiley Series in Forensic Clinical Psychology* is to produce texts that review research and draw on clinical expertise to advance effective work with offenders. We are both committed to the ideal of evidence-based practice, and we encourage contributors to the series to follow this approach. Thus, the books published in the series will not be practice manuals or 'cook books': they will offer readers authoritative and critical information through which forensic clinical practice can develop. We both continue to be enthusiastic about the contribution to effective practice that this series can make and look forward to continuing to develop it yet further in the years to come.

ABOUT THIS BOOK

Assessing an offender's risk is an important aspect of the forensic clinical psychologist's work. A large number of well-designed studies have been conducted into what features of offenders and offences predict reconviction. The best of these studies have identified cohorts of offenders and followed them over time to see who offends again and who does not. Information collected from the offender at the start of the process is analysed to see what predicts reconviction. Empirically identified predictors of reconviction have informed risk assessments, focusing the attention of clinicians on what really counts. However, there is one small problem: while group data tell us what is likely in general, using group data to tell us about any single individual within that group is less accurate. Hart et al. (2007) explain the problem of applying group data to an individual case using an example:

> Suppose a public opinion survey of 500 eligible voters found that 54% expressed their intent to cast ballots for candidate Smith in an upcoming election. This information allows one to forecast with reasonable confidence that candidate Smith will be elected by another group – namely, the general electorate. However, this same information does not allow one to predict the behaviour of a randomly selected voter with great confidence. Even though, in the absence

> of other relevant information, the most rational prediction is that every single voter will cast a ballot for candidate Smith, these individual predictions frequently will be wrong. (Hart et al., 2007, p. 61)

Predictors of risk derived from group data may need to be augmented by an individual clinical component. In this respect, 'offence paralleling behaviour' (OPB) provides one model of examining and tackling risk at an individual level. The idea of studying OPB has considerable appeal for professionals working with offenders whose problem behaviour (i.e. offending) is eliminated by external controls. Looking at functionally similar behaviours provides scope for both risk assessment and appropriately targeted interventions. However, there are significant challenges to the OPB model. Can functionally similar behaviours be accurately identified? Are they too not eliminated by the controlled environment? Suppose they can be identified, does working with these OPBs give added value in terms of risk reduction?

These questions are not easily answered. A considerable amount of research needs to be done to supply the scientist–practitioner with information about the validity, reliability and utility of the OPB model. This process can be begun only when OPBs can be accurately defined, reliably assessed and effectively changed. The editors and contributors to this book have set out their stall with regard to the OPB model. By sharing their scientific rationale, their current practices and their own critical appraisal of the model, they have set the scene for a new research agenda. We are pleased that they have chosen the *Wiley Series in Forensic Clinical Psychology* to disseminate their innovative and emerging approach.

Mary McMurran
Clive Hollin

REFERENCES

Andrews, D.A. & Bonta, J. (1994). *The Psychology of Criminal Conduct*. Cincinnati, OH: Anderson Publishing.

Hart, S.D., Michie, C. & Cooke, D.J. (2007). Precision of actuarial risk assessment instruments: evaluating the 'margins of error' of group v. individual predictions of violence. *British Journal of Psychiatry, 190*: s60–5.

Lösel, F. (1995). Increasing consensus in the evaluation of offender rehabilitation? *Psychology, Crime, and Law, 2*, 19–39.

McGuire, J. (Ed.) (1995). *What Works: Reducing Reoffending*. Chichester: John Wiley & Sons.

McGuire, J. (Ed.) (2002). *Offender Rehabilitation and Treatment: Effective Programmes and Policies to Reduce Reoffending*. Chichester: John Wiley & Sons.

EDITORS' PREFACE

Contemporary practice guidelines often recommend forensic practitioners adhere to formal treatment programmes, which have been developed for a range of offending behaviours, and use structured methods for appraising risk for future criminal behaviour (e.g. National Institute for Health and Clinical Excellence, 2009). These risk assessment methods and treatment programmes have clearly enhanced forensic practice. However, despite these improved treatment outcomes and increasingly accurate risk assessments, many offenders do not profit from treatment, and many risk assessment instruments lack predictive validity for particular groups of offenders or for offenders from different backgrounds or communities. As such, there is clearly an opportunity to enhance practice and a requirement to establish methods of assessment and treatment for those offenders who are unsuitable for structured group treatments or for whom structured risk assessment methods have not been validated. Furthermore, there is a need to enhance all treatments offered in secure settings so that the treatment environment is supportive of formal programmes and maximized outcomes.

The offence paralleling behaviour (OPB) framework has emerged as a useful adjunct to contemporary treatment and risk assessment approaches; it has the potential to supplement risk assessments, assist staff to identify treatment targets and opportunities for intervention, and contribute to the monitoring of progress for those offenders in treatment. The term 'OPB' was first introduced by Lawrence Jones, who was influenced by the scholarly work of psychologists working in Her Majesty's prison service (Clark et al., 1994; McDougall & Clark, 1991; McDougall et al., 1994), who recognized difficulties in assessing risk for violence in prisoners serving long periods of incarceration. The problem for assessors of these prisoners was that they may have adapted to the prison environment but not necessarily changed in a way that would reduce their risk of repeated criminal behaviour. Jones' earlier work (e.g. Jones, 2000) was also influenced by the principles of care underpinning traditional therapeutic communities (Jones, 1997). It was also influenced by strategies adopted by those behaviourally oriented psychotherapies that addressed in-session behaviours, which were considered to be proxies for problematic behaviours of interest, directly in treatment. Targeting these in-session proxies was undertaken so that new learning within session could hopefully be generalized to 'real-world' situations (e.g. functional analytic psychotherapy; Kohlenberg & Tsai, 1994).

In recent years the term 'OPB' has become common parlance amongst many forensic practitioners, no doubt because OPB seems to be an understandable and meaningful term. Staff who work in secure settings routinely consider in-session and in-custody behaviour to gauge treatment response and treatment need, and to assess risk for repeated criminal behaviour. Unfortunately, the introduction of the term may have inadvertently legitimized the practice of using so-called OPB before the framework was properly explicated and sufficient empirical evidence had accumulated. The very strong possibility that environmental factors and transient psychological issues may influence problem behaviours in custody and the fact that these problem behaviours may be misconstrued as persistent pathology (and thereby labelled OPB) led us, with several colleagues, to offer a refined definition of OPB (Daffern et al., 2007) and to pronounce a need for caution when invoking the OPB framework, particularly within the risk assessment context.

This book arose against a background of emerging interest in idiographic assessment methods and an increased interest amongst forensic practitioners in the OPB framework. The book was also conceived amidst concern (ours and others') about the potential for misapplication of the framework. To remedy this situation, we invited leading scholars and interested clinicians in the field to consider how they might conceptualize OPB and to suggest methods, where applicable, that might assist staff to identify and work with OPB. When reading the varied contributions that were received, we identified many similarities. Differences also exist and these are discussed in Chapter 20. Readers of this book are encouraged to critically examine the methods proposed. We hope this book presents an objective analysis of OPB, one that recognizes the opportunity the framework provides. We encourage clinicians and researchers to further refine the framework and evaluate the impact of using the framework in their assessment and treatment work.

Michael Daffern
John Shine
Lawrence Jones

REFERENCES

Clark, D. Fisher, M.J. & McDougall, C. (1994). A new methodology for assessing the level of risk in incarcerated offenders. *British Journal of Criminology*, *33*, 436–48.

Daffern, M., Jones, L., Howells, K., Shine, J., Mikton, C. & Tunbridge, V.C. (2007). Refining the definition of offence paralleling behaviour. *Criminal Behaviour and Mental Health*, *17*, 265–73.

Jones, L.F. (1997). Developing models for managing treatment integrity and efficacy in a prison based TC: the Max Glatt Centre. In E. Cullen, L. Jones & R. Woodward (Eds.). *Therapeutic Communities for Offenders*. Chichester: Wiley.

Jones, L.F. (2000). *Identifying and Working with Clinically Relevant Offence Paralleling Behaviour*. Paper presented at division of Clinical Psychology, Forensic Special Interest Group, Nottinghamshire.

Kohlenberg, R.J. & Tsai, M. (1994). Functional analytic psychotherapy: a radical behavioural approach to treatment and integration. *Journal of Psychotherapy Integration*, *4*, 175–201.

McDougall C. & Clark D.A. (1991) A risk assessment model. In S. Boddis (Ed.), *Proceedings of the Prison Psychology Conference*. London: HMSO.

McDougall, C., Clark, D.A. & Fisher, M. (1994). Assessment of violent offenders. In M. McMurran & J. Hodge (Eds), *The Assessment of Criminal Behaviours of Clients in Secure Settings* (pp. 68–93). London: Jessica Kingsley.

National Institute for Health and Clinical Excellence (2009). *Antisocial Personality Disorder: Treatment, Management And Prevention*. Retrieved 19 October 2009 from www.nice.org.uk/Guidance/CG77/NiceGuidance/pdf

ACKNOWLEDGEMENT

We are grateful for the opportunity to prepare this book for the *Wiley Series in Forensic Clinical Psychology* and in particular thank Professor Mary McMurran, the series editor, for her patience, wisdom and attention to detail – beyond the call of duty. We also thank Mr Chi Meng Chu for assistance with proofreading and Ms Lisa McGowan, who helped with formatting.

PART I

INTRODUCTION

Chapter 1

HISTORY OF THE OFFENCE PARALLELING BEHAVIOUR CONSTRUCT AND RELATED CONCEPTS

LAWRENCE JONES

Consultant Clinical and Forensic Psychologist, Lead Psychologist, Peaks Unit, Rampton Hospital, Nottinghamshire Healthcare NHS Trust, UK.

INTRODUCTION

Constructs related to offence paralleling behaviour (OPB) have been around in the literature for many years. Indeed, Haynes (2001) reminds us that for the most part psychological assessment is based on analogue measures. He writes:

> Most psychological assessment methods, such as questionnaires, interviews, and psychophysiological laboratory assessment, are analogue, in that inferences about a client are derived in an environment different from the environment of primary interest. (Haynes, 2001, p. 73)

Obviously, some forms of assessment involve direct observation of the phenomenon being studied. In the study and assessment of offending behaviour and the risk of offending, however, the context of assessment and intervention is generally significantly different from the context of the behaviour being examined. This difference between the context of assessment and the context of offending is a central problem for most assessments undertaken by forensic practitioners. Moreover, unlike many behaviours examined by psychologists, it is likely to be ethically problematic to deliberately create the contingencies that are liable to elicit the behaviour in the context of intervention or assessment.

A consequence of this is that forensic practitioners are presented with the problem of assessing something which they cannot observe or elicit deliberately in a context which is designed specifically to prevent the problem behaviour from being manifested. Both context and the phenomenon being assessed are out of bounds. Any solution to this problem is likely to be plagued with issues around validity and reliability. Faced with this problem, the practitioner can opt for one of two not mutually exclusive options:

Offence Paralleling Behaviour: A Case Formulation Approach to Offender Assessment and Intervention Edited by Michael Daffern, Lawrence Jones and John Shine

1. Find a proxy for the construct of interest.
2. Watch for naturally occurring contingencies – in the custodial setting – that mirror in some significant way the contingencies that were present at the time of the offence and see if these trigger offending behaviour or some functionally related behaviour.

Using self-report questionnaires makes the assumption that whatever construct is being assessed is a significant proxy measure for some process that contributed to the offence in the first place. It is usually a proxy for a criminogenic state or attitude/belief/intrapersonal process. As an assessment strategy, however, it does not attempt to mirror the contingencies that were around at the time of the offence or in any way assess the situational contribution to the state/attitude/belief being assessed.

The validity problems with using psychometric change as an index of clinically meaningful change in offending propensity are illustrated by Hanson and Wallace-Capretta (2000) who found that whilst most of the 'batterers' in their study showed significant in-treatment changes in criminogenic attitudes there was no relationship between positive changes in treatment and eventual reduced recidivism amongst male 'batterers'; indeed, they found the reverse. They write, 'Substance abuse and pro-abuse attitudes were positively related to recidivism at pre-treatment, but self-reported improvements were associated with increased (not decreased) recidivism'. Bowen et al. (2008) found a similar lack of correlation between in-treatment changes in psychometrics assessing criminogenic need with 'batterers' and eventual reconviction.

This is essentially a problem of validity. Is the proxy a valid measure of a propensity to offend (the hypothesized construct being measured)? When we examine this question more carefully, it becomes clear that the 'propensity to offend' is a nebulous construct and needs to be broken down into a set of hypothesized causal processes that drive offending before it can be usefully operationalized for an individual case.

Similarly with the behavioural observation solution, the question is one of the degree to which the custodial contingencies mirroring those at the time of the offence are actually a valid index of the contingencies that were around at the time of the offence. Typically, the validity of both measures of 'criminogenic factors' and risk assessments is established by predicting reconviction. Unfortunately, this is problematic in that reconviction is a poor measure of offending, particularly for individuals who have well-developed detection evasion skills (DES) (Jones, 2001, 2004) and in contexts where the clear-up rates are poor (Jones, 2001, 2004). What reconviction measures is detected – offending and as such it is biased towards identifying offenders who have failed to implement detection and conviction evasion skills (CES). Those individuals with these skills are not detected and do not get identified with the actuarial prediction paradigm. Much of the literature on clear-up rates for offending indicates that the majority of offending goes undetected (Jones, 2004).

Hanson and Wallace-Capretta (2000) also highlight this problem when they write:

> The apparent similarity of risk predictors for male batterers and general offenders, however, could be attributed to a common outcome criterion (arrest). Some of the risk factors, such as young age and low verbal IQ, could be substantially related to the probability of getting caught and processed by the criminal justice system. (Hanson & Wallace-Capretta, 2000, p. 75)

These two factors, young age and low verbal IQ, could be related to increased probability of getting caught in a number of ways:

1. Young age could be related to lack of experience of the criminal justice system (CJS) and thus absence of DES.

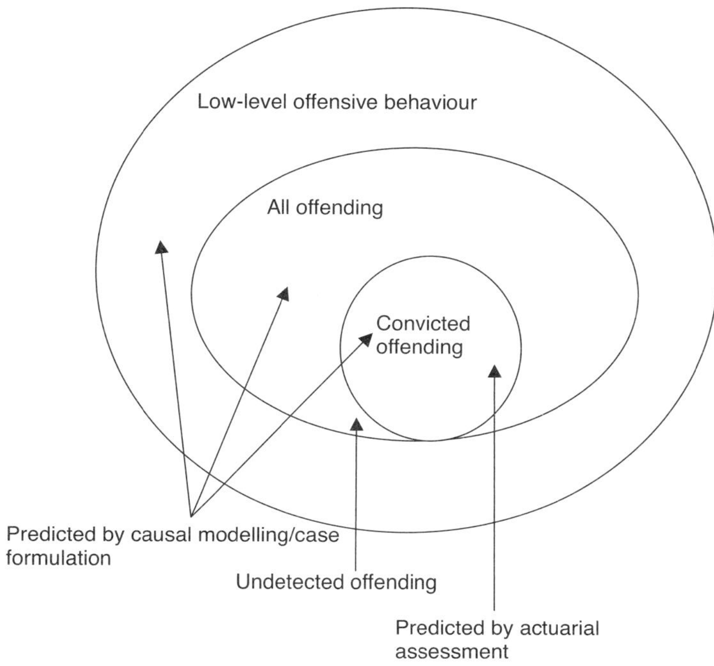

Figure 1.1 A set of all offensive behaviour, predicted by clinical judgement.

2. Young age could be related to a reduced detection evasion context; that is, younger people may be exposed to higher levels of supervision and older people to more opportunities to offend without being detected.
3. Low verbal intelligence may also be associated with lack of DES skills in presenting a case against conviction.

Figure 1.1 highlights a number of sources of confusion about what is being explained by different theoretical models of risk. For instance, the argument that because an individual does not have a history of violent (convicted) offending but then is found to behave violently in a custodial context means that this violent behaviour is situationally specific to custodial contexts may be missing the point. One possible alternative explanation for the lack of violent behaviour outside custody might be simply that the behaviour was not caught out-with the custodial context, but that, due to the increased levels of surveillance in custody, or simply the more specific surveillance of violence, the behaviour was detected and the individual's DES and CES were not effective in custody. The reliance by researchers on reconviction as an outcome measure has been driven by the relative accessibility of these kinds of data but may have had a distorting impact on practice because it has not taken fully into account the difference between detected and undetected crime. 'Effective' interventions, as well as changing offending behaviour, could be, in part, inadvertently shaped up by DES and CES (Jones, 2004), for example, by becoming more self-regulated and less impulsive in the way they offend.

In defence of conviction as an outcome measure, it might be argued that getting convicted is probably a good index of severity and persistence of offending because 'one off' offenders or infrequent offenders are less likely to get caught. Prolific offenders may also be more likely to get caught. Conviction might, clear-up rates notwithstanding, thus be a good index of general offensive behaviour, including offending. This is an empirical question and needs to be further explored.

Actuarial risk assessment methods do not typically take the step of developing an explanation for how psychological processes impact on offending and the risk of offending. The key feature of formulation-based attempts, some of which are explored in this chapter, at explaining offending and predicting risk – and essentially that is what an OPB account amounts to – is that they do make an effort to develop an account of the link between psychological processes and offending for the individual case, extrapolating from more general models developed to explain offending of a particular kind.

It is a curious phenomenon in the history of risk assessment and interventions targeting risk that intervention-based models of risk differ significantly from the models of risk used in the context of assessment. Most interventions targeting risk of reoffending use a combination of motivation, skill development, insight development and relapse prevention associated with developing approach goals (e.g. Marshall et al., 2005). The causal models of risk-related behaviour in this context differ significantly from the models implicit in risk assessments. Indeed, often the reasons for including variables in a risk assessment instrument are atheoretical and based on data-dredging exercises or meta-analyses of predictors of reoffending/reconviction. This lack of coherence between the two models of risk is puzzling. In this chapter the model of offence processes implicit in relapse prevention and related interventions will also be explored as they have much in common with the OPB construct. Types of risk assessment and offence analysis are first explored before the OPB construct is described and analysed.

TYPES OF RISK ASSESSMENT AND OFFENCE ANALYSIS

Actuarial Risk Assessment

Actuarial risk assessment focuses on one characteristic of the offender, their offence type, and then attempts to establish their risk of committing this offence again on the basis of a limited number of other defined variables using aggregated data for cases with the same characteristics. Actuarial risk assessment attempts to measure an underlying propensity using a number of historical (static) and more recently current changeable (dynamic) markers.

Anamnestic Risk Assessment

Anamnestic risk assessment makes use of individual data to identify factors contributing to risk. Elbogen and Tomkins (2000) write of anamnestic risk assessment as requiring the practitioner '. . . to determine unique risk factors and idiosyncratic patterns of relapse that are not captured by formal risk assessment instruments' (p. 436). They go on to argue:

> Anamnestic risk assessment supplements the actuarial based findings because the latter involve a fixed set of variables, which may not all apply in particular cases. Further, anamnestic assessments allow for clinicians to hone in on the specific circumstances that lead to relapse. For example, a patient might have a peculiar pattern of becoming increasingly anxious and paranoid after visiting a certain relative, which has, in the past, led to his becoming delusional, noncompliant with medications, and, subsequently, psychotic and dangerous. Anamnestic, but not actuarial, approaches to risk assessment would consider this type of important information. (Elbogen & Tomkins, 2000, p. 436)

Douglas and Kropp (2002) write of the anamnestic method:

> Some authors have referred to the anamnestic approach to risk assessment .... In this approach, the evaluator must 'identify violence risk factors through a detailed examination of the individual's history of violent and threatening behavior' (Otto, 2000, p. 1241). In this way, the examiner attempts to identify violent themes, pathways, and risk factors unique to the individual in question. . . . Hart (2001) has commented that the model assumes a behavioral chain that will repeat itself and thus be predictable. This assumption does not recognize the multifarious and dynamic nature of violence. That is, we should always remember that the same individual can be violent in many different ways and in many different circumstances. (Douglas & Kropp, 2002, p. 626)

The concerns identified here for anamnestic assessment are also true for OPB. The reification of a model of offending for an individual case can blind the clinician to alternative scenarios.

Relapse Prevention and Offence Cycle Models

The construct of an 'offence cycle' has been a central part of the way in which forensic practitioners have made sense of offending behaviour. This has typically been part of an intervention using the relapse prevention paradigm. A range of high-risk situations (involving external and internal stimuli previously associated with triggering a relapse process) are identified, and the individual is encouraged to develop alternative coping strategies for the situations identified. The relapse prevention model for intervening with offenders was originally developed for working with substance abuse by Marlatt and Gordon (1985) and later extended by forensic practitioners such as Laws (1989) to working with offenders. Essentially, this approach makes the assumption that the contingencies that were around at the time of the offence, if repeated, will increase the chances of relapse. It also makes the assumption that once an individual has offended in a particular way they can offend in the same way again in the future. Consequently, intervention focuses on developing strategies for pre-empting the range of factors that have been identified as antecedents to the offence, or offences in the case of multiple offenders, from happening again. Ward et al. (2007) have developed the emphasis of this model from one which was about 'avoidance goals', i.e. avoiding high-risk situations, to 'approach goals', setting up a lifestyle that enables the individual to meet the full range of their needs without offending. These models are similar to the OPB model in that they make links between a formulation of past offending and possible future offending. Any behaviour in the present that parallels that at the time of the offence can be seen as a high-risk situation and needs to be targeted for intervention.

Addiction to Crime

The 'addiction to crime' hypothesis, explored by Hodge (1997), highlights a pattern of increasingly repetitive offending characterized by the following processes: tolerance – the need for more to produce the same effect; withdrawal – distress after a period of non-engagement; craving – distress associated with desire to re-engage; salience – increasing importance of addiction in lifestyle; conflict – increasing awareness of negative consequences; relapse – reinstatement after a decision to stop or reduce. These developmental processes are very relevant to developing OPB hypotheses.

DIMENSIONS OF OPB ACCOUNTS

Whilst the term 'OPB' was first used by Jones (1997), there are a number of different ways in which the idea of current behaviour being similar to offending behaviour (or target behaviour in the context of other clinical problems) in a clinically significant way has been used in the literature. In this section a number of key dimensions differentiating different approaches to OPB are delineated.

WAYS OF ANALYSING EVENTS

Behaviour can be conceptualized as an event or as a sequence – a distinction similar to that between a categorical and a dimensional appraisal.

Single Events

Single-event accounts involve the identification of a simple event that was part of the development of the offence, which is also identified as occurring in the current context, for example, sexual arousal to children at the time of the offence and sexual arousal to children in custody associated with reading a catalogue with advertisements for children's clothes. This model is largely the one proposed by McDougall and colleagues (1994). Similarly, Neville et al. (2007) have developed a behavioural checklist containing 35 'single-event' variables that purportedly assists monitoring of both 'positive' and 'negative' behaviours throughout the course of therapy, paying particular attention to OPBs using content analysis of therapy notes.

Sequence of Events

A sequence of events and associated functions that were also evident in the development of the offence is also identified as occurring in the current context. An example of this could be a child sex offender in a relationship is rejected by his partner, becomes depressed and begins to seek out high-risk situations in which he might meet children, then meets a child and sexually offends against them. In custody they also experience rejection in a relationship, become depressed, seek out children's television programmes and masturbate whilst watching these.

Jones (2004) proposed that the term 'OPB' be used for sequences of behaviour that were repeated in the lead-up to the offence. He argued that sequences are important clinically as they capture a developmental process. In addition, the function of individual events in a checklist might be less clear than the function of behaviour in a repeating chain. This conceptualization derives from the behaviour analytic concept of chain or task analysis (e.g. Miltenberger, 2004) where behaviour is analysed as a sequence.

'LOW-LEVEL AGGRESSION' AS A RISK FACTOR FOR ESCALATION

Goldstein (2002) consistently argued that ignoring the manifestation of 'low-level aggression' (LLA) when rewarded develops into much more 'intractable high-level aggression' (HLA). He proposed that intervention needs to 'catch it small' to prevent this escalation process. So, for example, his model of intervention highlights the importance of intervening with LLA in schools.

In order of seriousness in a school context: 'horseplay', rule violation, disruptiveness, cursing, bullying, sexual harassment, refusal/defiance, threats, vandalism, out-of-control behaviour, student–student fights, attacks on teachers, use of weapons, collective violence.

In this model, LLA is seen as a lagged indicator of HLA and as generating HLA if it is allowed to be reinforced. The construct of LLA is similar to OPB in that it is a measure of the extent to which an individual's current state of learning is one that includes some degree of aggression as reinforcing. As such Goldstein's model is a sequential model of offending behaviour that highlights a 'within-incident chronology' where LLA 'escalates' to become HLA. This is a very specific theoretical model of an offence paralleling process.

KINDS OF LINKAGE

There are several linkage tasks required in undertaking an OPB analysis:

1. Linking offences committed by an individual, both within offence types and across offence types
2. Identifying links between behaviour at time of offence and behaviour in the current context
3. Proposing possible links between behaviour at the time of offence and the present context and behaviour in other possible (e.g. future post-release) contexts

Hollin (2002) writes:

> ... turning to the possibility of institutional behaviour to predict recidivism, the issue hinges on the degree of continuity of behaviour. In other words, does *offending* behaviour prior to imprisonment predict institutional (mis)behaviour? Then, does institutional behaviour predict recidivism post-release? (Hollin, 2002, p. 323)

The problem of 'continuity' of offending behaviour has been tackled in a number of different ways by clinicians engaged in risk assessment and interventions targeting risk, and by offender profilers trying to identify if offences belong to an offence series committed by a particular offender. In this section we explore different approaches to identify continuity.

Topological Similarity

Behaviour at the time of the offence is identified as being topographically similar to current behaviour simply because it has the same form or appearance as behaviour at the time of the offence. Checklist-based approaches such as McDougall and Clark's (McDougall & Clark, 1991) and Neville's (Neville et al., 2007) are topologically oriented and do not attempt to identify linkages based on function of behaviour or some other underlying psychological cause.

Statistical Linkage Analysis

There are a number of constructs in the forensic and clinical literatures that are similar to the construct of OPB. An individual's modus operandi (Canter, 1995), for example, is his way of conducting an offence that is clearly recognizable. In this work, a linkage is drawn between offences.

Linking offences using statistical procedures has increasingly been a feature of the offender-case linkage and profiling literature. This literature discusses two concepts: behavioural consistency and behavioural distinctiveness. A number of interesting suggestions have come out of this literature (Tonkin et al., 2008):

1. A distinction between situationally dependent and situationally independent behaviour (with the latter being more consistent across offences). It is suggested that situationally independent behaviours are also more in the 'control' of the actor.
2. Experience acts to increase some but not all offence behaviour.
3. Temporal proximity of acts enhances behavioural consistency.
4. Control behaviours (manner of getting control of victim) have been shown to have 'significant consistency' (Grubin et al., 2001; Woodhams & Toye, 2007).

Statistical procedures are used to identify if there is a link between the offences based on key topological characteristics of the offence. A number of linkage strategies have been identified in the literature, Jaccard's coefficient being the most common. This is a measure of similarity for variables where the presence or absence of a feature is recorded as binary data. As a measure it does not take into account joint non-occurrences of behaviour. It is argued that this is useful for data where non-occurrence does not mean non-existence. A taxonomic similarity measure has recently been suggested (Woodhams & Toye, 2007) as potentially less sensitive to missing data.

Psychological Similarity

In contrast to the topographical framework, it is also possible to look at patterns in psychological motivations for offending. Behaviour at the time of the offence is identified as being similar to current behaviour simply because it has the same function, or is driven by the same psychological process, as behaviour at the time of the offence. For example, at the time of the offence the offender was experiencing humiliation in the context of a relationship. The offender then rapes a stranger, and this results in him experiencing relief from humiliation and a sense of power. In custody the offender experiences humiliation from a peer, and then he goes back to his room and fantasizes about raping a woman; this results in a reduction in the feelings of humiliation and an increase in feelings of power. Jones (2004) argued that functional similarity was a critical task to the practitioner attempting to validate a pattern of behaviour as OPB. Jones also highlighted the importance of a number of psychological drivers, such as interpersonal status and relationship projects, and psychological and cognitive states. Daffern et al. (2007a) and Miller and Fritzon (2007) also made the case for functional as opposed to topographical similarity.

Jones (2004) proposed that structural similarity, with behavioural sequences, was likely to reflect functional similarity. If a chain of behaviour has been repeated, then it is more likely that each step in the sequence has a similar function to similar steps in other chains. Jones (2004) also identifies the possibility that components of behaviour chains, aimed at other functions, may be similar to those at the time of the offence.

Funder (2008) cites Allport (1961) on personality traits as having 'the capacity to render many stimuli functionally equivalent' (p. 347). This highlights the role of personality in shaping the ways in which functional similarity is generated for different individuals. Personality traits of dominance, for example, might be linked with an increased tendency to see others as trying to challenge an individual's authority or status.

Similarity in Single or Multiple Domains

Similarities can be drawn in a number of ways between sequences of behaviour. The number of different domains explored to identify possible parallels between offending behaviour and current behaviour is clearly dependent on the theoretical model of offending processes used by the practitioner.

One Domain OPB (e.g. Just Thoughts)

Behaviour at the time of the offence is identified as being similar to current behaviour in one domain only (e.g. just thoughts, just emotions or just behaviour). An example of this might be just identifying the behaviour of looking at a section of children's clothing catalogues as OPB for a child sex offender in prison.

Multiple Domains (Thoughts, Feelings, Behaviour)

Behaviour at the time of the offence is identified as being similar to current behaviour in multiple domains only (e.g. thoughts, emotions or behaviour). An example of this, building on that used in the previous section, might be the *behaviour* of looking at the section of children's clothing catalogues, *feelings* of being powerful and *thoughts* of the children in the images wanting to have sex with an adult, as OPB for a child sex offender in prison. This notion was developed by Shine and Morris (2000) in their paper describing the version of OPB they used as part of the prison service therapeutic community-accredited model, to include parallels in attachment themes evidenced by individuals undergoing therapy.

Jones (2004) highlighted the utility of identifying interpersonal processes and emotional states (proposing the use of instruments such as the (Gerald et al., 1990) University of Wales Institute of Science and Technology Mood Adjective Check List – see also Daffern et al., 2009 – or the standardized affective headings from Hermans, 1995) and cognitive (e.g. quality of attention) states in generating hypotheses about the function of behaviour during an offence process.

OFFENCE PARALLELING SITUATIONS

Ross and Nisbett (1991) argue that lay people tend to offer dispositional explanations for behaviour as opposed to situational ones in explaining others' behaviour (an error sometimes called the 'fundamental attribution error'; Ross, 1977). Developing an understanding of both the importance of situational factors in offending behaviour and ways in which dispositional thinking could bias the clinician is an important task for the clinician; however, it is equally important not to have situationist bias (see Chapter 6).

To make inferences about a particular behaviour being functionally similar to another behaviour, the context of the behaviour needs to be taken into account. Jones (2004) described the possibility that custodial contexts that do not have the same or similar features to that in which the offending behaviour evolved might be seen as 'damping' the possibility of OPB (see also Daffern et al., 2007b).

An offence paralleling situation is therefore a context that in some significant sense parallels that in which the offence originally occurred. Shoda and Lee Tiernan (2002) describe situations as having both an *internal* ('what one is thinking, feeling and doing at any given moment', p. 266) and an *external* component. From this perspective the internal component (what the situation/stimulus context means and how it is perceived by the individual) is most important.

The literature on what kinds of situations impact on behaviour in what ways is suggestive of ways in which behavioural consistency could be greater or less in different circumstances. Buss (1989) presented evidence, for example, to support the contention that situations that were more novel, formal, public, with detailed/complete instructions where there is little choice of behaviour and which were of brief duration had a greater impact on behaviour than personality; whereas situations that were more familiar, informal, private, general or did not have instructions, with a considerable choice of behaviour and which last for a long time, were more conducive to the expression of personality traits and therefore behavioural consistency.

Mischel and Shoda (e.g. 1995, 1999) developed a framework for analysing situational contribution to behaviour as 'if. . .then' profiles. This involved developing an individual's behavioural 'signature' using a series of 'if. . .then' statements of the form 'if situation x then behaviour y'. Alison et al. (2002) argue persuasively to use this paradigm in offender profiling work.

Swann and Selye (2005) comment that a 'full implementation of Mischel and Shoda's (1999) innovative approach clearly requires the development of a comprehensive taxonomy of situations' and go on to indicate that analysis of situations has made little progress since the early work of Wright and Barker (1950). However, more recent work on taxonomy of situations has been developed. Yang et al. (2006) suggested that people distinguish between situations in terms of goal processes, or what happened to people's goals. Edwards and Templeton (2005) identified five factors from people's assessments of qualities of situations: positivity, negativity, capacity to foster or hinder goal-related activities and ease of negotiation. Ten Berge and De Raad (2002) identified the following as qualities of situations: situations of pleasure, situations of individual adversity, situations of interpersonal conflict and situations of social demand. Saucier et al. (2007) suggested the following domains of description for situations: locations, associations, activities and passively experienced processes.

Work on the relationship between situations and behavioural consistency is essential to the task of identifying persistent offending. There are clear links to be made between the concepts of situationally dependent and independent behaviour from the behaviour linkage literature and the literature on types of situations (see above), particularly in terms of the extent to which situations inhibit or dampen an individual's 'agency' or capacity to pursue goals that are internally as opposed to externally driven. In addition, the fundamentally interpersonal nature of situational impact on behaviour (suggested by Jones, 1997, 2004) needs to be recognized in a more systematic way (cf. Fournier et al., 2008).

Contrived Analogue Situations and Analogue Behavioural Observation

A particular kind of offence paralleling situation is one deliberately engineered by practitioners to test specific hypotheses about an individual's behaviour. Haynes' (Haynes, 2001; Haynes et al., 2008) extensive work on *analogue behaviour* exemplifies this approach. In this approach the practitioner deliberately engineers situations that parallel those in which the target behaviour occurred:

> Analogue behavioral observation methods involve measurement of behavior and functional relations, often in multiple response modes (usually measuring overt/observable behavior but may focus on emotional, cognitive, and/or physiological events) in a contrived

> setting .... To strengthen the generalizability of the findings to a subject's natural environment, the observation situation incorporates elements that are similar to elements that are important in the subject's natural environment .... As Heyman and Slep noted, ABO is primarily useful as a hypothesis-testing strategy. It allows researchers to observe low frequency or socially sensitive behaviors, or behaviors that are unlikely to occur in the presence of the assessors without establishing settings to increase their likelihood. The main object is to discover interactions that maintain behavior problems. (Haynes, 2001, pp. 27–28)

An early example of the idea that offence-related behaviour is likely to recur in analogous current settings is found in the work of Aichorn (1951). Aichorn was working with young offenders in the 1920s and set up a home for 'wayward youth'. One of the clients in this home had been caught repeatedly stealing. Aichorn intentionally gave him work in the shop and monitored the money in the till anticipating that the problem would re-emerge in this context. When the young person eventually did steal money, he sat him down and discussed it with him in a non-punitive manner. In this intervention Aichorn was using past behaviour as a means of generating predictions about how the problem behaviour would manifest in the current contrived (treatment) setting and then testing this prediction.

Deliberately contriving situations in which offending behaviour can occur is generally ethically questionable. Clinicians should look at changing offending behaviour, not provoking it. As such forensic practitioners have to rely on observation of natural behaviour in situ. It is however conceivable that analogue situations can be ethically explored, particularly if they focus on setting up contingencies that were around in the *lead-up to the offence* as opposed to contingencies that were *around at the point of the offence itself*. Role-play, for instance, can be used to work on offence paralleling situations.

BASIC CONSISTENCY AND HIGHER ORDER CONSISTENCY

Work on consistency within intra-individual variation in behaviour has generated two concepts relevant to the study of OPB. The traditional idea of personality, which emphasizes temporal consistency, contrasts with the recent construct of higher order consistency (Shoda & Lee Tiernan, 2002). Larsen (1990) proposed the term 'second-order consistency' for the characteristic frequency with which an individual's behaviour changes over time, and Shoda and Lee Tiernan (2002) offer the term 'higher order consistency' to describe both 'second-order consistency' and consistency in the way individuals vary their behaviour across situations. Mischel and Shoda (1995, 1999) and Shoda and Mischel (1998, 2000) developed the concept of a 'behavioural signature' which captures an individual's characteristic way of evidencing variability and higher order consistency in behaviour across temporal and situational contexts.

Shoda and Lee Tiernan (2002) write:

> Just as individuals' responses to particular medications can be understood more fundamentally by considering the specific active ingredients rather than brand names, our analysis of situations focuses on the psychologically active features of situations. (Shoda & Lee Tiernan, 2002, p. 246)

Kinderman (2005) and Morton (2004) argue that psychological processes are the final common pathway mediating between biological, social and circumstantial factors and mental (and other) disorders. McGuire (2008) proposes that this claim can be extended to understanding violence by arguing that psychological processes are the final common pathway between biological, social and circumstantial factors and violence. In the context of risk assessment, this highlights the importance of identifying the psychological processes mediating the impact of other variables on behaviour.

THE EXTENT TO WHICH THE VALIDITY OF THE OPB HYPOTHESIS HAS BEEN TESTED

A critical test of validity of a construct is to establish the degree to which it has predictive validity. An OPB that has been identified but has not been subjected to any test of veracity has a different clinical value from one that has not been subjected to this kind of testing. There are different ways in which this can happen:

1. A formulation that has been used to make very specific predictions about OPB and which has then been shown to be accurate in that the predicted behaviours have actually happened should warrant more confidence than one which has not been through this kind of testing process.
2. A formulation where a number of offences and offence-related episodes have been used to accumulate evidence in its support. This could indicate a higher degree of confirmation than examples based on just one offence. In the philosophy of science, the 'degree of confirmation' solution to the problem of induction is not without problems. If however we reframe it using Popper's criteria of falsifiability, further evidence supporting the hypothesis would indicate that the hypothesis had survived exposure to the possibility of refutation on a number of occasions. Further, Epstein (1983) in responding to the situationist position argues that the 'personality coefficient' rises from 0.29 to 0.65 when aggregating over several occasions.

UNUSUAL BEHAVIOUR IS MORE USEFUL FOR DEVELOPING OPB FORMULATION

Behaviours that are relatively frequent and are exhibited by many individuals are often less likely to be more clinically useful than behaviours that are atypical and relatively infrequent. Behavioural sequences are more likely to be low frequency and atypical than individual behaviours because there is much more scope for variation in that context.

Funder (2008) describes Gilbert's (1998) thinking on this in the following excerpt:

> . . . dispositional attributions should be made only for an individual's behavior that is unusual; that is, different from what most other people do. Thus, if everybody puts on a coat on a cold day, the cause of any one person's behavior can be safely said to be the cold weather situation. The odd person (perhaps literally) who fails to wear a coat is doing so, presumably, because of something distinctive about himself or herself (e.g. an unusual immunity to or eccentric liking for cold). (Gilbert, 1998, p. 573)

Daffern et al. (2009) indicate that behaviour that is common is relatively useless for the purposes of OPB (e.g. he was breathing before and during the offence and he is breathing now; therefore, he is engaged in an OPB).

EMPHASIS ON SINGLE CASE HYPOTHESIS TESTING AND AVOIDING BIAS

In addition to the fundamental attribution bias identified by Nisbett and Ross (1980), there is a range of biases (cf. e.g. Tversky & Kahneman, 1974) that any clinical judgement is susceptible to that need to be systematically offset in work identifying OPB. Jones (2007) outlined some of these biases and suggested that clinicians need to be trained about them and about how they can be offset in the context of developing OPB formulations. Little work has been done on this, and this issue is further addressed in the final chapter.

RELATED CONSTRUCTS IN OTHER FIELDS OF APPLIED PSYCHOLOGY

Relapse Prodromes

Birchwood (1994) in work with psychosis has developed an intervention based on identifying, on a case-by-case basis, a 'relapse prodrome' or relapse signature. This pattern of behaviour can be then used by the individual to monitor the individual's own behaviour with a view to intervening pre-emptively if some of the early warning signs are apparent. This literature is particularly interesting in that it raises the possibility that there are some moderate changes in cognitive capacities (such as attention and mood regulation), which could be interesting sources of hypotheses for predictors of offending/OPB. Birchwood does not place any emphasis on asking why a particular prodrome is relevant for a particular individual (he does not look for the function of a change in attentional capacity, for instance). Individualized prodrome markers are drawn initially from a checklist developed out of interviews with numbers of service users and which had been shown to have some degree of predictive validity.

Enactments

An enactment is a construct that has been developed within the psychodynamic literature (e.g. Ellman & Moskowitz, 1998; Shur, 1994). The enactment is a sequence of behaviours in an interpersonal context, which is repeated in a number of different contexts throughout an individual's life. It is hypothesized that the repeating pattern is related to traumatic experiences which are played out in the present, sometimes with critical role reversals, such as the offender enacting aspects of their own abuse but in the role of the perpetrator. Therapists and staff are seen as unwittingly playing out and taking on aspects of the patient's problems. The function of this behaviour, it is argued, is for the victim to experience in some way the trauma that the perpetrators experienced when they were victimized/traumatized (Pollock et al., 2006; Stoller, 1986). The experience of the trauma is passed on to the victim by the perpetrator, and this then temporarily alleviates a sense of being alone. Repetition of these role-reversal events is understood as an attempt on the part of the offender to process or overcome the trauma.

The literature on interpersonal theory also highlights the way in which offenders treat staff in custodial or residential settings as if they are (often abusive or neglecting) parents or significant people from their pasts (see Jones, 1997, 2004) in a way that sometimes provokes them into behaving in a reciprocating way (i.e. behaving abusively).

SCHEMA THERAPY 'REPISODES'

Young et al. (2003), in discussing patterns of repeating behaviour associated with particular schemas (core beliefs), describe a pattern of repeating episodes or 'repisodes' (e.g. that constitute an individual's maladaptive response to relationships and difficult life events). The hypothesized mechanisms for generating repetition in Young's framework are underlying 'schemas' and 'modes'; essentially, these are core ways of thinking and states that each individual holds and which then shape that individual's behaviour. Schema therapists in the UK have used these constructs to develop an understanding of an individual's offending and OPB (see Table 1.1).

THE RANGE OF CURRENT USES OF OPB

Using the Milieu and Identifying Positive Alternative Behaviours

The initial work on identifying offence-related behaviour in custody did so as a part of a risk assessment strategy (Clark et al., 1994). Jones (1997) advocated the utility of this kind of case conceptualization for interventions. Jones (2004) drew on the work of Kohlenberg and Tsai (1994) who had developed an intervention strategy called functional analytic psychotherapy (FAP) which advocated the use of in-session behaviour as a way of targeting clinically relevant behaviour. In this, they advocate working with various forms of 'clinically relevant behaviour', behaviours that reflect the presenting problem, but which emerge in the session, whether it is the problem behaviour itself or some form of changed behaviour emerging in the session; behaviours that evidence change in the underlying problem and finally behaviour that evidenced insight into the problem behaviour. FAP was also advocated, building on Jones (2004) by Daffern et al. (2007a) as a framework for working with OPB.

Jones (2004) highlighted the importance of working with positive behaviour that was not offence paralleling in a context where it might have been expected (more recently called positive alternative behaviour and given the acronym PAB; Daffern et al., 2007a). In the context of discussion related to analysing interpersonal behaviour associated with offending Jones (2004) wrote:

> [This] allows people to ensure that the interpersonal project is explored and alternative behaviours introduced. It is also important that appropriate, non OPB behaviour is recognised and validated (Kohlenberg & Tsai, 1994; Linehan, 1993). This kind of attunement to the clinical relevance of behaviour can only be developed through building a milieu culture where **all behaviour,** on and off groups and individual interventions, are seen as relevant to the change initiative. (Jones, 2004, p. 61)

CONTEXTS IN WHICH THE CONSTRUCT OF OFFENCE PARALLELING BEHAVIOUR IS CURRENTLY BEING USED IN THE UK

The initial development and usage of the OPB construct was in the Max Glatt Centre, a small therapeutic community based in HMP Wormwood Scrubs. It was developed initially as a model to try to focus the interventions in the unit on the aim of reducing reconviction and as a way of articulating aspects of the way in which the therapeutic community functioned in order to

Table 1.1 Differences in key dimensions of different assessment procedures

Authors	Historical idiographic data used as a source of hypotheses	Usage	Frame of analysis	Kind of linkage between offence and current behaviour	Number of domains	Emphasis on single case testing and explicit procedures for avoiding bias	Contrived situations
McDougall et al. (1994)	Yes	Risk assessment	Event sequences	Form	Unspecified multiple	Predictions	None
Jones (1997)	Yes	Risk assessment and intervention addressing positive and problematic behaviour		Form and function		Prediction	None
Jones (2004)				Themes			
Shine and Morris (2000)	Yes	Intervention	Sequences	Unspecified	Specified multiple	Not emphasized	None
Neville et al. (2007)	Standardized list of in therapy behaviours	Intervention shaping 'positive and negative' behaviour	Event	Function	Unspecified	Not emphasized	None
Woodhams and Toye (2007) Linkage analysis	Lists of behaviours in offences	Offender profiling	Sequences as lists of behaviour	Statistical analysis of linkage between offences	Multiple	Not emphasized	N/A
Daffern et al. (2007a)	Yes	Risk assessment and intervention addressing positive and problematic behaviour	Sequences	Function	Multiple	Emphasized Predictions and clinical awareness of bias	None
Haynes (2001)	Yes	Intervention	Sequences and event	Not used for offence behaviour	Emphasis on behaviour	Some emphasis	Yes
Analogue assessment				But uses function			
Anamnestic assessment	Yes	Risk assessment	Not specified	Themes	Multiple	Not emphasized	None
Relapse prevention	Yes	Intervention addressing positive and problematic behaviour	Sequences	Function	Multiple	Not emphasized	None
Functional analytic therapy	Yes	Intervention addressing positive and problematic behaviour	Not specified explicitly	Not used solely for offence behaviour	Multiple	Not emphasized	Yes (role-play)
Kohlenberg and Tsai (1994)			'Clinically relevant behaviour'	But uses function			

enable the unit to go through a process of accreditation. Following the departure of the author from this unit, the model was not sustained. However, it was incorporated into the accredited treatment model for prison-based therapeutic communities, starting with HMP Grendon and later HMP Dovegate and HMP Gartree.

The most recent account of the use of OPB in therapeutic community settings is Morris (2004) (building on earlier work by Jones, 1997, and Shine & Morris, 1999) who describes OPB as attenuated offence re-enactment and highlights the way in which this behaviour is repeated in the treatment setting and used as a focus for group intervention. He describes two components of this work: firstly, the identification of the OPB, and secondly, the 'lateral linkage' of behaviour across different settings (e.g. in community meetings and on the football pitch). 'The notion of offence re-enactment' proposes that the resident's actual offences are not isolated events, but rather are a single manifestation of a longer cyclic repetitive process. The offence is one element of the cycle that has been more extreme or has come to the attention of the law. 'Because the cycles are part of the characteristic repertoire of the individual, they can be expected to exhibit themselves in the resident's everyday life' (Morris, 2004, p. 81). Interestingly, Morris attempts to integrate behavioural with more psychodynamic constructs in an attempt to describe the complexity of the therapeutic community model of intervention with offending behaviour.

The model has been used to some extent by individual clinicians at Rampton Hospital (a high secure hospital in the United Kingdom) and has been included in the Rampton Hospital risk assessment documentation. OPB has been used as a tool for motivational assessment (Jones, 2002). The Offending Behaviour Programmes Unit, England and Wales prison service, has incorporated a version of the model into the structured assessment of risk and need for sex offender intervention needs and has recently developed some in-house training to implement this (Simone Wakama, personal communication). Some work using an OPB model has been undertaken at HMP Littlehey as part of the risk assessment reporting on lifers at the end of their tariffs.

UK SCHEMA THERAPY

The construct of OPB has been adopted, following Jones (1997), by the schema therapy model used at HMP Whitemoor (Murphy & McVey, 2010) and by the schema therapy model implemented at the Rampton Hospital personality disorder directorate (Beckley and Gordon, 2010). Central to both these models is work on current OPB, or offence paralleling processes, as it emerges in group settings. Unlike work in therapeutic community settings, this is then linked to core schemas which are seen to be driving the behaviour.

MISUSE OF THE MODEL AND ATTEMPTS TO REFINE THE DEFINITION OF OFFENCE PARALLELING BEHAVIOUR

Due in part to recent interest in the model (evidenced above) and in the light of possible misapplication, an attempt has been made to refine the definition to preclude some of the possibilities for misuse (Daffern et al., 2007a). In particular, more emphasis was placed on the importance of testing out hypotheses about OPB by making specific predictions and then monitoring to see if the predictions would materialize. This volume has been written partly to refine the practitioner's clinical skills in developing testable hypotheses about OPB.

There are a number of ways in which the model is potentially open to misuse:

1. In its current state of development, it is more useful as a model for developing individualized treatment targets (alongside models such as the risk needs responsivity framework, developed by Andrews & Bonta, 2003) and as part of a risk management and intervention package. To use the model to make probabilistic statements about risk is probably unwarranted; however, it does have a role in informing risk assessment, management and scenario planning (e.g. Hart, 2009) assessments.
2. Making predictions of high frequency, naturally occurring behaviours is problematic (Daffern et al., 2009) in that the chances of confirmation of the hypothesis would be high. So, for example, saying that somebody would get angry after being told that they cannot have something on the ward because at the time of the offence they became angry when they were refused something is likely to be a behaviour that would be observed in just about any individual in a custodial setting at some time. If, however, there was a particular way in which the individual expressed their anger which was unique to them (e.g. threats to kill) and which was very much a feature of the offence, then this might warrant further exploration.
3. There is a danger of clinicians forcing everyday normal reactions to custody, or indeed any behaviour, in a procrustean manner into an OPB mould in a way that is potentially damaging for the client and which reinforces some of the more unpleasant aspects of seeing a person as their offence. This is also potentially true of the seemingly more positive psychology-oriented approach of looking at when an individual has been meeting needs in a prosocial manner, because this is still seeing a person in terms of their offending, not as a person who has offended.

CONCLUSIONS

The use of in-custody behaviour as a source of information about risk assessment, intervention and management is not a new concept; it is at the heart of what forensic practitioners do, and there is evidence of it being used in a number of ways by clinicians working in forensic contexts. Like other formulation (see e.g. Garb, 1998; Kuyken, 2006) strategies, behavioural analysis of offending behaviour has not yet been subjected to the same kinds of evaluation of validity and reliability as, for example, psychometric assessments (but cf. Daffern et al., 2009, for a recent exception).

The use of the term 'offence paralleling behaviour' is increasingly being used in different ways by different practitioners. The usage of the term in Jones (1997), and more particularly in Jones (2004) and Daffern et al. (2007a), was to describe an analysis of behaviour with a number of specific features:

1. Looking at sequences of behaviour, not single events
2. Using case formulation and functional analysis to identify the function of the behaviour or to look at the causal factors driving the behaviour in the offence and in the custodial context and attempting to justify the links between behaviour in the different contexts using this analysis
3. Identifying examples of behaviour that do not repeat past problematic behaviour
4. Making specific predictions and testing these to see if the formulation is robust
5. Intervening to address any factors identified as potentially problematic

It is hoped that further clinical and empirical work can be done to refine this construct with a view to rendering it more clinically useful and reducing the twin possibilities of taking an overly dispositional or situational perspective (cf. Funder, 2008).

Useful constructs about what kinds of behaviour are likely to be linked across situations are suggested by the offender profiling literature on 'linkage', the personality literature and the recently emerging literature on attempting to identify taxonomies of situations and identifying what aspects of situations dampen or facilitate the expression of personality traits and other 'person' variables. In addition, the literature on working with 'prodromes' in psychosis is likely to offer useful suggestions for developing pre-emptive intervention strategies in the future.

REFERENCES

Aichorn, A. (1951). *Wayward Youth*. London: Imago.

Alison, L., Bennell, C., Ormerod, D. & Mokros, A. (2002). The personality paradox in offender profiling: a theoretical review of the processes involved in deriving background characteristics from crime scene actions. *Psychology, Public Policy, and Law, 8*, 115–35.

Allport, G.W. (1961). *Pattern and Growth in Personality*. New York: Holt, Rinehart, & Winston.

Andrews, D.A. & Bonta, J. (2003). *Psychology of Criminal Conduct* (3rd edition). Cincinnati, OH: Anderson Publishing.

Beckley, K. & Gordon, N. (2010). Schema therapy within a high secure setting. In A. Tennant & K. Howells (Eds), *Using Time, Not Doing Time: Practitioner Perspectives on Personality Disorder and Risk*. The Wiley Series in Personality Disorders. Chichester: Wiley.

Birchwood, M. (1994). Cognitive early intervention. In G. Haddock & P. Slade (Eds), *Cognitive Behavioural Approaches to Schizophrenia*. London: Routledge.

Bowen, E., Gilchrist, E. & Beech, A.R. (2008). Change in treatment has no relationship with subsequent re-offending in U.K. domestic violence sample: a preliminary study. *International Journal of Offender Therapy and Comparative Criminology, 52*, 598–614.

Buss, A.H. (1989). Personality as traits. *American Psychologist, 44*, 1378–88.

Canter, D. (1995). *Criminal Shadows*. London: HarperCollins.

Clark, D., Fisher, M.J. & McDougall, C. (1994). A new methodology for assessing the level of risk in incarcerated offenders. *British Journal of Criminology, 33*, 436–48.

Daffern, M., Howells, K., Manion, A. & Tonkin, M. (2009). A test of methodology intended to assist detection of aggressive offence paralleling behaviour within secure settings. *Legal and Criminological Psychology, 14*, 213–26.

Daffern, M., Jones, L., Howells, K., Shine, J., Mikton, C. & Tunbridge, V.C. (2007a). Refining the definition of offence paralleling behaviour. *Criminal Behaviour and Mental Health, 17*, 265–73.

Daffern, M., Ogloff, J.R.P., Ferguson, M., Thomson, L. & Howells, K. (2007b). Appropriate treatment targets or products of a demanding environment? The relationship between aggression in a forensic psychiatric hospital with aggressive behaviour preceding admission and violent recidivism. *Psychology, Crime and Law, 13*, 431–41.

Douglas, K.S. & Kropp, R.P. (2002). A prevention-based paradigm for violence risk assessment: clinical and research applications. *Criminal Justice and Behavior, 29*, 617–58.

Edwards, J.A. & Templeton, A. (2005). The structure of perceived qualities of situations. *European Journal of Social Psychology, 35*, 705–23.

Elbogen, E.B. & Tomkins, A.J. (2000). From the psychiatric hospital to the community: integrating conditional release and contingency management. *Behavioral Sciences and the Law, 18*, 427–44.

Ellman, S.J. & Moskowitz, M. (1998). *Enactment: Toward a New Approach to the Therapeutic Relationship*. Northvale, NJ: Jason Aronson.

Epstein, S. (1983). Aggregation and beyond: some basic issues on the prediction of behavior. *Journal of Personality, 51*, 360–92.

Fournier, M.A., Moskowitz, D.S. & Zuroff, D.C. (2008). Integrating dispositions, signatures, and the interpersonal domain. *Journal of Personality and Social Psychology, 94*, 531–45.

Funder, D.C. (2008). Persons, situations and person-situation interactions. In O.P. John, R. Robins & L. Pervin (Eds), *Handbook of Personality* (3rd edition, pp. 568–80). New York: Guilford Press.

Garb, H.N. (1998). *Studying the Clinician: Judgment Research and Psychological Assessment*. Washington, DC: American Psychological Association.

Gerald, M., Jones, D.M. & Chamberlain, A.G. (1990). Refining the measurement of mood: the UWIST Mood Adjective Checklist. *British Journal of Psychology*, *81*, 17–42.

Gilbert, D.T. (1998). Ordinary personology. In D.T. Gilbert, S.T. Fiske & G. Lindzey (Eds), *Handbook of Social Psychology* (4th edition, Vol. 2, pp. 89–150). New York: McGraw-Hill.

Goldstein, A.P. (2002). Low-level aggression: definition, escalation, intervention. In J. McGuire (Ed.), *Offender Rehabilitation and Treatment: Effective Programmes and Policies to Reduce Offending* (pp. 169–92). Chichester: Wiley.

Grubin, D., Kelly, P. & Brunsdon, C. (2001). *Linking Serious Sexual Assaults through Behaviour*. Home Office Research Study 215. London: Home Office Research, Development and Statistics Directorate.

Hanson, R.K. & Wallace-Capretta, S. (2000). *Predicting Recidivism among Male Batterers*. Ottawa, Canada: Department of the Solicitor General. Retrieved from: http://www.sgc.gc.ca (accessed 21 November 2009).

Hart, S.D. (2001). Assessing and managing violence risk. In K.S. Douglas, C.D. Webster, S.D. Hart, D. Eaves & J.R.P. Ogloff (Eds), *HCR-20 Violence Risk Management Companion Guide* (pp. 13–25). Burnaby, British Columbia: Mental Health, Law, & Policy Institute, Simon Fraser University, and Department of Mental Health Law and Policy, Florida Mental Health Institute, University of South Florida.

Hart, S.D. (2009). *Violence Risk Assessment Using the HCR-20: A Scenario Planning Approach*. Thoresby Hall, Nottinghamshire: Nottinghamshire National Health Service Trust.

Haynes, S.N. (2001). Clinical applications of analogue behavioral observation: dimensions of psychometric evaluation. *Psychological Assessment*, *13*, 73–85.

Haynes, S.N., Pinson, C., Yoshioka, D. & Kloezeman, K. (2008). Behavioral assessment in clinical psychology research. In D. McKay (Ed.), *Handbook of Research Methods in Abnormal and Clinical Psychology* (pp. 125–40). Los Angeles, CA: Sage.

Hermans, J.M. (1995). From assessment to change: the personal meaning of clinical problems in the context of the self-narrative. In A. Neimeyer & M.J. Mahoney (Eds), *Constructivism in Psychotherapy* (pp. 247–72). Washington, DC: American Psychological Association.

Hodge, J.E. (1997). Addiction to violence. In J.E. Hodge, M. McMurran & C.R. Hollin (Eds), *Addicted to Crime* (pp. 87–106). Chichester: Wiley.

Hollin, C. (2002). Risk-needs assessment and allocation to offender programmes. In J. McGuire (Ed.), *Offender Rehabilitation and Treatment: Effective Programmes and Policies to Reduce Reoffending* (pp. 309–32). Chichester: Wiley.

Jones, L.F. (1997). Developing models for managing treatment integrity and efficacy in a prison based TC: The Max Glatt Centre. In E. Cullen, L. Jones & R. Woodward (Eds), *Therapeutic Communities for Offenders* (pp. 121–57). Chichester: Wiley.

Jones, L.F. (2000). *Identifying and Working with Clinically Relevant Offence Paralleling Behaviour*. Paper presented at Division of Clinical Psychology. Nottinghamshire: Forensic Special Interest Group.

Jones, L.F. (2001). *Anticipating Offence Paralleling Behaviour*. Birmingham: Paper presented at Division of Forensic Psychology Annual Conference.

Jones, L.F. (2002). An individual case formulation approach to the assessment of motivation. In M. McMurran (Ed.), *Motivating Offenders to Change* (pp. 31–54). Chichester: Wiley.

Jones, L.F. (2004). Offence paralleling behaviour (OPB) as a framework for assessment and interventions with offenders. In A. Needs & G. Towl (Eds), *Applying Psychology to Forensic Practice* (pp. 34–63). Oxford: Blackwell and British Psychological Society.

Jones, L.F. (2007). Offence paralleling behaviour (OPB): the relevance of in-treatment behaviour to risk assessment, management and intervention. Paper presented at the Annual Conference of the International Association for Forensic Mental Health, Adelaide, Australia.

Kinderman, P. (2005). A psychological model of mental disorder. *Harvard Review of Psychiatry*, *13*, 206–17.

Kohlenberg, R.J. & Tsai, M. (1994). Functional analytic psychotherapy: a radical behavioral approach to treatment and integration. *Journal of Psychotherapy Integration*, *4*, 175–201.

Kuyken, W. (2006). Evidence-based case formulation: is the emperor clothed? In N. Tarrier (Ed.), *Case Formulation in Cognitive Behaviour Therapy: The Treatment of Challenging and Complex Cases*. London: Routledge.

Larsen, R.J. (1990). Spectral analysis of psychological data. In A. Von Eye (Ed.), *New Statistical Methods in Longitudinal Research, Vol. 2: Time Series and Categorical Longitudinal Data* (pp. 319–49). San Diego, CA: Academic Press.

Laws, D.R. (1989). *Relapse Prevention with Sex Offenders*. New York: Guilford Press.

Linehan, M.M. (1993). *Cognitive Behavioural Treatment of Borderline Personality Disorder*. New York: Guilford Press.

Marlatt, G.A. & Gordon, J.R. (1985) *Relapse Prevention: Maintenance Strategies in the Treatment of Addictive Behaviors*. New York: Guilford Press.

Marshall, W.L., Ward, T., Mann, R.E., Moulden, H., Fernandez, Y.M. Serran, G.A. & Marshall, L.E. (2005). Working positively with sex offenders: maximizing the effectiveness of treatment. *Journal of Interpersonal Violence*, *20*, 1–19.

McDougall, C. & Clark, D.A. (1991). A risk assessment model. In S. Boddis (Ed.), *Proceedings of the Prison Psychology Conference*. London: Her Majesty's Stationery Office.

McDougall, C., Clark, D.A. & Fisher, M. (1994). Assessment of violent offenders. In M. McMurran & J. Hodge (Eds), *The Assessment of Criminal Behaviours in Secure Settings*. London: Jessica Kingsley.

McGuire, J. (2008). A review of effective interventions for reducing aggression and violence. *Philosophical Transactions of the Royal Society Biological Sciences*, *363*, 2577–97.

Miller, S. & Fritzon, K. (2007). Functional consistency across two behavioural modalities: fire-setting and self-harm in female special hospital patients. *Criminal Behaviour and Mental Health*, *17*, 31–44.

Miltenberger, R.G. (2004). *Behavior Modification: Principles and Procedures* (3rd edition). Pacific Grove, CA: Wadsworth.

Mischel, W. & Shoda, Y. (1995). A cognitive-affective system theory of personality: reconceptualizing situations, dispositions, dynamics, and invariance in personality structure. *Psychological Review*, *102*, 246–68.

Mischel, W. & Shoda, Y. (1999). Integrating dispositions and processing dynamics within a unified theory of personality: the cognitive-affective personality system. In L.A. Pervin (Ed.), *Handbook of Personality: Theory and Research* (2nd edition, pp. 197–218). New York: Guilford Press.

Morris, M. (2004). *Dangerous and Severe: Process, Programme, and Person: Grendon's Work*. London: Jessica Kingsley.

Morton, J. (2004). *Understanding Developmental Disorders: A Causal Modelling Approach*. Oxford: Blackwell.

Murphy, N. & McVey, D. (Eds) (2010). *Treating Personality Disorder: Creating Robust Services for People with Complex Mental Health Needs*. New York: Routledge.

Neville, L., Miller, S. & Fritzon, K. (2007). Understanding change in a therapeutic community: an action systems approach. *Journal of Forensic Psychiatry and Psychology*, *18*, 181–203.

Nisbett, R.E. & Ross, L.D. (1980). *Human Inference: Strategies and Shortcomings of Social Judgment*. Englewood Cliffs, NJ: Prentice-Hall.

Otto, R.K. (2000). Assessing and managing violence risk in outpatient settings. *Journal of Clinical Psychology*, *56*, 1239–62.

Pollock, P.H., Stowell-Smith, M. & Gopfert, M. (2006). *Cognitive Analytic Therapy for Offenders: A New Approach for Forensic Psychotherapy*. London: Routledge.

Ross, L. (1977). The intuitive psychologist and his shortcomings: distortions in the attribution process. In L. Berkowitz (Ed.), *Advances in Experimental Social Psychology* (Vol. 10, pp. 173–220). New York: Academic Press.

Ross, L. & Nisbett, R.E. (1991). *The Person and the Situation: Perspectives of Social Psychology*. New York: McGraw-Hill.

Saucier, G., Bel-Bahar, T. & Fernandez, C. (2007). What modifies the expression of personality tendencies? Defining basic domains of situation variables. *Journal of Personality*, *75*, 479–504.

Shine, J. & Morris, M. (2000). Addressing criminogenic needs in a prison therapeutic community. *Therapeutic Communities*, *21*, 197–218.

Shoda, Y. & Lee Tiernan, S. (2002). What remains invariant? Finding order within a person's thoughts, feelings, and behaviors across situations. In D. Cervone & W. Mischel (Eds), *Advances in Personality Science*, *1*, 241–70.

Shoda, Y. & Mischel, W. (1998). Personality as a stable cognitive-affective activation network: characteristic patterns of behavior variation emerge from a stable personality structure. In S.J. Read & L.C. Miller (Eds.), *Connectionist and PDP Models of Social Reasoning and Social Behavior* (pp. 175–208). Mahwah, NJ: Lawrence Erlbaum.

Shoda, Y. & Mischel, W. (2000). Reconciling contextualism with the core assumptions of personality psychology. *European Journal of Personality*, *14*, 407–28.

Shur, R. (1994). *Countertransference Enactments: How Institutions and Therapists Actualize Primitive Internal Worlds*. Northvale, NJ: Jason Aronson.

Stoller, I. (1986). *Perversion: The Erotic Form of Hatred*. London: Maresfield.

Swann, W.B., Jr & Seyle, C. (2005). Personality psychology's comeback and its emerging symbiosis with social psychology. *Personality and Social Psychology Bulletin*, *31*, 155–65.

Ten Berge, M.A. & De Raad, B. (2002). The structure of situations from a personality perspective. *European Journal of Personality*, *16*, 81–102.

Tonkin, M., Grant T.D. & Bond, J.W. (2008). To link or not to link: a test of the case linkage principles using serial car theft data. *Journal of Investigative Psychology and Offender Profiling*, *5*, 59–77.

Tversky, A. & Kahneman, D. (1974). Judgment under uncertainty: heuristics and biases. *Science*, *185*, 1124–31.

Ward, T., Mann, R.E. & Gannon, T.A. (2007). The good lives model of offender rehabilitation: clinical implications. *Aggression and Violent Behavior: A Review Journal*, *12*, 87–107.

Woodhams, J. & Toye, K. (2007). An empirical test of the assumption of case linkage and offender profiling with serial commercial robberies. *Psychology, Public Policy, and Law*, *13*, 59–85.

Wright, H. & Barker, R.C. (1950). *Methods in Psychological Ecology: A Progress Report*. Oxford: Oxford University Press.

Yang, Y., Read, S.J. & Miller, L. (2006). A taxonomy of situations from Chinese idioms: goal processes as a central organizing principle. *Journal of Research in Personality*, *40*, 750–78.

Young, J.E., Klosko, J.S. & Weishaar, M.E. (2003). *Schema Therapy: A Practitioner's Guide*. New York: Guilford Press.

Chapter 2

CASE FORMULATION IN FORENSIC PSYCHOLOGY

PETER STURMEY

Department of Psychology and the Graduate Center, City University of New York, New York, USA

Case formulation is a generic clinical skill that abstracts key features of a case to guide the selection of the most effective treatment for each specific person (Haynes & O'Brien, 2000). Eells (2007a) suggested that it also serves to integrate diverse client information, assist clients understand their own problems and enhance the therapeutic relationship. Clinicians have applied case formulation to a wide range of mental health problems in children, adolescents and adults (Eells, 1997, 2007b; Hersen & Rosqvist, 2008; Sturmey, 2007, 2008, 2009a, 2009b). Mental health professionals also use case formulation in forensic settings. In addition to the functions that case formulation serves in any context, forensic case formulation serves two functions specific to forensic contexts. Firstly, case formulation may summarize the development of offending and related behaviour (Gresswell & Hollin, 1992). Secondly, it may predict the most effective treatment and (re)habilitation programme for this particular client (Haynes & O'Brien, 2000) and, thus, may reduce the likelihood of future reoffending. The term 'case formulation' may have somewhat distinct meaning within forensic services. In forensic contexts, the term is sometimes used when a mental health professional presents a case formulation to a lawyer or judge and gives an opinion concerning issues such as treatability, risk assessment and likelihood of reoffending.

Forensic clinicians formulate a wide range of mental health problems. Some of these problems are long-standing, severe and dangerous and more commonly encountered in forensic than other settings, such as severe, low-frequency aggression, arson, sexual offending, suicide and self-harm. Forensic mental health professionals also formulate common clinical conditions, such as anxiety, depression and relationship-related problems.

Forensic case formulation is of central importance to professional practice. Job advertisements and description may refer to it. Professional training, such as generic master's degrees in forensic studies, or traditional mental health professional training, such as social work, nursing, psychiatry and psychology, may include training in case formulation. Continuing professional education may also include training in forensic case formulation.

This chapter reviews the definitions and general features of case formulation. It then goes on to discuss forensic case formulation, including using case formulation to understand offending histories, current offending behaviour and current mental health problems. The last section

Offence Paralleling Behaviour: A Case Formulation Approach to Offender Assessment and Intervention Edited by Michael Daffern, Lawrence Jones and John Shine

reviews outstanding issues in case formulation generally, specific challenges in formulating cases in forensic settings and future directions for forensic case formulation.

DEFINITIONS AND CHARACTERISTICS OF CASE FORMULATION

Case formulation is often contrasted with alternative ways to describe cases and to predict optimum treatment. These alternative approaches include diagnosis, actuarial prediction of treatment response and, in the context of forensic services, risk assessment. Typically, proponents of case formulation begin by pointing out that clinicians often use psychiatric diagnosis to predict optimal treatment. Hence, proponents of psychiatric diagnosis often suggest that a psychiatric formulation is necessary to determine the underlying disease, and that once the clinician has done this, the correct diagnosis will accurately predict treatment. We see evidence for this assumption when we refer to classes of psychotropic medications as antidepressants, anxiolytics and antipsychotics. We also see it when therapists organize treatments around diagnoses, for example, when they have specific treatment protocols enshrined in treatment manuals for depression, anorexia, etc., and when they organize group treatment around a particular diagnosis, such as anxiety management. We can also see this assumption when researchers and government agencies organize reviews, expert panels, research funding and meta-analyses of outcome research and treatment guidelines around diagnoses, for example, when the British National Institute for Health and Clinical Excellence publishes treatment guidelines organized around psychiatric diagnoses. So, psychiatric diagnosis is often used to predict the best treatment.

Proponents of case formulation then recite the limitations to psychiatric diagnosis as a predictor of the most effective treatment. These include (a) the unreliability of psychiatric diagnosis; (b) the limited validity of psychiatric diagnosis; (c) the differential response to treatment within a diagnostic group; (d) the lack of external validity of randomized controlled trials based on or around psychiatric diagnoses; (e) the large number of clients who meet multiple diagnoses, and hence the problem of selecting which diagnosis to use to predict treatment; (f) the large number of clients who apparently have already had treatment based on psychiatric diagnosis who have failed to respond to diagnosis-based treatment; (g) the large number of psychiatric diagnoses for which evidence-based guidelines are not yet available; and (h) the large number of unique clients whose clinically significant problems do not fit easily into psychiatric diagnoses. Hence, some books on case formulation refer to case formulation as 'beyond diagnosis' (Bruch & Bond, 1998), imply the limitations of diagnosis by referring to the complexity of cases (Tarrier et al., 1998) or note the importance of function rather than topography as a predictor of effective treatment (Sturmey, 1996, 2007, 2008).

Drake and Ward (2003) noted such problems in relationship to forensic case formulation. They suggested that case formulation might be especially useful in forensic contexts in four situations. Firstly, when an offender presents with multiple, complex problems and the focus of treatment is unclear, for example, when an offender presents with substance abuse, other psychiatric disorders and problematic offending behaviour. Secondly, case formulation might be especially helpful in situations where relatively little is known about a problem, such as internet pornography users or unique constellations of problems. Thirdly, case formulation might be especially helpful in forensic settings where standard treatments have failed to produce a socially significant change in the client's behaviour. They cite the example of an offender who had attended a group treatment programme for sexual offenders. Although he reportedly did well, the treatment was ineffective. This man's problems resulted from unusual sexual experiences when young which may have resulted in erectile dysfunction and premature ejaculation with adult partners. Consequently, he avoided adult sexual relationships. Instead, he turned to sexual behaviour with his partner's children. Only when his clinician correctly identified this problem and implemented treatment to address his sexual dysfunction with adult partners did his deviant sexual behaviour with children decrease. Finally, Drake and Ward suggested that forensic case formulation might be helpful when working with offenders who fail to progress, are disruptive within group treatment or are unmotivated to change because of shame or other personal issues that impede treatment progress.

Let us now move on to consider what case formulation is.

Definitions

Eells (2007a) offered the following definition of case formulation: 'A psychotherapy case formulation is a hypothesis about the causes, precipitants and maintaining influences of a person's psychological, interpersonal, and behavioural problems' (p. 4). Such a definition is theory-neutral and could be used to apply to a variety of approaches to case formulation. In fact, authors have made formulations from behavioural, cognitive, psychodynamic, humanistic, psychiatric and eclectic approaches (Dallos & Johnstone, 2005; Eells, 1997, 2007b; Hersen & Rosqvist, 2008; Sturmey, 2007, 2008, 2009a). Sturmey (2009b) noted that these different approaches share five features. First, case formulations are relatively brief. They are unlike an extensive, narrative history or detailed list of all of a client's presenting complaints and problematic situations. Rather, case formulations abstract certain cardinal features of a case that are given precedence over other information. For example, cognitive formulations might give precedence to identifying underlying cognitive schemas, rather than each and every instance of cognitive misattributions. Second, case formulations attempt to integrate or unify diverse information into a few key concepts. For example, a behavioural formulation might suggest that several topographically different forms of both adaptive and problematic behaviours all serve the same function, since the same establishing operations, discriminative stimuli and contingencies all control several topographically distinct adaptive and problematic behaviours. Third, formulations often attempt to account for both the development of the problem and the current factors that maintain the problem. For example, a psychodynamic formulation might suggest that relationship patterns during early development parallel the presenting problems and the client–therapist interactions. Fourth, formulations direct idiographic treatment. For example, a psychiatric formulation might indicate that the client's problems result from an underlying biological illness called schizophrenia and that treatment should consist of antipsychotic (rather than anxiolytic or antidepressant) medication and adjunctive treatments, such as education about the disease and input from a multidisciplinary team. Finally, most approaches to case formulation note that formulations are tentative, have boundaries and may be revised in the light of new information. For example, a failure to respond to the first intervention based on an initial formulation might provide additional information concerning family interaction patterns that inadvertently maintain a client's problems that was not available during initial assessment. This would result in a revised formulation and a new treatment plan that would take this new information into account and lead to a second treatment plan.

Clinicians have made case formulations from a variety of theoretical perspectives. Most books in this area discuss case formulation from cognitive (Persons, 1989, 2008) and cognitive–behavioural perspectives (Bruch & Bond, 1998; Gauss, 2007; Nezu et al., 2004; Persons, 1989, 2008; Tarrier, 2006; Tarrier et al., 1998). There are also publications on case formulation from behavioural (Dougher, 2000; Sturmey, 1996, 2008; Turkat, 1985, 1990), psychodynamic (McWilliams, 1999) and eclectic perspectives (Weerasekera, 1996). Finally, Sturmey (2009a) provided illustrations of case formulations of the same cases made from a variety of perspectives; Dallos and Johnstone (2005) also contrasted alternative approaches to formulating the same case. The next subsections discuss these different approaches to case formulation.

Behavioural Approaches

There is a long history to behavioural approaches to case formulation, which date back to Skinner's (1953, 1971) generic case formulations of depression, the role of learning in psychopathology and behavioural models of therapeutic change. Skinner (1953) speculated that mental health problems resulted from a variety of factors, but gave the greatest prominence to learning processes. One example of learning that might result in acquisition and maintenance of psychopathology relates to fear. Stimuli that in the past have been associated with punishment often disrupt ongoing adaptive behaviour and learning. Anxiolytic drugs often attenuate the disruptive effects of these stimuli on adaptive behaviour (Estes & Skinner, 1941). These observations suggested that this experimental model may be a behavioural model of fears and anxiety disorders. Another example of a learning mechanism that may result in the acquisition of psychopathology may be the effects of the loss of opportunities to emit previously effective adaptive behaviour and the loss of opportunities for reinforcement of previously reinforced adaptive behaviour. For example, common stressful life events, such as changes in residence, new jobs, new social roles, such as retirement, and losses, such as bereavement, all involve these two key features. For example, after bereavement, the bereaved person can no longer engage in social activities with the deceased person, and the deceased person can no longer reinforce the survivor's adaptive behaviour (Skinner, 1971). When multiple stressful life events occur, such as marriage, change in residence and a new job, then the multiple losses of opportunity to emit previously effective behaviour and multiple losses of reinforcers may place the person at particular risk for psychopathology.

Skinner (1953) suggested that a key aspect of intervention for psychopathology was the acquisition of a generalized repertoire of self-control skills. Skinner described self-control as merely one example of control of behaviour of other people, but in this case the person doing the controlling and being controlled was one and the same. Thus, we might leave a note for a family member to pick up the laundry or leave a note for oneself to pick up the laundry. In both examples, the person presents an antecedent stimulus (the note) to increase the likelihood of someone picking up the laundry; in the first example, the person being changed is a family member, and in the second example, the person leaving the note and picking up the laundry is one and the same. Skinner suggested that two classes of responses were involved in self-control: the controlling and the controlled responses. The controlling response (leaving a note) is a response that changes the probability of a controlled response (picking up the laundry). The focus of behavioural analysis is on the variables that influence the emission of the controlling response. The behaviour analysis of self-control focuses on the environmental variables that influence the emission of the controlling response, such as social and non-social antecedents and consequences that influence the likelihood and effectiveness of the controlling response. For example, a behaviour analyst might ask what variables make it most likely that a person will leave a note for themselves and what kind of note will be most effective in changing the probability of picking up the laundry.

Skinner (1953) gave numerous everyday examples of self-control. We sugarcoat pills and chase them down with a glass of water to reduce the likelihood of choking and increase the likelihood of swallowing. We make undesirable behaviour more difficult when we leave our credit card at home or only take a few cigarettes to work. We make alternative desirable behaviour more likely when we take a healthy lunch to work, instead of eating unhealthy and expensive restaurant food. We sometimes modify our own behaviour through consumption of caffeine, alcohol and other substances. We even punish our own inappropriate behaviour when we reprimand ourselves and slap our own face for talking out of turn or slap our own hand when reaching for a third biscuit.

Perhaps the most interesting and clinically relevant might be suicide as an example of self-control. Skinner (1953) observed that by killing oneself (the controlling response) one reduces the future probability of all behaviour, including painful and aversive behaviour (the controlled responses) to zero. The example is not facetious. Subsequent work with suicidal clients, such as dialectical behaviour therapy (DBT) and cognitive–behavioural interventions, can readily be interpreted as examples of teaching clients a generalized repertoire of controlling responses. For example, in DBT, the therapist identifies and teaches the client to discriminate response chains that result in suicidal gestures and attempts. Various interventions, such as engaging in alternative behaviour early in the response chain, can be described as controlling responses that make suicidal behaviour less likely. Intervention strategies, such as splashing one's face with ice-cold water, might be construed as an example of punishment of one's own behaviour early in the response chain, which again reduces the future probability of suicidal behaviour. The DBT therapist instructs their client to apply these strategies to all new challenging situations and reinforces their client's appropriate use of these skills. In this way, the DBT therapist teaches their client a generalized repertoire of controlling responses that can be applied to novel situations without direct teaching.

Skinner further elaborated on self-control and the role of the therapist. He suggested that therapists should not present the clients with solutions to their problems, even if the therapist believes that they have an effective solution. Skinner gave two reasons for this. The first, a pragmatic one, is that many clients may reject such solutions out of hand. A second more subtle reason is this. Skinner suggested that the therapist's job was to teach their clients to discriminate the relationship between the environment and their own adaptive and problematic behaviour, in effect, to generate their own behavioural formulation of their problem. In so doing the therapist will have done two things. They will have subtly begun the process of behaviour change before a formal treatment plan is begun. By teaching their client to discriminate and articulate the relationship between the environment and their own behaviour, they will have begun to teach them a generalized repertoire of self-control that the client may emit when novel, future problems arise and the therapist is no longer available. For example, suppose a client learns to discriminate that they often stay in bed and feel depressed during weekends. They might also notice that on some weekends when they engage in physical activity they get out of bed and feel less depressed. If they figure out to get a friend to call them early on Saturday mornings to meet up for a jog (the controlling behaviour), then they are much more likely to engage in mood-elevating exercise (the controlled response).

Skinner's work was very influential in subsequent behavioural conception and treatment of psychopathology, especially depression (Ferster, 1973), including contemporary work on behavioural activation (Hopko et al., 2003) and other behavioural accounts of depression (Kohlenberg & Tsai, 1994). Turkat (1985) expanded the application of behavioural approaches to case formulation to address such diverse problems as anxiety, depression, substance abuse and a variety of personality disorders (Turkat, 1990). Sturmey (2007) provided examples of the application of behavioural formulations to a wide range of psychopathology, including schizophrenia, substance abuse, and so on. Thus, clinicians and researchers have applied behavioural approaches to case formulation to a wide range of common clinical problems.

Cognitive and Cognitive–Behavioural Approaches

Persons (1989, 2008) wrote two highly influential volumes on cognitive approaches to case formulation. She suggested that cognitive case formulation involved collecting evidence about the client's behaviour, thoughts and emotions and using this to infer problems in the underlying cognitive schemas that influence the client's maladaptive thinking that resulted in the client's presenting problems. Her approach was greatly influenced by Beck. In Persons' approach the therapist draws up a problem list with the client to specify target problems and priorities for treatment. The cognitive model uses observations of client's behaviour and self-report of cognitions and emotions to infer underlying maladaptive cognitive schemata and automatic thought processes and the environmental triggers that precipitate them. By using techniques such as Socratic reasoning and behavioural experiments to test and hopefully disconfirm these maladaptive thinking patterns, cognitive therapy aims to change these underlying beliefs and thereby change current behaviour.

Some approaches to cognitive formulation incorporate to varying degrees of explicitness elements of behavioural approaches to case formulation. These may include the operant nature of symptoms and alternative behaviour, such as the importance of avoidance in anxiety and depression in maintaining these symptomatic behaviours. Cognitive–behavioural formulations generally eschew the technically correct language and conceptual foundations of behaviour analysis. So, cognitive–behavioural formulations may hint at operant mechanisms maintaining symptomatic behaviour by saying 'Mary is avoidant of other critical people and cries a lot' rather than 'Mary's crying and feigning minor illnesses are negatively reinforced by avoidance of interaction with others, especially criticism'.

Cognitive and cognitive–behavioural approaches to case formulation are currently the dominant approach to case formulation; most case formulation books adopt this approach. Cognitive and cognitive–behavioural approaches have expanded to account for such diverse problems as a wide variety of anxiety disorders, eating disorders, psychoses and substance abuse disorders. An important controversy remains over what the effective elements of cognitive–behavioural approaches are and the role of behavioural mechanisms in change in cognitive and cognitive–behaviour therapy (Sturmey, 2008).

Psychodynamic Approaches

Messer and Wolitzky (2007) defined psychodynamic case formulation as:

> A hierarchically organized set of clinical inferences about the nature and a patient's psychopathology, and, more generally, about his or her personality structure, dynamics, and development ... generated in the course of the psychoanalytically informed interview include the presumed reasons for the patient's experience and behaviour such as symptoms, dreams, fantasies, and maladaptive patterns of interpersonal relationships. (Messer & Wolitzky, 2007, p. 67)

There are several good resources that illustrate psychodynamic approaches to formulation including McWilliams' (1999) volume and several psychodynamic case formulations in Eells (1997, 2007b) and Sturmey (2009a). Psychodynamic case formulation takes current symptoms as symbols of unconscious fears and assumes the patient is unaware of their meaning and developmental origin. For example, fear of being trapped in a crowded elevator between floors might be taken as a symbol of an underlying fear of being trapped in a relationship, which would result in a loss of personal identity. This approach to case formulation assumes that many clients are unaware of the meanings of their symptoms and so the therapist's job is to infer these hidden meanings and their likely developmental sequence and to make them known to the client by providing interpretations of their symptoms and other aspects of their behaviour. Psychodynamic approaches to case formulation assume that this revelation of the meaning and symptoms disclosed during the special client–therapist relationship is the vehicle for symptom relief and behavioural change.

One approach to psychodynamic case formulation is Luborsky's Core Conflictual Relationship Theme (CCRT; Luborsky & Barrett, 2007). The CCRT method is used to define the common themes that run across many relationships that the patient describes in psychotherapy sessions. The therapist transcribes and analyses the session to identify the patterns of patient's wishes and other people's responses and the patient's responses. The therapist codes each relationship episode using a standardized coding system and analyses the pattern of responses across many such relationship episodes to identify the CCRT. The therapist uses this information in session to make interpretations. For example, Luborsky and Barrett (2007) reported a CCRT of a depressed 32-year-old woman who had a history of alcohol abuse. Analysing her response episodes leads to one interpretation, which was 'I see you get depressed after you deal with people who won't give you what you need' (p. 118).

Psychodynamic approaches differ markedly from behavioural and cognitive and cognitive–behavioural approaches to case formulation. Psychodynamic approaches see the vehicle for change as being the therapeutic relationship and interpretation, rather than learning, changes in current behaviour or changes in cognitive processes. Psychodynamic approaches also place more weight on history than these other approaches.

Eclectic Approaches

In *Multiperspective Case Formulation*, Weerasekera (1996) presented one systematic approach to eclectic case formulation that summarizes predisposing, precipitating, perpetuating and protective factors from each of eight individual and systemic factors. Individual factors include biological, behavioural, cognitive and psychodynamic factors, and systemic factors include couple, family, occupational/school and social factors. Weerasekera suggested that the therapist formulates cases from each of these eight perspectives and then integrates each of the eight formulations into one unified, eclectic formulation, which the therapist uses to develop an individual treatment plan, which typically involves several different kinds of interventions. Weerasekera presented this information in a grid (pp. 276–7).

Weerasekera (1996) illustrated this method by formulating the case of Susan who has a two-year history of vomiting, anxiety symptoms, which mostly occur outside the home, and avoidance of large social gatherings. These events were relatively recent and began after a break-up of a relationship with a married man. It is not possible to summarize all of this formulation here, but a partial illustration follows. Examples of biological factors included predisposition towards anxiety from a family history and biological protective factors included good general health. Examples of family precipitating factors included imminent separation from her family and leaving her mother alone, and family perpetuating factors included parental marital discord. Formulation from the eight perspectives suggested many possible treatments. Examples included behavioural treatments, such as exposure therapy. Formulation of couples of factors suggested that these issues should be addressed later, rather than immediately.

Weerasekera is but one eclectic approach to case formulation. Other eclectic approaches to case formulation include cognitive analytic approaches (Dunn, 2009), which blend psychodynamic, cognitive and other approaches. Some forms of cognitive–behavioural therapy also blend behavioural, cognitive and sometimes psychodynamic concepts.

COMMENTARY

These approaches to case formulation share a number of features and agree on a number of functions of case formulation. These differences include (a) which variables are given importance; (b) which variables are the causes of the client's problems; (c) the relative weight given to history; (d) the variables which can be manipulated to result in change in the client's behaviour; and (e) the relative importance and function of the therapeutic relationship (Sturmey, 2009b). Integrationists see these differences as relatively unimportant; others see them as fundamental and irreconcilable differences in approaches to behaviour.

Formulations of Common Forensic Problems

Clinicians in forensic services work with a very wide range of problems some of which relate to offending behaviour, some of which may be independent of offending behaviour and some of which may result from interaction with the justice system. In addition to formulating mental health problems, practitioners in forensic settings also make formulations of offending behaviour itself. This may include understanding how offending behaviour developed and the influence of the current environment on offending behaviour in order to develop treatment plans that address reoffending.

Formulations of Development of Offending Behaviour

There are several examples of formulations of the development of offending behaviour. These include Gresswell and Hollin's (1992) formulation of the development of multiple murder, Daffern et al.'s (2007b) formulations of a violent offender's behaviour (p. 269) and Drake and Ward's (2003) pathway model of sexual offending.

Multiple Murder Formulated

An interesting account of the development of an apparently senseless attempt to murder two people and a formulated plan to kill a further 20 people comes from Gresswell and Hollin (1992). They organized historical case material from 300 pages of records and 16 hours of interviews into seven interlocking ABC formulations which attempt to account for the gradual evolution of behaviour over the person's lifespan. The man had cold and insensitive parents, and embarrassing medical problems, such as undescended testicles and acne. During his teenage years, his peers rejected him and he learnt to search through his parents' papers in an attempt to get to know them; he also attempted suicide three times. He began to engage in problematic covert behaviour, such as revenge fantasies, and beliefs that he was better than other people which resulted in his feeling better. When he began to work, he learnt to cover up his social problems by lying and presenting himself as socially successful, while simultaneously being anxious concerning dating women. During this time he had one unsuccessful date and attempted suicide again. Later, when he was 29 years old, a plastic surgeon told him that his acne was untreatable, which led him to feel angry towards the surgeon and humiliated. His mother also died at this time, and this resulted in him ruminating on death and fantasizing about having friends when he was dead. These problems resulted in yet further social isolation. He then moved to public housing, was overtly hostile at work and was anxious and depressed. He began to have revenge fantasies about work and also began taking a knife with him to work. Subsequently, he began to believe that customers who came into the place where he worked knew about his sexual inadequacy, only ate his lunch in the car and began taking a wooden doweling to work, again as part of a revenge fantasy. Following another overdose and admission to a psychiatric hospital, he was told nothing could be done to stop him committing a massacre.

The next key trigger was the Hungerford massacre, an event covered extensively in the UK national media, in which one man killed many people. He then began to prowl at night searching for potential victims. He found prowling to be exciting and it made him feel confident. Repeating earlier behaviour with his parents, he now stalked specific victims and opened their mail; however, prowling eventually seemed to be pointless.

The final formulation related to the events leading up to the two attempted murders. Firstly, his painting was rejected for an exhibition and, secondly, the police interviewed him about an assault that someone else had committed. These two events led him to conclude that if someone else could do it, so could he. Subsequently, he obtained a crowbar and committed some acts of minor vandalism. At the one-year anniversary of him telling his general practitioner about his fantasies, he broke into an elderly woman's house, beat her with a dowelling club, went home, felt that he had done well and that his victim could never have peace. That night he slept well. A week later after a counselling session, he began stalking for another victim in order to slash their face, but could not find any victim and felt dissatisfied. So, he waited several hours outside a victim's house and stabbed the victim when he got out of his car. The police arrested him when the victim's wife called the police.

Gresswell and Hollin (1992) summarized the very large quantity of clinical material they collected in only seven tables using an ABC format. This formulation is also notable because the final, apparently incomprehensible attempted murders are understandable as the outcome of learning over the perpetrator's lifespan. No transition from one formulation to another is dramatic, but the final outcome was the learning of a behavioural repertoire which resulted in (a) the failure to acquire many adaptive behaviours, such as social problem-solving and self-regulation skills; (b) a failure to acquire typical secondary social reinforcers, such as those related to friendship and intimacy; (c) an unusual range of secondary negative reinforcers, such as reduction in unpleasant internal states through revenge fantasies; and (d) the acquisition of problematic cover behaviour, such as revenge fantasies, and overt behaviour, such as stalking and attempting to kill two people. The final formulation that encapsulated the presenting problem was that minor social events triggered massacre and revenge fantasies, which were a pleasurable way of coping with extreme despair. Gresswell and Hollin noted that this formulation had implications for treatment and rehabilitation including teaching him a range of skills to cope with social disappointments, social intimacy and triggers for violence.

A Violent Offender

Daffern et al. (2007b) provided a second example of a history-oriented formulation of Paul, which was part of a formulation that included formulations of current factors which are discussed below. Paul had been adopted with his twin sister, but he felt that his adoptive parents had always ignored him in favour of his sister. He spent much of his time daydreaming. After leaving home for college, he left a home-made bomb in a shopping centre and called the police to tell them it was there. Later, he committed a prolonged and sadistic attack on a young woman who was unknown to him. Paul reported that he withdrew into a fantasy world before both offences after he believed no one had noticed him. In this fantasy world, he thought about shocking and frightening people in order to let them know he existed.

A Typology of Sexual Offending

Drake and Ward (2003) developed the pathway model of sexual offending behaviour. This model proposed that there are five typologies of sexual offences, each associated with a characteristic developmental pathway. Pathway 1 was characterized by offenders with deficits in intimacy and social skills due to insecure attachment, resulting in problems trusting others, difficult adult relationships, low self-esteem and reduced personal autonomy. Pathway 2 was characterized by deficits in sexual scripts, such as seeking sex in inappropriate places with inappropriate partners or engaging in inappropriate behaviour. These deficient sexual scripts come from early deviant learning or inappropriate sexual experiences. Pathway 3 was characterized by the development of emotional dysregulation. These offenders failed to learn to recognize and name emotions, have learnt poor or inappropriate coping strategies, may use sex inappropriately as a coping strategy, and engage in acting out, which results in sexual offences. Pathway 4 was characterized by cognitive distortions, which may be specific to sexual behaviour or part of a more general set of beliefs about the world. Finally, Pathway 5 was characterized by deficits in all of the above.

Commentary

History-based formulations are tempting, perhaps even more so in forensic than other cases, since clinicians must account for often extreme and intense behaviour and sometimes seemingly random acts of violence. Plausibly accounting for the development of such behaviour may be useful to team members in trying to understand offending behaviour, and it might be a useful clinical tool with some offenders to develop a rational treatment plan.

Different approaches to case formulation place different emphases on history; indeed, some, such as psychodynamic approaches (McWilliams, 1999), place great weight on revealing links between developmental history and presenting problems, since psychodynamic approaches see it as the vehicle for change (Malan, 1979). In contract, other approaches place emphasis only on those variables that can be changed, that are causal to the presenting problems and that can be readily manipulated (Haynes & O'Brien, 2000). History *may* parallel the presenting problem. For example, Wolpe's approach to case formulation often involved a careful search for potential conditioning events; however, these historical conditioning events are useful, not only because they reveal the history of the presenting problem, but also because they reveal relevant conditioned stimuli *in the current environment* that sometimes clients are unable or reluctant to report and that could be incorporated into treatment (Wolpe & Turkat, 1985). Thus, not all approaches place value on history.

History-based approaches to forensic case formulation have significant limitations. These include (a) the likelihood that sometimes relevant clinical material may be incomplete and/or unavailable; (b) offenders may lie, distort and omit relevant clinical material and are sometimes highly skilled at doing so; (c) third parties, such as professional and non-professional staff and family members, may also have a variety of motivations to report history inaccurately; and (d) the offender's presenting problems may sometimes reflect their history, but this is not always the case. Thus, forensic clinicians should be cautious when making history-based case formulations.

Current Offending Behaviour

Forensic case formulations may also include current factors. Examples of these kinds of formulations include Nezu et al.'s (1997) formulation of aggressive sexual behaviour in a man with low average intelligence and acquired brain damage and Daffern et al.'s (2007a, 2007b) formulation of an offender with multiple problems.

Nezu et al. (1997) described a problem-solving, behavioural formulation of a 27-year-old male sexual offender (DJ) referred because of multiple problems whom services had referred for a psychological evaluation, risk assessment and treatment recommendations. DJ's problems included sexually aggressive behaviour, such as beating a women and attempted rape of a 12-year-old girl when he was 18 years old. His records indicated that he had been injured in a hit-and-run accident, having attended special education classes, and was labelled as 'emotionally disturbed', 'neurologically impaired' and 'borderline retarded'. Recent problems included an extended period of hospitalization, social withdrawal, agitation, suicidal gestures and attempting to choke a social worker. These problems had fluctuated during hospitalization, but had not stabilized. He also took carbamazapine for a seizure disorder.

Nezu et al. (1997) stated that the aims of their assessment were:

> '(1) to identify internal and external conditions affecting the probability of DJ's behaviour problems;
>
> (2) to identify the behavioural, cognitive, and affective topographical components of the client's presenting problems;
>
> (3) to identify various client-specific biological, developmental, social learning, and environmental variables that may have been functionally related to his current difficulties; and
>
> (4) to develop clinical hypotheses and a C[linical] P[athogenesis] M[ap] of the functional relationships among these variables. (Nezu et al., 1997, p. 390)

A clinical pathogenesis map (CPM) is a tool to organize the information about a case and predict the most effective treatment. A CPM is a pictorial representation which includes the developmental history, recent stressful events, relevant stimuli and current dysfunctional system that is similar to a path analysis or causal model. Thus, a CPM integrates history and current environmental variables into the formulation.

To obtain the information necessary to construct the CPM of DJ's problems, Nezu et al. (1997) collected assessment information from multiple sources. The use of multiple sources of information is a key feature of some behavioural approaches to case formulation (Haynes & O'Brien, 2000; Lappalainen et al., 2009). In DJ's case the multiple sources of information included a semi-structured interview with the client, staff interviews, a review of records, a reevaluation of his intelligence, self-report psychometric assessments of social problem-solving skills, role-play assessment of assertive and heterosexual skills and of anger-arousing situations, a cognition scale and group staff and therapists' collected ABC and other behavioural records of problem behaviour.

Intellectual assessment revealed that he functioned in the low average range, had no significant difference among subscale scores and had relative strengths in comprehension and relative weakness in abstract thinking. On self-report measures, he reported feelings of inadequacy, helplessness, loneliness, fear, hypersensitivity, hostility to others, especially women, sadness and depression and prominent anxiety. He declined to answer questions about sexual matters, other than admitting to fantasies about the same-aged women. His problem-solving skills were generally weak in all areas, including identifying situations as problematic, the consequences of his actions, strong use of avoidance coping and impulsivity in response to stress. His responses to assertive role-play situations were aggressive and sexualized, but there was some indication that he had some knowledge of socially assertive behaviour. He also displayed loud and aggressive behaviour in anger-provoking situations. His cognition assessment indicated beliefs consistent with paedophilia, such as a belief that a child who does not resist wants to have sex. Observational data indicated that antecedents for aggression were often misinterpretation of other people's behaviour. Consequences included staff attempting to calm him down, leaving him alone and threats of loss of privileges. Perceived losses and failure to change the topic when others constructively discussed his difficulties often triggered suicidal talk.

Nezu et al. (1997) combined all this information, summarized it in a CPM and provided the following narrative case formulation of aggressive behaviour:

> . . . cognitive deficits in areas such as concrete thinking . . . appeared to represent significant obstacles for coping effectively with various emotional triggers . . . behavioral difficulties appeared to be functionally related to a combination of organic processing deficits, emotional dysregulation, and an often idiosyncratic and cross-situational way of misinterpreting environmental events . . . several caregivers . . . had historically reacted to his distortion of events in argumentative or verbally combative ways . . . [which] served as antecedents to escalations of aggressive behavior . . . there has been consistent and reinforcing consequences . . . in that people . . . often became frightened by such episodes and tended to increase social attention by attempting to calm him down. (Nezu et al., 1997, p. 393)

Nezu et al. (1997) also provided a formulation of his sexual problems. They suggested that his skill deficits in areas such as social problem-solving, withdrawing into work and denying problems contributed to the development of this problem. Triggers in the current environment included criticisms at work and women he was attracted to rejecting him, even though he insisted he has no interest in sex. Finally, they also noted that DJ probably met diagnostic criteria for depression, reflected in labile mood and suicidal gestures.

Based on these two formulations, Nezu et al. (1997) made the following treatment recommendations. First, DJ should learn emotional regulation and problem-solving skills, perhaps through group and individual therapy, to expose him to stressors, such as perceived insults and rejection, in order to provide opportunities to reinforce tolerating distress and effective coping. Second, therapists and staff should react to his angry behaviour, not by challenging him, but by empathic statements, such as 'it must be frightening to have such thoughts' and redirecting him to other strategies to deal with distress. Finally, there should be a plan in place to deal with emergencies, such as major losses, which would be a day off from programming to avoid further triggers at a high-risk time. Nezu et al. also noted the tentative nature of the formulation and plan and the need to revise both as treatment proceeded.

A second forensic case formulation based on current factors comes from Daffern et al. (2007b) who reported case formulations of current offending and offence paralleling behaviour (OPB) of Paul, the case discussed earlier related to history-based formulations. Some of Paul's current problems included unassertiveness and retreating into a fantasy world. Staff described him as being a 'model patient', in that he was almost invisible; however, his problems became apparent when he wrote sadistic letters to female staff on three occasions. Interviews with him revealed that he enjoyed shocking practitioners with his violent sexual fantasies and enjoyed other people's shocked and fearful reactions to them. He also reported spending extensive periods fantasizing how to do this and that when he acted on these fantasies he briefly felt relieved.

Daffern et al. (2007a, 2007b) used this information to develop a treatment plan based on this formulation, which included five elements. First, Paul should recognize and express feelings of being neglected by others. Second, when staff and others neglected him he should assert himself, for example, after other patients had been shown unfair preference. Third, when he felt frightened or non-existent, he should talk and interact with people, rather than engage in deviant and isolated fantasy. Fourth, his therapy should include further exploration with him as to how this pattern of behaviour had been learnt. Finally, his plan should not include telling Paul to stop engaging in problematic behaviour, as this might only teach him not to report problematic behaviour, such as covert fantasizing.

Offence Paralleling Behaviour

OPB is one recently developed approach to formulating current offending behaviour (Jones, 1997). An obvious problem for forensic clinicians is the extreme difficulty in observing offending behaviour and the subsequent reliance on potentially inaccurate verbal reports of behaviour from the client and others. In response to this problem, Jones (1997) proposed the notion of OPB as a surrogate for offending behaviour. He defined OPB as:

> Any form of offence related behavioural (or fantasised behaviour) pattern that emerges at any point before or after an offence. It does not have to result in an offence; it simply needs to resemble, in some significant aspect, the sequence of behaviours leading up to the offence. (Jones, 2004, p. 38)

This chain of offence behaviour is conceived functionally rather than structurally (Sturmey et al., 2007). Daffern et al. (2007b) offered a more limited notion of OPB further by restricting its use to behavioural chains. They defined OPB as:

> a behavioural sequence incorporating overt behaviours (that may be muted by environmental factors), appraisals, expectations, beliefs, affects, goals and behavioural scripts, all of which may be influenced by the patient's mental disorder, that is functionally similar to behavioural sequences involved in previous criminal acts. (Daffern et al., 2007b, p. 267)

They noted that OPB does not have to be topographically similar to offending, but needs only to have functional equivalence to the chain of offending behaviour. They suggested that sequences of observed behaviour in clinical settings may be useful in making formulations of clinical and offending behaviour and in determining treatment, especially interventions early in the response chain. They illustrated this principle with the example of self-mutilation observed in a secure setting which may have served the same function as a violent index offence. Although the clinicians could not have observed offending behaviour because of the lack of opportunity to do so in secure settings, they could observe self-mutilation. To the extent that these two topographically different behaviours are functionally equivalent, formulation of self-mutilation might inform formulation and intervention with future violent offences.

OPB makes note of two other response classes that are relevant to conducting a forensic case formulation. These are prosocial alternative behaviours (PABs) and detection evasion skills (DES). A PAB is a behaviour that is functionally equivalent to the offending behaviour. For example, if the offending behaviour results in sexual arousal, then a PAB should also result in sexual arousal, but in an acceptable way, such as private masturbation to adult pornography. DES refers to a repertoire of behaviour that makes detection of an offence or OPB difficult. For example, when asked if the sexual offender touched a female staff, the offender might reply, 'Not really, I just slipped. She didn't understand that I slipped so she made a mistake when she said I tried to touch her'. The OPB of touching a female staff might be positively reinforced by sexual arousal, and the DES of lying may be negatively reinforced by avoidance of the negative consequence of detection. If the sexual offender replied that actually he had touched the female staff member, then he may have lost privileges, including access to female staff, and been reprimanded by staff and other inmates. Thus, OFB and DES would have been maintained and honest reporting of OPB weakened.

During an intervention, a clinician might attempt to increase a PAB in order to decrease an OPB. Given the history of many offenders to evade detection of their offending effectively, an apparent reduction in an OPB must also be accompanied by an increase in PAB. For example, if a formulation of aggressive behaviour indicated that aggression was maintained by a lack of assertive skills, then an effective treatment should result in both reductions in aggressive behaviour and simultaneous increases in assertive behaviour in settings and situations that provoke aggression.

Offence Paralleling Behaviour and Case Formulation

Like other functional approaches to case formulation, the OPB approach may be useful in making formulations and translating them into treatment plans. Forensic services often cannot intervene directly with highly dangerous offending behaviour and/or very low-frequency, intense behaviour, which may never occur in the treatment setting. An OPB formulation may be useful because it may identify behaviour in the current environment that clinical teams can address on a daily basis that may be related to offending. An OPB formulation may be helpful in identifying alternative functionally equivalent behaviour (PABs) that can be strengthened in the forensic setting. It may also allow reduction and weakening of responses that are early members of a response chain in which the offending behaviour is the terminal response. Identifying and weakening DES responses might also be a useful function of an OPB formulation and treatment plan. To the extent that forensic services are effective in doing so and promoting generalization of change from the forensic setting to the natural environment, then OPB formulations might lead to effective intervention plans.

OPB formulation plans might have a more indirect benefit to both service and clients. Some forensic services are often conflicted between their role in protection of the public from future potential harm, punishing the client (in the vernacular sense) for previous offences and providing an active and meaningful (re)habilitation service. In some situations where treatment options seem unavailable or hopeless, service may slip into custodial care and only pay lip service to the (re)habilitation functions that forensic services may play. OPB formulations are one way in which forensic service can address this problem since OPB formulations may give forensic services something to work on, a focus of (re)habilitation and a rationale for an overall treatment plan. Finally, an OPB formulation also has the potential to assist the client in making sense of their own problems, giving them a rationale for their own plan of (re)habilitation and perhaps encouraging their participation in making the formulation and treatment plan.

CONCURRENT MENTAL HEALTH PROBLEMS

Behavioural Approaches to Aggressive Behaviour

As noted earlier, forensic practitioners make case formulations of the full range of clinical problems. Discussion of such a wide range of applications is beyond the scope of one chapter, but the reader may refer to several sources of case formulations illustrating the application of behavioural, cognitive, cognitive–behavioural, psychodynamic, psychiatric and eclectic approaches to case formulation (Eells, 1997, 2007b; Sturmey, 2009a, 2009b). Although there are examples of forensic case formulations of other common problems, such as arson, personality disorders, sexual offending and substance abuse, this section focuses on one problem commonly encountered in forensic setting – aggressive behaviour.

It is difficult to define aggressive behaviour for several reasons. First, authors use a variety of terms with overlapping connotations, such as violence, anger, disturbed behaviour and disruptive behaviour. Some authors restrict these terms to physical aggression between people, such as throwing a chair at staff and hitting the staff. Others use these terms more broadly to include verbal behaviour, such as threats and cognitions, and emotions, such as angry thoughts. The term is also used to refer to property destruction, such as throwing furniture against walls. Many authors also offer distinctions based on its putative causes, rather than topography. Common examples here include two types of aggression, a first, variously referred to as angry, reactive, affective, hostile, impulsive, retaliatory and emotional aggression, and a second, referred to as instrumental aggression (Daffern et al., 2007b). Another common distinction regarding the putative causes of aggressive behaviour is that between so-called illness-related and behavioural aggression. The former connotes involuntary aggression due to a possible mental illness with a biological cause for which the client is not responsible and which must be treated with medical interventions, such as psychotropic medication. The latter connotes aggressive behaviour that is voluntary, which the client could have controlled, that service providers can treat using learning-based interventions and that could reasonably result in punishment (in the vernacular sense of this word). When defining aggressive behaviour, some authors have included other relevant behaviour, such as social skills (Frederiksen et al., 1976), coping, problem-solving, relaxation or other replacement behaviours. Other such analyses include precursor behaviour or, more recently, OPB (Daffern et al., 2007a; Jones, 1997).

Aggressive behaviour is significant to both the client and society. It is a common problem in some forensic populations. It may also result in the likelihood of more restrictive sentencing, longer, more restrictive sectioning under mental health legislature and more restrictive interventions methods, such as treatment in locked facilities, restraint, seclusion, multiple psychotropic medication and PRN ('as needed') medication.

Several recent papers have attempted to conduct assessments of aggressive behaviour in forensic settings that produce information that could inform case formulation. For example, Shepherd and Lavender (1999) analysed the antecedents and management strategies of 130 incidents in a psychiatric hospital that took place over a five-month period. Records included the behaviour, its antecedents and consequences, severity ratings and the location. There were marked effects of location: 93% of incidents took place on the ward and 75% took place in the day room, whereas *none* took place during therapeutic activities, such as groups. Approximately one-third of patients accounted for two-thirds of all incidents. Although there were approximately equal proportions of staff and patients as victims, 72% of victims were male. Interestingly, 58% of victims were male nursing auxiliaries, but only 37% of victims were male staff nurses. External antecedents were more common than internal antecedents. For example, arguments with others, provocation by others, staff insisting on activities, lack of cigarettes and ward restrictions were common social antecedents. Most intrapersonal antecedents were unspecified and only a few were related to delusions and voices. Physical interventions, such as control and restraint procedures and PRN medications, were more common than verbal consequences, such as counselling.

McDougall (2000) conducted a survey of the antecedents and consequences of violent incidents in a forensic adolescent unit. He analysed records of 219 violent incidents in a medium-secure inpatient unit for 20 boys and seven girls detained under the British mental health legislation. The participants' median age at the time of admission was 15 years (range 12–18 years). The most common mental health diagnoses were schizophrenia (44%) and conduct disorder (22%). Over half had been convicted of offences prior to admission, including grievous bodily harm ($N = 7$), murder ($N = 2$), attempted murder ($N = 1$), arson with intent to endanger life ($N = 1$), sexual offences ($N = 1$), possession of a firearm ($N = 1$) and damage to property ($N = 1$). The remainder were detained because of high risk or dangerous behaviour.

McDougall (2000) reported both inter- and intrapersonal antecedents to violent incidents. The most common interpersonal antecedents to violent incidents were hostility, threats of violence, anger, touch and limit setting, each of which occurred in approximately half of all incidents.

Intrapersonal antecedents were less common. The most common intrapersonal antecedent was being 'bored', which occurred in 31% of incidents. Less commonly occurring intrapersonal antecedents included preoccupation, positive psychotic symptoms and anxiety, each occurring in approximately 10% of incidents. McDougall also reported consequences of violence. The three most common consequences were increased observation (90%), separation (57%) and control and restraint (48%). Other consequences included individual sanction, physical restraint, counselling, PRN medication and medical intervention – all of which occurred in approximately one-third of incidents.

Daffern et al. (2007a) reported similar data from a secure, forensic inpatient psychiatric unit. They took data during a one-year period. After each aggressive incident, nurses completed the record of aggressive behaviour, a standardized measure of aggressive behaviour. Nursing staff and patients were then taken through a semi-structured interview, designed to elicit the purpose of the aggression. The purposes included demand avoidance, to force compliance, express anger, reduce tension, enhance status or social approval, compliance with instruction, to obtain tangibles, attention seeking and to observe suffering. Daffern et al. (2007a) based their analyses on a sample of 502 incidents of aggressive behaviour. They observed that 105 of 232 patients exhibited at least one act of aggression. Functions were elicited in 95% of incidents. Finally, they classified incidents as aggression to staff and to other patients.

The most commonly identified functions were to express anger and to reduce tension, and the least frequent category was to observe suffering. The difference in reasons for aggression to staff and patients is interesting. Aggression to staff was more likely than aggression to patients because of demand avoidance, forced compliance and reduced tension. Aggression to other patients functioned to express anger, enhance social status and for compliance with instruction. Finally, there were no differences related to tangibles, seeking attention and observing suffering.

These three studies are interesting and potentially valuable to forensic case formulation. They are strongly suggestive that aggression is not a property of the person, their diagnosis or personality, but rather is a property primarily of interpersonal situations (Sturmey et al., 2007). Both McDougall's study of adolescents and Daffern et al.'s (2007a) study of adults suggest that anger, hostility and threats of violence from others, demands and compliance issues with staff are common environmental correlates of aggression. Covert behaviour, such as fantasy prior to violent behaviour, might also be an important part of a formulation, but accessing covert behaviour accurately remains challenging, so its inclusion in formulations raises difficult problems unless it is accompanied by public behaviour, such as withdrawal.

These data are also strongly suggestive of the kinds of interventions that might be appropriate. The social nature of aggression suggests that clinicians should consider teaching skills to forensic patients, such as anger management, relaxation, social and problem skills. Similarly, since demands and requests for compliance from staff may be common environmental correlates of aggression, teaching staff interaction skills may also be potentially effective. These skills might include (a) differentially reinforcing alternative client's behaviour, such as compliance or acceptable forms of refusal; (b) making requests skilfully and in a less provocative manner; (c) reducing the frequency of demands and then fading demands in, either in terms of frequency of demands or in terms of the degree of provocation of the demand. McDougall's data also suggest that, since 'boredom' was a common correlate of aggression, provision of meaningful, reinforcing activities and/or teaching clients to self-manage their own leisure time more effectively (Skinner, 1953) may also be important in some contexts.

These survey studies also have significant limitations. They are all, with the exception of some incidents in Daffern et al.'s (2007a) study, based on staff reports, which may be inaccurate or incomplete. Further, although these studies reported some reliability data, the authors often only described these data incompletely; sometimes reliability data relate to only a portion of the entire data set, such as one session. More importantly, since all these data were correlational, it is unclear if the relationships between the environmental correlates were actually causal. For example, although staff demands were often correlated with client's aggression, it is uncertain if demand avoidance might be the cause of aggression. It is possible that demand reduction was merely a correlate of some other unobserved environmental event, such as removal from a noisy, overstimulating environment. Only a true experimental analysis of behaviour, in which the experimenter directly manipulated the independent variable, can answer this question.

Experimental Analyses of Aggression

There is a considerable number of experimental analyses of aggressive behaviour, which may inform forensic case formulation of aggression. These include both experimental analyses of prosocial skills related to aggression and analyses of aggressive behaviour itself.

Frederiksen et al. (1976) conducted an experimental analysis of social skills in two psychiatric inpatients with significant histories of aggression. The first participant was a 48-year-old man with ten previous psychiatric admissions. His aggressive behaviour was often related to failure to elicit help from others, such as asking for help, and other people interrupting his ongoing behaviour, such as asking him to stop smoking. The second participant was a 26-year-old man who had lost six jobs in the preceding eight months. He was often aggressive following supervisor criticism. Although, initially, he complied with his supervisor's requests, he subsequently became verbally abusive to his supervisor.

Intervention consisted of specific instruction, modelling, rehearsal and feedback to teach social skills, such as looking at others and appropriate requests. The authors observed these target behaviours as well as irrelevant comments, hostile comments and inappropriate requests in both role-play and situations on the psychiatric ward. Intervention took place in role-play situations which included both generic situations and situations specific to each client that the authors identified from observations on the ward.

Using a multiple-baseline design across participants, the authors demonstrated that social skills training not only improved the specifically targeted social behaviour but also resulted in generalized reduction in undesirable social skills. This was true both in role-play situations and in generalization probes on the ward and with novel people who were not involved in the training. After social skills training, ward staff who were unaware that the participants had been involved in social skills training reported that the participants exhibited improved functioning on the ward.

Matson and Stephens (1978) conducted a similar analysis of aggression in four chronic psychiatric patients. In baseline the patients emitted arguments and fights 0–4 times per day. During baseline they also showed unusual social behaviour, such as gaze avoidance, odd posture and facial mannerisms, inappropriate laughing, lack of appropriate content of speech and poor physical appearance. The authors used social skill training sessions, which lasted 10–40 minutes. Each session began with praise and instructions for appropriate grooming and dress. Then there were six role-play scenes in which the trainer praised improvement in specific skills. The trainer reviewed all skills in each scene. Social skills improved dramatically after training, both during training and at one-two and three-month follow-ups. Impressively, arguments and fights reduced to zero on almost all days during social skill training. During maintenance two patients showed no aggression and a third showed only one incident of arguments and fights. The fourth patient showed some regression at follow-up. This study suggests that the absence of appropriate social behaviour is highly predictive of aggression. Further, social skill training is an effective intervention for people with even the most severe psychiatric disorders. Although maintenance over time may occur, this should be carefully monitored and some patients may need additional training and booster sessions for maintenance to occur.

There is an extensive literature on experimental analysis of aggressive behaviour, primarily with children and adults with intellectual and other developmental disabilities. This literature might inform forensic case formulation of violent behaviour by drawing conceptual parallels between the analyses and treatments with people with developmental disabilities and forensic populations and adopting some of the methodologies used with people with developmental disabilities with forensic populations. One example comes from Marcus et al. (2001) who reported a functional analysis of aggressive behaviour in eight children and adolescents aged 3–13 years with intellectual disabilities and/or autism, all of whom attended preschool or school. Aggressive behaviour included hitting, kicking, biting others, etc. The experimenters identified the functions of their aggression by exposing the students to six conditions, such as attention and escape (the reader should consult the original article for details of the protocol).

Marcus et al. identified the function of aggression in seven of eight participants. For example, Matt almost only emitted aggressive behaviour in the escape from demand condition. Joe also only emitted aggression in the escape condition, but only when he had to remain in place at work. Marty displayed no aggression during his first analysis; however, his parents reported that he only aggressed to other children. When the experimenter conducted a descriptive analysis in the classroom for 3.5 hours over six days, they observed that the probabilities of aggression were unaffected by the teacher's attention, escape and access to materials; however, the probability of peer attention was much increased after aggression compared to the overall probability of aggression. This suggested that his aggression was differentially reinforced by peer attention rather than adult attention or any other consequence.

THE IMPLICATIONS OF THE FUNCTIONAL NATURE OF AGGRESSION

Taken together, these and other studies strongly suggest the functional and social nature of aggressive behaviour in a wide range of clinical and non-clinical populations and in different contexts, including formulation of aggression in forensic cases. Variables that control aggression vary from one person to another; they may vary one person's history, and they may vary from context to context within one person. These variables may also have crucial value in predicting indicated and contraindicated treatments for each person.

The following two examples illustrate the importance of individual differences in the variables that control aggression. The first person's aggression may be more likely when there is little activity, which may result in the person seeking stimulation. When there are a few staff present, the availability of an irritating potential victim may be the immediate trigger for threats and escalation to aggressive behaviour that terminates the victim's irritating behaviour. Putting it another way, lack of activity is an establishing operation for aggression. This establishing operation (a) temporarily increases the reinforcing value of removing other irritating people, and (b) temporarily increases the likelihood of all behaviour previously reinforced by the termination of other people's irritating behaviour, including seeking out potential victims. The discriminative stimulus of the potential victim's irritating behaviour has previously been paired with the termination of aversive stimuli in the past, such as the person not whining or leaving the area. This discriminative stimulus sets the occasion for a response chain that leads to aggressive behaviour that results in the victim removing themselves and staff intervening to tell the victim to be quiet. Perhaps temporary reductions in whining or the client backing off a little functioned as differential negative reinforcement of earlier members of the response chain. Thus, this person's treatment plan might include several potential elements based on this formulation including (a) teaching him to schedule interesting activities when there is nothing going on; (b) revising the facility's programme to reduce periods of inactivity; and (c) teaching this person a more effective way to terminate another person's irritating behaviour, such as politely asking him to be quiet or walking away to ask a staff for assistance. For a second person, who shows topographically similar aggression, the formulation and implied treatment plan might be quite different. For example, a person who is highly anxious and who finds social occasions very aversive might show aggressive behaviour that is negatively reinforced by removal of other people and subsequent reduction in anxiety. In this case, one might teach the person some form of relaxation, gradually expose him to progressively more anxiety-provoking situations and teach him an alternative way to terminate these situations. Thus, even modest differences in case formulation may lead to significantly different treatment plans for the same topography.

The variables that relate to the onset of aggression and its maintenance might differ. For example, a young child might learn to aggress to other children as an effective way to obtain toys from others. This might reflect the lack of opportunities to acquire typical effective social and language skills due to lack of learning opportunities in the home and school. Later on, especially during adolescence, if the person continues to fail to learn other effective communication, social and self-control skills, this person might learn to aggress to obtain money and food from others. If this person learns good vocational skills as an adult, then they may not need to use aggression to obtain money and food; however, if they fail to learn effective self-control skills and/or alternative sociosexual behaviour, aggression may now function to obtain sex from others. Thus, during this person's lifetime, aggression has been variously positively reinforced by toys, money and food, and sex. The treatment plans at these various times are conceptually quite similar – namely, strengthening alternative ways to obtain positive reinforcers and decreasing the motivation for access to these positive reinforcers by non-contingent access to them – although the precise form of the treatment plan would vary. It is also possible, of course, that the function of aggression may change during the lifespan. Aggressive behaviour that a child learns by removing parental demands may later function to access attention and reassurance as an adult.

The variables that control aggression may also change from context to context. For example, aggressive behaviour may serve more than one function for one person. It might reduce interaction from staff and associated aversive work demands in a vocational setting, whereas on the ward it might serve to obtain attention from staff at times of low staffing. If this were the case, the treatment plan would require two elements. At work, one might reduce the aversive properties of the work environment, for example, by reducing noise or the frequency of staff requests, teach the person to ask for a break appropriately and/or give non-contingent breaks, etc. In contrast, at home one might remind staff to talk to this patient more frequently, teach him some social skills to ask for staff attention, teach tolerance of delay for staff interaction, etc.

Note that the preceding section addressed neither diagnosis nor topography of aggression. A functional approach would produce a similar formulation and treatment of aggression maintained by termination of other people's irritating behaviour if the person has a diagnosis of obsessive–compulsive disorder, dementia or schizophrenia. Likewise, if the person's aggressive behaviour were either verbal threats, throwing furniture or threatening someone with a weapon or striking them, the formulation and the treatment plan would be similar, although some practical details might vary from instance to instance.

OUTSTANDING ISSUES AND FUTURE DIRECTIONS

General Challenges to Case Formulation

Despite the popularity of case formulation, there have been several critiques. These include problems with its reliability (Wilson, 1996) and validity, professional performance in case formulation

(Kuyken, 2006), how to use formulations with clients, economic aspects of case formulation and the role of biological variables in case formulations (Sturmey, 2008).

Reliability

Despite the popularity of case formulation, there has been surprisingly little research into some of the basic aspects of case formulation, including its reliability. For example, some authors have found mixed agreement among practitioners on such basic aspects of case formulation as identifying the target behaviour(s) of interest and the putative cognitive mechanisms underlying clinical problems. The paucity of such research and the mixed results that these studies have reported have led some to suggest that case formulation should be abandoned in favour of standardized, evidence-based manuals (Wilson, 1996); others to question if case formulation is, in fact, just another case of the emperor's new clothes (Kuyken, 2006). Undoubtedly, future research should address the reliability of all aspects of case formulation, including the reliability of identifying the elements of a case formulation and translating it into a treatment plan. More importantly than merely documenting the (un)reliability of case formulation, future research should also investigate what can be done to train clinicians to make more reliable case formulations. Several papers have suggested that many professional training programmes do not adequately prepare clinicians in this regard (Eells & Lombart, 2003; Eells et al., 2005); it is largely unknown how professional training courses do prepare clinicians to perform this important task. One potentially productive approach to this problem might be to (a) develop reliable and valid measures of writing case formulations, and (b) investigate those training variables that educators can manipulate, such as the number and varieties of cases to practise writing formulation.

Validity

The main purpose of case formulation is to predict the most effective treatment for each specific client (Haynes & O'Brien, 2000). Hence, a key test of the validity of case formulation is a demonstration that case formulation leads to treatment that is more effective than the treatment *that would otherwise have been implemented.* The emphasized text is important. Merely showing that treatment resulting from case formulation is better than chance or placebo control conditions is insufficient. For example, if sexual offenders respond to a standard package of sex education, and training in skills, such as assertiveness and social–sexual skills, merely showing that case formulation resulted in some effective treatment would be insufficient. Rather, a group that received treatments matched to the functions of their target problems should do *better* than a group receiving standard treatments or a group that receives treatments that do not match the function of their problem. For example, offenders might be violent because they lack skills to negotiate social problems or because they are easily provoked to violent behaviour by minor social stimuli, such as criticism. In this example, two treatments are possible – social skill training and some form of respondent extinction, such as desensitization to cues for violence. If that is the case, there should be a function by treatment interaction. Thus, those clients with social skill deficits should benefit from social skill training, but not desensitization to cues for violent behaviour, and those clients who overrespond to minor cues should respond to desensitization, but not social skills training. It is this treatment by function interaction which is the key test of the validity of case formulation.

Several outcome studies have investigated if there is such as treatment by function interaction; the results have been mixed. One example comes from Schulte et al. (1992), who conducted an experimental evaluation of function-based treatment for anxiety disorders. There were three groups. One group received function-based treatment. A second group was a matched control group, which also received individually tailored treatment based not on their own functional assessment, but on the functional assessment of a yoked-control subject. The third group received standardized flooding, which was not based on any individual case formulation. The group that received standardized flooding had better outcomes than the other two groups. Further, participants in the two other groups who received flooding had good outcomes, even when the flooding was based on a yoked subject's formulation, rather than the formulation of the client that received flooding.

Better news for formulation comes from McNight et al. (1984), who conducted function-based treatment of depression and did find evidence of a treatment by function interaction. That is, participants who received treatment based on the function of their depression had better outcomes than those that did not. Ghaderi (2006) found that individuals with bulimia had better outcomes with individual-based treatments than those that received standard, manualized treatment. There is also extensive evidence from the field of intellectual disabilities that interventions based on functional assessments are superior to those that are not. These studies include some problems that are relevant to forensic settings, such as aggression and sexual offences. Further, those studies that were based on an experimental functional analysis, rather than a descriptive analysis, had the largest effect sizes (Didden et al., 1997, 2006). There are currently no studies evaluating the validity of case formulation in forensic services.

The evidence for the treatment validity of case formulation is limited and mixed. One may choose to dismiss Schulte et al.'s negative results on several grounds. Perhaps their clinicians were not adequately trained in case formulation and hence their formulation-based treatments were invalid or weak. Further, one might argue that the use of flooding as the control group was indeed a tough comparison, since flooding is a very effective treatment for anxiety disorders. (The counterargument to the latter point might be, that is exactly the point of effective, manualized treatments.) The remaining studies that found positive effects of case formulation are simply too few: we need more such studies in a variety of contexts, populations and problems.

Using Formulations with the Client

Several authors have advocated using formulations collaboratively with clients. As noted at the beginning of this chapter, Skinner (1953) recommended that therapist should enable the client to discover their own formulation, rather than deliver it to them cold, in order to avoid having one's good advice rejected to begin behaviour change as soon as possible. Others have recommended doing so simply from the position of respect for client autonomy, and because developing a formulation together can be one aspect of a respectful, collaborative approach to helping the client. Such papers often imply that a collaboratively developed formulation and treatment plan might be more acceptable to the client and perhaps more effective than other approaches to develop case formulations.

Despite the various recommendations to do so, there is little evidence on using formulations with clients. Chadwick et al. (2003) reported that the majority of (a small sample of) clients with psychoses were positive about receiving their own formulations. Yet, some clients reported that receiving their formulations was demoralizing when their problems were presented as long-standing and related to early learning experiences, and, hence appeared apparently intractable to the client. Chadwick et al.'s results are not the last word on sharing case formulations with clients. There are many ways in which this could be done, and future research might evaluate these different approaches.

Economic Aspects

Making a formulation takes time, costs money in professional and support staff time and delays implementation of treatment. When is it worth it?

There may be some situations when diagnosis alone predicts effective and ineffective treatments quite well. If making an accurate diagnosis is quick and cheap and effective manualized treatments are available, the additional costs of case formulation and the limited or absence of client benefits may not be justified. On the other hand, if diagnosis is expensive and unreliable and if response to standard treatments is weak, then the cost of case formulation might be justified, especially if it leads to substantive benefits of formulation-based treatments. An interesting example of this question comes from Ghaderi (2006), who found that both manualized and individualized treatments of bulimia were effective compared to baseline, but that individualized treatment produced greater client gains than manualized treatments. Research has not yet answered the important question of what the costs and benefits of these two approaches to treatment. An additional consideration is the essential practical question of whether there are enough competent practitioners available to deliver each kind of treatment and the relative costs of training practitioners in each treatment approach.

Biological Variables

Some clinicians are happy to include biological variables, such as genetic predispositions, physical illnesses and socially acceptable substances, such as caffeine, alcohol, prescribed medications and illicit drugs, in case formulations. Such biological variables may sometimes be quite important, such as the potential role of caffeine in panic disorder, or of a painful physical condition limiting movement in someone with depression. That said, clinicians should be cautious in calling on biological variables as causes of behaviour on at least two counts. First, clinical judgement may be inaccurate in identifying biological variables that influence clinical problems. Second, it is often, but not always, difficult to manipulate the potential independent variables; hence, even when a correlation between a biological variable does truly exist, its status as a causal variable remains uncertain (Haynes & O'Brien, 2000).

Special Challenges to Forensic Case Formulation

Forensic case formulation faces some special challenges compared to case formulation in non-forensic mental health settings. First, the quantity of clinical material may be voluminous, incomplete and inaccurate. Relevant personal history may extend over decades. Distortions through simple poor memory, myths and exaggerations among clients and staff, and motivation to present a case either negatively or positively may all limit the accuracy and completeness of available information. A second problem for forensic case formulation is that the range of environments available to the client and clinician may be very limited. Some authorities emphasize the importance of sampling all the relevant environments and methods of assessment as essential for case formulation (Haynes & O'Brien, 2000; Lappalainen et al., 2009), but often in forensic case formulation the client is in an unusual environment which may have little relevance to understanding their offending behaviour. A clinician may attempt to understand offending behaviour by identifying current behaviour that may be related to previous offending, but this may be difficult. (This problem can be contrasted with formulating ongoing clinical problems that occur within the forensic settings.) A third challenge to the clinician in conducting forensic case formulation is that a clinician may have to formulate a wide range of clinical problems, whereas some mental health professionals may specialize in specific disorders. Thus, mental health professionals in forensic settings must have flexible, generic case formulation skills as well as specialized knowledge of forensic issues. Finally, formulating current problems may bring the clinician up against practices in forensic settings that may contribute to the onset or maintenance of clinical problems. Identifying such practices and integrating them into a clinical formulation are one clinical skill; raising them in team or management meetings and attempting to modify these practices through staff training and modification of current programmes are perhaps more challenging.

Future Directions

Reliability and Validity

The evidence on the reliability and validity of case formulation is at best mixed and sometimes negative (Kuyken, 2006). Future research can address these issues by conducting further reliability trials on the elements of case formulation, such as identifying the target behaviour; the reliability of identifying current and historical variables that affect the target behaviours; and on the reliability of translating a formulation into an idiographic treatment. Of course, the toughest test of the reliability of case formulation is that clinicians must perform all three of these tasks reliably. Reliability is only important insofar as it is a requirement for validity; without validity, it is of little interest. Researchers can evaluate the treatment validity of case formulation in randomized controlled trials in which interventions based on case formulation are compared to treatment as usual.

Related to this issue are concerns expressed in the literature that professional training and performance in case formulation are sometimes inadequate. Several authors have now developed generic criteria to assess the adequacy of case formulations (Eells & Lombart, 2003; Eells et al., 2005; Kuyken, 2006) that researchers could use when evaluating professional performance and professional training in this area.

Forensic Case Formulation

The literature on forensic case formulation is notable because of its relatively small size; the problems of case formulation in regular clinical practice that this chapter identified are amplified in forensic case formulation because of a lack of research in all areas of forensic case formulation. Forensic clinicians need more models of forensic case formulations and more research to address the generic issues in case formulation as applied to this particular context.

Offence Paralleling Behaviour

OPB is a recent development in forensic case formulation of special interest, in particular because it is conceptually analogous to other functional approaches to case formulation (cf. Sturmey et al., 2007). Thus, other functional approaches to case formulation can inform and refine OPB approaches. For example, Daffern et al. (2007b) suggested that OPB could be conceived specifically as chains of behaviour that sometimes result in offending behaviour. This notion can be further refined. Applied behaviour analysis has conceptualized response chains as sequences of responses that terminate in some final reinforcer (Cooper et al., 2007). Each member of the response chain has two functions: they are secondary reinforcers for preceding members of the chain and they act as a discriminative stimulus for the next member of the response chain. Researchers have used this model to demonstrate such relationships among members of the response chain (Lalli et al., 1995); to analyse the functions of earlier members of response chains in lieu of analysing potentially dangerous later members of the response chain (Borrero & Borrero, 2008; Smith & Churchill, 2002); and to develop interventions such as applying contingencies to early members of the response chain to eliminate the later, most problematic members of the chain indirectly (Deaver et al., 2001; Lalli et al., 1995). This model and the interventions in people with developmental disabilities may be applicable to offenders. Perhaps we can conduct functional analysis of non-dangerous OPB, examine the relationship between early members of response chains in offenders, and perhaps interventions to reduce the frequency of early members of response chains will be effective in eliminating dangerous offending behaviour at the end of a response chain. Future research should address these issues.

OPB may not only consist of response chains, which are organized linearly. Response chains are but one example of a response class – a group of topographically dissimilar responses that share the same establishing operations, antecedents and contingencies. Sometimes members of a response class are not organized linearly, but may substitute one for another as independent variables that control each member of the response class change (Cooper et al., 2007). For example, for some people offending behaviour might be reinforced by thrilling exhilaration experienced during offending, especially after extended periods of boredom. Such a person might also gamble, use illegal drugs, get into loud arguments and drink and drive – all of which may be reinforced by exhilaration. These responses may not be organized in a response chain, but may constitute a class of functionally similar responses that may substitute for one another depending on other as yet unspecified factors, such as the availability of material and circumstances necessary for each response and the effort required to engage in each response. Such an analysis might suggest alternative forms of case formulation and intervention. For example, case formulation of such response classes might involve identifying all the problematic and non-problematic forms of thrill-seeking, their establishing operations, discriminative stimuli and contingencies. Intervention options might include (a) abolishing the establishing operation by providing frequent, safe and appropriate forms of thrill-seeking; (b) teaching and supporting other functionally equivalent, safe and appropriate behaviour; and (c) devaluing the consequence maintaining the entire response class by non-contingent access to exhilarating behaviour.

A final area for future research is verbal behaviour and private verbal behaviour ('cognition') in particular. The traditional solution to incorporating cognition into case formulation and treatment comes from cognitive and cognitive–behavioural approaches to case formulation, which accepts client self-reports of attributions and thoughts processes as veridical and evidence of disordered thinking that is the cause of the problematic behaviour. Radical behaviourism construes thinking and feeling as private behaviour, observable only to one person, but which has no other special status and may potentially be subject to the same kinds of analysis as overt behaviour (Skinner, 1953, 1957). Such an analysis has been the productive basis for a variety of new behavioural therapies, such as acceptance and commitment therapies and also shares similarities with dialectic behaviour therapy. Such approaches to verbal behaviour also accept self-report of private behaviour, but rather than construing it as the cause of the problem, they construe it as behaviour to be changed through interventions such as acceptance and mindfulness training. There is little research on forensic case formulation and radical behavioural approaches to verbal behaviour. Forensic practitioners and researchers might usefully explore this option.

SUMMARY

Case formulation is a generic clinical skill that all mental health practitioners, including those in forensic services, should perform competently. Case formulations are concise abstractions that summarize the unique features of each individual and that guide the design of an idiographic treatment that is superior to the best alternative treatment. They can be made from many theoretical approaches.

There are several examples of forensic case formulation that address presenting problems and may also address historical aspects of the case. OPB is a new form of case formulation, which may be useful in forensic case formulation.

Research on case formulation is limited in quantity. Data on the reliability and validity of case formulations are contradictory. We have limited knowledge of professional performance in this area, but there are indications that it may be problematic. Future research should begin to address the application of case formulation to forensic settings and populations and address the unique challenges of forensic case formulation.

REFERENCES

Borrero, C.S.W. & Borrero, J.C. (2008). Descriptive and experimental analyses of potential precursors to problem behavior. *Journal of Applied Behavior Analysis, 41*, 83–96.

Bruch, M. & Bond, F.W. (1998). *Beyond Diagnosis. Case Formulation Approaches in CBT*. Chichester: Wiley.

Chadwick, P., Williams, C. & Mackenzie, J. (2003). Impact of case formulation in cognitive behaviour therapy for psychosis. *Behaviour, Research and Therapy, 41*, 671–80.

Cooper, J.O., Heron, T.E. & Heward, W.L. (2007). *Applied Behavior Analysis* (2nd edition). Upper Saddle, NJ: Merrill Prentic Hall.

Daffern, M., Howells, K. & Ogloff, J. (2007a). What's the point? Toward a methodology for assessing the function of psychiatric in patient aggression. *Behaviour, Research and Therapy, 45*, 101–11.

Daffern, M., Jones, L., Howells, K., Shine, J., Mikton, C. & Tunbridge, V. (2007b). Editorial. Redefining the definition of offence paralleling behaviour. *Criminal Behaviour and Mental Health, 17*, 265–73.

Dallos, R. & Johnstone, L. (2005). *Formulation in Psychotherapy*. London: Brunner-Routledge.

Deaver, C.M., Miltenberger, R.G. & Stricker, J.M. (2001). Functional analysis and treatment of hair twirling in a young child. *Journal of Applied Behavior Analysis, 34*, 535–38.

Didden, R., Duker, P. & Korzilius, H. (1997). Meta-analytic study of treatment effectiveness for problem behaviors with individuals who have mental retardation. *American Journal on Mental Retardation, 101*, 387–99.

Didden, R., Korzilius, H., van Oorsouw, W. & Sturmey, P. (2006). Behavioral treatment of problem behaviors in individuals with mild mental retardation: a meta-analysis of single-subject research. *American Journal on Mental Retardation, 111*, 290–98.

Dougher, M.J. (2000). *Clinical Behavior Analysis*. Reno, NV: Context Press.

Drake, C.R. & Ward, T. (2003). Treatment models for sex offenders: a move toward a formulation-based approach. In T. Ward, D.R. Laws & S.M. Hudson (Eds), *Sexual Deviance: Issues and Controversies* (pp. 226–43). Thousand Oaks, CA: Sage.

Dunn, M. (2009). A cognitive analytic formulation. In P. Sturmey (Ed.), *Varieties of Case Formulations* (pp. 199–21). Chichester: Wiley.

Eells, T.D. (1997). *Handbook of Psychotherapy Case Formulation*. New York: Guilford Press.

Eells, T.D. (2007a). History and current status of psychotherapy case formulation. In T.D. Eells (Ed.), *Handbook of Psychotherapy Case Formulation* (2nd edition, pp. 33–2). New York: Guilford Press.

Eells, T.D. (Ed.). (2007b). *Handbook of Psychotherapy Case Formulation* (2nd edition). New York: Guilford Press.

Eells, T.D. & Lombart, K.G. (2003). Case formulation and treatment concepts among novice, experiences, and expert cognitive-behavioral and psychodynamic therapists. *Psychotherapy Research, 113*, 187–204.

Eells, T.D., Lombart, K.G., Kendeljelic, E.M., Turner, L.C. & Lucas, C. (2005). The quality of psychotherapy case formulations: a comparison of experts, experiences, novice cognitive-behavioral and psychodynamic therapists. *Journal of Consulting and Clinical Psychology, 73*, 579–89.

Estes, W.K. & Skinner, B.F. (1941). Some quantitative properties of anxiety. *Journal of Experimental Psychology, 29*, 390–400.

Ferster, C.B. (1973). A functional analysis of depression. *American Psychologist, 28*, 857–70.

Frederiksen, L.W., Jenkins, J.O., Foy, D.W. & Eisler, R.M. (1976). Social-skills training to modify abusive verbal outbursts in adults. *Journal of Applied Behavior Analysis*, *9*, 117–25.

Gauss, V.L. (2007). *Cognitive Behavioral Therapy for Adults with Asperger Syndrome*. New York: Guilford Press.

Ghaderi, A. (2006). Does individualization matter? A randomized trial of standard (focused) versus individualized (broad) cognitive behaviour therapy for bulimia nervosa. *Behaviour, Research and Therapy*, *44*, 273–88.

Gresswell, D.M. & Hollin, C.R. (1992). Toward a new methodology of making sense of case material: an illustrative case involving attempted multiple murder. *Clinical Behaviour and Mental Health*, *2*, 329–41.

Hersen, M. & Rosqvist, J. (2008). *Handbook of Psychological Assessment, Case Conceptualization and Treatment. Vol. 1. Adults*. Hoboken, NJ: John Wiley & Sons.

Hopko, D.R., Lejuez, C.W., Ruggiero, K.J. & Eifert, G.H. (2003). Contemporary behavioral activation treatments for depression: procedures, principles, and progress. *Clinical Psychology Review*, *23*, 699–717.

Jones, L.F. (1997). Developing models for managing treatment integrity and efficacy in prison based TC: the Max Glatt Center. In E. Cullen, L. Jones & R. Woodward (Eds), *Therapeutic Communities for Offenders*. Chichester: Wiley.

Jones, L.F. (2004). Offence paralleling behaviour (OPB) as a framework for assessment and interventions with offenders. In A. Needs & G. Towl (Eds), *Applying Psychology to Forensic Practice*. Oxford: BPS Blackwell.

Kohlenberg, R.J. & Tsai, M. (1994). Improving cognitive therapy for depression with functional analytic psychotherapy: theory and case study. *The Behavior Analyst*, *17*, 305–19.

Kuyken, W. (2006). Research and evidence base in case formulation. In N. Tarrier (Ed.), *Case Formulation in Cognitive Behaviour Therapy: The Treatment of Challenging and Complex Clinical Cases*, (pp. 12–35). London: Brunner Routledge.

Lalli, J.S., Mace, F.C., Wohn, T. & Livezy, K. (1995). Identification and modification of a response-class hierarchy. *Journal of Applied Behavior Analysis*, *28*, 551–59.

Lappalainen, R., Timonen, T. & Haynes, S.N. (2009). The functional analysis and functional analytic clinical case formulation: a case of anorexia nervosa. In P. Sturmey (Ed.), *Varieties of Case Formulation* (pp. 157–78). Chichester: Wiley.

Luborsky, L. & Barrett, M.S. (2007). The core conflictual relationship theme: a basic case formulation method. In T.D. Eells (Ed.), *Handbook of Psychotherapy Case Formulation* (2nd edition, pp. 105–35). New York: Guilford Press.

Malan, D.H. (1979). *Individual Psychotherapy and the Science of Psychodynamics*. London: Butterworth.

Marcus, B.A., Vollmer, T.R., Swanson, V., Roane, H.R. & Ringdahl, J.E. (2001). An experimental analysis of aggression. *Behavior Modification*, *25*, 89–213.

Matson, J.L. & Stephens, R.M. (1978). Increasing appropriate behavior of explosive chronic psychiatric patients with a social-skills training package. *Behavior Modification*, *2*, 61–76.

McDougall, T. (2000). Violent incidents in a forensic adolescent unit: a retrospective analysis. *Nursing Times Research*, *5*, 87–88.

McNight, D.L., Nelson, R.O., Haynes, S.C. & Jarret, R.B. (1984). The importance of treating individually assessed response classes in the amelioration of depression. *Behavior Therapy*, *15*, 315–35.

McWilliams, N. (1999). *Psychoanalytic Case Formulation*. New York: Guilford Press.

Messer, S.B. & Wolitzky, D.L. (2007). The psychoanalystic approach to case formulation. In T.D. Eells (Ed.), *Handbook of Psychotherapy Case Formulation* (2nd edition, pp. 67–105). New York: Guilford Press.

Nezu, A.M., Nezu, C.M., Friedman, S.H. & Haynes, S.N. (1997). Case formulation in behavior therapy: problem solving and functional analytic strategies. In T.D. Eells (Ed.), *Handbook of Psychotherapy Case Formulation* (pp. 368–401). New York: Guilford Press.

Nezu, A.M., Nezu, C.M. & Lombardo, E. (2004). *Cognitive-Behavioral Case Formulation and Treatment Design. A Problem-Solving Approach*. New York: Springer.

Persons, J.B. (1989). *Cognitive Therapy in Practice. A Case Formulation Approach*. New York: Norton.

Persons, J.B. (2008). *The Case Formulation Approach to Cognitive-Behavior Therapy: Guides to Individualized Evidence-Based Treatment*. New York: Guilford Press.

Schulte, D., Kunzel, R. Pepping, G. & Scholte-Bahenbert, T. (1992). Tailor-made versus standardized therapy of phobic patients. *Advances in Behaviour, Research and Therapy*, *24*, 67–92.

Shepherd, M. & Lavender, T. (1999). Putting aggression into context: an investigation into contextual factors influencing the rate of aggressive incidents in a psychiatric hospital. *Journal of Mental Health*, *8*, 159–70.

Skinner, B.F. (1953). *Science and Human Behavior*. New York: Macmillan.

Skinner, B.F. (1957). *Verbal Behaviour*. Acton, MA: Copely.

Skinner, B.F. (1971). *Beyond Freedom and Dignity*. New York: Knopf.

Smith, R.G. & Churchill, R.M. (2002). Identification of environmental determinants of behavior disorders through functional analysis of precursor behaviors. *Journal of Applied Behavior Analysis*, *35*, 125–36.
Sturmey, P. (1996). *Functional Analysis in Clinical Psychology*. Chichester: Wiley.
Sturmey, P. (2007). *Functional Analysis in Clinical Treatment*. Burlington, MA: Elsevier.
Sturmey, P. (2008). *Behavioral Case Formulation*. Chichester: Wiley.
Sturmey, P. (2009a). *Varieties of Case Formulation*. Chichester: Wiley.
Sturmey, P. (2009b). Case formulation: a review and overview of this volume. In P. Sturmey (Ed.), *Varieties of Case Formulation* (pp. 3–32). Chichester: Wiley.
Sturmey, P., Ward-Horner, J., Marroquin, M. & Doran, E. (2007). Structural and functional approaches to psychopathology and case formulation. In P. Sturmey (Ed.), *Functional Analysis and Clinical Treatment* (pp. 1–22). New York: Elsevier.
Tarrier, N. (Ed.). (2006). *Case Formulation in Cognitive Behaviour Therapy: The Treatment of Challenging and Complex Clinical Cases*. London: Brunner Routledge.
Tarrier, N., Wells, A. & Haddock, G. (1998). *Treating Complex Cases. The Cognitive Behavioral Therapy Approach*. Chichester: Wiley.
Turkat, I.D. (1985). *Behavioral Case Formulation*. New York: Pergamon.
Turkat, I.D. (1990). *Personality Disorders. A Psychological Approach to Clinical Management*. New York: Pergamon.
Weerasekera, P. (1996). *Multiperspective Case Formulation: A Step Toward Treatment Integration*. Malabar, FL: Krieger.
Wilson, G. (1996). Manualized-based treatments: the clinical application of research findings. *Behaviour, Research and Therapy*, *34*, 295–314.
Wolpe, J. & Turkat, I.D. (1985). Behavioral formulation of clinical cases. In I.D. Turkat (Ed.), *Behavioral Case Formulation* (pp. 5–36). New York: Pergamon.

Chapter 3

DISTINCTIONS WITHIN DISTINCTIONS: THE CHALLENGES OF HETEROGENEITY AND CAUSALITY IN THE FORMULATION AND TREATMENT OF VIOLENCE

KEVIN HOWELLS

Institute of Mental Health, University of Nottingham, and Peaks Academic and Research Unit, Rampton Hospital, Retford, UK

In this chapter, I address three broad approaches to understanding and formulating (and hence subsequently treating) violent behaviour in forensic settings. In particular, there is a focus on the issue of heterogeneity of the patient or offender population. My (or any other) perspective is inevitably shaped by the particular context within which the clinical work is conducted, by the specific characteristics of the offender population receiving attention and by the philosophy, assumptions and policy objectives of the organization within which the clinical work occurs. The particular context that most informs the discussion in this chapter is that of the 'Dangerous and Severe Personality Disorder' initiative in England (Howells et al., 2007a), which is described in more detail below.

A brief clarification of appropriate terminology is required at the outset. Individuals whose serious violent behaviour has brought them into conflict with the law may subsequently be dealt with, assessed and treated (or rehabilitated) either within the criminal justice system or within forensic mental health services. Although there are areas of common purpose and practice within these two systems, for example, risk reduction, there remain substantive differences in underlying philosophies, assumptions, cultures and ways of conceptualizing problems of violence (Howells et al., 2004). The distinction between 'normal' and 'mentally disordered' offenders, with possible underlying assumptions that the two categories of person have fundamentally different causal antecedents for their violent acts, and hence different therapeutic needs, has been questioned and provides another example of the heterogeneity to be discussed in detail below. In this case 'offenders' and 'patients' may be *less* different than traditional thinking might lead us to expect (Howells et al., 2004). For now, the point to be emphasized is that many violent individuals may be characterized as 'offenders' or 'patients' or both. For purposes of brevity and convenience, I use the term 'offenders' throughout the discussion to follow, rather

Offence Paralleling Behaviour: A Case Formulation Approach to Offender Assessment and Intervention Edited by Michael Daffern, Lawrence Jones and John Shine

than 'patients' or 'offender-patients'. The use of terms such as a 'clinical approach' or reference to 'clinicians' or 'treatment' does not imply a medical model, nor should it be taken to imply that professional work is exclusively the province of mental health professionals, rather than criminal justice professionals such as forensic psychologists, criminologists or probation and prison staff.

DANGEROUS AND SEVERE PERSONALITY DISORDER AS AN ILLUSTRATIVE CONTEXT

In February 1999, the British Government announced plans to introduce a comprehensive Dangerous and Severe Personality Disorder (DSPD) pilot programme to deal with a category of individuals who were a source of public and professional concern and who were seen as falling between two stools – the criminal justice system and mental health services. The full background and nature of the proposed new service are described in Howells et al. (2007). At the time of writing, this initial government proposal has led to the existence of four new high-security treatment sites and services, two within the prison system and two within the forensic mental health system. In addition, a range of lower security and community services has been developed. These DSPD facilities now provide intensive assessment and treatment services for individuals who meet three criteria: they pose a high risk of harm; they suffer a severe personality disorder; and a functional link exists between the personality disorder and the behaviours that constitute high risk. The risk and personality disorder criteria are operationalized in some detail, though the functional link criterion has proved more problematic and difficult to specify with precision (Duggan & Howard, 2009; Howells et al., 2007). In practice, the people admitted to these services typically have histories of serious violence, including sexual violence, and meet the criteria for *Diagnostic and Statistical Manual of Mental Disorders*, 4th edition (DSM-IV) – personality disorder, particularly antisocial (ASPD) and borderline personality disorders (BPD), with a substantial minority meeting the criteria for psychopathy, as assessed by the Psychopathy Checklist–Revised (PCL-R; Hare, 2003).

THE STRUCTURAL/DIAGNOSTIC APPROACH

This population of offenders is a useful one to consider for the present chapter in that they illustrate the strengths and weaknesses of the three approaches to assessment, formulation and treatment to be discussed: the structural/diagnostic, the offence/topographic and the functional/individual (see below). Such offenders have clearly been classified as having a severe personality disorder diagnosis; however, they are also subject to offence-based categorization; typically, they are labelled as 'violent offenders' or 'sex offenders', though a minority would have histories of both types of offending. The issue arises of which of these three approaches has most utility in assessment, formulation and treatment.

In an ideal world, the diagnosis of personality disorder would be useful in that it would have explanatory and predictive value and would point to treatment approaches for personality disorder that have demonstrated effectiveness. However, the extent to which personality disorder explains and predicts violence remains uncertain, notwithstanding the functional link criterion specified for DSPD services (Duggan & Howard, 2009; Howells et al., 2007).

The complex issue of criteria to establish causality between mental health and other variables has been usefully analysed by Haynes (1992) and in relation to personality disorder and violence by Duggan and Howard (2009). The latter authors, following Haynes (1992), point to four necessary conditions for a causal relationship: covariation between variables, temporal precedence of the causal variable, exclusion of alternative explanations and establishing a logical connection between variables. They argue, persuasively, that Haynes' conditions have not yet been met in relation to personality disorder as a cause of violence: 'The evidence, such as it is, suggests that any relationship that exists between PD and violence is weak, and that PD, including ASPD, probably accounts for only a very small proportion of the variance in violent behaviour' (Duggan & Howard, 2009, p. 29). This sceptical view, if correct, has considerable implications for treatment interventions. It would suggest that change in personality disorders per se should not be a major target for treatment interventions when the major objective of treatment is to reduce risk of future violence. In other words, personality disorder has not yet been unequivocally demonstrated to be what has been termed a *criminogenic need* (Andrews & Bonta, 2006). This does not preclude, however, treating personality disorder as a *responsivity factor*; that is, deciding personality disorder should be addressed therapeutically because it is likely to interfere with, for example, engagement or compliance with treatment (Howells & Tennant, 2007; Ward et al., 2004). Equally, it could be argued that treatment interventions are not intended exclusively to reduce risk and that reducing the person's distress and poor social functioning is a worthwhile task in itself (Ward & Maruna, 2007), though it is implausible that the alleviation of the distress of perpetrators of violence was a major impetus to the DSPD initiative, which appears to have been instigated by a wish to reduce risk of violent assaults (Howells et al., 2007).

If it is accepted that personality disorder contributes, at best, modestly to variance in violent behaviour, there are clear implications for the process of *formulation* of the individual case. A formulation provides the basis for treatment planning (Sturmey, 1996, 2007). There is a clear need to identify in the formulation other variables (apart from structural diagnostic ones such as personality disorder) which are likely to be functionally linked to violence. To limit the formulation task to the identification only of the functional link between personality disorder (or any other disorder) and violence would be a travesty of the normal formulation process. Fortunately, the scientific and empirical literature on causes of violence is a substantial one, far more robust than that relating to personality disorder (Cavell & Malcolm 2007; Gannon, 2009; Howells et al., 2008; Sestir & Bartholow, 2007). The formulation would need to involve a large array of variables, including factors such as information-processing deficits, anger and affect regulation problems, impulsivity and low empathy (Day, 2009; Gannon, 2009; Howells, 2009).

Some of the reasons for the putatively weak power of personality disorder in the explanation of violence may derive from the fact that the construct of personality disorder, and of personality traits in general, may be at too high a level of generality, prone to inferential and measurement errors and insufficiently linked to core and genuinely explanatory brain and psychological processes and mechanisms (Blackburn, 2007; Duggan & Howard, 2009; Haynes, 1992; Mischel, 2004). It may be that, in clinical practice, it is the core processes associated with particular personality disorders that should become the target for assessment and intervention, particularly when there is independent evidence as to their being criminogenic needs. Poor anger regulation (Novaco, 2007), impulsivity (Jolliffe & Farrington, 2009) and paranoid cognition (Bentall & Taylor, 2006) provide examples of this sort of mechanism.

The above discussion of personality disorder–violence links is based on *nomothetic* studies, in which the overlap between the two populations – those with personality disorder and those who show violent behaviour – is investigated. However, the issue of the functional link has also to be dealt with *idiographically*. For a particular offender (as in DSPD admission), the question arises whether this person's violence is functionally linked to their personality disorder. There are several methodological problems in trying to answer this question. The fact that an individual belongs to two populations that overlap (the personality disordered and violent offenders) does not prove that personality disorder is a functional (causal) antecedent for that person's offending.

There are two ways, in theory, for establishing whether a functional link exists for the individual. Firstly, the link could be demonstrated by changing the personality disorder by treating it and demonstrating an effect on the occurrence of violence. Unfortunately, the evidence, as yet, that personality disorder, at least personality disorder in a forensic setting, can be effectively treated is lacking (Duggan et al., 2007). Secondly, the approach to establishing a functional link might be to investigate covariation between personality disorder and violence within individuals over time. Do periods in which personality disorder symptoms are evident tend to precede episodes of violence? In practice, this sort of covariation information is almost impossible to obtain in that, by definition, personality disorders are stable over time and not expected to show marked temporal variation. This state of affairs can be contrasted with, for example, that existing for substance abuse in relation to violence. Substance abuse is often episodic and thus it would be possible to demonstrate that periods of high substance abuse co-vary with violent episodes within an individual, making it reasonable to infer that a causal relationship is present. Should personality disorder prove to be less stable than previously believed, covariation may become feasible as a method.

One danger of the overemphasis on structural/diagnostic approaches is that the attention of the clinician is distracted away from the most pressing problem leading to admission to the service, towards less central features of the personality disorder. In the DSPD setting, for example, the most important factor leading to admission to such a high-security facility is the perceived high risk of future violence. Equally, discharge from such a setting, typically to a lower security mental health service, is more dependent on reduction in risk than on reduction of the severity of the personality disorder (Duggan, 2007). Thus, the propensity for violence itself needs to be the central problem addressed by the formulation. The existence of a personality or any other disorder may play a role in such a formulation, but it would constitute only one amongst an array of causal influences. Offence paralleling behaviour (Daffern et al., 2007b) becomes a core rather than a peripheral phenomenon, once attention is focused on violence itself rather than on the accompanying disorder.

STRUCTURAL/DIAGNOSTIC HETEROGENEITY

The problem of heterogeneity exists for both the structural/diagnostic approach and the offence/topographic approach (covered below). Personality disorders, for example, are of various types, with indications that it is only particular personality disorders, particular combinations of them or particular trait clusters that are linked to violence. In the general population, it appears that Cluster B personality disorders are most associated with offending (Coid et al., 2006), while in forensic groups antisocial and borderline personality disorders have the strongest link to offending and to violence (Howard, 2009). Howard (2009) and Howard et al. (2008) have proposed that it is the combination of antisocial and borderline traits that is 'toxic' and likely to be associated with violent offending and that this combination is more frequent in forensic patients in secure institutions than in community groups. For the identification of such subgroups and constellations of traits to be clinically (therapeutically) useful, the mechanisms underlying the traits/disorders need to be identified, so that they can feature as treatment targets. Affective self-regulation in general (Howard, 2009), for example, and in particular, anger regulation (Howells, 2009), has been suggested to be critical mechanisms, both of which have associated therapeutic strategies.

Thus, the broad category of personality disorder requires finer distinctions to be made. Psychopathy clearly constitutes a meaningful subgroup (Hare, 2003, 2006). However, evidence appears to be accumulating that it, in turn, is heterogeneous (Blackburn, 2009), with continuing debates as to what the subcomponents of psychopathy might be, as operationalized by the PCL-R (Cooke et al., 2004; Hare, 2003; Hare & Neumann, 2006). Blackburn's in-depth review of these issues leads him to conclude:

> Attempts to understand psychopaths have been hindered by the assumption that they represent a homogeneous group ... The 'classical' distinction between primary and secondary psychopaths now has empirical support but ... there may also be other significant subtypes research and practice can no longer afford to ignore these variations (Blackburn, 2009, pp. 128–29).

SIMILAR ISSUES IN AXIS I DISORDERS

The issues of the causal role of mental disorder in violent behaviour and of diagnostic category heterogeneity have a wider range of relevance than the diagnosis of personality disorder. Similar issues may arise in relation to Axis I disorders (Daffern & Howells, 2002). For illustration, the problems of causality and heterogeneity arise also in relation to schizophrenia and its impact on violence. The putative links between mental disorder and violence have been a focus of heated debate for more than 30 years. There is little doubt that violence and mental disorder are significantly correlated with each other, but, until relatively recently, establishing causality in this relationship has been highly problematic.

The schizophrenia and violence issue is most relevant to the implementation of violence programmes in forensic mental health settings or in prison programmes in which individuals with a history of psychotic disorder are not excluded. Hodgins (2008a) has argued that the link between schizophrenia and violence is robust and that it has been demonstrated in different countries, using different methodologies and designs. She suggests that people with schizophrenia have an elevated risk compared to the general population for conviction for non-violent criminal offences, a higher risk again for conviction for a violent offence and an even higher risk for conviction for homicide (Hodgins, 2008b). The elevated risk produced by schizophrenia is greater for females than for males. There is also evidence that high rates of criminality, particularly violent offending, are a precursor of schizophrenia.

Hodgins (2008a, 2008b) has produced a typology of schizophrenia–violence links. Thus, the heterogeneity issue is endemic. She states that a reason 'for the inconsistent results concerning the association of psychotic symptoms and violence is that studies have compared offenders with schizophrenia to non-offenders with schizophrenia, thereby assuming that the offenders constitute a homogeneous group. The evidence, however, does not support this assumption' (Hodgins, 2008b, p. 2508). Hodgins defines three groups (subtypes) that differ in relation to aetiology (causal factors) and response to treatment. They also differ in relation to age of onset and persistence of antisocial behaviour:

- *Type 1: 'Early starters'.* This group has an early onset of antisocial behaviour, which remains stable over lifetime. These individuals are usually convicted of crimes prior to the onset of illness. For this group the illness itself cannot be regarded as causal.
- *Type 2: Antisocial behaviour not present prior to onset of schizophrenia prodrome.* This group is consistent with the notion of schizophrenia as causal, though the association may be explained in other ways. Conduct disorder is a precursor of both schizophrenia and adult antisocial

behaviour, particularly violent behaviour. Conduct disorder is also a precursor of antisocial personality disorder.
- *Type 3: A late-onset group.* Chronic schizophrenia linked to antisocial behaviour does not occur until late thirties or early forties, and violence tends to be serious.

This work on schizophrenia demonstrates, again, the complexity of possible links between mental disorder and violence and the major difficulties in establishing that a disorder is definitely causal rather than being a consequence or merely a correlate. There is a need for idiographic, more detailed analysis and formulation of the individual case, as a precursor to treatment planning, at least when a major objective of treatment is to reduce the risk of violence.

THE OFFENCE/TOPOGRAPHIC APPROACH

It is not uncommon for therapeutic interventions for violence in criminal justice and forensic mental health services to be organized in terms of offence topography rather than causal mechanisms or criminogenic needs. Thus, we find treatment programmes for *violent offenders* or *sexual offenders*. While such categories may be administratively convenient, they may not be psychologically meaningful in that the similarity between offenders within the category may be entirely topographic (the form the violent behaviour takes) and not functional (the antecedents and needs underlying the behaviour). Topography is not a guide to what variables the treatment should target. Thus, two men may both have killed a family member by stabbing them, but the causal influences may be entirely different for the two people. For person A, the relevant antecedents might include characterological poor anger control, trait impulsivity and violence-supportive beliefs, while for person B, depressed mood following major life stressors, a prolonged period of alcohol misuse and the emergence of sadistic fantasy may be relevant. Putting both men in the same violence programme together may make little sense in that the content of the programme is unlikely to be suited to the needs of both. The options are either to make the range of needs covered by programmes very broad indeed, so that all participants find some element of the programme relevant, or to restructure therapeutic programmes along functional lines, so that only individuals with common needs are treated together, for example, a programme for men whose violence has been disinhibited by alcohol use or who share a severe anger regulation problem. This is the problem of the heterogeneity of violence and how this is to be accommodated, a problem that parallels those identified for structural/diagnostic approaches above.

IN WHAT WAYS IS VIOLENCE HETEROGENEOUS?

The treatment of violent offenders must ultimately be based on an understanding of the factors giving rise to violent acts or violent actors. There is substantial evidence that both violent acts and actors are not homogeneous categories.

Many clinicians, theorists and researchers have come to the conclusion that violent acts can be subdivided into more useful categories. One of the most long-standing distinctions, for example, has been between *hostile* and *instrumental* violence. Despite the pervasive nature of this distinction, it has suffered from poor definitions and a bewildering array of terms, for example, angry versus non-angry, hot-blooded versus cold-blooded, reactive versus proactive, defensive versus offensive and impulsive versus planned (McEllistrem, 2004). For simplicity, I use the term 'hostile versus instrumental' for the purposes of this chapter. Hostile and instrumental violence can be distinguished in terms of antecedent conditions, ongoing cognition and affective states and the functions or goals of the act. Some robberies, for example using violence to induce a bank cashier to hand over money, are instrumental in the sense that they may involve no obvious aversive or frustrating antecedents, an absence of affective, particularly angry arousal and hostile cognition, and the goal pursued is the instrumental one of obtaining money. This can be contrasted with homicides in which, for example, the violent perpetrator is reacting to perceived provocation and frustration by the victim; the perpetrator makes hostile appraisals of the victim ('they are insulting me'), feels angry and engages in violence for the purpose of hurting or harming the provoking victim.

The hostile/instrumental distinction is a very influential one in clinical contexts in that offenders whose violent acts can be characterized as hostile are likely to be construed as requiring therapeutic interventions to help them self-regulate violent impulses arising from anger, using an array of cognitive, affective and behavioural methods (Cavell & Malcolm 2007; Howells, 2008; Novaco, 2007). Typically, the therapeutic needs of instrumentally violent offenders are less clearly specified but are likely to involve challenging violence-supportive beliefs ('violence is acceptable to get what you want') and assisting the perpetrator to find alternative means to achieve desired instrumental outcomes. Recent work by Polaschek et al. (2008) has clarified the nature of violent offence-supportive cognitions of this sort, using implicit theory analysis. The latter are networks of beliefs organized around a dominant theme or theory that guide behaviour either implicitly or explicitly. In a qualitative study of violent offenders, Polaschek and colleagues identified four violence-related implicit theories ('beat or be beaten', 'I am the law', 'violence is normal' and 'I get out of control'). Chambers (2006) also identified three separate pathways to violent offending which she referred to as honour offences (following a perceived threat to status or safety, characterized by situational violent reactions to perceived threats), punishment offences (concerning either revenge or retribution towards a victim perceived to have committed a norm violation) and denial offences (involving extreme emotion occurring under conditions of extreme stress).

There are a number of problems with the angry versus instrumental distinction (Bushman & Anderson, 2001; Howard, 2009). Firstly, the distinction is most appropriately applied to acts than to actors. A violent individual may engage in both forms of violence, though a particular type of offence may still predominate in his history. Secondly, the distinction between the two forms is often difficult to make in practice (Barratt & Slaughter, 1998; Bushman & Anderson, 2001). Thirdly, hostile aggression appears to be mistakenly confounded with impulsive aggression and instrumental with planned violence (Bushman & Anderson, 2001). Many crimes of violence indicate that angry reactions to a provocation can be carefully rehearsed and nurtured over time until a planned retaliation or delayed revenge is enacted. Howard (2009) has usefully described a 2 × 2 typology of violence, which accommodates this latter observation and the general critique of Bushman and Anderson. In Howard's typology, *impulsivity–control* and *hostile–instrumental* (the latter is also termed *appetitive*) dimensions are orthogonal, generating four possible violent groups: *impulsive–hostile*, *impulsive–appetitive*, *controlled–hostile* and *controlled–appetitive*. Howard usefully introduces the notion of positive affect-driven violent behaviour, for example in the form of excitement or exhilaration. While some clinicians might readily equate instrumental violence (Howard's impulsive–appetitive group) with 'cold' psychopathic characteristics, Patrick's (2006) analysis suggests a complex picture emerging on the role of angry emotion in psychopathy (Howells, 2009).

Current neurobiological and developmental studies of violence appear to concur and to support the importance of the hostile/instrumental distinction. In the recent authoritative review of the neurobiology of violence published by the Royal Society (Hodgins et al., 2008), for example, Rutter (2008) concludes that violence is heterogeneous and that angry, instrumental and sadistic forms of violence should be distinguished. Blair's work on brain systems suggests different neuro-anatomical pathways for hostile and instrumental violence (Blair, 2004, 2008), and observed different developmental pathways to violence (see below) are broadly consistent with this way of dividing up the violent offending category. Dadds and Rhodes (2008) also point to heterogeneity of response to behavioural interventions with antisocial and violent children. In this case, callous and unemotional traits in boys were associated with poor responsiveness to behavioural programmes.

The existence of two types of aggressive behaviour is also suggested by large-scale empirical investigations of the links between personality and aggression. In such studies *aggression* has a broader meaning than *violence* and includes acts not necessarily leading to physical injury. Bettencourt et al. (2006) have also demonstrated that there are different personality correlates for aggression under neutral and under provocation conditions. Aggression under provocation conditions (AUPC) can probably be equated with hostile or angry aggression, as discussed above, while aggression under neutral conditions (AUNC) is similar to instrumental aggression. Personality correlates of AUPC include trait anger, anger intensity, anger frequency, duration of anger, rumination and narcissism, while correlates of AUNC include trait aggressiveness and its cognitive, physical and verbal components (Bettencourt et al., 2006). Bettencourt et al. summarize their findings in terms of *aggression-prone* versus *provocation-sensitive* personalities.

DEVELOPMENTAL TRAJECTORIES LEADING TO VIOLENCE

The developmental literature also reinforces the utility of the hostile/instrumental distinction discussed above. Hubbard and colleagues (2007), in reviewing this area, conclude:

> [I]n our opinion, the distinction between reactive and proactive aggression is critical . . . some episodes of children's aggressive behaviour are strongly driven by anger, whereas other instances of aggression are markedly lacking in anger, being driven instead by a desire to achieve an instrumental or social goal. (Hubbard et al., 2007, p. 270)

Hubbard et al. (2007) point out not only that hostile and instrumental aggressions are strongly correlated in children but also that the two forms of aggression have different correlates. Hubbard et al. interpret the developmental literature as revealing that children's level of hostile aggression is related to particular social, cognitive and emotional characteristics (hostile attributional biases, depression, rejection by peers) while instrumental aggression has different correlates (positive outcome expectancies) for aggression, instrumental goal orientation and deviant peer friendships (see Hubbard et al., 2007, pp. 270–71; cited in Bettencourt et al., 2006).

The importance of emotional functioning for some aggressive children, though not for all, is being increasingly acknowledged by those studying developmental antecedents for aggression and violence. Delays in important socio-emotional skills are linked with aggressive behaviour. Bierman (2007) points to critical skills: labelling of own feelings, recognizing the feelings of others, empathy and interpersonal understanding, regulation of emotional and behavioural reactivity, coping with frustration and distress and effective communication of emotion in problem-solving. Emotional arousal, particularly anger activation, interacts with cognitions and interpersonal contingencies in influencing subsequent aggression.

The hostile/instrumental distinction and the extension of it to impulsivity by Howard (2009) do not exhaust work suggesting heterogeneity. Work on gender differences suggests that males and females differ in the pattern of and antecedents for aggression and violence (Archer, 2000, 2004; Campbell, 2006; Graves, 2007). Women may have:

- A stronger association of aggression with internalizing conditions (see below) such as depression
- A greater inhibition of aggression as a result of socialization (see discussion of development below)
- A stronger association of aggression with physical and sexual victimization and subsequent post-traumatic stress disorder (PTSD) (Graves, 2007)

The gender difference may be best explained by improved acquisition of self-regulatory behaviours in females rather than by instigatory differences (see Campbell, 2006 and discussion of development above). These differences would appear to suggest that a violence intervention for women would require a different focus from one for men.

The heterogeneity of violent offenders has not gone unnoticed by those evaluating violence programmes. Serin (2004), for example, suggests 'violent offenders are sufficiently heterogeneous that endeavours to distinguish among types of offenders should be strongly encouraged . . . current strategies to assign all violent offenders to anger management programs is inefficient and ill-advised'. Similarly, in his comprehensive review of treatment outcomes for violence programmes, McGuire (2008) concludes that heterogeneity is important and that different subgroups may be differentially responsive to existing treatments. Similarly, Hollin (2006, p. 38), in a critical review of (sex) offender treatment, has commented:

> Clinical treatment focuses . . . on the individual, so that traditionally cognitive-behavioural treatment incorporates individual assessment and case formulation, leading to an individually tailored treatment plan . . . . the use of programmes may separate fine-grained clinical assessment from the planning and process of treatment . . . it seems likely that individual assessments would yield different targets for different . . . offenders. In which case, why have a[n] . . . offender treatment programme with fixed treatment targets for all . . . offenders?

THE INDIVIDUAL/FUNCTIONAL APPROACH

Sturmey (1996, 2007) and Haynes (1998) have described functional as opposed to structural approaches to psychopathology and social deviance, the former being characterized by a focus on the current context of the problem behaviour, on identifying controlling variables, operationalization of behaviour and an idiographic approach to assessment and treatment. All these components of the functional approach are relevant to the assessment and treatment of violent behaviours. The operationalization of problematic behaviour is particularly important in this context (see the discussion of defining the mental disorder as the problem, above). Daffern has pioneered the application of functional approaches to violence in forensic mental health settings (Daffern & Howells, 2002, 2009; Daffern et al., 2007a).

Function–analytic assessments (Daffern & Howells, 2002, 2009; Sturmey, 1996, 2007) seek to clarify the factors responsible for the development, expression and maintenance of problem behaviours. Such methods may be of assistance in understanding the factors contributing to the development, expression and maintenance of violence. Function–analytic assessments are typically achieved through assessment of the behaviour of interest, assessment of the individual's predisposing characteristics and consideration of the antecedent events, which are important for the initiation of the behaviour, and the consequences of the behaviour, which maintain and direct its developmental course (Haynes, 1998). Factors that should be considered in an adequate functional analysis of a patient's aggression (and which assist in the determination of function) include (Howells, 1998) (a) the frequency, intensity, duration and form of aggression; (b) environmental triggers (including background stressors); (c) cognitive antecedents (including biases in appraisal of events, dysfunctional schemas, underlying beliefs and values supporting aggression); (d) affective antecedents (emotions preceding aggressive acts, e.g. anger or fear); (e) physiological antecedents; (f) coping and self-regulatory skills; (g) personality dispositions (e.g. anger proneness, impulsivity, psychopathy, general criminality, overcontrol and undercontrol); (h) mental disorder variables (mood, brain impairment, delusions, hallucinations, personality disorders); (i) consequences/functions of aggressive acts (for perpetrator and others, short-term and long-term, including emotional consequences such as remorse and peer group or institutional reinforcement); (j) buffer factors (good relationships, family support and achievement in some area); and (k) opportunity factors (weapons and victim availability).

It can be seen that the variables identified as relevant antecedents for aggression are considerably broader than those identified in the personality trait approach and include many of the factors discussed as important within the anger/instrumental distinction. An exclusive reliance on trait personality descriptors as a means for understanding why a patient has been aggressive is clearly limited (see Mischel, 2004, for a more detailed account).

An assessment framework for analysing the functions of aggressive actions (assessed through review of proximal antecedents and consequences within the context of the individual's predisposing personal attributes and limitations) has been proposed by Daffern and colleagues (Daffern & Howells, 2007, 2009; Daffern et al., 2007a). This classification system, the 'assessment and classification of function' (ACF; Daffern et al. 2007a), acknowledges that multiple functions may be present for any particular act and that perpetrators may have different goals for different acts. These functions are *demand avoidance, to force compliance, to express anger, to reduce tension (catharsis), to obtain tangibles, social distance reduction (attention-seeking), to enhance status or social approval, compliance with instruction* and *to observe suffering*. For the ACF, each function is recognized through its characteristic antecedents and consequences and scored as present or absent for a particular aggressive behaviour. The ACF acknowledges that violence may have multiple functions and goals for the individual as well as for the group. Indeed, any one violent act may have multiple functions, suggesting it is unhelpful to think of functions as necessarily characteristic of the individual offender. Thus, methods such as the ACF classify acts rather than actors.

So far, the major applications of the ACF have been to mentally disordered violent offenders (Daffern et al. 2007a) and to personality disordered offenders (Daffern & Howells, 2009). In a study of 502 aggressive incidents in a high-security forensic psychiatric hospital in Victoria, Daffern et al. (2007a) found that anger expression was the most frequent function of aggression, but that functions differed for aggressive behaviours towards staff and those towards fellow patients. Demand avoidance was a common function for aggression towards staff but rare for aggression towards patients. To obtain tangibles (an instrumental function) was rare for all incidents. Daffern and Howells (2009) have recently extended this work to high-risk offenders with personality disorders in Rampton Hospital in the United Kingdom and added two further categories of function to the original nine functions, namely 'sensation seeking' and 'sexual gratification', to capture apparent sexual/sadistic functions occurring in this very high-risk and complex population. In the latter study the function of the violent offences leading to admission (index offences) proved to differ substantially from the functions of violent behaviours within the institution. The presence of sexual gratification as a function for non-sexual (topographically speaking) offences reinforces the argument, above, that there is a need to go beyond topography in understanding violent offences.

This method would seem to hold promise for assessing violent offenders in the criminal justice system. In ongoing work in the United Kingdom (Howard et al., 2009), for example, we have used the ACF to analyse the functions of violence in violent juvenile offenders whose violent acts occurred in the context of alcohol use. The functions of the violent acts were assessed from transcripts of 149 structured interviews with the violence perpetrator focused on the antecedents for the act on the day on which it occurred. Functions could be reliably rated. As in previous work, anger expression was the most common function, though other functions, such as sensation seeking and obtaining tangibles, were also found.

The importance of functional assessments of this sort is that they clearly suggest different therapeutic strategies for different violent offenders, depending on the exact functions of their violence. An offender who is predominantly 'anger expressive', for example, would have different needs from someone who is mainly seeking sensation or sexual arousal. The general direction of therapy would be to develop alternative, adaptive means of achieving personal functional goals and to change circumstances and other factors within the person in such a way that the need to pursue the problematic goal is reduced.

Idiographic methods of this sort are not necessarily incompatible with collecting nomothetic data. The clinician, for example, may describe common patterns of need in the population receiving the service (Hammond & O'Rourke, 2007). A nomothetic need analysis might suggest, for example, that alcohol misuse and hostile cognitive beliefs about others are known antecedents of aggression and that, therefore, treatment programmes to address these problems are required as part of service delivery to aggressive patients with personality disorders. An idiographic analysis of an individual (rather than the group), on the other hand, might suggest that a particular person's aggression is influenced by exposure to humiliating provocations and subsequent paranoid ideation. Population analyses are essential in service planning, while individual analysis is required to plan treatment for the individual patient. Both population and individual analyses would need to be informed by validated theories of the causes of the problem at hand, in this case violence, and by the findings of empirical studies as to what factors are aetiologically important. Idiographic assessment of causal influences allows for the likelihood that some influences will be idiosyncratic and specific to the individual under consideration. Such analysis is likely to be particularly important in complex populations, such as those with DSPD (Davies et al., 2007; Howells et al., 2007).

An individual/functional approach brings with it a sharpened focus on what offenders have actually done that leads to admission to a high secure service such as DSPD (for example, repeated stabbings of strangers in a public context), rather than on their general 'risk' or psychiatric classification. Individual/functional data can clearly inform judgements of the probability of the person engaging in these specific violent behaviours again in the future and suggest ways in which future risk can be assessed and managed. From this perspective, the assessment of offence paralleling behaviour (OPB) is a critical task, arguably a more important task than conventional assessments of risk and psychiatric status. Making clinical use of OPB would require a very detailed functional analysis of the index offence or pattern of offences leading to admission to a service and an equally detailed analysis of subsequent behaviours, particularly those within forensic institutions. Conventional risk assessments rarely involve such fine-grained idiographic analysis, though the increasing advocacy of greater attention to dynamic risk factors (Douglas & Skeem, 2005) is compatible with this individualized approach.

THE LIMITATIONS OF THE INDIVIDUAL/FUNCTIONAL APPROACH

Individual formulation tends to be labour-intensive and expensive initially. Unravelling the variables that have led an individual to commit, for example, a homicide may require extended work by a psychologist or other behavioural professional. This person would require a wide range and depth of skills, knowledge and expertise in both mental health and criminological fields, attributes which some have argued are often absent in contemporary 'what works'-influenced, 'packaged' rehabilitation programmes in which the emphasis is on standardized and manualized programme delivery, rather than on the appreciation of the diversity of those in treatment (Thomas-Peter, 2006). The major weakness of the individual/functional approach is that we know little about the reliability and validity of individual formulations in this particular field of practice. Formulations of clinical cases have particular requirements if they are to be regarded as scientific (Kuyken, 2006; Sturmey, 2009); not least they need to be stated with precision, tentative, capable of revision over time, based on adequate measures and potentially falsifiable (Haynes et al., 2009). The need for formal professional guidelines for formulation and standardization of methods is apparent if real progress is to be made in the forensic context.

The individual/functional approach also requires the provision of a wide-ranging and potentially complex array of therapeutic programmes to address the myriad, and sometimes idiosyncratic, areas of need identified for the individual – a far cry from the notion of the 'violence programme' being the solution for the 'violent offender'.

SUMMARY AND CONCLUSIONS

In this chapter, it has been proposed that there are three broad approaches to understanding, assessing and planning services for violent offenders, including offender-patients. The first is structural/diagnostic, the second is offence/topographic and the third individual/functional. All three approaches have strengths and limitations. The structural/diagnostic approach has the potential to deflect attention from the central behaviours that have led to admission to a particular therapeutic service (typically, serious violent offending or sexual offending), so that the clinical focus becomes one of treating the disorder per se as the major focus and judging improvement largely in terms of clinical change in the structural factor (for example, a reduction in personality disorder or schizophrenia). This problem is amplified when the functional link between the disorder and the violent behaviour is unclear, weak in effect or unproven, as may, arguably, be the case for personality disorders (Duggan & Howard, 2009). Although structural diagnoses, for example, personality disorders, may be a useful, broad-brush admission criterion for a service (as in DSPD), they rarely indicate a shared treatment need, largely because of the demonstrated heterogeneity of such groups. Finer distinctions are required to assemble a group of individuals who could be treated together in a group setting (most treatments in such settings are group-based). Finer distinctions may involve specifying particular disorders (for example, borderline personality disorder or psychopathic disorder) and then further specifying subcategories within these disorders (Blackburn, 2009). Ultimately, the making of finer and finer discriminations only ceases when some shared clinical need is established (for example, a problem of impulsivity or poor emotional self-regulation). At that point, an impulsivity programme or a self-regulation programme, for example, can be set up.

The offence/topographic approach shares many of these weaknesses, particularly the problem of lack of homogeneity. Topographic similarity of offences does not mean functional similarity exists. Thus, violent offenders, as described above, have diverse criminogenic and other needs, and the distinction-making task continues until a shared functional need is identified. The increasing evidence for the heterogeneity of these forensic populations is insufficiently recognized in clinical practice and in the organization of services.

The individual/functional approach is based on individual formulation of the case, thus dealing to a degree, with the problem of heterogeneity. The constant collapse of structural classifications of types of disorder and types of offending into smaller units leads inevitably to the assessment of the individual in terms of a multiplicity of potential causal antecedents. Allocating offenders to treatment in terms of broad structural classifications such as 'personality disorder' or 'violent offender' is unlikely to be productive (though this is an empirical question). The individual/functional approach shows promise, though this too has weaknesses that need to be addressed.

REFERENCES

Andrews, D. & Bonta, J. (2006). *The Psychology of Criminal Conduct* (3rd edition). Cincinna, OH: Anderson.

Archer, J. (2000). Sex differences in aggression between heterosexual partners: a meta-analytic review. *Psychological Bulletin, 126*, 651–80.

Archer, J. (2004). Sex differences in aggression in real-world settings: a meta-analytic review. *Review of General Psychology, 8*, 291–322.

Barratt, E.S. & Slaughter, L. (1998). Defining, measuring and predicting impulsive aggression: a heuristic model. *Behavioral Sciences and the Law, 16*, 285–302.

Bentall, R.P. & Taylor, J.L. (2006). Psychological processes and paranoias: implications for forensic behavioural science. *Behavioral Sciences and the Law, 24*, 277–94.

Bettencourt, B.A., Talley, A., Benjamin, A.J. & Valentine, J. (2006). Personality and aggressive behaviour under provoking and neutral conditions: a meta-analytic review. *Psychological Bulletin, 132*, 751–77.

Bierman, K.L. (2007). Anger and aggression: a developmental perspective. In T.A. Cavell & K.T. Malcolm (Eds), *Anger, Aggression and Interventions for Interpersonal Violence* (pp. 215–38). Mahwah, NJ: Lawrence Erlbaum.

Blackburn, R. (2007). Personality disorder and antisocial deviance: comments on the debate on the structure of the Psychopathy Checklist–Revised. *Journal of Personality Disorders, 21*, 142–59.

Blackburn, R. (2009). Subtypes of psychopath. In M. McMurran & R. Howard (Eds), *Personality, Personality Disorder and Risk of Violence* (pp. 113–32). Chichester: Wiley.

Blair, R.J.R. (2004). The roles of orbital frontal cortex in the modulation of antisocial behaviour. *Brain and Cognition, 55*, 198–208.

Blair, R.J.R. (2008). The amygdala and ventomedial prefrontal cortex: functional contributions and dysfunction in psychopathy. *Philosophical Transactions of the Royal Society B, 363*, 2557–65.

Bushman, B.J. & Anderson, C.A. (2001). Is it time to pull the plug on the hostile versus hostile versus instrumental aggression dichotomy? *Psychological Review, 108*, 273–79.

Campbell, A. (2006). Sex differences in direct aggression: what are the psychological mediators? *Aggression and Violent Behavior, 11*, 237–64.

Cavell, T.A. & Malcolm, K.T. (Eds). (2007). *Anger, Aggression and Interventions for Interpersonal Violence*. Mahwah, NJ: Lawrence Erlbaum.

Chambers, J. (2006). *The Violence Situation: A Descriptive Model of the Offence Process of Assault for Male and Female Offenders*. Unpublished doctoral thesis. Melbourne, Victoria, Australia: University of Melbourne.

Coid, J., Yang, M., Roberts, M., Moran, P., Bebbington, P., Brugha, T., Jenkins, R., Farrell, M., Lewis, G. & Singleton, N. (2006). Violence and psychiatric morbidity in a national household population – a report from the British Household Survey. *American Journal of Epidemiology, 164*, 1199–208.

Cooke, D.J., Michie, C., Hart, S.D. & Clark, D. (2004). Reconstructing psychopathy: clarifying the significance of antisocial and socially deviant behaviour in the diagnosis of psychopathic personality disorder. *Journal of Personality Disorders, 18*, 337–57.

Dadds, M.R. & Rhodes, T. (2008). Aggression in young children with concurrent callous-unemotional traits: can the neurosciences inform progress and innovation in treatment approaches? In S. Hodgins, E. Viding & A. Plodowski (Eds), *The Neurobiology of Violence: Implications for Prevention and Treatment. Philosophical Transactions of the Royal Society, 363*, 2567–76.

Daffern, M. & Howells, K. (2002). Psychiatric inpatient aggression: a review of structural and functional assessment approaches. *Aggression and Violent Behaviour*, *3*, 1–21.

Daffern, M. & Howells, K. (2009). The function of aggression in personality disordered patients. *Journal of Interpersonal Violence*, *24*, 586–600.

Daffern, M., Howells, K. & Ogloff, J.R.P. (2007a). What's the point? Towards a methodology for assessing the function of psychiatric inpatient aggression. *Behavior Research and Therapy*, *45*, 101–11.

Daffern, M., Jones, L., Howells, K., Shine, J., Mikton, C. & Tunbridge, V. (2007b). Refining the definition of offence paralleling behaviour. *Criminal Behaviour and Mental Health*, *17*, 265–73.

Davies, J., Howells, K. & Jones, L. (2007). Evaluating innovative treatments in forensic mental health: a case for single case methodology? *Journal of Forensic Psychiatry and Psychology*, *18*, 353–67.

Day, A. (2009). Offender emotion and self-regulation: implications for offender rehabilitation programming. *Psychology, Crime and Law*, *15*, 119–30.

Douglas, K.S. & Skeem, J.L. (2005). Violence risk assessment: getting specific about being dynamic. *Psychology, Public Policy and Law*, *11*, 347–83.

Duggan, C. (2007). To move or not to move – that's the question! Some reflections on the transfer of DSPD patients in the face of uncertainty. *Psychology, Crime and Law*, *13*, 113–22.

Duggan, C. & Howard, R.C. (2009). The 'functional link' between personality disorder and violence: a critical appraisal. In M. McMurran & R. Howard (Eds), *Personality, Personality Disorder and Risk of Violence* (pp. 19–37). Chichester: Wiley.

Duggan, C., Huband, N., Smailagic, N., Ferriter, N. & Adams, C. (2007). The use of psychological treatments for people with personality disorder: a systematic review of randomized controlled trials. *Personality and Mental Health*, *1*, 95–125.

Gannon, T.A. (2009). Social cognition and aggressive offending: an overview. *Psychology, Crime and Law*, *15*, 97–118.

Graves, K.N. (2007). Not always sugar and spice: expanding theoretical and functional explanations of why females aggress. *Aggression and Violent Behavior*, *12*, 131–40.

Hare, R.D. (2003). *The Hare Psychopathy Checklist–Revised* (2nd edition). North Tonawanda, NY: Multi-Health Systems.

Hare, R.D. (2006). Psychopathy: a clinical and forensic overview. *Psychiatric Clinics of North America*, *29*, 709–24.

Hare, R.D. & Neumann, C. (2006). The PCL-R assessment of psychopathy. In C.J. Patrick (Ed.), *Handbook of Psychopathy* (pp. 58–88). New York: Guildford Press.

Haynes, S.N. (1992). *Models of Causality in Psychopathology*. New York: Macmillan.

Haynes, S.N. (1998). The changing nature of behavioural assessment. In A. Bellack & M. Hersen (Eds), *Behavioral Assessment: A Practical Handbook* (pp. 1–21). Boston, MA: Allyn & Bacon.

Haynes, S.N., Yoshioka, D.T., Kloezeman, K. & Bello, I. (2009). Clinical applications of behavioural assessment: identifying and explaining behaviour problems in clinical assessment. In J. Butcher (Ed.), *Oxford Handbook of Clinical Assessment*. New York: Oxford University Press.

Hodgins, S. (2008a). Criminality among persons with severe mental illness. In K. Soothill, M. Dolan & P. Rogers (Eds), *The Handbook of Forensic Mental Health* (pp. 400–23). Cullompton, Devon: Willan.

Hodgins, S. (2008b). Violent behaviour among people with schizophrenia: a framework for interventions of causes and effective treatment and prevention. *Philosophical Transactions of the Royal Society B*, *363*, 2505–18.

Hodgins, S., Viding, E. & Plodowski, A. (Eds). (2008). The neurobiology of violence: implications for prevention and treatment. *Philosophical Transactions of the Royal Society B*, *363*, 1503.

Hollin, C.R. (2006). Offending behaviour programmes and contention: evidence-based practice, manuals and programme evaluation. In C.R. Hollin & E.J. Palmer (Eds), *Offending Behaviour Programmes: Development, Application and Controversies* (pp. 33–67). Chichester: Wiley.

Howard, R. (2009). The neurobiology of affective dyscontrol: implications for understanding 'Dangerous and Severe Personality Disorder'. In M. McMurran & R. Howard (Eds), *Personality, Personality Disorder and Risk of Violence* (pp. 157–74). Chichester: Wiley.

Howard, R., Howells, K., Jinks, M. & McMurran, M. (2009). A quadripartite typology of violence (QTV): relationships with functions of aggression. In I. Needham, P. Callaghan, T. Palmstierna, H. Nijman & N. Oud (Eds), *Proceedings of the 6th European Congress on Violence in Clinical Psychiatry* (pp. 342–45). Amsterdam: Kavanagh.

Howard, R.C., Huband, N., Mannion, A. & Duggan, C. (2008). Exploring the link between personality disorder and criminality in a community sample. *Journal of Personality Disorders*, *22*, 589–603.

Howells, K. (1998). Cognitive-behavioural therapy for anger, aggression and violence. In N. Tarrier, A. Wells & G. Haddock (Eds), *Complex Cases in Cognitive-Behavioural Therapy*. Chichester: Wiley.

Howells, K. (2008). The treatment of anger in offenders. In A. Day, M. Nakata & K. Howells (Eds), *Anger in Indigenous Men*. Annandale, NSW: Federation Press.
Howells, K. (2009). Angry affect, aggression and personality disorder. In M. McMurran & R. Howard (Eds), *Personality, Personality Disorder and Risk of Violence* (pp. 191–212). Chichester: Wiley.
Howells, K., Day, A. & Thomas-Peter, B. (2004). Treating violence: forensic mental health and criminological models compared. *Journal of Forensic Psychiatry and Psychology*, *15*, 391–406.
Howells, K., Daffern, M. & Day, A. (2008). Aggression and violence. In K. Soothill, M. Dolan & P. Rogers (Eds), *The Handbook of Forensic Mental Health* (pp. 351–74). Cullompton, Devon: Willan.
Howells, K., Krishnan, G. & Daffern, M. (2007). Challenges in the treatment of dangerous and severe personality disorder. *Advances in Psychiatric Treatment*, *13*, 325–32.
Howells, K. & Tennant, A. (2007). Ready or not they are coming: dangerous and severe personality disorder and treatment engagement. In E. Sullivan & R. Shuker (Eds), *Issues in Forensic Psychology No. 7: Readiness for Treatment* (pp. 11–20). Leicester: British Psychological Society.
Hubbard, J., McAuliffe, M.D., Rubin, R.R. & Morrow, M.T. (2007). The anger–aggression relation in violent children and adolescents. In T.A. Cavell & K.T. Malcolm (Eds), *Anger, Aggression and Interventions for Interpersonal Violence*. Mahwah, NJ: Lawrence Erlbaum.
Jolliffe, D. & Farrington, D.P. (2009). A systematic review of the relationship between childhood impulsiveness and later violence. In M. McMurran & R.C. Howard (Eds), *Personality, Personality Disorder and Violence* (pp. 41–62). Chichester: Wiley.
Kuyken, W. (2006). Research and evidence base in case formulation. In N. Tarrier (Ed.), *Case Formulation in Cognitive Behaviour Therapy: The Treatment of Challenging and Complex Clinical Cases* (pp. 12–35). London: Brunner Routledge.
McEllistrem, J.E. (2004). Affective and predatory violence: a bimodal classification system of human aggression and violence. *Aggression and Violent Behavior*, *10*, 1–30.
McGuire, J. (2008). A review of effective interventions for reducing aggression and violence. *Philosophical Transactions of the Royal Society B.*, *363*, 2577–97.
Mischel, W. (2004). Towards an integrative science of the person. *Annual Review of Psychology*, *55*, 1–22.
Novaco, R.W. (2007). Anger dysregulation. In T.A. Cavell & K.T. Malcolm (Eds), *Anger, Aggression and Interventions for Interpersonal Violence* (pp. 3–54). Mahah, NJ: Lawrence Erlbaum.
Patrick, C.J. (2006). *The Handbook of Psychopathy*. New York: Guilford Press.
Polaschek, D.L.L., Calvert, S.W. & Gannon, T.A. (2008). Linking violent thinking: implicit theory based research with violent offenders. *Journal of Interpersonal Violence*, *23*, 259–75.
Rutter, M. (2008). Introduction to the papers. *Philosophical Transactions of the Royal Society B*, *363*, 2485–90.
Serin, R.C. (2004). Understanding violent offenders. In D.H. Fishbein (Ed.), *The Science, Treatment and Prevention of Antisocial Behaviors. Vol. 2: Evidence-Based Practice*. Kingston, NJ: Civic Research Institute.
Sestir, M.A. & Bartholow, B. (2007). Theoretical explanations of aggression and violence. In T.A. Gannon, T. Ward, A.R. Beech & D. Fisher (Eds), *Aggressive Offenders' Cognition*. Chichester: Wiley.
Sturmey, P. (1996). *Functional Analysis in Clinical Psychology*. Chichester: Wiley.
Sturmey, P. (2007). *Functional Analysis in Clinical Treatment*. Burlington, MA: Elsevier.
Sturmey, P. (Ed.). (2009). *Clinical Case Formulation: Varieties of Approaches*. Chichester: Wiley.
Thomas-Peter, B. (2006). The modern context of psychology in corrections: influences, limitation and values of 'What Works.' In G.J. Towl (Ed.), *Psychological Research in Prisons* (pp. 24–39). Oxford: Blackwell.
Ward, T., Day, A., Howells, K. & Birgden, A. (2004). The multifactor offender readiness model. *Aggression and Violent Behavior*, *9*, 645–73.
Ward, T. & Maruna, S. (2007). *Rehabilitation*. London: Routledge.

PART II

THE APPLICATION OF OPB TO ASSESSMENT AND TREATMENT OF CRIMINAL BEHAVIOURS

Chapter 4

APPROACHES TO DEVELOPING OPB FORMULATIONS

LAWRENCE JONES

Consultant Clinical and Forensic Psychologist, Lead Psychologist, Peaks Unit, Rampton Hospital, Nottinghamshire Healthcare NHS Trust, UK.

INTRODUCTION

> ... it is always fallacious to infer a causal linkage between thematically kindred events from their mere thematic kinship. Yet it *may* happen that *additional* information will sustain such a causal inference in certain cases. (Grünbaum, 2004, p. 158)

Offence paralleling behaviour (OPB) is potentially useful for developing formulations relating to risk and for devising interventions targeting idiographically identified criminogenic needs. Clinicians use formulation all the time but may not systematize the way in which they do this. The quote from Grünbaum (2004) above identifies the dangers inherent in this activity. The all too common occurrence of practitioners unthinkingly seeing all behaviour as offence paralleling needs to be addressed. Recent work on case formulation highlights concerns about the validity and reliability of formulation that have been largely overlooked historically (e.g., Garb, 1998; Kuyken, 2006). In this chapter, it is argued that case formulation procedures are similar to qualitative methodologies and that strategies developed to address validity and reliability in qualitative research can be profitably used for the generation of hypotheses in case formulation. Single case methodology can then be used for more systematic exploration of these hypotheses (see Chapter 18).

Practitioners increasingly acknowledge that there are problems with a mechanical reliance on actuarial instruments in risk management. This kind of approach is based on group data and is less helpful for predicting the behaviour of individuals (Berlin et al., 2003; Bickley & Beech, 2001; Grubin, 1999; Hart et al., 2007). Recent developments in risk assessment reaffirm the utility of case formulation in risk assessment, for example, Hart's (e.g. 2008) concept of scenario planning. The OPB paradigm offers a framework for case formulation. As discussed in Jones (2004), there are problems with reconviction based actuarial assessments, primarily because the reconviction rate does not necessarily index actual rate of offending. This is essentially a

Offence Paralleling Behaviour: A Case Formulation Approach to Offender Assessment and Intervention Edited by Michael Daffern, Lawrence Jones and John Shine

problem with construct validity of actuarial assessments (e.g. Sizmur, 2008). While it cannot be used to make probabilistic statements about risk, OPB offers a useful approach to identifying risk-relevant current behaviour and significant possible risk events.

OPB is also clinically relevant and helps to make causal hypotheses about the links between change in current context and possible future performance. Jones (2004; see also Shingler & Strong, 2003) identified the utility of Kohlenberg and Tsai's (Kohlenberg & Tsai, 1994; see also Tsai et al., 2009) functional analytic psychotherapy (FAP) as an integrative behavioural model for developing OPB formulations. Many interventions addressing offending have focused primarily on developing insight and skills; Kohlenberg and Tsai's work highlights the importance of working on current behaviour reflecting the presenting problem or any change away from it. The OPB paradigm proposes a radical refocus of intervention towards working with offence and change-relevant behaviour in the here and now as well as exploring the past.

All forensic assessment is assessment of parallel functioning because clients' offending cannot be observed. However, it is not clear how comprehensive interventions based on this kind of assessment really are. Theorists argue that there are a number of different pathways to change. Multi-level psychological models (e.g. Barnard & Teasdale, 1991; Power & Dalgleish, 1997) highlight the possibility of change in more than one cognitive system, a propositional system, which is constituted by conscious reasoning processes, and an implicational system, which uses a more abstract holistic schematic representation, which integrates sensory, conceptual and bodily inputs and so accounts for affective states. Forensic interventions typically address offending by going through accounts of the offence and using this to develop an understanding of what situations are potentially high-risk. These interventions are focusing on change processes linked primarily with the propositional system. This does not address the full constellation of psychological factors that were around at the time of the offence. Looking at OPB is potentially a way of doing this. It enables formulation of and interventions with behaviour in the here and now using interventions that do not just address insight, but also address some of the less obviously conscious or language-based kinds of cognitive and behavioural processes described by the multi-level theorists.

DEVELOPING A FORMULATION OF RISK BEHAVIOURS FOR INDIVIDUAL CASES

Practice algorithms are a step-by-step procedural account of current best practice in a particular area. Jones (2002, 2007b) suggested a model for their use in forensic psychology. A diagram illustrating a practice algorithm for developing an OPB case formulation is presented below. The component parts of this practice algorithm will be described in more detail (Figure 4.1).

It is not possible to develop an OPB model if there is no formulation for the individual's offence(s). This *reference formulation* (see Jones, 2010 for a model of integrative case formulation) is then used to establish whether or not other behaviours can usefully be seen as offence paralleling. There are two kinds of formulation: the specific functional analysis or formulation of different individual offences, and the analysis of themes and common processes underpinning different offences. This can take the form of a series of hypotheses about common factors (e.g. personality traits, relationship problems, depressed mood) identified through thematic analysis of offence formulations. Looking at the function of specific offence-related behaviours is also useful. The offence is often best analysed as a sequence, rather than as a single 'event' with 'a function'. The steps in the practice algorithm are as follows.

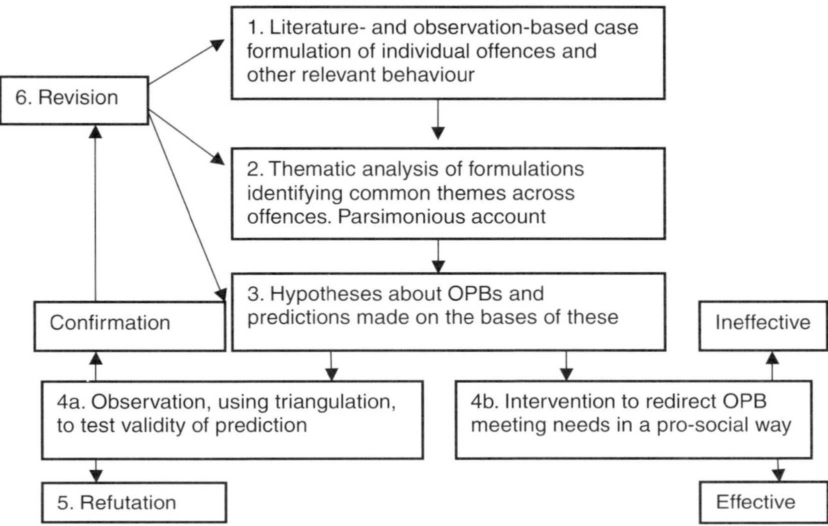

Figure 4.1 Practice algorithm for identifying offence paralleling behaviour.

The clinical literature relevant to the offence and individual case is reviewed in developing the formulation. It is also important to test whether the generic models of offending behaviour described in the literature (e.g. the integrated theory of sexual offending (ITSO) Ward & Beech, 2004, 2006) match the information available for the individual case; is this individual similar enough to the cohort researched in the literature to warrant using the same model with the individual case – a form of validation called 'pattern matching' (Campbell, 1966; Trochim, 1985; Yin, 2003). Causal models of offending in the literature are of necessity for a generalized offender – for example, for the ITSO model, 'a sex offender'. The clinical task is akin to content analysis where predefined categories are used to organize clinical data; the categories deriving from the literature are imposed on the data (e.g. looking at the case material for a specific sex offender and analysing it in terms of the different causal factors outlined in the ITSO).

The validity of this formulation is dependent upon (a) the extent to which the theoretical model it is based on has been validated; (b) the extent to which the individual case is deemed to be a good 'fit' to the model described in the literature; and (c) the extent to which interventions and predictions based on the formulation are effective. Examples of specific theoretical models described in the literature include Ward and Beech's (2006) ITSO, the range of psychological causal 'explanatory mechanisms' suggested by Persons (2009), and more generic models, such as Morton's (2004) suggestion that factors can be divided into domains of discourse (environmental, brain mechanisms, cognitive/affective and behavioural), which have more heuristic value in that they are not specific to a particular kind of task and are avoiding an overly parochial framework.

A contrasting 'bottom-up' approach, involving identifying themes for the particular offender in the clinical data can also useful. This involves analysing a range of problematic behaviours, especially any offending behaviour, and looking for themes that run through them. This method is more akin to 'grounded theory' (Strauss & Corbin, 1990), where the model is developed specifically for the individual case. The final formulation should be an integration of the two approaches and needs to be assessed against the criteria suggested later in this chapter. Figure 4.2 illustrates the relationship between idiographic and nomothetic approaches.

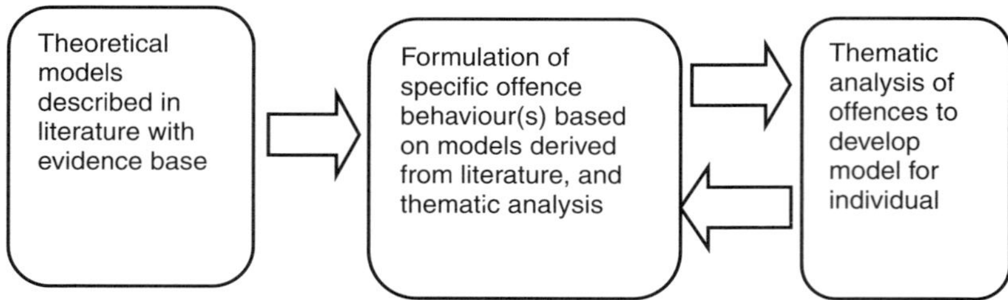

Figure 4.2 Linking theoretical model to individual case.

At this stage, the clinician should test the formulation against a series of offences, behavioural try-outs and near offences to see if it explains these events accurately. If it does, then it may be appropriate to proceed to making predictions. If it does not, then the model should be revised until it incorporates an account of the themes that underpin a range of different offences (though it must be recognized that there may be different functions for different kinds of offending). The next step is to make specific testable predictions of OPBs on the basis of the resultant reference formulation and see if these predictions come about. If they do not, then the model needs to be revised again. If they do, then it is appropriate to develop an appropriate intervention.

WHY A SEQUENCE OF BEHAVIOURS?

It is a clinical imperative that targetable antecedents need to be identified in order to intervene to prevent offending. There is also an identified requirement for lagged indicators of relapse. In a relapse prevention approach, it is generally agreed that processes that are closer to the offence may be more difficult to manage compared with more distal processes. For these reasons behaviour is better construed as a process than as an event. Different components of an offence sequence can have very different functions and yet they can still be part of a coherent, consistently repeating pattern of behaviour. Focusing on one function at the expense of the sequence of changing functions can get in the way of a clinically useful offence analysis.

Multiple data points in a developmental sequence also afford greater opportunity for testing the formulation being used. Trochim (1985) highlights the importance of having a number of predictions with a high degree of specificity in order to test the match between theory and tests of the prediction. The *non-equivalent dependent variable design* looks at more than one outcome measure and has specific predictions about how the different variables will change. In working with OPB, it is the match between a formulation and the predictions that are made on the basis of the formulation that is being evaluated. Having several observations with different predictions made about each is critical to this task. Trochim argues that predicting more complex patterns reduces the chances of finding plausible alternative explanations. This is an attempt to address the problems of under-determination (e.g. Klee, 1997); that is, the problem of choosing among competing theories that can each account for the same data.

Yin (2003) developed these ideas in his work on case study research. He highlighted the utility of explanation building in explanatory case studies (see the negative case analysis below), time-series and logic models where the investigator 'stipulates a complex chain of events over time. The events are staged in repeated cause-effect–cause-effect patterns, whereby a dependent variable (event) at an earlier stage becomes the independent variable (causal event) for the next stage' (p. 127). Sequential models of OPB, as well as being clinically more meaningful, lend themselves to more robust testing than one-stage models.

STRUCTURING A SEQUENTIAL ANALYSIS

Whilst an analysis of behaviour that is grounded in the data available should come up with unique sequential features for each individual, it is sometimes useful to look for particular kinds of feature in an offence process. These features include: (a) identifying the stressor or the triggering of the anticipated reward, since these establishing operations determine the kinds of function the behaviour has; (b) social context variables; (c) self-regulation changes in the lead-up to the offence; (d) the detection evasion skills (DES) used and their functions; (e) the offence procedures and offence functions; and (f) the procedures the individual uses to escape and withdraw from the crime scene.

SOURCES OF DATA

Data come from a range of sources, for instance, the offender's accounts of his or her past, observations of day-to-day behaviour recorded in case notes, accounts of custodial offences in depositions, social reports and clinical assessments. Ideally, any analysis should be done in collaboration with the individual offender and those who know them well. Gathering information about all offences from file information and collating different accounts of the same offence, social history, information about development of offending and accounts of 'try-outs' and OPB in the community can all be useful. Fantasies and plans that are about offending or that are associated with urges to offend are often very relevant.

Naturalistic observation of behaviour in custody is a useful source of information on which hypotheses about offending behaviour can be based. This can be done in a very detailed way (looking at the step-by-step sequence in a fight, for instance; who said what beforehand, whether the individual was trying to self-regulate or inciting themselves at some stage, what kinds of punching, kicking, biting, etc. were used and why...) or in a more broad-brush way (has visit, withdraws, becomes depressed, assaults). Whatever level of detail is used, a systematic review of offending skills needs to be undertaken.

Therapy interfering behaviours (Linehan, 1993) can be useful as a source of information about commitment-corroding processes for the individual. Goldstein's (1999, 2002) emphasis on non-offending offensive behaviour as offering an opportunity to intervene is useful in this context. It is also important to identify what detection and conviction evasion skills have emerged. Linked with this the extent and function of their secrecy skills repertoire is important to explore.

There is often a useful reciprocal relationship between considering the offence and current behaviour. Observations of offending patterns in OPB can be used to generate hypotheses about what happened at the time of the offence. So, for instance, if on the ward the OPB was preceded by an episode where the individual experienced a trauma flashback, they could then be asked if there was a similar pattern in the antecedents to their offending. This process of making links between current and past behaviour is summarized by the following two questions:

1. He/she was doing X in the lead-up to the offence. Is s/he doing this now on the ward/landing?
2. He/she was doing X on the landing/ward prior to OPB. Was this part of his/her offence process?

This process of linking can also be extended to looking at past experiences of abuse that may be recapitulated in the context of offending (Parker, 2004) and current offence-related fantasies.

1. He/she was doing X in the lead-up to the offence and OPB. Is s/he doing this now in fantasies? Is this a recapitulation of a theme from their experience of abuse?
2. He/she was doing X in fantasies or experienced this at time of being abused. Was this part of his/her offence process and OPB?

OFFENCE PARALLELING CONTINGENCIES

The analysis of offence paralleling situations is a critical task in the identification and interpretation of OPB. The ways in which custodial damping, a term used to describe the inhibitory effect of custody on the propensity to offend (Gentry & Ostapiuk, 1988; Jones, 2004), impacts on the possibility of OPB are important to analyse. One of the key sources of variance is the extent to which situations allow the individual to access and achieve goals and, conversely, the extent to which situations prevent the attainment of key goals or goods (Ward et al., 2007).

Surveillance and punishment have the effect of driving behaviour underground by increasing DES, i.e. skills repertoire in evading detection of offending. The more these factors are evident, the less likely it is that the individual will exhibit OPB. The coincidence of offence paralleling contingencies and systemic surveillance and punishment (or its anticipation) makes it more likely that OPB becomes secretive. Much of the process of becoming independent is about establishing sources of reinforcement that are not subjected to the control of surveillance (secrecy skills) and is often predicated on being able to obtain resources and pleasure without this being taken away by others with more power (see also Harrop & Trower, 2003). The function of secrecy is not just about evading detection, but it is also about establishing a sense of agency, dignity and independence. Contexts can be OPB supportive or inhibiting. An understanding of the relationship between the context and the individual's needs can be helpful in the analysis of OPB.

IDENTIFYING THEMES

In generating hypotheses through cross-situational analysis, *functional analysis* is a critical tool (e.g. Haynes & O'Brien, 2000). The offender profiling literature on *linkage analysis* and *modus operandi* is useful in this context. Unique 'developmental additions', often involving 'escalation', may also be useful to track across a behavioural series. Gresswell and Hollin (1992) suggested that offences in an offence series can be helpfully analysed in terms of what is repeated from the previous offence and what is uniquely developed in the current offence.

Thematic analysis requires some form of parsing of the behavioural sequence. Card sort techniques are a useful approach to the task, whether done literally with cards or 'on paper'. Identifying themes using this method is a process that involves sorting parsed behavioural components into a number of piles and then describing the criteria that has been used to sort into that pile. Sturmey's (2008) discussion of 'chaining' and 'task analysis' is a useful introduction to this kind of analysis from a behavioural perspective.

In the task of parsing behaviour, Jones (2004) pointed out that the action systems approach to behavioural modelling is potentially relevant (Clarke & Crossland, 1985; see also Fritzon & Miller, 2010, Chapter 8). Serial analysis of offending involves identifying behaviours that may have a similar function, psychological meaning or developmental structure. In doing this, it is useful not to simply look at single events (e.g. 'an offence') but to try to capture the various steps antecedent to the behaviour and to describe these as a sequence of discrete episodes. Establishing what constitutes a 'step' or 'parsing' behaviour into units needs to be done systematically, either using a theoretical model (perhaps trying to identify the stages of a standard developmental model of offending) or using Clarke and Crossland's (1985) suggestion of 'judging where the greatest discontinuities of form or function lie within the behavioural stream, sometimes by combining the views of a number of judges. . . ' (p. 103) as a strategy for parsing behaviour. It is also possible to use a criterion of episodes being clinically and psychologically meaningful to the investigator. This approach is particularly useful in thinking about how to break down behaviour into meaningful chunks. In the clinical context, this task can be done collaboratively with the client. Other clinicians can also be used as a source of hypotheses or as a way of testing the reliability of a particular parsing attempt. It is useful to include both antecedent and subsequent or consequent behaviours in the behavioural frame being investigated.

These sets of behaviours are taken from a number of contexts in an individual's life story. Contexts that have been clinically useful include childhood play behaviour, behavioural 'try-outs' and pre-offence OPB. An offending behaviour itinerary where offending skills in setting up, planning, gaining victim access, prosecuting an offence and fleeing from an offence can also be considered. In addition, detection and conviction evasion skills are important.

An example of a thematic analysis and the behavioural sequence underpinning is described for the fictional case of Peter in Box 4.1.

BOX 4.1 PETER (FICTIONAL CASE)

Themes

The following thematic sequence was derived from accounts of childhood experiences, offences and custodial experience.

Experiences or anticipates loss or rejection → feels abandoned → becomes distressed and then angry (anger offsets negative affect) → fantasises about drawing blood from woman → finds victim → acts out violent fantasy involving drawing blood → feels powerful, sexually aroused, and offsets feelings/fears of rejection.

Incidents from childhood

- When he was being evaluated for going into care at eight years of age, he reported an incident where he cut the arm of a girl in his class, first with a compass point but also was reported to have bitten her. He reported that he remembers her bleeding.
- Soon after this, he cut a girl's clothes at school with scissors for 'fun'. This was preceded by his being unsettled after being moved into care.
- At the age of 11, he reportedly stabbed a girl in his class with a pen 'for fun'.

Function: excitement, alleviation of anxiety, possibly expression of anger

(continues)

Offences

Childhood/adolescence:

- Had a fight and was restrained by a teacher who held him on the ground. Reports biting her and 'getting a buzz' out of the experience of fighting.
- Stabbed a paperboy with a knife. Reported feeling that he was going to be attacked so attacked first.
- Believed that a gang of 'skin-heads' were going to attack him. Threatened them with a knife.

Early twenties:

- A series of eight robberies of women on the street. Offences took place in context of a long-standing relationship that was deteriorating. All involved threatening victim with a knife for handbag. Described getting a sexual 'buzz' from doing this and on occasions going home and having sex with his partner thinking about what happened.
- Final offence involved cutting himself 'accidentally' during the course of a street robbery of a woman. He reportedly found the sight of blood sexually arousing. Reported cutting himself to avoid cutting the victim during the offence.

In custody

Reported current fantasies about making women bleed and becoming sexually aroused by this. An incident was reported by staff where he self-harmed, drawing blood, in the context of losing a significant relationship with a female nurse. He was reported to have made threats about her.

Exploration with Peter

When the sequence was explored with Peter, he agreed that this was a pattern that made sense to him (face validity). He indicated that he sometimes would fantasize about drawing blood without having experienced any obvious interpersonal stressors. He felt that this was because he had begun to find thoughts of drawing blood intrinsically sexually arousing. He also discussed feeling angry as giving him permission to fantasize in an aggressive way. He went on to explore the feelings of background anger he was currently feeling about rejection in his life and the way this had fed into violent retributive thoughts about women. He also indicated that the weapons incidents involving men were serving a different function. In these episodes he was much more concerned with self-defence.

The underlying sequence was a single-step sequence involving the generation of negative affect followed by offsetting it by generating feelings of anger and power. However, further exploration identified that Peter would also attempt to re-establish relationships when he felt that they were threatened. At times, however, his attempts to re-establish relationships

(continues)

were clumsy, based on imagined losses not real ones, desperate or had the opposite effect to that intended. (This represents the *reference formulation or functional analysis.*)

Predictions

It was predicted that if Peter were to re-enter this pattern of behaviour then:

- He would continue to fantasize about drawing blood both sexually and non-sexually.
- That these fantasies would become stronger when he was feeling rejected or when there was a significant absence (e.g. holiday of therapist or significant staff member) or loss (e.g. bereavement).
- Any situations that triggered attachment issues reminiscent of those that antedated the offence would precipitate a crisis and that the urge to act on the fantasies would become stronger at these times.
- Acting on the fantasies would either involve self-harm or attempts to draw blood from others.

The pattern was shared with Peter and he agreed that these were possibilities.

Outcomes

In the year following the predictions, Peter did not engage in any self-harm. He reported on two occasions getting very close to self-harming and on one occasion, fantasizing about acting on fantasies about cutting a female member of staff to draw blood. He continued to disclose having sexual fantasies involving drawing blood, not all of which had an obvious precursor of rejection or abandonment. During this period, Peter had not, however, experienced any significant relationships coming to an end. He had had a consistent relationship with his therapist (i.e. there were no changes in therapist or named nurse during the period). One of the episodes where he had nearly assaulted somebody was linked with him discussing his feelings about having been taken into care and the angry feelings this had triggered for him. This work appeared to trigger significant issues around abandonment for him and he described entering into a state similar to those in which he had offended.

Peter also had one episode of drug use during the year. He reported that drug use exacerbated both his feelings of anger at being rejected and his anticipation of excitement at the thought of engaging in blood-drawing behaviour on himself or victims in the context of sexual arousal.

Revisions

The OPB pattern was revised to take into account the additional steps (optional) of attempting to frantically repair the relationship and drug use, both as a way of trying to break out of the pattern and as a way of adding fuel to the process of self-incitement to offend associated with anticipating intense arousal if he acted on his fantasies.

CUSTODIAL BEHAVIOUR

Custodial behaviour that is not offence paralleling needs to be clearly distinguished from that which is. In addition, any behaviour that is evidence of positive change needs to be recognized and rewarded.

Prosocial Alternative Behaviour

Prosocial alternative behaviour (PAB) was highlighted by Jones (2004) and further developed as a construct by Daffern et al. (2007). This is the behaviour that evidences changes in past patterns of offence-related behaving. Analysis of PABs can be diagnostically useful in identifying at what point in a possible offence process an individual has managed to implement self-regulation skills. If this is late in the sequence, then it suggests that further work introducing self-regulation earlier in the sequence would be useful.

Unique Custodial Reactions

A unique custodial reaction (UCR) is behaviour provoked by the abnormality of the custodial context that is not evident outwith custody. This is difficult to identify as it can be pathologized as indicating that an individual is still exhibiting behaviours that are evidence of risk. An example of a UCR is expressing anger about loss of freedom and/or any obstacles to the possibility of moving towards liberty. Indeed, a significant component of any offender's experience in custody is likely to involve a range of reactions to the custodial experience and their loss of liberty. The concept of skills atrophy in custodial settings highlights the importance of identifying custodial responses that may be seen as normal reactions to custody (Benn, 2002). The clinical task is to try to separate out the extent to which an individual's presentation is due to a UCR as opposed to some form of OPB. The chances are that the presentation is a combination of both. Moreover, there may be some aspects of the custodial experience that exacerbate the underlying tendency to offend or evidence OPB. For example, an individual who offended violently due to feelings of anger about people in authority, with a history of being a victim of sexual or violent abuse in institutional settings, may become extremely violent in a custodial setting. Tarrier (2007) describes a similar dilemma in working with people diagnosed with psychosis: 'The patient needs to be able to discriminate between an actual relapse prodrome and normal mood fluctuations that do not signal a relapse. This is done through a process of discrimination training whereby the patient monitors mood and experience over a number of weeks with a goal of learning to distinguish a real prodrome from a false alarm' (p. 487). With an offender, a similar task might be differentiating between everyday anger, anger linked specifically to the custodial experience and offence-paralleling anger processes.

Once an offence-related psychological risk factor has been identified, a critical task is to identify what is happening to it currently – is it being expressed as an OPB, has it changed or is it being inhibited either through lack of opportunity or through self-regulation?

VALIDITY AND RELIABILITY

The construct of OPB, or similar constructs, has been critiqued by a number of commentators. Alison et al. (2003) suggested that ambiguous statements in offender profiles can be accepted as accurate, in the same way as the 'Barnum' effect, where people accept ambiguous accounts (e.g. in horoscopes) as being true about themselves. Others, for example Towl and Crighton (1995), have argued that it is prone to the kinds of bias identified by Kahneman et al. (1982), namely the representativeness, availability and anchoring/adjustment biases. The representativeness bias refers to the tendency to see surface issues (A) as representative of another set of issues (B), enabling what we know about B to be applied to A. In the Rosenhan study (1973) in which Rosenhan and his colleagues presented to psychiatrists as normally functioning people reporting only one symptom (a voice saying 'dull,' 'thud' and 'empty'), the psychiatrists misapplied the representativeness heuristic and admitted the researchers to psychiatric hospital, often with a diagnosis of schizophrenia. Practitioners need to be trained in the nature of this and other biases. Peer review (see below) can be structured in such a way so as to check on the different sources of bias in a systematic manner.

The availability bias is the tendency to use more readily available information in decision-making. Information that comes more readily to mind is more likely to be regarded as salient and used. Availability is determined by frequency, recency, vividness and effectiveness of search set. Several empirical studies have found evidence of the availability bias and suggest that it is particularly powerful because practitioners are often unaware of its effects. Following a protocol requiring inspection of a full range of data sources can go some way to offsetting this.

The anchoring and adjustment bias refers to the tendency to organize judgements around either an initial hypothesis or an otherwise overriding attributional bias. For example, the fundamental attribution error refers to a basic tendency to attribute people's behaviour to dispositional qualities rather than their situation. Requiring the practitioner to try a range of hypotheses from a range of domains (see Morton, 2004), including situational with dispositional hypotheses, can help to offset this bias. In addition, practitioners need to be encouraged to see hypotheses as provisional.

Formulation generally can be given warranty through two routes: either it identifies a psychological process that has been shown in the literature to be associated with reconviction or as offence-related, or it has been shown in the *individual case* to be consistently associated with offending behaviour. So, for example, having antisocial attitudes such as glorifying offending behaviour might be identified in an individual's OPB. This could be justified on the grounds that it has been shown in meta-analyses of predictors of reconviction to have a degree of predictive validity. The validity of the empirical evidence is passed on to the individual case if the assumption can be made that the individual case is a representative of the population upon which the evidence was based. It can, however, also be justified if, in the individual case, there was a history of specific antisocial cognitions (such as denigration of people in authority or justifications for treating people as objects) as being antecedent to offending. Through a process of induction (and failure to find a counter-example/refuting example) repeated episodes where the same antecedents are followed by the same consequences confer a higher degree of confidence in this combination as being likely to be repeated.

Testing the validity of any OPB predictions and the formulation that they are based on is a significant task for the practitioner. Subjecting the formulation to some form of test will result in a greater degree of confidence in its validity as long as it is a valid test and the test supports the formulation.

Kuyken (Kuyken, 2006; Kuyken et al., 2009) proposed the following guidelines for judging the validity of formulations. First, a top-down criterion is whether the theory on which the formulation is founded is evidence-based. Second, bottom-up criteria relate to the reliability and validity of the formulation. (Was the formulation process adequate? Can clinicians agree? Does the formulation triangulate with the client's experience, any standardized measures, professional/expert/panel consensus and clinical supervisor's impressions?) The practitioner is advised to follow a number of practice rules: (a) generate provisional formulations; (b) hold alternative formulations in mind; (c) provide adequate tests for formulations; (d) triangulate by testing hypotheses with client, individuals in the client's network, supervisor and standardized assessments; (e) have sensitivity to the impact of factors known to affect judgement (e.g. task complexity, practitioner competence and time pressures); (f) justify formulations through case notes and/or supervision; (g) follow contemporary practice guidelines; and (h) formulate using best available cognitive–behavioural theory and research.

If OPB is being used in an argument not to release somebody, then it needs to be well evidenced and tested. In the context of an intervention, on the other hand, it may be appropriate to see more behaviours as offence-related in order to encourage a habit of looking for this possibility.

QUALITATIVE STRATEGIES FOR IDENTIFYING THEMES AND ADDRESSING VALIDITY AND RELIABILITY

In this section, strategies for hypothesizing themes that can be used to make predictions about future possible OPBs will be explored and evaluated. Cassar, Ward and Thakkar (2003) used grounded theory to identify themes across *different* offenders' accounts of homicides. These were then used to develop a generic model of the offending process. The identical techniques used by these authors can be used ideographically, using an individual series of offences, near-offences and functionally similar behaviours. The unit of analysis is behaviour episodes and their psychological drivers (i.e. function) for an individual case, not offences across different offenders.

Jones (2004, 2007a) proposed using a range of strategies for identifying and testing themes in OPBs. He indicated that a structured approach to identifying patterns and themes in individual case narrative data was preferable to leaving it to intuition. Jones (2004) suggested a process of 'serial deviant case analysis' based on Kelly and Taylor (1981); this involves repeatedly revising the model in the face of cases that do not fit, until the model describes all new presentations. Indeed, case formulation is based on a qualitative methodology that is not necessarily spelt out by the practitioner. The clinician attempts to analyse a specific problem by identifying themes in the way that problem presents for the individual. Different practitioners will do this in different ways by trying to see if the data they have can be fitted to a theoretical template in a procrustean manner. So, for a behavioural analysis, all behaviour is analysed as being driven by reinforcement or punishment. A cognitive behavioural analysis would attempt to identify themes in the kinds of self-talk or schemas and modes that an individual has in order to develop a case formulation. The process of categorization used by the clinician is thus *theory-laden*. The nearest qualitative methodology to this is content analysis, in which a pre-existing schema is used to make sense of the data. This does not, however, allow for a 'bottom-up' identification of themes that emerge from the data, as might be sought in analyses such as grounded theory (Strauss & Corbin, 1990) or Interpretative Phenomenological analysis (IPA) (Smith & Osborn, 2003).

Qualitative methodologies offer a range of strategies for identifying themes with accompanying tests of validity. Useful constructs derived from this literature include looking for unusual or unique behaviours, either to a particular offender or to a particular offence series, adapting a model in light of instances that do not fit and actively seeking out refutation, and looking at 'similarities and differences' within and between offences in order to identify themes.

A number of strategies to improve reliability and validity are suggested in the qualitative literature (e.g. Lincoln & Guba, 1985). They include adequate information-gathering through systematic reviews of file data of all kinds, interviews with the individual and with staff who have observed the individual and prolonged observation of the individual. This helps to avoid developing formulations too quickly on the basis of little evidence. Triangulation is also highlighted as a validation strategy in the qualitative literature, including data triangulation (i.e. obtaining data from different sources), observer triangulation (i.e. obtaining data from different observers) and method triangulation (i.e. using different methods for observation) (Flick, 1992). If some degree of agreement is obtained across the different sources, more credence can be given to the hypothesis being tested.

Checking the OPB formulation with the person concerned is useful, although this strategy needs to take into account the position that the individual takes in relation to the therapeutic process. If they are actively opposed to therapy, then it is possible that they will react badly to this process. If, on the other hand, they are sympathetic to the clinical task, then this approach can be very useful both in terms of improving validity and in terms of the therapeutic impact of conducting the interview and exploring the issues with them. Initial questions about OPB can be explored with the individual to see if they cover all the relevant domains. They may respond by indicating that there are a number of other areas of their life where this same pattern of interacting or behaving was evident and these new contexts can then be systematically explored to see if they offer any new information about the underlying pattern of behaviour being analysed. Jones (2007a) suggested that asking staff and the patient's peer group about whether the behaviour identified as OPB is in a real sense offence paralleling can be useful.

Peer review might involve theme identification with one or more peers who are blind to each other's conclusions. The outcomes of this process can then be compared and contrasted to identify reasons for agreement and or disagreements.

Testing OPB formulations to see if they are effective at predicting behaviour is a procedure that adds significantly to the clinical validity of the formulation. A hypothesis that has been exposed to the possibility of refutation but which has withstood this is more credible than one which has not been through this process. Predictions are a way of testing the construct validity of the OPB model that has been generated. As with tests of construct validity in other contexts, it is useful to identify a range of different implications falling out of the model and test out whether reality matches these.

Predictions about specific OPBs based on an analysis of the individual's offence repertoire are useful. A clear indication of the time-frame within which the expected OPBs would occur is important. If the predictions do not actually come about, then the hypothesis needs to be revised. In this sense, the process is potentially continuous and iterative.

An example of a prediction for a male offender who committed a sadistic assault during a 'one-night stand' following a failed business deal might be as follows. Developmental antecedents might be experiencing sadistic sexual assault in school and bullying girls in school while being seemingly oblivious to the possibility of this being inappropriate. This, in conjunction with an assessment indicating high levels of arousal to sadistic sexual behaviour, might lead to a hypothesized underlying process of a sadistic interest in seeing others suffering and an absence of aversive reactions to seeing others in distress. Where there is increased arousal in relation to a stressor (an establishing operation), seeing others suffering might be used as a way of offsetting distress. In this case, predicted OPBs would be enjoyment of behaviour with a sadistic theme and this enjoyment would be magnified in times of stress. The specific behaviours one might look for are expressions of interest in sadistic sexual fantasies and an admission of using such fantasies to manage difficult interpersonal situations.

Several of these strategies echo the formulation guidelines proposed by Kuyken (Kuyken, 2006; Kuyken et al., 2009).

STRESS, STATE AND PLANNING AS ANTECEDENTS FOR ENACTMENT OF OPB

Stupa and Waters (2005) provided evidence of the relationship between state and schema activation. Different states are associated with different worldviews and act as establishing operations changing reinforcing and punishing properties of the environment. Emotion and mood, then, can be usefully seen as offence paralleling establishing operations or setting events. They are discrete events, or states, that prime the individual, for a limited period of time, to find some behaviours more reinforcing and some more punishing. For example, anger may make the possibility of reinforcement through physical attack more reinforcing.

Ressler et al. (1988) identified stressors, such as conflict, financial difficulties, marital problems, birth of a child, physical injury, legal problems, employment problems and bereavement as triggers for acting out fantasies about offending. These stressors trigger a 'frame of mind' – equivalent to state in the model above – such as frustration, hostility, anger or agitation and excitement. The stimulus context can thus be seen as activating an underlying trait or propensity, which results in a state which acts as the establishing operation for the offending (or paralleling) behaviour. Identifying traits and propensities and then exploring what kinds of stimuli trigger off states associated with them that lead to OPB can be useful in developing an individualized formulation.

SYSTEMIC PROCESSES

The importance of social contextual or systemic factors has often been neglected in case formulation (cf. Tarrier & Calam, 2002). An OPB can often be evidenced in the pattern of behaviours emerging in the social network around the individual. In the following fictional example, the individual ends up behaving with a member of staff in a similar way as they did with their mother. The individual's behaviour 'pulls' a reciprocating collusion from the member of staff (see Jones, 1997). In childhood, the individual formed a close relationship with his mum (enmeshed), to the exclusion of dad, who lost any authority in the family. He went on to offend, in his teens, using violence in the context of extortion. Following custody, he formed a cosy, idealized relationship with a female hostel worker who 'turned a blind eye' to warning signs of offending. In custody, he got 'perks' as a cleaner and formed a very close relationship with a member of staff. Staff generally feel charmed by him and do not respond to his strong-arming of other inmates on the wing. The predictions for future OPB for this individual might include staff being pulled into collusive relationships where things that others might be challenged about are ignored.

Behaviour that 'pulls' either overly cosy and collusive behaviour or overly punitive and retaliatory responses from practitioners is a useful focus for exploring OPB. Collusive behaviour from peers or authority figures can be associated with decreased fear of getting caught and has the effect of increasing the chances of offending. Punitive responses have the effect of driving behaviour 'underground' and increasing the implementation of DES.

A common pattern for OPB enactments, highlighted by Jones (2004, 2007a) is a reminder of a traumatic *or* intensely pleasurable experience, which then precipitates a relapse process

The social contexts associated with these experiences can become precipitants or maintenance factors for OPB in the current context.

CONCLUSIONS

An approach to developing and testing out OPB formulations has been introduced. The utility of qualitative methodology in developing themes for individual case formulation has also been explored. Some of the pitfalls that confront any formulation-driven, idiographic, applied psychology enterprise have been addressed. In particular, it is hoped that practitioners expose their OPB hypotheses to a testing framework and seek to validate and establish reliability of the observations that they make.

The potential for constructive use of OPB formulations in risk assessment to identify risk potential and possibilities (not probabilities) and therapeutic activities has been highlighted. The radical shift for intervention work from analyses of past offending as a medium for gaining insight to working with 'live' or 'hot' behaviour in the current milieu as offence-related presents practitioners with a challenge to work more with live contingencies. The recent recovery (e.g. Jacobson & Greenley, 2001) and related good lives models of rehabilitation and intervention (e.g. Ward et al., 2007) also highlight the importance of interventions being delivered in the full 24 hours, not just in therapy sessions. The focus here, in forensic custodial settings, is to build an anticipatory 'custodial good life' as a rehearsal for a future 'good life' in the community. In non-custodial settings, it is about building a 'good life', through interventions targeting the whole lifestyle of the individual, which maximizes the extent to which the individual is meeting their needs in prosocial and non-offending ways. This requires forensic practitioners to develop milieu-focused conceptual frameworks and research agendas as well as focusing individual and group interventions on building a 'good life'.

REFERENCES

Alison, L.J., Smith, M.D. & Morgan, K. (2003). Interpreting the accuracy of offender profiles. *Psychology, Crime and Law*, *9*, 185–95.

Barnard, P.J. & Teasdale, J.D. (1991). Interacting cognitive subsystems: a systemic approach to cognitive-affective interaction and change. *Cognition and Emotion*, *5*, 1–39.

Benn, A. (2002). Cognitive behavioural therapy for psychosis in conditions of high security: cases 13 (Malcolm) and 14 (Colin). In D. Kingdon & D. Turkington (Eds), *The Case Study Guide to Cognitive Behaviour Therapy of Psychosis*. Chichester: Wiley.

Berlin, F.S., Galbreath, N.W., Geary, B. & McGlon, G. (2003). The use of actuarials at civil commitment hearings to predict the likelihood of future sexual violence. *Sexual Abuse: A Journal of Research and Treatment*, *15*, 377–82.

Bickley, J.A. & Beech, A.R. (2001). Classifying child abusers: its relevance to theory and clinical practice. *International Journal of Offender Therapy and Comparative Criminology*, *45*, 51–69.

Campbell, D.T. (1966). Pattern matching as an essential in distal knowing. In K.R. Hammond (Ed.), *The Psychology of Egon Brunswick* (pp. 81–106). New York: Holt, Rhinehart & Winston.

Cassar, E., Ward, T. & Thakkar, J. (2003). A descriptive model of the homicide process. *Behaviour Change*, *76*, 76–93.

Clarke, D.D. & Crossland, J. (1985). *Action Systems: An Introduction to the Analysis of Complex Behaviour*. London and New York: Methuen.

Daffern, M., Jones, L., Howells, K., Shine, J., Mikton, C. & Tunbridge, V.C. (2007). Refining the definition of offence paralleling behaviour. *Criminal Behaviour and Mental Health*, *17*, 265–73.

Flick, U. (1992). Triangulation revisited: strategy of or alternative to validation of qualitative data. *Journal of the Theory of Social Behavior*, *22*, 175–97.

Fritzon, K. & Miller, S. (1010). Functional consistency in female forensic psychiatric patients: an actions systems theory approach. In M. Daffern, L.F. Jones & J. Shine (Eds), *Offence Paralleling Behaviour: A Case Formulation Approach to Offender Assessment and Intervention*. Chichester: Wiley-Blackwell.

Garb, H.N. (1998). *Studying the Clinician: Judgment Research and Psychological Assessment*. Washington, DC: American Psychological Association.

Gentry, M. & Ostapiuk, E.G. (1988). The management of violence in a youth treatment centre. *Clinical Approaches to Aggression and Violence: Issues in Criminological and Legal Psychology*, No. 12. Leicester: British Psychological Society.

Goldstein, A.P. (1999). *Low Level Aggression: First Steps on the Ladder to Violence*. Champaign, IL: Research Press.

Goldstein, A.P. (2002). Low-level aggression: definition, escalation, intervention. In J. McGuire (Ed.), *Offender Rehabilitation and Treatment: Effective Programmes and Policies to Reduce Offending*. Chichester: Wiley.

Gresswell, D.M. & Hollin, C.R. (1992). Towards a new methodology for making sense of case material: an illustrative case involving attempted multiple murder. *Criminal Behaviour and Mental Heath, 2*, 329–41.

Grubin, D. (1999). Actuarial and clinical assessment of risk in sex offenders. *Journal of Interpersonal Violence, 14*, 331–43.

Grünbaum, A. (2004). The heurmeneutic versus the scientific conception of psychoanalysis. In J. Mills (Ed.), *Psychoanalysis at the Limit: Epistemology, Mind, and the Question of Science* (pp. 139–60). New York: State University of New York Press.

Harrop, C.E. & Trower, P. (2003). *Why Does Schizophrenia Develop at Late Adolescence?* Chichester: Wiley.

Hart, S.D. (2008). The future of violence risk assessment and management: from prediction to prevention, from formula to formulation. Keynote speech, International Association for Forensic Mental Health Conference. Vienna.

Hart, S.D., Michie, C. & Cooke, D.J. (2007). Precision of actuarial risk assessment instruments: evaluating the 'margins of error' of group v. individual predictions of violence. *British Journal of Psychiatry, 190*, 60–65.

Haynes, S.N. & O'Brien, W.H. (2000). *Principles and Practice of Behavioral Assessment*. New York: Plenum.

Jacobson, N. & Greenley, D. (2001). What is recovery? A conceptual model and explication. *Psychiatric Services, 52*, 482–85.

Jones, L.F. (1997). Developing models for managing treatment integrity and efficacy in a prison based TC: the Max Glatt Centre. In E. Cullen, L. Jones & R. Woodward (Eds), *Therapeutic Communities for Offenders*. Chichester: Wiley.

Jones, L.F. (2002). An individual case formulation approach to the assessment of motivation. In M. McMurran (Ed.), *Motivating Offenders to Change*. Chichester: Wiley.

Jones, L.F. (2004). Offence paralleling behaviour (OPB) as a framework for assessment and interventions with offenders. In A. Needs & G. Towl (Eds), *Applying Psychology to Forensic Practice*. Oxford: Blackwell.

Jones, L.F. (2007a). Offence paralleling behaviour (OPB): the relevance of in-treatment behaviour to risk assessment, management and intervention. Paper presented at the Annual Conference of the International Association for Forensic Mental Health, Adelaide, Australia.

Jones, L.F. (2007b). Individual case formulation approach to assessment and intervention with engagement. In E. Sullivan & R. Shuker (Eds), *Readiness for Treatment*. Issues in Forensic Psychology, No. 7. Leicester: British Psychological Society.

Jones, L.F. (2010). Case formulation. In K. Howells & A. Tennant (Eds), *Using Time, Not Doing Time: Practitioner Perspectives on Personality Disorder and Risk*. Chichester: Wiley-Blackwell.

Kahneman, D., Slovic, P. & Tversky, A. (1982). *Judgement under Uncertainty: Heuristics and Biases*. Cambridge: Cambridge University Press.

Kelly, D. & Taylor, H. (1981). Take and escape: a personal construct study of car 'theft'. In H. Bonarius, R. Holland & S. Rosenberg (Eds), *Personal Construct Psychology: Recent Advances in Theory and Practice*. London: Macmillan.

Klee, R. (1997). *Introduction to the Philosophy of Science: Cutting Nature at its Seams*. London: Oxford University Press.

Kohlenberg, R.J. & Tsai, M. (1994). Functional analytic psychotherapy: a radical behavioral approach to treatment and integration. *Journal of Psychotherapy Integration, 4*, 175–201.

Kuyken, W. (2006). Evidence-based case formulation. Is the emperor clothed? In N. Tarrier (Ed.), *Case Formulation in Cognitive Behaviour Therapy: The Treatment of Challenging and Complex Cases*. London: Routledge.

Kuyken, W., Padesky, C.A. & Dudley, R. (2009). *Collaborative Case Conceptualization: Working Effectively with Clients in Cognitive Behavioral Therapy*. New York: Guilford Press.

Lincoln, Y.S. & Guba, E.G. (1985). *Naturalistic Inquiry*. Beverly Hills, CA: Sage.

Linehan, M.M. (1993). *Cognitive Behavioral Treatment of Borderline Personality Disorder*. New York: Guilford Press.

Morton, J. (2004). *Understanding Developmental Disorders: A Causal Modelling Approach*. Oxford: Blackwell.

Parker, M. (2004). Violence, sexual offending and sexual abuse: are they linked? A qualitative research study. In D. Jones (Ed.), *Working with Dangerous People: The Psychotherapy of Violence*. Oxford: Radcliffe Medical Press.

Persons, J.B. (2009). *The Case Formulation Approach to Cognitive-Behaviour Therapy*. New York: Guilford Press.

Power, M.J. & Dalgleish, T. (1997). *Cognition and Emotion: From Order to Disorder*. Hove: Psychology Press.

Ressler, R.K., Burgess, A.W. & Douglas, J.E. (1988). *Sexual Homicide: Patterns and Motives*. Lanham, MA: Lexington Books.

Rosenhan, D.L. (1973). On being sane in insane places. *Science*, *179*(70), 250–58.

Shingler, S. & Strong, L. (2003). Putting the 'B' Back into CBT: The Use of Behavioural Contingencies in Sex Offender Treatment – Summary of Paper Presented at the Annual NOTA Conference 2002, Lancaster. *NOTA News*, 45.

Sizmur, S. (2008, July). Construct validity and risk assessment for serious offending. Paper presented at the 8th International Association of Forensic Mental Health Services, Vienna.

Smith, J.A. & Osborn, M. (2003). Interpretative phenomenological analysis. In J.A. Smith (Ed.), *Qualitative Psychology*. London: Sage.

Strauss, A. & Corbin, J. (1990). *Basics of Qualitative Research: Grounded Theory Procedures and Techniques*. London: Sage.

Stupa, L. & Waters, A. (2005). The effect of mood on responses to the Young Schema Questionnaire: short form. *Psychology and Psychotherapy: Theory, Research and Practice*, *78*, 45–57.

Sturmey, P. (2008). *Behavioural Case Formulation*. Chichester: Wiley.

Tarrier, N. (2007). Schizophrenia and other psychotic disorders. In D.H. Barlow (Ed.), *Clinical Handbook of Psychological Disorders: A Step-by-Step Treatment Manual*. New York: Guilford Press.

Tarrier, N. & Calam, R. (2002). New developments in cognitive-behavioural case formulation. Epidemiological, systemic and social context: an integrative approach. *Behavioural and Cognitive Psychotherapy*, *30*, 311–28.

Towl, G. & Crighton, D.A. (1995). Risk assessment in prisons: a psychological critique. *Forensic Update*, *40*, 6–14.

Trochim, W. (1985). Pattern matching, validity and conceptualisation in programme development. *Evaluation Review*, *9*, 575–604.

Tsai, M., Kohlenberg, R.J., Kanter, J.W., Kohlenberg, B., Follette, W.C. & Callaghan, G.M. (2009). *A Guide to Functional Analytic Psychotherapy: Awareness, Courage, Love, and Behaviorism*. New York: Springer.

Ward, T. & Beech, A.R. (2004). The integration of etiology and risk in sexual offenders: a theoretical framework. *Aggression and Violent Behaviour*, *10*, 31–63.

Ward, T. & Beech, T. (2006). An integrated theory of sexual offending. *Aggression and Violent Behavior*, *11*, 44–63.

Ward, T., Mann, R.E. & Gannon, T.A. (2007). The good lives model of offender rehabilitation: clinical implications. *Aggression and Violent Behavior*, *12*, 87–107.

Yin, R.K. (2003). *Case Study Research: Design and Methods* (3rd edition). Thousand Oaks, CA: Sage.

Chapter 5

OFFENCE PARALLELING BEHAVIOUR AND MULTIPLE SEQUENTIAL FUNCTIONAL ANALYSIS

DAVID M. GRESSWELL

University of Lincoln, and Consultant Clinical Psychologist, Peter Hodgkinson Centre, Lincoln, UK

DAVID L. DAWSON

Mid Yorkshire Hospitals NHS Trust and Lincolnshire Partnership Trust, Lincoln University, Lincoln, UK

INTRODUCTION: THE PROBLEM OF ANALYSING OFFENDING BEHAVIOUR

Formulation of client behaviour is one of the key clinical skills of applied psychologists but remains one of the most difficult aspects of their role. In general clinical practice, developing a formulation that incorporates psychological research and theory whilst simultaneously providing a parsimonious and accurate account of a client's difficulties, is an intricate task. However, the formulation of offending behaviour presents its own specific challenges.

Although challenging, formulation remains an essential step in facilitating an understanding of offending behaviour and allows the forensic practitioner to assess the level of risk (in terms of seriousness and form) an individual presents. Without a formulation, forensic practitioners will struggle to predict the circumstances under which risk is likely to be most salient, or provide recommendations as to how those risks can be effectively managed through intervention.

Formulating offending behaviour, within both community and institutional settings, however, has its difficulties. As Jones (2004) has indicated, the behaviour under scrutiny has typically occurred months, if not years, before the forensic practitioner begins an assessment. Clients often deliberately minimize, distort or deny their offences to maintain status, to increase self esteem or avoid threats to it, or to avoid further legal proceedings. Offences may have taken place under the influence of drugs or alcohol, or in high states of arousal, both of which can affect recall. Finally, the criminal justice process itself, in which a client has been subject to repeated interviews and assessments, may also sensitize or desensitize an individual to the emotional impact of their offence in idiosyncratic ways. Given these influences, even cooperative, well-motivated individuals may struggle to give an accurate account of their offending behaviour or the emotional and cognitive factors they experienced during the commission of the offence.

Offence Paralleling Behaviour: A Case Formulation Approach to Offender Assessment and Intervention Edited by Michael Daffern, Lawrence Jones and John Shine

A further issue that arises when the forensic practitioner attempts a preliminary analysis of complex behavioural chains is how to classify behaviours that may appear to have a role in the offence sequence but also occur frequently within the 'normal' range of behaviours for the average member of society. These behaviours have a high baseline frequency and are therefore very poor single predictors of offending (Daffern et al., 2009).

In this chapter, we demonstrate how some of these difficulties and challenges can be addressed through the use of a multiple sequential functional analysis (MSFA) approach. Two case examples are presented – one in which the offender was highly motivated to cooperate openly with the assessment and intervention, and one in which the individual did not appear to be entirely forthright and in which the clinicians were faced with poor and contradictory information. This case material will be used to demonstrate the utility of MSFA for:

- Providing a theoretically sound framework to understand the development, instigation and maintenance of offending behaviour
- Generating explicit hypotheses about the functional relationships between events and offending
- Highlighting gaps in an offence analysis and contradictions in the available evidence
- Correctly identifying and increasing our understanding of offence paralleling behaviours (OPBs)
- Discriminating *actual* OPBs from behaviours that merely *appear* to be offence-related (e.g. topographically similar but functionally discrete)

Offence Paralleling Behaviour

Daffern et al. (2007) have described an OPB as:

> [A] behavioural sequence incorporating overt behaviours (that may be muted by environmental factors), appraisals, expectations, beliefs, affects, goals and behavioural scripts, all of which may be influenced by the patient's mental disorder, that is functionally similar to behavioural sequences involved in previous criminal acts. (Daffern et al., 2007, p. 267)

The definition offered by Daffern et al. is broad and encompasses both the topography and function of behaviour. In considering the application of this type of definition to forensic practice involving complex offence analyses, a number of issues emerge:

1. The definition suggests that the forensic practitioner should consider not only topography (i.e. behaviours that 'resemble' behaviours within the offence sequence) but also behaviours that can be demonstrated to be *functionally* related to the offence under analysis.
2. If the emphasis is primarily on topography, the forensic practitioner may have difficulty discriminating behaviours that are offence paralleling from behaviours that literally occur in parallel to the offence; that is, behaviours that co-occur but are not functionally related to offending.
3. Finally, a topographically similar behaviour may be benign in one context yet malevolent in another. If the forensic practitioner therefore focuses on topography and resemblance rather than context and function, there is a high risk of specific behaviours being misidentified or 'overvalued' within the OPB analysis, introducing additional error into the risk assessment process and leading to potential misallocation of intervention resources.

The aim of this chapter is to consider the role of MSFA in providing a framework for offence and OPB analysis in order to address a number of the practical and clinical issues that may arise when applying the concept of OPBs to real-life cases.

MULTIPLE SEQUENTIAL FUNCTIONAL ANALYSIS

An MSFA is essentially a series of functional analyses linked together to account for complex chains of historical behaviour (Gresswell & Hollin, 1992). Within a typical functional analysis, discrete behavioural events are analysed by undertaking what is often referred to as an A:B:C analysis (Sturmey, 1996, 2008). In such an analysis, the 'A' refers to environmental events *a*ntecedent to 'B', the *b*ehaviour being analysed, which in turn is followed by 'C', events *c*onsequent to the behaviour. Components 'A' and 'C' are therefore events in the environment, whilst 'B' includes observable and covert behaviours (such as emotions, thoughts, feelings and physiological activity). Such analyses use the form A:B:C rather than A > B > C to indicate that it is not necessarily possible to establish causal relationships within an A:B:C chain, but that the events in question tend to occur in a particular order and are therefore likely to have some form of functional relationship.

In addition to the A:B:C analysis, an individual functional analysis should include an explicit statement of *key learning*, as set out in Table 5.1.

MSFA uses multiples of the standard A:B:C format to help the practitioner to structure case material and facilitate understanding of historical events. The process is linear (as the MSFA represents a developmental process), emphasizes the fluid nature of an individual's learning history and highlights how an individual changes as he/she moves towards the commission of an offence. Thus, in an MSFA, the initial A:B:C sequence explicitly contributes to the antecedents in the next A:B:C sequence, and so on, whilst highlighting the discrete and subtle influence of prior events on current behaviour as the client moves through time (illustrated in Figure 5.1).

Table 5.1 Key learning established through functional analysis

A (Antecedents): including environmental events/offence triggers/cues

Although in a conventional behavioural functional analysis all antecedents should be events within the environment, there are exceptions. For example, some clients experience and respond to auditory hallucinations (internal events) as if they were coming from outside the body – these may also be included within this section.

B (Behaviour): including observable behaviours (such as verbal behaviour and physical actions), covert behaviours (such as self-reported cognitions, beliefs, fantasies) and other physiological behaviour (such as feelings and emotions which have both internal and external components and therefore need to be self-reported in addition to having the potential of being observed).

C (Consequences): these are environmental events or changes which follow the behaviour and as such reinforce, shape, maintain and affect the probability of the behaviour recurring in the future.

Key learning: In this section, the practitioner should make explicit statements about how the individual in question has been changed by the sequence of events outlined in the analysis. Importantly, the practitioner should also make explicit hypotheses about how the key learning outcomes contribute to the overall development of the offending behaviour.

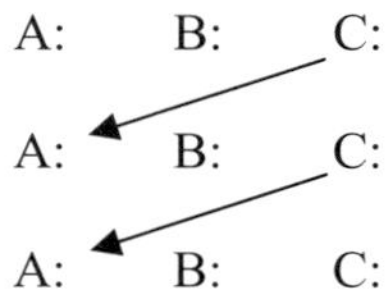

Figure 5.1 MSFA.

This linear, developmental approach has a distinct advantage over typical cyclical, diagrammatic or systemic formulations:

- MSFA highlights development and lends itself at each stage to forming hypotheses about functional relationships.
- MSFA explicitly emphasizes that new information must be added at each developmental stage of the formulation and highlights when insufficient information is known in relation to both antecedent (triggering) events and contextual consequences.
- MSFA facilitates consideration of learning outcomes and helps the practitioner to make an explicit statement about how the individual has *changed* as a result of the analytical sequence. For example, how some behaviour, such as pro-offending thinking, deviant fantasy or offence rehearsal has been reinforced, whilst other behaviours, such as previously held inhibitory controls or prosocial relationships, may have been weakened.
- MSFA aids understanding of the context in which the original offence occurred and thereby allows for explicit predictions regarding the nature and context of future offending or OPB to be made. The process thus helps to guide risk prediction, intervention and management.

In order to illustrate the utility of MSFA in facilitating understanding of the development of offending behaviour and how the methodology helps orient the forensic practitioner to functionally based treatment interventions, the following case of 'Paul', an offender who was motivated to cooperate with assessment and intervention, is offered.

Case Example 1

Paul

Paul, a 25-year-old man, was admitted to a secure hospital following a conviction for attempted murder against a female stranger. He received a diagnosis of 'delusional disorder'.

Paul had a five-year history of hypervigilance regarding women covering their breasts (either with their coats or arms) when they approached him in the street. He began to interpret this act as hostile, insulting and purposefully directed at him. The women could be of any age and did not need to be looking at Paul when the 'covering up' movement occurred. Paul's negative interpretation of the behaviour provided the motivation for the index offence. He stabbed a female stranger in the street after deciding to attack the next woman who 'insulted him' by covering herself up.

Paul's offence could be formulated using a number of psychological models, for example, Finkelhor's four preconditions model of sexual offending (Finkelhor, 1984) and Wolf's cycles of offending (Wolf, 1984, 1985). Although widely used within forensic practice, these models do not emphasize the linear developmental aetiology of the offending behaviour and do not make explicit statements about functional relationships between the individual's learning history and offending (or offence paralleling) behaviour. Such models are thus limited in their utility for predicting specific risk, identifying functionally related OPBs and highlighting potential treatment targets within specific contexts.

In order to emphasize how MSFA can help to address the limitations associated with less explicit methods, an MSFA of Paul's offending and potential OPBs is presented below. This analysis draws on information gained from extensive clinical interviews and previous file information.

Early Development

Paul was the oldest of three siblings brought up in a small port town. He described his parents as strict Christians with a strong moral code and frequently attended church as a child. He described himself as a 'very moral person'.

Paul reported that he felt 'different' from others at school. He had a mild jaw deformity, spoke rapidly with a mild stammer and could be difficult to understand. He felt self-conscious about speaking to people and described himself as a 'loner'. He left school at 16 years old and initially started an apprenticeship. However, he did not complete the training and remained unemployed up to the time of his offence. He did not have any friends, remained socially isolated and had no relationship experiences until he began to use prostitutes in his early 20s.

These factors can be consolidated into sequence one of the MSFA illustrated below:

MSFA 1: Early Development

A: Brought up with strict moral code
Teased by peers because of mild facial disfigurement and stammer
Unemployed
B: Feels different/sense of alienation from others
Socially avoidant
C: No relationships
Reduced opportunities for social contact

Key Learning Outcomes:

1. 'Internalized moral code' acquired from parents.
It was hypothesized that this learning outcome was key in the development of Paul's offending behaviour. His apparent strong 'moral code' seemed to be a powerful factor in eliciting feelings of self-consciousness and shame when he began to use prostitutes (see MSFA 2 below) and contributed to his tendency to interpret the behaviour of others as condemnatory (this later became an asset in developing an intervention strategy – see MSFA 4 below).
2. Beginnings of alienation and sense of 'being different'.
3. Development of using isolation to cope with feelings of alienation and difference.
The hypothesis here was that these two learning outcomes combined to increase Paul's sensitivity to the negative reactions of others whilst also leading to significantly reduced opportunities to experience evidence contradictory to his developing belief system. Being teased and made to feel unattractive and socially incompetent by peers at school significantly impacted on his willingness and ability to form appropriate adult relationships.

Origins of Pro-offending Thinking

At age 20, Paul began to visit prostitutes in his home town and reported that these were his only sexual experiences. He was initially frightened to approach the women and only went with a prostitute after she approached him. He reported that he believed the woman knew he was a virgin.

After this incident Paul started to use prostitutes regularly. He began to feel very self-conscious in the dockland 'red-light area' and surrounding streets and noticed that women covered themselves up when he approached them in the street: he began to have thoughts that other people knew he had been with prostitutes and that he was sexually inadequate and a 'loser'. He thought people were looking at him and started to spit at and jostle women who appeared to be covering themselves when he approached. He began to believe that his sexual behaviour had become widely known in the community and decided to move to another town. These factors can be consolidated into MSFA sequence 2:

MSFA 2: Origins of Pro-offending Thinking

A: Experiences from sequence 1
Approached by prostitute in the street
Women cover themselves up in the street as he approaches them
B: Uses prostitutes
Feels self-conscious about using prostitutes and about virginity/sexual inexperience
Believes people are looking at him in red-light area
Feels angry and judged
Begins to scan the streets and spit at and jostle women who he thinks are covering themselves up when he approaches
Moves town
C: Women covering themselves up
The behaviour of the women he has threatened (e.g. they may look intimidated, protest and turn away)

Key Learning Outcomes:

1. Can obtain sexual gratification from prostitutes, but feels shameful, guilty and very self-conscious.
2. Notices women covering themselves up when he approaches and interprets their behaviour as being a critical response to him and his sexual behaviour (using prostitutes).

In this sequence, the hypothesis was that as Paul started to feel self-conscious following his use of prostitutes (violation of his internalized moral code) he started to assume that people could tell what he had done and began to expect some form of condemnation and judgement from others, particularly women (who he thought would see him as sexually inadequate or deviant).

Inevitably, because Paul began to actively look (scan the street) for evidence of condemnatory behaviour, he 'saw' more of it. Although he experienced this perceived criticism (the women covering themselves in the street) as aversive and punishing, paradoxically, the punishment, rather than suppressing his 'scanning' behaviour, actually increased his anxiety and thereby increased the behaviour. So although visiting prostitutes was reinforcing in that it provided sexual gratification and social contact, the deferred consequences were that Paul felt ashamed, exposed and expectant of disapproval following the act. When he perceived that he had received such disapproval (women covering themselves), he reacted angrily.

This sequence highlights the need for the A:B:C structure (as opposed to the A > B > C structure) in that the women covering themselves up in the street was almost certainly *non-contingent* (i.e. not directly related) to the fact that Paul had visited prostitutes. However, because Paul noticed the behaviour after he had visited prostitutes, when feeling ashamed and exposed, for him, the events became associated. The sequence also demonstrates the paradox of aversive (punishing) stimuli having the function of increasing anger and anxiety-based behaviours.

Offence Sequence

Whilst living in a bedsit after moving town Paul bought himself a telescope in order to watch women both in the street and in the houses opposite for sexual gratification. He stopped visiting prostitutes, believed he heard other residents in his accommodation block talking about him in a derogatory manner and became almost completely socially isolated.

When Paul did venture out of his bedsit, he continued to notice women covering themselves up and believed that, in addition to the previous negative evaluations, the women also now judged him to be a 'peeping Tom'. Paul consequently experienced feelings of increased anger and continued to jostle women and spit at them, again if he thought they were being insulting.

After a number of these incidents, Paul decided to attack the next woman who 'insulted' him. He armed himself with a knife and attacked a female stranger in the street after she covered her breasts as she approached him. Paul was apprehended and received a conviction for attempted murder. His admission to a secure psychiatric hospital concludes the events presented in MSFA 3.

MSFA 3: Offence Sequence

A: Experiences from sequence 2
   Hears residents talking about him in a derogatory manner
   Women continue to cover themselves up in the new town
B: Stops using prostitutes
   Spies on women using telescope
   His interpretation of women's behaviour incorporates his own voyeuristic behaviour
   Increasing feelings of anger
   Arms himself with a knife
   Makes decision to attack next woman who 'insults' him
   Scans the street for the next woman who covers herself up and attacks her
C: Women continue to cover themselves up
   Is arrested, convicted of attempted murder and admitted to a psychiatric hospital

Key Learning Outcomes:

1. Despite no longer visiting prostitutes, people continued to say derogatory things about Paul and women continued to 'insult' him. He experienced increased feelings of frustration at his inability to control the negative responses of others and attributed the responses of the women as being due to their awareness of his other sexual activities (e.g. using the telescope for sexual gratification).

2. Paul found that even though he had changed his behaviour (e.g. moved town and stopped visiting prostitutes) he was still being 'judged' in the street by women. This increased his feelings of anger and frustration and he also attributed the women's behaviour as related to his voyeurism.

From this sequence, it can be hypothesized that Paul's offence is driven by frustration and anger rather than a specific delusional or psychotic episode. This sequence demonstrates the advantages of MSFA over a standard single cognitive–behavioural ABC formulation (e.g. Chadwick et al., 2003), overdescriptive formulations (e.g. Finkelhor, 1984) and overcyclical models of offending (e.g. Wolf, 1984, 1985). Although widely used, these models tend to offer a 'static' global formulation of the offence process rather than stressing the dynamic learning and change that has taken place on the pathway to offending. Although it can be argued that much of the behaviour leading up to the offence is motivated by delusional thinking, the offence itself appears to be driven primarily by frustration, shame and anger at his inability to stop women insulting him.

The sequence demonstrates the strength of an MSFA approach in facilitating understanding of sudden changes in an individual's behaviour in a way that diagrammatic or systemic models are unable to do. In this case, the question arises as to why Paul's behaviour suddenly escalated from spitting and jostling to a potentially lethal knife attack. The analysis presented leads to the hypothesis that the answer can be found in the spitting and jostling behaviour effectively being placed on an extinction schedule; that is, the behaviour may have been effective in changing the behaviour of individual women, but was ineffective at reducing the behaviour of women in general – if anything, to Paul, the women's behaviour appeared to increase as he became more frustrated, angrier and more focused on seeking out the 'offensive behaviour'. The sudden change in Paul's behaviour from spitting and jostling to what was, to the casual observer, a seemingly random knife attack, can be attributable to an increase in frustration and anger and to what could be described in behavioural terms as an 'extinction burst'.

MSFA and Offence Paralleling Behaviour

The above analysis facilitates an explicit, defendable formulation that shows Paul's offending was the end point of a sequence of behaviours and learning experiences that can be separated into analytical units. The analysis demonstrates that Paul's thoughts and behaviour were developed, shaped and maintained by his environmental context and provides the forensic practitioner with a collection of hypotheses that can be used in the process of predicting risk, planning interventions and, importantly, assessing whether other behaviours are offence paralleling.

This is demonstrated in the final functional analysis of the MSFA presented below in which three behaviours are hypothesized to be OPBs, and in particular, how similar cues on the ward (such as female nursing staff covering their breasts) appeared to elicit comparable overt and covert behaviours:

MSFA 4: Post-offence Behaviour/Offence Paralleling Behaviour

A: Experiences from sequence 3
Female nursing staff on the ward cover themselves up
Women on street (seen during escorted community leave) cover themselves up

B: *OPB 1*: Isolates self on ward and does not report feelings about women covering themselves up
OPB 2: Scans the street for women covering themselves up whilst on escorted leave (this behaviour is evident to escorting staff and is associated with poor engagement with escorts, limited conversation and 'staring' fixedly ahead)
OPB 3: Interprets behaviour of both nurses and women in the street (covering themselves up) as purposefully offensive
Subsequent poor relationships with female nurses

C: Paul was managed as a high-risk patient due to his non-disclosure of presenting difficulties
Offered psychology assessment and intervention

OPB Analysis

Paul's self-isolation on the ward was identified as OPB 1 in that it was both topographically similar to his behaviour prior to his offence and appeared to serve a similar function (e.g. reducing social anxiety) whilst also increasing the risk of reoffending by reducing the opportunity for Paul to have his pro-offending beliefs and assumptions disconfirmed.

OPBs 2 and 3 were identified as being topographically and functionally similar to Paul's behaviour in the street prior to his index offence. The behaviours have been separated into two OPBs because of the need to measure them and address them therapeutically in distinct ways. OPB 2 is a cluster of overt directly observable behaviours, whist OPB 3 identifies covert behaviours which can only be accessed and measured through self-report.

Given the above, the concept of OPB can be seen as potentially very helpful to the practitioners working with Paul in that it offers explicit, identifiable behaviours that can be addressed and measured in vivo and by self-report.

The above analysis demonstrates that MSFA can provide the forensic practitioner with a robust framework for identifying potential OPBs. As has been discussed previously, the MSFA approach allows for explicit functional statements to be made about the relationship between specific environmental triggers and subsequent presentation and behaviour. The emphasis on linking specific relations between environmental events throughout the individual's life course with the development of pro-offending beliefs, covert and overt behaviours, and currently observable triggers, allows the forensic practitioner not only to generate functionally based treatment interventions, but also to assess their efficacy and validity.

Intervention

Intervention with Paul was multidimensional and targeted the factors identified in the MSFA and the associated OPBs. A number of intervention strategies were used which could be assessed by observing changes in the frequency and intensity of the OPBs and the contexts in which they occurred.

The underlying hypothesis drawn from the MSFA was that the primary triggering event (a woman covering herself up when Paul approached, highlighted in MSFAs 2 and 3 and OPB 2) was an independent variable and more than likely occurred at a consistent level in the environment, irrespective of Paul's presence. The first intervention was therefore aimed at OPB 2 to demonstrate that the behaviour of the women was non-contingent to Paul's presence. This was achieved through Paul and ward staff observing women entering and leaving a busy shopping centre having previously established with Paul that the women could not see him (he was on a different floor level). Over multiple in vivo sessions, Paul began to accept that women did indeed cover themselves even when he was out of their sight. In addition, Paul began to display a number of other behavioural changes, including reduction in anxiety symptoms (overt), reduction in self-reported anxiety (covert) and an increase in social interaction with his escorts as his scanning behaviour reduced (overt). In addition, it was predicted that there would be an associated reduction in anxiety and therefore a decrease in Paul's self-isolation (OPB 1).

The second major treatment strategy was to draw upon Paul's 'internalized moral code' (identified in MSFA sequence 1) to challenge his pro-offending attitudes (OPB 3). Essentially, the treatment in this stage involved using Paul's established moral code to build on the uncertainty that had been generated about whether all women covering themselves up were doing so in response to him. This was achieved in two ways. Firstly, drawing on the initial intervention, Paul had accepted that women did appear to cover themselves independent of his presence and therefore he could not be certain that a woman covering herself in his presence was making comment or directing an insult at him. OPB 3 was also addressed by Paul observing other aspects of the female nurses' behaviour towards him (e.g. they did not treat him as a sexual threat or sexually inadequate) and having Paul directly question the nurses' motivation if he saw them making the movement.

Having addressed and created doubt around Paul's interpretation of the women's behaviour (identified in MSFA 2 and 3 and OPB 3), further work could then be undertaken to challenge Paul's belief that it was justifiable to attack women who 'insulted' him. Given this new uncertainty, Paul began to agree that launching a potentially lethal knife attack on someone who could be innocent was unfair and 'immoral' (MSFA 1). Secondly, through therapy, Paul began to accept that although being 'labelled' by women in the street as a sex offender or sexual inadequate may be hurtful and offensive, attempting to kill the 'perpetrator' was a disproportionate and therefore immoral response.

The third strand of the intervention was to help Paul to reduce his hypervigilant scanning behaviour (MSFA 2 and 3 and OPB 2) and thus his feelings of frustration and anger. A number of strategies were used to attempt to reduce this behaviour, but these were largely ineffective until intervention one (in vivo sessions) began to increase in effectiveness and Paul's general anxiety about being 'insulted' reduced, with further reductions in self-isolation and self-reported social anxiety on the ward (OPB 1) and in the street.

The efficacy of the intervention was assessed using a combination of overt and covert behavioural indices linked to the original MSFA. Changes in overt behaviours included observable reductions in scanning behaviour whilst in the street, reduced observable symptoms of anxiety and anger, improved social interaction and engagement with escorting staff, and closer therapeutic relationships with female staff on the ward. Changes in covert behaviour included reduction in self-reported anxiety, increased self-reported doubts in the previous belief system, increased belief in the 'randomness' of the women's covering up behaviour and a reported decrease in 'noticing' the behaviour whilst on community leave. The positive changes outlined above were sustained following Paul's discharge from hospital.

The Role of MSFA in Addressing Difficulties with Offence Analysis and the Identification of Offence Paralleling Behaviours

Paul's case highlights the benefit that MSFA can bring to case analysis in terms of deriving functional relationships between an individual's learning history, environmental stimuli and offending (or offence paralleling) behaviour. This MSFA, however, was undertaken with a motivated client with whom rapport could be established over a significant period and who was motivated to engage in treatment.

The defensibility and confidence in the analysis was increased by the addition of a detailed analysis of extensive witness statements, interviews with relatives, observation on escorted leave and on the ward, and scrutiny of previous professional reports. However, this amount of information is not always available to the forensic practitioner: the client may be unmotivated to address their offending (or alleged offending) behaviour, witness statements and professional reports can often be contradictory, and, given these difficulties, the forensic practitioner may find it very difficult to produce a robust offence analysis and thereafter correctly identify valid, reliable OPBs.

Case Example 2

A second case (Brian), an alleged sexual offender, illustrates some of these difficulties and shows how an MSFA methodology is used to identify significant limitations in both a provisional offence analysis and an actuarial risk assessment, as well as the associated difficulties in correctly identifying OPBs.

'Brian' was an alleged sexual offender who denied committing any offences. Although the alleged victims (a prepubescent boy and girl) gave vivid (but contradictory) accounts of his alleged offending, and despite supportive medical evidence, Brian was acquitted of the charges and continued to deny any wrongdoing. The question remained, however, whether Brian presented a risk to the young children in a new family he had become involved with, and whether the sexual behaviours that were still evident in his behavioural repertoire were offence paralleling or were merely behaviours that literally occurred in parallel to the alleged offending. Many of these behaviours have high base rates within the 'normal' non-offending population and therefore could not be considered as OPBs without being tied to a robust functional analysis. We therefore use Brian's case to demonstrate the role of MSFA in highlighting gaps and incongruities in a provisional offence and OPB analysis.

Brian

Brian was referred for an assessment in regards to the potential risk he presented to his current partner's children. Brian had previously been married to a woman who was clinically obese, of low intelligence and who had two children from a previous relationship. The relationship broke down, following which the children (a prepubescent boy and girl) alleged that Brian had sexually abused them.

Early Development

Consideration of Brian's early life came from extensive interviews with Brian and other family members but failed to reveal anything that the sexual offending research would identify as typical risk-increasing factors (e.g. he had not been sexually abused as a child; he had not been in the care system; he did not have any previous convictions or display any evidence of conduct disorder, affiliation towards children or signs of sexual deviance).

However, a number of less-specific factors emerged. These included a history of sexual abuse within the family (his father had been abused as a child); he had been bullied by an older brother, and a combination of his own bullying behaviour, poor school attainment and attendance led to him being placed in a special educational establishment, which was later investigated following allegations of sexual abuse (Brian denied any victimization). Another factor which was of interest but which was non-specific was Brian's social isolation and apparent lack of interest in social interaction or intimate relationships until he met his first partner (and mother of the alleged victims) when he was aged 31. Prior to this, Brian claimed that he had little interest in sex and denied the use of pornography. He reported that this partner introduced him to a number of diverse sexual practices, including oral and anal sex, and urophilia.

Brian claimed that his partner was highly sexualized and that, as the relationship progressed, she would leave him alone with her children (a prepubescent boy and girl). He reported that he began to hear rumours that she was having sex with other men whom she met whilst out drinking.

These factors can be consolidated into sequence one of an MSFA as illustrated below:

MSFA Sequence 1: Early Development

A: History of sexual abuse in family of origin (no allegations that Brian was abused)
Subject to bullying and violence at hands of older sibling

B: Social isolation in childhood and adolescence
Allegations of bullying other children in school
History of special education (school staff members later investigated for alleged sexual abuse – Brian denies having been victimized)
No sexual experience before first partner (denies use of pornography)

C: Introduced to a variety of sexual practices (including anal and oral sex and urophilia) by first partner
Partner is allegedly unfaithful and leaves Brian alone with children whilst out with other men

Key Learning Outcomes

It is difficult to establish the key learning outcomes from this sequence. Although in a retrospective analysis (taking an a priori assumption that Brian did abuse the children), it is possible to hypothesize that certain behaviours were indicative of potential risk (e.g. social isolation, history of bullying and difficulties in forming relationships). By contrast, if Brian did not abuse his partner's children, then it is very difficult to assess the functional relationships amongst the behaviours without his cooperation (which was not forthcoming).

Alleged Offence Sequence and Offence Paralleling Behaviours

The children disclosed sexual abuse to a family relative after the relationship between Brian and their mother had broken down. It emerged during the assessment process that the children had previously made allegations to their mother before her relationship with Brian had ended but that she had not taken action to protect her children. The children alleged that Brian had engaged in oral and anal sex with them and coerced them to perform oral sex on him. There was some medical evidence to support the allegations. However, although a police prosecution was initiated, Brian was acquitted and had by then formed a second relationship with a new partner who also had two prepubescent children from a previous relationship.

Again, Brian's new partner was morbidly obese and of comparatively low intelligence. By this time Brian was aged in his 40s, had been married, had no previous convictions or court appearances for any offences, had never been in care and had a stable work record. Consequently, actuarial risk prediction measures assessed him as presenting a low risk to his second partner's children.

Brian vehemently denied the offences, and consequently a detailed functional analysis of the alleged offences (if they occurred) using Brian's account was impossible: he denied any wrongdoing, asserted that the alleged victims and their mother had fabricated the allegations and denied that he presented any risk to his new partner's children.

During interview, Brian initially denied enjoying any sexual activity other than consenting heterosexual vaginal penetrative sex with his adult female partner. He claimed that although he found oral sex and urophilia distasteful, his previous partner (the mother of the alleged victims) had insisted on it and that he also performed oral sex on his current partner. In response to direct questioning, Brian also denied enjoying anal sex, claiming he found it repellent, although he admitted that he had engaged in anal sex with both his current and previous partners, despite him stating that his current partner also disliked the activity.

Although social services had alerted his new partner to the allegations that had been made against Brian and she had agreed to await the outcome of the assessment before allowing Brian to reside in the family home, it emerged during the course of the assessment that she had been colluding with Brian to allow him unsupervised access to the children and had actively tried to hide his presence from visiting social workers.

Upon initial analysis, then, it may appear that Brian's current behaviour parallels the previous alleged offending: he has again chosen a partner who is obese, of low intelligence and has two young children from a previous relationship; he engages in oral and anal sex with his new partner (despite indicating that he enjoyed neither activity and having disclosed that his current partner does not enjoy anal sex either).

This information can be placed into MSFA sequences 2 and 3, which are presented adjacent to each other below in order to emphasize how Brian's behaviours in his new relationship (described in sequence 3) *parallel* his behaviours in his first relationship (described in sequence 2). If Brian did abuse his first partner's children, then it could be hypothesized that the behaviours presented in MSFA sequence 3 are *offence paralleling* (i.e. OPBs).

MSFA Sequence 2: First relationship	MSFA Sequence 3: Current relationship
A: Events in sequence 1	Events in sequence 2
	Actuarial risk assessment: low risk
B: Chooses obese partner with limited intellectual ability and two young children	Chooses obese partner with limited intellectual ability and two young children
Oral sex with partner	Oral sex with partner
Anal sex with partner	Anal sex with partner
Alleged sexual abuse of children	
C: Partner colludes to cover up allegations of sexual abuse of children	Partner colludes to cover up
	Brian's presence in family home
Relationship breaks down and children make allegations	
Brian is acquitted of offence	

Key Learning Outcomes

At face value, it would appear that Brian has a predilection for the sexual activities described by his alleged victims (oral and anal sex) and admitted to engaging in these sexual behaviours with his current adult partner (who shares some of the features of his previous partner). Brian's current sexual behaviour and relationship choices therefore hypothetically parallel his alleged sexual offending behaviour, and thereby suggest that he may well be guilty of the original allegations of sexual abuse and therefore present a risk to the children in his new family.

However, when consideration is given to the baseline rates for oral sex (approximately two-thirds of adult males and females) and anal sex (approximately a third of adult males and females; Mosher et al., 2005), a number of difficulties begin to arise. It can be seen that this form of sexual behaviour (e.g. oral and anal sex) is common within non-offender populations and therefore, in isolation, has little predictive or discriminative validity in identifying sexual offenders from non-offenders.

Similarly, Brian's choice of obese female partners with low intelligence cannot of itself be seen as a risk factor without a detailed functional analysis to indicate that he is selecting these women based on their vulnerability or reduced ability to protect their children. It may be that Brian simply has a sexual preference for obese females.

Brian admitted (with an expression of distaste) that he had had anal sex with both the alleged victims' mother and his new partner. The occurrence of anal sex in the new relationship could therefore be seen as an OPB as it appears to validate the children's allegations that Brian has a predilection for anal sex. Unfortunately, for the assessing practitioner, anal sex is a common sexual behaviour within the non-offending population and therefore lacks sensitivity or specificity as an OPB: if Brian does have a predilection for anal sex, it does not logically follow that he wishes to have (or has had) anal sex with children.

Are these behaviours therefore 'offence paralleling' or do they simply reflect high non-offending community base rates? Equally, are the behaviours 'offence paralleling' in the sense that they resemble the alleged offending, or do they simply indicate obvious sexual preferences for anal sex and large women that literally parallel (but are functionally independent of) the alleged offending?

In principle, the specificity of these high baseline sexual behaviours can be increased by detailed analysis of the context in which they occur, by their place in a behavioural sequence and by their hypothesized function. For example, did Brian only engage in anal sex with his partner in the context of feeling frustrated? Was he more likely to want anal sex after spending the day with children? Did having anal sex with his partner function as an alternative to offending against children?

Unfortunately, Brian was not cooperative with a request for a full sexual history, thus the role of these sexual behaviours (i.e. whether they are OPBs) remains speculative. Furthermore, in the case of Brian, the key learning outcomes for MSFA 2 are intrinsically linked to whether Brian sexually abused the children. The hypothesized learning outcomes will therefore be divided firstly, on the basis that he did abuse the children (guilty) and secondly, on the basis that he did not (not guilty).

Guilty

If Brian is guilty of the allegations, then it would appear that he has learnt that he is able to gain access to children by targeting vulnerable women, he can persuade the women to collude with him to avoid disclosure and that with very young children (even with medical evidence to suggest otherwise) he can avoid the negative consequences of his offending. These consequences suggest that Brian is at an increased risk of reoffending in the future (and would certainly place him at a higher rate of recidivism than actuarial risk assessments suggested) and when paired with the hypothesis that the offending reflects a deviant sexual interest in children, he should not have contact with his current partner's children.

Not Guilty

If Brian is not guilty of the allegations, then the analysis would seem to suggest that Brian simply has an attraction to large women, is able to form adult heterosexual relationships and enjoys slightly unusual but largely unremarkable sexual practices. He does not appear to have been significantly affected by the break-up of his previous relationship or the allegations made against him.

However, the MSFA sequence above raises a number of outstanding questions which are difficult to reconcile with the *not guilty* analysis, but which can be subjected to further functional analyses in order to increase confidence in the resulting risk assessment and in its defensibility. Firstly, the question remains as to why the children would make such plausible allegations against Brian which were consistent with medical evidence. Brian's explanation was that the children's mother, motivated by revenge following the breakdown of the relationship, had made up the allegations and manipulated the children to relay them to the authorities. In a functional A:B:C analysis of this behaviour, the inherent inconsistencies in this explanation could be highlighted (for example, the young age and therefore lack of sophistication of the children, the corresponding medical evidence, the mother's intellectual ability, her questionable capacity to create a believable allegation and influence the children to repeat the claim across different settings). A second issue is Brian's denial of being the instigator of anal and oral sex with his second partner in the context of both parties apparently finding the activity distasteful. Denial is a behaviour that is also amenable to functional analysis, and the question as to what function the denial may serve in this context could be further explored (e.g. impression management or shame and embarrassment). However, detailed expositions of these events are beyond the scope of the current chapter but are underscored here simply to demonstrate the utility of the MSFA approach in identifying inconsistent and missing information.

Brian was considered to be a high risk of sexual offending by a child protection case conference and was denied access to his new partner's children. Despite this, his partner continued to collude and hide his presence in the family home, and her children were consequently removed into care.

CONCLUSIONS

In this chapter, we have attempted to highlight the benefits of adopting a functional approach to offence analysis and to the identification of OPBs. The functional approach is at the core of MSFA, a method which allows the forensic practitioner to chart the development of offending behaviour, to identify how environmental events help to elicit, shape and maintain behaviour, whilst assisting the practitioner to generate explicit hypotheses regarding the relationships between context, learning and behaviour.

The two presented cases clearly demonstrate the inherent weaknesses of focusing solely on behavioural topography, and show how the MSFA approach can be used to contribute to defensible risk assessment, to highlight inconsistencies in evidence and to draw attention to aspects of the analysis where there is missing or incomplete data.

MSFA can provide a framework for discriminating between OPBs and behaviours that merely parallel offending (those which have high baseline rates within non-offending populations) but which are not *functionally related* to previous or future offending. By adopting an MSFA approach,

OPBs can be placed within the context of a developmental understanding of the offender's progression to an offence, can increase confidence in the validity of the OPBs identified and can therefore increase the forensic practitioners' confidence in the assessments of risk and of therapeutic change.

REFERENCES

Chadwick, P., Birchwood, M. & Trower, P. (2003). *Cognitive Therapy for Delusions: Voices and Paranoia*. Chichester: Wiley.

Daffern, M., Jones, L., Howells, K., Shine, J., Mikton, C. & Tunbridge, V. (2007). Refining the definition of offence paralleling behaviour. *Criminal Behaviour and Mental Health, 17*, 265–73.

Daffern, M., Howells, K., Mannion, A. & Tonkin, M. (2009). A test of methodology intended to assist detection of aggressive offence paralleling behaviour within secure settings. *Legal and Criminological Psychology, 14*, 213–26.

Finkelhor, D. (1984). *Child Sexual Abuse: New Theory and Research*. New York: Free Press.

Gresswell, D.M. & Hollin, C.R. (1992). Towards a new methodology for making sense of case material: an illustrative case involving attempted multiple murder. *Criminal Behaviour and Mental Health, 2*, 329–41.

Jones, L. (2004). Offence paralleling behaviour (OPB) as a framework for assessment and interventions with offenders. In A. Needs & G. Towl (Eds), *Applying Psychology to Forensic Practice*. Oxford: Blackwell.

Mosher, W.D., Chandra, A. & Jones J. (2005). *Sexual Behaviour and Selected Health Measures: Men and Women 15–44 Years of Age, United States, 2002*. (Advance Data from Vital and Health Statistics No. 362). Hyattsville, MD: National Centre for Health Statistics.

Sturmey, P. (1996). *Functional Analysis in Clinical Psychology*. Chichester: Wiley.

Sturmey, P. (2008). *Behavioral Case Formulation and Intervention: A Functional Analytic Approach*. Chichester: Wiley.

Wolf, S.C. (1984). A model of sexual aggression/addiction. *Journal of Social Work and Human Sexuality, 7*, 131–48.

Wolf, S.C. (1985). A multi-factor model of deviant sexuality. *Victimology, 10*, 359–74.

Chapter 6

A STRUCTURED COGNITIVE BEHAVIOURAL APPROACH TO THE ASSESSMENT AND TREATMENT OF VIOLENT OFFENDERS USING OFFENCE PARALLELING BEHAVIOUR

MICHAEL DAFFERN

Centre for Forensic Behavioural Science, School of Psychology and Psychiatry, Monash University, Clayton, Melbourne, Australia; Victorian Institute of Forensic Mental Health (Forensicare), Fairfield, Australia; Peaks Academic and Research Unit, Rampton Hospital, Retford, Nottinghamshire, and Division of Psychiatry, Forensic Mental Health Section, Nottingham University, Nottingham, UK.

> 'I should have thought that a pack of British boys ... would have been able to put up a better show than that.'
>
> William Golding, *Lord of the Flies*

INTRODUCTION

Seizing opportunity for effective intervention, evaluating treatment progress and determining readiness for release are critical tasks for mental health professionals involved in the care and treatment of violent offenders. To assist those concerned with these tasks, to enhance integrity and to ensure comprehensiveness, treatment programmes and structured risk assessment methods have been developed and promoted. The offence paralleling behaviour (OPB) framework has emerged as a potential adjunct to these risk assessment methods and structured treatment programmes (Daffern et al., 2007a; Jones, 2004). The OPB framework is however in its infancy. This chapter introduces the rationale for structured methodology that may be used to examine similarity in aggressive behaviours across situations and in particular whether aggressive behaviours occurring within custody are offence paralleling. Assessment of similarity is central to the OPB framework. Mental health professionals working within institutions must determine whether behaviours observed within institutions can legitimately be referred to as offence paralleling and therefore whether they are relevant to treatment planning and release decision-making. Although OPB may occur prior to a criminal act (e.g. the emergence of stalking during a period of prior hospitalization; Daffern, 2010), this chapter focuses on aggressive acts occurring

Offence Paralleling Behaviour: A Case Formulation Approach to Offender Assessment and Intervention Edited by Michael Daffern, Lawrence Jones and John Shine

during incarceration subsequent to an act of aggression. This chapter also explores the potential for the OPB framework to be used as an adjunct to structured treatment programmes and risk assessment methods.

Before proceeding, there are two important assumptions implicit to the OPB framework and relevant to aggressive behaviour that require scrutiny:

1. Behaviour within institutions is similar, albeit muted by environmental constraints and opportunity, to past aggressive behaviour occurring outside the institution or in an environment of interest (e.g. a less secure psychiatric setting or supported residential facility).
2. It is possible to reliably identify OPB.

Behaviour within Institutions is Similar, Albeit Muted by Environmental Constraints and Opportunity

Although the notion of behavioural consistency presents discomfort for some behaviourists, and the notion has been criticized (Mischel, 1973), there is both theoretical and empirical support for cross-situational consistency in criminal behaviour. Grubin et al. (2001) identified behavioural consistency in serial sexual offenders. Zamble and Porporino (1990) showed that prisoners responded similarly to a range of prison difficulties as they had problems outside the prison, and McDougal and colleagues (Clark et al., 1994; McDougal & Clark, 1991; McDougal et al., 1994) reported that prisoners reveal comparable behaviour within the prison to their index offence. In a classic review, Olweus (1980) argued that it was both 'defensible and natural to assume the "existence" of some kind of relatively stable, individual-differentiating aggressive reaction tendencies within ... individuals' (p. 377). Theoretically, behaviour analysts have attended to the consistency issue (Vyse, 2004); the concept of behavioural momentum (Nevin & Grace, 2000) implies that under certain circumstances, including high rates of response-dependent or response-independent reinforcement, consistent cross-situational behaviour may be observed.

However, in contrast to the consistency perspective and the aforementioned evidence and argument (and some contrasting views; see e.g. Bartol & Bartol, 2004), our recent research has shown how unique demands operating within institutions contribute to the emergence of some aggressive behaviours (e.g. low-severity sexual aggression; see Daffern et al., 2008). Furthermore, the functions of aggressive behaviour in institutions may differ from the functions of aggression in the community (Daffern & Howells, 2009). These findings highlight the complexities involved with identification of OPB. Within custodial settings, aggression may be perpetrated by offenders and psychiatric patients who do not have a history of aggression. Similarly, some offenders with a history of serious violence may not be overtly aggressive during incarceration. In a study of consistency, Daffern et al. (2007b) examined the relationship between forensic psychiatric patients' aggressive behaviour prior to hospitalization, as well as their convictions for aggressive behaviour following hospitalization, and their aggression during hospitalization. Results showed that aggression in the community (before and after hospitalization) was related but that neither was related to aggression during hospitalization. These findings demonstrate temporal but not cross-situational consistency. Also highlighted is the critical importance of both psychological factors, particularly symptoms of psychiatric illness that influence aggressive behaviour in mentally ill offenders, as well as the opportunity and environmental constraints, and instigators of aggression. These results also show that characteristics within the individual, which are related to aggressive behaviour, persist during hospitalization. However, these persistent vulnerabilities do not necessarily manifest in overt aggression during hospitalization. The task for clinicians is to determine how these persistent vulnerabilities manifest in behaviour within custody. These behaviours, in spite of dissimilar topography, are still offence paralleling.

Clues for the identification of OPB and support for its existence may be seen in recent commentary by Walter Mischel, one of the early critics of behavioural consistency and an advocate of the *situationalist* perspective. According to Mischel (2004), only when there is continuity in important 'psychologically active' (p. 195) environmental contingencies (i.e. those that activate characteristic social cognitive person variables) will behaviour be maintained across different environments. Accordingly, for aggression observed in an institution to be considered offence paralleling, it would be necessary to demonstrate that equivalent psychological features (e.g. schemas of abuse and mistrust) played a functional role in the generation of previous aggressive behaviour and remain operative and causal to current aggressive behaviour (e.g. 'rejection' by a partner in the community and subsequent 'rejection' by unit staff during hospitalization).

As such, to determine whether aggressive behaviour is offence paralleling the task for clinicians is to understand which social cognitive variables are causal and should be considered in an OPB analysis. The general aggression model (GAM; Bushman & Anderson, 2001) provides guidance for this task. According to the GAM, aggression occurs because individuals acquire and apply aggression-related knowledge structures (scripts and schemas). Bushman and Anderson (2001) argue that these structures develop through observation and interactions with others and that, with repeated exposure, hostile knowledge structures become more complex, differentiated and difficult to change. In this way, repeated exposure to aggression can make hostile knowledge structures chronically accessible, establishing a repertoire of aggressive behaviour. A focus on the acquisition and rehearsal of aggressive scripts and violence-related schema in the assessment of an offender's index offence and prior aggressive behaviour helps assessors determine whether there is consistency in the aggressive behaviour observed within an institution. Other parts of the aggressive behaviour will also be of interest (e.g. function), and these are discussed later in the chapter. There will be similarities in an array of characteristics of the individual across settings; some will be causal and important (e.g. activated schemas and scripts) and others will be correlated, but neither causal nor important. Importantly, because opportunity (e.g. supervision and limited access to weapons) and constraint (i.e. rapid intervention from staff) dramatically alter the nature of expressed behaviour, topography (i.e. the form of the overt behaviour) should not be the exclusive focus of attention.

It is Possible to Identify Offence Paralleling Behaviour

A second assumption central to the OPB framework is that it is possible to reliably identify OPB. Determining whether any behaviour, whether overtly aggressive or not, is offence paralleling is complicated by the important role of the environment and changes over time to an individual's aggressive behavioural repertoire, whether through maturation or effective treatment. Misapplication of the OPB framework or application of simplistic analogue models based exclusively on topographical similarity sometimes occurs (Daffern et al., 2007a). Improper use of the OPB framework may result in inconsistent and idiosyncratic assessments that are detrimental to patients. These misapplications may be invoked to justify incapacitation and imposition of unnecessary treatment, based on the presence of a so-called OPB.

Unstructured assessment and classification of behaviour has the potential to be compromised by well-known observer biases (Nisbett & Ross, 1980; Tversky & Kahneman, 1974); these include the tendency for observers to emphasize stable dispositional factors while underemphasizing situational factors (the so-called *fundamental attribution error*; Ross, 1977). Observers may attribute the causes of an offender's aggressive behaviour within an institution to characteristics of the person (e.g. they lack empathy, are cruel or impulsive) rather than consider transient (state) factors within the individual or characteristics of the social environment (e.g. the person was under stress and perceived that limit setting or demands made of them were provocative).

Identification of OPB essentially requires comparison of two functional analyses, the initial analysis describing the criminal behaviours of interest and then the analysis of the behaviour suspected to be offence paralleling. Valid and reliable functional analyses are requisite for this task. It is important to acknowledge that studies testing the reliability of unstructured clinical case formulations have tended to show low levels of agreement. In an attempt to explore the reliability of clinical case formulations, Kuyken et al. (2005) studied the reliability and quality of cognitive therapists' case formulations. Consistent with previous studies (Mumma & Smith, 2001; Persons et al., 1995), Kuyken and colleagues (2005) noted high agreement between raters on the descriptive aspects of the case formulation. However, agreement on those aspects of formulation, which was dependent on theory-driven inference, was poor. Given these findings it is important, if functional analyses are to be compared, that methods to enhance the reliability and quality of the functional analyses are considered.

Others (Luborsky & Diguer, 1998) have argued that reliability of case formulations is improved when assessors are provided with (a) appropriate training and (b) structured case formulation methods. To this end, and in an endeavour to be comprehensive, Daffern et al. (2009) developed structured methodology to assist mental health professionals determine whether aggressive behaviours occurring within institutions paralleled violent acts preceding incarceration. This method (the structured aggressive behaviour analysis schedule – SABAS) is based on function analytic principles (Haynes, 1998), the criteria for conducting a functional analysis of violent behaviour (Howells, 1998) and the functions of aggression (Daffern et al., 2006). Through examination of various antecedents and consequences, sequences of behaviour could be compared. Indeed, functions were clarified through analysis of the behaviour in relation to antecedents and consequences. Analysis of sequences is necessary for OPB assessment (Daffern et al., 2007a; Jones, 2004).

The SABAS includes assessment of victim characteristics, environmental context and triggers (distal and proximal), affective and cognitive antecedents (including thoughts, appraisals and maladaptive schemas), psychophysiological activation, symptoms of major mental illness, disinhibitors and opportunity factors conducive to violence, weapon use and the function of the behaviour (see Table 6.1).

In the first test of the SABAS, we (Daffern et al., 2009) examined whether aggressive behaviours occurring during hospitalization were similar to past violent acts perpetrated by patients of a high-secure Dangerous and Severe Personality Disorder Unit. In this study, 26 patients' violent index offences were analysed with the aid of the SABAS by a trained and experienced clinical forensic psychologist. Independent and blind to this analysis, a maximum of five aggressive behaviours occurring during hospitalization that were perpetrated by each patient were reviewed (a corresponding total of 86 aggressive behaviours). The similarity of each inpatient aggressive behaviour and corresponding violent index act was then compared with three different methods: (1) clinical assessment of similarity made by a research assistant reviewing the completed SABAS for each index act and in-hospital aggressive act; (2) comparing a count of comparable components in the sequence; and (3) using a coefficient of similarity called Jaccard's coefficient, a statistical procedure that has gained prominence in case linkage research (Woodhams & Toye, 2007).

Results of all three methods showed that only about half of all pairs of aggressive acts were similar. Clinical appraisals resulted in 38.5% of incidents being considered 'somewhat similar'; 11.5% were described as 'very similar'. According to the count of equivalent parts 64.52% of aggressive behaviours occurring during hospitalization were considered similar to index acts.

Table 6.1 Schedule of violent behaviour

- Narrative description of the index offence.
- Victim characteristics (classification of sex and relationship to the victim, whether the victim was an acquaintance, friend, intimate or stranger).
- Narrative description of environmental triggers (distal and proximal).
- Narrative description of cognitive antecedents including thoughts and appraisals immediately prior to the offence. Determination as to whether common maladaptive schemas (Young, 1990) were activated prior to the offence. Five schemas were scored as present or absent: (a) emotional deprivation, (b) abandonment, (c) mistrust/abuse, (d) social isolation/alienation and (e) defectiveness.
- Classification of affective antecedents – made by rating whether adjectives from the UWIST Mood Adjective Checklist (Matthews et al., 1990) were used by others or the patient to describe the patient's affective state within three days prior to the aggressive behaviour. A rating was then made, after reading the file notes describing the aggressive behaviour, as to whether there was evidence that any of the adjectives from the UWIST Mood Adjective Checklist could be used to describe the patient's affective state in the three days after their aggression.
- Psychophysiological activation – tense arousal was rated on a five-point ordinal scale from 1 (*calm*) to 5 (*tense/irritable*); energetic arousal was rated on a five-point ordinal scale from 1 (*passive/tired*) to 5 (*active/energetic*).
- Whether active symptoms of major mental illness were present and, if present, these were described.
- The environmental context (within an institution, public place or domestic).
- The role of disinhibitors, specifically whether alcohol or drugs were used in the three days prior to the aggressive behaviour and then a narrative description of the type of drugs or alcohol used. It was also necessary in this section to identify whether the offence occurred with a willing accomplice and to describe whether there was evidence of other impairments of self-regulation (internal or external).
- A narrative description of opportunity factors conducive to violence.
- A classification of whether weapons were used and a description of the type of weapons used.
- A determination of the function of the behaviour. Function was assessed using the assessment and classification of function (ACF; Daffern et al., 2006). The functions assessed in this classification system are demand avoidance, to force compliance, to express anger, to reduce tension (catharsis), to obtain tangibles, social distance reduction (attention seeking), to enhance status or social approval, compliance with instruction and to observe suffering.

In the test of similarity using Jaccard's coefficient, randomly paired index acts and incidents of aggression during hospitalization that were known to have been committed by different patients were compared with the Jaccard's coefficients for matched index act and in-hospital aggressive behaviours. No statistically significant difference was found between the mean Jaccard's score for the matched index–inpatient pairs and the random index–inpatient pairs. In other words, aggressive behaviours occurring within hospital were no more similar to a patient's index act than randomly selected aggressive behaviours perpetrated by a completely different patient. Although this final result contrasts markedly with expectations, there are several plausible explanations, all of which highlight the complexity of OPB assessments, and all of which require appreciation before the OPB framework should be applied:

1. There may be considerable within-subject variation in the determinants and functions of aggressive behaviour over time. The absence of significant differences in Jaccard's scores between matched and random pairs may be because similarity in some pairings was obscured by dissimilarity in other pairings. Some aggressive behaviours occurring during hospitalization may be offence paralleling, whereas others may occur within the context of certain general predispositions towards aggression but consequent to unique environmental events.
2. Similarly, certain patients may not ever show entrenched or consistent aggressive behaviour, whereas some patients may be consistent in their behaviour. This hypothesis raises the

possibility that the OPB framework may only be useful for violent offenders showing entrenched idiosyncratic behaviour. Versatile offenders who are indiscriminate in their aggressive behaviour may not necessarily benefit from the additional resources dedicated to treatments inspired by OPB assessment.

In conclusion, a reliable method to identify and monitor aggressive OPB that may be utilized clinically is yet to be stringently tested and widely applied. Results of the aforementioned study highlight that similarity to index acts is observed in some but not all topographical similar aggressive behaviours occurring during hospitalization. This reinforces the need for comprehensive and structured appraisal of institutional behaviour, sensitivity to environmental factors and a thorough functional analysis and formulation of the patient's history of aggression, perhaps using an aid such as the SABAS; these are conditions of the OPB framework and necessary for adequate formulations from which comparisons of similarity may be undertaken.

USING OPB TO ASSESS AND TREAT VIOLENT OFFENDERS

Treatment Using OPB

OPB is targeted for treatment presumably because reinforcing or shaping (Skinner, 1957) new prosocial behaviours and extinguishing other undesirable and relevant behaviours within the institution will result in a reduced likelihood of subsequent problematic behaviour at liberty. This therapeutic notion is not new. Several therapies are premised on the assumption that long-standing problem behaviours targeted for treatment will emerge within psychotherapy, that these in-session behaviours are of the same general 'class of behaviours emitted with others' (Follette et al., 1996, p. 627), and that contingent responding to these behaviours may create new learning that may generalize to other settings. According to Hafkenscheid (2003), several forms of psychotherapy, including Yalom's interpersonal model of group psychotherapy (Yalom, 1985; cited in Hafkenscheid, 2003), function analytic psychotherapy (FAP; Kohlenberg & Tsai, 1991) and Kiesler's interpersonal therapy (Kiesler, 1988, 1996; cited in Hafkenscheid, 2003), assume that a patient's interpersonal problems reside in 'self-perpetuating, overlearned maladaptive (self-defeating) transaction cycles with significant others, including the therapist' (Hafkenscheid, 2003, p. 32).

Importantly, however, in confined and contrived settings such as prisons or secure psychiatric hospitals, the actual overt behavioural problems (e.g. overt violence) that may be the focus of treatment in the aforementioned therapies (e.g. social withdrawal) may not emerge in therapy or in the institution. However, so long as the environment activates equivalent social cognitive variables associated with the patient's aggression, then OPB should occur. For this reason targeting OPB (rather than the overt and topographically equivalent problem behaviour) is critical. Previously, Jones (2004) and Daffern et al. (2007a) argued that the OPB is similar to the principles used within FAP. However, unlike FAP, the OPB framework focuses on functionally equivalent behaviours observed by unit staff as well as observations made inside psychotherapy sessions. Within FAP, idiographically defined problem behaviours occurring within session (clinically relevant behaviour 1s; CRB1s) and in-session improvements (clinically relevant behaviour 2s; CRB2s) are the therapist's focus for treatment. FAP also takes note of problem behaviours occurring outside of session, outside problems (O1s) and outside improvements (O2s), which are functionally (and possibly topographically) similar to CRB1s and CRB2s. These O1s and O2s are not subjected to the same contingencies of therapist's response because they are reported by the patient rather than observed directly (Callaghan et al., 2003). Within institutions, behaviours may be observed (and correspondingly responded to by staff) when they occur both within psychotherapeutic sessions and during the course of the patient's daily activities on the ward. OPBs therefore resemble CRBs rather than outside behaviours (O1s and O2s), although within a secure institution many O1s and O2s may be observed and responded to by staff.

For FAP, the task for clinicians is 'contingent responding to naturally reinforce and increase the frequency of CRB2s while ignoring, punishing, or otherwise decreasing the frequency of CRB1s' (Follette et al., 1996; cited in Mulick et al., 2005; p. 229). In the OPB framework, the task is for therapists and all other unit staff to intervene when an OPB is emerging so that the sequence is not reinforced, or that it is altered so prosocial adaptive behaviour (PAB; Daffern et al., 2007a), the equivalent of in-session improvements or CRB2s, emerges and is reinforced (e.g. schemas associated with previous violent acts are activated and the patient is showing signs of or reporting rehearsal of aggressive scripts or fantasy). Intervention would be required at this point so that aggression does not occur and that aggressive scripts are not rehearsed or satisfying. To implement an OPB treatment model, staff would need to identify, early in treatment, close approximations of the desired PAB and shape these accordingly. According to Follette et al. (1996) therapists (or all institutional staff in the case of OPB) should be 'differentially reinforcing approximations to client improvements by beginning with very general behaviours and necessary responses (e.g., staying in therapy through the first session) before beginning to shape effective client responses more specifically' (p. 628). For instance, in the aforementioned example, upon detection of emergent rehearsal of scripts, staff would intervene in an attempt to reduce or alter OPBs either by interfering with the possibility of reinforcement (e.g. obtaining satisfaction through violent fantasy/script rehearsal and planning) or by facilitating rehearsal of alternative behaviours incompatible with aggression (e.g. relaxation and forgiving). Aggression might also be met with aversive consequences and prosocial replacement behaviours reinforced.

The OPB framework emphasizes the social reinforcing and therapeutic role that all unit/prison staff have in the treatment of the violent offender. Such a framework emphasizes the need for all staff to be actively engaged in the treatment process and for treatment to be conceptualized as something that occurs within formal treatment sessions (group and individual) as well as during all other activities (the so-called *immersion model*; A. Gordon & S. Wong, unpublished manuscript). Typically, offence-related programmes are delivered in a group and/or individual format (traditional therapeutic communities the exception) with general therapeutic guidelines offered to assist staff outside of these formal programmes (e.g. assist offenders complete homework, provide opportunities to rehearse new skills and promote general prosocial behaviour). However, these programmes rarely provide an explicit framework for how the informal environment is to operate so as to be conducive to change, tailored to an offender's specific needs, and maximally effective. The OPB framework offers a way for unit staff to understand and integrate the informal treatment work conducted between formal programme activities. It provides a structure that helps staff explore opportunities to support, shape and reinforce PABs and to intervene therapeutically with OPBs.

Confrontation and correction, including punishment, of aggressive behaviour during imprisonment and hospitalization, are, of course, standard practice. However, OPBs, which may be dissimilar in form to the actual offence, may not be regarded as relevant to the offender's treatment plan; they may go unnoticed or responded to inconsistently; inconsistent responses may consolidate problem behaviours. Additionally, low-severity aggressive behaviour or other forms of aggression which are prominent in institutions (e.g. subversion and non-compliance), but which may also be OPB, may not be appreciated as relevant to past or future offending because of topographical dissimilarity. The OPB framework highlights the need for staff of secure facilities to inquire as to whether a particular behaviour is offence paralleling (a condition of which is a shared multidisciplinary team formulation of the individual's offence history) and worthy of intervention.

According to FAP, reactions to CRBs should be natural (similar to the responses others may have in the community) rather than arbitrary so as to improve generalizability (Follette et al., 1996). However, providing natural responses to aggressive acts is compromised within secure psychiatric hospitals and prisons. Firstly, some immediate natural reactions to aggressive behaviour may be punitive (even violent); these are clearly unethical and unacceptable in the institutional environment. Staff may need to moderate their reaction and ensure it is consistent with treatment, yet still be 'real'. Furthermore, reactions within the unit may be mixed in spite of therapeutic confrontation and sanctions from staff, and some patients may reinforce the offender's aggressive behaviour. When a patient's aggression is reinforced by co-residents, the unit and its staff must ensure they also provide an additional response, nullifying the positive reinforcement offered by the offender's peers.

Assessment of Risk for Violence: A Role for OPB

Questions surrounding the capacity of mental health professionals to accurately identify risk for aggression are long-standing; a multitude of scholars have entered the risk assessment field, resulting in a burgeoning literature and an imposing and sometimes overwhelming array of risk assessment methods, tools, checklists, instruments and measures. Early risk assessment studies, which predominantly relied on review and follow-up of clinicians' unaided clinical appraisal of risk, revealed extremely poor predictive validity. There are many reasons for the inaccuracies observed in early research into clinical appraisals of risk; these include clinicians' failure to consider base rates for aggression (Monahan, 1981), errors in assessing clinicians' appraisal and decision-making (Tversky & Kahneman, 1974) and overestimates of risk due to concerns about Type II errors.

Demands on mental health professionals to improve predictive accuracy have resulted in the development of numerous risk assessment methods and instruments. Two particular approaches have developed: one relying on *actuarial models* (e.g. the Violence Risk Appraisal Guide (VRAG); Webster et al., 1994), the other focusing on *structured clinical appraisals* (e.g. the HCR-20; Webster et al., 1997). It is generally accepted that these methods have comparable predictive accuracy and that they are both superior (in terms of their predictive accuracy) to unaided clinical appraisals. However, there exists ongoing concern about their relative merits and limitations.

Actuarial methods are criticized because they neglect idiosyncratic but important characteristics of the individual that pertain to risk, and that they may lack generalizability and applicability beyond the development sample (Douglas et al., 2003). Actuarial methods have received additional criticism following Hart et al.'s (2007) reanalysis of data used in the development samples of various actuarial risk assessment instruments. Hart et al. (2007) concluded that these instruments' margin of error was too high to allow specific predictions to be applied to individuals. Concerns about the lack of completeness of actuarial methods and their exclusive focus on risk assessment rather than risk management have resulted in revisions of common risk assessment methods so that assessors are encouraged to draw upon clinical case formulations to enhance risk assessment procedures and risk management planning. In this regard, actuarial instruments should 'support, rather than replace, the exercise of clinical judgement' (Monahan et al., 2001, pp. 134–5).

Many contemporary risk assessment instruments invite clinical adjustments of actuarially derived risk scores based on clinical observations of important idiosyncratic risk-related characteristics of the individual or their environment. For instance, in the Level of Service/Case Management Inventory: An Offender Assessment System (Andrews et al., 2004), 'Barriers to Release' section, community supervision may be deemed inappropriate because '... while in prison, the offender has been extremely disruptive, noncompliant in treatment, or has made threats to people in the community' (p. 25). The OPB framework is clearly relevant to those adjustments of violence risk assessments that take into account issues arising during treatment and incarceration. Monitoring OBPs and PABs over the course of incarceration may clarify whether a patient has made positive progress indicative of decreased risk.

Many of the difficulties in determining whether behaviour is truly offence paralleling are relevant to the application of the OPB framework to risk assessment. Application of the OPB framework to risk assessment must therefore be cautious. However, many risk assessors are already evaluating episodes of problem behaviour within institutions and assigning them significance to their risk assessment. It is hoped that this chapter will encourage people already incorporating problematic and supposedly relevant in-custody behaviours to consider the complexities of their assessment and cautiously draw conclusions about the relevance of the in-custody behaviour to the offender risk assessment. The OPB framework may be useful because it sensitizes risk assessors to the possibility of OPB; this may ensure important indicators of persistent risk-related psychopathology arising during incarceration are not ignored, particularly when there is an absence of topographically similar problem behaviour.

In concluding, though the current trend in the risk assessment literature is to be more inclusive of clinical case formulation, unaided risk assessment methods have historically lacked predictive validity. Presently there is no validated OPB-informed risk assessment method. Nevertheless, the framework (with its documented limitations) is a significant advance over the ill-informed judgements that are made about the relevance of behaviours occurring during secure care, which are often ignorant of situational factors. When idiographic assessment is indicated then the OPB assessment must be protected from the same errors in clinical decision-making that tarnish anamnestic and other unaided clinical formulations. Knowledge of situational factors and the typical patterns and determinants of aggressive behaviour within institutions will assist assessors use the OPB framework as a useful adjunct to more traditional structured risk assessment instruments.

ADDITIONAL COMPLICATING FACTORS FOR OPB: FUTURE OPPORTUNITIES AND NEEDS

The Situationalist Perspective and the Immeasurability of Environmental Contributors to Violence

The principal barrier to creating a valid and reliable measure for identifying and measuring OPB is the difficulty measuring the extent of environmental antecedents and facilitators of aggressive behaviour. The traditional *dispositional* perspective locates the causes of violence exclusively within the individual. However, behaviourists (and probably most mental health professionals) appreciate the important role of the environment and its capacity to interact with the individual to influence aggression. As previously discussed, there will be some patients who will be aggressive during secure care who have not previously behaved aggressively (Daffern et al., 2006). This may be due to transient psychological states (e.g. irritability and negativity aroused by positive psychotic symptoms) activated by environmental factors (e.g. demanding behaviour by treatment providers within an institution) and situational crises (e.g. death of a family member). The crucial role of the environment in the elicitation of aggressive behaviour has been observed repeatedly (e.g. Milgram, 1974; Zimbado, 2004). In Zimbado's Stanford prison experiment, 24 community subjects were recruited and randomly assigned to the role of guard or prisoner. Prisoners were arrested, taken to a police station and then transferred to a mock prison environment in the basement of the Psychology Department at Stanford University where it was planned they would remain for the two-week study (Zimbado, 2004). Results of this experiment are famous and striking; the study had to be terminated after six days because of the pathology expressed by prisoners, guards and even Philip Zimbado, who acted as a prison superintendent for the study. Guards behaved sadistically, and they were violent and degrading in their treatment of prisoners; prisoners showed high levels of stress.

The criminological concept of *prisonization* (Clemmer, 1940), which in part reflects adaptation to the prison environment and adoption of subcultural normative behaviour, is also relevant to the dispositional perspective. Although some have argued that *prisonization* is reflective of 'inmates' lives prior to incarceration' (Irwin & Cressey, 1962; Slosar, 1978; Thomas & Foster, 1972; cited in Carr et al., 2006, p. 571), a widely held view is that adoption of customary prison behaviours is due to environmental deprivation; in other words, the isolation from liberty, goods, services and relationships contributes to novel antisocial behaviour and opposition to administration (Jiang & Fisher-Giorlando, 2002; see also Zimbado, 2004). The emergence of homosexual behaviour, and specifically rape in prisoners with no history of same, is an example. According to Knowles (1999), the need for power, dominance, sexual release and masculine identification may drive homosexual behaviour and sexual aggression in secure facilities. Although these are general needs, environmental deprivation may encourage their expression in the form of rape in the prison. Homosexual behaviour first occurs in many men during incarceration (Sagarin, 1976). In general, homosexual behaviour in prison is recast as 'transient, highly physical and unemotional' (p. 270); its function is to establish status and dominance (Knowles, 1999).

According to Ibrahim (1974, cited in Knowles, 1999, p. 272):

> Several factors in the social structure of the prison community may be functional in producing deviant sexual behaviour. These include: (i) the prison is a one-sex, closed society that stops heterosexual activity; (ii) deviant sexual behaviour is tolerated among prisoners, wardens, and administrators; (iii) insufficient work opportunities and recreation programmes leave prisoners with too much idle time; (iv) privacy is often impossible due to shared cells and dormitories, showers and rest rooms; (v) provision is usually not made for separation of sex offenders and homosexuals; (vi) decreased communication from the world outside the prison reduces identification with the sexual norms of society.

The *situationalist* perspective is in direct contrast with the dispositional perspective. It highlights the important and causal role of environmental factors in the emergence and maintenance of aggressive behaviour. The quote appearing at the introduction to this chapter is drawn from Golding's (1954) *Lord of the Flies*, which describes the transformation of British choirboys shipwrecked and isolated from adult supervision. Contrary to past behaviour the boys, under trying conditions, behave like brutal savages.

Clearly, radical (extreme) situationalist and dispositional perspectives are erroneous. Situation and predisposition interact (Blass, 1991); character and temperament influence the likelihood of aggressive behaviour across the lifespan; situational factors will dramatically affect the emergence, form and maintenance of the individual's aggressive behaviours. Mental health professionals utilizing the OPB framework must account for the role of the environment in determining whether improvement (emergent PAB) has occurred or why it is that aggressive behaviours have reduced in frequency or severity; situational factors are clearly relevant to this analysis and require consideration. Unfortunately, the inability of experts in human behaviour to estimate the role of situational factors (which would be helpful for OPB assessors) is highlighted through Stanley Milgram's obedience studies (see Zimbado, 2004, for a review of pertinent issues). In one of the obedience studies, 40 psychiatrists were provided with a basic description of the study and asked to estimate the percentage of subjects who would give the maximum 450 volts. On average they estimated that less than 1% and that only sadists would act in such a manner. This was a clear demonstration of ignorance of situational factors; in these experiments compliance rates as high as 90% were observed.

New Learning and Evolution in Violent Offenders

Within institutions offenders have the opportunity to benefit from treatment and to change. Unfortunately, in prisons and secure hospitals, offenders may also worsen, develop new skills to offend and behave violently. Observation of other offenders behaving aggressively and rehearsal of novel aggressive behaviours may expand an offender's aggressive repertoire. In a review of studies employing behavioural technologies to examine the social learning contingencies existing in prisons, Bukstel and Kilmann (1980) claimed that each study found 'overwhelming positive reinforcement' (p. 472) by the peer group for a variety of antisocial behaviours. Although this review occurred prior to widespread adoption of offender rehabilitation programming the capacity for aggressive offenders to acquire new skills, including antisocial attitudes supportive of violence, needs to be considered and constantly guarded against. Further to the acquisition of new offending skills is the possibility that aggressive offenders may also acquire detection evasion skills (DES; Jones, 2004; i.e. skills that allow criminal behaviour to persist with a reduced likelihood of apprehension).

Given possible changes to the offender's OPB over the course of an admission, it may be that the aggressive OPBs occurring soon after incarceration will show greater semblance to an aggressive index act, as their repertoire of aggression may not have altered, and they may not have acquired DES or new offending skills. As the offender acquires DES or novel ways of behaving aggressively (e.g. subverting authority, sexually abusing and self-harming), OPB may vary to a greater extent. Again, offenders with an established history of consistent violent action are most likely to show consistent OPB throughout their sentence. Finally, a developmental perspective, which takes account of the offender's history of aggressive behaviour prior to incarceration, is required. This allows for the offender's repertoire and trajectory of aggressive behaviour to be established prior to admission and compared with new learning and behaviour during incarceration; MSFA (see Chapter 5) appears to be a useful method that is consistent with this approach.

Adaptation to Prison

Research on the impact of imprisonment consistently shows the importance of individual and institutional differences in coping and adjustment; prison does not appear to be universally detrimental (Bonta & Gendreau, 1990; Zamble & Porporino, 1988), even for prison inmates subjected to long-term incarceration (Bolton et al., 1976). In one study, Zamble and Porporino

(1988) used structured interviews to interview 133 male prison inmates to learn how they coped with their environment. Although external and internal factors determined individual behaviour, many inmates reported severe distress at the beginning of their prison term but less during later stages of their prison sentence. Although some prisoners continued to be disturbed well into their prison term, these findings suggest that most prisoners will settle into their environment and experience less distress. Behavioural manifestations of distress (including aggression, self-harm and other problem behaviours) will typically lessen over the course of a prison sentence. Zamble and Porporino (1988) also revealed only modest positive behavioural change in prison. In another study of long-term prison inmates, most of whom were serving life sentences for homicide-related offences, Zamble (1992) found that prisoners became more involved in work and other structured activities, and less involved in casual socializing with other inmates. These changes were accompanied by evidence of improved adaptation, including decreases in dysphoric emotional states and stress-related medical problems. The number of disciplinary incidents also decreased.

Adaptation to prison is less consistent for mentally ill offenders, specifically those with schizophrenia. These offenders tend to adapt to prison less well, as measured by disciplinary infractions, ability to obtain a job in prison and ability to obtain release from prison (Morgan et al., 1993). Increased disciplinary problems should therefore not necessarily be associated with increased risk and criminogenic need; rather, these increased problems may reflect specific illness-related issues. The adaptation of offenders with personality disorder to prison and to psychiatric hospitals is less well known. However, given the substantial literature examining response to prisoners generally, and the high proportion of prisoners with antisocial personality disorder, patients with this form of personality disorder presumably adapt to prison relatively well. Offenders with other forms of personality disorder may have greater difficulty coping with incarceration. This may mean an increase in problematic behaviour consequent to exacerbation of personality pathology caused by environmental demands. The impact of these environmental demands on the problems observed during imprisonment and their relevance to the offender in the community needs to be carefully considered.

The work of Zamble (1992) and Zamble and Porporino (1988) seems to suggest a consistent pattern of adaptation that needs to be considered when examining possible change in psychological functioning and behaviour that would suggest meaningful change related to a reduction in risk rather than superficial adaptation to treatment and custodial circumstances. Prisoners not in effective offender rehabilitation programmes should be expected to adjust but not to improve. They should appear more emotionally and behaviourally settled as their sentences progress. In this situation prisoners should continue to show OPB throughout their sentence. In the early stages of their sentence, their OPB would more closely resemble (topographically) their typical offence patterns in the community, as has been suggested by Daffern and colleagues (2009). Later in the sentence, the OPB may be topographically dissimilar. For instance, violent offenders may behave in an overtly violent manner early in their sentence, and later they may become dismissive of staff, subversive or intimidatory. For example, in one study of aggressive and self-harming behaviour over the course of hospitalization, Daffern and Howells (2009) found that offenders initially behaved aggressively, but that as their hospital stay progressed they increasingly self-harmed. In this case, self-harm may have assumed the functions previously served by aggression. Finally, prisoners who are not exposed to effective treatments would be unlikely to show evidence of PAB, although an increase in compliance and adaptation would need to be carefully scrutinized to determine whether it is PAB or simply superficial adaptation. Long-term offenders may show and could be expected to develop DES. Offenders serving shorter sentences are more likely to persist with problem behaviours during imprisonment. They may be more willing to accept aversive reactions to their misbehaviour in the short term, knowing they will soon be released. For short-term offenders, it seems that the norm then is to expect persistent topographically similar OPB and not DES or PAB.

CONCLUSION

The OPB framework promotes comparison of two or more sequences of behaviour to determine similarity. Similarity is seen by comparing functional analyses to determine whether psychopathology associated with offending, either past or future, is maintained, and therefore necessitating intervention, either psychotherapeutic or risk management. Comparison of behaviour within hospital with a single index act, as is typically done, is problematic as this act may not be representative of the offender's entire repertoire or their prototypical aggressive behaviour. It is more important to compare the offender's entire repertoire of aggressive behaviour and their trajectory of action prior to incarceration with their current behaviour.

Assuming reliability and validity, several possible outcomes arise when comparing functional analyses: (1) some parts of the sequences will co-occur in both of the analyses; (2) no parts of the sequences will co-occur; and (3) all parts of the sequences will co-occur. The last option is unlikely because of the evolving nature of behaviour generally, and because situational factors inevitably alter the form of aggressive behaviour. The two most likely options are that there will be an insignificant level of similarity or that there will be sufficient similarity to justify labelling one of the behaviours offence paralleling. Results of our previous research (Daffern et al., 2009) revealed that very few parts of a sequence were similar during clinical appraisal, yet over 50% were deemed somewhat or very similar. This is most probably due to the presence of important, causal and remarkable parts of the sequence that were evident in both sequences.

Ascertaining whether there is sufficient similarity to warrant labelling a behaviour offence paralleling is a difficult task when there is some but not total similarity. The inclusion of high base-rate characteristics (e.g. anger arousal and physiological arousal) would result in overidentification and mislabelling of aggressive behaviours as offence paralleling. Similarly, high base-rate characteristics do not reflect persistent habits that are peculiar to the individual or indicative of unique behavioural patterns. (Note: Norms for aggressive behaviour and high base-rate characteristics are not established, and future research should clarify these to assist OPB assessment.)

So where does this leave the OPB assessor? Rather than creating an artificial threshold devoid of clinical sophistication and judgement, OPB should be determined based on the presence of sufficient similarity in important causal social cognitive variables; and functional similarity. Similarity in peculiar or significant idiosyncratic causal variables (e.g. sexual arousal when behaving aggressively) may also be evidence of a unique behavioural pattern. To determine whether the parts of the aggressive behaviour sequence are unique, clinicians and researchers would have to be mindful of the nature of aggression in different contexts and the base rates of these characteristics within secure settings. Finally, rather than establishing a threshold number of parts that are required for classification, assessors should determine what the trajectory is (both prior to and during incarceration) in terms of new learning. For example, is the offender demonstrating improvement (evident in acquired and rehearsed PAB), stability (evidenced by persistent OPB and DES but no PAB) or worsening (evidenced by ongoing OPB and DES but also an expansion of the aggressive repertoire)? Improvement should not be assumed in the context of absent OPB; environmental factors may suppress OPB; the offender may have acquired DES, and the characteristic activators of the offender's aggression may not be evident within the institution.

In summary, although the OPB framework is in its infancy, there is evidence of longitudinal and cross-situational consistency in aggressive behaviours; the task for the future is to validate methods that may be used to identify and monitor OPBs, PABs and DES. Ignoring OPB impairs comprehensiveness in risk assessments and reduces opportunities for contingent responding that supports treatment. It is clear from the research we have conducted thus far that not all topographically similar aggressive behaviours are offence paralleling. Comprehensive, structured functional analyses, grounded in models of aggressive behaviour and informed by empirically derived knowledge about aggressive behaviour within institutions, are required to limit misidentification and misapplication of the OPB framework. Whether they are independent of or adjunctive to structured methods, risk assessments drawing upon the OPB framework must be structured to limit observer error. The OPB framework has more immediate application to violent offender treatment where liberal application offered in a collaborative therapeutic relationship has the potential to increase opportunity for meaningful and immediate interventions and provide a framework that supports and informs all unit staff about their role in the violent offender's treatment.

REFERENCES

Andrews, D., Bonta, J. & Wormith, J.S. (2004). *Level of Service/Case Management Inventory*. Toronto, ON: Multi-Health Systems.

Bartol, C.R. & Bartol, A.M. (2004). *Introduction to Forensic Psychology*. Thousand Oaks, CA: Sage.

Blass, T. (1991). Understanding behavior in the Milgram Obedience Experiment: the role of personality, situations, and their interactions. *Journal of Personality and Social Psychology, 60*, 398–413.

Bolton, N., Smith, F.V., Heskin, K.J. & Banister, P.A. (1976). Psychological correlates of long-term imprisonment. *British Journal of Criminology, 16*, 38–47.

Bonta, J. & Gendreau, P. (1990). Reexamining the cruel and unusual punishment of prison life. *Law and Human Behavior, 14*, 347–72.

Bukstel, L.H. & Kilmann, P.R. (1980). Psychological effects of imprisonment on confined individuals. *Psychological Bulletin, 88*, 469–93.

Bushman, B.J. & Anderson, C.A. (2001). Is it time to pull the plug on the hostile versus hostile versus instrumental aggression dichotomy? *Psychological Review, 108*, 273–79.

Callaghan, G.M., Summers, C.J. & Weidman, M. (2003). The treatment of histrionic and narcissistic personality disorder behaviours: a single-subject demonstration of clinical improvement using functional analytic psychotherapy. *Journal of Contemporary Psychotherapy, 33*, 321–39.

Carr, A., Rotter, M., Steinbacher, M., Green, D., Dole, T., Garcia-Mansilla, A. & Rosenfeld, B. (2006). Structured assessment of correctional adaptation (SACA): a measure of the impact of incarceration on the mentally ill in a therapeutic setting. *International Journal of Offender Rehabilitation and Comparative Criminology, 50*, 570–81.

Clark, D., Fisher, M.J. & McDougall, C. (1994). A new methodology for assessing the level of risk in incarcerated offenders. *British Journal of Criminology, 33*, 436–48.

Clemmer, D. (1940). *The Prison Community*. New Braunfels, TX: Christopher Publishing House.

Daffern, M. (2010). The emergence and persistence of stalking behavior in psychiatric units: application of the offence paralleling behavior framework. *Journal of Behavior Analysis of Offender and Victim – Treatment and Prevention*, 2, 133–142.

Daffern, M. & Howells, K. (2009). The function of aggression in personality disordered patients. *Journal of Interpersonal Violence, 24*, 586–600.

Daffern, M., Howells, K. & Ogloff, J.R.P. (2006). What's the point? Towards a methodology for assessing the function of psychiatric inpatient aggression. *Behaviour Research and Therapy, 45* (1), 101–11.

Daffern, M., Howells, K., Stacey, J., Hogue, T. & Mooney, P. (2008). Sexually abusive behaviour in personality disordered inpatients of a high secure psychiatric hospital: implications for the assessment of offence paralleling behaviours. *Journal of Sexual Aggression, 14*, 123–33.

Daffern, M., Howells, K., Manion, A. & Tonkin, M. (2009). A test of methodology intended to assist detection of aggressive offence paralleling behaviour within secure settings. *Legal and Criminological Psychology, 14*, 213–26.

Daffern, M., Jones, L., Howells, K., Shine, J., Mikton, C. & Tunbridge, V.C. (2007a). Refining the definition of offence paralleling behaviour. *Criminal Behaviour and Mental Health, 17*, 265–73.

Daffern, M., Ogloff, J.R.P., Ferguson, M., Thomson, L. & Howells, K. (2007b). Appropriate treatment targets or products of a demanding environment? The relationship between aggression in a forensic psychiatric hospital with aggressive behaviour preceding admission and violent recidivism. *Psychology, Crime and Law, 13*, 431–41.

Douglas, K.S., Ogloff, J.R.P. & Hart, S. (2003). Evaluation of a model of violence risk assessment among forensic psychiatric patients. *Psychiatric Services, 54*, 1372–79.

Follette, W.C., Naugle, A.E. & Callaghan, G.M. (1996). A radical behavioural understanding of the therapeutic relationship in effecting change. *Behavior Therapy, 27*, 623–41.

Golding, W. (1954). *Lord of the Flies*. London: Faber and Faber.

Grubin, D., Kelly, P. & Brunsdon, C. (2001). *Linking Serious Sexual Assaults through Behaviour* (Home Office Research Study No. 215). London: Home Office Research, Development and Statistics Directorate.

Hafkenscheid, A. (2003). Objective countertransference: do patients' interpersonal impacts generalize across therapists? *Clinical Psychology and Psychotherapy, 10*, 31–40.

Hart, S.D., Michie, C. & Cooke, D.J. (2007). Precision of actuarial risk assessment instruments: evaluating the 'margins of error' of group *v.* individual predictions of violence. *British Journal of Psychiatry, 190*, s60–65.

Haynes, S. (1998). The changing nature of behavioural assessment. In A. Bellack & M. Hersen (Eds), *Behavioral Assessment: A Practical Handbook* (pp. 1–21). Boston, MA: Allyn & Bacon.

Howells, K. (1998). Cognitive behavioural interventions for anger, aggression and violence. In N. Tarrier, A. Welsh & G. Haddock (Eds), *Treating Complex Cases: The Cognitive Behavioural Approach* (pp. 295–318). Chichester: John Wiley & Sons.

Ibrahim, A.I. (1974). Deviant sexual behavior in men's prisons. *Journal of Crime and Delinquency, 20*, 38–44.

Irwin, J. & Cressey, D.R. (1962). Thieves, convicts and the inmate culture. *Social Problems, 10*, 142–55.

Jiang, S. & Fisher-Giorlando, M. (2002). Inmate misconduct: a test of the deprivation, importation, and situational models. *The Prison Journal, 82*, 335–58.

Jones, L.F. (2004). Offence paralleling behaviour (OPB) as a framework for assessment and interventions with offenders. In A. Needs & G. Towl (Eds), *Applying Psychology to Forensic practice*. Chichester: BPS Blackwell.

Kiesler, D.J. (1988). *Therapeutic Metacommunication: Therapist Impact Disclosure as Feedback in Psychotherapy*. Palo Alto, CA: Consulting Psychologists Press.

Kiesler, D.J. (1996). *Contemporary Interpersonal Theory and Research: Personality, Psychopathology, Psychotherapy*. New York: John Wiley & Sons.

Knowles, G.J. (1999). Male prison rape: a search for causation and prevention. *The Howard Journal, 38*, 267–82.

Kohlenberg, R.J. & Tsai, M. (1991). *Functional Analytic Psychotherapy: Creating Intense and Curative Therapeutic Relationships*. New York: Plenum Press.

Kuyken, W., Fothergill, C.D., Musa, M. & Chadwick, P. (2005). The reliability and quality of cognitive case formulation. *Behaviour Research and Therapy, 43*, 1187–201.

Luborsky, L. & Diguer, L. (1998). The reliability of the CCRT measure: results from eight samples. In L. Luborsky & P. Crits-Christoph (Eds), *Understanding Transference: The Core Conflictual Relationship Theme Method* (2nd edition, pp. 97–108). New York: Basic Books.

Matthews, G., Jones, D.M. & Chamberlain, A.G. (1990). Refining the measurement of mood: the UWIST mood adjective checklist. *British Journal of Psychology, 81*, 17–42.

McDougal, C. & Clark, D.A. (1991). A risk assessment model. In S. Boddis (Ed.), *Proceedings of the Prison Psychology Conference*. London: Her Majesty Stationery Office.

McDougal, C., Clark, D.A. & Fisher, M. (1994). Assessment of violent offenders. In M. McMurran & J. Hodge (Eds), *The Assessment of Criminal Behaviours of Clients in Secure Settings* (pp. 68–93). London: Jessica Kingsley.

Milgram, S. (1974). *Obedience to Authority: An Experimental View*. New York: Harper & Row.

Mischel, W. (1973). Toward a cognitive social learning reconceptualization of personality. *Psychological Review, 80*, 252–83.

Mischel, W. (2004). Toward an integrative model for CBT: encompassing behaviour, cognition, affect and process. *Behavior Therapy, 35*, 185–203.

Monahan, J. (1981). *The Clinical Prediction of Violent Behavior*. Rockville, MD: National Institute of Mental Health.

Monahan, J., Steadman, H.J., Silver, E., Applebaum, P.S., Robbins, P.C., Mulvey, E.P., Roth, L., Grisso, T. & Banks, S. (2001). *Rethinking Risk Assessment: The MacArthur Study of Mental Disorder and Violence*. Oxford: Oxford University Press.

Morgan, D.W., Edwards, A.C. & Faulkner, L.R. (1993). The adaptation to prison by individuals with schizophrenia. *Bulletin of the American Academy of Psychiatry and the Law, 21*, 427–33.

Mulick, P.S., Landes, S.J. & Kanter, J.W. (2005). Contextual behaviour therapies in the treatment of PTSD: a review. *International Journal of Behavioral Consultation and Therapy, 1*, 223–38.

Mumma, G.H. & Smith, J.L. (2001). Cognitive-behavioural-interpersonal scenarios: interformulator reliability and convergent validity. *Journal of Psychopathology and Behavioral Assessment, 23*, 203–21.

Nevin, J.A. & Grace, R.C. (2000). Preference and resistance to change with constant-duration schedule components. *Journal of the Experimental Analysis of Behavior, 74*, 79–100.

Nisbett, R.E. & Ross, L. (1980). *Human Inference: Strategies and Shortcomings of Social Judgement*. Englewood Cliffs, NJ: Prentice Hall.

Olweus, D. (1980). The consistency issue in personality psychology revisited – with special reference to aggression. *British Journal of Social and Clinical Psychology, 19*, 377–90.

Persons, J.B., Mooney, K.A. & Padesky, C.A. (1995). Interrater reliability of cognitive-behavioral case formulations. *Cognitive Therapy and Research, 19*, 21–34.

Ross, L. (1977). The intuitive psychologist and his shortcomings: distortions in the attribution process. In L. Berkowitz (Ed.), *Advances in Experimental Social Psychology* (Vol. 10, pp. 173–220). New York: Academic Press.

Sagarin, E. (1976). Prison homosexuality and it effect on post-prison sexual behaviour. *Psychiatry, 39*, 375–87.

Scacco, A. (1982). *Male Rape: A Case Book of Sexual Aggressions*. New York: AMS Press.

Skinner, B.F. (1957). *Verbal Behaviour*. Acton, MA: Copley.

Slosar, J. (1978). *Prisonization, Friendship and Leadership*. Lexington, MA: Heath Lexington.

Thomas, C.W. & Foster, S.C. (1972). Prisonization in the inmate contra-culture. *Social Problems, 20*, 229–39.

Tversky, D. & Kahneman, A. (1974). Judgement under uncertainty: heuristics and biases. *Science, 185*, 1124–31.

Vyse, S. (2004). Stability over time: is behaviour analysis a trait psychology? *The Behaviour Analyst, 27*, 43–53.

Webster, C.D., Harris, G., Rice, M., Cormier, C. & Quinsey, V. (1994). *Violence Prediction Scheme: Assessing Dangerousness in High Risk Men*. Toronto, ON: Centre of Criminology, University of Toronto.

Webster, C.D., Douglas, K.S., Eaves, D. & Hart, S.D. (1997). *HCR-20: Assessing Risk of Violence (version 2)*. Vancouver, BC: Mental Health Law & Policy Institute, Simon Fraser University.

Woodhams, J. & Toye, K. (2007). An empirical test of the assumptions of case linkage and offender profiling with serial commercial robberies. *Psychology, Public Policy, and Law, 13*, 59–85.

Yalom, I.D. (1985). *Theory and Practice of Group Psychotherapy* (3rd edition). New York: Basic Books.

Young, J. (1990). *Cognitive Therapy for Personality Disorders: A Schema-Focused Approach*. Sarasota, FL: Professional Resource Exchange, Inc.

Zamble, E. (1992). Behavior and adaptation in long-term prison inmates. *Criminal Justice and Behavior, 19*, 409–25.

Zamble, E. & Porporino, F. (1988). *Coping, Behavior and Adoption in Prison Inmates*. New York: Springer.

Zamble, E. & Porporino, F. (1990). Coping, imprisonment, and rehabilitation. *Criminal Justice and Behavior, 17*, 53–70.

Zimbado, P. (2004). A situationist perspective on the psychology of evil: understanding how good people are transformed into perpetrators. In A. Miller (Ed.), *The Social Psychology of Good and Evil: Understanding our Capacity for Kindness and Cruelty*. New York: Guilford Press.

Chapter 7

APPLYING THE CONCEPT OF OFFENCE PARALLELING BEHAVIOUR TO SEX OFFENDER ASSESSMENT IN SECURE SETTINGS

Ruth E. Mann

National Offender Management Service, London, UK

David Thornton

Sand Ridge Secure Treatment Center, Wisconsin, USA

Simone Wakama

HM Prison Whatton, UK

Maisie Dyson

National Offender Management Service, UK

David Atkinson

HM Prison Full Sutton, York, UK

INTRODUCTION

In this chapter, we consider how the concept of offence paralleling behaviour (OPB) applies to treatment and risk management work with sexual offenders. By treatment, we mean any endeavour involving collaborative therapeutic techniques that aims to assist men convicted of sexual offences to find a lifestyle that does not involve further offending. By risk management, we mean any endeavour, collaborative or uncollaborative, that aims to reduce the likelihood of further offending. Thus, treatment is a subtype of risk management work, but risk management work also includes some activities that might not be considered therapeutic. Criminal justice personnel who work with sexual offenders may take a rehabilitative approach or a risk management approach. Frequently, they are required to take both approaches, which can sometimes lead to uncomfortable moments when the needs or wishes of the offender conflict with the demands of public protection.

Offence Paralleling Behaviour: A Case Formulation Approach to Offender Assessment and Intervention Edited by Michael Daffern, Lawrence Jones and John Shine

Risk assessment – which we define as any process (but preferably a structured one) that identifies the factors which raise the risk of reoffending, and which leads to a conclusion about the level and nature of risk that the offender presents – is, in our view, a necessary precursor to both rehabilitation and risk management activity. While static risk scales are currently the most accurate form of risk assessment, most jurisdictions supplement static risk scales with an assessment of the changeable, psychological factors that are presumed to have played a causal role in the offending, and which can, at least theoretically, be addressed as a way of reducing risk. A proper risk assessment enables prioritization of treatment and risk management resources, and provides clarity about the specific targets on which those resources should be focused for a given offender.

Several structured risk assessment schemes for use with sexual offenders are now available. However, Mann et al. (2008) concluded that there is still considerable room for improvement in sexual offender risk assessment. Current schemes are limited because they lack a cohesive theory of sexual offender risk, focus on factors that raise risk but not 'protective' factors that enable successful desistance, and fail to incorporate neurobiological influences on behaviour (e.g. neurobiological consequences of early childhood trauma). There is also no currently validated process to accurately identify when risk has been reduced (especially, but not solely, by treatment).

We first consider how the concept of OPB fits with other theoretical developments in sexual offender risk assessment. We suggest how to incorporate OPB into risk assessment frameworks, and we examine different methodologies for monitoring offenders' OPBs. We then consider the practical matters of how to train staff in recognizing OPBs within risk assessment, and we discuss the ethical issues associated with observing institutional behaviour and interpreting it within the OPB framework. Our overarching aim is to encourage those who work with sex offenders to adopt the OPB framework safely and appropriately within their practice.

Elsewhere in this volume, Jones suggests that the concept of OPB can make a useful contribution to risk assessment, writing that 'Whilst [OPB] cannot be used to make probabilistic statements about risk, [it] offers a useful approach to identifying risk relevant current behaviour and significant possible risk events'. Daffern (this volume, Chapter 6) similarly suggests that 'the Offence Paralleling Behaviour (OPB) framework has emerged as a potential adjunct to these risk assessment methods and structured treatment programmes'. He adds later that 'Many of the difficulties in determining whether behaviour is truly offence paralleling are relevant to the application of the OPB framework to risk assessment. Application of the OPB framework to risk assessment must therefore be cautious', but then concludes that the OPB framework has plenty to offer to risk assessment, if correctly understood and applied.

It is certainly the case that the notion of OPB is attractive to risk assessors, who realize they lack tools to identify continuing risk or, conversely, reductions in risk. Unfortunately, assessors have sometimes, in our experience, used the language of OPB to justify labelling any antisocial behaviour as 'offence paralleling'. Jones and Daffern unite in condemning this usage of the OPB terminology. They note that, particularly in cases of incarcerated offenders, the demands of the institution, rather than any antisocial propensity, can contribute to the emergence of aggressive behaviour. It is important, therefore, not to over-assign the label 'offence paralleling' to any antisocial behaviour exhibited by a known offender. A behaviour can only be categorized as an OPB if it has functional similarity to behaviours leading up to the offence. A functional similarity is a similarity in the purpose of the behaviour, rather than a similarity in the behaviour itself (Daffern & Howells, 2002).

An example illustrates the difficulty in identifying functional similarity. An imprisoned sex offender, regarded as moderate risk, asked for a move to a different residential unit, but the prison authorities refused his request. Some days later, he asked again, this time explaining that he feared for his safety from other prisoners housed near him. On this occasion he obtained the move. However, it later emerged that he had not been at any risk from other prisoners. A member of staff then called for the prisoner to be regraded to a higher risk category, arguing that his 'manipulative behaviour' paralleled behaviours leading up to his offence, where he had groomed a child and his mother into accepting him into their family circle.

It seems likely that in this case the offender was lying to obtain a desired outcome. However, the risk assessment assumed that this lie paralleled his manipulation of others in order to access a victim. While there is topographical similarity between the two purposes, the consideration of the case did not encompass the 'assessment of environmental, cognitive, physiological and behavioural variables' (Daffern & Howells, 2002, p. 487) necessary to ensure functional similarity. In this case, the assumption that a lie told in prison bore functional similarity to previous manipulative behaviours led ultimately to the prisoner concerned serving considerably longer in prison. The case exemplifies Daffern's (this volume, Chapter 6) concern that 'Improper use of the OPB framework may result in inconsistent and idiosyncratic assessments that are detrimental to patients. These misapplications may be invoked to justify incapacitation and imposition of unnecessary treatment, based on the presence of a so-called OPB, which may be mistakenly construed as evidence for persistent pathology associated with known criminal aggressive behaviour'.

Furthermore, in the case above, not only was there no attempt to establish the underlying function of the behaviour, there was no attempt to integrate institutional observed behaviours into a structured risk assessment framework. In fact, grooming a child or a parent is not a cause of offending or a risk factor; it is a part of the offence process. Therefore, even if the observed institutional behaviour did mirror behaviour prior to offending, this could not automatically be considered to be a manifestation of a risk factor. It is, therefore, important to set out exactly how OPB should be conceptualized when assessing risk. In the next section, we propose an integration of OPB into a broader theory of sexual offender risk.

OPBs AND A THEORY OF SEX OFFENDER RISK

In our theory of sex offender risk assessment (Mann et al., 2008), we have suggested that risk factors exist as both propensities and manifestations. A propensity is equivalent to a psychological trait – an enduring vulnerability that leads to consistent expressions of certain thoughts, feelings or behaviours. For a propensity to be a risk factor, there must be robust empirical evidence that the factor predicts recidivism, and there should be a theoretically plausible justification that the factor could be a cause of sexual offending. There should also be a reason to believe that the propensity is amenable to change, and that a change in this propensity would reduce the likelihood of recidivism. Using the first of these criteria, Mann et al. (2008) proposed a list of well-supported risk factors for sexual recidivism, including sexually deviant interests, offence-supportive attitudes, poor adult attachment, impulsivity and a grievance schema. As yet, there is little published work to propose theoretically plausible accounts of how risk factors cause sexual offending, and there is similarly little published research which has investigated a relationship between changes on a risk factor and changes in risk.

Propensities reveal themselves through manifestations. A manifestation is an observable behaviour, which signifies the presence of a currently active underlying propensity. The concept of a manifestation, therefore, bears remarkable similarity to the concept of an OPB. Application of the OPB framework, with its emphasis on the importance of establishing functional similarity, provides a frame of reference by which a behaviour can be designated as a manifestation, or not.

Also consistent with OPB theory is our proposal that environments differ in how strongly they trigger propensities (see Thornton et al., 2008). The strength of a manifestation depends on the strength of the underlying propensity but also on the extent to which the environment triggers that propensity. For example, an exclusive-type paedophile, who only has a sexual interest in children, may manifest this propensity when living in the community by following, observing or engaging with children in his neighbourhood. His social and physical choices are relatively unconstrained by his environment, and so these manifestations of his propensity are possible and observable. Subjective sexual arousal may also be a manifestation of his sexual interest in children, although this is more likely to be constrained in an environment where other adults are present, and therefore would likely be less visible to others. In prison, a confined environment where no children are present produces few triggers for this propensity, and manifestations consequently are less likely, or may be weaker. The underlying propensity has not necessarily changed in its intensity, but the strength of the manifestations has changed because of the environment. In particular, the constraint of the environment will reduce the manifestations that are *observable to others*. The offender may experience sexual arousal to private fantasies of a child, which is a manifestation of sorts, but this arousal is not likely to be evident to observers.

Figure 7.1 provides a diagrammatic illustration of the relationship between propensities, manifestations and the environment. This diagram shows that the strength of manifestations is a function of both the strength of the underlying propensities (P1 to P4) and the extent to which the environment triggers each propensity (T1 to T4). Thus, a weaker propensity (in this case, P3) can, in a particular context, result in as strong a manifestation as a stronger propensity (in this case, P1) because the environment triggers the weaker propensity but not the stronger one. For example, a prison environment may trigger grievance thinking, even if this propensity is relatively weak, because prisons frequently disregard the rights of their inmates and frequently involve processes that are perceived as unfair which antagonize inmates. Furthermore, displays of aggression are common in some prison environments, so that the aggressive manifestation of grievance thinking is permitted. For these reasons, even a weak propensity to grievance may be frequently activated in a prison and may lead to observable manifestations of anger. However, if the environment suppresses particular manifestations of other propensities, such as sexual behaviour, then even a strong and currently active propensity (in this case, P1) will not result in an observable manifestation.

Knitting together this theory of risk with the concept of OPB, it can be argued that, for a sexual offender, an OPB is an observable manifestation of a propensity that is a risk factor for sexual offending. Adopting this definition may enable clearer thinking about OPBs in sexual offending and may guard against misuse of the OPB framework, as exemplified in the case description

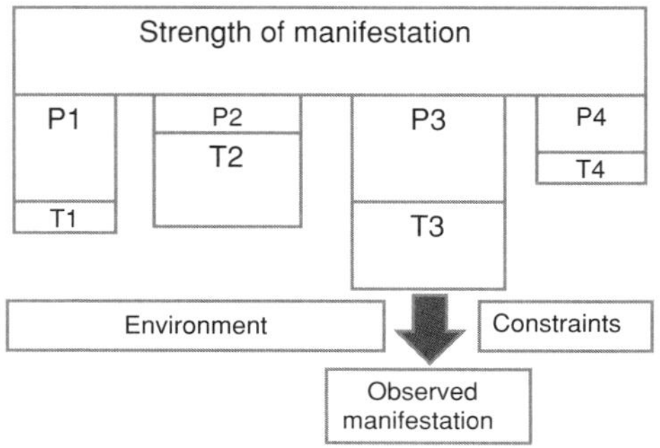

Figure 7.1 Relationship between propensities, manifestations and the environment.

given at the beginning of this chapter. As lying to achieve a desirable end is not a propensity unique to, or predictive of, sexual offending, the prisoner who (possibly) lied to obtain a move to another residential unit was not exhibiting OPB. Most likely, he was exhibiting a goal-directed behaviour, which was rational given the constraints of his environment (given that making a polite request for a change had proved ineffective). Therefore, to guard against misusing the OPB framework with sexual offenders, it is necessary to have a clear understanding of what does and does not constitute risk factors for sexual offending.

Mistakes in assessing sexual offenders arise when people work from an instinctive, rather than evidence-based, position on the nature of risk factors for sexual recidivism. For instance, Maruna and Mann (2006) pointed out that criminal justice systems often place heavy emphasis on 'taking responsibility for one's offence'. However, there is no empirical evidence that failure to take responsibility for past offending is a risk factor for recidivism. Rather, the existing research would point to the opposite conclusion: that failing to take responsibility for one's offending may be a desistance factor (see also Maruna, 2001). The risk assessor who understands this evidence will avoid interpreting failures to take responsibility as signs of persistent risk.

Similarly, a lack of victim empathy is not a risk factor for sexual recidivism (Hanson & Morton-Bourgon, 2005). Manifestations of poor empathy for others in sex offenders cannot be regarded as OPBs. But it is a popular belief – among clinicians and criminal justice professionals as well as lay people – that victim empathy and victim awareness are crucial aspects of sexual offender rehabilitation.

The concept of OPB fits nicely with contemporary theories about sex offender risk. But so far, there has been no attempt to develop a systematic scheme for identifying OPBs and incorporating them into risk assessments. We now turn to a discussion of whether this is possible, and consideration of some of the methodologies that could be adopted for such a purpose.

POSSIBLE METHODOLOGIES FOR SYSTEMATICALLY ASSESSING OPBs IN SEXUAL OFFENDERS

If OPBs represent manifestations of active risk factors, then their identification should provide important assistance to the assessment of current risk. At present, risk assessment frameworks (and clinical practice) for sex offenders are stronger at identifying what were risk factors in the past (i.e. identifying what led up to offending), but weaker at identifying which of these risky propensities remain currently active. Various possible methodologies include self-report through psychometric tests (e.g. Allan et al., 2007), clinician ratings of treatment progress (e.g. the 'got it' scale proposed by Marques et al., 2005), ratings of currently active propensities based on interviews (e.g. STABLE and ACUTE scales; Hanson et al., 2007) and psychophysiological measures such as the polygraph or penile plethysmograph. Some of these methods have yielded reasonable results in terms of predictive validity, but they all have limitations. For instance, self-reporting via psychometric tests is liable to impression management bias (faking good). Clinician ratings of treatment progress are usually based on the knowledge of the offending in one specified setting and may not be able to take into account the extent to which 'new' attitudes and behaviours have generalized across settings. Ratings of currently active propensities based on interviews capture only a small segment of offender behaviour, in one constrained environment. According to our theory, it is likely that the environment of the parole officer's office would constrain the manifestation of many risky propensities. While polygraph and penile plethysmograph have strong followings, both are hampered by lack of systematic implementation schemes and reliability/validity problems.

Given the limitations of self-report and other assessment technologies, it is perhaps quite surprising to find that there are currently no structured schemes for behavioural observation of sexual offenders' manifestations of risk factors. When we searched for possibly unpublished schemes in use by individual clinicians or agencies, we found no examples of structured schemes whatsoever. It is important to ask why this might be, and if, indeed, such an approach is feasible.

A likely explanation is simply that risk assessment researchers have not yet turned to this question because first it was necessary to clarify the nature of risk factors of sexual offending. The risk assessment literature has so far focused on identifying individual risk factors and establishing schemes for combining risk factors to improve predictive validity. Once this stage is completed, which is about where we are now, researchers will next turn their attention to properly trialling various different ways of measuring current activity of risk factors and identifying ways of establishing when a risk factor changes. We are not far off the time when large-scale studies of change against risk factors will begin to emerge, taking us forward into the next stage. This is therefore an excellent time to begin to think about ways in which the concept of OPB could aid the identification of currently active risky propensities.

Behavioural observation is a popular psychological assessment approach. Behavioural observation is, for obvious reasons, going to be easiest with offenders in residential settings such as prisons, hospitals or youth homes. In these contexts, staff have access to information about offenders' behaviour for 24 hours a day, seven days a week. On the other hand, the very nature of residential environments restricts the full range of social and physical activities that an offender can engage in, and this restriction will reduce the observable manifestation of risky propensities. Furthermore, as so clearly described by Jones et al. (Chapter 20), residential environments may trigger apparently antisocial behaviours which are not, in fact, the manifestation of risky propensities but which on the surface look like they might be. Staff who work with offenders in residential settings need to be very cognisant of the danger of pathologizing the behaviours that they observe by interpreting them as offence paralleling when they are not.

How, then, can OPBs be ethically identified in an incarcerated offender population? There are two issues. First, who monitors the behaviours? The staff who have most opportunity to monitor behaviours in a variety of contexts are likely to be residential staff such as prison officers or nurses. These staff tend not to have the training necessary to conduct full risk assessments and tend not to have the time to be able to follow up their observations with functional assessments for the purpose of the behaviour they observed. Hence, it might be expected that residential staff would be asked to report behaviours back to risk assessment staff such as psychologists.

The second issue relates to the degree of structure placed around the behavioural monitoring. The literature on behavioural assessment in residential settings identifies a variety of approaches to observing behaviour. One approach is to utilize structured, routine reporting. In this approach, residential staff would be instructed to return regular (e.g. daily) monitoring forms on residents (e.g. patients or prisoners). The monitoring forms would usually be in the style of a checklist, asking the staff member to report any observations of predefined behaviour since the last monitoring occasion. A typical question might be, 'In the last 24 hours, have you observed [the resident] raise his voice in anger to another person?' The checklist continues presenting suggested behaviours of interest, to which the assessor replies with a simple 'yes' or 'no' (alternatively, 'seen' or 'not seen').

As no such scale has been utilized with sex offenders, an example from another field is used to illustrate this approach. The Cohen-Mansfield Agitation Inventory (CMAI) is a highly structured behavioural monitoring scale, designed to be completed by residential staff (Cohen-Mansfield, 1986, 1988). The CMAI was developed for use by nursing staff with nursing home residents. The scale requires staff to rate the presence of 29 possible behaviours, such as wandering, pacing, screaming, biting and fighting, on a seven-point scale. The scale is completed for every resident every two weeks, with ratings relating to the extent to which the behaviours have been manifest over that period. Shah et al. (1998) noted that nursing staff tended to like this sort of scale because they are quick, easy, simple and brief to complete. However, the two-week observation period risks under-reporting of aggressive behaviours, and in practice these sorts of scales often need to be supplemented with attention to nursing and medical case notes, ward rounds and informal nursing discussions (Shah et al., 1998).

At the other end of the continuum is the approach which instructs staff members to report behaviours they see which they feel to be relevant, without being prompted to do so and without any required structure to their report. While theoretically less demanding on staff time, this approach does require residential staff to have an appreciation of what behaviours may be relevant to risk. For such a system to work well, staff must be able to differentiate risky behaviours from benign behaviours, and motivated to report the behaviours that they see. As residential staff frequently work in shifts, it is unlikely that one offender will be consistently observed by the same member of staff, which may mean that reporting is more related to the observer than the observed. It is likely that reporting rates will vary, depending on how busy, interested and conscientious an individual staff member is, both generally and at any specific point in time. And a specialist will probably then need to check the reports, reflect on whether the behaviours reported are likely to be OPBs or not, and then work with the offender to examine the functional meaning of each behaviour in more detail. Overall, this type of system is likely to be both costly and insufficiently consistent to be fair.

The two approaches described above represent quite markedly different methods for recording behaviours that are potentially OPBs. Another option is for residential staff to report certain specific behaviours when they arise rather than routinely, but to use a structured format in doing so. Daffern et al. (2007) reported on the record of aggressive behaviours, which is completed whenever an aggressive incident occurs and which requires certain set pieces of information to be recorded. In order to keep staff motivated to complete these records, Daffern et al. (2007) described the following procedures:

> A folder containing blank record sheets was left within the nursing station on each ward. An instruction sheet was left with the folder and the first author visited the ward at least three times every week to collect completed incident forms, review the recording process, maintain staff interest in the project, and assist in the completion of forms when these had not been completed by staff by asking staff whether there had been aggressive incidents that had not been reported. (Daffern et al., 2007, p. 105)

The extent to which the researchers in this study had to continually prompt staff to fill out the records indicates that behavioural reporting was inconsistent and liable to bias – with perhaps some staff more inclined to report problems than others, and with inclination to report likely to fluctuate according to other factors, such as workload. Daffern et al. (2007) further found that it was difficult to then determine the functions of the aggressive behaviours because 'few patients were willing to participate in interview following their aggressive behaviour' (p. 107).

The difficulty in deciding upon the function of individual aggressive incidents is a limitation for all the methodologies examined so far. Another limitation common to these approaches is that they all place some constraint on the behaviours recorded. That is, if staff are only required to report aggressive behaviours, the monitoring system will fail to identify non-aggressive OPBs. For sexual offenders, the range of behaviours with the potential to be offence paralleling, and which therefore ought to be monitored, is almost limitless and will include sexual behaviours, aggressive behaviours, socially isolating behaviours, vengeance, poor problem-solving, impulsivity and expressions of offence-supportive attitudes. Only a few of these (e.g. expressions of offence-supportive attitudes) will automatically be OPBs; most will require functional analysis to establish whether they are OPB. It is therefore likely that any routine monitoring system is mainly likely to record irrelevant events, and this wastes staff time, is demotivating, and ultimately is likely to lead to the demise of staff cooperation.

One way to maximize the likelihood of only functionally equivalent behaviour being recorded is for specialist staff to examine the records of a particular offender and to predict the kinds of behaviours that may occur which would constitute OPBs for that prisoner. This approach is exemplified in the Wakefield risk assessment model (WRAM) developed by Clark et al. (1993). In the WRAM, specialist staff examined individual cases, identified psychological risk factors and then predicted how these factors might be manifested in the secure setting (effectively, predicted the likely OPBs for each offender). Residential staff were co-opted to monitor offenders against the individualized list of predicted OPBs. Because the functional analysis was completed before, rather than after, the event, as it were, such a system should be more efficient by enabling staff to ignore behaviours that are not OPBs and encouraging a more directed form of observation. On the other hand, this system may fail to notice relevant behaviours if these had not been predicted beforehand.

Our examination of the literature indicates that there is no clearly superior way to routinely monitor offenders for OPBs. Whichever method is chosen, the risk assessor needs to be aware of reporting biases, reporting lethargy and the difficulty in ensuring that any reported behaviour is actually an OPB.

ETHICAL ISSUES IN MONITORING OPBs

It could be argued that when an offender enters a prison or other secure residential system, there is an implicit understanding that his or her behaviour is being observed and monitored. However, the processes involved, and the purposes and outcomes of the monitoring, may not always be completely transparent. While many staff who work within prison systems are unconcerned about the idea that processes are not transparent, psychologists are bound by ethical codes which usually see transparency as fundamental to ethical practice. How, then, should a psychologist, working in a prison system, participate in behavioural observation of prisoners without falling foul of ethical standards? In this section, we consider some of the ethical dilemmas that psychologists might face in implementing behavioural observation and reporting on OPBs for the purposes of risk assessment. Risk assessment presents complex ethical questions for psychologists, and we do not presume here to offer clear solutions as much as to raise awareness and promote discussion of the issues that a psychologist needs to reflect upon.

Consent

Professional codes of ethics – for example, the British Psychological Society (BPS) Code of Ethics and Conduct (BPS, 2006) – suggest that ideally prior to any psychological intervention a psychologist should seek and record informed consent from the client of the intervention. Two questions immediately arise in relation to the monitoring of OPBs. First, does such monitoring constitute an intervention? Second, is the offender the client? It could be argued that, if risk assessment is essential to public protection, the need to protect the public outweighs the offender's wishes. This argument concludes that observing an offender's behaviour without consent and including observation data within risk assessment may be justifiable. The BPS Code does allow for information to be withheld 'when necessary to preserve ... the efficacy of the professional service or in the public interest' (Standard 1.3 xi).

Haag (2006) considered these issues. He noted that there is an argument that risk assessment is a service provided for society at large, and that this differs from traditional psychotherapeutic activity with offenders where the offender is more obviously seen as the primary client. Haag noted the ruling in the Federal Court of Canada (Inmate Welfare Committee, 2003), which found that risk assessment could legally be conducted without the consent of the offender, because risk assessment was not provided for the benefit of the offender. However, Haag's conclusion, having considered this argument, was that even if risk assessment is legally permissible without consent, this does not make it ethical. In Haag's view, conducting a risk assessment on an offender without his or her consent constitutes disrespect for the dignity of the person and additionally carries a likelihood that incorrect information will be considered. Haag concluded that the only occasion where it may be ethical to assess an offender's risk without his consent is when a court or other legal authority orders such an assessment. Even in such an instance, according to Haag, a psychologist should probably not provide an opinion without having interviewed the offender and/or having access to the full file.

Similarly, Bonner and Vandecreek (2006) asserted that psychologists need to avoid making a distinction between offenders and the rest of society when it comes to considering an offender's rights and dignity, including the right to refuse consent. However, it is easy to imagine scenarios where an offender refuses consent to behavioural monitoring, yet observations of behaviour clearly indicate risk factors and so should be reported. Consider, for instance, a scenario where a staff member overhears two offenders discussing an intention to commit further sexual offences. It would clearly be ludicrous if the offenders were able to withhold consent for this information to be reported because they had not given permission for their conversations to be monitored. No one would argue that to be ethical, a psychologist should disregard this information in forming a parole recommendation, and that they should further discourage others from recording it or passing it on to the police or the parole board. We therefore suggest that it may be useful to distinguish between *consent*, where the offender is able to give or refuse permission for behaviour to be observed, and *transparency*, where the offender is made aware that in a secure setting his behaviour is open to observation and reporting at any time.

Even with this distinction, it is necessary to consider whether full transparency would harm the efficacy of the process – the key criterion, according to the BPS – that might justify withholding information from the offender client. It could be argued that if an offender is informed that his behaviour is being monitored, he will simply raise his guard and take more care not to reveal any risky behaviour. If a monitoring system operates that involves searching for predicted behaviours, he may particularly subdue his behaviours if he is informed of the exact manifestations that have been predicted. Returning to our earlier theoretical description, informing an offender that he is being monitored increases the extent to which the environment will constrain manifestations of risky propensities. This possibility has not been tested and so the concern remains an empirical question. That is, do offenders behave differently when informed that their behaviour is being monitored? It would be an interesting experiment to create a regime in which staff were trained to carry out an advanced level of observation and to offer inmates the choice as to whether they were held within such a regime.

Based on the exploration of the ethical issues above, we are led to conclude that conducting risk assessment that includes a specific exercise in behavioural monitoring, without informing the offender *at least in general terms* that his behaviour is being monitored, may be ethically problematic for psychologists. On the other hand, it is less ethically problematic for a psychologist to use information that others have reported as part of general monitoring, as long as the psychologist has made a reasonable effort to confirm the authenticity of the report. Specifically, we suggest that an inmate's consent is properly required for interviews, tests, etc. where he is an active participant, but that he should be informed that the totality of his conduct in prison may be observed and used in risk assessment. Further, all prison staff, including psychologists, have an obligation to carry out the fairest and most accurate risk assessments they can, regardless of whether the inmate agrees to being the subject (note: not the client) of the risk assessment. As part of this, psychologists should normally offer the inmate the opportunity to contribute to his or her own assessment by providing his or her perspective on others' observations.

Criminal justice personnel from other professions who conduct risk assessments may need to consider their own ethical codes in the same way. It is overly simplistic to argue that the *only* client in a risk assessment is the general public, or that the public and the offender can be easily distinguished in forensic practice. On the other hand, it is also unrealistic to suggest that the public and the offender always prioritize the same issues in risk assessment. There are some circumstances in which the risk assessment offers a service to the offender (by providing information about what she or he needs to do to earn release or to live more successfully in the community), but it is very common for the interests of the public and the interests of the offender to diverge (the offender wishing to be released despite continuing risk while the public interest in him/her is only being released if the risk is reduced).

Bonner and Vandecreek (2006) suggested that 'when the primary inmate client is failed, so is the public' (p. 559). By this we understand that the public is better served when risk assessors establish a more cooperative relationship with the subjects of their assessment, akin to a therapeutic alliance in which both parties agree on common goals that, among other things, serve public safety. Failure to establish this cooperative relationship could be seen as failing both the offender's and the public's interests. Arguably, then, it is good practice to seek to establish such a cooperative relationship, but if this attempt fails, then we are left falling back on humane management of the offender while prioritizing public safety. In the latter circumstance, a key issue is the relative weight given to the offender's interests versus the public's interests. At this point, the risk assessor enters into complicated territory that is likely to differ from case to case (and which, in the best traditions of ethical codes, should lead to professional reflection in each case). Does even a minor public interest trump a much more major interest of the offender? Automatically weighting public interest over the offender's interest would lead to a system that was littered with 'false positives' (offenders being designated as more dangerous than they really are) and potentially abusive in terms of human rights (which in turn makes it harder to establish cooperative relationships). The crucial ethical requirement for psychologists, case by case, is to find an appropriate balance between the rights/interests of the offender and those of the public.

Honesty and Accuracy

Another ethical imperative for psychologists is to ensure that their interventions are grounded in clarity, honesty, accuracy and fairness. This means that psychologists are bound to ensure that their interventions have integrity. This can be particularly pertinent when an intervention might have varying outcomes for the different clients and when not all clients will experience the outcomes as positive, as might well happen in the course of risk assessment.

First, in terms of behavioural monitoring, this ethical imperative suggests that the information-gathering process itself needs to be balanced. Information about behaviours indicative of risk reduction should be gathered, as well as information about OPB. This need for balance has already been considered in the OPB literature. Daffern et al. (2007) and Jones (2004) both discussed the importance of balancing OPB assessment with recognition of prosocial alternative behaviours (PABs). Likewise, Mann et al. (2008) proposed that the future of sexual offender risk assessment must include an equal focus on assessing protective factors as well as risk factors.

Second, the information-gathering process must be systematic (Maguire, 1997). Arcaya (1987) suggested that the assessor pay attention not just to the quantity of information gathered but to presenting and addressing contradictions, as if they were a lawyer in a courtroom.

Third, the information gathered must be fairly presented. As discussed earlier, it would be a misuse of behavioural monitoring to overpathologize observed behaviours by assuming they represent risky propensities when, in fact, they are normative responses to a particular environment. Staff who report behavioural monitoring information as part of a risk assessment must, therefore, be able to differentiate between OPBs that are topographically similar to offending behaviour, antisocial but environmentally adaptive behaviours, and more subtle offence paralleling behaviours that are functionally similar but topographically different from offending behaviour sequences. Currently, most of the behavioural observations that are recorded in secure settings come from staff who may not have had the opportunity to be trained in these concepts. Indeed, their focus may not be on recording a balanced account of an individual's behaviour, but may arise from a different set of objectives, such as recording behaviour which suggest an offender is a risk to himself or others or to the security of the environment. A psychologist who reports this information within a risk assessment needs to be mindful that the information was reported for a different purpose or by an untrained staff member. Assessors should incorporate an evaluation of the limitations of the evidence into their risk assessment reports (see BPS, 2006, Standard 4.2, iii).

This ethical imperative is also valid when an assessor uses information reported in previous risk assessment reports as evidence for continuing risk. Again, such information was not observed directly by the risk assessor, and so the risk assessor cannot personally vouch for the information being accurate and complete. Clear caveats must be given when referring to information where the authenticity cannot be (or has not been) confirmed.

Role Conflict

The way in which an offender behaves within rehabilitative treatment sessions can be a particularly rich source of behavioural evidence for continuing risk factors. Treatment staff are in an excellent position to observe how offenders respond to complex or demanding interpersonal situations such as direct challenge, emotional strain and interactions with peers. However, if an offender's behaviour in treatment is reported as relevant to risk assessment, the therapist making the report has entered into a dual role, and the two aspects of therapist and risk assessor present ethical problems, particularly if they are not discussed openly with the offender client. The role of risk assessor can compromise the trusting therapeutic relationship needed for effective treatment. Additionally, the role of therapist can compromise the objectivity needed for a balanced risk assessment. To manage these tensions ethically, a psychologist who treats offenders must reflect on the biases inherent in a dual role and develop awareness of how these biases are likely to affect their personal practice in each case. A psychologist who incorporates evidence from the treatment setting into a risk assessment report, but who did not observe this evidence first-hand, must reflect on their ability to provide an opinion on what that behaviour may or may not mean for the individual offender. At the least, when behaviour from a treatment setting is incorporated as evidence of a risky propensity into a risk assessment, the assessor should seek to speak with the offender and the treatment staff about the cognitive, motivational and emotional drivers behind the behaviour. The offender's perspective should be included within any report, although the assessor must remain aware that offenders quite commonly describe the context and function of their misbehaviours in the group inaccurately. Sometimes this is because their schemas were strongly activated during the original incident and sometimes it is more deliberate misrepresentation. The demand on the risk assessor is to seek all possible explanations of a behaviour, reflect fairly on all perspectives and reach a conclusion about whether the behaviour was or was not an OPB.

Confidentiality

OPB data are likely to be sought from multiple sources. This could mean that potentially sensitive and confidential information is handled by a number of different staff, not all of whom may subscribe to professional codes about the respectful use of information. Transparency is one of the cornerstones of ethical practice, so the limits to confidentiality must be fully explained to the offender when information about behavioural observation is provided. Ideally, there would be an explicit, written agreement between all involved parties relating to information sharing, confidentiality and its limits (see BPS, 2006, Standard 1.2, iii–vii).

However, it is likely (indeed desirable) that a range of behaviours will be recorded during a period of behavioural observation, and that not all of these behaviours will actually be related to the individual's risk. Some behaviours will be of a sensitive and personal nature. For example, an offender who is HIV-positive may not wish this information to be made generally available, but the risk assessor may feel that this medical condition is relevant to the offender's risk. In situations such as this, the risk assessor is responsible for ensuring that sensitive personal information is not released to others without good reason and that it is always treated with respect. This goes beyond the psychologist's own practice by requiring the psychologist to seek to influence and monitor the practice of others, including non-psychologists.

In conclusion, if behavioural monitoring is to be incorporated into risk assessment, with the aim of identifying OPBs and drawing conclusions about risk, psychologists (or others practising in line with professional ethical codes) face a range of possible ethical dilemmas. It is not sufficient to brush these away by arguing blithely that public protection outweighs all normal ethical considerations. On the other hand, sexual offending risk assessments do present some special circumstances where normal ethical imperatives may need to be adjusted. However, the risk assessor who draws conclusions about risk from behavioural monitoring information is ethically bound to ensure that they gather their data fairly, accurately and transparently.

TRAINING STAFF TO USE THE OPB FRAMEWORK WITH SEXUAL OFFENDERS

So far in this chapter, we have discussed why it is important that criminal justice workers, especially psychologists, who wish to employ the concept of OPB within risk assessment and treatment, have a sophisticated understanding of the concept so they can translate it into ethical practice. It cannot be assumed that this knowledge already exists in assessment and treatment practitioners. Indeed, our experience of introducing the concept of OPB into a risk assessment framework for sexual offenders quickly illustrated that, without training, assessors were likely to make the error of mistaking topographically similar behaviour for functionally similar behaviour. In informal communication, psychologists indicated they were unsure about what was expected of them, and when we reviewed risk assessment reports for routine quality assurance, we found that this topic was consistently poorly completed. We therefore conducted a training needs analysis (S. Wakama, unpublished document) to underpin the design of a training course aimed at forensic psychologists.

The training needs analysis involved semistructured interviews with ten prison psychologists who routinely completed risk assessment reports on sexual offenders. The interviews enquired about their understanding of the concept of OPB and their experiences of identifying OPBs and reporting on them. The interview transcripts were analysed using content analysis.

The majority of the interviewees described OPB as 'behaviour that was similar to the offence' (S. Wakama, unpublished document). There was a lack of recognition of the importance of establishing functional similarity to offending. Only two of the interviewees understood that OPBs could include emotions, thoughts and fantasies as well as overt behaviours.

Generally, the interviewees sought information about OPBs by seeking out and speaking to various staff members in the prison setting who interacted with the subject of their assessment. They recognized the need for a holistic picture of the prisoner's behaviour, and understood that they needed to compensate for the limited contexts in which they could directly observe behaviours. However, none of the psychologists interviewed had then discussed their reported behaviours with the prisoner concerned in order to reach a conclusion of functional similarity. We saw this as a crucial area to address in training, as both Jones (1997) and Bitsika (2006) have emphasized the importance of including the client in the process of identifying whether a behaviour is an OPB.

The psychologists interviewed recognized that the prison environment probably constrained the expression of risky propensities. They also recognized that they were in danger of confusing OPBs with environmentally adaptive behaviours and that they may not recognize some OPBs at all. Although the interviewees were generally confident about the ways in which OPB information would aid the risk assessment process, they also voiced some discomfort over the various ethical dilemmas inherent in OPB (as above) and communicated that they would welcome the opportunity to explore and resolve their ethical concerns.

The training needs analysis showed that training in the application of the OPB concept is essential, even for professionals who are highly experienced at risk assessment, to help them better identify, monitor and report on manifestations of risky propensities in incarcerated sex offenders. The main objectives for such training should be to increase understanding of the OPB construct (i.e. a knowledge-based objective), to improve confidence at establishing functional similarity (i.e. a clinical objective) and to improve the way in which risk assessors write about OPB (i.e. a skill objective). We concluded that training in OPB should cover five areas:

1. Exploration of the definition and theoretical underpinnings of OPB. In particular, we found that practitioners struggled with the complexity of the published definitions of OPB. They responded better to Wakama's (S. Wakama, unpublished document) simplified definition that 'Offence Paralleling Behaviour occurs when an individual demonstrates a sequence of behaviours, thoughts and/or feelings that have the same meaning for him as the behaviours, thoughts and/or feelings that were present in the lead up to their offence' (p. 19).
2. Advice on identifying OPBs and distinguishing OPB from topographically similar but functionally different behaviours. In particular, the training should explain that OPB is not synonymous with criminal behaviour or antisocial or anti-authority behaviour. Case examples help to illustrate this point. For example, an offender who was convicted of downloading indecent images of children, who refuses a direct instruction from a prison officer, can be said to be engaging in anti-authority behaviour but not OPB. An offender who has used cannabis for relaxation purposes in the past and fails a mandatory drug test in prison has committed an offence but is not necessarily demonstrating OPB in relation to sexual offending. A simplified model adapted from Jones (2007) assists trainees to understand how to identify potential OPBs in their caseloads and how to relate OPBs to treatment goals.

3. Developing awareness of the limitations of OPB and the limitations of the information available. Training should clarify that OPB is not in itself a risk assessment tool and that there is currently no predictive validity established for OPB assessments. OPB cannot therefore be used to define somebody's level of risk, and should only be reported in conjunction with other risk assessment processes to make a comprehensive assessment of risk and treatment need. A helpful training exercise might be to present trainees with a case example of a prisoner who appeared to demonstrate no antisocial or problematic behaviours in prison and asked them to consider the full range of explanations for his conformity. This exercise encourages trainees to think about detection evasion skills, the role of environmental constraints and the concept of prosocial alternative behaviours; and highlights the difficulty in concluding which of these three explanations is most likely. Case studies can help trainees think about how to weigh up the likelihood of each explanation in individual cases.
4. An opportunity to explore the ethical considerations related to incorporating the OPB concept within risk assessment. Here, trainees can be encouraged to work through a series of steps to test out assumptions about OPBs and to generate and investigate all other possible explanations for a behaviour. A particularly powerful exercise involves a case study of a prisoner who felt he had been the victim of a misguided 'diagnosis' of OPB – with the case discussion taking the approach of a trial or professional conduct hearing where the trainees are required to reach a verdict on the appropriateness of the assessor's conclusions about OPB.
5. Consideration of appropriate ways to report on OPBs within risk assessment reports. Training may need to offer specific advice and exercises about how to convey information on OPBs fairly and honestly, so that all those receiving the report (including the offender) understand how the observed behaviour paralleled the original offending and why the OPB is therefore problematic. Reports should explain how other hypothesized causes of the behaviour were tested and discounted. Reports should assist treatment by suggesting examples of prosocial alternative behaviours that the offender could use instead to meet the same functions; and recommending interventions that could assist him in developing these PABs. Lastly, reports should contain clear caveats about the quality, source and possible bias of the information used.

CONCLUSION

Current approaches to risk assessment of sexual offenders usually involve an assessment of the presence of both static and dynamic risk factors. Dynamic risk factors are potentially changeable and, theoretically, a reduction in the strength of these propensities would indicate that risk has reduced. Currently, risk assessors lack validated ways of identifying the extent to which risky propensities continue to exist. Application of the OPB concept provides some ideas here, if we assume that OPBs represent manifestations of underlying risky propensities, and that positive alternative behaviours represent an underlying weakening of a risky propensity in favour of a more functional or prosocial character trait. There are various ways in which OPBs and PABs may be monitored and recorded in secure settings, but all approaches have limitations. Furthermore, there is no approach, which can substitute for the clinical expertise needed to conduct functional analysis, yet the very need for functional analysis to underpin any system threatens its reliability. Monitoring behaviours in secure settings, and drawing conclusions about risk from the observed behaviours, poses both clinical and ethical challenges for the risk assessor. Even the most experienced users of structured risk assessment frameworks will greatly benefit from training in the OPB concept, and its ethical application.

REFERENCES

Allan, M., Grace, R.C., Rutherford, B. & Hudson, S.M. (2007). Psychometric assessment of dynamic risk factors for child molesters. *Sexual Abuse: A Journal of Research and Treatment*, *19*, 1079–632.

Arcaya, J.M. (1987). Role conflicts in coercive assessments: evaluation and recommendations. *Professional Psychology, Research and Practice*, *18*, 422–8.

Bitsika, V. (2006). Limitations of functional analysis: the case for including valued outcomes analysis in the investigation of difficult behaviour. *Behaviour Change*, *23*, 250–59.

Bonner, R.L. & Vandecreek, L.D. (2006). Ethical decision making for correctional mental health providers. *Criminal Justice and Behavior*, *33*, 542–64.

British Psychological Society (2006). *Code of Ethics and Conduct*. Leicester: British Psychological Society.

Clark, D., Fisher, M. & McDougall, C. (1993). A new methodology for assessing the level of risk in incarcerated offenders. *British Journal of Criminology*, *33*, 436–48.

Cohen-Mansfield, J. (1986). Agitated behaviours in the elderly: II. Preliminary results in the cognitively deteriorated. *Journal of American Geriatrics Society*, 34, 722–727.

Cohen-Mansfield, J. (1988). Agitated behaviour and cognitive functioning in nursing home residents. *Clinical Gerontologist*, 7, 11–22.

Daffern, M. & Howells, K. (2002). Psychiatric inpatient aggression: a review of structural and functional assessment approaches. *Aggression and Violent Behavior*, *7*, 477–97.

Daffern, M., Jones, L., Howells, K., Shine, J., Mikton, C. & Tunbridge, V. (2007). Redefining the definition of offence paralleling behaviour. *Criminal Behaviour and Mental Health*, *17*, 265–73.

Haag, A. (2006). Ethical dilemmas faced by correctional psychologists in Canada. *Criminal Justice and Behavior*, *33*, 93–109.

Hanson, R.K., Harris, A.J.R., Scott, T-L. & Helmus, L. (2007). *Assessing the Risk of Sexual Offenders on Community Supervision: The Dynamic Supervision Project*. Report 2007-05. Ottawa: Public Safety Canada.

Hanson, R.K. & Morton-Bourgon, K. (2005). The characteristics of persistent sexual offenders: a meta-analysis of recidivism studies. *Journal of Consulting and Clinical Psychology*, *73*, 1154–63.

Inmate Welfare Committee (2003). *William Head Institution v. Canada (Attorney General)*, 2003 FC 870 (Federal Court of Canada 2003).

Jones, L. (1997). Offence paralleling behaviour as a framework for assessments and interventions with offenders. In A. Needs & G. Towl (Eds), *Applying Psychology to Forensic Practice*. Oxford: BPS Blackwell.

Jones, L.F. (2004). Offence Paralleling Behaviour (OPB) as a framework for assessment and interventions with offenders. In A. Needs & G. Towl (Eds.). *Applying psychology to forensic practice*. Blackwell: British psychological Society.

Jones, L. (2007). *Offence Paralleling Behaviour: The Relevance of In-treatment Behaviour to Risk Assessment, Management and Development*. Rampton, Nottinghamshire: Rampton Hospital.

Maguire, J. (1997). Ethical dilemmas in forensic clinical psychology. *Legal and Criminological Psychology*, *2*, 117–92.

Mann, R.E., Hanson, R.K. & Thornton, D. (2008). *What Should Be Assessed in Sexual Offender Risk Assessment?* Paper presented at the Conference of the Association of the Treatment of Sexual Abusers, Atlanta, Georgia.

Marques, J.K., Wiederanders, M., Day, D.M., Nelson, C. & van Ommeran, A. (2005). Effects of a relapse prevention program on sexual recidivism: final results from California's sex offender treatment and evaluation project (SOTEP). *Sexual Abuse: A Journal of Research and Treatment*, *17*, 79–107.

Maruna, S. (2001). *Making Good: How Ex-convicts Reform and Rebuild Their Lives*. Washington, DC: American Psychological Association.

Maruna, S. & Mann, R.E. (2006). A fundamental attribution error? Rethinking cognitive distortions. *Legal and Criminological Psychology*, *11*, 155–77.

Shah, A., Evans, H., & Parkash, N. (1998). Evaluation of three aggression/agitation behaviour rating scales for use on an acute admission and assessment psychogeriatric ward. *International Journal of Geriatric Psychiatry*, 13, 415–420.

Thornton, D., Mann, R.E. & Hanson, R.K. (2008). *The Future of Risk Assessment*. Paper presented at the annual conference of the National Organisation for the Treatment of Abusers, Cardiff.

Chapter 8

FUNCTIONAL CONSISTENCY IN FEMALE FORENSIC PSYCHIATRIC PATIENTS: AN ACTION SYSTEM THEORY APPROACH

Katarina Fritzon

Psychology Department, Bond University, Gold Coast, Queensland, Australia

Sarah Miller

HM Prison Shotts, Scotland, UK

INTRODUCTION

It has always been a challenge to assess the extent to which treatment outcome in a forensic setting might result in a reduction in risk for repetition of the offending behaviour that has been the focus of treatment. Can we say with any confidence that participating in and completing treatment within the institutional setting equal a reduced likelihood of the undesirable behaviour recurring? Usually, the key behaviour does not and cannot occur within the institution; therefore, we cannot measure its reduction until months or possibly years after treatment has ended. Unlike in clinical settings, where certain symptoms are more readily observable and measurable, the 'symptoms' being treated in the forensic setting are nebulous and hidden, and often not disclosed in self-report. What if there were other more obvious behaviours that acted as close proxies to the offending behaviour – behaviours that served the same underlying function as the individual's offending behaviour? These might be behaviours that occur more frequently, or with greater intensity, than the offence behaviours, and more importantly, within the institution it might be possible to readily observe changes to these behaviours occurring as a direct consequence of treatment. The possibility of such functionally consistent behaviours is encapsulated within the concept of offence paralleling behaviour (OPB) as defined by Jones (2004):

> Any form of offence related behavioural (or fantasized behaviour) pattern that emerges at any point before or after an offence. It does not have to result in an offence; it simply needs to resemble, in some significant respect, the sequence of behaviours leading up to the offence. (Jones, 2004, p. 38)

Offence Paralleling Behaviour: A Case Formulation Approach to Offender Assessment and Intervention Edited by Michael Daffern, Lawrence Jones and John Shine

Therefore, OPB is not just a single event, but rather a culmination of a process or chain of events (Jones, 2004). Consequently, it is possible to have OPBs that are not obviously similar to the offence in terms of the eventual action taken, but which have similarities in terms of *'the pattern of behaviours, thoughts and emotions leading up to the offence'* (Jones, 2004, p. 39).

More recently, as interest in the OPB model has grown, Daffern et al. (2007) sought to refine this definition to prevent contradictory and idiosyncratic applications of the framework. They suggest: 'OPB is a behavioural sequence incorporating overt behaviours (that may be muted by environmental factors), appraisals, expectations, beliefs, affects, goals and behavioural scripts, all of which may be influenced by the patient's mental disorder, that is functionally similar to behavioural sequences involved in previous criminal acts' (p. 267).

This latest definition stresses that OPBs are not merely similar behaviours that are functionally unrelated. Daffern et al. (2007) also point out that OPBs should be distinguished from criminal behaviour occurring within the institution. They give the example of a patient with a history of sex offending behaving aggressively in custody: this individual could be said to be engaging in criminal behaviour but not necessarily OPB.

The thinking behind OPBs has much in common with the idea of an offence cycle, as well as with the literature on personality disorder, which both stress the way in which some people find themselves repeating the same self- or other harming behaviour over time. Recent thinking on behavioural regulation (Carver & Scheier, 1998) describes this sort of pattern, using models drawn from chaos theory, as a *behavioural attractor* – 'no matter what the starting point, the pattern of behaviour gets drawn towards a particular repeating configuration' (p. 27). In offender profiling literature, this is similar to the criminal consistency argument outlined by Canter (1995, 2000). Indeed, Jones (2004) has suggested that a way to generate and test hypotheses about OPBs would be to map the OPBs in the same space as the offence, and has explicitly likened this to the 'behavioural mapping methodology used by Canter' (p. 43), giving examples of research utilizing a behavioural action system framework, proposed by Shye (1985; see e.g. Canter & Fritzon, 1998).

This chapter proposes the action system framework, together with the methodology outlined in several studies employing this framework (e.g. Miller & Fritzon, 2007; Neville et al., 2007) as a way of exploring hypotheses about OPB, such that patterns existing within the offence style of the individual can be mapped onto similar patterns existing within the hypothesized paralleling behaviour. The chapter also outlines the evidence for self-harming as a parallel to fire-setting offence behaviour, following our previous research in this area (Miller & Fritzon, 2007).

MEASURING OPBs AND BEHAVIOURAL CONSISTENCY

It is often stated and widely accepted that past behaviour is the best predictor of future behaviour, especially within the field of forensic risk assessment. The underlying assumption is that all individuals retain their relative positions on certain dimensions or characteristics across various situations or sources of data. Therefore, one can predict how an individual will behave in a different situation from the one he or she is in at present. Indeed, recent theorizing about personality and change suggests that stability and change in personality are complementary to each other rather than in opposition (Duggan, 2004). In his discussion, Duggan (2004) refers to the model of personality originally put forward by Costa and McCrae (1994) that distinguishes between *basic tendencies* and *characteristic adaptations*. Costa and McCrae (1994) suggest that basic tendencies are largely innate, fixed dispositions that produce the characteristic adaptations, which are highly variable and depend on interactions with others and differing environments.

Clark et al. (1993) contributed early empirical evidence for cross-situational consistency by conducting a study in which predictions were made about the institutional behaviours of a sample of 65 violent offenders, based on their previous offending behaviours. These predicted behaviours were then compared to the offenders' actual institutional behaviours, and results indicated a reasonably high (60%) degree of predictability of prisoners' behaviours. Similar findings were achieved by Zamble and Porporino (1990) in their longitudinal study in Canadian prisons. They found that prisoners responded to a range of prison difficulties in a similar way as they had to problems outside prison.

Daffern et al. (2007) advocate that empirically validated methods should be established to help clinicians carry out 'systematic' and 'objective' function-analytic assessments from which OPBs and their functionally equivalent prosocial variants (prosocial alternative behaviours – PABs) can be identified. In a recent piece of research drawing on OPBs, Neville et al. (2007) found that the majority of prisoners (84%) in a democratic therapeutic community (TC) could be classified as having an overall behavioural 'style', which characterized their interactions with therapists and co-residents within the community. The behavioural variations in therapeutic interactions were found to conform to a hypothesized model based on concepts derived from behavioural action system research (Shye, 1985). This model is described in greater detail in the following section. Paired sample *t*-tests of residents' behaviours at the beginning and end (63% of participants completed at least a year in the TC) periods of therapy suggested that as residents progress through therapy they exhibited a move from the antisocial to the prosocial behaviours (or PABs) from within each of the four functional components of the model. Unfortunately, there has been no longer-term follow-up of the participants from this study, and so the results of this study are limited to observing behavioural change within the time-frame of institutional treatment. This research provides a possible framework for allowing decisions to be made about whether *offence-relevant* change has taken place as a result of treatment at an individual and group level.

THE *ACTION SYSTEM* MODEL AS A FRAMEWORK FOR UNDERSTANDING VARIATIONS IN OPBs

Shye's action system model (1985) hypothesizes that whilst all individuals' behaviour naturally varies from occasion to occasion, there is a core of consistency, which defines an individual's 'true nature' or 'style' (Matthews & Deary, 1998). This 'consistency' in behavioural style will be moderated by the sources and targets (e.g. desired locus of effect) of actions, both of which can be internal or external to the individual. Shye (1985) has illustrated in a number of studies that the combination of (a) the internal and external sources of action with (b) the agent or environment, as the targets of the action, gives rise to four basic modes of functioning action systems: *adaptive*, *expressive*, *integrative* and *conservative*. These are described in Table 8.1. In *adaptive* functioning the

Table 8.1 Summary of action system modes of functioning

Source of action in relation to the agent	Locus of effect in relation to the agent	Mode
External	External	Adaptive
Internal	External	Expressive
Internal	Internal	Integrative
External	Internal	Conservative

individual responds to the external environment by making adjustments to the environment; in the *expressive* mode, the individual demonstrates internal psychological aspects to the external world; whereas in the *integrative* mode, adjustments take place within the system, so that an action has an internal basis and is also directed at changing an internal state. Finally, the *conservative* mode refers to the way in which the individual relates to events that originate externally and are internally assimilated (Shye, 1985).

Shye's action system theory draws heavily on approaches developed in the behavioural and social sciences based on *action systems* (e.g. Parsons, 1953) or *living systems* (e.g. Miller, 1978; Shye, 1985). Unlike *closed systems* (Bertalanffy, 1976), *open systems* are so-called because they come into mutual interaction with the environment, and by the prevalence of complex interactions between internal elements of the system. Thus, systems are 'active' insomuch as they are 'open', 'organized' and 'stable' (Shye, 1985). In the case of human systems, being active involves being 'open' to maintaining transactions with the environment, including other humans. These interactions are 'organized' in the sense of following an internal logic to effect the intended consequences, and the behaviour is 'stable' in so far as it evolves out of existing and continuing processes within the individual and his or her surroundings. Buckley (1967) reiterates the point that personality theorists have repudiated a static view of personality, and draws attention to Allport's (1960) writings on personality as an open system. Miller and Gwynne (1972) also recognized this and stated:

> [D]ynamically, the individual may be regarded as having the characteristics of an open system. The individual lives in an environment to which he has to relate in order to survive . . . [and he must] regulate transactions across the boundary between the inside and outside.

Other writers point out that any system (i.e. individual) must evolve and improve its ability to interconnect with itself internally, as well as with its environment (Land & Kenneally, 1977). Jones (1982) writes that any open system 'not only has negative feedback (the self-regulation component in which errors are corrected, thus maintaining the status quo or "homeostasis" – equilibrium); but it must also have positive feedback' (p. 151). Not only must it know what it has done wrong, but also what it has done right. It must not only have feedback, but also feed-forward; that is, new information must be taken from its environment in order to meet continuously the needs of properly connecting with a changing environment (Land & Kenneally, 1977, p. 18).

Much of the literature and clinical case studies discussing OPBs to date have focused on interpersonal violence and its corollary within the institution. It has also focused on a male forensic population. Perhaps one of the key challenges in working with a female forensic population is the high incidence of self-directed rather than other-directed harm, which by its very nature is less observable and manageable. In terms of treatment, if the functions of self-harm can be better understood, then interventions can be directed at building an alternative skill repertoire, or PABs. The functional consistency between arson and self-harm identified by Miller and Fritzon (2007) provides a methodological example of how consistencies between offence behaviour and OPBs can be modelled, as well as providing treatment implications derived from this model.

Self-Harm

Distinguishing between self-harm and attempted suicide can be problematic. Babiker and Arnold (1997) point out that suicide attempts may not involve an intention to die (persons may have complex/confused views of exact intent), and frequent self-harmers may sometimes also injure themselves with suicidal intent. As such, Miller and Fritzon (2007) recommend utilizing the term *deliberate self-harm* (or simply *self-harm*), as first put forward by Morgan (1979), to refer to self-injury/self-mutilation (e.g. cutting, scraping, burning and banging) *and* attempted suicide (e.g. overdosing, attempted hanging and wrist cutting).

The high prevalence of self-harm in clinical settings, prisons and special hospitals is of particular concern. Briere and Gil (1998) estimate that clinical groups self-harm at five times the rate of the general population. Most recent figures from the UK prison service show that incidents of self-harm have risen from 16 393 in 2003 to 22 459 in 2007 (Howard League, 2008). Self-harm rates among women prisoners have risen most dramatically, with a 48% increase in recorded incidents between 2003 and 2007 (Howard League, 2008). High rates of self-harm have also been recognized amongst female special hospital patients. For example, Bland et al. (1999) found that 94% of women at Broadmoor Hospital self-harmed. Amongst clinical samples, the most common form of self-harm appears to be cutting of arms/hands (74%) and legs (44%), and less commonly abdomen (25%), breasts (18%) and genitals (8%) (Babiker & Arnold, 1997). However, some individuals burn themselves, bang themselves against something, bite themselves, and insert sharp objects under skin or into bodily orifices and swallow objects (Babiker & Arnold, 1997).

Coid et al. (1992) in an examination of the phenomenology of female prisoners' self-harm behaviour identified two subgroups. In the first group, behaviour appeared reactive to external factors such as stressful life-events. In the second group, behaviour appeared to be a symptom-relieving mechanism in women with borderline personality disorder and a range of impulse disorders. These two subgroups mirror the distinction drawn within the action system framework between the source of behaviour as either external or internal (Shye, 1985), thus indicating that this model appears to be relevant and applicable to distinguishing acts of self-harm.

Applying this model to the self-harming behaviour engaged in by a group of 50 mentally disordered female patients from a forensic hospital population, Miller and Fritzon (2007) found that their acts could be distinguished according to the source and target of the behaviour, as either internal or external to the individual. We applied a content analysis methodology to extract information from case files regarding the self-harming behaviours engaged in by the women (see Miller & Fritzon, 2007, for more information regarding the content analysis procedure, including inter-rater reliability and full definition of variables). Using multidimensional scaling methodology, we found that the correlations among self-harming behaviours clustered into four distinct regions of the multidimensional scaling (MDS) plot, shown in Figure 8.1.

MDS allows for the correlations of every variable against every other variable to be plotted, such that items that appear close together on the resulting output have higher correlations and therefore are assumed to be conceptually similar. In this way, groups of variables are understood to represent functionally distinct styles or 'types' of behaviour. As stated previously, the action system model proposes that there are four such groupings of ways in which individuals interact with their environment. In Miller and Fritzon's (2007) study, the four groupings were identified as below. The *integrative* form of self-harm involved acts that were planned and took varying forms, for example, hitting self, inserting objects into the body and targeting the genital area. These acts tended to be serial and to involve anger directed towards the self. The *expressive* form contained variables, suggesting an acting out of internal motives, as a form of communication. These acts involved verbal and physical aggression to others, reporting of the self-harm to another person, making threats and the event occurring around significant dates. The *conservative* region of the MDS plot contained variables, suggesting that the person was

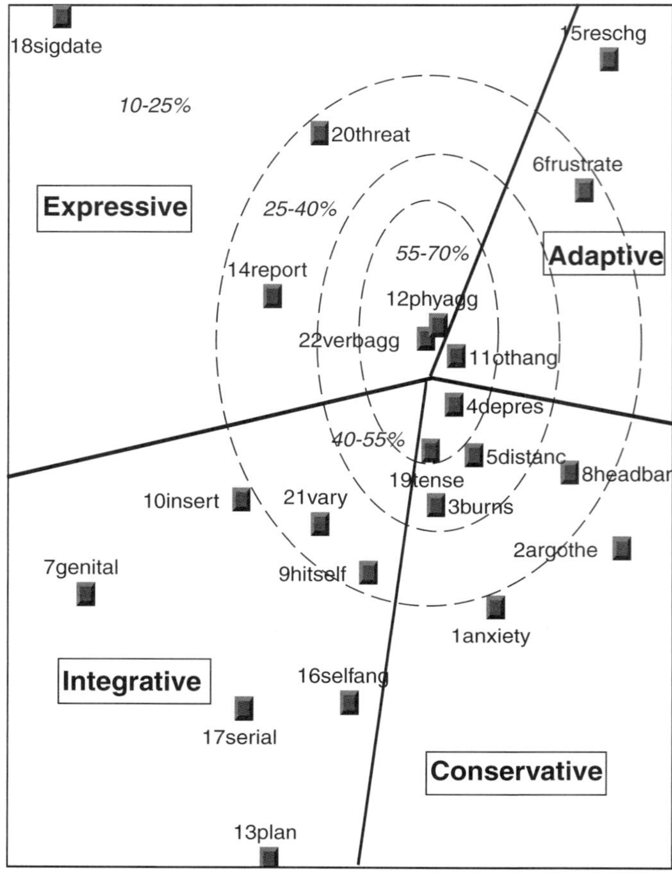

Figure 8.1 SSA of self-harm actions showing modal divisions. From Miller and Fritzon (2007).

self-harming in response to environmental events, such as an argument with another person, in response to which the individual distanced themselves from others, and engaged primarily in acts involving burning and head banging. The individuals involved were often diagnosed with depressive illness and anxiety. Finally, in the *adaptive* region of the MDS, acts of self-harm occurred when the individual was angry with another person, felt frustrated and had expressed a desire for residential change. These variables therefore indicate an element of manipulation of environmental contingencies.

Miller and Fritzon's (2007) paper focused on the self-harming behaviours of women who had all committed an index offence of arson. The self-harm was therefore hypothesized to be an OPB, which bore a functional similarity to the original offence behaviour of arson. In order to explore the consistencies between these two behaviours, the fire-setting incidents were also subject to MDS analysis. The theoretical links between fire-setting and self-harm in women are discussed in the following section.

Fire-Setting

Legally, fire-setting is referred to as arson, and defined as an act of destroying or damaging property with fire, without lawful excuse (Criminal Damage Act, 1971). Within the psychological literature, Puri et al. (1995) define fire-setting as the deliberate setting alight of any property which might or might not endanger life. Blumberg (1981) makes the useful distinction between non-psychologically motivated arson (those who commit arson for profit, crime concealment, to facilitate another crime or for sociopolitical protest) and arson in which an underlying psychological disturbance is assumed.

The high prevalence of arson among female patients and prisoners has been noted by researchers (e.g. Liebling et al., 1997; Lumsden et al., 1996). Some researchers note that female fire-setters are more disturbed than their male counterparts, manifesting higher rates of psychosis (32% of the women and 20% of the men, Lewis & Yarnell, 1951), mental retardation (68% of the women and 48% of the men, Lewis & Yarnell, 1951) and more self-harm tendencies (McKerracher et al., 1966).

Canter and Fritzon (1998) identified four behavioural themes of arson based on the target of the attack (either person or object) and motivational category (either instrumental or *expressive*). Each theme reflected an action system (Shye, 1985) mode of functioning: *despair arson* corresponded with *integrative* functioning because both the source and the target of the behaviour were internal to the arsonist; the source being emotional experiences, and the target being the arsonist's own home or body; *display arson* represented the *expressive* mode of fire-setting because of its emotionally driven, attention-seeking form, which is directed at buildings of significance; *destroy arson* corresponded with *conservative* functioning because it was an act involving revenge but fundamentally geared towards changing the internal state of the arsonist; finally, *damage arson* appeared *adaptive* as it was directed at property where some instrumental gain was involved, such as concealing a crime (Canter & Fritzon, 1998).

The fire-setting behaviours of the 50 women studied by Miller and Fritzon (2007) were also subjected to an MDS analysis, and the resulting plot is reproduced in Figure 8.2.

Essentially, the same four forms of fire-setting were identified by Miller and Fritzon (2007). The *integrative* mode comprised a suicidal act; the *expressive* mode involved acting out of psychological pressures; and the *conservative* mode was used to alter an angry/frustrated inner state seen to be caused by another. However, some key differences observed between this sample of only female arsonists, and the previous study by Canter and Fritzon (1998) as well as subsequent reproductions of the MDS analysis on other samples of arsonists (e.g. Almond et al., 2005; Santtila et al., 2003), were found within the *adaptive* mode of functioning. In other samples, whether from police data or male mentally disordered samples, the *adaptive* form of fire-setting tends to involve opportunistic manipulation of the environment, with the offenders often engaging in other concurrent forms of criminal activity. Within the female sample of mentally disordered fire-setters, however, the *adaptive* mode involves a different form of manipulation in the form of serial use of fire as a way of drawing attention to environmental needs, e.g. wishing to change residence.

Link between Fire-Setting and Self-Harm

Current OPB thinking stresses that there needs to be evidence that the identified OPB is problematic for the patient or others. Daffern et al. (2007) present the example that in controlled environments, where significant behavioural control is exerted, a patient may have little

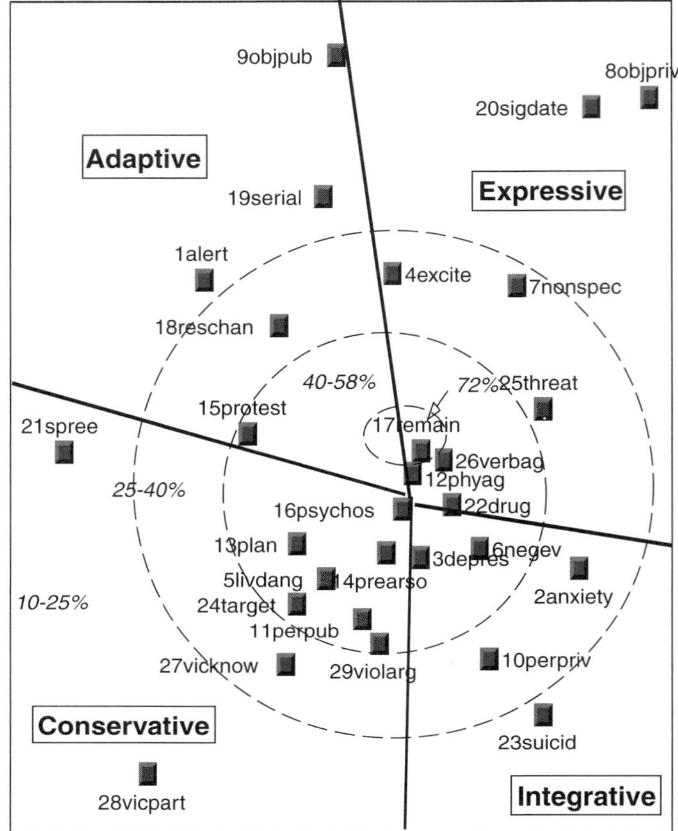

Figure 8.2 SSA of fire-setting actions showing modal divisions. From Miller and Fritzon (2007).

opportunity for violence and that '[s]elf-mutilation may operate within the same response class (in that it serves the same functions, has the same meaning(s) or meets the same needs) and may legitimately be classified as an OPB even though it is not similar in form' (p. 267).

Associations have been found in previous literature between self-harm and fire-setting behaviours. For example, compared to other psychiatric patients, suicidal and self-harm behaviours have been more commonly identified among fire-setters (Repo et al., 1997). O'Sullivan and Kelleher (1987) found a history of suicide attempts in over a third of their sample of incarcerated fire-setters. In particular, links have been found between self-harm and fire-setting behaviours amongst female offenders (Coid et al., 1999; Noblett & Nelson, 2001; O'Sullivan & Kelleher, 1987). Additionally, Coid et al. (1999) found that female prisoners with a co-morbid history of fire-setting and self-harm had severe personality disorder, early environmental disadvantage and extensive criminality. The researchers found that the relationship between fire-setting and self-harm was mediated through antisocial personality disorder and an underlying mood disorder. Table 8.2 summarizes the behaviours for each of the four modes of action within the acts of self-harm and fire-setting from the Miller and Fritzon's (2007) study.

Table 8.2 Summary of variables representing the four modes of action system functioning

Action system mode	Fire-setting	Self-harm
Integrative	Suicide attempt, person-private (own home), anxiety, negative event, depression ($\alpha = 0.52$)	Varying forms, insert, hit self, self-anger, serial; genital location, planned ($\alpha = 0.70$)[a]
Adaptive	Protest, residential change, alert, serial, object-public (car, business) ($\alpha = 0.42$)	Residential change, frustration and other anger ($\alpha = 0.46$)
Expressive	Remain/return to scene, drug and/or alcohol misuse, object-private,[b] physical aggression, verbal aggression, threat, excitement, emotional trigger, significant date ($\alpha = 0.53$)	Report, physical aggression, verbal aggression, threat, significant dates ($\alpha = 0.52$)
Conservative	Psychosis, planned, previous arson, lives endangered, targeted person-public,[c] violence/argument, victim known, victim partner, spree ($\alpha = 0.64$)	Depression, distance, tense, burns, headbang, argument other and anxiety ($\alpha = 0.60$)

[a]Cronbach's alphas are generally assumed to reflect the inter-item consistency of a scale, although there is debate about this (see Boyle, 1991). For psychometric tests, alphas of 0.70 are generally acceptable, whereas for research, 0.60 has been used as a less conservative cut-off. The lower alpha values found in this table can be reflective of fewer item numbers in the scale, small sample size as well as some negative correlations among items.

[b]For example, private area within a non-residential property.

[c]For example, known residential or public building.

Miller and Fritzon (2007) tested the functional consistency hypotheses with their data in two different ways. Firstly, correlations among the four behavioural clusters identified that the *integrative* form of fire-setting correlated with the *integrative* form of self-harm ($r = 0.37$, $p < 0.001$), and the *adaptive* form of fire-setting with the *adaptive* self-harm ($r = 0.37$, $p < 0.001$); however, non-significant correlations were found for the other two modes of behaviour. The second method by which consistency was examined was to classify the women according to their predominant mode of functioning for each of the two behaviours. Cross-tabulations then identified that women who engaged in *integrative* fire-setting also self-harmed using the *integrative* behaviours ($\chi^2 = 9.76$, $p < 0.001$) and so on for each of the four modes of functioning (χ^2 expressive $= 5.36$, $p < 0.05$; χ^2 conservative $= 7.51$, $p < 0.005$; and χ^2 adaptive $= 15.71$, $p < 0.001$).

This chapter therefore provides a methodological example whereby hypothesized links between offence behaviours and OPBs can be tested. It is important to understand the underlying functions of the behaviour and thereby to recognize that not every person who commits the same *type* of offence does so for the same reason. Equally, the links between offences and OPBs are not always going to be the same. For example, whilst self-harm might be an OPB for some fire-setters, for others the OPB link might be with a different behaviour altogether.

CASE STUDY

The following case study is described to illustrate qualitatively the functional similarities between fire-setting and self-harm. The patient attended a group for female fire-setters in a regional secure unit (RSU) in the United Kingdom.

Angela was raised in a single-parent family by a mother whom she reported as having struggled for all of her life with major depression. Because of this, Angela had taken responsibility from a young age for her own care, as well as the care of her sister and her mother. Despite this, Angela was a highly functioning individual who had a professional career. Following her mother's death, however, Angela's mental health began to deteriorate and she began consuming a large amount of alcohol. She stated that she was plagued by extremely disturbing thoughts of self-loathing around feeling responsible for her mother's death. When she was in this frame of mind, she would consume alcohol to 'shut out the thoughts'. She began self-harming by cutting her arms and punching walls. After several months of escalating alcohol dependence and self-harm, Angela began setting fires. These would always occur after she had consumed a large quantity of alcohol and after she had engaged in an act of self-harm (usually cutting). Her fires mostly involved litter receptacles and cars. She would frequently report these fires to the police and expressed a desire to be punished for her acts as well as to be hospitalized to receive care for her mental health concerns. She recalled a sense of satisfaction when she was arrested and held overnight in the cells. She reported that the police tried several times to have her admitted to hospital as they recognized that she needed help. She had a positive attitude to the police and felt 'looked after' by them. She began attending a psychiatric hospital as a day patient, and set fire there in the toilets, which she also self-reported. She was eventually convicted of several counts of arson and admitted to the regional secure unit. Her diagnoses upon admission were *major depressive disorder with psychotic features* and *borderline personality disorder*. Her behaviour at the RSU has included acts of verbal and physical aggression towards staff and fellow patients. When angry, Angela will sometimes scratch the skin on her arms, burn herself with cigarettes and punch walls. She has not set any fires since coming to the RSU.

FORMULATION OF FIRE-SETTING BEHAVIOUR

Table 8.3 provides examples of how Angela's behaviours were classified according to Miller and Fritzon's (2007) framework.

Table 8.3 Summary of Angela's actions within Miller and Fritzon's (2007) framework

Miller & Fritzon's (2007) behavioural code	Examples from Angela's case file
Negative events trigger fire-setting	Death of Angela's mother triggered fire-setting behaviour. Each individual fire triggered by episodes of Angela thinking about her mother's death, and her feelings of responsibility regarding this
Depression	Angela was diagnosed with *major depressive disorder with psychotic episodes*
Excitement	Angela reported that she found setting fires to be an 'exciting' experience, especially in the context of her social isolation and bereavement
Drug use	Angela reported that she always consumed alcohol prior to starting a fire
Public place, object target	The majority of Angela's fires took place in public places and involved rubbish bins and cars parked on the street
Alert police	Angela would frequently report the fires to the police herself
Residential change	Angela's mental health was deteriorating, and she reported a sense of being 'looked after' by the police, who made efforts to have her admitted to hospital. She reported that she agreed with their perception that she needed to be hospitalized
Serial	Angela set several fires over a period of months

To summarize, Angela's fire-setting behaviours include the following features: negative events trigger fire-setting, depression, excitement, drug use (includes alcohol), public place object target, alert police, residential change and serial. As can be seen in Figure 8.2, the majority of these are identified as adaptive behaviours. These acts have an external source and target and are described as a form of protest (Miller & Fritzon, 2007). The function of this fire-setting in the sample of women studied by Miller and Fritzon (2007) was to change an aspect of the personal environment of the individual, and they are described as seeking public awareness of their predicament. This seems to fit quite well as a clinical interpretation of Angela's fire-setting behaviour.

In terms of Angela's self-harming, these involved the following behaviours: *hitting self, serial verbal aggression, frustration, other anger* and *residential change*. The last three of these behaviours are also described within the Miller and Fritzon's (2007) framework as *adaptive* forms of self-harm. Angela's self-harming also contains two variables from the *integrative* classification and one (verbal aggression) from *expressive*. Both the fire-setting and self-harming behaviours therefore can be described as fulfilling primarily *adaptive* functions. In other words, Angela sought to change an aspect of her personal environment by behaving in these ways. In the case of her self-harming within the institution, she has made a number of requests to move wards, usually resulting from frustration or conflict with other patients. It is interesting that Angela's behaviour also has an element of the *expressive* function in relation to both the fire-setting and self-harming. In terms of gaining a full clinical picture of her behaviour, we would want to include this *expressive* element because the precipitating triggers for the behaviour are not just located in the physical environment, but also relate to the disturbing thoughts that she was having about being responsible for her mother's death. This case study is an illustration of the offence paralleling nature of self-harming within an institution, following admission for fire-setting.

To some extent, the functional consistencies between offence behaviours and OPBs will always be best understood at an individual level. However, the creation of models to explore links between commonly occurring OPBs and offence types is an important step towards developing better targeted treatment programmes and risk prediction models.

For example, currently the most common approaches to self-harm reduction within prison settings are dialectical behaviour therapy, problem-solving and/or drug-based interventions (Crighton & Towl, 2008). The results of the Miller and Fritzon's (2007) study indicate that all these interventions may be appropriate, but not necessarily for the same subgroups of self-harming individuals. For the *integrative* group, these individuals appear to have difficulty with emotional regulation, with both self-harming and fire-setting representing ways of processing strong emotions. For these individuals, therefore, dialectical behaviour therapy would appear to be most appropriate as one of its key group skills training is 'emotion modulation', which provides a way of changing distressing emotional states as well as learning 'distress-tolerance skills', that is, techniques for tolerating emotional states if they cannot be changed when wanted (Linehan, 1993).

For the *expressive* group, there is similarly an element of emotional regulation, although this is expressed in an outward rather than inward direction. Therefore, a problem-solving approach, encompassing elements of assertiveness and interpersonal therapy, could be beneficial (National Institute for Health and Clinical Excellence, 2007). In terms of fire-setting, this group does pose a challenge for intervention in that such individuals appear to receive reinforcement from aspects of the fire itself, and as such can be understood to have a 'pathological fascination' for fire (Fineman, 1995). This aspect is difficult to treat, but might respond to approaches derived from the addictions field and to some extent the treatment approach used with sexual offenders (e.g. sex offender treatment programme), as both focus on developing awareness of risk triggers and the best way to manage these.

The *adaptive* form of behaviour appears to be a product of a generally delinquent lifestyle (for fire-setting) and a characteristic way of achieving environmentally based goals (for self-harm). Thus, the focus of intervention might be on the cognitive structures and attitudes that allow the maintenance of such patterns of behaviour. Social skill training and interpersonal problem-solving would also be important behavioural modalities for promoting different strategies of achieving goals. Accredited UK offender behaviour programmes such as Enhanced Thinking Skills (ETS) programme which address thinking and behaviour associated with offending (impulse control, flexible thinking, social perspective-taking, values and moral reasoning) would be particularly useful for *adaptive* fire-setters because of their criminal lifestyles.

Finally, the *conservative* form of both fire-setting and self-harm appears to involve triggers occurring within the interpersonal social environment, and as such individuals may benefit from anger management approaches to intervention. Dialectical behaviour therapy might work well with *conservative* individuals as one of the core elements of skill training, *interpersonal effectiveness*, focuses on asking 'what one wants' effectively and maintaining relationships and self-esteem in interactions with other people (Linehan, 1993). Another UK offender behaviour programme, 'Controlling Anger and Learning to Manage It' (CALM), may be useful given its aim to enable participants to reduce the intensity, frequency and duration of negative emotions (such as anger, anxiety and jealousy), which are associated with their offending.

CONCLUSION

Identification of behaviours that serve the same underlying function as the individual's offending behaviour has proved to be a useful approach for treatment providers and treatment evaluators. Using Shye's action system model (1985), which is in keeping with the theoretical underpinnings of OPB (Jones, 2004), to test the hypothesis that there is a core consistency defining an individual's 'style', female fire-setters who engaged in self-harm were found to belong to one of the main action system types for both behaviours, signifying an underlying behavioural consistency (Miller & Fritzon, 2007). This methodological approach offers avenues for future research to explore not only the function of, but also potential consistency across, a wide range of criminal and non-criminal behaviours within the individual.

REFERENCES

Allport, G.W. (1960). The open system in personality theory. *Journal of Abnormal and Social Psychology, 61*, 301–10.

Almond, L., Duggan, L., Shine, J. & Canter, D. (2005). Test of the action system model in an incarcerated population. *Psychology, Crime and Law, 11*(1), 1–15.

Babiker, G. & Arnold, L. (1997) *The Language of Injury: Comprehending Self-mutilation*. Leicester: BPS Books.

Bertalanffy, L.V. (1976). *General Systems Theory: Foundation, Development, Applications*. New York: Braziller.

Bland J., Mezey, G. & Dolan, B. (1999) Special women, special needs: a descriptive study of female special hospital patients. *Journal of Forensic Psychiatry, 10*, 34–45.

Blumberg, N. (1981). Arson update: a review of the literature on firesetting. *Bulletin of the American Academy of Psychiatry and the Law, 9*, 255–65.

Boyle, G. (1991). Does item homogeneity indicate internal consistency or item redundancy in psychometric scales? *Personality and Individual Differences, 12*, 291–94.

Briere, J. & Gil, E. (1998). Self-mutilation in clinical and general population samples: prevalence, correlates and functions. *American Journal of Orthopsychiatry, 68*, 609–20.

Buckley, W. (1967). *Sociology and Modern Systems Theory*. Oxford: Prentice-Hall.

Canter, D. (1995). *Criminal Shadows*. London: HarperCollins.

Canter, D. (2000). Offender profiling and criminal differentiation. *Legal and Criminological Psychology, 5,* 23–46.

Canter, D. & Fritzon, K. (1998). Differentiating arsonists: a model of firesetting actions and characteristics. *Legal and Criminological Psychology, 3,* 72–96.

Carver, C.S. & Scheier, M.F. (1998). *On the Self-Regulation of Behaviour.* Cambridge: Cambridge University Press.

Clark, D.A., Fisher, M.J. & McDougall, C. (1993). A new methodology for assessing the level of risk in incarcerated offenders. *British Journal of Criminology, 33,* 436–48.

Coid, J., Wilkins, J., Chitkara, B. & Everitt, B. (1992). Self-mutilation in female remanded prisoners: II. A cluster analytic approach to identification of a behavioural syndrome. *Criminal Behaviour and Mental Health, 2,* 1–14.

Coid, J., Wilkins, J. & Coid, B. (1999). Fire-setting, pyromania and self-mutilation in female remanded prisoners. *Journal of Forensic Psychiatry, 10,* 119–30.

Costa, P.T. Jr & McCrae, R.R. (1994). Set like plaster? Evidence for the stability of adult personality. In T.F. Heatherton & J.L. Weinberger (Eds), *Can Personality Change?* (pp. 21–40). Washington, DC: American Psychological Association.

Crighton, D. & Towl, G. (2008). *Psychology in Prisons.* London: BPS Blackwell.

Daffern, M., Jones, L., Howells, K., Shine, J., Mikton, C. & Tunbridge, V. (2007). Refining the definition of offence paralleling behaviour. *Criminal Behaviour and Mental Health, 17,* 265–73.

Duggan, C. (2004). Does personality change and, if so, what changes? *Criminal Behaviour and Mental Health, 14,* 5–16.

Fineman, K.R. (1995). A model for the qualitative analysis of child and adult fire deviant behavior. *American Journal of Forensic Psychology, 13*(1), 31–60.

Howard League (2008). *Suicide Rates in UK Prison Service.* Retrieved from http://www.howardleague.org/index.php?id=231#c91 (accessed 2 September 2008).

Jones, L. (2004). Offence paralleling behaviour (OPB) as a framework for assessment and intervention with offenders. In A. Needs & G. Towl (Eds), *Applying Psychology to Forensic Practice.* Malden, MA: Blackwell.

Jones, M. (1982). *The Process of Change.* Boston, MA: Routledge & Kegan Paul.

Land, G. & Kenneally, C. (1977). Creativity, reality and general systems: a personal viewpoint. *Journal of Creative Behaviour, 11*(1), 12–35.

Lewis, N.D.C. & Yarnell, H. (1951). Pathological firesetting (pyromania). *Nervous and Mental Disease Monographs, 82,* 28–33.

Liebling, H., Chipchase, H. & Velangi, R. (1997). Why do women harm themselves? Surviving special hospitals. *Feminism and Psychology, 7,* 427–37.

Linehan, M.M. (1993). *Cognitive-Behavioral Treatment of Borderline Personality Disorder.* New York: Guilford Press.

Lumsden, J., Wong, M.T.H., Fenton, G.W. & Fenwick, P.B.C. (1996). Violence ratings of female patients in Broadmoor Hospital. *Psychology, Crime and Law, 3,* 51–62.

Matthews, G. & Deary, J. (1998). *Personality Traits.* London: Routledge.

McKerracher, D.W., Street, D.R.K. & Segal, L.J. (1966). A comparison of the behaviour problems presented by male and female subnormal offenders. *British Journal of Psychiatry, 112,* 891–97.

Miller, E.J. & Gwynne, G.V. (1972). *A Life Apart.* London: Tavistock.

Miller, J. (1978). Attaining freedom in existential group therapy. *American Journal of Psychoanalysis, 38*(2), 179–83.

Miller, S. & Fritzon, K. (2007). Functional consistency across two behavioural modalities: fire-setting and self-harm in female special hospital patients. *Criminal Behaviour and Mental Health, 17,* 31–44.

Morgan, H.G. (1979). *Death Wishes? The Understanding and Management of Deliberate Self-Harm.* Chichester: John Wiley & Sons.

National Institute for Health and Clinical Excellence (2007). *Depression: Management of Depression in Primary and Secondary Care.* London: NICE.

Neville, L., Miller, S. & Fritzon, K. (2007). Understanding change in a prison therapeutic community: an action systems approach. *Journal of Forensic Psychiatry and Psychology, 18*(2), 181–203.

Noblett, S. & Nelson, B. (2001). A psychosocial approach to fire-setting – a case controlled study of female offenders. *Medicine, Science and Law, 41,* 325–30.

O'Sullivan, G.H. & Kelleher, M.J. (1987). A study of fire setters in the South-West of Ireland. *British Journal of Psychiatry, 151,* 818–23.

Parsons, T. (1953). Some comments on the state of the general theory of action. *American Sociological Review, 18,* 618–31.

Puri, B.K., Baxter, R. & Cordess, C.C. (1995). Characteristics of fire-setters: a study and proposed multiaxial psychiatric classification. *British Journal of Psychiatry*, *166*, 393–96.

Repo, E., Virkkunen, M., Rawlings, R. & Linnoila, M. (1997). Suicidal behaviour among Finnish fire setters. *European Archives of Psychiatry and Clinical Neuroscience*, *247*, 303–7.

Santtila, P., Hakkanen, H., Alison, L. & Whyte, C. (2003). Juvenile fire-setters: crime scene actions and offender characteristics. *Legal and Criminological Psychology*, *8*, 1–20.

Shye, S. (1985). Nonmetric multivariate models for behavioral action systems. In D. Canter (Ed.), *Facet Theory Approaches to Social Research*. New York: Springer Verlag.

Zamble, R. & Porporino, F. (1990). Coping, imprisonment and rehabilitation. *Criminal Justice and Behavior*, *17*, 53–69.

Chapter 9

THE ASSESSMENT AND TREATMENT OF OFFENCE PARALLELING BEHAVIOURS IN YOUNG OFFENDERS: ADDED COMPLICATIONS OR GREATER OPPORTUNITIES FOR CHANGE?

Zainab Al-Attar

Head of Psychology, Programmes & Sex Offender Clinical Services, HMP Wymott, UK; G-MAP, Greater Manchester, UK

INTRODUCTION

This chapter explores the range of factors that add to the complexity of identifying and monitoring *offence paralleling behaviours* (OPBs) in young offenders in secure settings, and predicting their future risk as adults in the community. It starts by highlighting some of the distinguishing features of the young offender population compared to adult offenders and exploring the numerous developmental processes that need to be considered when identifying OPBs in this group. Adding to these complexities is young offenders' unique response to environmental contingencies within a custodial environment, the potency of peer group norms and the developmental window for the renegotiations of identity. Consequently, predicting community behaviours in adulthood, once these environmental contingencies and peer norms are changed, is a particular challenge for risk assessors working with young offenders. This leads to the conclusion that a developmentally sensitive focus on the functional equivalence rather than the topography of antisocial behaviours, within the context of environmental contingencies, is more important in this group of offenders than any other. Finally, the complexity of variables shaping young offenders' evolving behaviours can be balanced against the greater milieu for change and development of prosocial alternative behaviours in this patient population.

Clinicians working with young offenders (broadly defined as 13–21 years old) will often remark on the volatility and versatility of their behaviours, especially when followed up from early or mid-adolescence to early adulthood. Conquering the complex challenge of identifying custodial and predicting future community offence OPBs is a challenge for all custodial clinicians. However, clinicians working with young offenders additionally have to contend with the uncertainty brought about by the developmental changes, and emotional and psychosocial

Offence Paralleling Behaviour: A Case Formulation Approach to Offender Assessment and Intervention Edited by Michael Daffern, Lawrence Jones and John Shine

fragility of this age group. In many instances, OPBs are defined on the basis of the functions and behavioural sequences of offences committed during early adolescence. Custodial behaviours spanning the developmental journey from early adolescence to early adulthood are then compared with the childhood/early adolescent behaviours that unfolded during the offence, in the quest to identify OPBs. The period separating an early adolescent offence and the adulthood behaviour in question will see the young offender exposed to changes in the environmental contingencies of the custodial setting, staff and fellow prisoner responses to the young offender's behaviour, and occasionally, rehabilitative interventions. In addition to such dynamic factors, this time window will also capture an array of developmental changes in physiological, cognitive, emotional and psychosocial functioning. Thus, functional analysis of potential OPBs will necessarily need to take into account developmental changes. Indeed, not only will some behaviours become developmentally outdated ways of serving a given function as the youngster gets older, but the function in question may become void due to developmental maturity, in early adulthood. Inversely, prosocial alternative behaviours also need to capitalize on developmental opportunities. Hence, the developmental journeys travelled by incarcerated adolescents both add to the complexity of assessing and treating OPBs and offer valuable opportunities for prosocial change or developing what has been termed *prosocial adaptive behaviours* (PAB; Daffern et al., 2007), which are functionally equivalent prosocial alternative responses that come to replace the OPBs.

This chapter aims to explore the developmental processes potentially impacting on the behaviour of young offenders as they transition from adolescence to early adulthood, and examine ways that such developmental processes may complicate the assessment and targeting of OBPs, as well as ways that they may facilitate greater opportunity for rehabilitation. Each area of potential developmental change is examined, in turn, including neurophysiological/neurocognitive, sociocognitive, psychosocial, psychosexual, emotional and personality development. Case examples from the author's clinical work with young offenders are presented to illustrate the key arguments. The overall implications of developmental changes for individualized assessment methodologies and treatment plans used with young offenders are discussed, before conclusions are drawn.

DEVELOPMENTAL CHANGES AND THEIR IMPLICATIONS FOR OPBs

Neurobiological/Neurocognitive Development

Neurobiological development and functioning may impact negatively or positively on the behaviour of young offenders and attempt to change it. Each of these potential effects is now highlighted.

Negative Impacts

Psychological as well as physical trauma can impact on early brain development, which can in turn adversely affect social and emotional development (Elliott, 1999). Aggression has been linked to dysfunctional corticolimbic activity (Coccaro et al., 2007). Biological risk factors to aggression, through their interaction with social risk factors, have been highlighted to mediate early-onset aggression in children and young adolescents (Brennan et al., 2003). Thus, to some extent adverse neurological processes may unfold before the young offender comes into custody, and if one accepts the 'early-onset persistent' aggression typology of young offenders (Moffitt, 1993), it may be argued that such adversity would be difficult to overcome and may continue to shape antisocial behaviour and hence OPBs in later life. On the basis of such an argument, one implication of neurological disadvantage is that youngsters will continue to display similar levels of OPBs as they age, that their OPBs may be more resistant to change and in some sense more difficult to contain or manage through traditional psychological therapies. Furthermore, early neurocognitive markers of risk may in fact forecast an escalation of violence in adulthood, with one mechanism being the progression from childhood attention deficit hyperactivity disorder (ADHD)/oppositional defiant disorder/conduct disorder to the later development of antisocial personality disorder (discussed in detail in later sections).

One case illustrating the continuity of aggression and its parallels into adulthood in youngsters with neurobiological vulnerability is Patient M. This patient was an adolescent who had received a diagnosis of temporal epilepsy and was serving a custodial sentence for grievous bodily harm committed against a similar-aged peer who had verbally aggressed against him, sending him into a 'rage'. Three years later, at the age of 20, despite 'successfully' completing numerous rehabilitative, cognitive–behavioural interventions, this young man continued to display sudden violent outbursts in response to teasing by other prisoners, sending him into a rage and leading to his physical restraint. In his case, the violence during the index offence and in custody bore hallmarks of intermittent explosive disorder, a mental disorder defined in DSM-IV and a condition associated with abnormal brain activity (Koelsch et al., 2008). It is worthy of note that an analysis of OPBs in this case tapped into critical risk information that general indicators of custodial behaviour or psychometric testing did not offer. Another case is Patient R, a young man who had experienced severe physical abuse as a child (leading to psychological and possible physical/neurological trauma) and later received brain injury during a high-speed chase as a teenager. This young man was serving a custodial sentence for attempted murder following a robbery. He described his behaviour during the offence as being driven by an uncontrollable impulse to hurt someone. This young man, two years into his prison sentence, was segregated for suddenly stabbing his peers in the prison classroom. When I interviewed him about the incidents, he once more described experiencing sudden surges of violent impulse, even though there was no objective provocation. Two years after his release, at the age of 23, this young man was charged with the violent and sadistic murder of two strangers he set out to rob, with the violence being described as unprovoked and frantic. Sadly, the OPBs were not only topographically predictable but also seemingly resistant to change through custodial interventions. A third case is Patient J, an adolescent with Asperger's syndrome, whose violence was characterized by sudden-onset, frantic acts of aggression, with sudden offset. Triggers commonly included perceived injustice. Three years into his custodial sentence, at the age of 20, this young man reacted with sudden-onset aggression in response to perceived injustice perpetrated by fellow inmates, despite gaining impressive insight into his aggression and its triggers through two years of individual therapy. Whether there was a causal link between the three aforementioned young men's neurological status and their violence cannot be conclusively established and is a highly complex clinical question. But, what is clear is that these cases highlight the complexities in predicting OPBs in patients with brain injury (in one sense the triggers to their behaviour may be vast and unclear to the observer, and in another sense their violent behaviours may be repetitive, similar in form and hence more predictable). Such cases also raise the question of whether OPBs may be more resistant to change through traditional cognitive–behavioural custodial interventions. This reinforces the argument for individually tailored interventions that either replace or operate as an adjunct to traditional criminogenic custodial interventions, so as to ensure responsivity to the individual's complex needs.

Positive Impacts

Developmental immaturity and consequent plasticity in neurological and neuropsychological functioning can, inversely, serve as an advantage in the rehabilitation of young offenders. Development in the nervous system (e.g. completion of myelination, a cellular maturational event) is attained by the third decade of life, particularly where brain regions implicated in aggression are involved (Benes et al., 1994; Elliott, 1999). Post-adolescent and early adulthood maturation in the frontal structures and functions, specifically executive functioning, has been documented (Romine & Reynolds, 2005; Sowell et al., 1999), and hence it could be argued that even if index offence behaviours were exacerbated by frontal immaturity, this problem may be easier to compensate for in young offenders by comparison to adults, whose cortical development has reached its conclusion.

Learning from errors and adapting behaviour in response to *these* errors is associated with frontal functioning, and this function has been found to improve post-adolescence (Hogan et al., 2005), suggesting that psychological therapies and a prosocial environment may impact markedly on young offenders as they approach adulthood. Both natural developmental maturity and prosocial learning and rehabilitative therapies may lead to better developed frontal processing, which in turn may serve to reduce impulsivity, risk-taking and behavioural/emotional disinhibition, and enhance consequential thinking, empathy and sociomoral reasoning. Mullin and Simpson (2007) found a reduction in negative behaviours in offenders with impaired executive functioning following completion of the enhanced thinking skills, although this effect was smaller in younger adult offenders. Such changes clearly have implications for changes in expected OPBs, some of which may no longer serve a necessary function for the young adult (e.g. the function of sensation-seeking may be overtaken by the function of relating to others, and revenge behaviours may no longer be necessary if hostile cognitive biases were not activated). Nevertheless, one cannot assume that prosocial behaviours (PABs) emerge simply by virtue of matured executive functioning, with such interventions as enhanced thinking skills for offenders with impaired executive functioning failing to produce an increase in positive behaviours in some studies (Mullin & Simpson, 2007). Thus, whilst a reduction in OPBs may be expected with short-term interventions targeting cognitive and neurocognitive maturity, the development of PABs could require relearning through environmental reinforcement (e.g. by residential staff) and intensive therapy (e.g. therapeutic community, sex offender treatment programmes and violence reduction programmes). Such environmental and therapeutic interventions need to take into account complex psychosocial variables that are more pertinent to the young, as discussed later in this chapter.

In addition to frontal structural and functional development, changes in cortisol levels may also impact on changes in behaviour. For example, morning and evening cortisol levels and their relative levels have been implicated in antisocial behaviour, rule-breaking, attention behaviour problems and conduct disorder symptoms in boys and relational aggression in girls (Susman et al., 2007). Morning increases in cortisol levels can be lower in children than in adults (Rosmalen et al., 2003), offering one example of how neurochemical changes through maturation may impact on changes in levels of aggression. Other examples include changes in hormone levels such as levels of androgen/testosterone, with high levels of these hormones being associated with aggression and acting-out behaviour, especially in boys (Susman et al., 1987). Other neurobiological maturational changes that may have implications for aggression and its paralleling forms, which include the reduction in the hyperactivity–impulsivity symptoms (though not the remaining symptoms) of ADHD in adulthood (Ingram et al., 1999). Nevertheless, secondary problems, such as substance misuse, academic underachievement and co-morbid mood and anxiety disorders (Clarke et al., 2005; Ingram et al., 1999), may have long-lasting effects unless they are targeted in young adult offenders. Furthermore, aggressive adolescents with ADHD are more likely to befriend fellow aggressive adolescents with ADHD (Mariano & Harton, 2005), highlighting the need to target peer relationships in youth custody, as well as facilitating natural developmental maturity, if ADHD and related aggressive OPBs are to be reduced. Thus, neurobiological and psychosocial factors interact to shape a reduction of aggression and the development of prosocial behaviours in young offenders, and an assessment of OPBs and PABs needs to consider such interactions.

Cases illustrating the optimistic prognosis of young offenders with neurocognitive impairments include Patient C who was convicted of a string of violent, arson and sexual offences by the age of 16. He had received diagnoses of ADHD and conduct disorder during childhood, and there were clear signs of neurocognitive impairments, possibly due to numerous head injuries received during fights and long-standing polydrug use. Patient C's behaviour during the early stages of his incarceration was impulsive, oppositional and violent. Over the course of four years, following environmental reinforcers of positive behaviours and the absence of negative behaviours, peer challenges of negative behaviours, individual therapy and cognitive–behavioural interventions targeting his problem-solving skills and sexual offending risk, and opportunities for structured purposeful activity (including full-time education, employment and gymnasium sessions), Patient C's behaviour became markedly less impulsive, more prosocial and stable. There was no reason to believe that Patient C had acquired *detection evasion skills* (DES; Jones, 2004) and hence was simply continuing to exhibit OPBs without getting apprehended. Instead, he was displaying PABs, indicating that it was possible to reduce OPBs in a young man with such neurobiological vulnerabilities.

Neurobiological development may only impact on OPBs if the functions of offence behaviours include psychological processes that are mediated by neurobiological correlates, or at least when the development of PABs is contingent on neurobiological maturity. When this is not the case, neurodevelopmental changes may merely serve to alter the manifestation of OPBs, for example by giving way to less impulsive expressions of OPBs, or more sophisticated and carefully planned OPBs. Furthermore, as levels of impulsivity decrease and learning and social processing become more sophisticated, so may evasion detection skills in young offenders. Therefore, it is important to note that OPBs may be more difficult to spot and be topographically very versatile in young offenders, due to the very neurobiological maturation that may unfold in youth custody.

In conclusion, neurobiological and neurocognitive developmental processes may either complicate or facilitate the process of reducing OPBs and developing PABs in young offenders, as they transition from adolescence to young adulthood. Both developmental stage and plasticity need be borne in mind, as well as the possible changes in behavioural manifestation due to such developmental processes when assessing and targeting OPBs through rehabilitative interventions.

Sociocognitive Development

Perspective-Taking, Egocentricity, Empathy and Moral Development

Young adolescents may still be developing their perspective-taking ability and moral sophistication (Kohlberg, 1985; Piaget, 1965, 1970). Selman (1971a, 1971b) in fact postulated that only at stage 3 (age 9–15) does the individual have the capacity to consider an interpersonal interaction through the third person's perspective, and only at stage 4 (beyond age 15) do they recognize that one may not be aware of the consequences of their actions for others. According to

Selman, as the individual transitions from adolescence into adulthood, they continue to develop their understanding of complex social interactions and moral perspectives. Thus, on the basis of healthy sociocognitive development alone, young offenders are expected to potentially undergo change and a possible change in risk and OPBs. Nangle et al. (2003) argued that interventions for youth should be sensitive to dynamic developmental processes, proposing a case for applying this to the development of perspective-taking in juvenile sex offenders.

Delinquent adolescents are likely to show even greater egocentricity, a delay or immaturity in moral development, and social skill deficits (Gibbs et al., 1996) by comparison to their non-delinquent peers, and are more likely to attribute blame to others when confronted with ambiguous problem situations, with such external blame attributions being linked to aggression (Foundaccaro & Heller, 1990). Delinquent youths' empathy deficit is a potentially strong predictor of delinquency and antisocial behaviour (Robinson et al., 2007; Thompson & Gullone, 2008). Indeed, remedial programmes for adolescent offenders such as the EQUIP intervention (Gibbs et al., 1995) have traditionally focused on addressing such deficits and facilitating maturity in sociocognitive and sociomoral development. Where offence behaviours are driven by such deficits or developmental delays, maturation (spontaneous or through successful interventions) would be expected to bring about a reduction in OPBs. However, where offending is unrelated to such sociocognitive deficits or developmental immaturity, OPBs are not expected to reduce. Depending on the underlying risk factors and functions of the OPBs, they may become more sophisticated, especially if the young offender uses his or her more mature sociocognitive functioning to better evade detection or enact more subtle forms of OPBs. This is an important consideration for clinicians and custody staff, who only too often become impressed with how mature and cooperative the young adult has become by comparison to his or her teenage years, yet may overlook the relevance, or lack thereof, of such maturation for OPBs.

Other complications in relating cognitive maturity with OPBs and risk include findings that behavioural improvements may not always follow on from cognitive maturation (Kohlberg, 1985), and therefore behavioural practice of PABs should be equally central to rehabilitative interventions as cognitive skill facilitation. Furthermore, moral development should not be confined to an individual's internal world. The importance of the custodial environment for young people's moral development and antisocial behaviour is illustrated by Brugman and Aleva's (2004) study, which found that the moral atmosphere of a custodial facility was more strongly correlated with self-reported antisocial behaviour in the young than their stage of moral development or competence. Thus, OPBs may be targeted for change through enhancing the moral atmosphere of the residential and therapeutic settings in youth custody. Finally, there is growing evidence that empathy may not be linked to adolescent delinquency (Larden et al., 2006) or sexual recidivism across ages (Hanson & Morton-Bourgon, 2005), suggesting that the development of greater empathy may not be a relevant dimension of OPBs and PABs for all offenders, and therefore interventions with a strong focus on empathy may, for some offenders, not directly address OPBs, as commonly assumed.

Psychosocial Development

Key developmental tasks for adolescents include developing a sense of autonomy, alongside a connectedness with others, rebellion, independence and a sense of identity (Bailey, 1993). Adolescents break away from their parental influences and test out ways of relating with their peers, with the peer group also serving as a key platform for establishing a sense of mastery and obtaining social acceptance, particularly when the adolescent's prosocial interactions outside his peer group are limited. Identity renegotiation through the peer group and attitudes towards authority are two dimensions of psychosocial development that need to be considered by forensic practitioners working with the adolescent offender, as they may have direct relevance for continuity of criminality into adulthood, as well as for custodial behaviour. Achieving psychosocial maturity in late adolescence/early adulthood is critical to breaking the cycle of offending, and there are many challenges and obstacles to facilitating such healthy development in custodial settings (Steinberg et al., 2003). Two of these challenges are now discussed.

Identity Negotiation and Autonomy – the Peer Group

Identity formation theories purport that, as the adolescent moves through various developmental stages to achieve a positive ego identity, identity and role confusion can be associated with a failure to successfully complete a developmental stage (Erikson, 1959, 1968) and consequently delinquency (Muuss, 1988). One may argue, therefore, that risk may be reduced if custodial regimes and interventions help the adolescent progress successfully through their developmental stages. Inversely, one may argue that an antisocial identity may be enforced through incarcerating young people with other more criminally minded peers, who are likely to strongly reinforce antisocial behaviour (Bukstel & Kilmann, 1980), and hence risk may be exacerbated as they move through their developmental tasks in custodial settings. This is especially pertinent as the peer group becomes the primary forum for identity negotiation during adolescence, at a time when the adolescent is striving towards an individual identity and autonomy (the latter itself stifled by incarceration). Identity is constructed through relationships, and this can be argued to be most potent when amidst equal peers, with whom the adolescent feels autonomous and compares himself or herself against (Piaget, 1965; Pugh & Hart, 1999). The prison environment may thus generate a greater stifling of autonomy (Greve, 2001) and in turn a greater need for peer-oriented socialization. Once affiliated to a peer group, an adolescent offender adopts their norms and values, at least publicly. Whereas peer deviance has been found to interact with parenting practices and community/neighbourhood organization shaping delinquency, outside of prison (Chung & Steinberg, 2006), in custody the two latter factors may be argued to diminish in their potency in the individual's day-to-day life, leaving more scope for peer deviance to shape the adolescent's delinquent as well as prosocial behaviour and identity.

In addition to the inevitability of being exposed to antisocial peers in prison, another factor mediating young people's choice to affiliate to antisocial peers in custody is their fear of threat and need for acceptance and autonomy. Upon entering custody, the young person may seek to affiliate to and internally identify with a group that is recognized to have power and status amongst prisoners. Assignment to a peer group may be partly based on reputation or desired reputation, and the young affiliate may alter his identity with changes in his peer group activity (Pugh & Hart, 1999). The implications of such findings are that the young offender makes a critical choice of peer group, which then comes to affect the development of his/her values, norms and behaviours, in custody and beyond. Thus, in between the index offence and custodial OPBs may emerge new developments in the adolescent offender's identity and values, mediated by peer group affiliation and activity, and changes in these. Where the peer group values and 'reputation' were similar prior to and during incarceration, OPBs may be easier to spot. Where the adolescent offender affiliates to different peer groups (more or less antisocial) in custody, changes in his behaviour may either lead to masking of more severe or sophisticated forms of OPBs (i.e. a change in their manifestation) or their reduction. No more is this pronounced than in scenarios where the adolescent joins a violent gang for the first time in prison, or when they leave behind their precustodial gang norms and affiliate to a prosocial but relatively high status group in prison. In the former scenario, they may transition from stealing to impress peers to extreme acts of violence, to serve the same function. In the latter scenario, they may transition from violence as a form of control and anger expression to fitness and sports, to serve the same functions (hence demonstrating PABs and a reduction in risk, in such cases where behaviour towards their peers and trainers during the sporting/fitness activity is prosocial). In addition to changes in stable behavioural patterns, a further complication is that adolescents often behave differently when in the presence of their peers compared to when alone, for example adopting riskier decisions and behaviours when amidst their peers (Gardner & Steinberg, 2005). Thus, they may demonstrate PABs when alone and OPBs when with peers. Thus, in some contexts, a young offender's risk and OPBs may be reduced, whereas in others they may be heightened, by virtue of the adolescent's marked susceptibility to psychosocial influences. Two of the most concerning facets of peer group influences on violence in prisons are the high rates of bullying in youth custody and gang affiliation. Each is now commented on.

Bullying has been shown to be more prevalent amongst young than adult offenders, and young offenders are more likely to employ direct forms of bullying (Ireland, 1999, 2002). One explanation put forward for this phenomenon is that relationships amongst young offenders revolve around dominance, power and control, with these dynamics promoting bullying (Connell & Farrington, 1996; Ireland, 1999; Palmer & Farmer, 2002). Thus, bullying generally appears to serve to establish control, status and gain acceptance from peers, and the need for such processes is amplified in young people. Other factors that may mediate young offenders' greater engagement in bullying may include their greater egocentricity, less well-developed moral reasoning, and greater impulsivity and levels of aggression. The implications of such findings and explanations include the likely increase in OPBs in custody by offenders whose offending and bullying serve similar functions. Furthermore, some young people may have histories of offences which did not function to gain control, status and acceptance by peers but who may acquire such behaviours in custody. In this sense, their risk of aggression may be raised, but this may not be marked by an increase in OPBs. One case example is Patient D whose index offence was indecent assault of a toddler but who persistently bullied his peers or 'soldiered' for more dominant bullies in custody, in order to gain protection, avoid victimization and restore status following the social stigmatization generated by his index offence. Finally, as offenders enter adulthood, their bullying (and OPBs, where the two serve comparable functions) may become subtler, consistent with studies of self-reported bullying in prisons (Ireland, 1999, 2002). Thus, bullying needs to be explored in relation to OPBs, when conducting risk assessments.

Gangs and their impact on adolescent identity and offending have formed the focus of policy makers, researchers, clinicians and prison authorities alike for decades. Traditionally, most gang members are aged between 12 and 24, although gang membership has been reported to be ageing (Curry & Decker, 1998). Research has established a clear mediating effect of gang/peer violence on an individual adolescent's use of violence (see Henry et al., 2001, for a review). Given the importance of the peer group for identity formation, the autonomy and mastery that is commonly associated with gang membership within prisons and the adolescent's increased need for such autonomy and mastery, young offenders' gang involvement cannot simply be deconstructed using generic prosocial modelling approaches used with adults. The very psychosocial influences that operate during adolescence to shape violent gang activity need to be deployed to facilitate prosocial change. Group therapy may be one way of achieving this with young people, and may potentially have greater utility for young offenders than adults, due to the very developmental potency of peer group influences. This was recognized by McCorkle et al. (1958), who referred to this approach as 'guided group interaction' and later refined into what came to be known as 'positive peer culture' (Vorrath & Brendtro, 1985). The group therapeutic setting (such as a therapeutic community) can offer a significant testing ground for both the assessment of OPBs and their reduction, so long as it addresses criminogenic needs. This is especially important for young people whose offending is gang- or peer-related. Without such an approach, it would be very difficult for such young people to robustly adhere to PABs and abandon OPBs if such changes attract rejection from their peers and a loss of perceived autonomy and status in an adult world that they experience as controlling and associated with authorities they do not view as legitimate.

Finally, given that the peer group becomes decreasingly influential as the young person transitions into adulthood, do we need to be overly worried about peer group influences when the young offender is detained into their adulthood? For example, adults are less likely to adopt risky decisions and behaviours than adolescents, even though they are still influenced by some peer factors (Gardner & Steinberg, 2005), and gang membership is commonly a time-limited behaviour (Esbensen & Huizinga, 1993). Nevertheless, there does seem to be cause for concern, in terms of the longer-term adult sequelae of antisocial peer group affiliations. Research has shown that affiliation with deviant peers predicted having an antisocial romantic partner as a young adult (Simons et al., 2002). This suggests that assessments of young offenders should not just assume inevitable developmental reductions in risk, and that consideration of antisocial associations needs to be broadened beyond the peer group or gang as the young offender transitions into adulthood. The young adult's OPBs may come to operate in or be influenced by different relationships and life domains, by comparison to their adolescent offence behaviours.

Attitudes towards Authority

Although young people's prosocial attitudes towards societal authorities (including the law and police) have traditionally been founded in their attitudes towards their parents (Freud, 1949; Piaget, 1951), such a correlation has not always been found, and this raises questions about using custodial behaviours or family ties as proxies of prosocial development in young offenders. One study showed that in early adolescence (age 13–15) positive attitudes towards authorities (police, teachers, army) and parents are strongly correlated, but in later adolescence (age 16–17) there were more positive attitudes towards authorities but less positive attitudes towards parents (Rigby & Rump, 1981). This suggests that negative attitudes towards the authority of parental figures may change in shape and significance as the adolescent gets older. Although the sample in this study consisted of non-criminal school pupils, it highlights the developmental fluidity and complexity of attitudes towards such authorities as prison staff and such adult role models as parents/carers. Indeed, negative attitude towards institutional authority not only is a concern in terms of custodial behaviour but has also been correlated with self-reported delinquency in young people (Rigby et al., 1989; Tarry & Emler, 2007). Furthermore, institutionalized teenage delinquents have been shown to report positive attitudes towards some but not all authority figures (e.g. teachers and parents, but not police and the law). Thus, whilst assessing antisocial attitudes and their offence parallels is critical to risk assessment, one should be aware of the likely complexity and developmental changes in attitudes expressed, and exercise caution in linking all attitudes towards any authority and their changes to risk of offending.

An example of an apparent change in attitude towards authority that was unrelated to a reduction in risk is that of Patient K, a young prisoner who displayed frequent rule violations and a conflicted relationship with his parents whilst in a juvenile prison but whose behaviour became compliant, cooperative with his parents and that of the 'model prisoner' when he transferred to a young offenders institution at the age of 18. Nevertheless, security information suggested ongoing suspicions of covert bullying of peers and drug use, highlighting that expressed attitudes towards custody staff and parental figures may change without a corresponding change in OPBs, especially when such OPBs were not functionally linked to negative attitudes towards authority/parents.

A further example highlighting the complexity of young offenders' negative attitudes is Patient T, who was serving a life sentence for the murder of his mother. This young man displayed a positive attitude towards prison authority figures, male and female, even when he viewed them as harsh or punitive. Nevertheless, he continued to harbour anger at his mother and father, and indeed any family member close to him who 'let him down' in some way. Clearly, his attitudes towards his parents and his way of coping with stress in his relationships with parental figures were functionally linked to his index offence, but his interactions with custodial authority figures seemed to have no bearing on this. To a young person like Patient T, authority figures within the family and custody staff had different significance for him and his attitude to one should not be seen as a proxy for the other when assessing OPBs. Further evidence for such an argument includes cases such as Patient G, a gang-affiliated young man from an inner city neighbourhood. This young man, and indeed his peers, displayed model prosocial behaviours at home but led a disparate life on the streets, challenging the police and 'the system', which he viewed as excluding him and his family (who were from a minority ethnic and religious background). Patient G displayed empathy, respect and prosocial conflict resolution skills when interacting with his family, but at the same time challenged prison authorities, bullied more vulnerable prisoners outside of his gang and continued to engage in criminal activity and callous violence whilst in prison. He and his peers, interestingly, replicated this dynamic within the prison, adopting a positive and respectful attitude towards therapy staff (whom they considered to be akin to their family) but not discipline staff, whom they considered to represent a harsh exclusive 'system'. This echoes Levy's (2001) findings of the discrepancy between positive attitudes towards parental and some institutional figures (i.e. teachers) and negative attitudes towards authority figures associated with law enforcement. This illustrates the importance of assessing OPBs to identify such complex subtleties of custodial behaviour, which would otherwise be missed by standard attitudinal tests. The implications of such clinical case and research findings also extend to treatment planning, in that it could be argued that whilst, on the one hand, young offenders may respond more positively to interventions from professions seen as 'non-punitive' on the other hand, it is vital for discipline (officer) staff to be involved in treatments so as to help change negative attitudes towards the law and societal rules, which appear to be pivotal to reducing risk in some youth.

It appears that young people's attitudes towards and perceptions of authority figures require more complex analysis than perhaps those of adults, especially at a time when parents become less directly influential and prison staff become more directly involved in the young person's care, learning and discipline. This could offer a positive opportunity, given Rigby and Rump's (1981) findings, for some young people to relate more positively to prosocial adult role models in custody and as a result reduce their risk and OPBs, particularly if their negative attitudes to societal authorities played a functional role in their offending.

Psychosexual Development

Establishing intimacy and becoming comfortable with one's sexuality are amongst the developmental tasks of adolescence. Physiologically, the adolescent undergoes radical changes, with a substantial rise in testosterone levels in males around the time of puberty. Furthermore, intimacy transfers from similar-sex friendships to romantic partners, with new boundaries and experiences being tested by the adolescent. With the physical capacity to perform sexually, the cognitive ability to form an understanding of sexuality, and the emotional lability and intensity that may be nurtured within adolescent relationships, adolescence is a critical time for both adaptive and maladaptive development and change. The implications for the assessment and treatment of OPBs are numerous and warrant careful consideration in forensic settings, particularly when the behaviour under the microscope is inappropriate or abusive sexual conduct. That is not to say that continuing risk should be somehow overlooked in the hope that developmental plasticity may spontaneously reduce risk, for a history of adolescent offending increases risk of recidivism (Långström, 2002; Lee et al., 2003; Prentky et al., 2000; Ross & Loss, 1991). Rather, what constitutes OPBs and markers of risk reduction may be more complex to reliably measure.

Whilst puberty is commonly observed by clinicians to mark the onset of sexually deviant behaviours, the transition into adulthood may bring with it other changes for the incarcerated adolescent. With decreases in levels of impulsivity, stabilization of hormonal levels, cognitive and sociomoral maturation, and a better understanding of sexuality may emerge either as a reduction in the need for OPBs and an increase in PABs, or alternatively OPBs may transform topographically, being replaced with less overtly sexualized behaviours that serve a similar function. Thus, the function of past sexually abusive behaviours needs to be established, so as to spot topologically variant OPBs. Inversely, the adolescent may continue to experiment sexually, in custody, as he travels through the developmental journey to sexual maturity. Such experimentation may thus reflect otherwise healthy developmental processes confined to fellow prisoners by virtue of environmental restrictions, rather than OPBs, or it may signify low-level sexually abusive behaviour that may be functionally dissimilar to the index sexual offending, the latter being shown in secure settings and found to be partly triggered by environmental factors in adult sex offenders (Daffern et al., 2008). In fact, due to the experimental and risk-taking facets of adolescent sexual behaviour, victimology is difficult to predict, on the one hand (i.e. an offender with past underaged female victims may turn to similar-aged male peers in custody), and developmentally normative sexual behaviour may be misconstrued as or at least fused with OPBs, in custody, on the other hand.

Thus, any assessment and treatment of sexually abusive behaviour need to be embedded in a dynamic developmental context in order to be meaningful. For example, risk factors known to mediate sexual recidivism in adult sex offenders need to be measured through a dynamic developmental template. The presence of adult risk factors for sexual offending needs to be compared to similar-aged peer norms, and their origin needs to be considered as developmentally 'in progress'. This particularly applies to such risk factors as sexual preoccupation, sexual interest in underaged minors (who may be of a similar or slightly younger age than the perpetrator), egocentric attitudes of entitlement and offence justification, angry ruminations, lack of stable intimate relationships, greater relatedness to slightly younger individuals (who may be minors) and fragile self-esteem/loneliness/externalized control (which in adolescents may partly be coloured by the battle for autonomy). Consequently, risk assessment needs to be developmentally sensitive and dynamic. Treatment may be designed to facilitate the developmental progression necessary to reduce the operation of these risk factors. Both assessment and treatment content need to be continually updated in the light of the ongoing developmental changes.

Emotional Development

With adolescence come changes in hormonal activity associated with emotional dispositions such as anger, nervousness, sadness and impulse control (Susman et al., 1987). There is a shift towards externalized expression of emotions between the ages of 12 and 18 (O'Kearney & Dadds, 2004). Emotions may be experienced and displayed more frequently, intensely and for longer periods (Goodenough, 1931; Greene, 1990; Larson et al., 1980, 2002). Additionally, delinquent adolescents experience a wide range of more intense negative emotions by comparison to non-delinquents, and this is more pronounced when they have a history of trauma (Plattner et al., 2007). The role of poor emotional impulse control and intense explosive anger is commonly recognized by clinicians working with aggressive youngsters. Furthermore, the inability to cope with negative emotions and stress has been found to constitute a possible antecedent to sexual offending (Proulx et al., 1999). Developmental maturation may in some cases curtail the emotional intensity experienced by some young people and thus may diminish the need for aggression as a maladaptive emotional release mechanism. Nevertheless, less explosive emotions may lie underneath the surface and may find a release in more controlled, albeit equally abusive ways, later in life. Thus, overcoming the emotional turbulence of adolescence may either reduce OPBs or else give rise to different forms of OPBs or greater detection evasion capability.

Worthy of note, incarcerated adolescents may be exposed to increased levels of emotional distress in custody, and their healthy methods of release or self-soothing (e.g. intimate relationships and healthy risk-taking activities) may be curtailed. Additionally, for adolescents who previously used illicit substances to self-soothe, a reduction in substance misuse may bring about heightened levels of distress. Furthermore, research on adolescent–parent interactions has shown that adolescents' negative affect is related to the process of establishing autonomy and connectedness during interactions with parents (Allen et al., 1994), suggesting that interactions between adolescent offenders and custodial staff may be particularly emotionally charged. Thus, OPBs may increase in custody in response to environmental changes, and in such cases it is very important to recognize, validate and support the healthy expression of negative emotions. This is unfortunately not always considered a security-friendly approach in juvenile prisons, and prison rules often punish (non-violent) emotional expression. This can either lead the young person to dissociate or simply learn to evade detection whilst continuing to express their negative emotions in abusive ways (e.g. by sadistically bullying more vulnerable peers, out of sight of staff). Consequently, OPBs may not involve comparable forms of emotional expression in custody, due to any of the aforementioned reasons. Thus, assessments of OPBs should tease apart healthy developmental maturation linked to risk reduction from emotional masking or suppression, and treatment and management should, where possible, promote healthy expressions of negative emotions and avoid their suppression or covert redirection.

Personality Development

Problematic adolescent behaviour may or may not be significant in predicting longer-term personality development (particularly antisocial and borderline traits) and its criminogenic links. The case for and against continuity is now presented and the significance of each for OPBs explored.

Adolescent Conduct Problems as Predictors of Antisocial Personality

Although personality disorders are not diagnosed prior to the age of 18, a number of childhood and adolescent antecedents or precursors to adult antisocial behaviour have been identified, such as aggression, stealing and substance misuse (West & Farrington, 1977). Antisocial behaviour has been found to be persistent across the transition into adulthood, with the most antisocial 18-year-old individuals in the Cambridge study maintaining this status at age 32 (Farrington, 1991). Research has shown that the likelihood of adult narcissistic and antisocial personality disorders increased by more than six and five times, respectively, when individuals had a disruptive disorder during childhood (Ramklint et al., 2003). The temporal continuity between adolescent externalizing behaviour (including ADHD, oppositional defiant disorder and conduct disorder) and adulthood psychopathy, as young people transition into early adulthood, has been demonstrated in research (Loney et al., 2007).

Given the well-established link between antisocial/psychopathic personality and violence (Forth et al., 1990; Hill et al., 1996; Quinsey et al., 1995; Rice & Harris, 1992; Serin, 1991, 1996; Serin & Amos, 1995), it is pertinent to identify the mechanisms linking disruptive and externalizing behaviour in young offenders and antisocial personality in adulthood, and to target such mechanisms in an attempt to reduce the likelihood of strengthening antisocial personality traits and hence risk. For example, given that disruptive/externalizing behaviours are likely to disrupt healthy socialization (family and prosocial peer relationships, and education), it could be argued that custodial interventions for disruptive adolescents should focus on facilitating healthy socialization, particularly as custodial settings limit access to prosocial similar-aged peers and may exacerbate exposure to antisocial peer groups. In terms of assessment, where disruptive/externalizing behaviours were linked to a young person's offending, their recurrence in custody should be identified as offence paralleling and potentially predictive of adult offending rather than conceptualized as mere prison rule violation or a transitory adolescent behavioural phase, as such behaviour may potentially become integrated into stable aspects of the adult personality, if not addressed.

Lack of Continuity between Adolescent Conduct Problems and Adult Antisocial Personality

Childhood and adolescent antisocial behaviours have been argued by some to be 'phase-related discontinuities' which interact with other developmental factors along the childhood–adulthood antisocial behaviour trajectory, and it has been noted that whilst antisocial personality in adulthood is almost always preceded by antisocial behaviour in childhood, the converse is not true (Bailey, 1993). Robins (1991) purported that the trajectory from conduct disorder to chronic psychiatric disorder in adulthood can be aborted. One childhood–adulthood antisocial behaviour link that has been argued to be a potential target for intervention is attachment style. Avoidant, dismissing or any insecure and disorganized attachment styles are most likely to be linked to hostile and antisocial behaviour in adolescents (Bailey, 1993), and therefore attachment-based interventions and the establishment of healthy attachments with peers and adults may be central to reducing the risk of antisocial behaviour continuing into adulthood.

Given the potential developmental changes in how young people act out or relate to others, it could firstly be argued that risk of antisocial behaviour could be reduced with the developmentally appropriate interventions. A second implication of such developmental plasticity is the likelihood that OPBs may change in form, particularly if the functions of the antisocial behaviours are not directly addressed by interventions focusing on personality disorder (or its behavioural precursors) or attachment style. It may be that some traits or behaviours are more criminogenic than others and should be targeted in order to abort the trajectory to adult offending. As well as antisocial personality markers, borderline traits have also been highlighted to be potentially relevant for such a process.

Links between Borderline Traits in Adolescence and Adulthood

Research has shown mixed findings with regards to the continuity of borderline traits from adolescence to adulthood. Whilst childhood abuse, incest, affective instability, impulsivity, substance misuse and greater co-morbid Axis I and II disorders are associated with continuity of symptoms, discontinuity/remission has been associated with high IQ, low narcissistic entitlement and the absence of parental divorce (Sharp & Romero, 2007). Although not formally diagnosed before the age of 18, some clinicians have proposed the need to identify childhood manifestations of borderline symptoms (Goldman et al., 1992). Clinicians working with young offenders may commonly observe such traits in some, although the author's experience suggests that such symptoms are highly receptive to environmental changes and could be quickly stabilized and just as quickly destabilized.

Where functional links are established between an adolescent offender's borderline traits and violence, it is imperative that any stability or instability of borderline symptomatology is monitored. Furthermore, given the more chaotic and changeable nature of borderline patients' behaviour coupled with the developmental changes expected in adolescent offenders and their sensitivity to environmental contingencies, OPBs may present as topographically very different in custody and functional analyses are required to tease out what is an OPB and what is a spurious expression of borderline tendencies. A case study to illustrate such complexity is Patient F.

Patient F was convicted of the murder of his best friend. He described the trigger to his 'rage' as being perceived rejection by the victim (who taunted and laughed at him). He described having idolized and felt an intense need for the victim, and 'wanted to be like him'. Patient F also recollected violently assaulting his sister after she had dismissed his distress whilst he was confiding in her. Once again he had idolized his sister and viewed her as his only ally and confidante. Patient F reported feeling intensely angry towards his parents for 'not meeting his needs' and had frequently expressed his anger through smashing furniture in the house, taking overdoses and cutting his arms. Functional analyses of his various acts of aggression towards self and others revealed that he experienced an intense need for significant others, felt angry at their perceived abandonment, and once an interaction triggered his fear of abandonment, he experienced what he construed as intolerable rage, which he impulsively externalized through aggression or self-harm. In prison, Patient F presented as a 'model prisoner' albeit vulnerable and needy of staff time. Interestingly, when he felt or feared abandonment and experienced 'rage', he took to disclosing his suicidal intentionality to staff, securing more contact time with them. He did this more with particular staff and at particular times in the day (in the close lead-up to lock-up or 'patrol states' when prisoners are locked in their cells and staffing levels are minimal). His descriptions of his relationships reflected unstable, intense, all-or-nothing friendships with fellow prisoners. He wrote letters to a female school friend, expressing his romantic commitment to her and expressed suicidality when she informed him that she did not wish to pursue a romantic relationship with him. He also self-harmed when his 'favourite' officer had a day off and protested that he would only discuss his problems with this officer. Psychologically, there appeared to be clear OPBs, which were unhelpful behaviours triggered by perceived or feared abandonment and consequent anger/rage. Yet ironically he had no custodial records of aggression. After eight months of therapy addressing his borderline schemas, environmental contingencies rewarding healthy coping with perceived abandonment and psychosocial opportunities to interact with a range of peers and staff when not engaging in or disclosing suicidality, Patient F's OPBs dramatically reduced. He coped well with transition into the adult prison system and has continued to show good engagement in therapy. This case illustrates the topological changes in OPBs, the lack of direct correspondence between custodial misdemeanours and OPBs for some young offenders and the marked susceptibility of serious pathology rooted in borderline personality traits to change through even short-term therapy. This further highlights the need for both optimism and caution when addressing OPBs in young offenders with personality pathology.

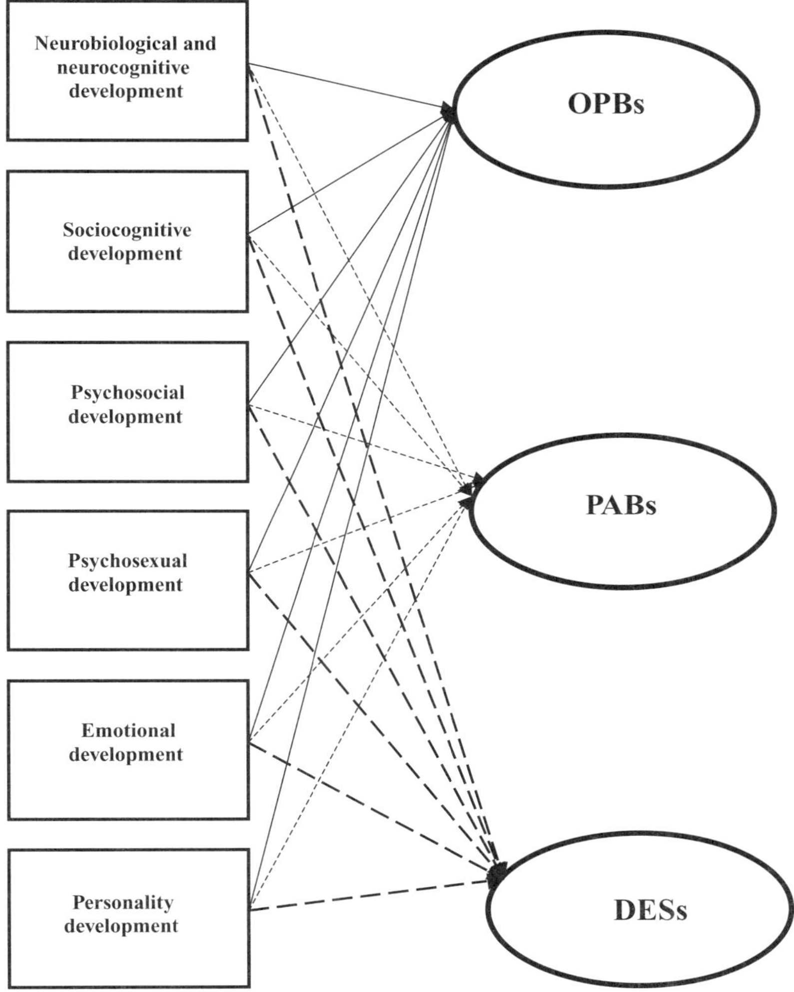

Figure 9.1 Examples of developmental factors impacting on offence paralleling behaviours (OPBs), prosocial adaptive alternatives (PABs) and detection evasion skills (DESs) in young offenders.

IMPLICATIONS OF ADOLESCENT DEVELOPMENT FOR ASSESSMENT METHODOLOGIES, MANAGEMENT AND TREATMENT PLANNING

The complexities of delineating what may constitute an OPB across changing developmental stages of a young offender's life have been highlighted throughout this chapter. Some of the developmental factors that impact on OPBs, PABs and DESs have been discussed in the previous section and are summarized in Figure 9.1. Whilst existent OPB frameworks already purport a focus on the psychological function of a behaviour rather than its topography (Daffern et al., 2007), this is of even greater importance in young offenders who are continuing to undergo bio-psychosocial developmental changes. Furthermore, in order to delineate how the very functions of antisocial behaviours may transform through the course of childhood–adolescence–adulthood, there is a need for 'multiple' sequential functional analytic methodology (Gresswell & Hollin, 1992) that tracks learning, changes in environment and changes in physiological, cognitive, emotional and behavioural responses to stimuli that come with natural human development.

The use of functional and multiple functional analytic methodology in clinical and forensic practice has been illustrated by numerous researchers and clinicians (Falshaw & Browne, 1999; Gresswell & Hollin, 1992; Jackson et al., 1987; Owens & Ashcroft, 1982) and is not detailed in this chapter. It also formed the focus of a study by the author (Al-Attar, 2004), which examined pathways from early trauma to adolescent arson, sexual offending and homicide. The latter study revealed that responses to trauma evolved over the course of development, and became increasingly aggressive in the young offenders studied. Critically, the behaviours that served a given psychological function changed in form as the young person developed and the forms of aggression varied over time, consistent with the escalation of 'overt behaviours' leading to homicide, reported by Gresswell and Hollin for their case illustration. This not only has clear implications for assessment of chronicity of a risk factor and indeed OPBs, but also for predicting its different manifestations and contexts. Furthermore, it has clear implications for treatment planning (Hayes & O'Brien, 1990), which should not be confined to focusing on the antecedents, behaviours and consequences of the index offence alone, but should address developmental precursors and post-offence behaviours, and their functions. For example, when treating a young person with an index sexual offence, intervention should focus equally on non-sexual precursors to the index offence (e.g. prepubertal robberies or arson that may serve similar functions) as well as post-offence functionally equivalent behaviours of all forms (e.g. bullying of peers and self-harm). Essentially, the emphasis should be on function, and not topography, in treatment. Finally, functional analysis may inform effective inpatient or custodial management planning. The centrality of functional assessments to planning effective management and avoiding inadvertent reinforcement of maladaptive behaviours has been argued for both adolescent and adult residential settings (Carbone & Lynch, 1983; Daffern & Howells, 2002; McDougall, 2000).

Clinicians will commonly see young offenders who display an array of different maladaptive behaviours against self and others, which may be functionally equivalent, for example arson and self-harm (as found by Millar & Fritzon, 2007, in adult women) as well as other acts of aggression, including hostage-taking, criminal damage and violence, with all behaviours being underpinned by similar functions. To this extent, functional analysis is critical in unpicking what may constitute an OPB amongst the numerous, evolving problematic behaviours of youngsters in custody, and distinguish it from newly learnt forms of maladaptive behaviours and developmentally normative behaviour that may simply be incongruent with institutional rules. Equally important is the dynamic adaptation of assessments to make them responsive to ongoing developmental changes and to daily changes in the young offender's social environment, to which he or she may be highly reactive. Finally, clinicians comparing young and adult offenders may appraise young people as at higher risk due to their less sophisticated DESs (Jones, 2004), which lead to a higher detection rate of OPBs in young offenders compared to older, less impulsive offenders. An understanding of developmental differences and changes will enable us to more accurately appraise and address OPBs and to cater for the range of aforementioned complexities.

CONCLUSIONS

Theories of adolescent delinquency and risk have increasingly moved towards a developmental framework (Tolan et al., 1995), and it follows that such a developmental framework, addressing progress in bio-psychosocial development over the course of incarceration, should be adopted when assessing and intervening to reduce OPBs and criminogenic risk. Such a framework needs to map the interplay of developmental changes, risk (and its manifestations) and protective factors in the young offender, and delineate how OPBs, evasion of their detection and PABs may be mediated through such an interplay. Risk factors and protective factors may vary by age, as may trajectories to offending at different ages, and therefore OPBs are bound to also, as the young offender transitions from adolescence into adulthood, generating complexity as well as optimism for clinicians assessing OPBs and planning rehabilitative treatments for youth in custody. This greater complexity, as well as opportunity for change, deserves greater attention and systematic, developmentally meaningful research over the coming years. The current chapter serves to unearth some of the many developmental questions that need to be posed by those adopting an individualized OPB approach to the assessment and treatment of young offenders. Such developmental questions and complexities point to the clear need for adopting an OPB framework that focuses on the functions of behaviour rather than topography, when assessing, managing and treating young offenders.

REFERENCES

Al-Attar, Z. (2004). *Developmental Trajectories from Early Trauma to Arson, Homicide, and Sexual Assault: Three Illustrative Cases from a Young Offender Prison Population*. Unpublished MSc Dissertation. Leicester: University of Leicester.

Allen, J.P., Hauser, S.T., Eickholt, C., Bell, K.L. & O'Connor, T.G. (1994). Autonomy and relatedness in family interactions as predictors of expressions of negative adolescent affect. *Journal of Research on Adolescence, 4*, 535–52.

Bailey, S. (1993). Personality development in adolescents. *Journal of Forensic Psychiatry, 4*(3), 415–19.

Benes, F.M., Turtle, M., Khan, Y. & Farol, P. (1994). Myelination of a key relay zone in the hippocampal formation occurring in the human body during childhood, adolescence, and adulthood. *Archives of General Psychiatry, 51*, 477–84.

Brennan, P.A., Hall, J., Bor, W., Najman, J.M. & Williams, G. (2003). Integrating biological and social processes in relation to early-onset persistent aggression in boys and girls. *Developmental Psychology, 39*, 309–23.

Brugman, D. & Aleva, A.E. (2004). Developmental delay or regression in moral reasoning by juvenile delinquents? *Journal of Moral Education, 33*, 321–38.

Bukstel, L.H. & Kilmann, P.R. (1980). Psychological effects of imprisonment on confined individuals. *Psychological Bulletin, 88*, 469–93.

Carbone, V.J. & Lynch, (1983). The functional analysis of behavior in a juvenile detention facility. *Counseling Juvenile Offenders in Institutional Settings, 6*, 21–41.

Chung, H.L. & Steinberg, L. (2006). Relations between neigborhood factors, parenting behaviors, peer deviance, and delinquency among serious juvenile offenders. *Developmental Psychology, 42*, 319–31.

Clarke, S., Heussler, H. & Kohn, M.R. (2005). Attention deficit disorder: not just for children. *Internal Medicine Journal, 35*, 721–5.

Coccaro, E.F., McCloskey, M.S., Fitzgerald, D.A. & Phan, K.L. (2007). Amygdala and orbitofrontal reactivity to social threat in individuals with impulsive aggression. *Biological Psychiatry, 62*, 168–78.

Connell, A. & Farrington, D. (1996). Bullying amongst incarcerated young offenders: developing an interview schedule and some preliminary results. *Journal of Adolescence, 19*, 75–93.

Curry, G.D. & Decker, S.H. 1998. *Confronting Gangs: Crime and Community*. Los Angeles, CA: Roxbury.

Daffern, M. & Howells, K. (2002). Psychiatric inpatient aggression: a review of structural and functional assessment approaches. *Aggression and Violent Behavior, 7*, 477–97.

Daffern, M., Howells, K., Stacey, J., Hogue, T. & Mooney, P. (2008). Is sexually abusive behaviour in personality disordered inpatients analogous to sexual offences committed prior to hospitalisation? *Journal of Sexual Aggression, 14*, 123–33.

Daffern, M., Jones, L., Howells, K., Shine, J., Mikton, C. & Tunbridge, V.C. (2007). Refining the definition of offence paralleling behaviour. *Criminal Behaviour and Mental Health, 17*, 265–73.

Elliott, F.A. (1999). A neurological perspective of violent behavior. In M. Hersen & V. Van Hasselt (Eds), *Handbook of Psychological Approaches to Violent Criminal Offenders*. New York: Plenum Press.

Erikson, E.H. (1959). Identity and the life cycle: selected papers. *Psychological Issues, 1*, 1–171.

Erikson, E.H. (1968). *Identity: Youth and Crisis*. New York: Norton.

Esbensen, F. & Huizinga, D. (1993). Gangs, drugs, and delinquency in a survey of urban youth. *Criminology, 31*, 565–89.

Falshaw, L. & Browne, K.D. (1999). A young man referred to specialist secure accommodation. *Child Abuse Review, 8*, 419–32.

Farrington, D.P. (1991). Antisocial personality from childhood to adulthood. *The Psychologist, 4*, 389–94.

Forth, A.E., Hart, S.D. & Hare, R.D. (1990). Assessment of psychopathy in male young offenders. *Psychological Assessment: A Journal of Consulting and Clinical Psychology, 2*, 342–44.

Foundaccaro, M.R. & Heller, K. (1990). Attributional style in aggressive adolescent boys. *Journal of Abnormal Child Psychology, 18*, 75–89.

Freud, S. (1949). *An Outline of Psychoanalysis*. New York: Norton.

Gardner, M. & Steinberg, L. (2005). Peer influence on risk taking, risk preference, and risky decision making in adolescence and adulthood: an experimental study. *Developmental Psychology, 41*, 625–35.

Gibbs, J.C., Potter, G. & Goldstein, A.P. (1995). *The EQUIP Program: Teaching Youth to Think and Act Responsibly through a Peer-Helping Approach*. Champaign, IL: Research Press.

Gibbs, J.C., Potter, G.B., Barriga, A.Q. & Liau, A.K. (1996). Developing the helping skills and prosocial motivation of aggressive adolescents in peer group programs. *Aggression and Violent Behavior, 1*, 283–305.

Goldman, S.J., D'Angelo, E.J., DeMaso, D.R. & Mezzacappa, E. (1992). Physical and sexual abuse histories among children with borderline personality disorder. *American Journal of Psychiatry, 149*, 1723–26.

Goodenough, F. (1931). *Anger in Young Children*. Minneapolis: University of Minnesota Press.

Greene, A.L. (1990). Patterns of affectivity in the transition to adolescence. *Journal of Experimental Child Psychology, 50*, 340–56.

Gresswell, D.M. & Hollin, C.R. (1992). Towards a new methodology for making sense of case material: an illustrative case involving attempted multiple murder. *Criminal Behaviour and Mental Health, 2*, 329–41.

Greve, W. (2001). Imprisonment of juveniles and adolescents: deficits and demands for developmental research. *Applied Developmental Science, 5*, 21–26.

Hanson, R.K. & Morton-Bourgon, K.E. (2005). The characteristics of persistent sexual offenders: a meta-analysis of recidivism studies. *Journal of Consulting and Clinical Psychology, 73*, 1154–63.

Hayes, S.N. & O'Brien, W.H. (1990). Functional analysis in behavior therapy. *Clinical Psychology Review, 10*, 649–68.

Henry, D.B., Tolan, P.H. & Gorman-Smith, D. (2001). Longitudinal family and peer group effects on violence and non-violent delinquency. *Journal of Clinical Child Psychology, 30*, 172–86.

Hill, C.D., Rogers, R. & Bickford, M.E. (1996). Predicting aggressive and socially disruptive behavior in a maximum security forensic hospital. *Journal of Forensic Sciences, 41*, 56–59.

Hogan, A.M., Vargha-Khadem, F., Kirkham, F.J. & Baldeweg, T. (2005). Maturation of action monitoring from adolescence to adulthood: an ERP study. *Developmental Science, 8*, 525–34.

Ingram, S., Hechtman, L. & Morgenstern, G. (1999). Outcome issues in ADHD: adolescent and adult long-term outcome. *Mental Retardation and Developmental Disabilities Research Review, 5*, 243–50.

Ireland, J.L. (1999). Bullying behaviours amongst male and female prisoners: a study of adult and young offenders. *Aggressive Behavior, 25*, 161–78.

Ireland, J.L. (2002). Do juveniles bully more than young offenders? A comparison of the perceived and actual bullying behaviour reported by juvenile and young offenders. *Journal of Adolescence, 25*, 155–68.

Jackson, H.F., Glass, C. & Hope, S. (1987). A functional analysis of recidivistic arson. *British Journal of Clinical Psychology, 26*, 175–85.

Jones, L.F. (2004). Offence paralleling behaviour (OPB) as a framework for assessment and interventions with offenders. In A. Needs & G. Towl (Eds), *Applying Psychology to Forensic Practice*. Oxford: BPS Blackwell.

Koelsch, S., Sammler, D., Jentschke, S. & Siebel, W.A. (2008). EEG correlates of moderate intermittent explosive disorder. *Clinical Neurophysiology, 119*, 151–62.

Kohlberg, L. (1985). The just community approach to moral education in theory and practice. In M.W. Berkowitz & F. Oser (Eds), *Moral Education: Theory and Application* (pp. 27–87). Hillsdale, NJ: Erlbaum.

Långström, N. (2002). Long-term follow-up of criminal recidivism in young sexual offenders. *Psychology, Crime and Law: Special Swedish Studies on Psychology, Crime and Law, 8*, 41–58.

Larden, M., Melin, L., Holst, U. & Långström, N. (2006). Moral judgement, cognitive distortions and empathy in incarcerated delinquent and community control adolescents. *Psychology, Crime and Law, 12*, 453–62.

Larson, R.W., Csikszentmihalyi, M. & Graef, R. (1980). Mood variability and the psychosocial adjustment of adolescents. *Journal of Youth and Adolescence, 9*, 469–90.
Larson, R.W., Moneta, G., Richards, M.H. & Wilson, S. (2002). Continuity, stability, and change in daily emotional experience across adolescence. *Child Development, 73*, 1151–65.
Lee, R.J., Cottle, C.C. & Heilbrun, K. (2003). The prediction of recidivism in juvenile sex offenders: a meta-analysis. Manual submitted for publication.
Levy, K.S.C. (2001). The relationship between adolescent attitudes towards authority, self-concept, and delinquency. *Adolescence, 36*, 333–46.
Loney, B.R., Taylor, J., Butler, M.A. & Iacono, W.G. (2007). Adolescent psychopathy features: 6-year temporal stability and the prediction of externalising symptoms during the transition to adulthood. *Aggressive Behavior, 33*, 242–52.
Mariano, K.A. & Harton, H.C. (2005). Similarities in aggression, inattention/hyperactivity, depression, and anxiety in middle childhood friendships. *Journal of Social and Clinical Psychology, 24*, 471–96.
McCorkle, L., Elias, A. & Bixby, F.L. (1958). *The Highfields Story*. New York: Henry Holt.
McDougall, T. (2000). Violent incidents in a forensic adolescent unit: a functional analysis. *Nursing Times Research, 5*, 346–62.
Millar, S. & Fritzon, K. (2007). Functional consistency across two behavioural modalities: fire-setting and self-harm in female special hospital patients. *Criminal Behavior and Mental Health, 17*, 31–44.
Moffitt, T.E. (1993). Adolescence-limited and life-course-persistent antisocial behavior: a developmental taxonomy. *Psychological Review, 100*, 674–701.
Mullin, S. & Simpson, J. (2007). Does executive functioning predict improvement in offenders' behaviour following enhanced thinking skills training? *Legal and Criminological Psychology, 12*, 117–31.
Muuss, R.E. (1988). *Theories of Adolescence* (5th edition). New York: Random House.
Nangle, D.W., Hecker, J.E., Grover, R.L. & Smith, M.G. (2003). Perspective taking and adolescent sex offenders: from developmental theory to clinical practice. *Cognitive and Behavioral Practice, 10*, 73–84.
O'Kearney, R. & Dadds, M. (2004). Developmental and gender differences in the language for emotions across the adolescent years. *Cognition and Emotion, 18*, 913–38.
Owens, R.G. & Ashcroft, J.B. (1982). Functional analysis in applied psychology. *British Journal of Clinical Psychology, 21*, 181–90.
Palmer, E.J. & Farmer, S. (2002). Victimising behaviour among juveniles and young offender: how different are perpetrators? *Journal of Adolescence, 25*, 469–81.
Piaget, J. (1951). *Play, Dreams and Imitation in Childhood*. New York: Norton.
Piaget, J. (1965). *The Moral Judgement of the Child*. London: Routledge & Kegan Paul.
Piaget, J. (1970). *Genetic Epistemology*. New York: Norton.
Plattner, B., Karnik, N., Jo, B., Hall, R.E., Schallauer, A., Carrion, V., Feucht, M. & Steiner, H. (2007). State and trait emotions in delinquent adolescents. *Child Psychiatry and Human Development, 38*, 155–69.
Prentky, R., Harris, B., Frizzell, K. & Righthand, S. (2000). An actuarial procedure for assessing risk with juvenile sex offenders. *Sexual Abuse: A Journal of Research and Treatment, 12*, 71–92.
Proulx, J., Perreault, C. & Ouimet, M. (1999). Pathways in the offending process of extra-familial child molesters. *Sexual Abuse: A Journal of Research and Treatment, 11*, 117–29.
Pugh, M.J.V. & Hart, D. (1999). Identity development and peer group participation. *New Directions for Child and Adolescent Development, 84*, 55–70.
Quinsey, V.L., Rice, M.E. & Harris, G.T. (1995). Actuarial prediction of sexual recidivism. *Journal of Interpersonal Violence, 10*, 85–105.
Ramklint, M., Von Knorring, A-L., Von Knorring, L. & Ekselius, L. (2003). Child and adolescent psychiatric disorders predicting adult personality disorder: a follow-up study. *Nordic Journal of Psychiatry, 57*, 23–28.
Rice, M.E. & Harris, G.T. (1992). A comparison of criminal recidivism among schizophrenic and non-schizophrenic offenders. *International Journal of Law and Psychiatry, 15*, 397–408.
Rigby, K., Mak, A.S. & Slee, P.T. (1989). Impulsiveness, orientation to institutional authority, and gender as factors in self-reported delinquency among Australian adolescents. *Personality and Individual Differences, 10*, 689–92.
Rigby, K. & Rump, E.E. (1981). Attitudes toward parents and institutional authorities during adolescence. *The Journal of Psychology, 109*, 109–18.
Robins, L.N. (1991). Conduct disorder. *Journal of Child Psychology and Psychiatry, 32*, 193–212.
Robinson, R., Roberts, W.L., Strayer, J. & Koopman, R. (2007). Empathy and emotional responsiveness in delinquent and non-delinquent adolescents. *Social Development, 16*, 555–79.
Romine, C.B. & Reynolds, C.R. (2005). A model of the development of frontal lobe functioning: findings from a meta-analysis. *Applied Neuropsychology, 12*, 190–201.

Rosmalen, L. Van, Stams, G.J.J.M., Brugman, D. & Dekovic, M. (2003). *The Moral Reasoning of Juvenile Delinquents: A Meta-analysis*. Unpublished manuscript. University of Amsterdam, Department of Education.

Ross, J. & Loss, P. (1991). Assessment of the juvenile sex offender. In G.D. Ryan & S.L. Lane (Eds), *Juvenile Sexual Offending: Causes, Consequences, and Correction* (pp. 199–251). Lexington, MA: Lexington Books.

Selman, R.L. (1971a). Taking another's perspective: role-taking development in early childhood. *Child Development*, *42*, 1721–34.

Selman, R.L. (1971b). The relation of role taking to the development of moral judgement in children. *Child Development*, *42*, 79–91.

Serin, R.C. (1991). Psychopathy and violence in criminals. *Journal of Interpersonal Violence*, *6*, 423–31.

Serin, R.C. (1996). Violent recidivism in criminal psychopaths. *Law and Human Behavior*, *20*, 207–17.

Serin, R.C. & Amos, N.L. (1995). The role of psychopathy in the assessment of dangerousness. *International Journal of Law and Psychiatry*, *18*, 231–38.

Sharp, C. & Romero, C. (2007). Borderline personality disorder: a comparison between children and adults. *Bulletin of the Menninger Clinic*, *71*, 85–114.

Simons, R.L., Stewart, E., Gordon, L.C., Conger, R.D. & Elder, G.H. (2002). A test of life-course explanations for stability and change in antisocial behavior from adolescence to young adulthood. *Criminology*, *40*, 401–34.

Sowell, E.R., Thompson, P.M., Holmes, C.J., Jernigan, T.L. & Toga, A.W. (1999). In vivo evidence for post-adolescent brain maturation in frontal and striatal regions. *Nature Neuroscience*, *2*, 859–61.

Steinberg, L., Chung, H.L. & Little, M. (2003). Reentry of young offenders from the justice system: a developmental perspective. *Youth Violence and Juvenile Justice*, *1*, 1–18.

Susman, E.J., Dockray, S., Schiefelbein, V.L., Herwehe, S., Heaton, J.A. & Dorn, L.D. (2007). Morningness/eveningness, morning-to-afternoon cortisol ratio, and antisocial behavior problems during puberty. *Developmental Psychology*, *43*, 811–22.

Susman, E.J., Inoff-Germain, G., Nottelmann, E.D., Loriaux, D.L., Cutler, G.B. & Chrousos, G.P. (1987). Hormones, emotional dispositions, and aggressive attributes in young adolescents. *Child Development*, *58*, 1114–34.

Tarry, H. & Emler, N. (2007). Attitudes, values and moral reasoning as predictors of delinquency. *British Journal of Developmental Psychology*, *25*, 169–83.

Thompson, K.L. & Gullone, E. (2008). Prosocial and antisocial behaviors in adolescents: An investigation into associations with attachment and empathy. *Anthrozoos*, *21*, 123–37.

Tolan, P.H., Guerra, N.G. & Kendall, P.C. (1995). A developmental-ecological perspective on antisocial behavior in children and adolescents: toward a unified risk and intervention framework. *Journal of Consulting and Clinical Psychology*, *63*, 579–84.

Vorrath, H.H. & Brendtro, L. (1985). *Positive Peer Culture* (2nd edition). New York: Aldine.

West, D.J. & Farrington, D.P. (1977). *The Delinquent Way of Life*. London: Heinemann.

Chapter 10

OFFENCE ANALOGUE BEHAVIOURS AS INDICATORS OF CRIMINOGENIC NEED AND TREATMENT PROGRESS IN CUSTODIAL SETTINGS

AUDREY GORDON

Regional Psychiatric Centre, University of Saskatchewan, Saskatoon, Saskatchewan, Canada

STEPHEN C.P. WONG

Personality Disorder Institute, University of Nottingham and Department of Forensic Mental Health Science, King's College, University of London, and the University of Saskatchewan, Canada

INTRODUCTION

Antisocial behaviours observable in the community may take on different appearances in controlled settings such as in prisons where close monitoring as well as swift and severe sanctions for misbehaviours are the norm. In a heavily controlled environment, the 'repackaging' or modifications of blatant antisocial acts, which otherwise would be easily observable in the community, could be due to restrictions of the environment, the absence of potential victims and precursors, or the unavailability of the tools of crime such as weapons or drugs. For example, a child molester, whose *modus operandi* has been to use the internet to lure his victims, may resort to viewing images of children in magazines and masturbating to them in prison. A violent young man, who enjoys getting into bar fights to show off his physical prowess, instead may resort to verbally intimidating and insulting others while doing time in prison. A psychopath who swindled and defrauded others may turn into a jailhouse lawyer. Many of these inappropriate, albeit marginally tolerable, behaviours in a custodial setting are similar or analogous to offences committed by such individuals in the past. Similarly, individuals who have been in custody for a long time may be so institutionalized that these offence analogue behaviours may be hard to detect. For example, an individual, whose offending pattern was due to a lack of structure in his daily living, may function and manage quite well in a structured prison regime. However, on his return to an open and unstructured community setting, without the necessary skills for independent living, he may decompensate quickly into his past antisocial patterns. Although we use the custodial setting here and in latter discussions as an exemplar to illustrate the nature of offence analogue behaviours, these behaviours could be observed in non-custodial settings

Offence Paralleling Behaviour: A Case Formulation Approach to Offender Assessment and Intervention Edited by Michael Daffern, Lawrence Jones and John Shine

with similar contingencies, such as in the community when the individual is electronically monitored or in other similar closely supervised circumstances.

The observations of these offence analogue behaviours within custodial settings are, in many instances, good indications that the root problems underlying the antisocial behaviours have remained intact. Without effective rehabilitation, when the 'appropriate' situations present themselves again and the sanctions and controls are lifted, such as when an individual is transferred to a less controlled low-security environment or released back to the community, the antisocial behaviour(s) will likely re-emerge. These analogues of criminal behaviours are idiosyncratic to the individual and are indications of the ongoing presence of offence-related problems. They can be considered as ongoing examples of 'crime in action' (so to speak) within custodial settings.

OFFENCE ANALOGUE BEHAVIOURS AND CRIMINOGENIC NEEDS

We have argued elsewhere that criminogenic needs or dynamic (changeable) risk factors linked to violence should be identified as treatment targets and can be used to guide risk reduction treatment (see Wong & Gordon, 2006; Wong et al., 2007). In this chapter, we introduce the term *offence analogue behaviours* (OABs) to specifically describe the here-and-now markers for the individual's criminogenic needs, that is, the current manifestations of the individual's problem areas within custodial settings. We propose that OABs are idiosyncratic to the individual, linked to the individual's criminogenic needs, and usually result from an interaction of the individual's criminogenic needs and the immediate environment. Whereas criminogenic needs are used to describe the individual's macrobehavioural problems as often seen in the general community, such as general antisocial attitudes (and associated criminal behaviours), the term 'OAB' is used to describe the individual's specific behavioural manifestations that are linked to his or her criminogenic needs as they may manifest within a controlled or custodial environment.

It is important to clearly identify an individual's OABs in custodial settings for a number of reasons. First, individuals who 'repackage' or temporarily suppress their antisocial behaviours while in custody are by no means problem-free, and they should not be misconstrued by staff as having been rehabilitated. The potential for institutional staff to be manipulated and conned into a false sense of comfort by some personality disordered and, in particular, highly psychopathic offenders has been repeatedly documented (for example, see Wong & Burt, 2007, pp. 477–8). In the community, psychopaths can behave like chameleons, changing their colours to suit the moment; just as much can be expected when they are in custody. Second, since OABs are closely linked to the individual's criminogenic needs, they can be considered as the person's here-and-now targets for risk reduction treatment. Also, recognizing and addressing OABs swiftly may avert problems spiralling out of control, thus resulting in improved risk management. Third, reduction in the intensity and frequency of OABs could be considered as one indicator of general improvement and, for those participating in risk reduction treatment, as possible indicators of treatment progress and risk reduction. Despite having participated in risk reduction treatment, those who continue to demonstrate significant OABs are likely the ones who are not responsive to treatment and correspondingly show little or no risk reduction. Our hypothesis is supported by results of a recent study showing that institutional misconducts/offences are significant predictors of recidivism in the community (French & Gendreau, 2006). Thus, a careful assessment of the change in OABs in relation to treatment involvement should provide some indication, *though not necessarily a complete picture*, of treatment progress. We revisit this point later.

INFORMING TREATMENT USING 'HERE-AND-NOW' BEHAVIOURS

The use of here-and-now behaviours to inform treatment is not a novel concept. For example, in many psychotherapeutic approaches, within the therapist–client relationship, expression of distress, the articulation of problem thoughts and the role-playing of problem behaviours are often encouraged so as to obtain information about the client's ongoing problems and general functioning and to formulate interventions (e.g. Callaghan et al., 1996; Kohlenberg & Tsai, 1994). Therapeutic community treatment models have also acknowledged the importance of addressing problematic behaviours as they manifest within the treatment milieu. The use of here-and-now behaviours to inform treatment is generally predicated on the notion that a client's behaviours during therapy can be observed and modified, and that his behaviours in the treatment context should be, at least in part, a facsimile of his behaviours in a wider context (Genders & Player, 1995).

Similarly, there is increasing recognition in the value of using here-and-now behaviours in assessment and interventions with forensic clients (see Daffern et al., 2007a, 2007b; Jones, 1997, 2000, 2001, 2004; Kennard, 2004; Neville et al., 2007). The term 'offence paralleling behaviours' (OPB; Jones, 1997, 2000, 2001, 2004) has been used to describe 'the pattern of behaviours, thoughts, and emotions leading up to the offence' (Jones, 2004, p. 39). In essence, OPB is similar to the concept of an offence chain or cycle, or the notion of 'behavioural attractor' (Carver & Scheier, 1998, cited in Jones, 2004, p. 39) and Birchwood's (1994) description of relapse signatures (cited in Jones, 2004, p. 39). Incorporating concepts from functional analytic psychotherapy (Kohlenberg & Tsai, 1994), the OPB framework places significant focus on the functional aspects of behaviour (Daffern et al., 2007b). Taken with the client's self-report and the third party observations by significant others and staff, Jones suggests that OPBs can be a very useful adjunct in case formulation and OPB-related work can be used to identify appropriate treatment interventions, evaluate treatment progress and assist with custodial decision-making (2004). Jones' OPB framework has also been used within prison-based therapeutic communities (Shine & Morris, 2000). Within a prison therapeutic community context, Lewis (1997) maintains that a key aspect of group therapy is working through re-enactments of repetitive and persistent patterns of thinking, feeling and behaving that could have originated in negative early relationships. Daffern et al. (2007b) suggest that interest in this framework may 'be related to its clinical utility, intuitive appeal, and face validity ... and lend credence to the daily observations of prisoners' behaviours by institutional staff' (Daffern et al., 2007b, pp. 265–6). However, Jones' (2004) definition of OPB may be 'too broad and potentially over-inclusive and this may result in inconsistent and idiosyncratic application of the framework that is incompatible with other risk assessment methods or validated treatment strategies' (Daffern et al., 2007a, p. 266). Also, Daffern et al. (2007b) concluded after reviewing the literature that there is no empirical evidence on the effectiveness of interventions based on the OPB conceptualization in reducing antisocial behaviours, criminality or violence.

OPB AND OAB: SIMILARITIES AND DIFFERENCES

There are obvious similarities between OABs and OPBs. Both are used to identify current behavioural patterns linked to past antisocial behaviours and offending. Current behavioural patterns may resemble previous incidents of violence and criminality explicitly or in more subtle ways, and such patterns could be used to inform case formulation and intervention. As well, multisource and convergent information should be used to determine the individual's OABs and OPBs.

However, there are important and significant differences in the theoretical underpinnings of OABs and OPBs. Jones (2004) draws on a number of theoretical frameworks to account for the offence process as depicted by the individual's OPBs. Jones appears to suggest that the interpersonal nature of the offending behaviours could be explained and understood, to a significant extent, within the interpersonal circumplex described by Blackburn (Blackburn, 1990; as cited by Jones, 2004). The attachment theory framework was also considered by Jones to be 'another useful framework, not inconsistent with the interpersonal paradigm ... [that can be used to explore the offender's] ... incompatible representation of the self and others described by Liotti (1999) ...' (Jones, 2004, p. 55). As well, Jones suggests that 'offence accounts can usefully be analyzed ...' (p. 55) within the Karpman triangle (Karpman, 1968, as cited in Jones, 2004) and the typology of roles described by narratologists (Greimas, 1966, 1970; Propp, 1968; Souriau, 1950; as cited in Jones, 2004). Of interest is that the theory of the Psychology of Criminal Conduct (PCC; Andrews & Bonta, 1994, 1998, 2003, 2007, 2010) was not used to explain OPBs. However, Jones did mention the PCC model as one of a number of models that could be used to account for 'developing repeating patterns of behaviour' (Jones, 2004, pp. 57–8). Whereas Andrews and Bonta argued strongly in favour of the careful and systematic assessment of offenders' risk, need and responsivity using valid and reliable risk assessment tools (see Andrews & Bonta, 1994, 1998, 2003, 2010), Jones (2004) suggested that 'the "what works" literature and third generation actuarial assessment strategies ... have been seriously compromised by their heavy use of reconviction as an outcome' since, by using reconviction as an outcome measure, it is estimated there is a large 'proportion of crime that (actuarial instruments such as) the PCL-R does not predict' (Jones, 2004, p. 37). It is not that actuarial instruments are not able to predict other criminal outcome measures such as unreported criminal acts or court proceedings, it is simply that these measures usually were *not chosen* by researchers as outcome measures to assess predictive efficacy because they are often difficult and very costly to collect reliably.[1] It is correct, as Jones suggested, that we should use actuarial risk assessment approaches but that consumers need to pay careful attention to what is being predicted when using actuarial tools to assess risk and predict recidivism.

In contrast, as discussed above, OABs are explicitly anchored to the theoretical underpinning of the PCC and the principles of effective correctional treatment, that is, the risk, need and responsivity principles (RNR; Andrews & Bonta, 1994, 1998, 2003, 2010). In brief, the PCC is based on a combination of social learning, cognitive–behavioural and social cognition theories. The PCC attributes the cause of antisocial behaviours to a combination of 'personal control through antisocial attitudes, interpersonal control through social support for crime provided by antisocial associates, nonmediated control established by a history of reinforcement of criminal behaviour, and/or personal predispositions' (Andrews & Bonta, 2003, p. 10). In assessing these factors, the origins and functionality of the antisocial tendencies also typically emerge. The use of RNR principles in designing and delivering correctional intervention has received considerable empirical support. RNR-based interventions have been found to be more effective in reducing recidivism than those that are not (see Andrews & Bonta, 2003, 2010; Andrews et al., 1990; Harland, 1995; McGuire, 1995; Motiuk & Serin, 2001). Recent writings, including meta-analytic and other reviews, have identified the 'risk-need-responsivity framework (Andrews & Bonta,

[1] When criminal justice outcomes such as institutional misconduct and parole violations or clinical variables programme drop out or treatment performance are used as outcome measures, actuarial tools such as the PCL-R, the HCR-20 or the violent risk scale were able to predict these higher base-rate events in contrast with lower base-rate reconvictions (see e.g. Dolan & Fullam, 1996; Hart et al., 2007; Olver & Wong, 2009; Serin, 1995; Shine & Hobson, 2001; Wong, 2009).

2003) [as] . . . currently the best validated model' (McGuire, 2008, p. 2591) for reducing aggression and violence.

The PCC essentially provides a theoretical basis for the identification of common criminogenic factors that can be targeted for treatment. According to this theoretical framework, effective correctional treatment should lead to positive changes in the criminogenic needs, resulting in risk reduction. Interventions directed at areas unrelated to recidivism (i.e. not criminogenically related) will not reduce the individual's recidivism risk.

Given that we define OABs as the here-and-now manifestation of the criminogenic needs of the individual, it follows that OABs should also be the logical theoretical extensions of criminogenic needs, from within the risk, need and responsivity framework. A key corollary of this theoretical link is that treatment directed at OABs, theoretically speaking at least, should result in the reduction of recidivism. On account of these theoretical and empirical linkages, OABs could be used, in particular, in custodial settings to guide the identification of the individual's here-and-now treatment targets linked to violence and criminality and, at least in part, to assess treatment change and risk reduction. In comparing the two theoretical frameworks, interventions based on OAB conceptualization would be guided by the RNR principles, whereas interventions based on OPB conceptualization, as suggested by Jones (2004), would be guided by functional analytic psychotherapy, interpersonal therapy or other similar approaches. However, as indicated above, there appears to be no empirical evidence to indicate that interventions based on the OPB framework are effective in reducing recidivism (see Daffern et al., 2007b).

Since there are significant differences in the theoretical underpinnings of OAB and OPB, we prefer to use the term 'OAB' rather than 'OPB' to describe the risk-need-responsivity principles and risk reduction treatment-based conceptualization of behaviours that are equivalent, similar or analogous to the pattern of offending behaviours.

LINKING OAB CHANGES TO TREATMENT CHANGES

As discussed above, the theory of PCC posits that the reduction in criminogenic need should result in the reduction of recidivism, and since OABs logically flow from criminogenic needs, it follows that a reduction in OABs should also lead to a reduction in recidivism. As such, reductions in OABs observed within institutional and custodial settings could be used as one of the indicators of risk reduction. In risk reduction treatment programmes, as treatment progress and improvements are made by participants, the intensity and frequency of occurrences of OABs are expected to decrease. An assessment of OAB changes in conjunction with programme participation could be used as an indicator of treatment progress. However, there is an important caveat.

The caveat is that the reduction of OABs may not *always* be a sufficiently accurate indication of the individual's true propensity for antisocial behaviour or his/her treatment progress. For example, triggers or challenges that usually precipitate the antisocial behaviours may be reduced or absent due to various reasons. For example, a wife abuser who is highly controlling towards women may appear to be quite well behaved in the absence of interactions with female staff. A man who had many problems with his peers may seem to be managing well when left alone or restricted to solitary confinement.

Daffern et al. (2007b) have suggested that treatment progress involves not only a reduction in OPBs but also an increase of prosocial alternative behaviours (PAB) other than those orchestrated purely for impression management or to avoid detection. We similarly posit that a more complete depiction of treatment progress should be represented by both an increase in positive or offence replacement behaviours (ORBs) and a decrease in OABs. In short, not doing the wrong things (fewer OABs) is good, but one has to do more of the right things instead (more ORBs). We define ORBs as the appropriate skills, usually newly acquired ones, an individual uses to manage past problems or situations that had culminated in criminality or violence. Observations of ORBs are particularly critical in controlled settings because of the many artificial situations that an individual may be subjected to that may inhibit and reduce problem behaviours.

Like OABs, ORBs should also be linked to the individual's criminogenic need areas and one size does not fit all. For example, what is often considered by custodial staff to be positive and constructive pursuits while incarcerated (and rightfully so), such as striving to improve one's education and work skills, may be risk-reducing for someone whose antisocial behaviours were related to a lack of steady employment but may be totally irrelevant for someone else who did not have such problems. Similarly, for someone with a passive-aggressive problem, who tended to suppress his anger and then act out violently, behaving assertively and standing his ground are his relevant ORBs, but not so for a psychopath who revels in showing off his verbal skills and having the last word. In fact, for the psychopath, the same behaviour may be his OAB.

Since treatment takes time, we suggest that in most cases the gradual decrease in OABs, together with a corresponding gradual increase in ORBs, should indicate positive treatment progress leading to risk reduction. Recent data suggest that an increase in ORBs together with reductions in OABs, as measured by the progression through the stages of change (as in the transtheoretical model of change, Prochaska & DiClemente, 1984; Prochaska et al., 1992), is linked to reductions in recidivism (Lewis et al., 2009). Further detail concerning this particular study is presented below. Further discussions on the covariations of OABs and ORBs and their theoretical implications will be elaborated more fully in a future paper. In this chapter, we focus on the discussion of OABs, links to criminogenic needs, and treatment progress and its measurement.

MEASUREMENT OF OABs

As noted above, concerns have been raised that the proposed OPB framework may be too broad, leading to too many OPBs being wrongly deemed to be offence-linked. As a result, individuals may be considered to be at a higher risk than warranted (Daffern et al., 2007b), that is, an overidentification of false positives. Daffern et al. then suggested that clinicians could use 'empirically validated methods . . . [as tools to] conduct systematic and objective . . . assessments . . . [to identify and monitor] OPBs and their functional equivalent pro-social variants . . .' (Daffern et al., 2007b, p. 271), thereby reducing subjectivity, observer biases and the reliance on fortuitous observations. Furthermore, clinicians may wish to try to predict which OPBs are likely to manifest as a part of the initial assessment process using analyses of the individual offence patterns and systematic observation of their behaviours in custody (Daffern et al., 2007b).

We have proposed that OABs are the here-and-now indications of criminogenic need, that is, dynamic or changeable risk factors. Reduction in the intensity and frequency of OABs should be one of the indicators of treatment progress. As suggested by Daffern et al. (2007b), systematic and reliable methods should be determined to identify and measure OABs and prosocial alternative behaviours or PABs.

For the purpose of illustration, the violence risk scale (VRS; Wong & Gordon, 1999–2003) will be used as a systematic and reliable method to identify dynamic risk factors and also as a means to measure treatment change (Wong & Gordon, 2006). We posit that, after a thorough review of the offender's criminal patterns and his community and institutional functioning, OABs and ORBs could be derived based on the dynamic risk factors and stage of change ratings that would be identified as part of the VRS assessment.

The VRS is an actuarial tool specifically developed to identify dynamic (criminogenic) risk factors linked to violence and to measure their change. The VRS uses six static and 20 dynamic variables to assess the risk of violence. It also uses a modified version of the stages of change (SOC) model to measure treatment change (Prochaska & DiClemente, 1984; Prochaska et al., 1992). Progression through the stages is translated into a quantitative measure of risk reduction for each criminogenic need area identified as a treatment target.[2] The VRS SOC ratings assess both the degree and the stability of treatment progress over time. The VRS has been shown to be a valid and reliable tool to assess the risk of violence (Wong & Gordon, 2006). Recent evidence also suggests that changes in the dynamic variables are linked to changes in violence based on a follow-up period of about five years in the community (Lewis et al., 2009).

Since OABs are the here-and-now markers of criminogenic needs, the VRS dynamic variables can be used to guide the identification of the individual's OABs. Changes in OABs also can be mapped onto the different SOC for the dynamic variables. The SOC ratings are largely based on whether the individual has been reducing OABs as well as implementing ORBs within the current and, if applicable, past controlled setting(s). The more the two dimensions are reduced and augmented, respectively, the more the individual would have progressed along the SOC. For example, those in the action stage of change would have far fewer and less serious OABs and more consistent ORBs than those in the preparation stage of change.

AN ILLUSTRATION OF ASSESSING OABs AND ORBs BASED ON VRS DYNAMIC FACTORS

One of the 20 VRS dynamic factors is *criminal attitudes* and the descriptions that characterize an individual with significant criminal attitudes is given below (Wong & Gordon, 2003, p. 36):

> The individual does not believe in the importance of prosocial behaviour and rules. Such an attitude is evidenced by the minimization of the need for maintaining law and order in society, repeatedly trying to find ways to circumvent laws or established rules, justifying and rationalizing antisocial behaviours, or refusing to accept responsibility for one's actions. Regular law-abiding ways of living may be considered by such individuals to be boring or beneath them. The prosocial and law-abiding world tends to be very alien to them. The individual's criminal attitudes facilitate the use of violence.

The above general description of Criminal Attitudes provides exemplars to illustrate the construct underlying this dynamic variable. These descriptions however are not exhaustive, and considerable variations are expected on how the characteristics may manifest among individuals. Some of the most frequently observed OABs that correspond to *criminal attitudes* are noted in the OAB example provided (see page 178); however, any additional/alternative OABs that the individual offender presents should also be captured using the general description exemplars as a guide. Similarly, identification of ORBs can be derived from the SOC maintenance stage exemplar, set forth in the VRS manual (Wong & Gordon, 2003), which delineates prosocial, risk reduction descriptors[3] for each of the VRS dynamic factors. Within a defined assessment period,

[2] The exception is the progress from precontemplation (denial) to contemplation (no denial) stage indicating only acknowledgement of problems but no behavioural change and therefore no risk reduction.

[3] Characteristics such as 'The individual consistently respects the rights and the needs of others. The individual actively challenges criminal attitudes that support the use of violence ...' (Wong & Gordon, 2003, p. 37) and so forth.

OABs and ORBs can be monitored to determine if any changes over the course of treatment have occurred. A rating guide for the identification and monitoring of OABs and ORBs has been developed and is available from the authors. An excerpt of the guide is provided below for illustration purposes.

Example of OABs that correspond to criminal attitudes:[4]

- Maintains attitudes that support aggression and violence
- Refuses to abide by or tries to circumvent institutional rules and policies (overtly or covertly)
- Acts as mouthpiece for anti-authority factions within the setting; plays the role of jailhouse lawyer
- Maintains anti-authority viewpoints and challenges institutional staff (overtly or covertly)
- Subscribes to the 'con-code': minimizes, justifies or rationalizes rule-breaking or antisocial behaviours

Additional OABs:

- ____________________________________
- ____________________________________
- ____________________________________

Examples of ORBs that pertain to Criminal Attitudes are listed below; additional/alternate ORBs should also be listed.

- Respects the rights and the needs of others
- Abides by rules and regulations rather than trying to break or circumvent them
- Actively challenges criminal attitudes and 'con-code' tendencies
- Accepts responsibility for actions
- Uses relevant skills to deal with conflicts and challenges (e.g. resolving differences appropriately, interpreting rules in socially appropriate manner)
- Avoids high-profile prisoners known to be confrontational with staff

Additional ORBs:

- ____________________________________
- ____________________________________
- ____________________________________

To illustrate the practical application of the OAB assessment in determining relevant OABs, consider the case of Mr Smith.[5]

During Mr Smith's pretreatment VRS assessment, a number of criminogenic factors were assessed as significant. File and interview information indicate that he holds strong anti-authority beliefs and consistently disregards rules and regulations. He regards socially appropriate behaviours as stupid and something that he does not need to pay attention to. He rationalizes and justifies antisocial behaviours, uses crime and violence to meet his needs, and even encourages his peers to join his cause. He also has problems managing his emotions which have often led to violence, in particular, when he feels disrespected, betrayed, rejected or anxious. Mr Smith

[4] General guidelines and corresponding OABs and ORBs for additional criminogenic factors are included in the rating guide available from the authors.

[5] Although the example is based on a real clinical case, substantial changes have been made to render it unrecognizable.

often relies on alcohol and the abuse of prescription medication to cope with his distress. He also isolates himself and ruminates over his predicaments which increase his distress. With the confluence of feeling disrespected, betrayed, rejected and anxious while being alone and having nowhere and no one to turn to, he has committed serious violent acts on number of occasions. During his incarceration, at times he has refused to participate and also has failed several urinalysis for banned substances.

He has shown a number of problematic behaviours since his admission to a treatment programme approximately one month ago. For example, he often monopolizes group therapy time while attempting to redirect the focus of the group towards his own issues. He questions the need for the group to start so early, complains about the group and the programme being too long, and the need to do so much homework. He frequently leaves group, claiming an urgent need to use the toilet. On more than a few occasions, staff members have detected a strong smell of smoke immediately after he used the toilet facility, a non-smoking area. When confronted, he repeatedly denies smoking, claiming someone else was smoking there before him. He also complains about the lack of time for recreational and leisure activities, claiming he has the right to have more time. He makes fun of 'square John' work, saying it is boring. He often makes derogatory comments about the 'system' and maintains that his sentence was unjust and the judge was overreacting. He often attempts to rally support from his peers. Early in the programme, he received a letter from his common law wife who told him that she had met someone else and could not wait for his release. Immediately afterwards, he tore up the letter and threw it in the garbage bin, kicking it as he went by. When confronted by staff, he yelled, 'Mind your f—ing business'. He then proceeded to his room and started smashing things. He subsequently isolated himself, refused to attend group or talk to staff or peers for several days, claiming he was ill. A few days later, he was found with a 'brew' in his room during a routine search.

Once Mr Smith's criminogenic needs have been determined using the VRS, the next step is to identify his corresponding OABs. For the purpose of illustration, only three of 20 VRS dynamic risk factors are examined: criminal attitudes, emotional control and substance abuse. In practice, OABs are determined, based on information obtained through a comprehensive assessment of the individual's personal, interpersonal and circumstantial factors, as well as environmental contexts. In this example, corresponding OABs were derived based on the above brief case description. For the purpose of brevity, only OABs are provided; corresponding ORBs for Mr Smith should also be determined.

Criminal attitudes:

- Maintains attitudes that support aggression and violence
- Breaks ward rules repeatedly after many warnings, such as making excuses to leave treatment groups
- Acts as mouthpiece for other anti-authority peers
- Undermines lawful way of making a living; thinks that law-abiding activities, such as maintaining a steady job, are just stupid and there are easier ways to make a living
- Subscribes to the 'con-code': minimizes, justifies or rationalizes rule-breaking and/or antisocial behaviours

Emotional control:

- Frequent angry outbursts directed at staff, peers and objects when feeling rejected, betrayed or treated unjustly
- Can become highly reactive when emotionally distressed: resorts to yelling and throwing things
- Isolates and ruminates about reasons for his distress

Substance abuse:

- Drug or alcohol use
- Hoarding 'brew'-making ingredients
- Ongoing cravings and attempts to 'self-medicate' (e.g. muscling peers for their prescribed medications)
- Positive urinalyses or refusal to be tested

The above OABs are clearly applicable to Mr Smith, very specific and relevant to him at this time in his treatment, and are closely linked to the three criminogenic or dynamic risk factors within the VRS. The three dynamic risk factors are obviously his 'macro' treatment targets with the OABs being more idiosyncratic and 'micro' behavioural manifestations of those targets. Both the treatment targets and the OABs can be shared with Mr Smith in a collaborative treatment approach such that both staff and the participant have a very clear appreciation of the problem areas and the outcomes expected, that is, the ORBs. The systematic determination of OABs early on in a treatment programme can alert and prepare staff to manage such behaviours and start influencing the client's offence-related tendencies from the very beginning of treatment. Staff can continue to monitor the OABs and ORBs as indicators of Mr Smith's progress in treatment. His list of OABs and ORBs can be amended as he progresses in treatment: some may be deleted while others are added as required.

There are some important points to note regarding the collection of 'data' to identify, monitor and amend OABs and ORBs. Given that both must be linked to the individual's criminogenic needs, the use of generic indicators of positive treatment change, such as regular and punctual group attendance and completion of homework assignments, is usually not specific enough for the individual. For example, a psychopath, incarcerated for committing fraud in an elaborate and complex scam, would likely have little or no difficulty in attending, or saying the right thing, in groups or completing required homework. For such an individual, using indicators of treatment progress such as homework completion or group attendance is probably irrelevant and erroneous. Along this same line, evaluations of treatment impact, that is, presence or absence of OABs and ORBs, should occur over time and place and not be restricted to time spent in 'formal' treatment interventions such as treatment groups. Observations based only on formal treatment activities may be highly biased and selective as clients usually spend less than 10% of their waking hours in formal treatment activities.[6] Using the array of day-to-day living situations and circumstances, there are a greater number of opportunities for the individual to practise what has been preached in the treatment room and for multistaff observations. For offenders unwilling to 'walk the treatment talk', one would anticipate very few ORBs and many more OABs despite efforts to fake good in formal treatment situations.

SUMMARY AND CONCLUSIONS

To reduce the risk of violence and criminality, there is a need for evidenced-based, clear, transparent and theoretically derived treatment targets for intervention. The need is even more acute within a custodial setting as misbehaviours may be 'repackaged' within a more controlled custodial environment. We proposed that OABs are the candidates for such treatment targets. The theoretical underpinning of OABs, that is the psychology of criminal conduct and the RNR,

[6] Two hours of treatment time per day over five working days compared to 16 waking hours per day over seven days.

clearly addresses offending, offending behaviour and the reduction of reoffending. The VRS, used to guide the identification of OABs, is also closely linked to RNR and possesses acceptable psychometric properties. OABs are behaviours that, potentially, could be influenced by therapeutic approaches, such as cognitive behavioural therapy, which has been shown to be efficacious for the treatment of offenders (Andrews et al., 1990; French & Gendreau, 2006). There is now preliminary evidence that changes in OABs and ORBs are linked to reduction in recidivism (Lewis et al., 2009). Briefly, in a sample of treated high-risk personality-disordered offenders, progression in the stages of change, which reflects reductions in OABs and increases in ORBs, was linked to reduction in violent recidivism in a six-year follow-up in the community. In addition to treating OABs to reduce recidivism in the long-term, identifying and intervening OABs for internal security reasons should also enhance short- to medium-term risk management within institutional settings. For example, information on the presence and changes to OABs should be useful for decisions related to the security placement and transfer of offenders and also to assist in subsequent rehabilitative recommendations. Rather than being restricted to formal treatment domains and personnel, the monitoring of OABs and ORBs should take place over time and contexts and involve a variety of institutional staff. Such an approach should provide more reliable and valid assessments of whether the individual is 'ready and willing to walk the talk' and can apply treatment learning to the management of analogous risk-related situations and circumstances.

REFERENCES

Andrews, D.A. & Bonta, J. (1994). *The Psychology of Criminal Conduct*. Cincinnati: OH: Anderson Publishing.

Andrews, D.A. & Bonta, J. (1998). *The Psychology of Criminal Conduct* (2nd edition). Cincinnati, OH: Anderson.

Andrews, D.A. & Bonta, J. (2003). *The Psychology of Criminal Conduct* (3rd edition). Cincinnati, OH: Anderson.

Andrews, D.A. & Bonta, J. (2007). *The Psychology of Criminal Conduct* (4th edition). Cincinnati, OH: Anderson Publishing.

Andrews, D.A. & Bonta, J. (2010). *The Psychology of Criminal Conduct* (5th edition). Cincinnati, OH: Anderson Publishing.

Andrews, D.A., Zinger, I., Hoge, R.D., Bonta, J., Gendreau, P. & Cullen, F.T. (1990). Does correctional treatment work? A clinically relevant and psychologically informed meta-analysis. *Criminology, 28*, 369–404.

Birchwood, M. (1994). Cognitive early intervention. In G. Haddock & P. Slade (Eds), *Cognitive Behavioural Approaches to Schizophrenia*. London: Routledge.

Blackburn, R. (1990). Treatment of the psychopathic offender. In K. Howells & C. Hollin (Eds), *Clinical Approaches to Working with Mentally Disordered and Sexual Offenders. Issues in Criminological and Legal Psychology*, Vol. *16* (pp. 54–66). Leicester: British Psychological Society.

Callaghan, G.M., Naugle, A.E. & Follette, W.C. (1996). Useful constructions of the client–therapist relationship. *Psychotherapy, 33*(3), 381–90.

Carver, C.S. & Scheier, M.F. (1998). *On the Self-Regulation of Behaviour*. Cambridge: Cambridge University Press.

Daffern, M., Ferguson, M., Ogloff, J., Thomson, L. & Howells, K. (2007a). Appropriate treatment targets or products of a demanding environment? The relationship between aggression in a forensic psychiatric hospital with aggressive behaviour preceding admission and violent recidivism. *Psychology, Crime and Law, 13*(5), 431–41.

Daffern, M., Jones, L., Howells, K., Shine, J. Mikton, C. & Tunbridge, V. (2007b). Editorial: refining the definition of offence paralleling behaviour. *Criminal Behaviour and Mental Health, 17*, 265–73.

Dolan, D. & Fullam, R. (2007). The validity of the Violence Risk Scale second edition (VRS-2) in a British forensic inpatient sample. *Journal of Forensic Psychiatry and Psychology, 18*, 381–93.

French, S.A. & Gendreau, P. (2006). Reducing prison misconduct: what works! *Criminal Justice and Behavior, 33*(2), 185–218.

Genders, E. & Player, E. (1995). *Grendon: A Study of a Therapeutic Prison*. Oxford: Clarendon Press.

Gendreau, P., Little, T. & Goggin, C. (1996). A meta-analysis of the predictors of adult offender recidivism: what works! *Criminology, 34*, 575–607.

Greimas, A.J. (1966). *Semantique Structurale*. Paris: Larousse.

Greimas, A.J. (1970). *Du Sens*. Paris: Seuil.

Harland, A.T. (Ed.). (1995). *Choosing Correctional Options that Work: Defining the Demand and Evaluating the Supply*. Thousand Oaks, CA: Sage Publications.

Hart, S.D., Kropp, P.R. & Hare, R.D. (1988). Performance of psychopaths following conditional release from prison. *Journal of Consulting and Clinical Psychology, 56*, 227–32.

Jones, L.F. (1997). Developing models for managing treatment integrity and efficacy in a prison based TC: the Max Glatt Centre. In E. Cullen, L. Jones & R. Woodward (Eds), *Therapeutic Communities for Offenders*. Chichester: Wiley.

Jones, L.F. (2000). *Identifying and Working with Clinically Relevant Offence Paralleling Behaviour*. Paper presented at Division of Clinical Psychology, Forensic Special Interest Group, Nottinghamshire.

Jones, L.F. (2001). *Anticipating Offence Paralleling Behaviour*. Paper presented at Division of Forensic Psychology Conference, Birmingham.

Jones, L.F. (2004). Offence paralleling behaviour (OPB) as a framework for assessment and intervention with offenders. In A. Needs & G. Towl (Eds), *Applying Psychology to Forensic Practice* (pp. 34–63). Oxford: BPS Blackwell.

Karpman, S.B. (1968). Fairy tales and script drama analysis. *Transactional Analysis Bulletin, 7*, 39–43.

Kennard, D. (2004). The therapeutic community as an adaptable treatment modality across different settings. *Psychiatric Quarterly, 75*, 295–307.

Kohlenberg, R.J. & Tsai, M. (1994). Functional analytic psychotherapy: a radical behavioural approach to treatment and integration. *Journal of Psychotherapy Integration, 4*, 175–201.

Lewis, K., Olver, M. & Wong, S.C.P. (2009). The Violence Risk Scale: validity, measurement of treatment changes and violent recidivism in a high risk and personality disordered sample of male offenders. Manuscript submitted.

Lewis, P.S. (1997). Context for change (whilst consigned and confined): a challenge for systematic thinking. In E. Cullen, L. Jones & R. Woodward (Eds), *Therapeutic Communities for Offenders* (pp. 71–89). London: Wiley.

Liotti, G. (1999). Disorganization of attachment as a model for understanding dissociative psychopathology. In J. Solomon & C. George (Eds), *Attachment Disorganisation*. New York: Guilford Press.

McGuire, J. (Ed.). (1995). *What Works: Reducing Reoffending, Guidelines from Research and Practice*. Chichester: Wiley & Sons.

McGuire, J. (2008). A review of effective interventions for reducing aggression and violence. *Philosophical Transactions of the Royal Society B, 363*, 2483–622.

Motiuk, L.L. & Serin, R.C. (2001). *Compendium 2000 on Effective Correctional Programming*. Ottawa, ON: Ministry of Supply and Services Canada.

Neville, L., Miller, S. & Fritzon, K. (2007). Understanding change in a therapeutic community: an action systems approach. *Journal of Forensic Psychiatry and Psychology, 18*(2), 181–203.

Olver, M. & Wong, S.C.P. (2009). Therapeutic responses of psychopathic sexual offenders: treatment attrition, therapeutic change, and long term recidivism. *Journal of Consulting and Clinical Psychology, 77*(2), 328–36.

Prochaska, J.O. & DiClemente, C.C. (1984). Toward a comprehensive model of change. In W.R. Miller & N. Heather (Eds), *Treating Addictive Behaviours: Processes of Change*. New York: Plenum Press.

Prochaska, J.O., DiClemente, C.C. & Norcross, J.C. (1992). In search of how people change: applications to the addictive behaviors. *American Psychologist, 47*, 1102–14.

Serin, R.C. (1996). Violent recidivism in criminal psychopaths. *Law and Human Behavior, 20*, 207–17.

Shine, J. & Morris, M. (2000). Addressing criminogenic needs in a prison therapeutic community. *Therapeutic Communities, 21*(3), 197–218.

Shine, J.H. & Hobson, J.A. (2000). Institutional behaviour and time in treatment among psychopaths admitted to a prison-based therapeutic community. *Medicine, Science, and the Law, 40*, 327–35.

Souriau, E. (1950). *Les Deux Cent Mille Situations Dramatiques*. Paris: Flammarion.

Wong, S.C.P. (1984). *Criminal and Institutional Behaviors of Psychopaths*. (Programs Branch User Report). Ottawa, ON: Ministry of the Solicitor General of Canada.

Wong, S.C.P. & Burt, G. (2007). The heterogeneity of incarcerated psychopaths: differences in risk, need, recidivism and management approaches. In J. Yuille & H. Herve (Eds), *The Psychopath: Theory, Research and Practice* (pp. 461–84). Mahwah, NJ: Erlbaum.

Wong, S.C.P. & Gordon, A.E. (1999–2003). *The Violence Risk Scale*. Unpublished manuscript, Saskatoon, Saskatchewan.

Wong, S.C.P. & Gordon, A.E. (2006). The validity and reliability of the Violence Risk Scale: a treatment-friendly violence risk assessment tool. *Psychology, Public Policy, and Law*, *12*(3), 279–309.

Wong, S.C.P., Gordon, A. & Gu, D. (2007). Assessment and treatment of violence-prone forensic clients: an integrated approach. *British Journal of Psychiatry*, *190*(Suppl.), s66–74.

Chapter 11

INSTITUTIONAL OFFENCE BEHAVIOUR MONITORING AS AN AID TO COMMUNITY SUPERVISION OF HIGH-RISK OFFENDERS: EXPERIENCE FROM MULTI-AGENCY PUBLIC PROTECTION ARRANGEMENTS

CYNTHIA MCDOUGALL

Centre for Criminal Justice Economics and Psychology and the Department of Psychology, University of York, UK

DOMINIC PEARSON

Durham Tees Valley Probation Trust, County Durham, UK

ROGER BOWLES

Centre for Criminal Justice Economics & Psychology, University of York, UK

JUDITH CORNICK

HMP Acklington, Northumberland, UK

This chapter describes the Multi-Agency Public Protection Arrangements (MAPPA), which provide a framework for supervision of high-risk offenders in the community in England and Wales. It illustrates from research evidence how knowledge of prison behaviour has the potential to improve the effectiveness of supervision in the community, and describes a project, ADViSOR, designed to systematically provide information on observed behaviour in prison to offender managers in the community. The method of evaluation of the project, including analysis of costs and benefits, is outlined, and ethical issues are discussed.

BACKGROUND

The process of assessing risk of reoffending has undergone a number of transformations in the last two decades and has developed into a sophisticated, theoretically driven and

Offence Paralleling Behaviour: A Case Formulation Approach to Offender Assessment and Intervention Edited by Michael Daffern, Lawrence Jones and John Shine

research-based methodology. It has long been recognized that the original concept of clinical judgement as the most appropriate means of risk assessment is seriously flawed, and that clinical judgement is susceptible to numerous biases (Blackburn, 1993; Hall, 1987; Tversky & Kahneman, 1974). Subsequent actuarial approaches, derived from analysis of large offender datasets, have demonstrated robust predictive validity, regularly providing evidence that statistically identified historical data are the best predictors of future reoffending (Grove & Meehl, 1996; Maden et al., 2006; Monahan et al., 2001; Quinsey et al., 1998). It has however been recognized that although actuarial assessment processes are reliable predictors of reoffending, they do not allow for any improvement to occur (Nuffield, 1989); history remains history and is unchangeable. Age at first offence or previous violent offences, for example, remain on record. Therefore, any interventions aimed at lowering an offender's risk levels do not diminish the actuarial measure, and the offender maintains or increases his or her original risk level (Andrews, 1989). A third generation of risk assessment tools has since been developed which incorporates the historically based actuarial measure, and additionally provides a structured clinical assessment, in order to reduce the judgement biases which previously beset clinical assessment methods (Blackburn, 2000). Based on research evidence of the dynamic factors most associated with reoffending (Bonta, 1996), clinicians are guided towards the kinds of questions that should be asked and incorporated into a clinical assessment. One of the best examples of a structured assessment tool is the HCR-20 which, as its acronym implies, includes historical, clinical and risk management information (Webster et al., 1995). The predictive validity of this structured assessment instrument has been found to be sound (Belfrage et al., 2000; Douglas et al., 1999a, 1999b; Gray et al., 2003, 2008) and allows a combination of historical and clinical assessments, leading to focused risk management of offenders on the basis of this framework of evidence.

An assessment methodology that has been somewhat neglected in the development of risk assessment tools is behavioural risk assessment. Although behavioural assessment is closely associated with functional analysis assessment techniques (Owens & Ashcroft, 1982) and the behavioural diagnosis model (Kanfer & Saslow, 1969), nowhere has observation of behaviour been systematically incorporated into a comprehensive risk assessment protocol, and this is long overdue.

BEHAVIOUR AS A PREDICTOR OF RISK

Over some years, past behaviour has been identified as the best predictor of future behaviour and a number of studies have demonstrated the links (Bonta et al., 1998; Borum, 1996; Farrington et al., 1998; Mossman, 1994). Although McDougall and colleagues (Clark et al., 1993; McDougall & Clark, 1991) identified and demonstrated experimentally that the underlying patterns of offence behaviour were linked to later prison behaviour, to the authors' knowledge, no one has yet demonstrated the continuity of the specific offence behaviour through the prison sentence and after release. The nearest examples of continuity from prison sentence to release have come from Hill (1985), who showed that disciplinary behaviour in prison was a strong predictor of reoffending behaviour after release, and Zamble and Porporino (1990), who showed in a longitudinal study that prisoners responded to problems inside prison as they did to problems outside, and that some behavioural measures predicted future offending. The paucity of research on behavioural risk assessment is an omission, particularly since behaviour in the present and the future could be seen as an extension of the behaviour in the past, which makes the actuarial measures so powerful in predicting future behaviour.

A positive aspect of using behaviour as a predictor is that behaviour is specific and reduces the amount of subjectivity and potential cognitive bias that exists in clinical interpretations, including judgements that are anchored in theory. Violent behaviour in an offence followed by violent behaviour in prison leaves little scope for doubt about the consistency of the behaviour. This contradicts the view of other authors that behavioural risk prediction is too open to cognitive bias (Towl & Crighton, 1995).

Contemporaneously with the development of risk assessment methods, the social demand for reliable risk assessment has also increased. The number of people imprisoned in the United Kingdom per head of the general population far outstrips that ratio in the rest of Europe (Walmsley, 2007), and hence there is pressure to reduce the UK prison population. Additionally, deficiencies in risk assessment processes have been illustrated in some high-profile cases of offenders who have been released from prison, only to go on to commit further serious offences (Her Majesty's Inspectorate of Probation – HMIP, 2006). In order to manage high-risk offenders effectively in the community, our risk assessment processes must be shown to provide defensible and credible approaches to minimizing risk and protecting the public, and these assessment processes must be applicable to the most serious offenders. MAPPA have been put in place for just this purpose.

MULTI-AGENCY PUBLIC PROTECTION ARRANGEMENTS

MAPPA have been in place in England and Wales since 2001 following the Criminal Justice and Court Services Act (2000). This placed a duty on the Police and the National Probation Service to work together to manage the risks posed by sexual, violent and other dangerous offenders in the community. The Criminal Justice Act (2003) was built on the earlier requirements and included provisions to make the prison service part of the 'responsible authority'. The prison service's role is critical to accessing information regarding the offender's behaviour in custody, information on his/her engagement in accredited programmes and other activities, and preparation for release into the community.

The prison service is required to ensure that information is shared with the community-based offender manager and is incorporated into the sentence planning process as part of 'end-to-end' offender management (HM Prison Service, 2004). The responsible authorities have a duty to ensure that any risks to the public identified pre- and post-release are managed robustly at the necessary level of MAPPA management.

Offenders eligible for MAPPA are registered sex offenders and violent offenders sentenced to 12 or more months' custody. MAPPA may also include offenders subject to hospital orders with restrictions, adult offenders that have already been formally cautioned for their behaviour, or those convicted of an offence in a MAPPA category while abroad. The responsibility for identifying MAPPA eligible offenders falls to each agency that has a statutory role in their supervision or care (National Offender Manager Service, 2009).

Strategies to address identified risks must be managed effectively across agencies. Level 1 cases, which are considered to present the lowest risk of reoffending, are likely to be managed involving liaison between at least police and probation service managers. Level 2 cases, which are considered to present a greater risk of harm, will involve regular multi-agency meetings of representatives of all involved agencies chaired by a senior manager in the probation service. Level 3 cases, which present the greatest risk of causing serious harm, again involve regular multi-agency meetings but will be chaired at Probation Director level. Agencies represented will be the police, probation service and prison service, and may include representatives from local authority social care services, health and mental health services, education, housing, employment, youth offending teams and victim support agencies. These MAPPA levels of offender management require the most accurate and relevant risk information possible on the offender under consideration.

The prison service additionally has a duty to contribute information to the Violent offender and Sex Offender Register (ViSOR), although creation and maintenance of the ViSOR record is generally the responsibility of the police and probation staff. ViSOR is a national secure database developed by the police and the national offender management service to help share confidential information and intelligence in relation to individual sexual and violent offenders.

MAPPA Supervision

The magnitude of the task of supervising some of our most violent and serious sex offenders should not be underestimated. Although communication between prisons and the community agencies and advice on risk management has greatly improved, there are still gaps in the information that is made available. Routinely, offender managers receive information from prisons on an individual's response to offending behaviour programmes, and they will be told about attitudes and relationships with family, friends and fellow prisoners. They will also hear about high-profile risk behaviours that may occur, for example, security issues such as attempting to contact a victim of their crime. What is missing, however, is routine information about offence-related behaviour in prison, which provides crucial insight into whether the offender is trying to change his or her offending behaviour or whether he or she is continuing with the patterns of behaviour that might lead to future offending. The majority of cases that are considered in MAPPA are serious sexual offences. This raises the question as to how an offender with such a strong sexual offending drive manages this sexual drive whilst in prison. The offender's sexual drive is not left behind with his or her property when he or she is received into prison, so what happens to it? Is this drive being managed in a prosocial way with offence behaviour being moderated whilst in prison or are deviant interests being pursued in prison providing evidence of a likely continuation of offending? This is valuable information from which to draw conclusions about the offender's motivation and capacity for controlling his offending behaviour. The ADViSOR project, described below, was initially a local attempt between HMP Acklington and Durham Probation Area to explore whether systematic provision of information on prison behaviour using the police ViSOR database (hence A-D-ViSOR) could add value to the supervision of risk-related behaviour and to the development of interventions that might assist those offenders who have the motivation to change.

DEVELOPMENT OF BEHAVIOURAL RISK ASSESSMENT

Although the cross-situational consistency of behaviours has been demonstrated by Hill (1985) and Zamble and Porporino (1990), relatively little use of this knowledge has been made in the supervision of offenders in the community. Within closed institutions, there has been much more interest in behavioural risk assessment development, primarily because there are limited means of assessing offenders who are spending long periods in custody. Offenders in prisons who have committed serious offences are interviewed in depth on numerous occasions by a variety of interviewers, and there is the danger that they will begin to produce learned responses to the repetitive questions from different interviewers over numerous interview occasions. Changes in psychometric measures of attitudes and emotional control can be used as a means of evaluation, but these are self-report measures and can only be viewed as interim measures which may or may not correlate with future actual behaviours.

It was the lack of adequate measures of change in level of risk in life sentence prisoners, and the observation that index offence behaviours emerged within the prison environment (McDougall & Clark, 1991), that prompted the experimental study of consistency in behaviour from offence behaviour to behaviour in prison (Clark et al., 1993). Although some studies had demonstrated consistency of behaviour across different environments, and disruptive institutional behaviour had been shown to predict future reoffending, the proposition of similarities in the nature of offence behaviour and subsequent prison behaviour had not previously been tested. The Clark et al. study sought to examine whether anecdotally observed offence-related behaviour could be consistently identified by independent observers and whether these behaviours could be linked to index offence behaviour. In the Clark et al. study in HMP Wakefield, two experienced prison psychologists independently examined the offence behaviour of life sentence prisoners from detailed police and court records, using a process similar to a functional analysis paradigm (Owens & Ashcroft, 1982), and predicted how the offence behaviour might be manifested in prison. Further, two experienced psychologists, who did not have knowledge of the offence behaviour, independently examined officer reports of prison behaviour, prison records, security information and other written information sources. They were asked to extract examples of reported behaviour and not to discriminate between positive and negative behaviours. In the final stage of assessment, the predicted behaviours were then compared with actual behaviours by three different experienced psychologists who did not work in HMP Wakefield. Accuracy of prediction was found to be greater for the sample of prisoners under study (65%), when compared to a control sample group of life sentence prisoners matched with a random selection of the behaviours (20%). These results were statistically significantly different. A further study (McDougall et al., 1995) described a process of operationalizing this risk assessment process so that changes in level of risk could be monitored by officers through behaviour monitoring in prisons that housed life sentence prisoners. This Wakefield risk assessment model was used in the prison service as the main means of life sentence prisoner assessment for some years, prior to a review of the life sentence planning system as a whole (HM Inspectorate of Prisons and Probation, 1999) and revision of the system.

In 1997, an offence paralleling behaviour model was developed by Jones (1997), which identified offence-related behaviour as an offence chain, with the potential for the chain to be broken or adapted by intervention. It was proposed that, if the links between thoughts, feelings and behaviours in the offence-chain could be adapted in a pro-social way, then the patient or offender could be assumed to have a reduced risk of reoffending. Jones (2004) has since distinguished offence paralleling behaviours from offence behaviours (i.e. specific offences committed in a closed establishment), detection evasion behaviours (i.e. covering up an offence by other apparently more pro-social behaviours) and positive behaviours, which could be described as pro-social (i.e. instead of punching an individual, the patient might choose to punch a wall). The development of the offence paralleling behaviour model, with its emphasis on links between thoughts, feelings and behaviours, makes the process more amenable to cognitive-behavioural intervention and evaluation of the impact of an intervention on future risk.

Community Risk Management

Both the Wakefield risk assessment model (McDougall et al., 1995) and the offence paralleling behaviour model (Jones, 1997) have attempted to monitor changes in risk behaviour of offenders whilst in custody. However, neither of the models has explored the utility of the models after release. This is an important development phase and is particularly valuable in provision of risk information to MAPPA. Other models have however taken account of risk management in the community.

The HCR-20 (Webster et al., 1995) and the SONAR (Hanson & Harris, 2000) have both attempted to provide valid risk management guidance based on research evidence. Studies of the HCR-20's predictive validity have shown promising results both for assessments of inpatient violence (e.g. Gray et al., 2003; Grevatt et al., 2004) and for assessments of community violent recidivism (e.g. Belfrage et al., 2000; Doyle & Dolan, 2006; Gray et al., 2008). Hanson and Harris (2000) have attempted to identify acute risk factors in the community on the basis of known research evidence on sex offenders, and proposed a set of acute risk factors, such as distress or anger, which were associated with the timing of reoffending. Following a prospective test of their risk assessment methodology, Hanson et al. (2007) concluded that although their measures collectively added predictive power above and beyond that provided by the best static risk assessment, the 'acute' factors did not reliably relate to the timing of reoffending.

Neither of the above frameworks specifically includes previous offence behaviour as a risk indicator. The ADViSOR project attempts to explore the value of knowledge of offence-related prison behaviour, such as seeking to make contact with the children of other offenders, being in possession of photographs of potential victims, and inappropriate behaviour with female staff, as possible risk indicators. The project aims to enhance risk management by identifying risk behaviours that relate to the individual offender.

THE ADViSOR PROJECT

As mentioned above, detailed information about offenders while in prison is passed on to multi-agency public protection units in their regular meetings. This can include specific information on offence-related behaviour, where it has come to the notice of the offender supervisor, and is considered to be of value to the offender managers in the community. Currently, a system does not exist for this information to be collected from wing staff on a regular basis and some behavioural information may be missed. The ADViSOR project was set up by the National Probation Service, County Durham, (now Durham Tees Valley Probation Trust) and HMP Acklington in order to systematically collect information from prison staff on relevant offence-related behaviours to inform offender supervisors and to assist community offender managers in planning public protection arrangements for offenders on release, with the ultimate intention of populating the ViSOR database with risk-relevant behavioural information from prisons.

The primary aim of ADViSOR is effective risk management through the MAPPA. A secondary aim is to seek to engender self-control behaviours in offenders, where the offender is motivated to cooperate, building on observed positive behaviours in prison (which Jones, 2004, would categorize as positive pro-social behaviours). The current intervention builds on an earlier project, which was aimed at operationalizing psychological risk assessment (McDougall et al., 1995), and does so by involving wing prison officers, offender supervisors in prison, education and instructional staff, officers supervising visits and security staff. It is recognized that prison staff are the first line of observation of offender behaviour, and it is important to involve them in the public protection process.

The Design of ADViSOR

The design of the ADViSOR project was a consultative process, as it is acknowledged that such a project can only succeed with the cooperation and commitment of those involved in the process.

The project began with consultation of offender supervisors, some of whom had previously worked as wing prison officers, about the kinds of offence-related behaviours that could be observed on wings. Offender supervisors confirmed that there was evidence of offence-related behaviours which were known to wing staff, but that there was no system in place for this kind of information to be recorded and communicated. Examples of the behaviours that wing staff and offender supervisors had noted were behaviours related to offending; for example, choosing to sit near children during visits, having photographs of children in their possession, exchanging depositions about their and others' offences, making contact outside of the prison with women with children, seeking to join fan clubs, maintaining correspondence networks with released sex offenders, grooming of prisoners and/or staff, and sexual bartering and coercion. This is just a selection from a wide range of behaviours, some of which involve actual offences such as rape and physical intimidation.

Although previous studies, which require behavioural observation, have used prison behaviour checklists (Cooke, 1998; McDougall et al., 1995), and indeed a behaviour checklist is used in evaluation of prison offending behaviour programmes (Nugent et al., 2005), offender supervisors recommended that we should not use checklists. In their view, checklists were rarely completed conscientiously, especially when repeated over long periods, and would be unreliable. Furthermore, to avoid unintended or intended bias, reports needed to record the evidence to back up reports of offence-related behaviour, and this would not be possible with checklists. It was recommended that the project would gain more cooperation if we used documentation already in existence, for example, completion of wing history sheets. Staff are required to write a comment in wing history sheets about each prisoner on a weekly basis, but the kinds of information recorded usually relate to behaviours that concern prison security as opposed to risk of causing harm on release. Indeed, wing staff training focuses mainly on security issues and it is a novel concept to them that they should be involved in assessment of risk of harm on release. This highlighted the need for awareness training for wing staff on risk of harm issues in order to alert them to the important contribution they can make. To reinforce this message, it was suggested that a guidance note be attached to the wing file indicating the kinds of behaviour that might be observed and which, if observed, should be recorded. A copy of the wing information sheet is shown in Figure 11.1. This lists a sample of the kinds of information that offender supervisors identified as being regularly observed in prison. The lists include behaviours described by Jones (2004) as offence behaviour (e.g. rape), detection evasion skills (i.e. grooming of staff) and positive behaviours (i.e. avoiding mixing with other sex offenders).

It is acknowledged that there is an emphasis in the behaviour monitoring form on offence-related behaviour and less emphasis is put on positive behaviours in the prison. It should be remembered however that the purpose of the behaviour monitoring form is not to assist decisions about release; the release date of the prisoner will have already been determined. At this stage the primary concern is about ensuring that the public is protected from further offences and that potential victims are safeguarded. It is for this reason that emphasis is placed on the risks relating to the prisoner's release. Positive behaviours will be sought and built upon by the offender manager in attempting to make an impact on the offender's offending behaviour, whilst at the same time being responsible for his or her safe management in the community.

Offender supervisors in the prison agreed to take responsibility for extracting information from wing history sheets when a prisoner was due for release. They also undertook to complete a behaviour monitoring form which would record the risk behaviours that had been observed on the wings, and would predict the likely behaviour following release. The behaviour monitoring form was designed to be as simple as possible to encourage its use and to minimize the additional work that could accrue from completing complicated forms. A copy of the front page of the behaviour monitoring form is shown in Figure 11.2,[1] and similar pages are provided for each

[1] Copies may be obtained from the Psychology Unit, Durham Tees Valley Probation Trust, UK.

Wing Information Sheet

TYPES OF INFORMATION TO INCLUDE ON THE HISTORY SHEET

We are interested in identifying behaviour in prison which is related to offence behaviour, so that we can provide information on level of risk, and advise on likely behaviour in the community. Please report on the *History Sheet* evidence of any relevant behaviour, examples of which are shown below. This will be followed up and collated by Offender Supervisors for use in Inter-departmental Public Protection meetings and MAPPA meetings.

Acquaintances	***Behaviour with other prisoners***
- Close friendship with offenders with similar offences - Always mixes with sex offenders - Grooming of other prisoner/s - Sexual relationship with other prisoner/s - Details of cell-mate	- Intimidating behaviour to other prisoners (including violence/ rape) - Sexual behaviour for payment - Victimized by other prisoners – injuries - Bullying – lack of, or lots of personal belongings
Behaviour in Work / Education - Involved in offence-related discussion with other prisoners - Inappropriate comments to instructor / teacher - Inappropriate behaviour with teachers - Selects unlikely reading materials - Attempted grooming of instructors - Interested in learning about skills related to own offending - e.g internet access, making soft toys	***Reading/Photographic Materials*** - Pornographic material - Unlikely reading material, such as women's magazines, material with pictures of children, young girls or boys, etc., catalogues - Offender depositions - Pictures and photos of concern on pin board
Hobbies/ Pastimes - Making soft toys - Choice of TV - interest in violent videos or video-games playstation. - 'Fetish'-like behaviours (e.g. collecting underwear) - Phone sex/compulsive masturbation - Excessive use of gym -'Legitimate' avoidance of offending behaviour Programmes	***Contacts with outside world*** *(by letter or phone)* - In touch with ex-prisoners/sex offenders - Wide range of contacts - Contacts with children - Female pen-friends/ grooming - Postal orders and transfers of money - Lots of small amounts of money to one address - Contact with minority groups, including religious
Visits - Drug trafficking - Inappropriate behaviour with visitor/s - Watching children on visits - Excessive applications to see children, e.g., nephews, nieces - Requests to see partner's children	***Behaviour with staff*** - Seeks out female members of staff - Seeks out specific member of staff - Grooming behaviour - Tries to 'bend the rules' - Seeks favours - Exposes self (even if seemingly by accident) - Excessive use of requests/complaints
Any other behaviour that concerns you – Please contact offender supervisor	***Positive Behaviours Related to Offending*** - Avoiding offenders with similar offences - Evidence of controlling offence-related interests - Positive alternative behaviours - Constructive plans for release

OFFENDER SUPERVISOR UNIT

Figure 11.1 Wing information sheet.

Behaviour Monitoring Form

OFFENDER SUPERVISOR PRISON BEHAVIOUR FORM

(ONLY FILL IN RELEVANT SECTIONS)

Release date No

Name of Offender	DOB PNC No
Name of Offender Supervisor	Name of Offender Manager
Signature	Today's date

1. ACQUAINTANCES	▪ Close friendship with offenders with similar offences ▪ Always mixes with sex offenders ▪ Grooming of other prisoners ▪ Sexual relationship with other prisoner/s ▪ Details of cell-mate
Behaviour with acquaintances causing concern – (include evidence) Give two examples if possible 1) 2)	
Likely behaviour on release indicated by behaviour with acquaintances	
APPROVED PREMISES (Complete if applicable)	
COMPLETED BY OFFENDER MANAGER AFTER RELEASE YES/NO (Describe)	**Behaviour evident in first three months**

Continue on extra page if necessary

Figure 11.2 Behaviour monitoring form.

category of behaviour of interest. The predicted behaviours section is included in order to be precise about the likely community behaviour based on the prison behaviour observed and to avoid the kinds of bias that could occur if the behaviours described were too general, leading to a wide range of possible interpretations.

The behaviour monitoring form is completed by the offender supervisor and sent electronically to the offender manager in the community to assist completion of public protection plans. It is recognized that an important factor in maintaining the behavioural monitoring system is feedback to the staff in the prison as to whether the behaviour recorded and predicted has in fact occurred. A section of the form therefore provides for the offender manager to record any behaviour in the community linked to the predicted behaviour to enable feedback to HM prison staff. Although it is the intention that this communication will take place via the ViSOR database, full use of ViSOR by the relevant agencies, at the time of writing, has not taken place.

Consultation with offender managers in the community confirmed the value of the behavioural information and the importance of its timing. Ideally, information should be available at required time-points throughout the offender's sentence so that changes in behaviour, and hence levels of risk, could be monitored, although it was recognized that this would place much pressure on already stretched prison resources. It was considered that, at a minimum, behavioural information should be provided at least 3–6 months before an offender's release date in order to contribute to MAPPA meetings.

It was identified that some of the most high-risk offenders are first released to approved premises (formerly known as hostels), and hence approved premises should be involved in the behaviour monitoring process. Approved premises add value by offering a perception of freedom in comparison to the regimes in prisons, with opportunities for access to social use of alcohol and a wider range of potential activities. Additionally, the responsibility of staff in approved premises in relation to MAPPA is clear; Probation Circular 35/05 (National Probation Service, 2005) states that, routine observation and daily assessments of patterns of behaviour, and reliable procedures for those assessments must be recorded'. There is therefore close supervision and observation at approved premises that can provide a valuable bridge between prison and community behaviour monitoring.

LEARNING FROM IMPLEMENTATION OF ADViSOR

Following the introduction of ADViSOR, we have found that it is essential to appoint a prison coordinator for the ADViSOR behavioural risk assessment process. Although there are many enthusiasts for the project, unless it is designated as someone's job to see that the monitoring forms are completed regularly, completion is likely to fall behind. It is also sometimes necessary to follow up Wing History Sheet comments with the individual officer to obtain more information or clarification.

Staff training is essential to the introduction of the project, as the concept of contributing information relevant to risk of harm after release has not previously been incorporated in prison officer training, although that may be due to change. Experience suggests that the following training processes should be adopted:

- The ADViSOR project should be introduced to senior level managers at the outset to ensure top-level managerial support for the project.
- Wing staff should be trained to recognize the kinds of behaviour that may be relevant to risk of harm after an offender is released from prison. Training should be given on how to record

this information on Wing History Sheets, together with supporting information on behaviour with evidence of instances.
- Offender supervisors need a minimum of half a day's training prior to implementation of the project to be made aware of the behaviours to be recorded, and predictions that may be made about likely behaviours on release.
- Education staff, works instructors and staff supervising visits should also receive awareness training.
- Offender managers in the community need a minimum of half a day's training prior to implementation of the project to explore the value that can be obtained from the behavioural information provided, and to consider how this information can be incorporated into sentence planning. They should be made aware of the importance of feedback to offender supervisors in prison and how this should be reported.

It is intended that manuals will be drawn up by the ADViSOR project team, in order to standardize the awareness training and offender supervisor/manager training, and to allow for cascading of training following the initial training schedule for the project.

Use of Wing History Sheets and Monitoring Forms in Practice

The project is in its early stages, and there is insufficient information to allow for a quantitative evaluation so far. The information is however interesting at a qualitative level. Some of the information obtained from behaviour monitoring is serious in nature and may have reached the MAPPA meeting without the existence of the ADViSOR project; for example, in one case, the offender manager had already been told that the offender had tried to get in touch with a member of his victim's family. Other types of information are however less likely to be reported, as they describe lower-level risk behaviour, but which may become important if maintained over a long time period. These can relate to who regularly visits the offender, who corresponds and who is on the offender's telephone list. This can raise questions about supervision, as in the case of an offender whose success on release was perceived to be dependent on strong family relationships but who, the behaviour monitoring revealed, had received no visits, letters or phone contact from his family throughout his sentence. This led the offender manager to take a closer look at the robustness of the family support. In another case, a victim had written to the prison asking how to arrange to visit the prisoner who had offended against her. The significance of this request might not have been recognized in the normal course of events, but was picked up by the offender supervisor in completing the behaviour monitoring form. Another case emerged where there were examples of inappropriate behaviour with different female members of staff in different parts of the prison. These separate pieces of information alone did not attract attention, until they were linked up in the ADViSOR monitoring process as a worrying pattern of behaviour. It is becoming evident that it may be such ongoing low-level risk behaviour that may not appear to be sufficiently serious to be raised in MAPPA meetings that are likely to come to the fore in the new monitoring system.

EVALUATION OF THE PROJECT

In order to assess the effectiveness of the ADViSOR project in reducing risk of harm, it is considered essential that the effectiveness and cost benefits of the project are analysed. The central hypothesis to be tested is that the provision of information on offence-related behaviour in prison, and the forwarding of this information to community offender managers using the new behaviour monitoring form, will improve the quality of offender management and thereby enhance public safety.

The first phase of the research has been the implementation of the project and an ongoing process evaluation of implementation. The second phase of the research will comprise qualitative and quantitative analysis and a cost-benefit analysis.

Choice of Outcome Measures

The longer-term objective of the project is to improve offender management to reduce the likelihood of reoffending. For longer-term evaluation purposes therefore the appropriate outcome measure will be the proportion of offenders reconvicted at one year and two years, respectively after release, supplemented by information about the length of time to reconviction and the type of offences committed.

Since data collection for such an analysis will take upwards of two years, there is a need to develop some interim indicators or intermediate outcome measures to inform policy development.

Proposed interim indicators for this purpose will include the proportion of offenders who are charged or cautioned, or who violate licence conditions or display behaviour giving cause for concern within 6–12 months of release from prison, with particular attention being given to behaviours identified by prison offence-related monitoring.

Methodology

Qualitative Analysis

1. Evidence will be sought from the prison, where the behaviour monitoring form is being piloted, on:
   - The quality of the information that is being obtained from behaviour monitoring recorded in wing information sheets and the behaviour monitoring form;
   - The time taken by prison offender supervisors to collect behavioural information from Wing History Sheets, and from individual officers, works instructors and teachers, including organizational aspects of data collection (such as securing prison officer and other staff cooperation, quality control of the data being collected);
   - The time taken by offender supervisors to input the data; and
   - The staff-training requirement.
2. The research will also examine the processes within the regional community probation services by which information from the pro forma is received and used to inform the drafting of sentence plans or licence conditions and other aspects of offender management. The degree to which licence conditions are linked to the content of behavioural information received is an example of the kind of summary measure of how the new information might be influential.
3. Impact of the supervision on interim measures, such as whether offenders are charged, cautioned or violate licence conditions, will be examined in relation to behaviour reported from the prison.
4. A further part of the evaluation will involve investigating the process by which the new information coming from the prison is incorporated into the police ViSOR database system.

Quantitative Analysis

The hypothesis to be tested is that the improved provision to community offender managers of information about offender behaviour in prison will support better risk assessment and management of offenders and help identify licence conditions that are more likely to prevent reoffending. The purpose of the quantitative analysis is to compare reconviction outcomes for the 'intervention' group released in early 2008 with those of the two 'comparison' groups, one comprising offenders released during the previous six months period and the second comprising comparable offenders released contemporaneously from a prison not running the prison behaviour monitoring scheme.

The characteristics of offenders in the three groups will be compared to establish how closely matched they are in relation to variables, such as age, type of offence for which they have been imprisoned, number of convictions to date, age at first conviction, OASys profiles, etc. The groups will then be compared on the number of charges, cautions and convictions within three, six and 12 months of release. The mean seriousness of any offences committed will also be recorded, as will involvement in other 'incidents' in which they are known to have been involved following release from prison.

COSTS AND BENEFITS

The qualitative and quantitative components of the evaluation will include a review of the cost-benefit characteristics of using the behavioural monitoring form. A full analysis of the benefits will only be possible once sufficient reconvictions data have been accumulated to make an assessment of the crime reduction impact of ADViSOR. But there is scope for considering the cost side of the project somewhat sooner.

The costs of ADViSOR are a mix of up-front capital costs and recurrent costs. The up-front costs involve staff training and the costs of setting up the organizational links needed to support the new information flows. Liaison between prisons, probation, police and other agencies is costly to establish. We will endeavour to make some estimates of the scale of the work entailed in training and liaison, and the resource costs associated with it.

The recurrent costs will fall on prison staff completing and collating the data on offenders and also on community offender managers who will have an additional stream of information to incorporate in files and decision-making. Once the project has been under way for three months and monitoring forms on a number of prisoners have been compiled, it should be feasible to investigate the amount of staff time (and thus costs) involved in running the system. Interviews with prison staff completing and/or collating the data on offenders and also with community offender managers will be used to explore these recurrent costs.

Project Design Costs

The 'project design' cost element, including the costs of this evaluation, is a 'one-off' cost that would not have to be met again. It covers items such as the basic design work and background research, along with the design of the forms to be used, the design and revision of the content of staff training and the production of training material. These costs are all 'sunk': they are irrecoverable irrespective of the impact of the project.

Project Initiation Costs

Some, but not all, of the initial costs incurred in ADViSOR would be incurred if the project were to be rolled out elsewhere. The project initiation costs that would arise if the project were being rolled out in a different setting would include the following:

- Governor or senior management involvement to make decisions about how the project is to be run, including allocation of responsibilities and briefing of middle managers and supervisory staff
- Middle manager time to set up the information collation system, appoint a coordinator, liaise with wing staff and offender supervisors, liaise with offender managers in the community
- Training of offender supervisors
- Training, or at least awareness raising, for wing staff
- Ensuring that existing methods of liaison with offender managers in probation are in place and are adequate for dealing with a new flow of sensitive information

Recurrent Project Costs

Once the system has been implemented over a period of a few weeks or months, it may require minimal support from senior staff. At this point the key requirements would be:

- Ensuring that an information coordinator in the prison spends an appropriate amount of time and effort collecting and monitoring the quality of information being collected in wing files

The principal costs associated with this will be salary and related costs of a coordinator in the prison and of a coordinator in the relevant probation offices.

Recurrent Benefits

The measure of benefits would rely primarily on a comparison of the reconviction outcomes for ADViSOR-supported offenders and a control group about whom the information was not being collected. This might be based on estimates of the economic and social costs of the offences for which the intervention group are responsible in relation to the corresponding costs for the control group.

An absolute minimum of several months would be required before any such estimates could be made, particularly in relation to sex offenders whose offence types tend to involve lower reconviction rates and longer intervals to reconviction than for other groups of prisoners.

Project Returns and Viability

The key determinant of the returns will thus be the benefits derived. These benefits are expected primarily in the form of reduced reoffending rates for discharged prisoners. But there may be additional benefits at offender management level. If it can be demonstrated that the increased flow of information from the prison offender supervisor to the community offender manager makes it easier to collect the information required for MAPPA purposes, then there might be some savings to police, probation and others.

ETHICAL CONSIDERATIONS

Although the value of behavioural risk assessment is generally recognized, some concerns have been raised about the ethics of monitoring behaviour in prison, and it has been proposed that it is necessary to inform the offender when a specific behaviour is being monitored. A contrary argument is that offenders in the public protection category are already informed by means of a printed leaflet (National Offender Manager Service – NOMS, 2007) that they are considered to present a serious risk of reoffending and that their actions are being continuously monitored and assessed to prevent their reoffending, The latter approach is supported by the British Psychological Society in its generic professional guidelines (2008), which allow for exceptions in obtaining permission to disclose information, that is:

> In exceptional circumstances, disclosure without consent, or against the client's expressed wish, may be necessary in situations in which failure to disclose appropriate information would expose the client, or someone else, to a risk of serious harm (including physical or sexual abuse) or death (p. 10). . . . There are a number of circumstances where this (disclosure) might not apply: for example where the health, safety or welfare of the client or someone else would otherwise be put at serious risk. (p. 9)

Similar guidance exists in clinical domains. Blackburn (1993) proposes that psychologists in a multidisciplinary context are professionally obliged to share information with other members. This is particularly so where there is a conflict between the interests of the public and those of the offender. Blackburn states that 'the guiding principles should be the maximum benefit and least harm with pride of place going to those interested parties whose lives are most negatively affected by the problem behaviour' (p. 412).

CONCLUSION

The ADViSOR project has required the cooperation and involvement of a wide range of people within both the prison and the regional community probation areas. This has been made particularly easy because the concept of observing and monitoring behaviour in prison as a means of predicting risk behaviour in the community is generally accepted among practitioners. It is not a difficult psychological concept and, when proposed, seems so logical that it is surprising that it has not been done before. Having introduced the idea of behaviour monitoring to wing staff, we immediately received requests to be involved in the project from other staff in the prison who come into contact with offenders in other domains, for example, in education and in work situations, whose environments present different opportunities in which to observe behaviour. There are however dangers in monitoring behaviour in that incorrect inferences might be drawn from behaviours which may not be linked to offending. This is why it is essential to give proper training in completion of the behaviour monitoring form and the use in sentence planning of the information provided to require that reports of prison behaviour and community behaviour are supported by evidence and to ensure that the ADViSOR project is properly evaluated. We have yet to demonstrate that offence-related behaviour in prison is related to offence behaviour after release, but if this can be shown, we will have a valuable means of enhancing the protection we give to the public through the MAPPA.

ACKNOWLEDGEMENTS

The project was commissioned and directed by Hazel Willoughby, Director of Public Protection for Durham and Teesside Probation Services. The authors thank Hazel for her enthusiastic contribution, commitment and support for the ADViSOR project. Thanks are also due to Kevin Dawson, North East Prison Service Area, MAPPA and OASys Coordinator, whose assistance in setting up and facilitating the project has been invaluable, and the North East Regional Offender Manager, who has funded the ADViSOR project. We thank Brian Halliday, Annmarie Taylor and Leila Sedgewick for providing project management and administrative support in making the systems work as they should.

REFERENCES

Andrews, D.A. (1989). Recidivism is predictable and can be influenced: using risk assessments to reduce recidivism. *Forum on Corrections Research*, *1*(2), 11–18.

Belfrage, H., Fransson, G. & Strand, S. (2000). Prediction of violence using the HCR-20: a prospective study in two maximum security correctional institutions. *Journal of Forensic Psychiatry*, *11*, 167–75.

Blackburn, R. (1993). *The Psychology of Criminal Conduct*. (pp 177–204) Chichester: John Wiley & Sons.

Blackburn, R. (2000). Risk assessment and prediction. In J. McGuire, T. Mason & A. O'Kane (Eds), *Behaviour, Crime & Legal Processes: A Guide for Forensic Practitioners*. Chichester: Wiley.

Bonta, J. (1996). Risk-needs assessment and treatment. In A.T. Harland (Ed.), *Choosing Correctional Options That Work* (pp. 18–32). Thousand Oaks, CA: Sage.

Bonta, J., Law, M. & Hanson, R.K. (1998). The prediction of criminal and violent recidivism among mentally disordered offenders. *Psychological Bulletin*, *123*, 123–42.

Borum, R. (1996). Improving the clinical practice of violence risk assessment: technology guidelines, and training. *American Psychologist*, *51*, 945–956.

British Psychological Society (2008). *Generic Professional Practice Guidelines* (2nd edition). Leicester: British Psychological Society.

Clark, D.A., Fisher, M.J. & McDougall, C. (1993). A new methodology for assessing the level of risk in incarcerated offenders. *British Journal of Criminology*, *33*(3), 436–48.

Cooke, D.J. (1998). The development of the prison behavior rating scale. *Criminal Justice & Behavior*, *25*(4), 482–506.

Douglas, K.S., Cox, D.N. & Webster, C.D. (1999a). Violence risk assessment: science and practice. *Legal and Criminological Psychology*, *4*, 149–84.

Douglas, K.S., Ogloff, J.R.P., Nicholls, T.L. & Grant, I. (1999b). Assessing risk for violence among psychiatric patients: the HCR-20 violence risk assessment scheme and the psychopathy checklist: screening version. *Journal of Consulting and Clinical Psychology*, *67*, 917–30.

Doyle, M. & Dolan, M. (2006). Predicting community violence from patients discharged from mental health services. *British Journal of Psychiatry*, *189*, 520–26.

Farrington, D.P., Lambert, S. & West, D.J. (1998). Criminal careers of two generations of family members in the Cambridge study on delinquent development. *Studies on Crime & Crime Prevention*, *7*(1), 85–106.

Gray, N.S., Hill, C., McGleish, A., Timmons, D., MacCulloch, M.J. & Snowden, R.J. (2003). Prediction of violence and self-harm in mentally disordered offenders: a prospective study of the efficacy of HCR-20, PCL-R and psychiatric symptomatology. *Journal of Consulting and Clinical Psychology*, *71*, 443–51.

Gray, N.S., Taylor, J. & Snowden, R.J. (2008). Predicting violent reconvictions using the HCR-20. *British Journal of Psychiatry*, *192*, 384–87.

Grevatt, M., Thomas-Peter, B., Hughes, G. (2004). Violence, mental disorder and risk assessment: can structured clinical assessments predict the short-term risk of inpatient violence? *Journal of Forensic Psychiatric Psychology, 15*, 278–92.

Grove, W.M. & Meehl, P.E. (1996). Comparative efficiency of informal (subjective, impressionistic) and formal (mechanical, algorithmic) prediction procedures: the clinical-statistical controversy. *Psychology, Public Policy, and Law, 2*, 293–323.

Hall, H.V. (1987). *Violence Prediction: Guidelines for the Forensic Practitioner*. Springfield, IL: Charles C. Thomas.

Hanson, R.K. & Harris, A.J.R. (2000). Where should we intervene? Dynamic predictors of sexual offence recidivism. *Criminal Justice and Behavior, 27*, 96–135.

Hanson, R.K., Harris, A.J.R., Scott, T-L. & Helmus, L. (2007). Assessing the risk of sexual offenders on community supervision: the dynamic supervision project. *Public Safety Canada*. Retrieved from www.publicsafety.gc.ca/res/cor/rep/cprmindex-eng.aspx.

Hill, G. (1985). Predicting recidivism using institutional measures. In D.P. Farrington & R. Tarling (Eds), *Prediction in Criminology*. (pp 96–118) Chichester: Wiley.

HM Inspectorate of Probation (2006). *An Independent Review of A Serious Further Offence Case: Anthony Rice*. London: Crown Copyright.

HM Inspectorates of Prisons and Probation (1999). *Lifers – A Joint Thematic Review by HM Inspectorates of Prisons and Probation*. Retrieved from http://www.justice.gov.uk/inspectorates/hmi-prisons/thematic-reports-and-research.htm.

HM Prison Service (2004). *Multi-agency Public Protection Arrangements* (Prison service order 4745). Retrieved from http://www.hmprisonservice.gov.uk/resourcecentre/psispsos/listpsos/.

Jones, L.F. (1997). Developing models for managing treatment integrity and efficacy in a prison based therapeutic community: the Max Glatt Centre. In E. Cullen, L. Jones & R. Woodward (Eds), *Therapeutic Communities for Offenders*. Chichester: Wiley.

Jones, L.F. (2004). Offence paralleling behaviour (OPB) as a framework for assessment and interventions with offenders. In A. Needs & G. Towl (Eds), *Applying Psychology to Forensic Practice* (pp. 34–63). Oxford: BPS Blackwell.

Kanfer, F.H. & Saslow, G. (1969). Behavioural diagnosis. In C. Franks (Ed.), *Behaviour Therapy: Appraisal and Status*. New York: McGraw-Hill.

Maden, A., Rogers, P., Watt, A., Lewis, G., Amos, T., Gournay, K., et al. (2006). *Assessing the utility of the Offenders Group Reconviction Scale-2 in predicting the risk of reconviction within 2 and 4 years of discharge from English and Welsh medium secure units* (Final Report to the National Forensic Mental Health Research Programme). Retrieved from http://www.nfmhp.org.uk.

McDougall, C. & Clark, D.A. (1991). A risk assessment model. In S. Boddis (Ed.), *Proceedings of the Prison Psychology Conference*. London: Her Majesty's Stationery Office.

McDougall, C., Clark, D.A. & Woodward, R. (1995). Application of operational psychology to assessment of inmates. *Psychology, Crime and Law, 2*, 85–99.

Monahan, J., Steadman, H.J., Silver, E., Appelbaum, P.S., Robbins, P.C., Mulvey, E.P., et al. (2001). *Rethinking Risk Assessment: The Macarthur Study of Mental Disorder and Violence*. New York: Oxford University Press.

Mossman, D. (1994). Assessing predictions of violence: being accurate about accuracy. *Journal of Consulting and Clinical Psychology, 62*, 783–792.

National Offender Management Service (2009). *MAPPA Guidance version 3.0*. Retrieved from http://www.probation.homeoffice.gov.uk/files/pdf/MAPPA Guidance 2009 Version 3.0.pdf.

National Probation Service (2005). *The Role and Purpose of Approved Premises* (Probation Circular 37/2005). London: National Probation Service.

Nugent, F., Geohagan, K. & Travers, R. (2005). *Cognitive Skills Assessment Test Battery Guide: Test Battery Guide Version 2*. London: Ministry of Justice, Offending Behaviour Programmes Unit.

Nuffield, J. (1989). The SIR scale: some reflections on its applications. *Forum on Corrections Research, 1*, 19–22.

Owens, G. & Ashcroft, J.B. (1982). Functional analysis in applied psychology. *British Journal of Clinical Psychology, 21*, 181–89.

Quinsey, L., Harris, G.T., Rice, M.E. & Cormier, C.A. (1998). *Violent Offenders: Appraising and Managing Risk*. Washington, DC: American Psychological Association.

Towl, G.J. & Crighton, D.A. (1995). Risk assessment in prisons: a psychological critique. *Forensic Update, 40*, 6–14.

Tversky, D. & Kahneman, A. (1974). Judgement under uncertainty: heuristics and biases. *Science, 185*, 1124–31.

Walmsley, R. (2007). World Prison Population List. Retrieved from the International Centre for Prison Studies, King's College London, website: http://www.prisonstudies.org.

Webster, C.D., Eaves, D., Douglas, K.S. & Wintrup, A. (1995). *The HCR-20 Scheme: The Assessment of Dangerousness and Risk*. Vancover, BC: Simon Fraser University and Forensic Psychiatric Services Commission of British Columbia.

Zamble, R. & Porporino, F. (1990). Coping, imprisonment and rehabilitation. *Criminal Justice and Behaviour*, *17*(1), 53–69.

Chapter 12

WORKING WITH OFFENCE PARALLELING BEHAVIOUR IN A THERAPEUTIC COMMUNITY SETTING

JOHN SHINE

The Millfields Unit, Centre for Forensic Mental Health, London, UK

> What is important is that complex systems, richly cross-connected internally, have complex behaviours, and that these behaviours can be goal-seeking in complex patterns.
>
> W. Ross Ashby (1957)

INTRODUCTION

The term *offence paralleling behaviour* (OPB) originated from the work of Jones (1997, 2004) who developed the construct whilst working at the Max Glatt Centre, a therapeutic community (TC) based within Wormwood Scrubs prison. The development of the OPB construct was influenced by the work of Clark et al. (1994), who developed a methodology that linked behaviour in the prison environment to the risk of recidivism. Although the OPB construct is most closely associated with behavioural approaches in psychology, particularly, functional analytical psychotherapy (FAP) (Kohlenberg & Tsai, 1991), the central notion underlying OPB of behavioural consistency across time and across situations is not the sole preserve of behaviourism. As Daffern points out in this volume, there is a long history of applying concepts of behavioural consistency within different psychological traditions as diverse as psychodynamic therapy (see Chapter 19), interpersonal therapy, cognitive therapy and cognitive analytic therapy.

The OPB construct was used specifically in a forensic context to assist in risk assessment in terms of supplementing existing measures and in terms of setting treatment targets. Jones (2004) originally defined OPB as:

> Any form of offence related behavioural (or fantasised behaviour) pattern that emerges at any point before or after an offence. It does not have to result in an offence; it simply needs to resemble, in some significant respect, the sequence of behaviours leading up to the offence. (Jones, 2004, p. 38)

Offence Paralleling Behaviour: A Case Formulation Approach to Offender Assessment and Intervention Edited by Michael Daffern, Lawrence Jones and John Shine

A recent paper (Daffern et al., 2007) noted that use of the original definition provided by Jones was potentially overinclusive, leading to the potential for misuse. A revised definition emphasizing the functional equivalence between sequences of behaviour in institutions and offending behaviour was proposed:

> OPB is a behavioural sequence incorporating overt behaviours (that may be muted by environmental factors), appraisals, expectations, beliefs, affects, goals and behavioural scripts, all of which may be influenced by the patient's mental disorder, that is functionally similar to behavioural sequences involved in previous criminal acts. (Daffern et al., 2007, p. 3)

In this volume, a range of contributors from different theoretical and professional backgrounds have written on the potential application of the OPB construct in terms of its application in working with violent offenders, sex offenders, young offenders and in community settings. In this chapter, I will be highlighting the importance of the institutional environment for working with OPB. Specifically, I will argue that the principles derived from functional analytical therapy for working on an individual basis with clients can be applied to therapeutic environments. Building on earlier work (Shine and Morris, 2000) the model of a forensic TC will be used as a potential example of this approach.

PROBLEMS WITH APPLYING THE OPB FRAMEWORK IN TRADITIONAL FORENSIC SETTINGS

Interest in the OPB framework is expanding. Forensic settings that have used the OPB framework include prisons and high-secure special hospitals (see Daffern et al., 2007 for details). Some of the problems in working with the OPB framework in these settings have been highlighted in this edition. For example, Daffern highlights the problems with observer biases, the difficulties and the problems of separating situational from dispositional factors and identifies ways in which some of these behaviours may be addressed through a structured behavioural approach based on OPB. As I highlight later in this chapter, one of the difficulties with the model proposed by Daffern is the capacity of the institutional environment to lend itself to the observation and activation of OPB. As Daffern (see Chapter 6) notes: 'so long as the environment activates the *equivalent variables* associated with the patient's aggression, then OPB should occur' (emphasis added).

This raises the question of how equivalent variables associated with aggression are to be activated. A potential problem with this approach is that many forensic environments, such as prisons, are simply not geared to providing the types of environments that will assist in identifying and working with OPB. For example, Shine and Morris (2000) noted that the standard use of risk assessment and career planning for life sentence prisoners was hampered because of the sterility of the environment in terms of opportunities to observe and meaningfully reflect on the relationships among peers and between peers and staff.

The reasons for these difficulties in applying the OPB construct in institutional environments fall into two main areas:

1. Issues arising from the influence of the inmate subculture and
2. Overemphasis on within session therapy behaviour

Each of these areas will be discussed in turn.

The Influence of the Inmate Subculture

Criminal peer group influences have been repeatedly identified as falling within the major set of criminogenic needs in reviews of the literature on factors predicting recidivism (Andrews & Bonta, 1998). One of the factors influencing this finding was research indicating that the use of unstructured psychotherapy groups had poorer outcomes, including iatrogenic effects in terms of increased recidivism, a finding that was attributed to the influence of unregulated negative peer group influences (Harris et al., 1991). The importance of the institutional environment in maintaining criminal behaviour was highlighted in a series of papers reviewed by Bukstel and Kilmann (1980), who concluded that there was strong evidence for the influence of negative peer groups in reinforcing the beliefs and attitudes that underpin offending. However, particularly in the early days of implementing accredited programmes based on 'what works' principles, little attention was paid to the wider contingencies affecting inmate behaviour outside the therapy room – the environment and culture in which the programmes were delivered. Yet, as some observers noted (see, for example, Clarke et al., 2004), good progress on offender behaviour programmes may be impaired, or even reversed, if a well-delivered programme is conducted in an institutional environment and culture where there is widespread drug dealing, bullying, illegal trading in goods such as tobacco, illicit DVDs and other antisocial influences at work.

The use of prison officers as tutors and facilitators on accredited programmes may act as an important counterbalance to these processes, particularly if effective prosocial modelling is practised. However, they are unlikely by themselves to be of sufficient influence when compared to the pervasive and strongly reinforcing factors that occur within the environment outside of the therapy room. The institutional environment may be defined by the roles of prisoner and guard or doctor and patient (Goffman, 1991) and underpinned by powerful inmate subcultures that serve to reinforce antisocial beliefs and behaviours. Within the closed environments of prisons and high-secure hospitals, it is possible that some prisoners or patients may behave in one way in the confines of the therapy room and another outside of it. Jones (2004) has termed this process as the acquisition of detection evasion skills (DES) and this is explored further below.

Most of the facilitators who deliver accredited programmes are aware of this dynamic, and seek to encourage offenders to generalize their skills to different environments. Audit systems for accredited programmes have also been expanded to include factors that operate in the wider environment. However, without effective and therapeutically safe communication channels between the environment and the offender, this is often hampered. The wider inmate subculture, which operates throughout the day rather than the weekly few hours or so of the therapy session, may act as a strong deterrent against this process through the inmate taboo against 'grassing' (i.e. informing on fellow offenders or patients), or being seen as a 'Governor's nark' (someone who is behaving in a prosocial manner in order to curry favour with officials and acting against his fellow inmates).

Therapeutic Focus on Within-Session Behaviour

The expansion of offender behaviour programmes in the United Kingdom in the early 1990s was based on meta-analyses showing that properly implemented programmes were effective in reducing recidivism. In order to ensure proper implementation, it was important to pay attention to the factors that maintained programme and treatment integrity (Andrews & Bonta, 1994). This involved focusing close attention on areas such as the training of staff, the selection of offenders (based on principles of risk, need and responsivity; Bonta, 1997) and monitoring the delivery of the therapy in terms of factors such as programme adherence, treatment style, groupwork skills and responsivity.

As pointed out below, this was, and remains, a highly laudable aim. A recent review (Dowden & Andrews, 2004) identified that attention to such factors was one of the features that differentiated effective from non-effective interventions. Although the importance of treatment fidelity is well understood within clinical psychology, reviews have indicated that its application has been inconsistent across a range of interventions (see, for example, Moncher & Prinz, 1991). The large-scale use of methods such as video or audio monitoring used in prison and probation-based accredited programmes is also being used to promote treatment fidelity in the recent expansion of community-based CBT approaches to treat anxiety and depression and to aid effective supervision (see http://www.ucl.ac.uk/clinical-psychology/CORE/supervision_framework.htm).

The emphasis given to in-session behaviour by the therapist and the client has led to improved methods for monitoring the quality of therapy during offender programmes. However, with some important exceptions such as the *Chromis* programme for treating psychopathy (HM Prison Service, 2005), the methods for monitoring out-of-session behaviour have not been accorded the same level of attention as those occurring during the sessions themselves. Methods to monitor out-of-session mood state and behaviour, such as anger management diaries, and skills-based role playing, coaching and mentoring based on examples from such diaries, are common in forensic-institutional-accredited programmes. However, their effectiveness may be limited if the conditions for effective generalization of skills learned on programmes are not present in the wider environment. Indeed, Kohlenberg and Tsai (1991) provocatively argue that: 'Behaviour acquired via coaching, modelling, role playing and behaviour rehearsal during the session is functionally different from the behaviour that is supposed to occur in daily life, even though they may look the same' (p. 184).

Creating conditions for effective generalization is undertaken in two stages: firstly, by conducting a systematic functional analysis of a person's offending behaviour in order that the relevant affective, cognitive and behavioural variables associated with the person's previous offending behaviour are identified. The second stage involves identifying examples from the client's natural environment for recognizing examples of skill application and improvement. In order to be seen as valid examples of skills generalization using a functional analytical approach, these examples should be as close as possible to the stimulus conditions that bring about the symptoms.

For example, take the case of an offender whose index offence involved attacking another person. The assault followed an interaction when he was seen to 'lose face' in the eyes of other members of his gang and he attacked the person who provoked him to reassert his status within the peer group. During an anger management group, the offender learns skills such as assertiveness and challenging automatic thoughts to deal with anger. Following successful completion of therapy, he is seen to apply these skills both in the therapy sessions and in situations in the environment in dealing with frustrations with institutional prison officers. Such cases will often receive good reports from programme staff, however it is questionable whether the same skills can be seen to generalize to situations that are functionally equivalent. In this case, the stimulus conditions when the offender feels humiliated in front of a peer group containing people he feels a degree of attachment to are (arguably) those that are most clinically relevant in assessing whether the skills have been internalized and able to be transferred to future situations when he is at risk of relapsing.

An ideal test of the offenders internalization of skills learnt on an anger management group, would be exposure to interactions that activated similar emotional states and cognitions that occurred during his offence, rather than exposure to general examples of stimuli that might be similar, but not functionally equivalent, to the persons offending.

Given the difficulties of using OPB in traditional forensic settings, the question then arises of what types of environments are best suited to working therapeutically with OPB. From the above sections, optimal environments would appear to require the following characteristics:

1. They would, as far as possible, recognize and work within the pervasive influence of inmate subculture and have in place powerful methods to counteract this and replace it with a culture in which barriers between staff and offenders are minimized. Ideally, rather than being a barrier to effective therapy, the inmate subculture would be harnessed as a force that challenges traditional ways of relating to staff and other prisoners or patients. For example, rather than marginalizing sex offenders, they are seen as offenders with similarities to other types of offending such as violence. Rather than adhering to the role of not openly informing when examples of antisocial or criminal behaviour come to light (termed 'grassing' within the inmate subculture), antisocial behaviour would be a source of feedback identifying criminogenic needs to be worked on in therapy.
2. They would be based on a holistic model of therapy in which interactions that occur out of formal therapy sessions are seen as highly clinically relevant in terms of assessing risks and progress and have in place therapeutically safe and robust feedback systems to allow out-of-session behaviour to be communicated in as much detail as possible.
3. The patients/prisoners/offenders taking part in the treatment approach would be fully aware of the use of DES and be able to recognize genuine change and reinforce prosocial behaviour through the therapeutic communication channels when they occur.

In this author's view, the treatment model that meets these conditions is that of the forensic TC. The use of the OPB construct within this model is now explored.

THE USE OF OPB IN FORENSIC TCs

It was perhaps no coincidence that Jones developed the OPB construct whilst working in a prison-based TC. Within this environment, it is not unusual for observers and clinicians to observe that 'the attitudes, values, cognitions and patterns of behaviour that underpin offending behaviour to 'come to life' in a vivid manner' (Shine & Morris, 2000).

The TC approach to treatment is built around the principle of developing a 'culture of enquiry' – a place where day-to-day interactions form the core basis of the therapy and are explored within an expectation of reciprocal feedback between patients and between patients and staff (Norton, 1992). Residents play an active and leading role in organizing and regulating the therapy and the behaviour of members through processes such as democratization – group decision-making, empowerment and a high emphasis on communal participation and experience, in all aspects of therapy and community life.

There is a significant literature outlining the history of TCs (see, for example, Kennard, 1998). Within the last 10 years, forensic TCs have undergone considerable development in terms of accreditation and audit systems. In forensic services, this process began with the accreditation of 'A' wing at Grendon prison (a TC in Buckinghamshire), in 1998. The submission was based on criteria identified by the Correctional Services Accreditation Panel (CSAP) and involved specifying how criminogenic needs (individualized risk factors associated with recidivism) were addressed within a TC setting. The model of change identified offenders with personality disorder and specifically antisocial personality disorder, as the treatment group most likely to benefit from this approach.

The submission in 1998 highlighted how antisocial attitudes were specifically targeted by the TC model:

> In the therapeutic community, a multi-disciplinary and multi-dimensional approach specifically targets and challenges antisocial attitudes, values and beliefs; it specifically sets up an anti-criminal culture in which residents associate; it explores and challenges the antisocial history; explores in detail the problems of the family of origin and it provided residents with experiences of personal achievement as through experiences they become leaders of the community. At the same time, at another level, the internalisation of these new appropriate role models and experiences lead to structural change of personality, diminishing the temperamental and personality factors that are conducive to criminal behaviour and reducing the sense of personal distress. (Shine & Morris, 1999, p. 13)

OPB formed an important part of the accreditation submission based on the original work by Jones (1997) of establishing links between the individual's relapsing behaviour and patterns of relapse when at liberty. These ideas were incorporated into a model of change that involved developing insight into three domains: a resident's attachment history, his behaviour on the unit and his criminal behaviour. In addition to understanding connections between the domains in terms of a personal formulation of offending behaviour, the TC offered opportunities to work at different levels: fantasies, affect, cognitions and behaviour within each domain (see Figure 12.1 below). In this way the OPB construct is used as a dynamic and evolving process in which the therapeutic focus can move between an exploration of childhood events such as abuse, trauma, experiences of abandonment (attachments), recent examples of community interactions such as prison rule violations, angry outbursts or experiences of loss due to important staff members leaving (behaviour on wing) or accounts of previous offending preceded by similar affective stages or cognitive processes (criminal behaviour). This is illustrated in Figure 12.1 below.

Within this approach, OPB is not introduced in a planned manner but emerges naturally as part of residents' interactions within the community. A critical component of this model is the involvement of other residents in the process. This is undertaken in terms of helping identify and conceptualize relevant paralleling behaviour and providing feedback to help the residents both

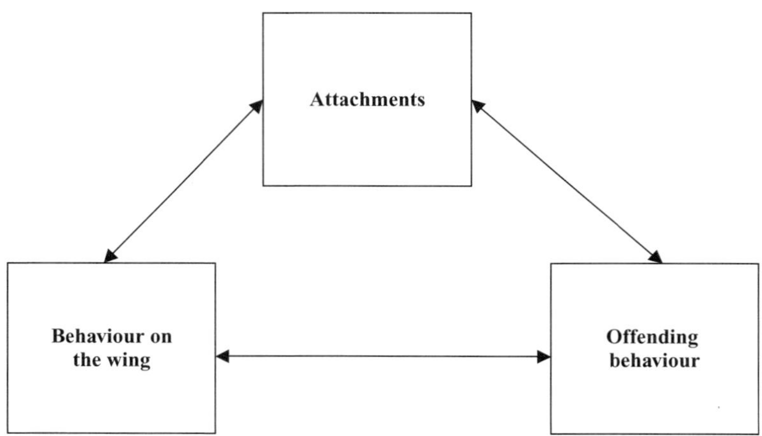

Figure 12.1 Offence paralleling behaviour: the three domains. From Shine and Morris (2000).

develop insight into these processes and reinforce prosocial change. An important criterion that distinguishes the TC approach is the use of connections between different therapeutic activities in which an individualized formulation of a person's difficulties can be monitored and explored in different therapeutic forums (these are termed lateral linkages by Morris, 2004). In this way, the TC approach potentially offers the opportunity of therapeutic synthesis in a way that other models may find more difficult because of the problems of the inmate subculture identified above.

These concepts have since been developed and incorporated into a model for prison democratic TCs which were accredited by the CSAP in 2004 (HM Prison Service, 2004). The developments in audit and accreditation for democratic TCs are outlined by Clark and Lees (2004).

FURTHER DEVELOPMENT OF THE OPB FRAMEWORK IN TC SETTINGS

The accredited model of change for democratic TCs drew upon a range of different therapeutic tradition: 'From cognitive behavioural through psychodynamic and expressive artistic therapeutic approaches and onto spiritual and educational dimensions' (Shine & Morris, 1999, p. 17.) In recent years, there has been a growth in therapeutic approaches that seek to integrate concepts from the cognitive behavioural, psychodynamic and humanistic literature. Examples include cognitive analytic therapy (Ryle, 1997) and schema-focused therapy (Young, 1994). It has become increasingly clear that for clients who are hard to treat and have multifaceted problems, such as those suffering from personality disorder, a pragmatic approach that seeks to address different therapeutic needs using the best available methods, perhaps offers the best approach. One such approach is FAP (Kohlenberg & Tsai, 1991), a form of radical behaviourism. FAP incorporates aspects of both psychodynamic theorizing (such as transference, the therapeutic relationship and the focus on here-and-now interactions) and cognitive therapy (the use of conditional assumptions and core beliefs about the self) but reformulates these within the principles of learning theory and utilizes primarily behavioural techniques as the treatment approach within the context of intense and curative therapeutic relationships.

FAP is based on the importance of utilizing clinically relevant behaviour (CRB) as a focus for therapeutic intervention. Three types of CRB are identified: CRB1 refers to examples of clients presenting problems that occur in the session, an example given by Kohlenberg and Tsai (1991, p. 19) is of a patient suffering from speech anxiety who shares the same experience of 'freezing up' during a therapy session when talking to his therapist.

CRB2 refers to instances of the client making progress on their clinical problems during the therapy session. For example, a patient who has low self-esteem and lacks assertiveness skills experiences feelings of being ignored by the therapist during a therapy session. Rather than this being the stimulus to repeat an established cycle of self-defeating thinking and avoidance, the client uses assertive behaviour to gain the therapists attention.

CRB3 are examples of the client talking about their own behaviour and its underlying causes. Kohlenberg and Tsai (1991) include 'reason giving' and 'interpretations' under this category of behaviour. CRB3 behaviours are therapeutically useful because they give the opportunity for clients to see 'functional connections' between what happens in session and in the client's life outside therapy and therefore help reinforce transfer of learning.

Although originally developed for clinicians involved in individual therapy with clients, FAP offers a framework that has much wider applicability. OPB is derived from FAP principles and, as described above, played a key role in the accreditation model for forensic TCs. However, further exposition of the FAP framework may be useful in terms of clarifying how the therapeutic environment can be harnessed to further enrich therapy by focusing on CRB. In the case of forensic TCs, this involves focusing on criminogenic needs as expressed through the framework of OPB. As stated at the beginning of this chapter, in order for OPB to occur, the equivalent variables have to be activated in the client's environment. Kohlenberg and Tsai (1991) identify some rules for applying FAP in psychotherapy; the relevant ones are reviewed below from the OPB perspective of the forensic TC environment.

Rule 1: Watch for CRB

The identification of CRB is seen as the 'core' principle of FAP, and its importance is derived from the notion that following this rule will enable the expression of intense emotional reactions and therefore lead to improved therapeutic relationships and outcomes. For this to occur, the individual therapist needs to monitor closely the clients' behaviour during the session; failure to do this could result in failure to reinforce improvements in the clients' problems.

Within the group-based culture of the TC, application of this rule involves generalizing from the individual relationship between patient and therapist to the relationship between the patient and the groups that form the TC. For this principle to be applied it is important that a well-functioning group should recognize OPB and PAB (prosocial alternative behaviours, Daffern et al., 2007) as they occur in the therapy sessions and use therapeutic opportunities to explore and reinforce PAB. Group feedback in this setting is potentially more powerful than feedback from an individual therapist since it originates from the inmate subculture. Clinical experience form those who work in forensic TCs attest to the power of group processes in challenging and modifying inmate behaviour; this is also borne out in inmate accounts of therapy (see, for example, Genders & Player, 1995).

The key to effective application of this principle is a comprehensive functional analysis of a person's offending behaviour and a case formulation incorporating examples of OPB. This involves an evidence-based examination of the factors in a client's background that led to his/her offending and the psychological processes that may serve to maintain his/her offending in the present day. To be effective, this should involve much more than an honest and factual account of offending with the community (although this is important), but include how the psychological processes that underpinned a person's offending are activated in parallel forms within interactions or behaviours that occur in the wider TC. It follows that to be effective in a TC, this should be shared with the whole community in order to enable other group members to give feedback on a client's behaviour in the therapy setting. Personal experiences of undertaking individualized case formulation incorporating OPB by other group members will help in the identification of OPB for other members and in the reinforcement of PAB when they occur.

Rule 2: Evoke CRB2

Within traditional FAP, the process for evoking CRB2 is the therapeutic relationship. Kohlenberg and Tsai (1991) argue that the important factor in therapist effectiveness in evoking CRBs is the nature of the client's presenting problems. From this rule it follows that to be effective, therapists need to adapt their style to that which best evokes therapeutically relevant CRBs within the therapy session. For some clients, this would be a 'blank screen'; for others it would be a warm and active therapist. Kohlenberg and Tsai also identify that environmental factors can be structured to evoke CRB, including techniques such as homework assignments and imagery exercises and psychodynamic techniques such as free association. However, as Kohlenberg and Tsai acknowledge, the problem with these techniques is that they were not specifically developed to evoke CRB and so may lose their therapeutic value: 'The problem with these techniques is that the therapist that uses them may be so intent on looking for alter egos, wise men within, unconscious material and dysfunctional cognition, that the CRB is not seen or viewed as incidental' (p. 28).

In contrast, the TC environment does not have to rely on specific therapeutic techniques to evoke OPB (although they may be very useful in adjunctive therapies such as art therapy or homework assignments from CBT approaches) as the environment itself is deliberately structured to create a framework where social learning can take place and thus evoke OPB. Shine and Morris (2000) identified that the main task of the multidisciplinary team in forensic TCs was to 'construct a social milieu which is conductive to the development of free social interaction and expression between inmates and staff' (Shine & Morris, 2000, p. 202). The natural environment of the TC therefore serves to evoke OPB because once a person enters a TC, he or she participates in a range of interconnected therapeutic activities that link together through processes of group and individual feedback.

However, it is important to note that for this process to be effective, there needs to be a shared case formulation within the MDT and for this to be discussed, agreed and understood with the client and the wider community. Finally, under this section the importance of the physical and psychological safety of clients and staff is paramount. Creating environments that evoke OPB carries potential risks. The prime responsibility for managing this process rests with the therapeutic team but is also shared by the residents of the community:

> The task of the therapeutic team is to set up a social environment where residents feel safe and able to relinquish their aggressive and paranoid attitudes that they have acquired in the prison system . . . Residents must feel they are in an environment safe enough to explore their criminal behaviour, and to be challenged and criticised about their rationalisations and avoidances of responsibility and . . . to tolerate the criticism and hostility that they may be faced with during their stay without resort to assaultative behaviour or other destructive activity which would undermine the work, (Shine & Morris, 1999, p. 203).

Reassuringly, the most recent research and the institutional climate of HMP Grendon, a TC that is accredited and includes attention to OPB as an important component of the model of change, indicates that across a range of measures such as the institutional climate and levels of assault, Grendon performs considerably better than comparable prisons with similar populations (Goodwin, 2008). This indicates that properly regulated TCs can work safely and effectively in an environment that evokes OPB.

Rule 3: Reinforce PABs

Kohlenberg and Tsai (1991) note that applying rule 3 in terms of CRB2s is difficult to put into practice because in traditional therapy the only natural reinforcers are the reactions between the individual therapist and client. In a holistic therapeutic model such as a TC, the range of reinforcers in the natural environment is considerably greater and includes: all members of the MDT, the patient's nursing team or personal officer/group officer, the members of his small psychotherapy group, the wider community group, social contact with visitors or peer reviews as part of the TC audit, as well as the range of staff he will come into contact with through activities such as occupational therapy groups. The main factor that differentiates the TC approach from a model such as that described by Daffern (see this volume, Chapter 6) is

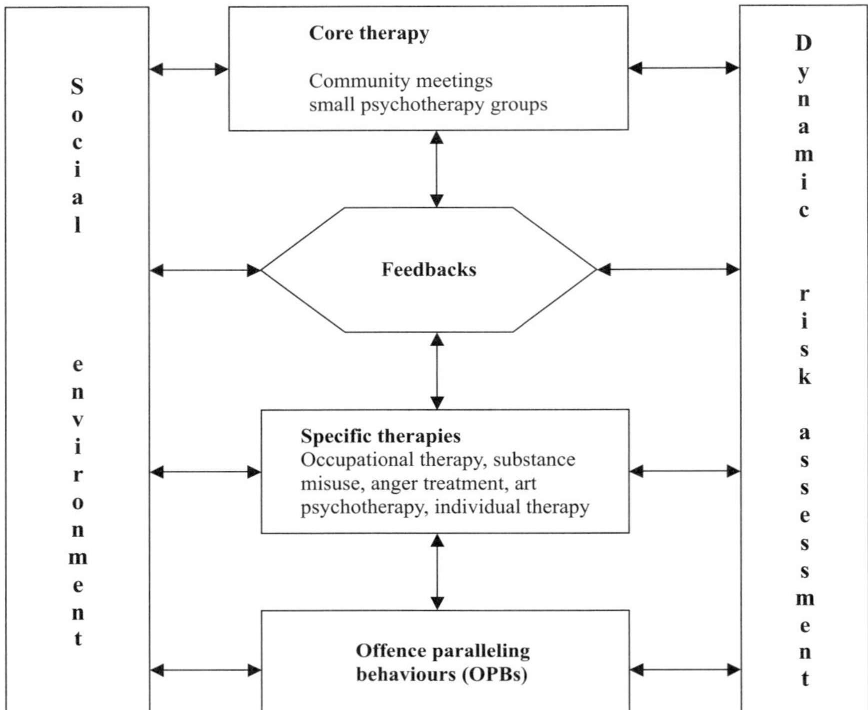

Figure 12.2 Role of OPB within an adapted forensic therapeutic community.

that as well as unit staff, the reinforcement comes from the patient's peer group. One area where patient feedback can be particularly helpful is in the awareness of avoidance behaviour from the client. In FAP the role of the therapist is to ask what the response avoids. In TCs, this can be done by the patient group to great therapeutic effect, particularly if the other patients have been through similar experiences and are alert to avoidance or other types of safety-seeking behaviours.

OPB IN A TC SETTING

The quotation at the start of this chapter was taken from Ashby (1957), in *An Introduction to Cybernetics*. Ashby illustrated how focusing on a few connections, such as feedback loops in cybernetics, is of limited use in understanding the functioning of the whole system when there are complex interconnections between parts of the system taking place. In a similar way, interactions between a patient and a single therapist, or a group session set within a traditional prison or secure hospital environment, may provide little information about how an offender is behaving outside therapy sessions and within his wider social and support network. Such interactions may serve to reinforce the offender's criminal or prosocial behaviour. The concept of OPB gives a useful theoretical framework to bridge this divide and potentially achieve a greater understanding of patterns of lapsing and relapsing behaviour. Institutional environments, such as TCs, that use this framework are able to identify and work with criminogenic treatment targets in a 'here-and-now' environment. However, for OPB to be useful, the environment itself needs to evoke equivalent variables to the client's offending behaviour. In this chapter, I have argued that the forensic TC can provide such an environment. However, in order to be useful, it is vital to consider the behaviour as part of a holistic approach rather than independent systems. In this way, validity and reliability in assessing OPB and PAB can be improved.

A model for an adapted TC has recently been described (Shine, 2010). This contains elements found in all accredited TCs (termed core therapies – small groups, community meetings and feedbacks) and specific therapies based on treatment need. In this model, OPB forms the link between the social environment and dynamic risk assessment through observation of a patient's behaviour in the environment. The important point is that the OPB is linked closely with all the elements of the model. In this way, OPB and PAB can be used to identify, practise and review treatment targets in the real-life setting of the TC such as community meetings, small groups and specific therapies, (Figure 12.2).

CONCLUSION

This chapter has described how OPB has played an increasing role in the development of forensic TCs in the last decade and how the concept could be elaborated further through the use of methods from integrative therapeutic approaches, specifically FAP. Finally, it should be noted that the OPB construct is, at this point in time, in the early stages of development. I have argued that, theoretically, the TC environment provides the ideal culture to assess and work with OPB. However, although this perspective may be strongly supported by clinical lore and anecdote, it is important to stress that it is, at this stage, a hypothesis and therefore open to confirmation or refutation. Research on OPB has only recently begun. An important question raised by this chapter is the types of institutional environments that are best suited to working with OPB. Future research needs to identify whether the propositions argued in this chapter are empirically supported. One way that future research could investigate this is by comparing the identification and capacity to work clinically with OPB in traditional forensic institutions and in forensic TC settings.

REFERENCES

Andrews, D.A. & Bonta, J. (1994). *The Psychology of Criminal Conduct*. Cincinatti, OH: Anderson.

Andrews, D.A. & Bonta, J. (1998). *The Psychology of Criminal Conduct* (2nd edition). Cincinnati, OH: Anderson.

Ashby, W.R. (1957). *An Introduction to Cybernetics*. London: Chapman and Hall.

Bonta, J. (1997). *Offender Rehabilitation: From Research to Practice*. Ottawa: Public Works and Government Services Canada.

Bukstel, L.H. & Kilmann, P.R. (1980). Psychological effects of imprisonment on confined individuals. *Psychological Bulletin*, *88*, 469–93.

Clark, D., Fisher, M.J. & McDougall, C. (1994). A new methodology for assessing the level of risk in incarcerated offenders. *British Journal of Criminology*, *33*, 436–48.

Clark, D. & Lees, J. (2004) Auditing prison service accredited interventions. In M. Parker (Ed.), *Dynamic Security – The Democratic Therapeutic Community in Prison* (pp. 255–70). London: Jessica Kingsley.

Clarke, A., Simmonds, R. & Wyatt, S. (2004). *Delivering Cognitive Skills Programmes in Prison: A Qualitative Study* (Research Findings No. 242). London: Home Office.

Daffern, M., Jones, L., Howells, K., Shine, J., Mikton, C. & Tunbridge, V.C. (2007). Refining the definition of offence paralleling behaviour. *Criminal Behaviour and Mental Health*, *17*, 265–73.

Dowden, C. & Andrews, D.A. (2004). The importance of staff practice in delivering effective correctional treatment: a meta-analytic review of core correctional practice. *International Journal of Offender Therapy and Comparative Criminology*, *48*, 203–214.

Genders, E. & Player, E. (1995). *Grendon: A Study of a Therapeutic Prison*. Oxford: Clarendon Press.

Goffman, E. (1991). *Asylums: Essays on the Social Situation of Mental Patients and Other Inmates*. London: Penguin Social Sciences.

Goodwin, C. (2008). HMP Grendon: A prison therapeutic community. *Forensic Update*, *94*, 29–34.

Harris, G.T., Rice, M.E. & Cormier, C.A. (1991). Psychopathy and violent recidivism. *Law and Human Behaviour*, *15*, 625–37.

HM Prison Service (2004). *Accreditation Manual Prison Therapeutic Communities*. London: Abell House.

HM Prison Service (2005). *Chromis Manuals*. London: Offending Behaviour Programme Unit, Abell House.

Jones, L.F. (1997). Developing models for managing treatment integrity and efficacy in a prison based TC: The Max Glatt Centre. In E. Cullen, L. Jones & R. Woodward (Eds), *Therapeutic Communities for Offenders* (pp. 121–57). Chichester: Wiley.

Jones, L. (2004). Offence Paralleling Behaviour (OPB) as a framework for assessment and interventions with offenders. In A. Needs & G. Towl (Eds), *Applying Psychology to Forensic Practice*, (pp. 34–63). Oxford: Blackwell and British Psychological Society.

Kennard D. (1998). *An Introduction to Therapeutic Communities*. London: Jessica Kingsley.

Kohlenberg, R.J. & Tsai, M. (1991). *Functional Analytic Psychotherapy: Creating Intense and Curative Therapeutic Relationships*. New York: Plenum Press.

Moncher, F.J. & Prinz, J. (1991). Treatment fidelity in outcome studies. *Clinical Psychology Review*, *11*(3), 247–66.

Morris, M. (2004). *Dangerous and Severe: Process, Programme, and Person: Grendon's Work*. London: Jessica Kingsley.

Norton, K. (1992). A culture of enquiry: it's preservation or loss. *Therapeutic Communities*, *13*, 3–25.

Ryle, A. (1997). *Cognitive Analytic Therapy and Borderline Personality Disorder: The Model and the Method*. Chichester: Wiley.

Shine, J. (2010). Towards a social analytical therapy. In R. Shuker & E. O'Sullivan (Eds), *Grendon and the Emergence of Therapeutic Communities: Developments in Research and Practice* (pp. 79–96). Oxford: Wiley.

Shine, J. & Morris, M. (1999). *Regulating Anarchy*. Aylesbury: Springhill Press.

Shine, J. & Morris, M. (2000). Addressing criminogenic needs in a prison therapeutic community. *Therapeutic Communities*, *21*, 197–218.

Young, J.E. (1994). *Cognitive Therapy for Personality Disorders: A Schema Focussed Approach* (revised edition). Sarasota, FL: Professional Resource Exchange.

Chapter 13

A QUALITATIVE EXPLORATION OF OFFENCE PARALLELING BEHAVIOUR: A PRISON-BASED DEMOCRATIC THERAPEUTIC COMMUNITY RESIDENT'S PERSPECTIVE

Natalie Bond

HMP Gartree, Leicestershire, UK

Gail Steptoe-Warren

Coventry University, Warwickshire, UK

INTRODUCTION

Exploring offence paralleling behaviour (OPB) from the perspective of the residents of a prison-based democratic therapeutic community (TC) is the focus of research described in this chapter. Within TCs the OPB framework has been advocated as a focus for both intervention and risk assessment of offenders with the potential to inform treatment planning and assessment of progress throughout an intervention (Jones, 2004; Jones & Shuker, 2004; Shine & Morris, 2000). An emphasis on interpersonal interaction as a basis for therapy allows the emergence of dynamic risk factors, providing a potentially ideal environment for OPBs to emerge, be identified and addressed (see Shine & Morris, 2000 for more details on the TC environment and process). In this context OPBs are both anticipated and contained.

TCs have been offered as an approach for the rehabilitation of offenders in UK prisons since the 1960s. In more recent years, there has been a growing demand to make tangible the evidence of their effectiveness to retain their credibility and funding (Jones & Shuker, 2004). The 'what works' literature has highlighted the importance of criminogenic risk factors in the treatment of offenders (Andrews & Bonta, 1994) and TCs are required to show they are able to address criminogenic need in a clearly defined manner (Shine & Morris, 2000). Measuring the progress of residents poses a formidable methodological challenge, but is crucial to understand the effective elements of the intervention and to demonstrate effectiveness of the TC approach.

Offence Paralleling Behaviour: A Case Formulation Approach to Offender Assessment and Intervention Edited by Michael Daffern, Lawrence Jones and John Shine

OFFENCE PARALLELING BEHAVIOUR IN A DEMOCRATIC THERAPEUTIC COMMUNITY

Morris (2004) proposed a model of change detailing how TCs target criminogenic need on the basis of four assumptions. Firstly, it is assumed that *offence re-enactment* occurs. This is described as minor infringement that in some way echo or mimic the index offence. It is assumed that criminogenic factors contribute to offence re-enactment during these infringements as they do actual offending (Lewis, 1997). Secondly, behaviour displayed in one context (work, sports field) is addressed in another (therapy group), termed *lateral linkage* (Morris, 2004). Thirdly, deeper understanding of criminogenic factors and offending is gained through exploration (Morris, 2004). The fourth assumption is that an individual's criminogenic factors or offending profile become common knowledge across both staff and residents who are able to recognize offence re-enactment in order to prompt exploration and change. Currently, no empirical research in the forensic literature exists to test these assumptions or the effectiveness of the strategy.

The concept of offence re-enactment is similar to the phenomenon of OPB, which has also been described as a framework for TC intervention (Jones, 1997, 2004; Shine & Morris, 2000). OPB had been defined as any form of offence-related behavioural pattern that emerges at any point before or after an offence (Jones, 2004). The behaviour does not have to result in an offence but significantly resemble the sequence of behaviours that did lead to an offence (Jones, 2004). Initially used with drug users, this strategy involved establishing links between an individual's relapsing behaviour in prison and, when at liberty, finding patterns or a parallel process to the offending behaviour. Jones (1997) reported that the strategy, utilized at the Max Glatt Therapeutic Community, was extended to target other offence-related behaviour. Behaviour was explored on four levels (behaviour, affect, cognitions and fantasy) within three domains including childhood, offending and current behaviour (Shine & Morris, 2000).

A revised definition (Daffern et al., 2007b) suggests that OPB is a behavioural sequence incorporating overt behaviours (that may be muted by environmental factors), appraisals, expectations, beliefs, affects, goals and behavioural scripts that is functionally similar to behavioural sequences involved in previous criminal acts. The revised definition was born from concern that the original definition was too broad, potentially overly inclusive and vulnerable to misapplication. Daffern et al. (2007b) aimed to encourage best practice and emphasized that behaviours being referred to as OPB should be functionally rather than topographically similar and might be 'muted' by contextual factors. The research described in this chapter was conducted prior to the revised definition yet also highlighted concern that the term OPB might be over-inclusive. Establishing the function of behaviour was important in confirming that a behaviour was offence paralleling. Further, consideration of personal and social factors was also deemed necessary as these might mute or modify the presentation of OPBs.

EMPIRICAL RESEARCH

With regards to previous research, there is one study that has focused on OPB, assessing and modelling behavioural change in a prison TC (Neville et al., 2007). In this study, a behavioural checklist was devised through content analysis of staff case notes of group therapy sessions and included both negative and positive behaviours. A multidimensional approach was then used to trace the presence of those behaviours and change over regular intervals for each participant.

A general shift from dysfunctional to functional behaviours in the therapy group was observed for those who remained in treatment for 18 months (Neville et al., 2007).

Assessing and monitoring observable behaviours may be a positive progression when compared to prior research, which has ordinarily demonstrated TC effectiveness through self-reported measures (Newton, 1998). Self-reported change may not translate into actual behaviour change and measures can be vulnerable to potential deception and self-presentation biases. Neville and colleagues (2007) research is also a positive shift from previous behavioural checklists that concentrate solely on problematic behaviours (Hobson et al., 2000). This trend is important given the significance of identifying and reinforcing positive behaviours to encourage change (Ward, 2002).

However, the checklist described by Neville and colleagues (2007) measures dysfunctional behaviour that is not necessarily OPB; these dysfunctional behaviours are not based on, or linked to, an assessment of the individual's offending behaviour pattern. Therefore, changes demonstrated might be positive but not necessarily offence-related. For example, the checklist would identify a reduction in the frequency of negative behaviours, such as arguing or disagreeing. However, the men could continue to respond aggressively to a parallel trigger pertinent in the index offence, therefore continuing to display OPB. As such, a focus on a discrete behaviour without context makes it difficult to assess whether it is the individual that has changed or merely that pertinent situational triggers are absent. Functional analysis, as described by Sturmey (1996), would help to identify the cycle of offending, to include situational factors and the function of behaviours, against which current patterns of behaviour might be measured. Methods proposed to assess if current behaviours are offence paralleling are further outlined in Jones (2004), although this remains an area that is underdeveloped and needs to be the subject to future research. Arguably, user-friendly checklists to measure offence-related behavioural change might only be useful if they are individually tailored and based on an adequate functional analysis (Daffern et al., 2007b).

Empirical research has highlighted the potential problems while focusing on offence-related behaviour as discrete behaviour, rather than a process (Daffern et al., 2008). Analogous models that infer continuing pathology and risk based on the presence of discrete behaviours analogous in form to offending behaviour have been shown to be misleading (Daffern et al., 2008). In a study of sexually abusive behaviours in patients in a dangerous and severe personality disorder (DSPD) unit, Daffern and colleagues (2008) revealed a high level of low-severity sexually abusive behaviour. Against expectations, the frequency of recorded sexually abusive behaviour was unrelated to seriousness of prior offending. Sexually abusive behaviours were observed in both those with and without prior sexual offending history. These results suggest that apparently comparable behaviours might not actually be indicative of sexual deviancy and as such, used as evidence of persistent or apparent risk, of sexual reoffending. Used properly, the OPB framework, which considers sequence and function of behaviour, may provide a more accurate assessment of risk for sexual recidivism.

Concern that the OPB framework has found its way into practice in several contexts well before empirical support and conceptual clarity has led practitioners to call for empirical research regarding this concept (Daffern et al., 2007b). Although intuitively and clinically appealing, lack of scrutiny of the feasibility of the framework for either treatment or risk assessment purposes was thought to increase the potential for misuse (Daffern et al., 2007b). Inappropriate use of this framework may have adverse implications for those to whom it is applied. As such, there is both the potential for prolonged detention or unwarranted treatment based on supposed 'OPBs' that are incorrectly considered to be evidence of persistent psychopathology (Daffern et al., 2007b).

CURRENT RESEARCH

Given the above concern, the current research set out to explore the offence paralleling construct from the perspective of those on whom the framework might be applied: offenders resident in a TC. Whilst practitioners have detailed their observations and assumptions regarding offence paralleling in the TC (Jones, 1997; Morris, 2004), current empirical research is limited. If these behaviours are used to indicate current risk or to measure progress, then methods of accurate identification would need to be devised and a thorough understanding of the issues that might undermine the accuracy of this approach would be beneficial. The current research was conducted in 2006, prior to the growing interest, revised definition and recent published research concerning OPB (e.g. Daffern et al., 2008; Daffern et al, 2009).

Applying grounded theory to TC residents' perspectives of OPB was considered an ideal opportunity to submerge the researcher in the phenomena of interest, without the constraints of 'expert' opinion. TC residents offer a unique insight into the potential function, motives and intentions behind their own offending and current behaviours, which might not be accessible from observation alone. As voluntary and active participants in the daily process of therapy, the TC resident's experience in identifying and exploring current and offending behaviour and the link between the two was thought to be an invaluable resource from which this research project hoped to gain. Knowledge of whether the concept of offence paralleling might be operationalized as an indicator of current risk and/or indicator of treatment progress might benefit from the experience of people who display and work with this concept on a daily basis. The aim of the current research was therefore to gain an insight into OPB, as a phenomenon and a focus for intervention, from those engaged in the TC process. The aim to explore behaviours that might be deemed offence paralleling by residents and how they are identified was hoped to unravel some of the emerging issues with this concept.

There is a paucity of literature concerning sex offenders within TCs and issues have been identified with monitoring sexualized behaviour within institutions (Daffern et al., 2008). Therefore, the current research aimed to explore offence paralleling from the perspectives of men who resided in a prison-based TC and have been convicted of a sexual offence(s). Focus groups are considered particularly suited to research exploring individuals' opinions, understanding and ideas (Wilkinson, 2003) and therefore were employed here. Focus groups benefit from the interaction between participants, which stimulated meaningful debate and discussion.

METHOD

Participants

Participants were 23 residents from the specialized sex offender wing at HMP Grendon. The majority had a current ($n = 19$) and/or a previous conviction ($n = 6$) for a sexual offence. A total of 17 were recorded as posing a risk to children. Participants' mean age was 38 years (standard deviation was 8.5 years) and age of participants ranged from 22 to 69 years. The majority were described as white ($n = 21$), two were described as minority ethnic. The mean length of time at HMP Grendon for participants was 22 months ($SD = 10$, range = 1–61 months).

Consent

All participants consented to take part in the research exploring the nature of OPB within the TC and agreed that any information gathered could be used for research purposes and published.

Procedure

Consistent with TC principles, residents democratically voted in favour of the research taking place on the wing, and 23 of the 42 community members volunteered to take part. Participants gave informed consent and were asked to attend one of the focus groups held in a private room on the wing. The focus groups were recorded in the form of field notes transcribed by the researcher. Focus groups lasted between 1 and 1.5 hours. Participants were asked to explain their understanding of offence paralleling, what behaviours they deemed to be offence paralleling and describe how these behaviours are identified. The researcher adopted a facilitator role with minimal direction to ensure the issues that arose were those deemed significant by the participants. Participants were debriefed after each focus group and advised to take any arising issues to their therapy group.

Analytic Strategy

All information gathered during the focus groups was subjected to grounded theory analysis (Charmaz, 1995; Strauss & Corbin, 1990). Grounded theorists advocate the use of a set of systematic procedures to inductively derive a theory, or set of categories, from the qualitative data (Strauss & Corbin, 1990). Each line of data was provided a concept code, termed *open coding*, and then similar concept codes were grouped, termed *axial coding*. These techniques were used to record, group and relate themes and concepts as they emerged from the data. Memo writing was used to record ideas during open coding to aid later analysis. Constant comparisons were made using the *flip-flop* technique to ensure categories devised matched the data and the notion of *category saturation* (Strauss & Corbin, 1990) was considered met when no more themes or categories could be found and all ideas had been thoroughly elaborated.

Results

Grounded theory analysis of the research transcripts resulted in the construction of the OPB model (OPBM) with three core and 15 sub-categories. Sub-categories are not necessarily mutually exclusive. All categories are evidenced by transcript extracts.

OFFENCE PARALLELING BEHAVIOUR MODEL

The OPBM comprises three core categories (definition, enactment and engaging). Exploring a resident's understanding of OPB provided contributions which naturally grouped into a resident's *definition* of OPB, which was the first core category established. *Enactment* grouped contributions regarding the behavioural manifestation or enactment of OPBs, which included examples of behaviours (*parallel behaviours*) and associated issues with the presentation of those behaviours (*modified manifestation*). Therefore, *enactment* was split into *modified manifestation* and *parallel behaviours*. *Modified manifestation* was the term attached to residents' comments concerning the issue that OPBs observed might be modified or distorted in some way within the prison environment. *Parallel behaviours* grouped contributions, which described behaviours that the residents thought were offence paralleling. The category was then subdivided into the types of behaviours discussed (*potentially all, grooming, fantasy/pornography, isolation and maladaptive coping*).

The third core category of *engaging* grouped comments which described the therapeutic process through which OPBs are identified and addressed within the TC. The sub-categories that emerged could be labelled *motivation, familiarity, monitor, challenge, link domains, develop insight* and *replace old behaviours*.

DEFINITION

The defining features of OPB described by the residents emphasized current, day-to-day behaviour resembling the offending behaviour process ('behaviour in here that is same as behaviour leading up to offence') manifested in a weaker form ('not as extreme') identifiable in themselves and others ('I recognise paralleling in others') observable across contexts ('same patterns in what we do, in work and leisure') representing core elements of themselves ('is all related to core beliefs') rooted in childhood experience (see Linking Domains) often observable in what they described as 'boundary pushing'. Parallel function was also emphasized giving consideration to intended use and victim ('depends who I apply it to . . . depends how I use it').

ENACTMENT

Enactment referred to the issues with, and the behavioural manifestations of, offence paralleling.

Modified Manifestation

A core facet of the OPBM described concerned the notion that OPB might be muted or modified in some respect, either by personal choice or environmental factors.

Conscious effort to adhere to community rules and motivation to change behaviour can mute or modify the behavioural presentation ('it is like still going on with stuff was doing outside but try to suppress it'). Attempts to avoid detection would also mute OPB. It is noteworthy, that whilst residents described attempts to avoid detection, the behaviours reported had ultimately been detected through the therapeutic process. One resident admitted 'dealing in pornography' which was discovered ('when it all came out and came on top I tried to get out of it'). He described how using pornography was not related to his offending, but criminal activities similar to this were. Various strategies to avoid detection described included 'lying', 'keeping quiet', 'keeping people away' and 'keeping a close clique of friends'.

The physical constraints of the prison environment were noted as a significant factor that could potentially mute or modify the manifestation of OPBs. Limited or no opportunity to directly offend was particularly emphasized by child sex offenders ('there is no access to directly offend', 'I can't actually offend in prison as I do not have access . . . you know to young girls'). Substituting elements of the offending process ('I could only use fantasy, not actually offend') or modifying the form was also described ('I used alcohol outside and went to self-harm inside'). In contrast, environmental constraints were seen to increase some forms of sexually related behaviour ('it is like a kettle on boil . . . there is a lot of sexual banter . . . haven't got outside stimuli').

Parallel Behaviours

Despite the strong notion that potentially all problematic behaviours might be considered offence paralleling, several behaviours consistently and strongly emerged as those considered to be identifiable as potentially OPBs by the residents.

Potentially All

The notion that potentially all problematic behaviour reflects core aspects of an individual's pervasive interpersonal and thinking styles was raised. Daily interactions were deemed to highlight deficits that were apparent in and contributed to their offending and therefore viewed as offence paralleling ('Asking for juice at the pod that you are not entitled to is like attitude why pay when can get it for free? . . . why pay for sex when can get it for free? . . . I feel entitled to it', 'look at the small things, not emptying bins, leaving the light on, inconsideration for others is parallel'). It was acknowledged that 'people have different views of what is relevant' and that it may be a benefit to interrogate all problematic behaviour to determine what is offence paralleling ('everything a benefit to look at', and 'need to scrutinize parts of you then put it all together').

Grooming

Behaviours described as 'grooming' were consistently referred to as offence paralleling. The most direct example of this was provided by one resident who described how, in his previous prison, he had befriended a young male, whom he had perceived as weak, with the intention to sexually and violently offend against him. This had paralleled the antecedents to the resident's index offence ('I chose my victim because I thought he was weak'). When this resident transferred to the therapeutic community, the inappropriate nature of this friendship was detected by wing staff through the monitoring of his mail ('The staff on the wing were reading my mail and they saw what I was writing and they confronted me about it'). Whilst there was a consensus that grooming was an OPB often observable in the community environment, they readily debated the fact that the function of the behaviour needed to be interrogated before assuming it as offence-related. Intention and recipient were considered significant factors when assessing whether grooming behaviours observed were offence paralleling:

> When [we] groom children get them involved in activities buying and giving them things, with people on wing . . . offering to give people things . . . is trying to buy their friendship. Depends who apply it to . . . with children was to get them into bed.

Fantasy/Pornography

Fantasizing about offending and use of pornography were often referred to in unison and are linked here purely for illustrative purposes and brevity; these distinct behaviours did not necessarily co-occur. The term pornography was used to describe both pornographic material and neutral material used to fuel offence-related fantasies. Sexual fantasy was described both as a parallel to the antecedents of offending and something which provided a replacement for offending.

Fantasizing about offending and using pornography were identified as pertinent antecedents to sexual offending and for some had manifested since coming to prison ('Getting caught watching porn in here, which I did, is related to offence', 'I was using material to fuel fantasies [prior to coming to therapeutic community] up to SOTP [sex offender treatment programme]'. Some felt that current use of pornography was not necessarily offence-related ('I didn't use this porn to fuel it for that'), whilst for others it was considered a problem and offence-related. The men described how this is explored further during the therapy.

Isolation

This category grouped behaviours such as being withdrawn, secretive, not communicating, not expressing emotions, becoming socially isolated and perceiving emotional isolation. Isolation was frequently commented upon and consistently deemed offence-related by the residents' apparent in the antecedents and a contributing factor to offending ('Isolated . . . why offend?' 'I was keeping friends away', 'It is like not being able to communicate to others and not expressing your emotions . . . this is all linked to offending', 'expressing self and confiding in people were problems which had prior to offending and were things that contributed to offending'). Many reported exhibiting these behaviours in the prison environment ('Always being secretive like was outside', 'offence paralleling behaviour is behaviour like becoming withdrawn and being secretive', 'what I carrying over is only isolation from my life outside', 'I can do that now, I shut my cell door, I do it emotionally, I shut myself off'). Some felt that isolating themselves was specific to those who committed sexual offence ('sex offenders have isolated personalities').

Anger and Aggression

Examples of institutional aggression included an attempted and an actual physical assault ('swung at member of staff', 'bit someone, cut someone with plastic knife'), incidents of verbal abuse ('called her a bitch', 'arguing and shouting', 'become verbally aggressive') an incident of aggression towards property ('he threw the chair') and passive aggressive behaviour ('would not even talk to or look at women, they were beneath me'). Many identified poor anger management as a 'big problem' and felt they had a 'bad temper', which was linked to their violent offending. Some identified parallels in the function of violence during offending and current incidents of aggression, which included using aggression to cope with other emotions or difficulties ('That is how I used to deal with things', 'look for a fight as a way of coping with emotions') and maintaining a violent image ('I had an image . . .').

Maladaptive Coping

Maladaptive coping strategies, often involving avoidant or defensive strategies, were highlighted as a significant antecedent to offending, which they felt are also paralleled in the prison environment ('I hurt people to stop how I felt', 'look for a fight as a way of coping with emotions', 'I masturbated to porn as a way of coping', 'I have used drugs in prison [previous prison]').

Residents highlighted how behaviour may take a different form but serve a similar function to offence-related behaviour. Examples included those who would manage emotions through aggressive or violent behaviours, who found other maladaptive methods to mange emotions, such as self-harming or obsessive behaviour ('I have self-harmed in prison [previous prison]', 'I am control freak . . . cleaning to cope').

ENGAGING

The core category, *engaging*, grouped residents' comments concerning how they engage with the TC process, which encouraged them to identify, challenge and replace OPB. Residents discussed the therapeutic factors, which encouraged the men to identify OPB and the stages they go through to explore OPB.

Motivation

Motivation on the part of the individual to explore their behaviour, disclose their own failings, monitor and challenge others whilst accepting challenge and responsibility for their own behaviour was described as a fundamental requirement ('We come here with the intention of looking at our behaviour . . . we have to own our behaviour, we have to take responsibility for it') to identify OPB and engage with the therapeutic process.

Familiarity

Small therapy groups provide a forum for self-disclosure through which individuals get to know each other. Telling their life story is an expectation of participants in TC and facilitates the identification of OPBs ('We become familiar with each other, each others' lives and offending . . . give a life story at the beginning of therapy when we feel comfortable', 'It is a lot easier to notice offence behaviour in those who are in our smaller group because we hear more of them'). Importantly, there is a reliance on self-disclosure to identify paralleling behaviours that might otherwise be hidden, such as sexual fantasy ('No one else knows what is in your head, only you can bring this stuff to the group'). Living in close proximity allows individuals to get to know each other well enough to identify what they described as OPB ('When people on your landing are not coping we know . . . You know when people are not coping because you get used to their normal behaviour. This is all part of our offending').

Monitor

Active monitoring was a fundamental aspect of the OPBM described ('We police ourselves'). The men explained how it was easier to identify and monitor behaviours in others than in themselves ('It is easier to recognize faults and flaws in each other, rather than yourself'). Some felt that they were in a better position than the staff to monitor behaviour ('We see more than the staff'), whereas others disagreed ('no difference in the type of behaviours identified by staff and prisoners').

Personal experience was considered a key aspect that facilitated active monitoring ('You think you are good at keeping secrets but they have been doing it twice as long as me', 'we can recognize these behaviours in each other as we have done it ourselves'). An element of seeing themselves in others was also described ('like when you see behaviours by others . . . see in self').

Challenge

Residents described how both they and the staff actively question individuals about their behaviour. Being 'challenged' was consistently referred to as an important strategy for identifying OPB and understanding what part it plays in the process of offending ('My small group challenged me over it [using pornography] . . . they asked me why I needed it . . . I didn't think that I had needed it, I didn't think it had been a problem, but I had a change of opinion').

Link Domains

This subcategory grouped residents' reflections of how they explore behaviour across domains (childhood, offending and current behaviour) and context to identify and understand OPB.

Many residents firmly identified the origin of their current and offending behaviour patterns to be rooted in their childhood developmental experiences. Many reported being victim to traumatic childhood experiences such as sexual abuse, physical abuse, neglect and bullying ('I was abused by my stepdad', 'I came from a very abusive family', 'I was sexually abused when I was in children's homes') and/or witness to abusive relationships ('parents argue, he would swear and shout but not hit her') from which most believed their own maladaptive behaviour evolved ('It comes from own abuse', and 'my behaviour related to my childhood').

Understanding the impact of childhood experiences on offending and current functioning was particularly emphasized. Some men identified that they had transferred negative emotions felt towards childhood abusers to current relationships and victims. One man described 'dehumanizing people', including the victim of his violent rape and, through verbal abuse, his current partner and female officers on the wing who, in doing so, he offended against. He stated, 'It relates to mum ... she is a cruel, evil bitch ... I have no love for mum ... have measured all women against my mum'.

Other residents described transferring the dominance of past abusers to themselves and/or through a process of social learning modelled abusive behaviour ('I think that when I attacked her [victim of rape and murder] I pictured myself and I was actually my mother ... like how she used to attack me').

Identifying OPBs required time ('When been here a while, have been here 12 months, begin to see patterns in behaviour') and exploration of behaviours across contexts ('we would still have the same patterns in what we do, in work and leisure', 'things did outside now doing inside like', 'the image we show on the wing is the image we put up outside').

Develop Insight

Identifying OPBs required personal insight which residents described as a fundamental aim, developed through the therapeutic process. Residents described a shift from awareness of a problem ('I have ... a deviant arousal to children', 'I had a bad attitude towards females', 'I can't emotionally trust', 'I get a buzz out of having power over someone') to an understanding of that problem. They described insight into contributing factors and antecedents to offending behaviour ('My wife was ill', 'at the time of my index offence my relationship was going downhill', 'I had groomed my victims, I had befriended their family'). Residents discussed their insight into their offending process, such as recognizing acute triggers and cognitive processes, insight they had acquired through the therapeutic process ('I start grievance thinking', 'if staff do something to disempower me', 'when people take the micky it is like stepping back to being at school'). The residents often described how they had developed insight into the function of their offending behaviour ('The anger and violence ... used it to mask how feeling', 'I hurt people to stop how I felt'). The insight gained was described as paramount in producing change but this insight was not always present ('I don't recognize why I am doing it and if I did, I would stop it').

Replacing Old Behaviour

Some residents were keen to emphasize how they were learning to replace their OPB with prosocial alternatives and more functional behaviours. This is consistent with the concept of positive alternative behaviours (PAB) described by Daffern et al. (2007b). Some residents considered that the most positive changes were appropriate expression and management of their emotions, replacing antisocial attitudes and negative feelings, communicating with others and asking for help ('I have started trying to express, expressing myself and confiding in people', 'I am learning ways to sit on feelings and deal with them', 'I am expressing self more appropriately', 'now I take a step back and calm down', and 'now have positive feelings and see a side to women I have not seen before'). Learning and encouragement from others were often referred to as essential aspects of the change process.

DISCUSSION

The aim of the research, to explore OPB as a phenomenon and focus for intervention through the eyes of those engaged in a TC intervention, was achieved. The research benefited significantly from residents' insight and openness about their lives, experiences and offending.

Residents' definitions of OPB showed an understanding and concern reasonably consistent with that described of clinicians and researchers (Daffern et al., 2007b; Daffern et al., 2008; Jones, 2004; Morris, 2004). The notion that *potentially all* negative behaviours may parallel offending in some respect is perhaps similar to the concern that the term OPB, without clarification, might be overinclusive (Daffern et al., 2007b). TC residents' implied sequences of behaviour were important and reported that they displayed 'patterns' of behaviours 'similar' to those in the lead-up to and commission of their offending, although typically in a 'less extreme' manner. Assessing the function of behaviour was also highlighted. Use of pornography and 'sexual banter' were examples of behaviours they felt could be potentially misinterpreted as pathological if considered out of context and without consideration of the function of that behaviour.

The OPBM provided insight into those behaviours which residents deemed potentially offence paralleling (parallel behaviours: potentially all, grooming, fantasy/pornography, isolation, anger/aggression and maladaptive coping) and the importance of exploring the function of behaviours and factors that might influence the presentation of those behaviours (modified manifestation). Additionally, residents described how the TC encouraged an environment where OPBs can be identified, contained, challenged and changed (engaging: motivation, familiarity, monitor, challenge, link domains, develop insight and replacing old behaviours). Residents described an environment that encouraged and supported them to replace old behaviours and develop and practise prosocial alternatives (replacing old behaviours).

The grounded theory approach was conducive to extracting themes without imposing preconceived ideas that may have restricted the level of insight and rich description gained. Residents provided a unique opportunity to view OPB from the perspective of the offender, which had been absent from the OPB literature to date. OPB, as a description, appeared to have face validity for residents' which perhaps aided the research.

It is encouraging that the validity of the OPBM is supported by consistency with the model of change proposed by Morris (2004) and the OPB framework outlined by Jones (1997, 2004). Residents described a process which benefited from *motivation* to address offending behaviour, self-disclosure and a sense of shared problems (*familiarity*), an active aim to *monitor* and *challenge* current behaviour in order to establish parallels (*link domains*) from which, with time, they *develop insight* necessary to make offence-related change (*replacing old behaviours*). This resonates with the therapeutic processes highlighted by prior research (Genders & Player, 1995; Miller et al., 2006).

The current research provided insight into the factors that facilitate the self-reported change of TC residents that has been observed by others (Genders & Players, 1995; Gunn et al., 1978; Newton, 1998). Encouragingly, the behaviours reportedly targeted by the OPB framework (replacing old behaviours) in this study are amongst the main criminogenic risk factors deemed treatment targets in the offender rehabilitation literature (Andrew & Bonta, 1994), including pervasive criminal personality, emotional management and criminal attitudes.

Previous research has highlighted the 'time-in-treatment effect' (Cullen, 1994; Genders & Players, 1995; Marshall, 1997; Taylor, 2000) where self-reported change and reduced reconviction rate are observed in those who remain in TC treatment for 18 months or more. Consistent with this, residents reported that time is needed for old behavioural patterns to emerge, be identified and challenged and allow for practise of new behaviours within the TC environment, some referring to 12 months. Residents also noted that time was needed for community members to establish the required level of familiarity with one another to recognize and challenge offence paralleling.

IMPLICATIONS FOR PRACTICE

The feasibility of using OPBs, as a focus for intervention, risk assessment, treatment planning or as a means to measure progress through an intervention, is dependent on valid and reliable observation and recording. The research findings here highlight some of the issues with identifying and monitoring behaviour within an OPB framework. These issues require consideration and include the notion that current behaviours might be muted or modified by personal and/or environmental factors and the need for clear criteria as potentially all negative behaviours could be deemed offence paralleling by staff and residents. Further, behaviours need to be explored to establish function. The importance of self-disclosure of behaviours not observable to others, such as fantasizing, and the importance of time to allow OPBs to emerge and be identified are also critical issues.

The notion that even trivial problematic behaviour may reflect core aspects of an individual's pervasive interpersonal or thinking style and that these may parallel their offending is potentially problematic. The suggestion that *potentially all* problematic behaviour might be offence paralleling suggests that accurate assessment is likely to be susceptible to subjectivity. Behaviours perceived as offence paralleling by one person might not be deemed as such by another. Subjective interpretation would threaten the validity and reliability of an assessment of current behaviours. Clear criteria of what constitutes 'offence paralleling' alongside staff training would be required to improve validity and reliability. In line with other practitioners (e.g. Daffern et al., 2007b; Jones, 2004), residents attributed significant importance to exploring the function of a behaviour for an individual and noted that presence of a discrete behaviour alone is insufficient to assume that paralleling is taking place.

The current findings confirm the concern that measuring discrete behaviours may lead to misidentification of treatment need. For example, 'isolation' was described both as a detection evasion strategy, where men said they would try 'keeping quiet', 'keeping people away' and 'keeping a close clique of friends' to avoid detection of various activities.

Accurately identifying function and comparable sequences is extremely complex. The function of behaviour might not always be apparent and most residents noted the importance of allowing time for patterns to emerge. Some reported having to explore behaviours to unravel their function and some required intimate self-disclosures to allow a thorough assessment. An example might be the use of pornography to fuel offence-related fantasy. Function is difficult to extract without the residents' cooperation and there is a reliance on motivation, self-disclosure and active enquiry (familiarity, monitor and challenge) to obtain this information, all of which would influence valid and reliable assessment. Functional analysis, as outlined by Sturmey (1996), might provide some guidance on how an assessment of offending behaviour patterns might be achieved, which might form the basis from which current behaviours might be compared. Daffern et al. (2007a) have developed methods for eliciting the purpose of violent behaviour in psychiatric inpatients, which might also be drawn upon.

Environmental and individual factors may modify or mute the parallel behaviour (see Modified Manifestation), which may hinder accurate observation. The current research provided some insight into how behaviours may be altered and these factors should be a consideration of an offence paralleling identification system or staff training protocol.

These results provide insight into those behaviours deemed significant by residents themselves. Whilst prior research has concentrated on monitoring behaviours observed during therapy groups (Neville et al., 2007) the current findings strongly suggest that behaviour throughout the community should be monitored. The residents draw attention to the extent to which they interact with others (isolation), the nature of their relationships with others and how they are formed (grooming), their use of pornography and fantasy, anger and aggression and maladaptive coping strategies as significant areas for exploration.

Despite discrete behaviours being consistently identified as offence paralleling, patterns of behaviour were deemed idiosyncratic. Strategies to identify and monitor personal OPBs would need to be based on thorough individually tailored functional analysis. Many residents identified childhood as the origin of their offending behaviour (link domains) and assessment procedures adopted might benefit from exploration of significant childhood experiences. Identifying personal triggers appears to be important to the OPB framework. Strategies to monitor OPBs would benefit from incorporation of situational factors to ensure that pervasive patterns of responding to triggers have changed rather than the triggers being merely absent.

Residents described the TC as an environment that permitted yet contained OPB and fostered a culture where behaviour is adequately explored to identify and make sense of those parallels. Therefore, the success of valid and reliable identification and monitoring of OPB appears to be dependent on the broader principles and ethos of a TC being upheld. An important underlying principle is that residents are curious about themselves and others, thereby creating a 'culture of enquiry' and a 'living-learning' environment (Campling, 2001; see also Kennard, 1998). The community further provided ideal opportunity for men to develop and practise new behaviours.

LIMITATIONS AND FUTURE RESEARCH

Generalizability of research findings from a population of adult men who have committed sexual offences to other offender populations is perhaps limited in some respects yet transferable to others. Some of the OPBs highlighted are specifically linked to sexual offending (grooming, use of pornography), and perhaps not relevant to other offence types, whilst some are perhaps as likely across offender types (maladaptive coping). The key issues, such as the importance of identifying function of current behaviour and assessing the impact of environmental and personal factors on the manifestation of behaviours, are perhaps relevant across offence types. Similarly, the therapeutic factors (*engaging*) involved in developing relationships and an environment where OPBs are identified, explored and addressed are as likely on TCs with a variety of offence types. Replication of this study with a different offender population might further clarify the validity of the OPBM across offender populations.

Reliance on self-report has been both an asset and limitation of the study. Particular caution is advised when working with self-report within a forensic population who may be inclined to deceive (Canter & Fritzon, 1998). High levels of psychopathy have been observed in the HMP Grendon population (Hobson & Shine, 1998), which might further exacerbate that concern. Future research may benefit from triangulation with other information and inclusion of staff opinion to explore the validity of findings derived from interviews with offenders.

Exploratory in nature, this research benefited from a broad scope of contributions facilitated by the focus group approach and provided valuable insight into the OPB framework from the perspective of offenders. Focus groups provided the opportunity to observe some of the key aspects discussed, such as challenging each other to encourage developed insight. Experience of group therapy is likely to have enhanced the quality of data revealed in this study as intimate and sensitive material was discussed. The design may have deterred some residents from taking part and the female researcher too may have influenced the data collected, although it is difficult to assess the impact of either. Replication of these research findings would validate the OPBM observed. The current findings might provide a basis for assessment on an individual level.

Residents of the TC were confident that the therapy they were engaged with was helping them make significant and positive changes to their lives. They reported that the focus on OPB was one aspect of the broader TC approach, which facilitated that change. Once clinicians and practitioners are able to monitor offence paralleling in a consistent manner, knowing when and how to intervene to encourage positive change will be an important aim. The next step would be to demonstrate that change in these behaviours is both linked to the intervention and a reduction in the risk of reoffending, thereby demonstrating effectiveness of the TC approach and the OPB framework.

REFERENCES

Andrews, D. & Bonta, J. (1994). *The Psychology of Criminal Conduct*. Cincinnati, OH: Anderson.

Campling, P. (2001). Therapeutic communities. *Advances in Psychiatric Treatment*, *7*, 365–72.

Canter, D. & Fritzon, K. (1998). Differentiating arsonists: a model of firesetting actions and characteristics. *Psychology, Crime and Law*, *3*, 73–96.

Charmaz, K. (1995). Grounded theory. In J.A. Smith, R. Harre & L. Van Langenhore (Eds), *Rethinking Methods in Psychology* (pp. 27–49). London: Sage.

Cullen, J.E. (1994). Grendon: the therapeutic community that works. *Therapeutic Communities for Offenders*, *14*, 301–11.

Daffern, M., Howells, K., Manion, A. & Tonkin, M. (2009). A test of methodology intended to assist detection of aggressive offence paralleling behaviour within secure settings. *Legal and Criminological Psychology*, *14*, 213–26.

Daffern, M., Howells, K. & Ogloff, K. (2007a). What's the point? Towards a methodology for assessing the function of psychiatric inpatient aggression. *Behaviour Research and Therapy*, *45*, 101–11.

Daffern, M., Howells, K., Stacey, J., Hogue, T. & Mooney, P. (2008). Sexually abusive behaviour in personality disordered inpatients of a high secure psychiatric hospital: implications for the assessment of offence paralleling behaviours. *Journal of Sexual Aggression*, *14*, 123–33.

Daffern, M., Jones, L., Howells, K., Shine, J., Mikton, C. & Tunbridge, V.C. (2007b). Refining the definition of offence paralleling behaviour. *Criminal Behaviour and Mental Health*, *17*, 265–73.

Genders, E. & Players, E. (1995). *Grendon: A Study of a Therapeutic Prison*. Oxford: Clarendon Press.

Gunn, J., Robertson, G., Dell, S. & Way, C. (1978). *Psychiatric Aspects of Imprisonment*. London: Academic Press.

Hobson, J. & Shine, J. (1998). Measurement of psychopathy in a UK prison population referred for long term psychotherapy. *British Journal of Criminology*, *38*, 504–15.

Hobson, J., Shine, J. & Roberts, R. (2000). How do psychopaths behave in a prison therapeutic community? *Psychology, Crime and Law*, *6*, 139–54.

Jones, D. & Shuker, R. (2004). Concluding comments: a humane approach to working with dangerous people. In D. Jones (Ed.), *Working with Dangerous People: The Psychotherapy of Violence* (pp. 191–99). Oxford: Radcliffe Medical Press.

Jones, L. (1997). Developing models for managing treatment integrity and efficiency in prison-based TC: the Max Glatt Centre. In E. Cullen, L. Jones & R. Woodward (Eds), *Therapeutic Communities for Offenders* (pp. 121–60). Chichester: Wiley.

Jones, L. (2004). Offence paralleling behaviour (OPB) as a framework for assessment and interventions with offenders. In A. Needs & G. Towl (Eds), *Applying Psychology to Forensic Practice* (pp. 34–63). Oxford: BPS Blackwell.

Kennard, D. (1998). *An Introduction to Therapeutic Communities*. London: Jessica Kingsley.

Lewis, P. (1997). Context for change: a challenge for systematic thinking. In E. Cullen, L. Jones & R. Woodward (Eds), *Therapeutic Communities for Offenders*. Chichester: Wiley.

Marshall, P. (1997) *A Reconviction Study of HMP Grendon Therapeutic Community*. Home Office Research Findings No. 53. London: Home Office.

Miller, S., Sees, C. & Brown, J. (2006). Key aspects of psychological change in residents of a prison therapeutic community: a focus group approach. *The Howard Journal of Criminal Justice*, *45*, 16–128.

Morris, M. (2004). Grendon's programme: model of change. In M. Morris (Ed.), *Dangerous and Severe: Process, Programme and Person: Grendon's Work*. London: Kingsley Press.

Neville, L., Miller, S. & Fritzon, K. (2007). Understanding change in a therapeutic community: an action system approach. *Journal of Forensic Psychiatry and Psychology*, *18*, 181–203.

Newton, M. (1998). Changes in measures of personality, hostility and locus of control during residence in a prison Therapeutic Community. *Legal and Criminological Psychology*, *3*, 209–23.

Shine, J. & Morris, M. (2000). Addressing criminogenic needs in a prison therapeutic community. *Therapeutic Communities*, *21*, 197–219.

Strauss, A.L. & Corbin, J. (1990). *Basics of Qualitative Research: Grounded Theory Procedures and Techniques*. Newbury Park, CA: Sage.

Sturmey, P. (1996). *Functional Analysis in Clinical Psychology*. New York: Wiley.

Taylor, R. (2000) *A Seven-Year Reconviction Study of Grendon Therapeutic Prison*. Home Office Research Findings No.115. London: Home Office.

Ward, A. (2002). *Good Lives*. Paper presented at Division of Forensic Psychology annual conference, Manchester.

Wilkinson, S. (2003). Focus groups. In J.A. Smith (Ed.), *Qualitative Psychology: A Practical Guide to Research Methods* (pp. 184–204). London: Sage.

Chapter 14

UNLOCKING OFFENCE PARALLELING BEHAVIOUR IN A CUSTODIAL SETTING – A PERSONAL PERSPECTIVE FROM MEMBERS OF STAFF AND A RESIDENT IN A FORENSIC THERAPEUTIC COMMUNITY

HELEN DOWDSWELL, GERALDINE AKERMAN AND LAWRENCE
HMP Grendon, Grendon Underwood, UK

INTRODUCTION

A democratic therapeutic community (TC) is based on the principle of a flattened hierarchy, in which all those involved have a say in how it runs. In line with this ideal, this chapter is written by staff and a resident from HMP Grendon: Helen has worked as a prison officer for seven years; Geraldine has worked as a forensic psychologist for 10 years; and Lawrence is a resident at Grendon who has been imprisoned for over 20 years. During that time we have experienced life behind bars from the perspective of staff members and as a resident in several different establishments. These include dispersal prisons (i.e. high-security prisons for prisoners who are considered to be a major threat to public safety), a Category B local male establishment (i.e. a medium-secure prison housing remand prisoners or those who have just been sentenced), prison landings, as facilitators of sex offender treatment groups, a young offender institute and a prison run as a TC.

In this chapter we describe the similarities and differences in offence paralleling from a clinical point of view in the different prison environments as described above, and then concentrate on HMP Grendon, a Category B prison that operates as a TC. In addition, the opportunities, challenges and dangers associated with assessing risk and measuring change using the concept of offence paralleling behaviour (OPB) are discussed.

The term OPB describes the way a person interacts with others in a similar pattern to that which has already led him (or her) to committing an offence, or is 'functionally similar to behavioural sequences involved in previous criminal acts' (Daffern et al., 2007, p. 267). It can be an internal process, such as ruminating on past injustices, or interpersonal, that is, how one person responds to another. OPB could be all-encompassing, for instance, demonstrating

Offence Paralleling Behaviour: A Case Formulation Approach to Offender Assessment and Intervention Edited by Michael Daffern, Lawrence Jones and John Shine

a minor act of aggression (such as the raising of a voice) or reacting in a negative manner, or it could be more specific (e.g. re-enacting particular aspects of an offence) (Jones, 1997). Similar patterns of behaviour and personality traits persist, often throughout a lifetime and across settings, and can be hard to change. Some traits may result in inappropriate expression of anger, or include the need to control, to have distorted attitudes, feelings of helplessness and the overwhelming need to be loved (Klein, 1993). Some feelings and needs are common to all of us, but it is the way that these needs have been met which causes some men to offend and find themselves in prison. Most people have experienced a problematic relationship or situation in their life, but some have crossed a line in meeting their needs in a way that results in serious harm to others and a prison sentence.

The concept of OPB in TCs was developed from the work of Jones (1997), who suggested that OPB might be represented by thoughts, feelings or actions that may have obvious similarities to the individual's offence. Whilst the concept has intuitive appeal and has high face validity for those who work in custodial settings, the labelling of custodial behaviour in this way can be problematic and could lead to over-inclusion of behaviours that may represent an adjustment to institutionalization rather than OPB. Jones suggests that the TC allows exploration and identification of the behaviours, situations and emotional states that may be relevant to offending. The TC promotes exploration and a culture of enquiry and debate. It also encourages individuals to behave as they would if they were at liberty (Cullen, 1997) as opposed to other prisons, which are characterized by a need for prisoners to project an image that may enhance self-protection. Cullen emphasized the need to provide a full range of opportunities within TCs, for instance work, education, leisure and domestic responsibilities, with each component integrated so that behaviour in each is linked and open.

The TC at HMP Grendon is an intervention accredited by the Correctional Services Accreditation Panel. The identification of OPB within the TC model was integral to gaining this status; Shine (this volume, Chapter 12) notes that attention to OPB is a key part of the TC model of change. Shine and Morris (1999) illustrate the concept of OPB with an example of a resident who, in the developmental domain, demonstrated borderline, avoidant and antisocial features, with a lack of trust of others, a high level of self-criticism and perceptions of himself as worthless and unlovable. His offence happened within an unstable relationship resulting in him feeling rejected and subsequently committing arson. In the TC he was isolated, volatile and barricaded himself in his cell. Fantasies of control and ruminative, revenge-seeking thoughts, precursors to his past offending, were recognizable and subsequently challenged.

The TC allows the internal world of the resident to become external through the continual exploration of current behaviour. It is therefore accessible and open for examination and change. As residents describe their thoughts and attitudes, underlying schemas (i.e. mental process used to organize and simplify views of the world and resulting belief) become evident and can be challenged by others. For example, a resident may have the belief that the world is hostile to him. This may have developed from feeling rejected and abused as a child and perceiving later behaviour from others as rejecting of him. This can activate hostile behaviour in him in a TC, as it did prior to offending. These beliefs and behaviours should be challenged and alternative thoughts and behaviour practised. However, labelling behaviour as offence paralleling may be problematic and subjective and not necessarily always accurate. The function of the TC is to explore, understand and challenge dysfunctional beliefs.

As residents increase their commitment to more prosocial behaviour, they become more knowledgeable about their own risk and the characteristics within themselves and others that need to change. Day-to-day behaviour is scrutinized and discussed with staff and other residents in order to identify distorted thoughts amenable to change through cognitive therapy and behavioural change with reinforcement of more functional and prosocial alternatives (prosocial alternative behaviour, PAB; Daffern et al., 2007), theoretically this reduces OPB. Jones (2009) highlights the need for triangulation of information; that is, seeking information from several sources, for example staff, the resident and others. This approach can also inform risk of relapse by identifying potential signs of it and developing robust plans by which these risks can be managed. Jones warned that punishment of OPB might increase detection evasion skills (DES; see this volume, Chapter 3), so it is important that there is dialogue between the multidisciplinary team to allow OPB to emerge and DES to be monitored.

THE PRISON WING

A prison wing is a discrete unit and a community in its own right. It contains a variety of people who differ in their cognitive, emotional and behavioural dimensions. Staff working in the unit have an impact on the atmosphere and its culture. Often, the presence of female officers (in a male prison) calms the atmosphere on a prison wing. Perhaps this is because, traditionally, women are thought to have a more caring attitude, or maybe simply men feel more comfortable with the gender balance. The presence of female officers may also provide an opportunity for men who have inappropriate attitudes towards women to express, question and challenge these and to practise more prosocial interactions.

Very often a man (or woman, but for this chapter, we shall speak of men) will behave in prison in a similar manner to how they did outside. A man who is feared on the streets is usually feared when he is in prison. Sometimes that fear is experienced by the staff with the job of looking after him in custody. This could include prisoners 'policing' the landings, creating a semblance of safety. Imprisoned men will often protect prison officers if those officers are considered to be fair and caring, especially if female. There is no 'street' credibility in assaulting female staff. Also, if officers of either sex are considered to be decent and respectful to them, prisoners will not want to see them given a hard time. It is in their own interests to keep those staff 'sweet' and keen to work there, behaviour that is clearly self-serving. Quite a few times whilst working with remand prisoners, I was told, 'Thank goodness you're back, Miss' after I had taken some leave. That was simply because my supervision of men was consistent and fair and I took no pleasure in making life harder than necessary for them. However, such comments should be questioned and possibly challenged within a TC, where staff should seek to understand the underlying behaviour and to question such comments.

Whilst working in a local Category B prison the differences between wings such as the remand, short- and long-term sentence wings were noticeable. Across these wings, men, who had committed different crimes and received various sentences, had to find their own particular niche or place in the community as they did prior to their offences. One prisoner was serving a sentence for armed robbery and was suspected of more than one murder. He was the 'king' of the landing; he cultivated fear around him so that his needs were met. He was especially charming and friendly to female officers. He often received preferential treatment from staff and should other prisoners upset these officers, they would be 'spoken to' by him and told not to do it again. As he walked down steps to join a line of men waiting for meals the queue would divide like 'Moses parting the waves'. He was greatly feared by the other prisoners, who were aware of his reputation. He was treated with caution (and feared) by many of the staff. He was a man who usually got what he wanted. It was easy to see how he was carrying on the same behaviour (i.e. instilling fear to achieve his needs) whilst in prison as he did outside. This was achieved in quite subtle ways, for instance mentioning contacts he had outside or when he spoke of past acts of violence. When he was released he moved in dangerous circles and rumours often circulated that he had been shot dead.

Another man was imprisoned for sexual offences against his own children. His life on the outside had involved dealing in drugs and he had been a so-called 'Mr Big'; he was obeyed, feared and respected by others. Despite his offences (which in the prison hierarchy are considered the lowest of the low), he managed to make friends with other strong characters, including prisoners serving time for non-sexual offences, who did not know what he was in for and did not choose to ask. On the wing his behaviour was similar to that on the outside in that he maintained control of those around him. He was a man who spoke quietly because he did not need to be more vocal. He always got his message across. In order to maintain this control, part of his OPB was to threaten staff with his solicitors when anything occurred which he did not like. In the group he treated female staff in a similar way to how he had treated his wife. Therefore, staff members needed to be aware of the extent to which their behaviour was being shaped by the residents. He had kept his wife quiet and prevented questions from her about her own children by supporting her drug habit. In the group the man attempted to keep female staff quiet in order to deflect questions. He did this with quiet determination or by trying to convince staff how well he had worked on his criminal behaviour. This pattern of behaviour could well have developed as a response to childhood circumstances, where the need to have control over his environment may have caused him to rely on aggressive interactions for self-protection. Interestingly, many men state that in their childhood, mixed messages were sent from significant adults. Perhaps one day they would be treated well whilst the next, for no apparent reason, shouted at and beaten cruelly. Not knowing what would happen on any given day, the men report that it was easier and more consistent to always behave badly. That way the attitude and treatment from the adults would be the same, albeit shouting, screaming and beatings. At least they knew what was coming and this was consistent and could be more easily dealt with and accepted. It is easy to see how the acquisition of an aggressive interpersonal style as a child could grow to a broad repertoire of criminal aggressive behaviour.

The man described above moved to a different prison after many years in a TC. He portrayed himself as someone who was able to do the work required of him; he constantly preached about how much he had changed. There were often suspicions about his underhand behaviour, but nothing could be substantiated. The 'reward' for him was to reduce his category, which is a measure of risk reduction. Having moved on to a prison with a lower security category, he soon established himself once again as 'Mr Big' and continued to rule the landings, suggesting that OPB was still present.

Both these men, like many others, behaved in prison in a similar way to how they had behaved outside, and the extent to which this is OPB or simply adjusting to life in such circumstances is not always straightforward. Their lifestyles had included criminal activities, which had led them step-by-step to offend. Their behaviour inside had paralleled their offence-related behaviour. They had both felt the need to use anger, threats and violence to achieve what they wanted, indicating that they were not likely to change this pattern of behaviour, and no doubt their behaviour got them what they wanted and so was functional; as such, they would need to have a good reason to change their behaviour. However, it is not always clear what is OPB as aggressive or manipulative behaviour can be functional in prison for some people and not lead to offending. Some offenders have behaved in an aggressive manner in prison in order to achieve their aim, but this does not necessarily lead to an offence once released. So it is the staff's role to identify OPB and what behaviour is simply adjusting to life in prison.

YOUNG OFFENDER INSTITUTIONS

Young offenders institutions (YOIs) house youths aged 18–21 years. It can be very sad to see youths imprisoned at such a young age and spending much of their time trying to maintain an image. Some of the youths have spent their lives involved in antisocial behaviour. For these, prison may be an inevitable outcome; it can also be a place where young people 'hone their craft' that is, develop skills related to criminality, including DES (see this volume, Chapter 3). Much of their image is dependent on glorifying their crimes, each wanting to seem 'harder' than the other, and they may see this as a way to survive in such a harsh environment. It is tempting to see these acts as offence paralleling, though it is also important to understand the environment's role in promoting antisociality and status associated with violent behaviour, that is, violence may be helpful and necessary for survival in the YOI. Helen's experience of working with young offenders in a TC was that there are some who will benefit from therapy at a young age if allowed to by their peers. The aim of the TC is to provide a prosocial environment and one in which challenging offence-supportive attitudes is encouraged. The problem lies with being able to identify appropriate candidates for the TC and protect them from negative influences. It is important that the environment in which the TC functions is supportive of its ideals.

Youths can be impulsive, have poor perspective-taking skills and be reckless in their thinking and behaviour. In custody these problems are targeted with the enhanced thinking skills programme, an accredited programme aimed at developing appropriate cognitive skills. For some, incarceration will be the 'wake-up call' they need, and they will take the opportunity to attend education and vocational training to try to improve their chances on release. But this will take a good deal of strength of character and expert intervention if it is going against a caustic culture of the wing. OPB is particularly evident in the maintenance of gang culture and bullying (see also Chapter 12). Clearly, YOIs need to spend time developing a prosocial culture supportive of change and positive behaviour.

SEX OFFENDER TREATMENT PROGRAMMES

As described elsewhere in this volume (see Chapter 7), observing the behaviour of prisoners participating in sex offender treatment programmes (SOTPs) can be enlightening. Some men think that attending a programme for those who have committed a sexual offence will 'tick the boxes' and give an impression that they are doing the work necessary to reduce risk and therefore hasten release. However, the work usually proves hard to fake because of close scrutiny from staff and fellow prisoners in his group. One comment often made to staff is that men will seem to be challenging their attitudes and offending behaviour in the group, but when they return to the landing they are looking at pornography, making abusive comments towards females, or watching programmes on television containing images of violence or other images that sexually attract them. Such behaviour may well have a functional link to their past offending. Jones (2004) defines OPB as any form of offence-related behavioural (or fantasized behaviour) pattern, so using pornography and displaying offensive attitudes towards women could qualify as part of the chain of events leading to offending. It is however important to ascertain whether the prisoners' current behaviour is relevant to their offending before labelling it as offence paralleling.

Most SOTPs involve looking at the antecedents to offending and also looking at the impact on the victim(s) and others who might have been affected. As a participant works to develop victim empathy, it is generally hard for offenders to avoid the feelings this procedure brings up. This is often seen as the most powerful part of the programme because the man has to look at what he has done to another adult or child, by putting himself 'in their shoes'. In SOTPs men also explore how their lifestyle, relationships, attitudes, emotions and sexual interests affected their life leading up to the offence in order to make links with why he felt motivated to offend, and identify OPB in the current location. As they identify the thoughts, feelings and actions preceding the offence, they identify how these recur in the present. This may well help to identify OPB and how and why it has developed. By monitoring himself and being observed by others, each participant can be made aware of behaviour when it repeats itself in the prison environment. It is important that staff facilitating programmes work closely with the officers on the wings to monitor behaviour on and off the group in order to recognize OPB and point it out to the prisoner. Within a TC there is ample opportunity to explore behaviour as it occurs, identifying thoughts and potential actions. During a therapy session or community meeting, men are frequently asked why they have responded in the manner they have and asked to link it back to previous behaviour.

Having looked at prison settings, we now discuss OPBs in therapeutic communities. As discussed elsewhere in this volume (Chapter 12), the subculture developed within prisons can mask more naturalistic behaviour and so a TC provides opportunities for OPB to emerge.

THE THERAPEUTIC COMMUNITY

The development and ethos of TCs have been described within this volume (see Chapters 12 and 13) and extensively (Akerman, 2002; Genders & Player, 1995; Shine & Morris, 1999) elsewhere. As such, this will not be repeated here; rather the ways in which TCs differ from other prison settings in terms of OPBs will be discussed. In a TC, each wing or unit develops its own culture, influenced by staff and residents. As such, the relationships between the two groups are the subject of constant discussion. Jones (2004) discussed the importance of recognizing the consequences of behaviour, which is possible within a TC because of this constant scrutiny of behaviour. If a resident breaks a rule, or acts in an aggressive or offensive manner, he is aware of the impact this has on others and is accountable for it. This is in contrast to their past when they have committed a crime and (usually) not seen the consequences. Then they are punished much later and asked to give accounts of it within the criminal justice system, which is far removed from the original site of the crime. Therefore, they are also often emotionally removed from the scene.

Dynamics similar to those within a family are often re-enacted through the close working relationships in a TC. Working in a TC prison gives staff the opportunity to observe the behaviour of prisoners across all situations. The behaviour of prisoners in therapy groups, the gym, in education and at work is all 'grist for the mill' of therapy, the men's behaviour in these different settings may also provide opportunity for OPB in a way that rigid, traditional prison settings do not. As others have commented (Daffern et al., 2007), it is important to understand the function of the behaviour and to differentiate between those behaviours that are truly OPB and those that indicate a propensity for criminal behaviour generally, and the need to be mindful of PABs and DES.

In TCs the expression of emotion is encouraged alongside developing the skills to do so in an appropriate manner. The close proximity of community living puts the person's behaviour under the microscope and prompts the phrase 'Therapy 24/7' as there is no getting away from it. However, it can take some discussion to decide whether behaviour is an example of paralleling that led up to the offence (see Chapters 6 and 10 for further discussion). For example, if a man has committed a violent crime and proceeds to be argumentative and aggressive with others in the prison community, this will be challenged and explored. This behaviour may be a response to a present situation or may be a persistent pattern of behaviour, which had contributed to past offending. If a man views the world as hostile and responds to others in that manner, he will be encouraged to examine and dismantle his thinking and relationship style, as well as seeking evidence to counter it. Group members and staff will discuss why he feels the need to act this way and what he gets from it. It could be that this behaviour helped him to achieve his aims in the past. As is the case with all people, men in prison have developed their personalities and behaviour as a response to the circumstances they find themselves in. Growing up in fear and deprivation leads to the development of defensive behaviour to help cope with these conditions. Living in a TC helps the residents to learn that these responses are no longer needed and also helps to develop reparative relationships with peers and those in authority.

Staff need to remain objective whilst developing close working relationships with each other and with residents. Marshall (2006) likened it to how we would treat a friend, in that if they were doing something that was unhelpful to them we would point it out to them rather than standing back and letting them hurt themselves and others. So, OPB is pointed out and, as always, it is up to the resident if they want to change it or not, but they get the chance to practise new behaviour within a safe and supportive environment.

In psychodynamic therapy groupwork a man discusses what his life was like from his earliest memories to the present day. He is encouraged to explore the feelings, attitudes, lifestyles, schemas and emotions of his past and, with the help of others, finally see for himself how he has arrived at where he is now. Patterns of relating may then be identified and OPB become more apparent. For some men, this can take a long time for a variety of reasons. He may not be fully committed to changing his behaviour, he may not care about what he has done or if he creates more victims. Alternatively, he may find it difficult to break down the pattern of behaviour and link with emotions that are painful to tolerate. During ongoing groupwork all these areas are spoken about in great depth.

SO HOW IS BEHAVIOUR AMENABLE TO CHANGE?

The answer is to alter the way the man thinks, feels and acts. Behaviour is learned and can be very hard to change. We all know how to go about getting what we want using the easiest method. Having worked with many men who manipulate others in order to get their own way (as they have done for many years), it can become second nature for them to 'groom' staff and others as they did with vulnerable others on the outside (this may be to their detriment, as reported Mann and colleagues, Chapter 7). For some men, the aggressive approach is undesirable, so they prefer the more gentle method of befriending and getting along with others. This is often the way they managed to befriend their victims and how trust was achieved. As with men who use aggression to achieve their aim, these men need to have their behaviour challenged over time.

Residents who do succeed in making changes are then able to reflect on their past and have the chance to alter future behaviour. In many cases, the man has managed this because he finally realizes that he has choices in life and can achieve what he wants without having to hurt others.

Often within a therapeutic setting, a resident can experience personal reactions to others that are shaped by past relationships, which means he sees in another person qualities that remind him of someone else. For instance, one resident felt totally shut down in the group because another group member reminded him of his father who had physically abused him as a child. He had also felt angry with his mother for not protecting him. He expressed his anger by returning to masturbating to inappropriate fantasies of raping a child, and he felt justified in doing so. As in the time leading up to his offence, he kept these feelings to himself, but his anger leaked out when he could no longer control it. He got angry with a female member of staff who challenged him and threatened to stab her. He recognized that this paralleled the anger he felt towards his mother and that it was being re-enacted in the TC.

Interestingly, one resident evoked emotions within a wide range of people including staff. His grandiose attitude and need to control made him a difficult individual to work with. However, it is clear that the man learnt this behaviour as a means of keeping others 'at arm's length' and to feel more powerful. This behaviour had served a purpose in his life but it was not what was required in the TC and so needed to change if he were to relate well to others. Jones (2004) suggests that behaviour develops over time into antecedent OPB and so it is useful to understand the pathway to the offending. It takes time and understanding to recognize what the dynamics are within each relationship and so each relationship must be scrutinized so that each can see their role in it and how the feelings evoked can be resolved in the here-and-now rather than responding to events from the past.

Another resident has a history of being focused on his own needs and not being aware of the impact this has on others. He demonstrates psychopathic traits (Hare, 2003), being manipulative, parasitic and lacking empathy. He describes having a group of people outside of prison who support him financially and emotionally. He stated that he asks them for money so that he can phone them and they would miss his phone calls if he were to stop calling. During conversations with them he tells them all his problems. He has distanced himself from his family who, he says, seek support from him and are not willing to provide it. He described how he could not 'be bothered to work' as he does not need the money because it is sent in to him. He would not want to work for the feeling of self-worth it evokes or to be able to support himself; rather, he prefers to rely on his friends for money. He has stated that he could not budget and always lives ahead of his means, buying cigarettes, CDs and clothes and then asking for extra money for phone calls rather than budgeting. His sexual preoccupation also continued in the TC with his use of pornography, sexual banter in conversations and frequent inappropriate sexual comments. Therefore, the task at hand is to identify which of his behaviours reflect general antisocial behaviour and which are OPBs. This requires functional analysis of the offending and determining the similarity of these offending behaviours with his current behaviour.

One resident remains completely sexually preoccupied in the TC. He has spoken in-depth about his sexual offending against a female child, an adult woman who he was in a relationship with and the rape of a stranger. He describes sexualizing animate and inanimate objects, having sex with a man in another prison and thoughts of sex with animals. He described a deep-seated fear of being hurt or rejected in a relationship; staying in a constant state of sexual arousal helps him avoid that. He states that being in relationships 'kills' and 'smothers' him, indicating the intensity of feelings evoked, and so for him to live in a TC in a prison must feel extremely intense. His OPB of sexual preoccupation continues in the TC evidenced by the television programmes he watches, using images in magazines for arousal and watching children's programmes to get more masturbatory stimulation. He reports masturbating three times a day and replays aspects of his sadistic offending through apparent pleasure at the distress his behaviour causes staff. He learned fantasy modification techniques on a complementary programme undertaken in the TC but still found it intensely difficult to curb his impulsive responses. Through keeping a diary and reporting ongoing behaviour to the therapy group his day-today behaviour can be monitored, whereas such behaviour would not be recognized or discussed in most prisons.

ASSESSING RISK IN A TC USING OPB

In order to progress through the prison system residents need to demonstrate that they have reduced their risk. This would usually be done through showing that they are more able to cope with difficult emotions and by acquiring PAB. TCs rely largely on dynamic security (that is, security resulting from the relationship between staff and residents, rather than the physical security of the establishment) and so the relationship between staff and residents is paramount. There can be tension between security and clinical staff when OPB begins to emerge because the standard prison response would be to prevent and punish it. However, in order to access, explore and change the OPB it needs to be seen. So, it is not always easy to assess risk in a TC as you must decide exactly what behaviour is OPB from each resident. All staff need to develop a working knowledge of the OPB for each individual and attempt to recognize when this is evident. This is not a straightforward task. Irreplaceable information can emerge from places other than the therapy group, for instance behaviour in a classroom, gym or chapel, and so all of these need to be fed back to wing staff routinely.

One example involved a man who had applied for an escorted day release to a nearby town. He had support from all the staff he worked with, but the day out was refused because a probation officer had not given their backing. The resident was greatly upset by this refusal and withdrew into himself for a short while. Other minor setbacks had contributed to his disappointment and he was seen to be displaying OPB, which included isolating himself and showing anger as a way of expressing his frustration and disappointment. In some individuals this could be seen as a natural response to disappointment but this man noted parallels to having lost his job, isolating himself and then offending against his daughter. Fortunately, he did recognize this and had developed the ability to talk about how he was feeling and resolve this within himself (and he did later get his day out).

YOUNG OFFENDERS IN A TC

It can be very difficult for young offenders to work successfully in a TC prison. Peer pressures often prevent the individual from giving their full attention to change. Even if a few youngsters want to participate, they can easily find themselves in the minority and may be targeted by those wishing to undermine the therapeutic culture. Insight-oriented therapeutic change requires that the individual understands how past behaviour has resulted in offending and how best to prevent doing so in the future. There needs to be a desire to link current behaviour to that leading up to their offending. Often this understanding is not present with youth as they have little on which to base their experiences. Jones (2004) emphasizes the need to provide an environment which provides situational cues to offending, that is, opportunities to offend. This would provide indicators of OPBs and the chance to challenge them. This is not so easy in a prison housing some of the country's most dangerous young offenders. Prison staff usually represent authority to young offenders, something 'to kick against', not a source of guidance and understanding, and so the young men need to be given time to adjust to this changing role.

During Helen's experience working with young offenders in a TC, it was very difficult to deal with one wing dedicated to therapy in the midst of a fully functioning high-security prison (usually prisons dedicate a solitary wing to therapy, and HMP Grendon is the only prison in the United Kingdom to consist completely of therapy wings). If a prison has only one wing promoting therapeutic values, problems can arise through ignorance of what happens in the unit and jealousy by both staff and other offenders for what they view as a unit receiving more resources. There was mistrust and envy constantly directed towards the TC and the continuing pressure to put 'bums on beds' in an ever-increasing prison population, an action not conducive to therapy. This could result in inappropriate offenders being moved into the unit and these offenders disrupting the therapeutic environment. Also, the youth were not adept at challenging each other on issues such as voting in new members for the community. Therefore, people were voted in for the wrong reasons (e.g. known drugs suppliers; known, that is, to the inmate population and not the staff).

ADJUSTING TO DIFFERENT ENVIRONMENTS

Working in a prison is a very interesting, intense and emotional experience. Coming to a TC environment from a traditional prison can be quite traumatic for staff and prisoners. When one is used to obeying rules, strict regimes, an officer-is-always-right attitude and a lack of flexibility, a TC is quite a challenge. In a TC everyone is entitled to an opinion, is treated with respect, is called by their first name and can challenge anyone (staff included) about their behaviour. This can help a resident to develop his opinion and ability to voice it appropriately. Residents learn to take responsibility, which may be very different from their past life when they have had no responsibility for themselves or others and lived on a day-to-day basis. OPB may occur through a resident reneging on a task assigned to him (for instance, cleaning). Each member would be challenged if he did not take his work seriously.

One example of behaviour challenged heavily in the community is the need for instant gratification rather than waiting to achieve a goal. Quite often this has been an attitude that has caused problems for a man in the past and it is pleasing when he begins to realize that his 'wants' affect other people. One example was a man requesting that staff ring the kitchen urgently for some 'bin bags' as we had run out. The kitchen staff frequently visited the wing and the man had had plenty of opportunities to make this request to them. He was encouraged to wait for the next visit from a kitchen worker but this was not the answer he wanted to hear. It was explained to him that everyone was busy and that if anyone needed bin bags when the shop was shut, they had to wait until it reopened. Three years later, after the man had been away at another establishment for a few months in order to do programmes, his attitude was very different. He was more thoughtful of others and was able to challenge his own behaviour as well as accept others' opinions. He accepted that he could wait to get what he wanted and that he could tolerate the emotions evoked.

One resident, Lawrence, who has experienced life in a variety of prisons, will now describe OPB from his perspective.

I am in my twenty-first year of imprisonment having been convicted of murder and rape in 1988. I have spent 18 years in high-security prisons as a Category A prisoner, and I have spent the last two and a half years in HMP Grendon TC.

While in the high-security estate I began to address my offence-related beliefs and challenge my OPBs (not very successfully on occasion), and to gradually reduce my level of risk through participation in the offending behaviour programmes (OBPs) available. Although I gained valuable insight into my behaviour, offending and the impact of my offending, the OBPs are mainly cognitive in approach, and so after discussion with psychologists I decided to come to Grendon to explore the emotional dimensions of my childhood experiences, and especially how my early emotional development had influenced my relationships and later offending.

During my sentence, I have experienced the similarities and differences that exist between a typical prison wing engaged in offender programmes and a full TC environment. The similarities are simply that both exist as communities populated by a diversity of maladaptive and criminally minded personalities, where the predominantly abusive and manipulative learnt behaviours are played out in the day-to-day relationships. The differences are threefold: in the 'system' (i.e. mainstream prison) there is a huge amount of peer pressure from those not engaged in programmes and so not challenging their OPBs, and it would take an exceptionally strong personality to successfully challenge and change their behaviour in those environments. The second difference lies in the ethos of the TC where the transition between wing, education, work and gym is seamless, in that the scrutiny and challenge of OPB is constant. Thirdly, although staff in the system can become targets for manipulation, the emphasis is usually on keeping them 'sweet' and at a distance, so as to pursue OPBs, and give the usual day-to-day criminal activities a chance of success. In a TC, staff work much more closely with residents and are therefore the main targets for manipulation or 'grooming'. This applies especially to female staff, and even more so if the female staff member is perceived to be influential, or a main report writer.

In my experience, OPBs can be obvious, while others are quite subtle. Examples of my own OPBs are bringing a pornographic DVD into the community, lending it to other residents, and also threatening another resident. In each case both behaviours reflected aspects of my offending – objectifying women, sexual preoccupation and violent behaviour. My actions with the DVD created a situation where everyone involved became compromised and unable to challenge each other. It also showed a lack of empathy and understanding towards others engaged in therapy in that it possibly fuelled their deviant fantasies. While in therapy, residents are encouraged to speak openly about the sexual and violent abuse inflicted upon them during their own childhood. My threat of violence towards another resident created a ripple effect in the community in that it left many residents feeling afraid and could have impeded their progress in therapy.

In my opinion, residents' relationships, especially with female staff, are an area where quite subtle OPBs can be observed. One resident (a former pimp and repeat violent sexual offender) had, in a previous establishment, expressed a desire to utterly dominate a professional woman. His behaviour would be to build a relationship with an influential female staff member. During conversation he would constantly identify with the staff member's partner and then proceeded to 'banter' with her in an apparently jovial and boisterous manner, giving the impression of friendliness and normality. If his part of the conversation was listened to carefully, it became quite apparent that within the seemingly innocent banter was a subtle and constant sexist monologue, quite derogatory, that basically stated, 'woman, know your place'. Although his offences were sexually violent, in my opinion, it was quite apparent that his need to dominate women still existed within his relationships.

In my own past and present relationships, what could be construed as an OPB or lead to OPB (deviant fantasy) became apparent in that I would 'close down' and ignore others rather than express my emotions, usually feelings of resentment or anger stemming from what I perceived as rejection. This behaviour became increasingly apparent after I formed quite a deep emotional attachment to a female member of staff who had shown me a lot of care, and who had given me a lot of her time to help me adjust after my long period in high security conditions. When I perceived that this relationship was under threat (by other staff who justifiably had become concerned with my feelings for her) I would withdraw emotionally, especially from her, perceiving her professionalism as a rejection of me. It took me a while to recognize that my behaviour was manipulative and controlling, in that my silence would eventually force her to come to me. This made me realize that even when I genuinely cared about someone I could still use their care against them, evidencing a lack of empathy within myself when emotionally confused. I linked this behaviour back to my early childhood, as this was the way in which my mother drew affection and attention from me, and then rejected me by becoming emotionally abusive and violent.

The therapy group relationship dynamic is also an area where OPBs can be observed. One resident (a repeat child sex offender) uses transference within the group as a justification to engage in deviant and offence-related sexual fantasy. He identifies many of the group members with his father, who totally dominated him and whom he allegedly greatly feared as a child. During groups, he is extremely defensive, emotionally evasive and continually frustrates any attempt by the group to access his feelings or gain any real understanding of his life and offending history. He then proceeds to take on a victim stance, believing that the group have not listened to him and emotionally attacked him. After the group session had ended, it was discovered that he would continually complain about his treatment on the group by choosing to seek out and complain to those residents who would reinforce his victim stance. He would then use these negative emotions as a justification to isolate himself and indulge in further offence-related sexual fantasy, which is a direct parallel to his prior offending pattern.

In conclusion, I have found that observing OPBs and their dynamics in others is so much easier than trying to see them in myself, although perceiving them in others usually indicates that I possess them myself! Even when I became aware of OPBs, or behaviour that could lead to OPB, I have found that the emotional weight that supports my belief can be so great that I will fight tooth and nail to justify my actions. Due to the complexity of some (if not all?) OPBs and their underlying attitudes/beliefs, experience has shown me that the full TC environment is essential for containing and supporting this process, and in my opinion, (though I fight the process every day) it is the only realistic chance of challenging OPBs and so making a genuine change for the better.

SUMMARY

This chapter has looked at the development of the concept of OPBs within a prison-based TC, and given examples of different prison environments and how staff and residents experience them. The differences between OPB and general criminal behaviour have been discussed and examples of how such behaviour is managed have been described. As stated, it can be difficult to differentiate between current management of emotions and behaviour and repetition of OPB. As noted elsewhere in this volume (see Chapters 6 and 7), it is important that training is provided to ensure as far as possible that a thorough case formulation is developed which is not over-inclusive of irrelevant behaviour.

It will be important to develop a framework that helps to formulate relevant OPB for each resident, how it could be monitored on a day-to-day basis and effectively challenged in the TC. As the TC provides an environment akin to living outside of prison in many ways, it provides the opportunity to reignite thoughts, feelings and behaviour, which is not accessible in a traditional prison, and therefore, to change them.

REFERENCES

Akerman, G. (2002). Development of a checklist to measure community-minded behaviour in a prison-based therapeutic community. *Forensic Update*, *69*, 17–29.

Cullen, E. (1997). Can a prison be therapeutic? The Grendon template. In E. Cullen, L. Jones & R. Woodward (Eds), *Therapeutic Communities for Offenders* (pp. 75–99). London: Wiley.

Daffern, M., Jones, L., Howells, K., Shine, J., Mikton, C. & Tunbridge, V.C. (2007). Refining the definition of offence paralleling behaviour. *Criminal Behaviour and Mental Health*, *17*, 265–73.

Genders, F. & Player, E. (1995). *Grendon: A Study of a Therapeutic Prison*. Oxford: Oxford University Press.

Hare, R. (2003). *Psychopathy Checklist – Revised* (2nd edition). Toronto, ON: Multi-Health Systems.

Jones, L. (1997). Developing models of managing treatment integrity and efficacy in a prison-based TC: the Max Glatt Centre. In E. Cullen, L. Jones & R. Woodward (Eds), *Therapeutic Communities for Offenders* (pp. 121–57). London: Wiley.

Jones, L.F. (2004). Offence paralleling behaviour (OPB) as a framework for assessment and interventions with offenders. In A. Towl & G. Towl (Eds), *Applying Psychology to Forensic Practice* (p. 38). Oxford: BPS Blackwell.

Jones, L.F. (2009) *Offence Paralleling Behaviour (OPB) and Risk Assessment Management and Intervention*. Portsmouth: University of Portsmouth.
Klein, J. (1993). *Our Need for Others and Its Roots in Infancy*. London: Routledge.
Marshall, W. L. (2006). *Approaches to Modifying Sexual Interests*. NOTA, 16th Annual conference, York.
Shine, J. & Morris, M. (1999). *Regulating Anarchy: The Grendon Programme*. Aylesbury: Springhill Press.

Chapter 15

PSYCHIATRIC NURSES WORKING WITH OFFENCE PARALLELING BEHAVIOUR

TRISH MARTIN

Forensicare, Australia

INTRODUCTION

This chapter has been written for psychiatric nurses: the largest group of mental health professionals providing assessment, treatment, management and care for patients that are identified as mentally disordered offenders (MDOs). Although psychiatric nurses are yet to develop a framework that can define their contribution to the rapidly developing practice in forensic mental health, there is evidence that models from other disciplines are proving to be effective and can be integrated with nursing theory and practice. Offending risk assessment tools, principles of risk management and offending treatment programmes have advanced in the last decade or so, but the involvement of nursing varies internationally.

Inpatient nurses do, however, provide leadership in a number of areas, including forming relationships with patients, observation and assessment, maintaining the therapeutic environment on the unit, and managing inpatient violence. For various reasons inpatient violence occurs regularly in forensic mental health settings and nurses have sound experience in the management of these situations. In this chapter, the developing offence paralleling behaviour (OPB) model is presented as a framework that complements existing nursing competencies and provide a link between inpatient violence and violent offending to assist nurses to enhance their role in addressing offending behaviour.

PSYCHIATRIC NURSING IN THE FORENSIC CONTEXT

Despite a long history of providing care in forensic mental health settings, the role of the psychiatric nurse in these settings has been difficult to define (Carton, 1998; Mason, 2002). A lack of consensus regarding the role of the forensic psychiatric nurse was apparent when Robinson and Kettles (2000) presented a range of international views. In terms of professional recognition, forensic psychiatric nursing is relatively new on the nursing landscape and has

Offence Paralleling Behaviour: A Case Formulation Approach to Offender Assessment and Intervention Edited by Michael Daffern, Lawrence Jones and John Shine

tended to develop in isolated pockets in response to local health and justice department policies, legislation and the other services and supports that are available.

For Benson (1992) the question of whether specific skills are required to work with MDOs in secure environments was unanswered. In the same period, Burnard (1992) suggested that forensic psychiatric nursing seemed to be concerned with a range of issues that were outside of the usual remit of nursing, including illness, crime, morality, treatment, containment and possibly punishment. Since then many authors have attempted to define the role of nurses in forensic mental health and what it was that they do that might be deemed as therapeutic. Carton (1998) described the therapeutic role of nurses as one in which they are required 'to form trusting relationships with offender-patients in order to be able to assess risk, to develop intervention strategies which address the patient's offending behaviour and mental state, and to be able to evaluate the effectiveness of these interventions' (p. 252).

The mainstream psychiatric nursing literature has consistently reported the value of the nurse–patient relationship (Dunwell & Hanson, 1998; Eckroth-Bucher, 2001; Jackson & Stevenson, 2000; Laskowski, 2001; O'Brien, 1999; Teising, 2000). Through the nurse–patient relationship nursing care is delivered, and teaching and counselling are accomplished (Pieranunzi, 1997). Forensic nursing authors also consider the nurse–patient relationship to be crucial (Hammer, 2000; Topping-Morris, 1992; Woods et al., 2002). According to Petenelj-Taylor (1998), the ability to establish a therapeutic relationship with a forensic patient is one of the most important forensic nursing competencies as it affects every aspect of the nursing process, and ultimately, the provision of quality care. Few authors, however, have identified what comprises quality nursing care or which psychiatric nursing interventions are effective in the forensic setting.

ADDRESSING OFFENDING BEHAVIOUR

The emphasis on offence behaviour is what differentiates forensic psychiatric nursing practice from that of mainstream colleagues. However, the subject of the nurse's therapeutic role in addressing offending behaviour has received little attention in the literature and remains undeveloped in practice (Burrow, 1993; Martin, 2001). Nurses may avoid addressing offence issues due to an absence of a forensic psychiatric nursing framework and a lack of education in this area.

Psychiatric nurses in one forensic mental health facility identified that they were reluctant to discuss patients' offences with them (Martin, 2003). The nurses argued that establishing rapport with a patient could be compromised if the nurse's thinking about the patient was tainted by thinking about the patient's offence, and by raising concerns about the offence with the patient, especially if the patient was unwilling to discuss them. Nurses could become judgemental and impose their moral and value standards on patients. Nurses documented the offence on admission, and then forgot about it and hoped that what was done with the patient was useful. Nurses were more likely to address issues with patients when a serious offence has been committed. The patient's mental illness could be assessed by observing him, but to assess the offence issues the nurse must talk to the patient. In the interviews, the nurses identified a social awkwardness and constructed the relationship with patients as a fragile process that could be damaged by exploring offence issues. The nurses' lack of willingness to identify the factors associated with the index offence and to assess the significance of these factors in relation to ongoing behaviour was a missed opportunity to contribute to risk assessment and development of the nursing contribution to forensic mental health practice.

Nurses in forensic settings have to face the fact that they carry a great responsibility for the welfare of the offender and the community and if they are to intervene effectively they must include assessment and treatment of the patient's offending behaviour (Prins, 1991). Too often in forensic settings nursing interventions have focused on the achievement of the patient in less significant areas, the offence is viewed as simply a matter of record and need not be considered in the present (Martin & Street, 2003; Prins, 1991; Vaughan & Badger, 1995).

Holistic assessment and treatment of patients who have been charged with a criminal offence is however the function of a forensic mental health service. Yet if nurses fail to demonstrate a willingness to assist patients to integrate the offence into their experience, then in this omission nurses also fail to represent their practice as holistic and therapeutic. Speedy (1999) contended that until nurses have an understanding of the meaning of a patient's behaviour from the patient's perspective they have a custodial role. Others have claimed that in the absence of effective nursing interventions nurses had been reduced to providing entertainment or diversion strategies in order to fill the patient's time (Mason & Mercer, 1998). Mason and Mercer also argued that it was inappropriate to suggest that these strategies were therapeutic in the absence of theoretical frameworks and evaluation.

Nursing assessment in forensic mental health necessarily includes information about the circumstances, the nature and consequences of the MDO's offence and this is integrated with a comprehensive health assessment for planning and implementing treatment and rehabilitation. The forensic psychiatric nurse works with MDOs and their carers to facilitate an understanding of mental illness and offending behaviour.

One component of offending risk assessment is the relationship of mental illness to the offending. The nature of the relationship between mental illness and offending is complex due to a number of mediating or confounding factors and because MDOs are a heterogeneous population. Research shows that mental illness is associated with increased rates of offending. However, mental illness is rarely sufficient to account for criminal acts. Of greater relevance to individuals and their treatment is the interaction between specific symptoms, personality, social factors and the context in which offending occurs (Mullen & Lindqvist, 2000).

Psychiatric nursing has traditionally been aligned with psychiatry but the medical model is insufficient to explain offending behaviour. Hodgins (2002) stated that most people with schizophrenia do not commit criminal offences but of those that do, some begin offending before they are symptomatic, others as they become psychotic for the first time and some after a long course of the illness; they concluded that there may be different subgroups of offenders with schizophrenia. Similarly, Wallace et al. (2004) proposed that offending reflected a range of factors that are operative before, during and after periods of active illness.

According to 'what works' principles (Andrews & Bonta, 2007), offender rehabilitation is most likely to have a positive impact if criminogenic needs – the dynamic risk factors that are directly associated with the probability of re/offending – are targeted in treatment. There is an overlap in the criminogenic needs for MDOs and non-MDOs. Criminogenic needs include pro-criminal attitudes, criminal associates, substance abuse, antisocial personality and negative emotionality. Non-criminogenic needs are also dynamic but are weakly associated with recidivism and include self-esteem, anxiety, group cohesion, emotional empathy and psychological discomfort (e.g. hostility, anger). For MDOs, it is important to address both sets of needs but recognition of the criminogenic needs in relation to offending is essential in order to reduce the potential for further offending.

While mental health assessment and treatment is fundamental, assessment and intervention related to offending behaviour are necessary components of nursing care in the forensic mental health context. Until forensic mental health nursing theory is developed, nurses will have to look to the theory and models of other disciplines to develop competence in this area of care.

The following section is presented as a revision of the common principles of risk assessment that can also be applied to risk assessment of inpatient violence. This framework is relevant to

OPB and inpatient violence and can assist nurses to assess risk and identify cases when OPB is evident.

RISK ASSESSMENT IN FORENSIC PSYCHIATRY

In relation to long-term risk predictions of violence, Monahan (1983) argued that psychiatrists and psychologists appeared to be wrong at least twice as often as they were right in their unaided clinical predictions of violence, although with further examination of existing studies he concluded that 'what little we do know is not entirely bleak' (p. 169). He argued that unstructured clinical prediction was inadequate and argued for a second-generation method of risk assessment that would incorporate actuarial tools capable of providing clinicians with additional information on which to base their clinical judgements. Importantly, he recommended the inclusion of more situational items such as characteristics of the family, environment, work environment and peer group environment.

Considerable research has been undertaken since Monahan (1983) published his work and there is now a third, perhaps even a fourth generation of risk assessment (Andrews & Bonta, 2007; Ogloff & Davis, 2005). The situation has evolved from a second generation of actuarial prediction, to a third generation of structured professional judgement. The third generation of violence risk assessment has moved beyond prediction of an adverse event to the identification of the risk factors that contribute to the likelihood of an adverse event and to the management of those dynamic factors in order to assist the patient with violence control and to reduce aggression (Mullen, 2000). An emerging fourth generation of risk assessment places more emphasis on responsivity factors, treatment planning and service delivery from initial assessment to case closure. Prevention and management of violence have become the foci of contemporary risk assessment in forensic mental health.

PRINCIPLES OF OFFENDING RISK ASSESSMENT

The offending risk assessment aims to be a transparent and accountable process that improves the consistency of those decisions that inform treatment and risk management. The process is useful to determine the appropriate setting for the MDO, to identify those MDOs requiring intensive interventions, and to inform leave and discharge decisions. The offending risk assessment facilitates effective communication between the people and agencies involved with the MDO, and forms the basis for advice or reports related to ongoing management.

The following principles provide direction for nurses undertaking a risk assessment:

1. *Gather information (static and dynamic factors) on multiple areas of functioning* – The risk under consideration is unlikely to be related to just one factor; many factors will interrelate to contribute to the risk. As much information as is possible needs to be collected.
2. *Obtain information via multiple methods and sources* – Comprehensive information needs to be collected in a systematic manner. To be included in the multiple methods and sources are the review of clinical files and other documentation (e.g. legal and incident reports), the use of relevant risk assessment tools, and interviews with the MDO, family/carers and any person with relevant information to contribute to the process. Risk assessment requires input from the interdisciplinary team. The other health professionals contribute expertise in specific areas, and criminal justice staff should also be consulted as they often have information about the MDO that augment the assessment.

3. *Evaluate the accuracy of information* – Information needs to be confirmed. Information given by individuals can be distorted for a number of reasons (memory, an affective response to the information, motivation and consequences of giving the information) and documentation can be inaccurate depending on factors such as omissions in content or authorship.
4. *Repeat the assessment at regular intervals* – Personal and situational circumstances will change. Therefore, risk assessment needs to be repeated at intervals that are dependent on these changes. Changes in mental state, substance use, relationships, changes in behaviour or attitude in relation to programmes completed, and where the MDO is situated (prison, hospital or community) are examples of the conditions that can influence changes in the MDO's risk status. Risk assessment is a dynamic process.
5. *Effective risk management works against being able to demonstrate prediction accurately* – When a risk is identified, risk management and interventions should be implemented, which, if successful, will prevent the potential adverse event.

FACTORS THAT MAY IMPINGE ON OR WEAKEN RISK ASSESSMENT

These are factors that the psychiatric nurse needs to consider when undertaking risk assessment with MDOs. Clinton et al. (2001) reported the inherent difficulties in engaging patients in assessment who are severely psychotic and/or aggressive, and who are also detained and feel angry and resentful towards staff, especially when staff are perceived as responsible for their loss of liberty. The psychiatric nurse also needs to understand that secure environments can mask risk due to high levels of surveillance and support. Factors that can weaken risk assessment include:

- Information about the MDO is not available, recorded or passed on, resulting in an ignorance of risk factors
- Minimization of historical events
- Over-reliance on recent events
- Extraneous factors, not openly recognized
- Infrequency or discontinuation of assessment
- Non-verification of statements made by patient and/or others
- Not taking into account evidence contrary to patient's assertions
- Not recognizing patient manipulation and consequent staff discord
- Lack of thorough investigation of assertions of 'insight' and 'remorse'
- Lack of openness between those involved in the patient's care and treatment
- Discounting information not supportive of hoped-for outcome
- Self-expectations by clinicians of being decisive and successful
- Avoiding confrontation with the patient
- Inadequate reporting of lesser incidents or incidents generally
- Response distortion by the MDO for the purpose of gaining privileges or avoiding consequences
- The MDO may not possess sufficient insight to effectively respond to questions
- Not giving enough attention to contextual and situational factors and relying too much on characteristics and of the MDO.

(from Arnetz & Arnetz, 2000; Clinton et al., 2001; McMahon & Knowles, 1997; Potts, 1995 as cited in Allen, 1997; Walters, 2006).

It is also problematic when nurses believe that they have a close relationship with a patient and become complacent in their assessment. Therapeutic optimism always must be balanced with vigilant assessment of the patient's risk potential and validation through corroboration. For nurses undertaking risk assessment in forensic settings, there is a professional responsibility for the safety and welfare for not only the MDO, who will suffer the consequences of further risk behaviour, but also potential victims and the community generally.

INPATIENT VIOLENCE

Violence in acute inpatient settings is a major international concern that has prompted many professional and industrial bodies to produce a plethora of policy documents and guidelines. Early research related to inpatient violence focused on personal characteristics of the perpetrator; later research has included a range of situational factors that have impacted on inpatient violence (see Gadon et al., 2006 for a comprehensive review of the literature). Daffern and Howells (2002) would identify the research studies contained in the literature review by Gadon, Johnston and Cooke as structural approaches, which emphasize the form of inpatient violence and would recommend an inclusion of functional approaches (which identify purpose). A risk assessment of inpatient violence requires inclusion of a functional analysis to identify the patient's purpose of violence. This can be of considerable value in guiding management strategies and psychological interventions aimed at reducing aggression.

No test or interview can predict violence with high accuracy (Scott & Resnick, 2006). Encinares et al. (2005) suggest that actuarial tools used to assess imminent inpatient violence contain inadequate and fragmented information and do not account for factors in a specific situation. The prediction of violence is complex and part of the complexity can be attributed to the multifaceted nature of violence. An act of violence can be characterized in terms of nature, frequency, imminence and severity, the characteristics of the perpetrator of violence, the context and antecedents of the act, and the circumstances of the assessment. In addition, global conceptualizations of violence are inadequate, and predictors of one form of violence may be quite different from predictors of another form (Daffern, et al., 2006; Mitchie & Cooke, 2006; Monahan & Steadman, 1994; Scott & Resnick, 2006).

Inpatient violence may also be more of a response to the contextual setting of a confined ward than to an individual's mental state (Daffern et al., 2006; Walsh et al., 2002). The study by Lancee et al. (1995) suggested that violence by inpatients was frequently associated with the quality of staff–patient interactions. They found an association between nurses' limit-setting styles and levels of patient anger. Whittington and Wykes (1994) suggested that when a patient is assessed as high risk then the clinicians feel stress, which can lead to behaviours such as avoidance, overcontrol and hostility, thereby increasing the risk of violence. These authors identified that the task of predicting inpatient violence needs to also consider aspects other than the characteristics of the perpetrator. The environment and staff culture and practice and situational antecedents also need to be taken into account. These factors will continue to confound clinicians' ability to predict inpatient violence when only individual patient characteristics are considered.

Two studies that have studied inpatient violence have found differences in staff and patients' views about the causes or functions of violence (Daffern et al., 2006; Duxbury, 2002). Duxbury hypothesized that the differences may have been due to a lack of recognition of contributory factors possibly resulting from a lack of training in precursors or lack of interaction with the patient prior to the violent act. Daffern et al. (2006) identified that having little time to analyse various factors, insufficient expertise of clinicians, a preference for viewing the cause of violence to illness and there being few guidelines or measures to help discriminate among the various functions of violence may be reasons. A lack of understanding regarding the functions of violence will limit nurses' ability to estimate the likelihood of violence and to provide intervention.

Linaker and Busch-Iversen (1995) undertook research to identify predictors of violence in psychiatric inpatients. Five factors were found which were later incorporated into the Brøset Violence Checklist (Almvik & Woods, 1998, 2003). Early testing of this tool found it to be effective (Abderhalden et al., 2004). In Australia, items from the Brøset Violence Checklist were tested and two were incorporated into another risk assessment tool – the dynamic appraisal of situational aggression (Ogloff & Daffern, 2006). The value of these tools is that they have a small number of items that can be quickly considered to identify patients at risk of imminent violence and to assist in identifying the function of the act of violence. Ogloff and Daffern (2006) investigated inpatient nurses' ability to predict aggression in the following 24 hours and found that their predictions of aggression improved with the use of a risk assessment tool.

By contrast, in a study of unaided clinical prediction, Haim et al. (2002) asked14 psychiatrists and nine psychiatric nurses to make short-term predictions of inpatient violence. Results showed that there was little difference between the accuracy of the two professions; 30% of their positive predictions were correct and 91% of their negative predictions were correct. Both the groups used unstructured clinical judgement citing criteria such as 'previous acquaintance with patient', 'patient threatens violence' and 'rater feels threatened'. An earlier study also found that there was a higher success in predicting non-violence than violence (Convit et al., 1998).

Elbogen et al. (2002) surveyed mental health clinicians from a range of disciplines to examine their perceptions of the relevance of factors derived from research on violence risk assessment. The findings indicated that while 'clinicians perceived research risk factors to be relevant, they perceived behavioural variables not subjected to empirical scrutiny as significantly more relevant for violence risk assessment' (p. 37). The authors referred to Webster et al. (1997) who had noted that the research on the prediction of violence and the clinical practice of assessment scarcely intersect. They hypothesized that clinicians may view certain risk factors as irrelevant to practise or difficult to utilize; they may also have been unaware of evidence-based factors, or were resistant to using instruments, or relied on other factors that they found to be more critical to inpatient violence risk assessment.

Other issues that limit clinicians' ability to estimate the likelihood of violence in individual patients have been identified. Information about the patient is not available, recorded or passed on, resulting in an ignorance of risk factors (McMahon & Knowles, 1997). Often there is inadequate reporting of lesser incidents or incidents generally (Arnetz & Arnetz, 2000). Walters (2006) identified that when engaging patients in the task of risk assessment, there may be response distortion for the purpose of gaining privileges or avoiding consequences and that patients may not possess sufficient insight to effectively respond to questions. It is difficult to recognize success in the prediction of the risk of inpatient violence as, if it was predicted, then presumably interventions would be put in place to prevent it (Allen, 1997; Haim et al., 2002; Reid, 2003).

OFFENCE PARALLELING BEHAVIOUR

Jones (2004) has defined OPB as 'any form of offence related (or fantasized behaviour) pattern that emerges at any point before or after an offence; it simply needs to resemble, in some significant respect, the sequence of behaviours leading up to the offence' (p. 38). Daffern et al. (2007b) offer a further definition of OPB:

> A behavioural sequence incorporating overt behaviours (that may be muted by environmental factors), appraisals, expectations, beliefs, affects, goals and behavioural scripts, all of which may be influenced by the patient's mental disorder that is functionally similar to behavioural sequences involved in previous criminal acts. (p. 267)

Under certain circumstances consistent cross-situational behaviour may be observed when the patient's thinking, feeling and behaviour have the same function and meaning and meet the same need (Daffern et al., 2007b). It is important to note, however, that it is sequences and not discrete behaviours that are of interest and are required before behaviour may be properly labelled as offence paralleling (Daffern et al., 2007a).

Lee-Evans (1994) proposes that not all people behave consistently and that behaviour is the product of previous experiences and an interaction between situational and individual influences (e.g. cognitions, skills, values and beliefs). Emphasis is placed on identifying environmental events that give rise to problem behaviours of interest. These behaviours should be capable of being observed and measured. Attention should also be given to current situational influences that help to maintain the problem behaviour. Explanation of the behaviour should be sought in terms of the functions it serves in a particular context; topographically dissimilar behaviours (behaviours that look different) may have the same function; therefore, the task of analysis is to understand behaviour in terms of the function (purpose) it serves rather than its form (what it looks like).

Recognition of OPB requires comprehensive information about the index offence and identification of the sequence of component parts (the offence chain). The context and other situational factors are clearly relevant to the OPB analysis and require consideration. Examination of the behavioural sequences leading to and following the index offence/problem behaviour of interest allows comparison with the analysed current behaviour to determine if sequences are sufficiently similar to represent OPB. Not all ongoing antisocial behaviour or misdemeanour is OPB; 'sometimes a cigar is just a cigar'.

Daffern et al. (2009) cautioned that, as a model, OPB lacks empirical support and conceptual clarity and may be inappropriately used. Daffern et al. (2007a) warn that without further theoretical development and skilful application, the OPB framework may experience the pitfalls of first-generation risk assessment. An unstructured assessment may lead to an incorrect conclusion and inappropriate labelling of behaviour as OPB. If inpatient behaviour is incorrectly identified as OPB, there are serious implications for the patient if leave or discharge decisions are negatively affected. Although it is a model in early development, there are sufficient implications for the enhancement of the nursing role in assessing and caring for patients that are also offenders.

THE RELATIONSHIP OF OPB TO INPATIENT VIOLENCE

Much of the literature examining inpatient aggression has taken a structural approach with a focus on the demographic and clinical characteristics of aggressive patients. Recently, there has been more emphasis on the environment and the interpersonal context. To understand whether or not a patient's violence in the inpatient setting is OPB, it is necessary to undertake a functional analysis of the offence and compare this with each incident of inpatient violence (Daffern et al., 2009).

A functional analysis attempts to identify the purpose of behaviour by identifying 'important, controllable, causal functional relationships applicable to a specified set of target behaviours for an individual client' (Haynes & O'Brien, 1998, p. 654). A complete functional analysis includes an assessment of the behaviour itself, the individual's predisposing characteristics, the antecedent events that are considered important for the initiation of the behaviour, and the consequences of the behaviour which maintain and direct its developmental course (Haynes, 1998; Jackson et al., 1987).

Lee-Evans (1994) advised that problem behaviour should be defined in terms of specific behaviours that can be observed and measured and attention paid to situational influences that help to maintain the problem behaviour and not to look for underlying pathology: that behaviour is an interaction of individual characteristics and environmental features. An explanation of the behaviour should be sought in terms of the functions it serves in a particular context. In other words, it should identify the environmental events that interact with characteristics (propensities, sensitivities, traits, etc.) to influence behaviour.

For an act of inpatient aggression to be labelled as OPB, the equivalent psychological features or sequences of behaviour that had a role in offending would have to be identified in the inpatient aggressive act (Daffern et al., 2007b). Daffern and colleagues have developed a structured aggressive behaviour analysis schedule (SABAS) that can be used to guide a functional analysis of events of inpatient and index offence violence occurring in the community to determine whether similarity exists (Daffern et al., 2009):

- Description of the index violent act
- Victim characteristics
- Description of distal and proximal environmental triggers
- Description of cognitive antecedents
- Classification of affective antecedents
- Assessment of psychological activation
- Presence and description of active symptoms of major mental illness
- Classification of the environmental context
- Role of disinhibitors
- Description of opportunity factors
- Weapon use
- Determination of the function of the behaviour

Using the SABAS, Daffern et al. (2009) examined the similarity of violent index offences and aggressive behaviour in patients hospitalized for treatment of personality disorder. They found that some patterns of aggression were consistent and entrenched, but not all. As such, some behaviour appeared to be offence paralleling, but not all. Frequency of violence allows more opportunity for patterns of reactions to be examined and for OPB to be identified or ruled out (McDougall et al., 1994).

OFFENCE PARALLELING BEHAVIOUR: IMPLICATIONS FOR PSYCHIATRIC NURSING

The OPB model is a useful adjunct to structured risk assessment methods and has the potential to suggest treatment strategies by identifying criminogenic needs. It may also assist staff determine whether current behaviour reflects an ongoing risk of reoffending and help staff identify treatment targets. The model can assist staff monitor progress by looking for a reduction in OPB and provide evidence for transparency in decision-making related to leave from the unit, transfer to a less secure environment or discharge (Daffern et al., 2007b; Daffern et al., 2009; McDougal et al., 1994).

One essential domain of inpatient nursing that the OPB model can provide credence is the observation of patients. In many ways the hospital environment can be described as artificial as patients are not exposed to the same experiences that they have in the community. However, in other ways patients are exposed to similar situations in which OPB can be observed. Nurses are well placed to observe patients in their daily living on the unit. An understanding of the offence and sensitivity to OPB would give structure to their daily observations.

Nurses are comfortable with their role as observers. Peplau (1952), one of the earliest psychiatric nursing theorists, described the aim of nursing observation as the identification, clarification and verification of impressions about patients as they occur. Peplau identified a process in which observations led to hypotheses about the patient's behaviour and were organized to identify the patient's needs, and to identify and evaluate helpful nursing intervention. When documented observations were not purposeful, they became what Peplau labelled random observations, which were not precise enough to be of value to colleagues or to the nurse delivering care to the patient.

Similarly, Schwecke (2003, p. 113) has also identified a number of factors to investigate when a psychiatric nurse assessed a patient's behaviour:

- The context or situation that precipitated the behaviour
- What the patient was thinking
- What the patient was feeling
- Whether the behaviour made sense in the context
- Whether the behaviour was adaptive or dysfunctional
- How this episode fitted with the total picture of the patient
- Whether a change was needed

Presumably, neither Peplau nor Schwecke was familiar with OPB but their views are included here to demonstrate how nursing has developed frameworks that, with further refinement, would provide sound analyses of inpatient and violent offending. The OPB model can provide nurses with a structure to their observations and assessments that would support their role in addressing offending behaviour. Inpatient nurses are best placed to observe patients but their observations are often fragments of daily activities of patients – what Peplau (1952) would label as 'random'. Under the OPB framework nurses would focus their observation, at least in part, on OPB and on evidence of change, so-called prosocial adaptive behaviour (Daffern et al., 2007a).

From the author's research (Martin, 2003) a series of case file entries for one patient is given as an example of possible OPB. The index offence of the patient was an assault on a female followed by an assault on a female officer in the prison. The patient's behaviour became a concern to nurses when he indicated an interest in female staff.

'. . . Also frequently asking questions regarding [female medical officer named] and a female member of nursing staff – when told this questioning was inappropriate he indicated he wanted to be "just friends" with the female nurse. . . . It was made clear to him that he would

(continues)

be nursed by male staff due to his behaviours with females (index offence and assault on female prison guard) – accepting of this after initially requesting a female nurse.'

'Request to see me in seclusion with [named nurse] present. [Patient named] wanting to have "private" discussion about [named female nurse] nurse. Wanting to talk to Unit Manager [named] to get her permission to have relationship with [named female nurse]. Informed [Patient named] of the inappropriateness of these types of requests. Need to continually reinforce the nurse–patient relationship and its boundaries. [Female nurse named] also informed of the situation.'

'... Throughout the course of the morning it was noticed that [Patient named] was quite focused on female nurse [named]. He was watching her intently during the mealtimes. Whilst in the lounge room he sat opposite her, then quite openly moved across and sat beside her. All his body language was focused at her, i.e., crossing of legs, leaning towards her. [Patient named] watched her closely when she moved away from him to speak with other patients or staff. *Close observation necessary.*'

The patient's behaviour, although of evident concern to nurses, was raised inconsistently in their case file entries. There was no exploration with the patient as to why he wanted to have a relationship with a nurse, though the nurses repeated in their reporting that such a relationship was 'inappropriate' and that the patient was 'informed' of this fact. The issue was documented but there was no sense that the nurses' observations were part of a systematic assessment or treatment plan.

One nurse reported a detailed account of the patient's behaviour, identifying ongoing interest in the female nurse in her presence and determined that ongoing observation was necessary. Knowledge of the OPB model and a functional analysis using the SABAS (Daffern et al., 2009) may have assisted the nurses to structure their observations to make a more accurate assessment and then identify relevant risk management strategies. The patient may have been demonstrating OPB, but further information about the victim and the sequence of behaviours surrounding the problem behaviour would be required to make that decision and to determine risk and treatment need. However, the tacit knowledge of the nurses was evident in their identification of a possible link between the patient's offence and his ongoing behaviour.

The goal of intervention is to avoid further offending by increasing personal effectiveness. Protecting the community is best achieved through returning MDOs to the community with the necessary skills, attitudes, opportunities and social supports to meet their needs in a more adaptive and prosocial manner. All interventions should focus on the construction or development of new social repertoires rather than simply the elimination of troublesome repertoires (Blackburn, 2002). With OPB an understanding of behaviour in terms of the functions it serves in a particular context, and being aware that topographically dissimilar behaviours may have the same function, also suggests that the goal of intervention is to teach new and appropriate ways of achieving desired goal treatment (referred to by Daffern et al., 2007b) as prosocial alternative behaviour or PAB) to facilitate adaptive means of achieving same end (Lee-Evans, 1994).

Nurses, because of their frequent contact with patients, also have a role in reinforcing what is done in formal programmes and shaping the environment to support pro-social behaviour (Daffern et al., 2007b). McDougall et al. (1994) noted that what is said by patients in groups is not always evident in their behaviour on the unit and the nurses' observations can be invaluable to programme staff who need to assess engagement, commitment to change and progress in treatment. Beyond observing, nurses can also take therapeutic advantage of contacts with patients by providing learning opportunities to assist patients acquire and practise adaptive and prosocial behaviour. In some ways the inpatient environment is contrived or artificial and it can be difficult to predict how the patient will function in the community. The identification of OPB can provide a way to monitor any change in offending behaviour and contribute to risk assessment, treatment and discharge planning.

Nursing care is delivered in the context of the therapeutic relationship with the patient – working collaboratively to develop mutual trust and respect and desired outcomes (Encinares et al., 2005). Care is based on a holistic assessment of the patient with emphasis in the forensic setting being placed on the offending behaviour and potential inpatient violence and any identified association between the two – OPB.

Nurses that are involved in the assessment and management of risk are often not adequately educated and trained to do so. Structured assessment tools have been demonstrated to be useful in assessing the risk of offending and the risk of inpatient violence. While these tools have been found to improve clinicians' ability to estimate the likelihood of violence, they are rarely used consistently or integrated into nursing care and management by nurses in inpatient settings.

Undertaking a structured risk assessment with patients can help them to understand their behaviour and can enhance their engagement in treatment. Ongoing assessment is necessary to ensure that the treatment and management plan is contemporary and that it promotes and organizes interventions in a way that promotes consistency and continuity in the treating team. The forensic psychiatric nurse works as a member of an interdisciplinary team drawing on the knowledge and skill of each discipline, and with the patient and carers, the psychiatric nurse undertakes assessment and delivers care.

The OPB model offers nurses in forensic mental health settings an opportunity to use their proficiency in the assessment and management of inpatient aggression and expand their contribution to offending risk assessment. As shown in the previous file entries, nurses are able and intuitively make useful observations and identify possible concerns. Knowledge of the OPB framework may give nurses the skill and confidence to organize their observations in a structure that can identify whether a patient's offending potential is increasing or decreasing, refine their treatment and evaluate whether their treatments are working.

CONCLUSION

Psychiatric nurses working in forensic contexts require knowledge of the factors that contribute to offending and inpatient violence, and skills in risk assessment. Engaging collaboratively with MDOs to analyse the circumstances of offending behaviour and assessing MDOs' personal reactions to offending behaviour can facilitate engagement and commitment to treatment. Though care should be taken, analysis of previous offending should not be avoided. Systematic and comprehensive risk assessment requires validated risk assessment tools and structured clinical judgement. These are needed to develop risk management strategies and to ensure that the level of intervention and supervision is appropriate to the MDO's risk profile.

In the absence of forensic mental health nursing theory, the nursing literature has been mired in the concerns of nurses trying to make sense of the context of care. It has only recently started to address the therapeutic potential of nurses. Other disciplines may be further advanced in forensic mental health theory and practice, but nurses have significant and established roles in forming relationships with patients, maintaining a therapeutic environment, observation and assessment, and managing inpatient violence. The OPB model complements existing nursing frameworks and offers an integrated framework for further development of the nursing role in managing inpatient violence and addressing the offending behaviour of patients.

REFERENCES

Abderhalden, C., Needham, I., Miserez, B., Almvik, R., Dassen, T., Haug, H.J. & Fischer, J.E. (2004). Predicting inpatient violence in acute psychiatric wards using the Brøset Violence Checklist: a multicentre prospective cohort study. *Journal of Psychiatric and Mental Health Nursing, 11*, 422–27.

Allen, J. (1997). Assessing and managing risk of violence in the mentally disordered. *Journal of Psychiatric and Mental Health Nursing, 4*, 369–78.

Almvik, R. & Woods, P. (1998). The Brøset Violence Checklist (BVC) and the prediction of inpatient violence: some preliminary results. *Psychiatric Care, 5*, 208–11.

Almvik, R. & Woods, P. (2003). Short-term risk prediction: the Brøset Violence Checklist. *Journal of Psychiatric and Mental Health Nursing, 10*, 236–38.

Andrews, D.A. & Bonta, J. (2007). *The Psychology of Criminal Conduct* (4th edition). Cincinnati, OH: Anderson Publishing.

Arnetz, J.E. & Arnetz, B.B. (2000). Implementation and evaluation of a practical intervention programme for dealing with violence towards health care workers. *Journal of Advanced Nursing, 31*, 668–80.

Benson, R. (1992). The clinical nurse specialist in forensic settings. In P. Morrison & P. Burnard (Eds), *Aspects of Forensic Psychiatric Nursing* (pp. 45–60). Aldershot: Avebury.

Blackburn, R. (2002). Ethical issues in motivating offenders to change. In M. McMurran (Ed.), *Motivating Offenders to Change: A Guide to Enhancing Engagement in Therapy* (pp. 139–56). Chichester: John Wiley & Sons.

Burnard, P. (1992). The expanded role of the forensic psychiatric nurse. In P. Morrison & P. Burnard (Eds), *Aspects of Forensic Psychiatric Nursing* (pp. 139–54). Aldershot: Avebury.

Burrow, S. (1993). The role conflict of the forensic nurse. *Senior Nurse, 13*, 20–25.

Carton, G. (1998). Nurse education: scribes and scriptures. In T. Mason & D. Mercer (Eds), *Critical Perspectives in Forensic Care Inside out* (pp. 244–55). Basingstoke: Macmillan.

Clinton, C., Pereira, S. & Mullins, B. (2001). Training needs of psychiatric intensive care staff. *Nursing Standard, 15*, 33–36.

Convit, A., Jaeger, J., Pin Lin, S., Meisner, M. & Volavka, J. (1998). Predicting assaultiveness in psychiatric inpatients: a pilot study. *Hospital and Community Psychiatry, 39*, 429–34.

Daffern, M., Ferguson, M., Ogloff, J., Thomson, L. & Howells, K. (2007a). Appropriate treatment targets or products of a demanding environment? The relationship between aggression in a forensic psychiatric hospital with aggressive behaviour preceding admission and violent recidivism. *Psychology, Crime and Law, 13*, 431–41.

Daffern, M. & Howells, K. (2002). Psychiatric inpatient aggression: a review of structural and functional assessment approaches. *Aggression and Violent Behavior, 7*, 477–97.

Daffern, M., Howells, K., Mannion, A. & Tonkin, M. (2009). A test of methodology intended to assist detection of aggressive offence paralleling behaviour within secure settings. *Legal and Criminological Psychology, 14*, 213–26.

Daffern, M., Howells, K. & Ogloff, J. (2006). What's the point? Towards a methodology for assessing the function of psychiatric inpatient aggression. *Behaviour Research and Therapy, 45*, 101–11.

Daffern, M., Jones, L., Howells, K., Shine, J., Mikton, C. & Tunbridge, V.C. (2007b). Refining the definition of offence paralleling behaviour. *Criminal Behaviour and Mental Health, 17*, 265–73.

Dunwell, F. & Hanson, B. (1998). Appraising a ward's 'philosophy of care' statement. *Mental Health Nursing, 18*, 18–22.

Duxbury, J. (2002). An evaluation of staff and patients' views of and strategies employed to manage inpatient aggression and violence on one mental health unit: a pluralistic design. *Journal of Psychiatric and Mental Health Nursing, 9*, 325–37.

Eckroth-Bucher, M. (2001). Philosophical basis and practice of self-awareness in psychiatric nursing. *Journal of Psychosocial Nursing, 39*, 32–39.

Elbogen, E.B., Calkins Mercado, C., Scalora, M.J. & Tomkins, A.J. (2002). Perceived relevance of factors for risk assessment: a survey of clinicians. *International Journal of Forensic Mental Health, 1*, 37–47.

Encinares, M., McMaster, J.J. & McNamee, J. (2005). Risk assessment of forensic patients. *Journal of Psychosocial Nursing and Mental Health Services, 43*, 30–36.

Gadon, L., Johnston, L. & Cooke, D. (2006). Situational variables and institutional violence: a systematic review of the literature. *Clinical Psychology Review, 26*, 515–34.

Haim, R., Rabinowitz, J., Lereya, J. & Fennig, S. (2002). Predictions made by psychiatrists and psychiatric nurses of violence by patients. *Psychiatric Services, 53*, 622–24.

Hammer, R. (2000). Caring in forensic nursing: expanding the holistic model. *Journal of Psychosocial Nursing, 38*, 18–24.

Haynes, S. (1998). The changing nature of behavioural assessment. In A. Bellack & M. Hersen (Eds), *Behavioral Assessment: A Practical Handbook* (pp. 1–21). Boston, MA: Allyn & Bacon.

Haynes, S.N. & O'Brien, W.H. (1998). Functional analysis in behavior therapy. *Clinical Psychology Review, 10*, 649–68.

Hodgins, S. (2002). Research priorities in forensic mental health. *International Journal of Forensic Mental Health, 1*, 7–23.

Jackson, H.F., Glass, C. & Hope, S. (1987). A functional analysis of recidivistic arson. *British Journal of Clinical Psychology, 26*, 175–85.

Jackson, S. & Stevenson, C. (2000). What do people need psychiatric and mental health nurses for? *Journal of Advanced Nursing, 31*, 378–88.

Jones, L.F. (2004). Offence paralleling behaviour (OPB) as a framework for assessment and interventions with offenders. In A. Needs & G. Towl (Eds), *Applying Psychology to Forensic Practice* (pp. 34–63). Oxford: BPS Blackwell.

Lancee, W.L., Gallop, R., McCay, E. & Toner, B. (1995). The relationship between nurses' limit-setting styles and anger in psychiatric inpatients. *Psychiatric Services, 46*, 609–13.

Laskowski, C. (2001). The mental health clinical nurse specialist and the 'difficult' patient: evolving meaning. *Issues in Mental Health Nursing, 22*, 5–22.

Lee-Evans, J.M. (1994). Background to behaviour analysis. In J.E. Hodge, M. McMurran & C.R. Hollin. (Eds), *The Assessment of Criminal Behaviours of Clients in Secure Settings* (pp. 6–34). London: Jessica Kingsley.

Linaker, O.M. & Busch-Iversen, H. (1995). Predictors of imminent violence in psychiatric inpatients. *Acta Psychiatrica Scandinavica, 92*, 250–54.

Martin, T. (2001). Something special: forensic psychiatric nursing. *Journal of Psychiatric and Mental Health Nursing, 8*, 25–32.

Martin, T. (2003). *Exploring the Relationship of the Nurse-Patient Relationship in an Acute, High Security Forensic Psychiatry Unit*. Unpublished doctoral thesis, Monash University, Melbourne, Victoria.

Martin, T. & Street, A. (2003). Exploring evidence of the therapeutic relationship in forensic psychiatric nursing. *Journal of Psychiatric and Mental Health Nursing, 10*, 543–51.

Mason, T. (2002). Forensic psychiatric nursing: a literature review and thematic analysis of role tensions. *Journal of Psychiatric and Mental Health Nursing, 9*, 511–20.

Mason, T. & Mercer, D. (1998). Rehabilitation: 'the ship of fools'. In T. Mason & D. Mercer (Eds), *Critical Perspectives in Forensic Care Inside out* (pp. 1–8). Basingstoke: Macmillan.

McDougall, C., Clark, D.A. & Fisher, M.J. (1994). Assessment of violent offenders. In J.E. Hodge, M. McMurran & C.R. Hollin. (Eds), (*The Assessment of Criminal Behaviours of Clients in Secure Settings* (pp. 68–93). London: Jessica Kingsley.

McMahon, M. & Knowles, A. (1997). Psychologists' and psychiatrists' perceptions of the dangerous client. *Psychiatry, Psychology and Law, 4*, 207–215.

Mitchie, C. & Cooke, D. (2006). The structure of violent behavior. *Criminal Justice and Behavior, 33*, 706–37.

Monahan, J. (1983). The prediction of violent behaviour: developments in psychology and law. In C. Scheirer, C. James & B.L. Hammonds (Eds), *Psychology and The Law: Master Lecture Series Vol. 2* (pp. 151–76). Washington, DC: American Psychological Association.

Monahan, J. & Steadman, H. (1994). Towards a rejuvenation of risk assessment research. In J. Monahan & H.J. Steadman (Eds), *Violence and Mental Disorder: Developments in Risk Assessment* (pp. 1–17). Chicago: University of Chicago Press.

Mullen, P.E. (2000). Dangerousness, risk, and the prediction of probability. In M.G. Gelder, J.J. Lopez-Ibor & N. Andreasen (Eds). *New Oxford Textbook of Psychiatry, Vol. 2.* (pp. 2066–2078). Oxford: Oxford University Press.

Mullen, P.E. & Lindqvist, P. (2000). Treatment and care in forensic mental health. In M. Gelder, J. Lopez-Ibor & N. Andreasen (Eds), *New Oxford Textbook of Psychiatry, Vol. 2* (pp. 2109–121). Oxford: Oxford University Press.

O'Brien, A.J. (1999). Negotiating the relationship: mental health nurses' perceptions of their practice. *Australian and New Zealand Journal of Mental Health Nursing, 8*, 153–61.

Ogloff, J.R.P. & Daffern, M. (2006). The dynamic appraisal of situational aggression: an instrument to assess risk for imminent aggression in psychiatric inpatients. *Behavioral Sciences and the Law, 24*, 799–813.

Ogloff, J.R.P. & Davis, M.R. (2005). Assessing risk for violence in the Australian context. In D. Chappell & P. Wilson (Eds), *Issues in Crime and Criminal Justice* (pp. 301–38). Chatswood: Lexis Nexis Butterworths.

Peplau, H.E. (1952). *Interpersonal Relations in Nursing*. Basingstoke: Macmillan Education.

Petenelj-Taylor, C. (1998). Forbidden love: sexual exploitation in the forensic milieu. *Journal of Psychosocial Nursing*, *36*, 17–23.

Pieranunzi, V.R. (1997). The lived experience of power and powerlessness in psychiatric nursing: a Heideggerian hermeneutical analysis. *Archives of Psychiatric Nursing*, *11*, 155–62.

Potts, J. (1995). Risk assessment and management: a home office perspective. In J. Crighton (Ed.), *Psychiatric Patient Violence Risk and Response* (pp. 35–43). London: Duckworth.

Prins, H. (1991). Dangerous people or dangerous situations? – Some further thoughts. *Medicine, Science and the Law*, *31*, 25–37.

Reid, W.H. (2003). Risk assessment, prediction and foreseeability. *Journal of Psychiatric Practice*, *9*, 82–86.

Robinson, D. & Kettles, A. (Eds) (2000). *Forensic Nursing and Multidisciplinary Care of the Mentally Disordered Offender*. London: Jessica Kingsley.

Schwecke, L.H. (2003). The nursing process. In N.L. Keltner, L.H. Schwecke & C.E. Bostrom (Eds), *Psychiatric Nursing* (pp. 111–19). St. Louis, MO: CV Mosby.

Scott, C.L. & Resnick, P.J. (2006). Violence risk assessment in persons with mental illness. *Aggression and Violent Behaviour*, *11*, 598–611.

Speedy, S. (1999). The therapeutic alliance. In M. Clinton & S. Nelson (Eds), *Advanced Practice in Mental Health Nursing* (pp. 59–76). Oxford: Blackwell Science.

Teising, M. (2000). 'Sister, I am going crazy, help me': psychodynamic-oriented care in psychotic patients in inpatient treatment. *Journal of Psychiatric and Mental Health Nursing*, *7*, 449–54.

Topping-Morris, B. (1992). An historical and personal view of forensic nursing services. In P. Morrison & P. Burnard (Eds), *Aspects of Forensic Psychiatric Nursing* (pp. 2–44). Aldershot: Avebury.

Vaughan, P.J. & Badger, D. (1995). *Working with the Mentally Disordered Offender in the Community*. London: Chapman & Hall.

Wallace, C., Mullen, P.E. & Burgess, P. (2004). Criminal offending in schizophrenia over a 25-year period marked by deinstitutionalisation and increasing prevalence of comorbid substance use disorders. *American Journal of Psychiatry*, *161*, 716–27.

Walsh, E., Buchanan, A. & Fahy, T. (2002). Violence and schizophrenia: examining the evidence. *British Journal of Psychiatry*, *180*, 490–95.

Walters, G.D. (2006). Risk-appraisal versus self-report in the prediction of criminal justice outcomes. *Criminal Justice and Behavior*, *33*, 279–304.

Webster, C.D., Douglas, K.S., Eaves, D. & Hart, S.D. (1997). *HCR-20: Assessing Risk for Violence (Version 2)*. Burnaby, British Columbia: Simon Fraser University and British Columbia Forensic Psychiatric Services Commission.

Whittington, R. & Wykes, T. (1994). An observational study of nurse behaviour and violence in psychiatric hospitals. *Journal of Psychiatric and Mental Health Nursing*, *1*, 85–92.

Woods, P., Collins, M. & Kettles, A.M. (2002). Forensic nursing interventions and future directions for forensic mental health practice. In A.M. Kettles, P. Woods & M. Collins (Eds), *Therapeutic Interventions for Forensic Mental Health Nurses* (pp. 240–45). London: Jessica Kingsley.

Chapter 16

OFFENDERS WITH SEVERE PERSONALITY DISORDER AND 'LIFESTYLE PARALLELING BEHAVIOURS'

CORINNE SPEARING

The Millfields Unit, Centre for Forensic Mental Health, London, UK

VICTORIA WASTENEY

The Millfields Unit, Centre for Forensic Mental Health, London, UK

PHIL MORGAN

Dorset Community Health Services, UK

INTRODUCTION

As occupational therapists considering the relevance of 'offence paralleling behaviours' (OPB; Daffern et al., 2007; Jones, 2004) in occupation-focused treatment, the exploration of the link between offending and lifestyle became interesting and highlighted an area for research. Through exploring this link, the notion of 'lifestyle paralleling behaviours' (LPB) emerged as a useful concept to consider in treatment.

This chapter focuses on the concept of LPB. We are approaching this concept from the perspective of occupational therapy, paying particular attention to the clinical application of the task of risk reduction and the community reintegration of patients residing in a dangerous and severe personality disorder (DSPD) pilot project, the Millfields Unit. The Millfields Unit is a National Health Service (NHS) pilot service established for men with serious emotional and personality difficulties who, as demonstrated by previous offending, pose a serious risk to the public.

The treatment approach used at the Millfields Unit is the therapeutic community. Within this framework a variety of different forms of psychological therapies are used, from cognitive behavioural to psychodynamic, to foster the skills needed to recognize and regulate emotion, to understand others, to control impulsive or destructive behaviour, to form relationships with others that are rewarding rather than damaging, and to spend personal time enjoyably and productively.

Offence Paralleling Behaviour: A Case Formulation Approach to Offender Assessment and Intervention Edited by Michael Daffern, Lawrence Jones and John Shine

Within the occupational therapy service, an emphasis is placed on the use of 'occupation' and lifestyle as a way to assess and manage risk. In this context the use of the word 'occupation' refers broadly to how individuals spend their time, rather than solely looking at vocational activity.

As per the Millfields Unit status as a pilot, we have been examining the occupational skills and needs of this group of patients and attempting to develop new ways of working in order to address them. It is using this experience that has informed this chapter. As such, this chapter aims to: (1) introduce LPB as a new concept; (2) provide a useful definition; (3) explore its relationship with OPB; (4) share how the notion has developed; and (5) examine its clinical relevance and application in reducing risk as well as supporting successful community reintegration for offenders. The chapter also includes an outline of current and relevant literature. This includes literature from Occupational Science (OS; Cronin-Davis et al., 2004; Molineux, 2004; Whiteford, 2000), occupational therapy and the Model of Human Occupation (MOHO; Kielhofner, 2002) and the Good Lives Model (Ward & Brown, 2004).

Although this chapter is written with an emphasis on occupational therapy, we feel that LPB needs to be considered when working with offenders with severe personality disorder and therefore it is a helpful concept for all professionals working with this group specifically, and possibly for all offenders.

THEORETICAL CONCEPTS UNDERPINNING LPB

The role of lifestyle in the rehabilitation of offenders has been previously documented, perhaps most clearly within the lifestyle performance model (Velde & Fidler, 2002), the model of human occupation (Kielhofner, 2002) and occupational science literature (Cronin-Davis et al., 2004; Molineux, 2004; Whiteford, 2000), and the good lives model (Ward & Mann 2004; Ward & Brown, 2004). One of the core assumptions of the 'good lives model' is that in order to rehabilitate offenders, it is necessary to provide them with the necessary resources, skills and knowledge to be able to live a better life. The good lives model suggests that offenders consciously or unconsciously work towards goals that enable them to obtain 'primary goods'. Primary goods are experiences, activities and actions that human being seek for their own sake and are intrinsically beneficial. The areas acknowledged include (Ward & Mann 2004):

- Mastery experiences
- Autonomy and self-directedness
- Emotional turmoil and stress
- Friendship, romantic and family relationships
- Meaning and purpose in life
- Happiness/pleasure creativity
- Healthy living and functioning

Ward (2004) argued that in order to shape the behaviour change process, individuals working to rehabilitate offenders must construct conceptions of a better and good life for the offender.

The good lives model has a similar conceptualization of the 'occupational' nature of people and their drive for purpose and meaning through activity as the occupational therapy and occupational science literature. Although occupational therapy models are not solely focused on offenders or people with personality disorder, they do provide a useful framework for the way people are shaped and define themselves through their lifestyle.

Velde & Fidler (2002) developed a lifestyle performance model that provided a framework for the study and use of activity in the daily lives of individuals in their environment and in society. Lifestyle has been described as a number of activity patterns that a person develops over time (Fidler, 1996). These patterns of doing are the result of a person's motivation to meet their intrinsic needs and the demands of their environment.

The model of human occupation (Kielhofner, 2002) provides clinicians with a theoretical model and standardized assessments and outcome measures to translate theory into practice. The core of this model is focused on the assertion that occupational performance is a central force in well-being, development, health and change. According to this model human beings engaging in activities of daily living (e.g. work) are able to maintain, reconstruct and increase their core constructs and capabilities (Parkinson et al., 2004). For example, an individual engaging in vocational work may be able to develop roles, responsibilities and self-esteem, and increase their ability to maintain a structured routine.

Occupational science offers a framework for therapists to acknowledge broader, external influences such as education, society, environment and government policies of a patient's current situation and psychopathology (Cronin-Davis et al., 2004). The focus of occupational science is to view humans as occupational beings (Wilcock, 1993; Yerxa et al., 1989). This suggests that as human beings, we have an innate drive to engage in some form of occupation and in the absence of, or disruption in, occupation we fail to thrive and function optimally.

Within the forensic environment, the developing concepts of occupational risk factors have been useful when identifying and treating occupational dysfunctions in the context of lifestyle.

Occupational risk factors have been defined as follows:

Occupational deprivation: 'The deprivation of occupational choice and diversity due to circumstances beyond the control of the individual' (Wilcock, 1998, p. 257).

Occupational disruption: A changeable or temporary inability to engage in occupation due to acute illness or injury and environmental or lifestyle changes (Whiteford, 2000).

Occupational imbalance: 'The loss of balance of engagement in occupations which lead to well-being' (Molineux, 2004, p. 173; see also Wilcock, 1998).

Performance deficits: Those dysfunctions that impact on an individual such as their cognitive, psychosocial and physical functioning (Molineux, 2004).

Occupational alienation: 'Isolation, powerlessness, frustration, loss of control, estrangement from society or self' (Wilcock, 1998, p. 257).

Attention to occupational risk factors has been useful when working with patients at the Millfields Unit as it has offered a means to examine the development of lifestyle and the key occupational risk factors that contribute to offending. For example, early experience of neglect and a lack of simulation through play within the home (occupational deprivation) and being reared in a social environment where lifestyle choices were predominately related to substance use, antisocial or criminal behaviour (occupational imbalance) may result in the person developing limited skills or enjoyment of broader options of activities (performance deficits). The key way for this person to develop a sense of skill or mastery may then be through engaging in violence or criminal activity (occupational alienation).

In examining the role lifestyle plays in the assessment and management of risk, it has been essential to consider offending as an 'occupation', albeit a criminogenic one, that is antisocial and which has both costs and benefits for the individual and forms an important part of their identity.

Against the background of the notion of occupational risk factors we are able to target our 'occupation-focused' treatment to enable our patients to develop a sense of identity away from their previous criminal lifestyle. For example, looking at the individual described (above) our treatment aims would be to: provide opportunities for the person to explore new occupational choices in a way that they feel safe and in control; support them in developing skills to be able to engage in a range of occupations; support them to develop a balanced routine that consists of a range of activities; and support the individual to gain a sense of mastery and control through engaging in prosocial activities.

By considering occupational risk factors and the literature on occupational science, occupational therapy, the model of human occupation, and the good lives model we began to develop our concept of LPB. Although the theoretical frameworks presented above offer an understanding of the relationship between lifestyle and offending, they do not provide clinicians with a unifying concept from which robust risk management and treatment plans could be formulated. As such, we looked to develop a concept that incorporated an understanding of offending in the context of 'lifestyle' that could be applied in a clinical setting which could evidence meaningful change to a person's lifestyle and the level of risk they pose.

DEVELOPING THE CONCEPT OF LPB

The notion of LPB developed following the introduction of formulation meetings at the Millfields Unit. The formulation meetings provide an opportunity for the multidisciplinary team (MDT) to examine the links between the development of personality disorder and offending behaviour and the psychological processes that maintain both and that led to the index offence. The formulation meeting also identifies treatment targets and OPBs that may be observed.

Within this process, the occupational therapy team built on the concept of 'occupational diagnosis' introduced by Rogers and Holm (1991). The concept of occupational diagnosis outlines a structure for practitioners to summarize their diagnostic reasoning. It includes four components: explanatory (likely cause of the problem), cue (signs and symptoms), descriptive (identifying the problem) and pathological (medical or psychiatric pathology underlying the problem; Roger & Holm, 1989). The concept of occupational formulations emerged from this notion and was developed as part of the MDT formulation. These formulations can be described as an analysis of an individual's past and present occupational functioning in relation to offending behaviour.

Through the formulation meeting process, we began to examine the relationship between each patient's lifestyle, offending behaviour and personality disorder. We observed that although patients were reporting psychological shifts (and superficially their attendance in the programme was bearing this out), there were limited shifts in how they were spending their time. Although they described apparently feasible prosocial future goals, there was little actual evidence with their participation in activities within the institution that these goals would be realized in the future. The concept of *impression management* (Paulhus, 1998) was considered important for many individuals in care. For example, a patient attended all psychological therapies and set goals for future employment, education and self-care that were all prosocial and encouraging when reviewing progress. However, his current lifestyle within the unit did not reflect these stated goals; he would not apply for a vocational post, he did not attend education programmes and he refused to engage in self-catering. He also discouraged peers from engaging in activities and, when questioned about this and his routine, he became verbally abusive, thereby showing that the prosocial goals he had set were somewhat unrealistic and not representative of his actual progress and presentation within the unit.

We also noticed that there were parallels between some patients' current lifestyles and how they participated in activities, and in general, their lifestyles, at the time of their index offences. For example, after a patient became unemployed in the community he became socially isolated and his behaviour became increasingly antisocial. Subsequently, he committed the index offence. Within the Millfields Unit there was a period of time where this patient disengaged from all occupational therapy groups and from his peer group; soon after it was observed that his antisocial behaviour (e.g. engaging in low-level intimidating behaviour) again increased and led to a more serious incident (e.g. attempting to assault a fellow patient).

Through observation and clinical review, we identified that some patients' engagement in activities within the unit would change prior to them becoming involved in incidents (e.g. engaging in substance misuse, self-harm and actual or threatened violence). For example, one patient disengaged from regular gym activity immediately prior to absconding. Previously, the gym sessions had helped this patient manage feelings of restlessness and agitation. An alternative occupational indicator of possible impending concern is when a patient suddenly engages in an occupational activity that provides access to 'weapons' or self-harming materials with the intention to use them.

In addition, the Millfields Unit has worked closely with Glen Thomas (see Chapter 17) in the delivery of its substance misuse programme. Through this work, the occupational therapy department has examined the relationship between habits, routines and addictive behaviour. We uncovered clear examples of patients engaging in substitute addictive behaviours such as using the gym, playing video games and obsessively preparing high caffeine-content drinks. We began to expand the idea of parallel behaviours and looked at how people's lifestyle may contribute to not only maintaining their addictive behaviour but also their offending behaviour.

What Are Lifestyle Paralleling Behaviours?

Within the occupational therapy literature there is little or no research examining LPB within forensic services. This would appear to be a new definition of an advanced perspective of treating the occupational and lifestyle needs of offenders with personality disorder. It is closely linked and developed following the emergence of the OPB concept.

Our working definition of LPB is as follows: lifestyle choices and related behaviours that manifest within institutional settings that have similarity or parity with behaviours that an individual engaged in prior to or during their index offence/offending behaviour and provided an occupational context which supported the offending to take place.

For example, a particular patient lived in a cultural and environmental context that included financial deprivation and minimal social support and family contact. Associates were predominantly antisocial (e.g. peers from the 'paid muscle'/debt collecting industry) and alcohol abuse and gambling were predominant issues. The index offence was the manslaughter of a debtor. His lifestyle prior to hospital admission was characterized by periods of isolation, instability within relationships and frequent violence and other antisocial behaviour. Most occupations engaged in were criminogenic. This lifestyle appeared to support the index offence. Possible parallels with this lifestyle emerged within the hospital setting. For example, he showed fluctuating motivation for treatment, spent excessive periods isolated in his bedroom, had few positive peer relationships, traded despite prohibition and intimidated others.

The notion of LPB is based on the premise that offending takes place within a context (in terms of routines, patterns, environment and interpersonal relationships) that exists independently of, but interacts reciprocally with, a person's psychological state. It also looks at the skills and functional abilities that an individual has and how these influence lifestyle choices. LPB should be looked at as a wider context for exploring OPB (Figure 16.1).

Predominant treatment approaches for offenders with personality disorder focus on psychological change, with lifestyle change a by-product of effective changes in thinking, feeling and

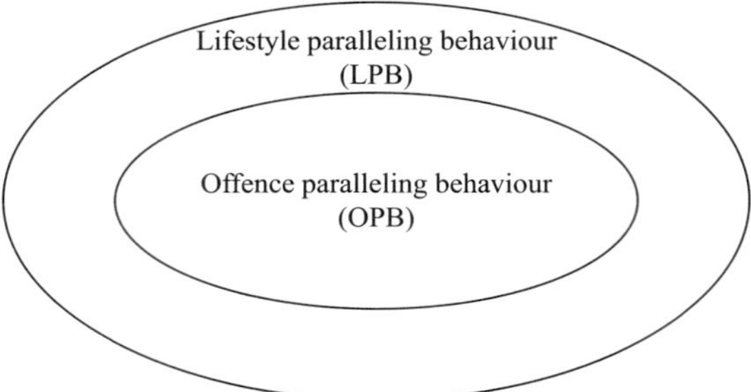

Figure 16.1 Representation of the context in which LPB and OPB take place.

relating. By addressing lifestyle alongside OPB the opportunity to work with the 'whole person' is created. This approach is consistent with the good lives model.

Evidence of LPB within forensic environments may be observed/highlighted by the following examples:

- Sleeping habits: choosing to sleep on the floor when previously being homeless, sleeping through the day when previous routine involved engaging in anti-social behaviour during the night
- Daily routine: the inability to structure time due to previously living a chaotic lifestyle without time boundaries, daily structure driven by substance needs i.e. a high number of caffeine loaded drinks throughout the day
- Eating patterns: eating primitively, secretively, overeating, storing food
- Activity choices: choosing isolative activities or activities that provide a sense of control
- Relationships/interactions with others: forming exploitative relationships, intimidating others
- Isolative behaviour: remaining in bedroom for prolonged periods of time, avoidance of group forums
- Tool use: seeking out sessions that offer the opportunity to use tools that may have been previously used as weapons, or items used as part of employment
- Trading: acquiring items that can be used to trade with i.e. Shower gel, tobacco, coffee
- Gym use: patterns of using the gym in an addictive fashion, used as a continuation of previous routine
- Gang culture: orientating to others who, together with themselves, provide a sense of safety against another force, groups that work to keep out those who are perceived to represent something weak or deficient
- Acquisition of goods (money, food): a need to gather items and possibly store them despite there being unrestricted access to them
- Self-care: varying degrees of attention to self, this may be observed to fluctuate with mood, it may become apparent that some may have never learned the process and skills involved in self-care i.e. not knowing how to wash, with what and when
- Domestic activity patterns: cleaning, laundry, either getting others to do this for them or irregular or obsessive patterns

The benefits of looking at LPB are twofold. They can be supportive in developing protective factors as well as informing risk assessments. These benefits are demonstrated throughout the remainder of the chapter.

The Links between OPB and LPB

The criticisms that can be levelled at OPB are also relevant, if not more so, to LPB. For example, OPB has been seen by some as controversial. There is a question as to whether observer bias influences the identification of OPB and also how the environment and the effects of restrictions and institutionalization influence an individuals' behaviour (Daffern et al., 2007).

OPB and LPB are similar in terms of their use within treatment planning. LPB can inform treatment plans, identify future goals and may indicate future success or limitations. For example, take the case of a patient who continues to be socially isolated, despite treatment attempts to create a prosocial alternative, in this case it is suggested that the individual would require further intervention within this area when returning to the community to prevent the possibility of resuming lifestyle patterns associated with offending behaviour.

One difference between OPB and LPB is that in LPB the offending is considered as part of, or within, the individual's lifestyle. As part of treatment, the offence/offending (depending on the meaning and value of the act to the individual and period of time over which it occurred) is considered to be an occupation.

This has an advantage in terms of its clinical application as it approaches the offending in the context of lifestyle. This may have the advantage of limiting defensiveness by making offence-focused work feel less threatening, thereby increasing the motivation of the patient to engage in emotionally and intellectually complex work.

In looking at lifestyle it is important to strike a balance between on the one hand addressing offending and dysfunctional behaviours whilst, on the other, not imposing a lifestyle that fails to meet the social, psychological and cultural needs of the individual. It is essential, when making decisions on risk and lifestyle, to ensure that they are not based on the value judgements of the clinician but on the likelihood of reoffending and are culturally congruent to the individual. It is also important to acknowledge that within institutions there are limited opportunities for different lifestyles, and the social environment does not always support change in regard to developing a prosocial lifestyle (see below for exploration).

Therefore, it is crucial that there is a rigorous approach to assessing lifestyle, that clear and demonstrable examples are presented and that the patient takes a central role in exploring links between lifestyle and offending and that any future plans are consistent with their own life narrative. The remainder of the chapter focuses on how we provide this rigorous approach and how it is crucial that the patient is central to work addressing their lifestyle issues.

Assessment

There is a dearth of research and standardized assessments that focus on lifestyle, personality disorder and offending. Thus, as occupational therapists attempting to assess an individual's LPBs, we have had to draw on a combination of theories, models and approaches, to enable us to understand and analyse these behaviours in the most effective way.

When assessing an individual's lifestyle within the unit, there are three phases that we acknowledge and examine in depth: exploration of their past lifestyle history; analysis of their current lifestyle pattern; and finally the relationship between the two.

Explanation of Individual Lifestyle History

To understand why an individual behaves the way they do, we first need to understand what influenced them to be the person they are. To do this we have found the MOHO Assessment

Occupational Performance History Interview (OPHI-II; Kielhofner et al., 1998) and the occupational risk factors developed from occupational science (occupational deprivation, alienation, disruption and imbalance; Cronin-Davis et al., 2004) to be useful.

While working with men with long histories of offending, it is crucial to consider past offending behaviour as occupation or activity. This is helpful for understanding criminal behaviour and for treating both mental health problems and the actual offending behaviour (Couldrick & Alred, 2003). Within the assessment process we have found, as Farnworth et al.'s (2004) work advises, that a more systemic approach to assessment, such as the use of OPHI-II and the analysis of previous lifestyle, to be helpful in both designing treatment programmes and engaging individuals in meaningful interventions.

The OPHI-II assessment includes three areas of occupational performance:

1. Exploring a patient's occupational lifestyle history through semi-structured interview
2. Rating scales that give an interval measure of a patient's occupational competence, identity and impact of their occupational behaviour settings
3. A life history narrative

The life history narrative has proved to be most useful when assessing offenders with personality disorder, particularly when trying to analyse historical information and establish links between a patient's occupational and offending history. Additionally, applying an occupational science perspective to this assessment has been beneficial when identifying if or when an individual has experienced, for example, occupational deprivation or alienation, and establishing causal relationships between such events.

Gathering this information has been crucial in finding out what meaning or value an individual derived from their occupation (including their criminal behaviour). This process highlights treatment targets and clarifies how the individual can be provided with opportunities to develop prosocial activities and occupations that provide the value and motivation that are specific to their occupational needs. This also enables us to establish what skills (e.g. organization) a patient may have used within a criminogenic occupation, such as dealing drugs, which can be channelled into a prosocial role (such as being the unit's activity coordinator). There are many skills that may have been used in previous criminal behaviours (e.g. social, organization, planning, time management, problem-solving and decision-making) that can be used in unit activities.

Analysis of Individual's Current Lifestyle Patterns

This phase of assessment is perhaps one which requires the most use of the core skills of an occupational therapist, that is to say, the ability to assess occupational functioning and deliver interventions that are creative and successful in engaging patients in the process of achieving occupational functioning.

We know that within secure environments the lives of residents are mostly dominated by personal care and leisure activities. Therefore, there are limited opportunities to develop roles as a worker or student, or to build relationships outside of the institutional setting. Farnworth et al.'s (2004) research confirmed that this was the case and that individuals in this environment were dissatisfied, describing themselves as 'killing time' or 'bored'. This highlights the challenge that occupational therapists face in their aim to 'enable individuals to experience occupational enrichment and achieve occupational functioning' (Hunter & McKay, 2008, p. 80) within the context of a restricted environment where risk is continually managed.

Within the context of our unit's treatment model, the therapeutic environment is such that there is a good opportunity to observe and assess current lifestyles, and to attempt to identify links with those lifestyles patients previously engaged in and that may have supported offending behaviour. At the Millfields Unit, assessment occurs continually. The daily routine of the unit begins with gym activities, a unit planning meeting and then either a community meeting or psychotherapy-based small group. For most patients, there are numerous other groups offered from lunchtime until 7 pm. These include cooking, gardening, sports, Tai Chi, education, reading, vocational roles and responsibilities, and programmes such as lifestyle planning, art therapy, anger treatment and substance misuse. As occupational therapists are involved in all aspects of the therapeutic community, we are in an ideal position to observe and assess lifestyle and LPB.

To record these observations, we have found the model of human occupation screening tool (MOHOST; Parkinson et al., 2004) to be helpful as a baseline assessment for individuals' functional ability. The MOHOST is an observational assessment that is 'based on the concepts from the model of human occupation, which addresses motivation, performance, and organisation of occupational behaviour in everyday life' (Parkinson et al., 2004, p. 4). This assessment identifies strengths and limitations in areas of functioning; motivation for occupation, pattern of occupation, communication and interaction skills, process skills and the environment. Although this tool has been useful in providing a standardized measure to identify strengths and limitations it is limited in assessing offending behaviour and acknowledging and understanding the impact of an individual's personality disorder on their overall occupational functioning.

The Relationship Between Past and Present Lifestyles

This phase of assessment is critical to treatment planning, setting targets that improve function and reduce risk. As previously mentioned, the unit established formulation meetings for all multidisciplinary team members to combine assessment findings and explore psychological processes and risk factors. This provided the occupational therapy team with a forum to analyse occupational and offending behaviour in the context of a patient's past and present lifestyle. Consequently, this became vital in terms of how we identified and explored patients' LPB.

A combination of historical, observational and self-report has provided the most valid assessments. Using this assessment information, the team and patient have collaboratively been able to construct specific and meaningful plans. This has been particularly beneficial in enabling patients to take responsibility for their own treatment.

Treatment

Within the context of the treatment model of the unit, the therapeutic community and the models for the practice of occupational therapy, we currently address the LPB needs of the patient group in the following ways.

The therapy programme includes three *community meetings* and two *small groups* (psychotherapy-based groups) per week. These forums target emotional well-being and criminal behaviour. However, they also form a vital part of the development of a prosocial routine (e.g. being responsible for attending appointments on time and for maintaining personal care when meeting with other people, both of which are essential requirements of future employment or participation in formal education).

Occupational therapy treatment takes place in a variety of settings: education session, gym, sports hall, unit kitchen, garden, in the ward, within vocational rehabilitation work and within the shared social area. The various settings in which treatment occurs are advantageous as they provide opportunities to see how people respond in a range of different social and physical environments.

As a condition of their stay, patients must attend the psychotherapeutic groups. Occupational therapy treatment is optional. As such, there is a very real opportunity to look at a person's motivation to change their lifestyle. On the unit there is a strong culture of peer challenge and as patients gain an understanding of the role lifestyle plays in their offending they are able to challenge each other about the need to make changes to how they participate in the entire programme and not just the seemingly compulsory psychotherapy groups.

The use of activity in work with offenders with personality disorder provides clinicians with a tool for assessing occupational functioning and for increasing self-awareness and exploration. It is also used as a way of achieving prosocial patterns of behaviour that can be rehearsed and used in the process of maintaining progress discharge (Couldrick & Alred, 2003). We would add that this process is the construction of a lifestyle that is prosocial, healthy and risk-reducing. It is this prosocial lifestyle behaviour that is hopefully paralleled in community living.

Reintegration into the community after a period of incarceration presents offenders with personality disorder with a range of problems and challenges. Intense preparation is required to ensure that this transition is as smooth as possible, with the ultimate goal being to enable the individual to function and progress through life as a prosocial and valuable member of society. Christiansen (1999) asserted that engaging in occupations not only contributes to the development of a person, but that it also maintains and creates an individual identity. When identities are built through occupation they provide the opportunity for developing a life that is meaningful. It is through this meaningfulness in life that wellness can be found.

Couldrick and Alred (2003) point out that engaging in any activity is not necessarily therapeutic. Individuals with antisocial personality disorder may, for example, dominate others in a group to increase their own sense of worth or they may superficially engage in tasks to give the impression that they are progressing when they are really just managing the impression others have of them to hasten discharge. Some activity can also provide an opportunity for individual's to avoid certain treatments, and others may choose to engage in tasks above their ability in order to reinforce problematic self-schemas (e.g. to experience rejection or feelings of incompetence). It is therefore important not just to provide activities, but to grade or structure the activities so that they provide the opportunity for change in relevant needs and that participation in the occupation being considered is measurable – this is important to determine change.

In order to increase the patient's skills and awareness of the importance of their engagement in activities, we have developed a lifestyle planning treatment group. This is specific to the needs of our patients, and complements the existing treatment programme. The group is designed to run for 12 sessions. It canvasses the following topics:

- Occupation and activity
- Occupation function and dysfunction
- Occupation and identity
- Occupation and offending
- Society, culture and environment
- Occupation and the process of change
- Budgeting and accommodation
- Work and education
- Hobbies – social/leisure and relationships
- Travel and health
- Goal planning
- Occupational formulation

Patients are selected for participation on the basis of their current treatment needs and their current stage of treatment. Those with community leave are given priority. The group draws on characteristics of other community living groups. It considers themes of work, accommodation and educational opportunities. However, the lifestyle planning group also focuses on three key aspects of lifestyle functioning:

1. Identifying and analysing the patients LPBs to enable them to acknowledge the impact of their previous lifestyle on offending and to draw on any functional aspects of that lifestyle that can be used to support the creation of a prosocial one
2. Enabling the patients to have the skills, knowledge and access to resources required to create a prosocial lifestyle in the community
3. For the patients to create their own occupational formulations, meaning that they would have an in-depth understanding of their offending, occupational experiences and personality disorder in the context of their lifestyle

At the time of preparing this chapter, the first lifestyle planning programme was one third complete. Our early observation and evaluation have found the following aspects to be useful:

1. Using practical exercises (e.g. carrying out everyday tasks such as making a sandwich or tying a shoelace in a different order to demonstrate the complex skills used in activity and the difficulties unlearning or changing skills and patterns that are already habitual. We have also staged debates and had educational speakers to work through tasks such as compiling a curriculum vitae and role-playing interviews). This has been particularly beneficial in assisting individuals to understand concepts and make links between activity, occupation, lifestyle and offending.
2. Discussions around identity and how this can be developed through activities and occupations. This topic generated much discussion and interest from the patients. We feel this is an area that could be developed further, particularly in relation to the benefits the patients perceived from their criminal identity and the perceived losses (e.g. loss of status) that living a different lifestyle would produce. When examining LPBs and activity choices, identity and peer acceptance played an important part in the decisions participants made. Therefore, it is probably important that these issues are made explicit so the patients are able to start thinking about and addressing them.
3. The variety of different media used was also helpful. For example, staging debates, using video and other visual aids to demonstrate seemingly difficult concepts, has proved helpful in maintaining motivation and engagement and in creating a non-threatening forum for participants to address aspects of the programme.

There has been optimum attendance to the group and members have indicated that the content is useful and relevant. In the future, the programme will be formally evaluated and translated into formal session plans for other clinicians. This enhances integrity and supports other clinicians undertake this type of programming.

CONCLUSION AND FUTURE DIRECTIONS

The concept of LPB is emerging, and although our recent work described here has been with offenders with personality disorder we believe it has relevance for work with offenders more generally. Presently, we are exploring ways of applying LPB in clinical practice by developing and adapting our approaches to assessment and treatment. The introduction of the concept of LPB has began to allow us, alongside the patient, to explore their internal motivation to offend and to examine how problematic patterns of behaviour are established, thereby assisting patients identify the role that lifestyle plays in their offending behaviour and supporting them to manage their own risk through participation in prosocial activity.

It is hoped that the use of the LPB concept in the development of these lifestyles will help to consolidate the psychological changes that patients have made through participating in the treatment programme. Also, it seems that the LPB concept could provide an additional unique and valuable contribution to the process of risk assessment in the MDT. It may also provide an opportunity for monitoring a patient's progress during treatment.

As stated previously, one of the major criticisms that could be levelled at the notion of LPB is that it is at this stage speculative and as yet not subjected to empirical scrutiny. Therefore, the focus of our work at present is on developing evidence for the validity of the concept and developing a more robust approach to its clinical application. In developing this evidence base, we are exploring a research opportunity to evaluate past and current lifestyle in relation to psychopathy. This would involve a study of scores of the MOHOST (Parkinson et al., 2004) and their association with psychopathy, in particular, facet 3 of the Psychopathy Checklist-Revised (PCL-R; Hare, 2003). This research is in development; as such results are not yet available.

In relation to the clinical application of LPB, the occupational therapy department at the Millfields Unit is continuing to develop the LPB approach and to apply it to assessment and treatment tasks. As stated earlier, there is a lack of choice of standardized assessments and outcome measures that specifically focus on the relationship between offending and lifestyle. Although some of the MOHOST assessments have been adapted for forensic patients, there remains room for development of assessments capable of examining the links between occupation and offending. The occupational therapy department is currently developing an assessment and outcome measure titled the assessment of the relationship between occupational functioning and offending behaviour (AOBOF). We are planning to pilot this instrument in the near future and disseminate the results when available. In addition, we will evaluate the efficacy of the lifestyle planning group and develop a programme that can be delivered by other clinicians.

REFERENCES

Christiansen, C. (1999). Defining lives: occupation as identity: an essay on competence, coherence, and the creation of meaning. *American Journal of Occupational Therapy, 53*, 547–58.

Couldrick, L. & Alred, D. (2003). *Forensic Occupational Therapy*. London: Whurr.

Cronin-Davis, J., Lang, A. & Molineux, M. (2004). Occupational science: the forensic challenge. In M. Molineux (Ed.), *Occupation for Occupational Therapists* (pp. 169–79). Oxford: Blackwell.

Daffern, M., Jones, L., Howells, K., Shine, J., Mikton, C. & Tunbridge, V.C. (2007). Refining the definition of offence paralleling behaviour. *Criminal Behaviour and Mental Health, 17*, 265–73.

Farnworth, L. Nikitin, L. & Fossey, E. (2004). Being in a secure forensic psychiatric unit: everyday the same, killing time or making the most of it. *British Journal of Occupational therapy, 67*, 430–38.

Fidler, G.S. (1996). Lifestyle performance: from profile to conceptual model. *American Journal of Occupational Therapy, 50*, 139–47.

Hare, R.D. (2003). *Manual for the Hare Psychopathy Checklist Revised* (2nd edition). Toronto, ON: Multi-Health Services.

Hunter, E. & McKay, E. (2008). Doing in secure settings. In E. McKay, C. Craik, K. Hean Lim & G. Richards (Eds), *Advancing Occupational Therapy in Mental Health Practice* (p. 80). Oxford: Wiley-Blackwell.

Jones, L. (2004). Offence paralleling behaviour (OPB) as a framework for assessment and interventions with offenders. In A. Needs & G. Towl (Eds.). *Applying Psychology to Forensic Practice* (pp. 34–63). Oxford: BPS Blackwell.

Kielhofner, G. (2002). *A Model of Human Occupation: Theory and Application* (3rd edition). Philadelphia: Lippincott, Williams & Wilkins.

Kielhofner, G., Mallinson, T., Crawford, C., Nowak, M., Rigby, M., Henry, A. & Walens, D. (1998). *A User's Manual for the OPHI-II: The Occupational Performance History Interview (Version 2.0)*. Chicago: Model of Human Occupation Clearing House.

Molineux, M. (Ed.) (2004). *Occupation for Occupational Therapists*. Oxford: Blackwell.

Parkinson, S., Forsyth, K. & Kielhofner, G. (2004). *The Model of Human Occupation Screening Tool*. Chicago: University of Illinois.

Paulhus, D.L. (1998). *Paulhus Deception Scales*. United States and Canada: Multi-Health Systems.

Rogers, J.C. & Holm, M.B. (1989). The therapist's thinking behind functional assessment, Part I. In C.B. Royeen (Ed.), *AOTA Self Study Series: Assessing Function*. Rockville, MD: American Occupational Therapy Association.

Rogers, J.C. & Holm, M.B. (1991). Occupational therapy diagnostic reasoning: a component of clinical reasoning. *American Journal of Occupational Therapy*, *11*, 1045–53.

Velde, B.P. & Fidler, G.S. (2002). *Life-Style Performance: A Model for Engaging the Power of Occupation*. Thorofare, NJ: Slack.

Ward, T. & Brown, M. (2004). The good lives model and conceptual issues in offender rehabilitation. *Psychology, Crime and Law*, *10*(3), 243–57.

Ward, T. & Mann, R. (2004). Good lives and the rehabilitation of offenders: a positive approach to treatment. In A. Linley & S. Joseph (Eds.), *Positive psychology in practice* (pp. 598–616). John Wiley & Sons.

Whiteford, G. (2000). Occupational deprivation: global challenge in the new millennium. *British Journal of Occupational Therapy*, *63*, 200–4.

Wilcock, A. (1993). A theory of the human need for occupation. *Journal of Occupational Science*, *1*, 17–25.

Wilcock, A. (1998). *An Occupational Perspective of Health*. Thorofare, NJ: Slack.

Yerxa, E.J., Clark, F., Frank, G., Jackson, J., Parham, D., Pierce, D., Stein, C. & Zemke, R. (1990). An introduction to occupational science: a foundation for occupational therapy in the 21st century. *Occupational Therapy in Health Care*, *6*, 1–17.

Chapter 17

SUBSTANCE MISUSE PARALLELING BEHAVIOUR IN DETAINED OFFENDERS

GLEN THOMAS
Rampton Hospital, Retford, UK

JOHN HODGE
Consultant Clinical and Forensic Psychologist

This chapter introduces the concept of parallel substance misuse behaviour and seeks to use theoretical constructs from the addiction literature to develop clinicians, understanding of how they can improve their knowledge of these issues in delivering substance misuse interventions in detained populations. The population to which this chapter mainly relates is a group of detained mentally disordered offenders within the Forensic Division of a large healthcare trust in England. However, similar substance misuse paralleling behaviours (SMPBs) have been observed in other detained offender populations (e.g. Murphy, personal communication, 2009). Numerous clinical examples are used to demonstrate how these parallel behaviours can aid the clinical decision-making process.

BACKGROUND AND RELEVANCE

It is well evidenced that there are high rates of substance use among mentally disordered offenders detained in forensic settings and that substance misuse is associated with serious violent offending in these populations (D'Silva & Ferriter, 2003; Quayle et al., 1998; Ritchie et al., 2003). In addition, substance misuse following discharge is the strongest predictor of relapse and reoffending in mentally disordered offender populations (Scott et al., 2004). While mentally disordered individuals misuse a variety of substances, it is noted that alcohol, stimulants and cannabis are the substances most commonly used (Bloye et al., 2003).

Like their colleagues in mainstream mental health services, the majority of healthcare professionals who work in forensic services have a limited knowledge of substance misuse-related issues (Barry et al., 2002). Strategies used to manage substance misuse in forensic environments are frequently dominated by interventions with a security rather than therapeutic emphasis

Offence Paralleling Behaviour: A Case Formulation Approach to Offender Assessment and Intervention Edited by Michael Daffern, Lawrence Jones and John Shine

(Dolan & Kirwan, 2001). Consequently, while some forensic services do experience significant problems with leakage of substances into their unit, many are relatively substance-free (D'Silva & Ferriter, 2003). The existence of a substance-free environment, coupled with the length of detention of many offenders, results in a perception that because individuals are not seen to be using substances the problem no longer exists (Kendrick et al., 2002). It can be argued that this is one of the main explanations as to why it has taken so long for practitioners to recognize and acknowledge the need for substance misuse interventions in medium and high secure forensic settings (Durand et al., 2006).

LINKS BETWEEN THE SUBSTANCE MISUSE LITERATURE AND OFFENCE PARALLELING BEHAVIOUR

There are many similarities between the concept of offence paralleling behaviours (OPB) and concepts within the substance abuse literature (e.g. *addiction* and *dependence*; Hodge et al., 1997). Like many concepts in the substance misuse literature, the concept of OPB has been criticized for being poorly operationally defined (despite a great deal of face validity) (Daffern et al., 2007). However, as in substance misuse, OPB implies a high level of salience of the paralleling behaviours involved (or at least their end point). However, OPB does avoid the use of value-laden medical concepts such as addiction and dependence, which have diverted a great deal of research energy in the substance misuse field without any obvious benefit.

Perhaps the closest concept within the substance misuse literature to OPB is that of *seemingly irrelevant decisions* (SIDs) found in Marlatt's (e.g. Marlatt & George, 1984) work on relapse. In the substance abuse literature, SIDs are postulated to be precursors to relapse in clients who have abstained but are at risk for returning to substance use. Although they are viewed as cognitive events (decisions) rather than as behaviours (although examples in the literature are often described in behavioural terms) they appear to be functionally equivalent to OPBs in terms of predicting future substance use in the same way as OPBs predict future offending. Despite the use of the term 'decision' and the implication or assumption of a conscious process in much of the relapse literature, it is unclear whether SIDs are a result of conscious intent to return to substance use or a set of overlearned habitual behaviours associated with substance use and engaged in with little conscious awareness. They can be interpreted either as a result of conscious decision-making or as risk behaviours engaged in without conscious intent of relapse, as can OPBs. Unfortunately, the SIDs concept, while useful in describing the similarities between the two fields, may not add a great deal to the OPB literature since it is as poorly operationally defined as is OPB and there has been relatively little research to develop or refine it. Indeed, the OPB concept may have advantages over the older SIDs concept in that it avoids the issue of deliberate intent by focusing on behaviour, rather than on decision-making.

Substance Misuse as OPB

The role of substance use and misuse in relation to offending is well recognized and incorporated within several risk assessment tools (Gray et al., 2008) as a risk factor for future criminal offending. Indeed, studies have consistently shown that those offenders most likely to reoffend seriously are those who demonstrated significant substance misuse prior to the original offence (Norris, 1984; Scott et al., 2004); both studies describe this relationship in patients with previous alcohol problems discharged from different levels of forensic services. For many offenders substance use or misuse is a regular feature of their offence pattern and as such the use, escalating use or particular use of substances can be recognized itself as an OPB in many clients. However, where access to substances is limited or prevented, as it is for many detained clients, complacency can develop and lead to the view that if clients have not had opportunity to use substances for significant periods of time, then the substance misuse problem is reduced or extinguished. Indeed, this view may be adopted by clients themselves – some offenders report that they have viewed a term of imprisonment positively as a way of their overcoming problems with substances (Cleland, 2007). Nevertheless, many offenders return to substance use and misuse in a relatively short period of time following release or discharge and sometimes even after very lengthy periods of incarceration or detention (e.g. Scott et al., 2004). This, together with the strong links between reuse of substances and recidivism, clearly indicates that addressing substance misuse should be a much higher priority for forensic settings than is currently the case.

Substance Misuse Paralleling Behaviours

With one exception, the concept of SMPBs has had little or no research attention. Most research on substance misuse focuses on community populations where access to substances is relatively uncontrolled and research therefore concentrates on conditions precipitating relapse and the consequences of this. SMPBs are unlikely to be demonstrated when the preferred substance is readily available (except in the case of voluntary abstinence where they may be expressed as SIDs as described above).

However one form of SMPBs has been recognized in the research literature – the strong physiological and/or psychological reaction to exposure to relevant substance-use cues has received considerable research attention. This *cue exposure* research has demonstrated that these involuntary reactions are linked to reports of intense craving for substances, as well as physiological symptoms, resembling physical withdrawal from the substances even after lengthy periods of abstinence, (Franken et al., 1999; Robinson & Berridge, 1993). These reactions are associated with a strong probability of relapse into substance use and abuse. Exposure to relevant substance and substance use cues in psychiatric and offender populations have demonstrated that many users exhibit these reactions (Kuntze et al., 2001; Smelson et al., 2002). Based on the assumption that cues are classically conditioned to the substance use, some studies have demonstrated that prolonged exposure to cues can help to diminish the reactions to them (Dawe et al., 1993). However, the evidence is still mixed on the long-term effectiveness of this as a reliable intervention.

There are obvious similarities here to a type of OPB where prisoners who have sexually offended against children may demonstrate sexual arousal on the penile plethysmograph to images of young children. There are obvious ethical difficulties in attempting to attenuate these responses using cue exposure techniques in sex offenders. Nevertheless, at least one study has attempted treatment of a young male fire-setter using cue exposure described in the study as stimulus satiation. This study had a positive outcome sustained over a six-month follow-up (Daniel, 1987).

This reaction to substance cues is involuntary and often surprises those who display it, since many had believed they had overcome their problems with substances. This is particularly the case where they have been denied access both to substances and the cues associated with their use for lengthy periods of time (e.g. after a period of inpatient treatment for substance abuse; Childress et al., 1986; Smelson et al., 2002). Indeed, many users report that they thought their substance use problems had been 'cured'. However, although the links between these reactions to substance use cues have been well recognized in the substance misuse literature for nearly 30 years, it is still relatively unknown for forensic settings to assess clients' reactions to substance use cues as a way of estimating future risk of relapse and thereby of future offending. The presence of a reaction would indicate positive risk, but the absence would not necessarily indicate lack of risk.

Work by Saladin et al. (2003) has suggested that the issue may be even more complicated in populations who may be experiencing post-traumatic stress disorder (PTSD) symptoms as a result of trauma. The relevance to offender populations stems from research indicating a high prevalence of PTSD symptoms in these populations (e.g. Collins & Bailey, 1990; Spitzer et al., 2006). Saladin's work has shown that there is an interaction between the cues relevant to the trauma and those relevant to substance abuse such that both trauma cues and substance use cues elicit strong craving for drugs. Speculatively, this link is probably due to the use/misuse of substances to self-medicate for PTSD symptoms, as described by Stewart (Stewart et al., 2000; Stewart et al., 1998). Thus, in these populations, individuals are likely to react to a much wider range of environmental cues and therefore are much more vulnerable and likely to relapse into substance use.

Although reactions to cue exposure are not yet used regularly as part of risk assessment in forensic settings, the research is well established and relatively uncontroversial (Smelson et al., 2002). However, other forms of SMPBs may also occur which have not, until now, been described in the research literature. The possible existence of these new SMPBs has emerged from observations by the authors in their work at Rampton Hospital, and in supervision of others delivering substance misuse programmes across a range of secure settings. This different set of SMPBs may be unique to people detained or incarcerated for long periods of time without any access or with very limited access to their substances of choice. Some of these individuals have reported continued preoccupation with substances even after many years of detention, and have expressed a clear intention to resume substance use whenever they are released or discharged. These individuals have often developed a range of SMPBs to keep alive their interest and focus on substance use. For example, one high-secure patient who, while drunk on alcohol, had committed murder in his late teens, reported to one of the authors *27 years later* and whilst still detained, that he still fantasized about drinking every day and brewed his coffee strong 'so that it tasted like Guinness'. Around the same time, the same patient was reported by staff to have behaved drunkenly after imbibing four cans of 'alcohol-free lager' (0.01% alcohol) at a social event within the hospital.

In the addiction research literature, maintenance of an 'alcohol addiction' problem over this period with little or no access to alcohol is unprecedented. This literature still mainly focuses on the properties of substances as being the responsible agent for long-term use and often assumptions are made about the need for continued use to maintain the 'addiction'. This view persists despite the evidence of relapse after periods of voluntary abstinence lasting many years. However, the patient described above is by no means unique. When asked, many other long-term detainees report that their interest in substances is relatively undiminished. As far as we can tell, clinicians and researchers rarely ask. If they do so, the question is often posed in settings where there is considerable pressure on the client to portray themselves in a 'good light' – for example, at Tribunals, Parole Boards or when close to discharge or release. Prisoners or patients when asked in less-pressurized circumstances can identify many strategies they employ to achieve some altered state of consciousness, previously achieved by their substance use and misuse. Included in these strategies are:

- Use of substances to which they still have access – for example, caffeine (in coffee – taken very strong and frequently, Coca Cola and other soft drinks; Fowler et al., 1998); psychiatric medication (by manufacturing 'symptoms' to ensure it will be prescribed, saved up if possible to achieve a 'hit', traded with other patients/prisoners: Buhrich et al., 2000), and excessive eating or cigarette smoking (Taylor et al., 1998).

- Engaging in behaviours associated with their previous substance use – for example, rolling tobacco into spliffs (reefers); smoking cigarettes in their bedroom with the lights down to resemble the way they used to take cannabis, and engaging in substance use fantasies (Cattano, 1996).
- Finding other methods of achieving altered states of consciousness, for example, drinking large quantities of fluids; this alters their electrolyte balance and can lead to 'water intoxication' (Cosgray et al., 1993) and violent behaviour (Hodge, 1997).

How these and other strategies can be accommodated in the daily routine and lifestyle of patients in a high-secure hospital are illustrated in the case studies below. These methods of maintaining substance use problems over the long term are important for OPB in two ways. Firstly, those strategies that seem to maintain an interest in substance misuse may provide insights into how interests in offending can be maintained by other OPB. Secondly, and more importantly, since (as we have argued above) continued interest in substance use and misuse may in itself be a key OPB, it is crucial that it and the strategies used to maintain it be identified and, if possible, challenged and diminished.

Case Studies

All of the behaviours we are going to discuss in this text are ones that we have either observed or alternatively ones that patients have personally disclosed and talked about whilst in treatment. The examples are not isolated cases; many have been observed repeatedly in different individuals. For the purpose of maintaining anonymity, only the behaviours will be described and pseudonyms have been used to illustrate particular case examples.

Case 1

Peter was a dependent drinker prior to his index offence and detention in hospital, regularly consuming in excess of 25 units of alcohol per day. His initial motives for drinking alcohol (beer) in such quantities were very much around the need to self-medicate his feelings. However, as his tolerance and dependence to alcohol increased, his drinking was focused primarily on avoiding withdrawal from alcohol. He experienced chronic anxiety, which was exacerbated by excessive alcohol misuse. Whilst in hospital, Peter attempted to engage in treatment for his previous substance misuse. During treatment, he complained of continually craving alcohol, tasting it in his mouth and needing to drink copious quantities of caffeinated drinks to help him take these feelings away. By this time, Peter had been in hospital for over 10 years and had last consumed an alcoholic drink at the time of his index offence four years prior to that date.

At this point in treatment, Peter was drinking between 35 and 40 cups of tea and coffee every day, and putting three spoonfuls of coffee or the equivalent in terms of tea bags into a pint-size mug. Whilst Peter initially made his drinks with hot water he would then cool these down so that he could take large gulps of his drink. He would consume a pint of tea or coffee in five to six mouthfuls. He complained of continually feeling anxious, regularly experiencing panic attacks and a poor sleep pattern for which he required regular night sedation. It was Peter himself whilst discussing his alcohol use with a substance misuse nurse who made the observation that his use of caffeinated drinks paralleled his use of alcohol in the community, his motive for drinking and the effects that he gained from it being the same in both instances.

Following a lengthy period of intervention from the substance misuse nurse, Peter reduced his use of caffeine completely, although he would have the occasional cup of decaffeinated tea or coffee. His anxiety problems disappeared, his sleep pattern became more normal, he stopped using night sedation, and, most importantly, his cravings for alcohol and feeling the taste of alcohol stopped completely. It was also noted that Peter's self-esteem and confidence to engage in therapeutic work increased significantly and within a year of this intervention he was moving on to a medium-secure setting.

Case 2

Jo has been detained in hospital for more than 11 years following an unprovoked violent assault on a member of the public. He was previously a heavy drinker and would consume five to six pints of alcohol on his way home from work every evening. On the ward, Jo does not eat the evening meal. Instead he drinks four pints of water and cordial very quickly, on average taking three minutes to drink the full four pints. He is ritualistic in how he does this and nurses on the ward are wary of trying to stop him drinking his squash quickly because it may trigger an aggressive incident. There have been a number of occasions when Jo has become aggressive towards his fellow patients if they try to interrupt his drinking.

Case 3

Jean has been in care for a considerable number of years. She was moved into high-secure care because she became a serious management problem at the medium-secure unit where she resided prior to transfer. When she was living in the community Jean regularly got drunk on vodka, ostensibly to cope with trauma-related memories. Her index offence (grievous bodily harm) was committed whilst she was intoxicated. Five years after her transfer to high-secure care, an attempt was made to reduce Jean's dependency on her medication. As her medication was reduced over the next 18 months, she began drinking water in larger and larger quantities. Jean described the water as tasting just like vodka and that it helped her cope with how she felt. Some 12 months after the initial reduction in medication, Jean was consuming up to 16 litres of water a day. Despite efforts by staff to reduce her high levels of water consumption, she continued to drink excessively. She regularly appeared intoxicated and became aggressive towards staff when in this condition. She also made several attempts to kill herself whilst in an intoxicated state.

Any attempts to help Jean reduce her water consumption resulted in her experiencing a withdrawal state in which she became anxious, irritable, agitated and so aggressive and threatening that she required extra medication to calm her down. Jean openly stated that the effect of drinking water in such large quantities was exactly the same as when she had drunk vodka in the community, albeit significantly cheaper.

Case 4

Lawrence has a serious mental health problem and has been a patient in a high-secure hospital for over 10 years following conviction for manslaughter. He was a heavy cannabis user in the community. One of his primary motivations for using cannabis was that it helped him relax when he felt stressed. In such instances, he would retire to his bedroom, close his curtains and lie on his bed smoking cannabis while listening to his favourite music. While attending a recent session of the substance misuse treatment group, Lawrence told the other group members that he regularly goes to his bedroom when he feels stressed, draws the curtains, listens to his favourite music and thinks back to when he used to smoke cannabis. When he does this Lawrence says that he can taste and smell cannabis; he also feels really chilled and relaxed. A number of his fellow group members then disclosed similar experiences. Independent validation through observations by ward staff and random drug testing clearly indicated that Lawrence has not had access to cannabis for many years. In addition, the hospital has operated a strict no-smoking policy for some considerable time.

Case 5

Paul was transferred to hospital following deterioration of his mental state while serving a lengthy prison sentence for murder. Paul had been an injecting heroin user for many years and there is evidence to suggest that he continued to use the drug whilst in prison. He was eventually diagnosed as suffering from a serious mental illness, namely schizophrenia, and he was placed on a depot injection of a common antipsychotic drug. This he received on a weekly basis. Paul became obsessed about getting his depot injection at the same time every Saturday morning. He insisted on seeing it being drawn up into the needle and watched intently while the nurse administered it. If there were any delays in his getting the injection, Paul would become increasingly agitated and demanding. He described his depot medication as his weekly 'fix'. After having received his injection, he would typically retire to his room and sleep for several hours.

Case 6

George is a popular patient on the ward. Every Friday night he organizes a get-together for a number of his peers and has a few drinks and nibbles. During these sessions, George and three of his peers would typically consume up to 16 litres of cola and several bags of crisps and similar nibbles. During a recent session of the substance misuse group, George described an incident where the four of them had been drinking at one of their Friday night parties. Unfortunately, one of the individuals concerned had either drunk or eaten too much and was sick in front of his peers. This incident upset another member of the party and a fight then developed. Fortunately, the situation was quickly brought under control by nursing staff, but not before one of the party had been placed in seclusion to help him calm down and compose himself. This experience however did not stop the concerned individuals from getting together the following week to repeat their Friday night get-together.

George also talked about how while his peers would bring two 2-litre bottles of cola to the party he would bring a comparable quantity in the smaller 500 ml bottles. George's previous drinking pattern had been to drink whisky alongside a beer 'chaser'. George described in detail how these smaller bottles reminded him of this drinking style. He would have two bottles at one time, one being his 'whisky' the other his 'chaser'. George also talked about how angry he had become on one occasion whilst visiting the patients' shop to purchase his weekly supply of cola when he had found the part of the shelf that normally held his small bottles of cola was empty. The remaining part of the shelf was full of 2-litre bottles of the same variety of cola.

Case 7

Walter used to be a polydrug user before he was sent to prison for a series of violent offences. However, this behaviour did not cease while he was in prison and eventually he was transferred to hospital as a consequence of repeated disciplinary problems. He was diagnosed as having personality disorder, including both antisocial and borderline types. Although Walter struggled to settle in hospital, he was eventually able to engage in treatment for his substance misuse. Prior to commencing the group, it was noted by the facilitators that Walter was being prescribed painkillers, benzodiazepines and night sedation for back pain, anxiety problems and difficulties in sleeping. It was also noted that there was a suggestion from his prison records that many of the difficulties he had experienced in prison had been linked to him using prescribed and illicit substances in that environment. During the early part of the treatment group, Walter disclosed that his substance use was primarily motivated by the need to help him cope with how he felt at that time. Some of the examples that Walter gave included using amphetamine and cocaine to help him feel happy and safe, and using alcohol and cannabis to cope with bad memories. During the early part of his treatment, Walter was experiencing a number of problems on the ward and it was noted by ward staff that he was becoming even more demanding for medication at times of increased stress. Some four months into the treatment programme, Walter started to question his use of prescribed medication. During this period, as part of the programme, Walter had been monitoring both his substance-related cravings and his concurrent emotional state. This information was fed back into the group at the start of every session and it was with the help of his peers and the group facilitators that Walter started to acknowledge that his substance use was continuing, albeit through the use of prescribed medication. Over the next few months, Walter was able to identify what thoughts and feelings would trigger the urge to take medication. He was able to develop a relapse plan to help him manage his emotions more effectively. At the same time he agreed to a slow and planned reduction of his prescribed medication in agreement with his clinical team.

It should be noted that although the clinical team questioned the necessity of Walter's prescribed medication, it was generally felt that it was at least helping him engage therapeutically with his treatment. Up to this point, any suggestion by the clinical team of a reduction in Walter's medication would have resulted in an escalation of his challenging behaviour and a threatened withdrawal from his treatment programme. Upon completion of the programme Walter had successfully ceased his medication. He had also developed a more sophisticated understanding of his own risk factors in relation to his mental health and substance misuse problems. In addition, Walter had practised and evidenced a range of coping responses to a number of potential relapse situations he had encountered on the ward, any of which could have resulted in him asking to be prescribed medication. Many of these experiences, it could be suggested, mirrored possible substance relapse situations he may face when back in the community and for which similar coping responses would be required.

SUMMARY

The case studies described above evidence that while many secure forensic establishments are generally free from substances, many patients are able to continue their substance using behaviour, albeit through a different substance and over a considerable period of time. There has been surprisingly little research into how an addiction to a specific substance can be maintained for long periods in the absence of the substance itself. Even in the extensive literature on substance misuse in the community, there is little attention paid to relapse after long-term abstinence. Clearly, further research is needed. In forensic settings, in particular, the link between resumed substance use and risk is well established (Scott et al., 2004). However, the evidence presented here calls into question the current view that the length of enforced abstinence in these settings is sufficient in itself to address the problem.

It is also possible to speculate that the same mechanisms and strategies, which keep alive a substance addiction over a lengthy period of time, may also be active in the relapse process after a long-term period of abstinence for substance misusers in the community. For example, Hser et al. (2001) found in a cohort of heroin addicts followed up over a 33-year period, that of those who had achieved abstinence, 25% relapsed after 15 years. Because of its community focus, what little research has been done has largely focused on passive processes such as the long-term maintenance of cue-reactivity (as described above). There has been little or no suggestion that long-term relapse may be due to active cognitive and behavioural processes which keep alive the experience of substance use.

The case studies above have illustrated that the motives and emotional states, which drive many forensic patients to use substances, continue whilst they are in hospital. It can be argued that many individuals are able to maintain an excessive and frequently dependent pattern of parallel behaviours, that like patterns of substance use some parallel behaviours can be very ritualistic in nature and that in some instances there may be a clear cultural element to these behaviours, for example, in case 6 George's drinking pattern was consistent with his cultural background. Moreover, any attempts by care staff to stop substance paralleling behaviours can induce withdrawal (note case 3). Similarly, that violence-related problems associated with intoxication, heavy use and withdrawal states from substances can and are frequently observed within the context of SMPBs in secure psychiatric environments. Furthermore, patients in these environments regularly make use of prescribed medication, which includes painkillers, some antipsychotic medication, anticholinergic medication, benzodiazepines and night sedation as substitute substances. Finally, even the administration of medication through such ritualistic means as intramuscular injection may be observed to be a parallel behaviour in those individuals who have a history of injecting drugs.

Relevance to Treatment

So what are the implications of identifying substance-related parallel behaviours within secure environments, and most importantly what benefits can be obtained from this source of information? It has already been noted that working with mentally disordered offenders on their substance misuse problems within secure forensic environments is a complex and challenging process, especially where the environment is free from illicit substances. In addition, many interventions used within mainstream community drug and alcohol services are simply not suitable with a population where any relapse into substance use presents an increased risk of violence-related recidivistic offending (Scott et al., 2004). Consequently, there is a paucity of evidence of effective substance misuse interventions with mentally disordered offenders in such environments (D'Silva & Ferriter, 2003). In the service where the first author works, a group programme has been developed (it is also facilitated on a one-to-one basis for patients who are unable to work in a group) and running for several years which seeks to address the relationship between the individual's mental disorder and substance misuse problems and how these link with the offending behaviour (see D'Silva & Ferriter, 2003, for an outline of the programme structure). The programme comprises 56 individual sessions that normally run over a 15-month time frame, with each session lasting about two hours. It appears to be highly effective in engaging patients in working on their substance-related problems and completion rates for the programme are well over 95%.

However, evaluation of substance misuse interventions within secure environments are notoriously difficult and tend to be overreliant on psychometric tools, which can be open to misinterpretation by the clinician and inaccuracy by the patient. We see substance-related parallel behaviours as a rich source of information, which can be beneficial both to the patient undertaking treatment and clinicians attempting to evaluate their interventions (e.g. case 7). It should be noted that patients starting to undertake any substance-related work in the group frequently self-report a considerable increase in the number of substance-related cravings they experience. This often results in an associated increase in the number of substance-related parallel behaviours exhibited by the individual, which in most instances diminish in intensity over the course of the programme.

The substance misuse programme mentioned above seeks to utilize substance parallel behaviours from two perspectives; firstly, that of the patient participating in the programme and secondly, that of the clinician attempting to formulate an assessment of the patient's substance risk profile and their ability to manage and cope with such risk areas in the future. In relation to patients participating in the programme it seeks to help them recognize, acknowledge and understand that while it may be many years since they last used alcohol or drugs, many of their substance behaviours are still present. It teaches patients that monitoring these behaviours and identifying any associated cues and triggers is a useful means to better understand personal risk factors related to substance relapse. Also, it enables patients to develop a more sophisticated understanding of the links between their use of substances and their offending. Most importantly, it enables patients to practise, rehearse and refine coping skills and strategies for their substance parallel behaviours in a safe environment prior to their return to the community.

From the clinician's perspective, substance-related parallel behaviours are useful in helping develop a more sophisticated understanding of the possible relationships that may exist between the patient's mental disorder, their substance misuse and their offending behaviour. They are also useful in assessing the level of risk still present and, more importantly, how patients are likely to react to community reintegration. It can be argued that this is a particularly important issue in secure establishments, which are predominately free from alcohol and illicit substances and where substance-related risk is otherwise difficult to observe. However, we would suggest it is from a treatment perspective that parallel substance behaviours have significant potential in that they enable the clinician to evaluate the patient's ability to implement relevant coping skills and strategies.

We have suggested that there are numerous benefits to recognizing and identifying parallel substance behaviours in forensic settings. Clearly, they present a unique opportunity for clinicians in several aspects of the treatment process. This is an important factor when considering the increasingly outcome-driven agenda which exists in today's health and social care environment.

REFERENCES

Barry, K., Tudway, J. & Blissett, J. (2002). Staff drug knowledge and attitudes towards drug use among the mentally ill within a medium secure psychiatric hospital. *Journal of Substance Use*, *7*, 50–56.

Bloye, D., Ramzen, A., Leach, C., Davies, L. & Hilton, R. (2003). Substance use disorders in patients admitted to a medium secure unit: a comparison of three assessment measures. *Journal of Forensic Psychiatry and Psychology*, *14*, 585–99.

Buhrich, N., Weller, A. & Kevans, P. (2000). Misuse of anticholinergic drugs by people with serious mental illness. *Psychiatric Services*, *51*, 928–29.

Cattano, J. (1996). The influence of unconscious fantasy process in addictions and relapse. *Clinical Social Work Journal*, *24*, 429–42.

Childress, A.R., McLellan, A.T. & O'Brien, C.P. (1986). Abstinent opiate abusers exhibit conditioned craving, conditioned withdrawal and reductions in both through extinction. *British Journal of Addiction*, *81*, 655–60.

Cleland, G. (2007). Prisoners flee drug culture of open jails. *Times Online*. Retrieved August 15, 2009, from http://www.timesonline.co.uk/tol/news/uk/crime/article2368664.ece.

Collins, J. & Bailey, S. (1990). Traumatic stress disorder and violent behaviour. *Journal of Traumatic Stress*, *3*, 203–20.

Cosgray, R., Davidhizer, R., Newman Giger, J. & Kreisl, R. (1993). A program for water-intoxicated patients at a state hospital. *Clinical Nurse Specialist*, *7*, 55–61.

D'Silva, K. & Ferriter, M. (2003). Substance use by the mentally disordered committing serious offences – a high-security hospital study. *Journal of Forensic Psychiatry and Psychology*, *14*, 178–93.

Daffern, M., Jones, L., Howells, K., Shine, J., Mikton, C. & Tunbridge, V.C. (2007). Refining the definition of offence paralleling behaviour. *Criminal Behaviour and Mental Health, 17*, 265–73.

Daniel, C.J. (1987). A stimulus satiation treatment programme with a young male firesetter. In B. McGurk, D.M. Thornton & M. Williams (Eds), *Applying Psychology to Imprisonment* (pp. 239–46). London: Her Majesty's Stationery Office.

Dawe, S., Powell, J., Richards, D., Gossop, M., Marks, I., Strang, J., Gray, J. & Jeffrey, A. (1993). Does post-withdrawal cue exposure improve outcome in opiate addiction? A controlled trial. *Addiction, 88*, 1233–45.

Dolan, M. & Kirwan, H. (2001). Survey of staff perceptions of illicit drug use among patients in a medium secure unit. *Psychiatric Bulletin, 25*, 14–17.

Durand, M., Lelliott, P. & Coyle, N. (2006). Availability of treatment for substance misuse in medium security psychiatric care in England: a national survey. *Journal of Forensic Psychiatry and Psychology, 17*, 611–25.

Fowler, I., Carr, V., Carter, N. & Lewin, T. (1998). Patterns of current and lifetime substance use in schizophrenia. *Schizophrenia Bulletin, 24*, 443–55.

Franken, I., de Haan, H., Van Der Meer, C., Haffmans, J. & Hendriks, V. (1999). Cue reactivity and effects of cue exposure in abstinent posttreatment drug users. *Journal of Substance Abuse Treatment, 16*, 81–85.

Gray, N., Taylor, J. & Snowden, R. (2008). Predicting violent reconvictions using the HCR-20. *British Journal of Psychiatry, 192*, 384–87.

Hodge, J.E. (1997). Addiction to violence. In J.E. Hodge, M. McMurran & C.R. Hollin (Eds), *Addiction to Crime* (pp. 87–104). London: Wiley.

Hodge, J., McMurran, M. & Hollin, C.R. (1997). *Addiction to Crime?* Chichester: Wiley.

Hser, Y., Hoffman, V., Grella, C.E. & Anglin, M.D. (2001). A 33-year follow-up of narcotics addicts. *Archives of General Psychiatry, 58*, 503–8.

Kendrick, C., Basson, J. & Taylor, P. (2002). Substance misuse in a high security hospital: period prevalence and an evaluation of screening. *Criminal Behaviour and Mental Health, 12*, 123–34.

Kuntze, M., Stoermer, R., Mager, R., Roessler, A., Mueller-Sphan, F. & Bullinger, A. (2001). Immersive virtual environments in cue exposure. *Cyber Psychology and Behavior, 4*(4), 497–501.

Marlatt, G.A. & George, W.A. (1984). Relapse prevention: introduction and overview of the model. *British Journal of Addictions, 79*, 261–73.

Norris, M. (1984). *Integration of Special Hospital Patients into the Community*. Aldershot: Gower.

Quayle, M., Clark, F., Renwick, S., Hodge, J. & Spencer, T. (1998). Alcohol and secure hospital patients: an examination of the nature and prevalence of alcohol problems in secure hospital patients. *Psychology, Crime and Law, 4*, 27–41.

Ritchie, G., Billcliff, N., McMahon, J. & Thomson, L. (2003). The detection and treatment of substance abuse in offenders with major mental illness: an intervention study. *Medicine, Science and Law, 44*, 317–26.

Robinson, T. & Berridge, K. (1993). The neural basis of drug craving: an incentive-sensitization theory to addiction. *Brain Research Reviews, 18*, 247–91.

Saladin, M., Drobes, D., Coffey, S., Dansky, B., Brady, K. & Kilpatrick, D. (2003). PTSD symptom severity as a predictor of cue-elicited drug craving in victims of violent crime. *Addictive Behaviours, 28*, 1611–29.

Scott, F., Whyte, S., Burnett, R., Hawley, C. & Maden, T. (2004). A national survey of substance misuse and treatment outcome in psychiatric patients in medium security. *Journal of Forensic Psychiatry and Psychology, 15*, 595–605.

Smelson, D., Losonczy, M., Kilker, C., Starosta, A., Kind, J., Williams, J. & Ziedonis, D. (2002). An analysis of cue reactivity among persons with and without schizophrenia who are addicted to cocaine. *Psychiatric Services, 53*, 1612–16.

Spitzer, C., Chevalier, C., Gillner, M., Freyberger, H. & Barnow, S. (2006). Complex posttraumatic stress disorder and child maltreatment in forensic inpatients. *Journal of Forensic Psychiatry and Psychology, 17*, 204–16.

Stewart, S.H., Conrod, P.J., Samoluk, S.B., Pihl, R.O. & Dongier, M. (2000). Posttraumatic stress disorder symptoms and situation-specific drinking in women substance abusers. *Alcoholism Treatment Quarterly, 18*, 31–47.

Stewart, S.H., Pihl, R., Conrod, P. & Dongier, M. (1998). Functional associations among trauma, PTSD, and substance-related disorders. *Addictive Behaviours, 36*, 797–812.

Taylor, P., Leese, M., Williams, D., Butwell, M., Daly, R. & Larkin, E. (1998). Mental disorder and violence. *British Journal of Psychiatry, 172*, 218–26.

Chapter 18

EVALUATING INDIVIDUAL CHANGE

JASON DAVIES

Intensive support and Intervention Service, Cefn Coed Hospital, Swansea, and School of Medicine, University of Swansea, UK

LAWRENCE JONES

Consultant Clinical and Forensic Psychologist, Lead Psychologist, Peaks Unit, Rampton Hospital, Nottinghamshire Healthcare NHS Trust, UK.

KEVIN HOWELLS

Institute of Mental Health, University of Nottingham, and Peaks Academic and Research Unit, Rampton Hospital, Retford, UK

Clinical approaches to assessing change often rely upon a clinical review of individual case material in order to make judgements about change and pre-post-change on psychometric assessment. However, these methods only allow simple answers to be provided to the questions 'Has this particular individual changed?', 'By how much?' and 'In what way(s)?' and typically they do not provide robust information about the nature, extent or possible causes of change. However, more sophistication in relation to change measurement is developing in the United Kingdom as others, such as the Parole Board and Mental Health Review Tribunals, ask specific questions with respect to change. This has also been reflected in mental health settings through the revisions to the system for coordinating care for those with wide-ranging needs or most at risk known as the care programme approach (Department of Health, 2008); and in developments such as the creation of the outcomes compendium (NIMHE, 2008) which provides clinicians 'who wish to gauge clinical effectiveness and recovery, in a balanced, culturally appropriate, ethical and respectful manner' (p. 7) with information on commonly used instruments for outcome measurement.

This chapter explores the use of idiographic approaches for assessing change in the context of forensic settings. Four key questions will be addressed in order to develop a template for assessing change. Consideration will be given to the ways in which offence paralleling behaviour (OPB) might be incorporated into this approach. Those interested in data at the group level are reminded that individual and group approaches should be seen as complementary and that the approach laid out here lends itself to case aggregation in order to develop group-based outcomes.

Offence Paralleling Behaviour: A Case Formulation Approach to Offender Assessment and Intervention Edited by Michael Daffern, Lawrence Jones and John Shine

INDIVIDUAL CHANGE IN FORENSIC SETTINGS

Context

Evaluating individual change in forensic settings poses great challenges for researchers and clinicians. Within the forensic literature, detailed individual evaluation is largely absent as researchers maintain their focus at the group level (i.e. what works for this type of problem). Whilst group-based designs are the obvious approach to such questions, the 'gold standard', randomized control trial (RCT), has many limitations (e.g. Davies et al., 2007; Sperry et al., 1996). Importantly, RCT and other group-based approaches are not designed with individual evaluation and outcome in mind. Therefore they offer little, if anything, to aid our evaluation and understanding of change at the level of the individual. Furthermore, outside of research settings, there is little programme evaluation undertaken routinely, individual change is typically the most common focus of attention. Indeed, the need for empiricism at the individual level within forensic services has never been greater. The increase in attention being paid to the quality and cost-effectiveness of treatment (e.g. Petermann & Muller, 2001; Sperry et al., 1996) has particular resonance in forensic settings where treatments are generally expensive and are limited in their availability (i.e. need outstrips provision). This is coupled with emerging evidence that treatment in forensic settings may make some offenders worse (Jones, 2007). Therefore, an individual-centric methodology is required to enable researchers and practitioners to answer critical questions for each individual about the degree of change (i.e. outcome measurement), to allow treatment effectiveness at the individual level to be monitored (i.e. outcome monitoring) and to enable modifications to treatments to be made in an appropriate and timely fashion (i.e. outcome management). Interested readers should consult Ogles et al. (2002), who explore these ideas in more detail. In addition, data can be accumulated to provide information at the service level, which can be used to influence and shape future service delivery as described by Sperry et al. (1996). However, the resources, training and expertise for systematic and routine evaluation are often overlooked.

Embedding assessment into clinical practice can help to manage a number of subtle processes, which can interfere with measurement including those outlined by Shulman (2007) in relation to educational assessment. Embedded assessment, for example, assessments that are used routinely by practitioners to help shape interventions, should be used often and from the earliest stages in order to guide, support, enrich and influence interventions without interfering with therapy. In contrast, occasional and 'external' assessments, that is, assessments used infrequently and solely for the assessment of change, may distort the therapeutic and evaluation processes they were intended to support. One example is the interventions for, and the measurement of, problem-solving skill. Here interventions are designed to teach an approach to problem-solving whilst many of the measures commonly used are based on 'scoring' knowledge of a specific problem-solving model.

It must be stated that individual change is generally very complex (Lambert, 1994) and often non-linear, with the result that identifying meaningful change is difficult. Therefore, key questions such as 'Did change occur and by how much?', 'What effort (dosage) was expended?' and 'Did the person's state(s) or levels of functioning stabilize?' (Newman, 1994) present numerous challenges for evaluation. These questions overlap with questions that are often raised in the context of trying to understand the process or shape of change (e.g. Hayes et al., 2007), knowing when to withdraw an intervention because it is harmful and deciding when to continue with a therapy because to stop might mean colluding with a problem such as avoidance.

OFFENCE PARALLELING BEHAVIOUR: SPECIAL CONSIDERATIONS

A number of recent articles have considered evaluation in forensic settings at the individual level (e.g. single case approaches, Davies et al., 2007; card sort methods, Hammond & O'Rourke, 2007). Such approaches have a long tradition and many texts exist to guide practitioners in their use (e.g. Bloom et al., 2006; Ottenbacher, 1986; Petermann & Muller, 2001). However, before considering a framework for outcome assessment, we must first consider the notion of OPB as an 'entity' to measure.

Practitioners and researchers must be mindful of the proxy nature of OPB – to state an obvious but a sometimes overlooked principle – 'they may not be actual offending behaviours (OBs)'. This is an important limitation when we consider change in OPBs. Identifying OPBs can be achieved in a number of ways (see other chapters in this volume), however it is itself an inexact process. Evidence from previous research that most people with quality 'x' behave in manner 'y' can provide one source. However, a second, and perhaps more important approach is one based on the careful and detailed analysis of an individual's previous offending in order that patterns in OB can be identified. In such a situation we might see that whenever this individual has manifested quality 'w', they have gone on to behave in manner 'y'. These two sources can help highlight our OPB sequences, that is, quality 'w' and 'x' leading to behaviour 'z' within the institution (see Figure 18.1). Thus we have directly comparable qualities leading to functionally equivalent behaviours that may be seen in institutional and other contexts. However, the OPB may also differ in critical ways from the OB, often when the context or other factors are different (e.g. drug being absent in the treatment setting, the lack of contact with 'significant others'). Additionally, with high-risk but infrequent behaviours, developing a meaningful and observable parallel may prove difficult, thus limiting our capacity for measurement. Large variability in the features being measured also needs careful attention and where this occurs, a reduction in variability may be an initial goal for intervention.

Where change in OPB can be demonstrated, the practitioner is faced with the task of explaining the meaning and significance of this. Where the OPB has considerable functional equivalence

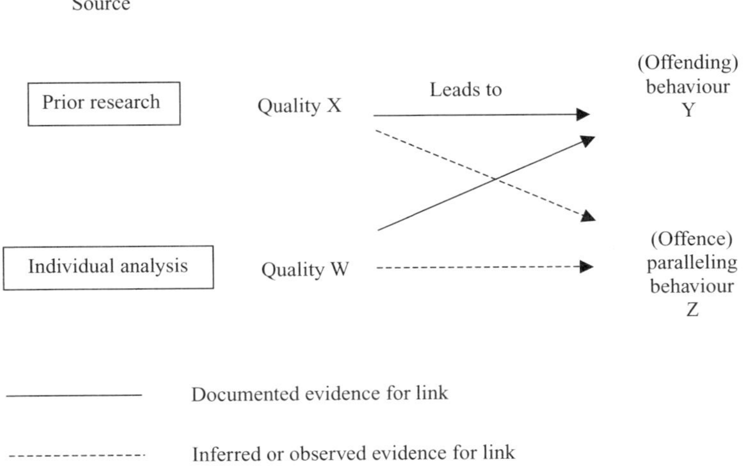

Figure 18.1 Basic sources for understanding offending and offence paralleling behaviour.

to the OB, the tendency would naturally be to draw confident conclusions about change in the risk of engaging in OB. However this raises another issue – is change in OPB generalizable to OB? In addition, it can be argued that many psychometric assessments of 'criminogenic factors' are measuring OPB or at least manifesting criminogenic needs and therefore we have to accept and acknowledge this limitation. However, evidence that a factor is causal can be derived from two main sources as shown in Figure 18.1.

A FRAMEWORK FOR OUTCOME ASSESSMENT

In order to develop a pragmatic and responsive approach to the individual assessment of change, four questions will be used. Each question posed concerns a different aspect of change. These questions may stand alone; however, the first question provides a starting point from which more specific issues may be addressed.

Question 1: Has Change Occurred?

The most basic but perhaps the most critical question to be asked is: Can we evidence whether or not clinically relevant change has occurred? The use of clinical opinion to answer this question (as is often relied upon) is susceptible to a range of biases such as the 'desire for change to occur' based on the need for positive outcomes to validate the effort expended during treatment. Therefore, answering this question needs independence and rigour in order to counter the range of biases that can be present in the individual and the practitioners working with them. In order to establish whether or not change has occurred, it is critical to focus on identifying what has changed and to quantify how much it has changed.

Several authors have provided frameworks for approaching the question 'has change occurred?' (e.g. Davies et al., 2007; Lambert, 1994; Ogles et al., 1996). These highlight a number of basic requirements:

- Clear specification of what is to be measured (with an acknowledgement of what can and cannot be measured (quantified) and what are the most important and relevant things to measure) using
- Measurement from multiple perspectives (e.g. psychometrics, behaviour, informant report, self report) and
- Using different methods (e.g. frequency counts, quality judgements) with
- Atheoretical measures (i.e. not uniquely related to a specific model of therapy) that can show
- Patterns of change over time and include
- Predictions or expectations about the nature and type of change that will be produced (i.e. what should(n't) change and what change should(n't) 'look like').

To address this latter point, the evaluation approach should be informed, before treatment begins, by specification of what needs to change. This should be based on: (1) a detailed individual formulation (e.g. Persons, 1989, 2008); (2) the careful study of possible OPB (e.g. Jones, 2004); (3) the existing evidence base from published research (evidence-based practice); and (4) the existing evidence base from clinician knowledge and experience (practice-based evidence).

Additionally, predictions can be made about reduction in the use of detection evasion skills (DES, Jones, 2004) following intervention. Change in the use of DES and secretiveness generally is seen as a positive outcome as it renders risk-related behaviours more manageable. Another useful outcome to make predictions about is an increase in positive adaptive behaviours (PAB;

Daffern et al., 2007), prosocial behaviours that serve the same function as OB but that do not result in distress to self or others.

In order to select outcome measures, practitioners should consider the criteria outlined by Newman and Ciarlo (1994). These include measures being relevant to the target group that have objective referents (i.e. concrete examples for each level of a measure), and that are useful (and minimally intrusive) in clinical services. The nature of what is to be measured could include target complaints (which could include OPBs), goal attainment or therapy process measures, which might include therapist evaluation and the measurement of moment-to-moment change (Ogles et al., 1996).

Once data are collected three principal approaches to analysis can be taken. The most simple is a clinical review of the raw data. In some circumstances, it may be possible to identify change just by looking at the information collected in its basic form such as behavioural frequency count data. For example, if an individual was observed to be aggressive at least three times per day prior to treatment and following treatment this observation reduced to 0 for 20 consecutive days, improvement would be evident just from the raw data. Such 'simple observations' can be useful, however they are prone to bias and are difficult to make confidently when the pattern of change in the data is more complex. A more robust method is to use graphical analysis (e.g. Morley & Adams, 1991). Plotting data over time either in their raw form or summarized in some way (e.g. plotting weekly means over time) may reveal patterns within the data. The use of methods such as the insertion of trend lines can also help identify changes that may have occurred. As can be seen in Figure 18.2, as the variation in the data reduces (as shown by the profile), the average level of anger reduces, and the trend within the data (shown clearly by the trend lines) shows a reduction in anger during the treatment phase that would not have been expected if no treatment had been provided (this can be estimated by extending the baseline trend line). Some data (e.g. psychometric pre- or post-test data and observational and self-report data) may also lend itself to statistical analysis (e.g. Bloom et al., 2006; Morley & Adams, 1989). Such approaches can help with decision-making and are most effective when used to supplement the other methods (Box 18.1).

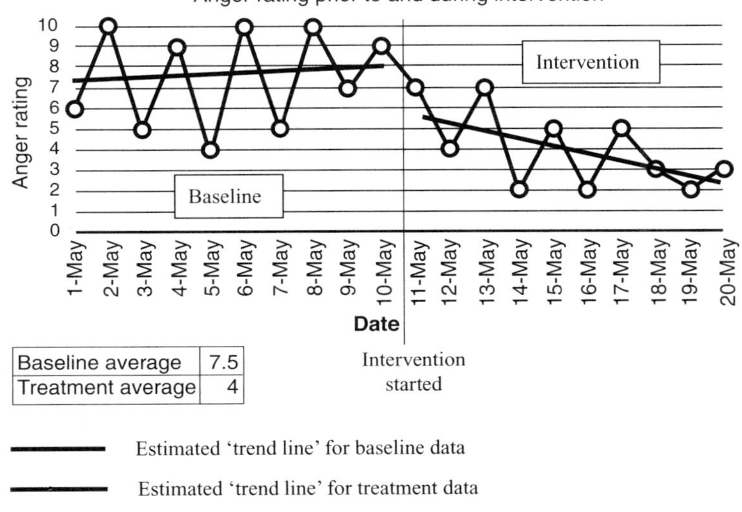

Figure 18.2 Basic graph showing daily anger ratings prior to and during intervention.

BOX 18.1

Has change occurred? – a case example.

Overview

Tom has a history of violence and aggression towards others in the community, which has included making numerous threats to kill and assaulting others on at least five occasions. Functional analysis revealed that all the behaviours occurred within the context of anger and that the threats to kill stemmed from 'not feeling listened to', whilst the assaults all followed an episode in which Tom reported 'being made to look stupid'. Within the service, in the six months prior to treatment, a number of 'problem behaviours' were observed, including shouting at others and walking very closely behind staff members during night shifts. These were reported by Tom to occur whenever he did not feel staff were listening to him. He was also observed to raise his fists to another person on 28 occasions, which he had done when he believed another individual was trying to humiliate him. He has been receiving treatment which has comprised an anger management intervention and developing a strategy to 'tackle not being listened to' for four months.

A formulation

The following simple formulation shows the possible relationships between perception, emotion and behaviour and indicates the points for the intervention as outlined above.

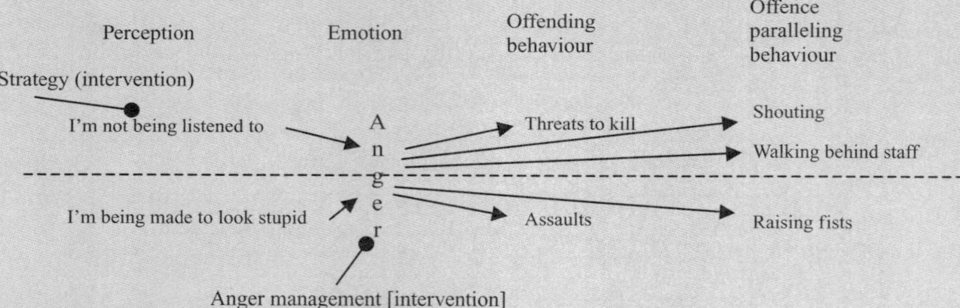

Within the formulation, the function of the behaviours (both offending and offence paralleling) appears to offset negative emotion (reported here as anger although other emotions such as shame may also be present). Based on the formulation, possible outcomes include all behaviours being reduced because of the intervention for the common emotional component, or a reduction only to the 'top line' of behaviours based on the strategy development for 'not being listened to'. Elements of both interventions being effective could lead to more complex outcomes.

Measurement

Measurement of change has been based on three sources of information:

(continues)

1. Psychometric measures – *State-Trait Anger Inventory-2 (STAXI-2)* (Spielberger, 1999) and the *Brief Symptom Inventory (BSI)* (Derogatis, 1993).
2. Daily self-ratings of highest experience of anger (0–10), highest experience of urges to hit (0–10), highest level of self-worth (0–10) and number of strategies used (checklist).
3. Daily staff observations of the frequency of: verbal threats to kill; assaultative behaviours (OBs); shouting, following staff and raising fists (OPBs); and observations of the sequence: (1) feels 'made to look stupid' in social interaction or feels that he is not being listened to; (2) becomes angry; (3) becomes threatening (a three-item checklist) or assaultative.

Predictions of change

Prior to starting treatment, the team predicted that change would be recorded as:

- A reduction in state and trait anger and in anger out on the STAXI-2; reduced hostility score (BSI)
- A reduction in daily rating for anger and urges and an increase in number of strategies used
- A reduction in observations of OBs and OPBs

These predictions were based on the expectation that if the interventions were successful, they should specifically target the measures of anger such as expression (anger out – STAXI-2, observed behaviours, self-reported urges) without specifically changing other factors, such as depression (BSI).

The Extent of Change

Psychometric change:

STAXI-2 – decrease on the S-Ang/V and increase in AC-I subscales
BSI – decrease on the hostility and depression subscales; increase on the paranoid subscale

Daily ratings:
Over the six months of available data (two months before treatment and four months over the period of treatment), the daily ratings of anger show a downward trend, no changes in urge to hit, increase in self-worth, increase in number of strategies used.

Observer reports:
Over the 10 months of data available (six months prior to treatment and four months over the period of treatment), there have been occasional threats to kill and two assaults (all of which occurred in the pre-treatment period), shouting has reduced, following staff has increased and there have been fewer episodes of raising fists. The three-step sequence of behaviours identified as part of OPB was observed in most OB and OPB episodes: (1) feels 'made to look stupid' in social interaction or feels that he is not being listened to; (2) becomes angry; and (3) becomes threatening/offends violently (thereby offsetting feelings of humiliation and lack of status).

(continues)

Comment

Based on the data reported, it would appear that Tom has changed in a number of the areas measured across all three modes of measurement used (psychometrics, daily self-report and daily observer report). In some areas, the change that has taken place has been in the opposite direction to that which was predicted. Some areas have shown no notable change over the period of measurement (some of which, such as some of the BSI subscales, were not expected to change). A few areas have not shown change where it was expected.

Question 2: Is Change Significant, Meaningful and Relevant?

Demonstrating that a quantifiable change has occurred is necessary but not sufficient for providing commentary on individual change in most circumstances. Therefore, it follows that if a quantifiable change has occurred, the next logical question to be addressed should be 'Is the change significant, meaningful and relevant?' To consider whether or not the magnitude of the change observed is worthy of further consideration, the chances of the change being due to random fluctuations or measurement error should be tested. Where psychometric test data are available, this is most easily achieved through measuring the *statistical significance* of the change observed. One of the most popular indices of statistical significance for individual change when using psychometric test data is the reliable change index (RCI) (e.g. Jacobson & Traux, 1991). The RCI allows an individual's change score to be tested to determine whether the change is likely to have occurred by chance. A simple calculation can be performed (RCI = (post-test score − pretest score)/standard error of measurement), although there are many tools and calculators available online to assist with this (e.g. http://www.psyctc.org/stats/rcsc.htm); http://www.leeds.ac.uk/lihs/psychiatry/courses/dclin/completed_research/RCI_Tramline_Display/RCI_main_page.html). Where data are derived from self or observer report, a range of statistical analyses, such as *t* tests, can be used (e.g. Bloom et al., 2006; Morley & Adams, 1989). Commonly used statistical software packages (e.g. SPSS) have options for time-series analysis although a number of specialist software packages are also available (e.g., Bloom et al., 2006). However, those undertaking statistical analysis of idiographic data should be mindful of the potential confounding problems with this such as autocorrelation (Bloom et al., 2006; Turpin, 2001). The next step is to assess how *clinically meaningful* the change observed is. There are many ways of addressing this (see Ogles et al., 2002 for a review) including qualitative questioning of the individual themselves (what do you notice that is different about yourself?), asking others (how has X changed in the last six months?) or by observing behaviour (e.g. absence of violence). Where 'norms' on psychometric tests are available, moving from one category to another (e.g. from a 'disordered level of functioning' to a more 'normal level of functioning') or by more than two standard deviations could be used to indicate clinically meaningful change. Often with self- and observer report data, change thresholds can be set before treatment begins. Again online calculators can be used (e.g. http://www.psyctc.org/stats/rcsc.htm). The final stage is to consider whether or not the change made is *relevant*. Due to the subjective nature of relevance, it is essential that 'what should change if treatment works' is identified before individual change is assessed. The relevance of change requires a return to the individual formulation to help assess how the measured change would be expected to impact on the problem behaviour directly or indirectly. For example, if we are trying to promote effective and socially skilful problem-solving, a reduction in anxiety symptoms may not be relevant whilst changes in ability to problem-solve would be relevant. Relevance is a particularly important question to consider when change is observed in OPBs – again, the formulation containing a functional analysis is critical if the clinician is to extrapolate a reduction in OPB to a predicted reduction in OB with any confidence (Box 18.2).

BOX 18.2

Is change significant, meaningful and relevant?

Statistically Significant/Reliable?

Returning to our example of Tom, several measures showed no change – those psychometric measures where change was evident were tested using the RCI calculation (as reported in Table 18.1).

Table 18.1 Data relating to those psychometric measures where change was observed

Measure	Baseline score	Current score	Difference	RCI	Comment
STAXI-2[a] – SAng/V	18 ($T = 78$)	13 ($T = 64$)	5	3.112	Reliable change
STAXI-2[a] – AX-I	10 ($T = 32$)	25 ($T = 56$)	15	5.801	Reliable change
BSI[b] – Hos	3.60 ($T = 77$)	2.52 ($T = 71$)	1.08	0.975	Reliable change
BSI[b] – Dep	3.84 ($T = 71$)	2.64 ($T = 60$)	1.2	1.235	Non-reliable change
BSI[b] – Par	1.59 ($T = 58$)	3.36 ($T = 75$)	2.11	1.157	Reliable change

[a]Male psychiatric test data.
[b]Male psychiatric inpatient test data.
STAXI, State-TRAIT Anger Expression Inventory; BSI, Brief Symptom Inventory; RCI, Reliable Change Index; HOS, Hostility; DEP, Depression; PAR, Paranoia.

Clinically Meaningful?

STAXI-2 – SAng/V – change is less than two standard deviations (7.1), AX-I change is larger than two standard deviations (9.36) and falls into the normal range for men Tom's age.

BSI – the change on the Par scale is larger than two standard deviations (1.74), neither of the other scales shows a change at or above two standard deviations nor fall below the 'caseness threshold' using community norms.

For the *self-report* data – mean scores were calculated. Anger ratings show a change of 3 points (mean during baseline – 8; mean during treatment – 5). This reduction reflects a qualitative change from *mostly very angry* to *occasionally quite angry*. Self-worth increased by an average of 2 points (mean during baseline – 2, mean during treatment – 4). The mean score on the daily ratings for number of strategies used shows a change of 2 points (mean during baseline – 0.5, mean during treatment – 2.5).

The *observer report* data for OB showed five threats to kill during the baseline and none during treatment, and two assaults during baseline with none during treatment. Decreases in two OPBs were evidenced (shouting reduced from an average of 15 episodes per week

(continues)

pretreatment to three during the treatment period, and raising fists reduced from an average of eight per week during pretreatment to one per week during treatment). Following staff increased from an average of three episodes per week pretreatment to six during the treatment period. Monitoring for the three-step sequence indicated that each of the episodes evidenced the same process. There were, however, several episodes where he experienced humiliation and coped with it in a more prosocial way (reporting it to staff).

Relevant?

Change on the two STAXI-2 scales are in the right direction however because of the nature of the treatment provided other scales were also expected to change. The change in the BSI Hostility score was predicted, however the increase in paranoia would not be anticipated from the intervention and would appear to be irrelevant to the focus of change in this case. The change in the daily self-report ratings show some expected changes, however the increase in self-worth cannot be attributed directly to the focus of the intervention. The increase in skills use suggests skills acquisition related to treatment content. The positive changes in the observer reports are consistent with the treatment goals, however this is only evident in some areas and in one area there appears to be an increase in OPB, which was not predicted and requires further analysis in order to understand.

Comment

For this discussion only the anomalies will be focused upon. The BSI Hostility scale shows a reliable change but at a level that fails to meet our predetermined criteria for clinical significance. Thus we would conclude that the change was reliable but not clinically meaningful. The changes to the BSI Paranoia scale would appear irrelevant to measuring outcome from treatment, however this may provide useful information about (1) the possible influence of other factors to the 'wanted' changes observed; and (2) the role these factors themselves may play in the changes observed. A careful reformulation and review of the OPB may help to disentangle this. The increase in following/walking behind staff is counter to expectation and coupled with the decrease in shouting and fist-raising requires a review of our formulation and original treatment predictions. The low incidence of the OB makes drawing any firm conclusions about change difficult without further data over time.

If we relied on pre-post-psychometric measurement alone we might be tempted to conclude that the intervention was a success. However, as we see above, this does not capture the full picture.

Question 3: Is Change Transient or Stable?

A major issue for clinicians and decision-makers is whether or not the change that has been measured will 'stand the test of time'. This is of particular concern in forensic contexts where the effect of the environment to 'damp down' or change behaviour may be great. Some changes, especially those that are still being developed, may 'come and go' or be affected by daily fluctuations in the environment or the individual. However, once the change appears stable across time in the same setting, the generalizability of the change can be explored (i.e. will the change(s) made remain in the face of different contexts, resources, demands and stressors). This is difficult to assess confidently, however, it may be tested to some extent by continuing to measure the key variables over time and when the individual is in different settings contexts or psychological states.

Settings should be viewed as falling into at least two categories: (1) settings that have some familiarity for the individual, such as other areas of the establishment or places they know from the past; and (2) new (and unfamiliar) settings such as new services or placements. The environment/context of the original OB may also be important to consider. The availability of known (familiar) people is also a factor in the way in which the setting can be categorized (see this volume, Chapter 3 on attempts to categorize situations and offence paralleling situations).

As part of considering the generalizability of a change, clinicians and researchers should return to the formulation (or reformulate) in order to try to predict which factors might influence and importantly support or 'reverse' change. These will be

a. Internal factors (stress; coping; impulsivity, etc.)
b. External factors (social networks; context/environment)

A return to the context of the original OB is a useful part of establishing some of these factors (Box 18.3).

BOX 18.3

Is change transient or stable?

Context

Following the intervention with Tom described previously, measurement was continued using the tools already described. After a period of three months, a routine event provided an opportunity to explore stability across settings. This arose when Tom was transferred to another ward. It is now two months since Tom moved ward.

Testing Stability of Change

The events described above provide two distinct periods within which to test stability:

- The first period could be characterized as one in which most factors have remained constant but the specific treatment being provided has ceased – this provides a test of stability across time.
- The second period could be characterized as one in which some of the context has changed (e.g. different staff, etc.) but some factors remain familiar (ward routine the same, access to gym and activities as before) – this provides a test of generalizability of change to a new but partly familiar environment.

Ongoing measurement provides the structure with which to assess the stability of change.

(continues)

Findings

Period one

Psychometrics were repeated in the week before Tom was (unexpectedly) moved. The findings were consistent with those at the end of treatment with the exception of the Depression scale (on the BSI), which had returned to near the level measured before treatment (3.88). On the self-report measure, self-worth was noted to have gone down to an average weekly score of 1; all other ratings remained as they were at the end of treatment. Observer reports revealed that Tom had threatened to kill a member of staff on two occasions during the period but that there had been no assaults. Shouting and following staff had increased slightly (average four and seven per week, respectively) whilst raising a fist had remained low (average 1.3 per week). Again, monitoring for the three-step sequence indicated that the same process was taking place in most of these episodes.

Period two

Measures taken two months after the move showed a reduction in the BSI Paranoia (0.99) and the BSI Depression (1.79) scales whilst all other scales remained as they were at the last time of measurement.

Self-reported self-worth increased to three and a slight reduction in urges (from eight to six) was reported. Observer reports revealed no further assaults or threats, a decrease in following staff (to four per week) and no episodes of shouting. Other measures remained the same.

Comment

It must be noted that whenever the observer providing a rating changes (and especially when an individual moves setting), special care must be taken to ensure that consistency in measurement is maintained (typically through training). It is possible that the observer ratings recorded here include measurement error due to this.

The picture at this point is complex with a number of measures fluctuating over time. From a cursory review, it could be possible that there are important interactions occurring between some of the fluctuating factors. Strictly speaking, in order to consider the question of stability over time, only those measures that have remained unchanged since the changes made during treatment should be considered at this point. In relation to Tom, the AX-I showed an initial change, which has remained evident throughout. Similarly, a decrease in raising fists since the commencement of the intervention is also evidence of a stable change.

Some practitioners would also include within their review of stability across settings and time those areas that have shown an ongoing change in the same direction since treatment started. In this case only shouting shows this pattern.

If we had ended our measurement at the end of the intervention, we would probably have concluded that the intervention had been successful. It is likely that we would also have missed the other relationships that have been revealed over time (see Box 18.4) and that require further assessment.

What Caused the Change?

The Holy Grail for services is to identify the 'cause of change', especially in services where treatments are extensive, intensive and costly. In many forensic services, the range of possible 'causes' is vast and the knowledge of natural remission/expected 'course' for any individual is not sufficient to allow anything other than the statement 'change appears to have taken place' to be made. Factors other than treatment, which can influence change, have been described by others (e.g. Bloom et al., 2006; Turpin, 2001). Therefore, the critical challenge is to attempt to isolate the causal factor from an array of possible causes (including the general environment). Possible service or treatment factors can be crudely grouped as internal factors (such as psychological treatments – both individual and group – direct neurological/biological interventions such as biofeedback, medication, surgery, electroconvulsive therapy, abstinence from drugs) and external factors (such as the context and environment). Measurement of these factors is critical if associations between change and the cause of change are to be shown. For example, the general environment (sometimes referred to as ward atmosphere) can be assessed using an array of tools which have grown out of the seminal work on the implications of the environment by Moos (1974). Those working in settings such as therapeutic communities will be familiar with the role that context and other individuals can play in relation to change. At the service level, understanding the cause of change is relevant because it helps to show what the service is able to do, what the service provides that works, what is offered that has limited utility and how services might be developed. What caused change is also highly relevant at the individual level as it will help address question 3 (above) and therefore aid in the assessment of risk and possibly the prediction of future behaviours. At the wider level, understanding what caused change is important for theory development.

The answer to the question 'what caused change?' is an inference based on understanding the type, nature and degree of change and the factors 'in play' at the time change began or took place. In order to achieve this, we need to be thorough in our documentation and assessment of all possibly influential variables. For example, relevant individual characteristics, treatment dosage and psychotherapeutic process (Sperry et al., 1996) may all may help answer this question. A range of possible non-intervention causes of change (commonly referred to as *threats to validity*) have been identified (e.g. Bloom et al., 2006; Turpin, 2001) and these should be carefully considered and, where possible, managed. A further possible challenge to making a link between cause (intervention) and effect (change noted) is when (as is often the case) change takes place some time after an intervention is begun (i.e. the 'treatment lag effect'). For interventions that are expected to be cumulative, the pattern of change may help show causality. Other ways to strengthen the confidence in the cause and effect link do exist and include 'tailoring and prescribing' treatments that allow us to know what was done and when. This can be achieved through specifying algorithms for treatment selection. These ideas have been presented generally (e.g. Sperry et al., 1996) and for specific presenting difficulties (e.g. Livesley, 2003) and could occur within a framework of controlled practice (Petermann & Muller, 2001). However, in many settings, careful and detailed recording of as many factors as possible (e.g. start date for new interventions, significant life events, changes in medication, change in environment) is the most realistic way of addressing this issue. Over time it may be possible to review change across a number of individuals to identify common patterns and thus draw aggregated conclusions about the cause of change (Box 18.4).

BOX 18.4

What caused the change?

The change profile in Tom's data is complex. It would be fair to conclude (in the absence of any other internal or external 'events/interventions') that the areas in which change was stable (see Box 18.3) were a result of the intervention. For example, change to the AX-I (and the point at which this change took place) could reflect the acquisition of skills to manage anger experiences learned during the anger management intervention. This would tie in with the continued evidence for skills use since intervention began. An alternative explanation would be that he was dealing with humiliation more effectively. Analysis of changes in the three-step sequence suggested that both hypotheses were true; there were several episodes where he had managed his humiliation by seeking support from staff, there were also episodes where he had taken the first two steps (i.e. humiliation followed by anger) but had managed to express his anger in a way that did not result in inappropriate behaviour. The findings provide partial support for the benefits derived from the intervention, however, it is clear that the intervention has significant limitations in terms of the changes brought about by it.

In reviewing the patterns within the data, it would appear that there is a relationship between mood (depression), paranoia and some of the behaviours being recorded. A review of the formulation, and further analysis of the OB and the OPBs in light of these factors could help to understand any role they might play more thoroughly. If they are important, then a reformulation would allow predictions to be made of the possible effect that addressing these could have on the target behaviours. However, it is also possible that this picture is further complicated by factors which link to depression and paranoia which themselves may need to be monitored and addressed. This could be added as an initial step to the three-step OPB (making a four-step sequence). These variables may operate as 'setting conditions' (i.e. establishing operation) for the sequence.

Although a range of measurement was used with Tom, it is clear that a number of potentially important variables were not measured. Most notably the perceptions (see Box 18.1) were not subject to daily self-report monitoring. Again, these may have played an important role in the changes and fluctuations seen.

Finally, the OBs remain in evidence periodically. Therefore a review of the relationship between the OBs and the OPBs is warranted especially given the substantial reductions seen with some of the OPBs.

CONCLUSION

A detailed approach to the evaluation of change can be developed at the individual level. Such an approach, if designed carefully, can help clinicians to address the questions of 'Has this individual changed?', 'In what way(s)?', 'By how much?' and 'Why?' It can also enable services to be clearer about the outcome of their work and therefore the effectiveness of the service. We should ask ourselves (especially when we are dealing with complexity, high stakes (and risks) and in expensive services) why such measurement of outcome is not routine in contrast to many physical health settings (Ogles et al., 1996). Clearly, there may be measurement issues (routinely taking biometric data such as blood pressure or pulse may be simpler); however, clinicians and researchers should work together to overcome such challenges to enable evaluation to be embedded and routine. This is not a new idea; arguments for integrating evaluation into practice have been made (e.g. Ryle, 1975), however, now is an opportune moment to do this. It is true that the actual 'gold' test of outcome in forensic settings (especially when OPB is the focus) will remain the absence or presence of OBs over time. However, unless we measure robustly we will never know what changes have occurred and why.

REFERENCES

Bloom, M., Fischer, J. & Orme, J.G. (2006). *Evaluating Practice: Guidelines for the Accountable Professional* (5th edition). Boston, MA: Allyn & Bacon.

Daffern, M., Jones, L., Howells, K., Shine, J., Mikton, C. & Tunbridge, V.C. (2007). Refining the definition of offence paralleling behaviour. *Criminal Behaviour and Mental Health, 17*, 265–73.

Davies, J., Howells, K. & Jones, L. (2007). Using single case approaches in personality disorder and forensic services. *Journal of Forensic Psychiatry and Psychology, 18*, 353–67.

Department of Health (2008). Refocusing the care programme approach: policy and positive practice guidance. Retrieved on April 22, 2010 from http://www.dh.gov.uk/en/Publicationsandstatistics/Publications/PublicationsPolicyAndGuidance/DH_083647.

Derogatis, L.R. (1993). *Brief Symptom Inventory: Administration, Dcoring, and Procedures Manual* (4th edition). Minneapolis, MN: National Computer Systems.

Hammond, S. & O'Rourke, M. (2007). The measurement of individual change: a didactic account of an idiographic approach. *Psychology, Crime and Law, 13*, 81–95.

Hayes, A.M., Laurenceau, J-P. & Cardaciotto, L. (2007). Methods for capturing the process of change. In A.M. Nezu & C.M. Nezu (Eds), *Evidence-Based Outcome Research: A Practical Guide to Conducting Randomized Controlled Trials for Psychosocial Interventions* (pp. 335–58). New York: Oxford University Press.

Jacobson, N.S. & Truax, P. (1991). Clinical significance: a statistical approach to defining meaningful change in psychotherapy research. *Journal of Consulting and Clinical Psychology, 59*, 12–19.

Jones, L. (2004). Offence paralleling behaviour (OPB) as a framework for assessment and intervention with offenders. In A. Needs & G.J. Towl (Eds), *Applying Psychology to Forensic Practice* (pp. 34–63). Oxford: BPS Blackwell.

Jones, L. (2007). Iatrogenic interventions with personality disordered offenders. *Psychology, Crime and Law, 13*, 69–79.

Lambert, M.J. (1994). Use of psychological tests for outcome assessment. In M.E. Maruish (Ed.), *The Use of Psychological Testing for Treatment Planning and Outcome Assessment* (pp. 75–97). Mahwah, NJ: Lawrence Erlbaum Associates.

Livesley, W.J. (2003). *Practical Management of Personality Disorder*. New York: Guilford Press.

Moos, R.H. (1974). *Evaluating Treatment Environments: A Social Ecological Approach*. New York: John Wiley & Sons.

Morley, S. & Adams, M. (1989). Some simple statistical tests for exploring single-case time-series data. *British Journal of Clinical Psychology, 28*, 1–18.

Morley, S. & Adams, M. (1991). Graphical analysis of single-case time-series data. *British Journal of Clinical Psychology, 30*, 97–115.

Newman, F.L. (1994). Selection of design and statistical procedures for progress and outcome assessment. In M.E. Maruish (Ed.), *The Use of Psychological Testing for Treatment Planning and Outcome Assessment*. Mahwah, NJ: Lawrence Erlbaum Associates.

Newman, F.L. & Ciarlo, J.A. (1994). Criteria for selecting psychological instruments for treatment outcome assessment. In M.E. Maruish (Ed.), *The Use of Psychological Testing for Treatment Planning and Outcome Assessment*. Mahwah, NJ: Lawrence Erlbaum Associates.

NIMHE (2008). *Mental Health Outcomes Compendium*. Crown Copyright. Retrieved on December 1, 2009, from http://www.dh.gov.uk/en/Publicationsandstatistics/publications/PublicationsPolicyandGuidance/DH_093316.

Ogles, B.M., Lambert, M.J. & Fields, S.A. (2002). *Essentials of Outcome Assessment*. New York: John Wiley & Sons.

Ogles, B.M., Lambert, M.J. & Masters, K.S. (1996). *Assessing Outcome in Clinical Practice*. Boston, MA: Allyn & Bacon.

Ottenbacher, K.J. (1986). *Evaluating Clinical Change*. Baltimore, MD: Williams & Wilkins.

Persons, J.B. (1989). *Cognitive Therapy in Practice: A Case Formulation Approach*. New York: Norton.

Persons, J.B. (2008). *The Case Formulation Approach to Cognitive-Behavior Therapy (Guides to Individualized Evidence-Based Treatment)*. New York: Guilford Press.

Petermann, F. & Muller, J.M. (2001). *Clinical Psychology and Single-Case Evidence: A Practical Approach to Treatment, Planning and Evaluation*. Chichester: John Wiley & Sons.

Ryle, A. (1975). *Frames and Cages*. London: Sussex University Press.

Shulman, L.S. (2007). *Counting and Recounting: Assessment and the Quest for Accountability*. Retrieved on July 23, 2009, from http://www.changemag.org/Archives/Back%20Issues/January-February%202007/full-counting-recounting.html.

Sperry, L., Brill, P.L., Howard, K.I. & Grissom, G.R. (1996). *Treatment Outcomes in Psychotherapy and Psychiatric Interventions*. New York: Brunner/Mazel.

Spielberger, C.D. (1999). *State-Trait Anger Expression Inventory-2 (STXI-2)*. Odessa, FL: Psychological Assessment Resources Inc.

Turpin, G. (2001). Single case methodology and psychotherapy evaluation. In C. Mace, S. Moorey & B. Roberts (Eds), *Evidence in the Psychological Therapies: A Critical Guide for Practitioners* (pp. 91–113). Philadephia: Brunner-Routledge.

Chapter 19

A PSYCHODYNAMIC PERSPECTIVE ON OFFENCE PARALLELING BEHAVIOUR

Cleo Van Velsen

The Millfields Unit, Centre for Forensic Mental Health, London, UK

INTRODUCTION

Daffern et al. (2007) have refined the definition of offence paralleling behaviour (OPB), in contrast to that of the originator of the concept (Jones, 2004), and this definition is the one I refer to in this chapter. It states that OPB is 'a behavioural sequence incorporating overt behaviours (that may be muted by environmental factors), appraisals, expectations, beliefs, affects, goals and behavioural scripts, all of which may be influenced by the patient's mental disorder, that is functionally similar to behavioural sequences involved in previous criminal acts' (Daffern et al., 2007, p. 267).

In this chapter, I would like to examine the ways in which the concept of OPB reflects aspects of a psychodynamic model of understanding and how this may contribute to a multidisciplinary approach to the assessment and management of mentally disordered offenders.

I use the term 'patient' in the text and examples, and have based the clinical vignettes on my experiences of treatment of men suffering from a variety of personality disorders. This is not to say that such an approach would not be useful for other groups of mentally disordered offenders, for example those suffering from a major mental illness such as schizophrenia. The vignettes are not of any individual patient but composites of encounters over many years of working within NHS forensic psychiatric settings, both as a forensic psychotherapist and alongside other disciplines, including forensic psychology, in multidisciplinary teams.

DEFINING THE PSYCHODYNAMIC MODEL

One problem in considering a psychodynamic or psychoanalytic approach is the diverse number of models that have emerged, since Freud first described what he called the new science of psychoanalysis at the beginning of the twentieth century. There are differences between countries, continents and between schools within any one country. There is ongoing debate as to whether psychoanalysis is an art, science, philosophy or some hybrid, and there tends to be a

Offence Paralleling Behaviour: A Case Formulation Approach to Offender Assessment and Intervention Edited by Michael Daffern, Lawrence Jones and John Shine

synonymous use of the terms 'psychoanalytic' and 'psychodynamic'. In this chapter, I do not have space to explore all the differences. I use the term 'psychodynamic', with the understanding that it derives from a branch of psychology 'initiated by Freud ... concerned with three distinct areas of study: the development of the mind and the influence of early experience on adult mental states; the nature and the role of unconscious mental phenomena, and the theory and practices of psycho analytic treatment particularly transference and counter-transference' (Bateman & Holmes, 1995, p. 17).

I further define the psychodynamic model, to which I refer in this chapter, as the way in which patterns of intra- and interpersonal functioning persist over time, reflecting an internal world, with an established pattern of object relationships (an object referring to an internalized relationship with important others in the person's development) which may not always be consciously available, either to the patient or those observing him. This leads to a repetition, over time, of relationships with people in the person's life (including victims in the case of forensic patients), and such repetition includes affects, thoughts (cognitions), fantasies and behaviour.

The psychodynamic model is based on a developmental understanding of intra- and interpersonal function. The basic assumption is that childhood experiences, particularly within relationships, affect the adult person due to the internalization of these relationships, creating an internal world with internal objects, representative of a pattern of relating. For example, a child who experienced a depressed and withdrawn mother may internalize a rejecting and unavailable maternal object, which will be reflected in the establishment of future relationships. However, taken too simplistically, this concept implies an old-fashioned notion of the 'tabula rasa' which suggests that the infant is a blank slate onto which the environment is imprinted, leading to an overemphasis on psychic determinism. This neglects the reality that babies are born, not only with innate characteristics of a genetic nature, but may also have been subject to more subtle environmental influences, for example, intra-uterine alcohol exposure, malnourishment and other obstetric complications. The result of addressing this reality has led to a more complex view, held, to a greater or lesser extent, by various schools of psychoanalysis and borne out by recent research in genetics, which has demonstrated a subtle interaction between genetics and environment, namely that the inherited aspects of the child or baby will, in turn, influence the environment (Moffitt, 2005). Perhaps paradoxically, therefore, there has been a confluence between genetic research and object relation-based psychoanalytic theory, leading to a more truly dynamic model of development. This moves away from the unhelpful stereotype regarding the psychodynamic model, namely that all 'blame' in later difficulties is located externally (e.g. in parents), rather than acknowledging the importance of a child's personality. Thus, in the above example, a baby might be difficult for its mother to attune herself to and thus will be *experienced* as unavailable rather than inherently being so. For further discussion, see Moffitt (2005), Moffitt et al. (2006) and Fonagy (2003).

I am referring to attachment theory which derives from the work of John Bowlby, and has been used as the basis for much recent research. Bowlby was trained as an analyst but was also influenced by developments in cognitive science (see Fonagy, 2001). Attachment theory describes the development of an internal working model, defined by Fonagy (2001) as:

> 1) expectations of interactive attributes of early care givers, created in the first year of life, and subsequently elaborated; 2) event representations by which general and specific memories of attachment related experiences are encoded and retrieved. (Fonagy, 2001, p. 13)

The internal working model integrates autobiographical memories and personal narrative leading to repetitive patterns of relating to others and thus repetitive patterns of behaviour. Blumenthal (2009) has summarized the recent research on attachment within forensic populations, which postulates that not only are there disturbed attachment patterns, but these are often denied by the person and linked to an impaired capacity to reflect upon their own minds and those of others, i.e. an impaired capacity to mentalize. This can predispose to violence because feelings, for example, associated with perceived threat or loss, cannot be thought about, but are instead acted out.

Internal cues such as mood, or aspects of temperament which have a genetic component, could be seen as relevant to the child's response to separation, as well as external events and social environmental contexts. Once again this model clarifies that it is not only early experiences on the part of the caregivers that are relevant to the re-creation of an internal model, but also innate aspects of the person.

As far back as 1914, Freud stated that 'the patient does not remember anything of what he has forgotten and repressed but acts it out. He reproduces it, not as a memory but as an action; he repeats it without, of course, knowing that he is doing it, that he is repeating it' (p. 150). I want to argue that this insight is closely linked to the concept of OPB. What differs is the definition of behaviour and the position of the observer.

PSYCHODYNAMIC MODEL AND OFFENDING

The very definition of personality disorder within the *Diagnostic and Statistical Manual of Mental Disorders*, Vol. IV (American Psychiatric Association, 2000) and International Classification of Diseases V10 (World Health Organization, 1992) contains the notion of long-standing and entrenched characteristics of behaviour and functioning. This implies repetitive patterns of behaviour and interpersonal relating which will be reflected, not only by the patients but by the institutions in which they are housed.

Recently in the UK there has been the development of units working with dangerous and severe personality disorder, not itself a diagnosis but a description of those, within the criminal justice system, whose offending appears to be functionally related to a personality disorder such as antisocial, borderline and narcissistic (Hawes, 2009).

Psychodynamic theory posits that all the mechanisms that have been described are present in us, in differing proportions and extent, but that there are a group of people found in forensic institutions who concretize fantasy into action, leading to a concretization of responses, for example, by society, the legal system and even therapeutic institutions. Acknowledging and describing thoughts and affects not only in our patients, but in ourselves, can reveal repetitive patterns of behaviour and relating which can then be tackled.

When considering such offenders from a psychodynamic view point, it is (as in other models) necessary to consider what might lie behind the offence; for example, stealing from somebody may not be solely acquisitive, but may involve a range of other motivations, some of which are unconscious.

One model of considering criminal activity, which is useful, derives from Glasser (1996) who describes two main types of offending:

1. There are those criminal acts due to fear of attack or intrusion, which reflect a state of psychic self-defence; i.e. there is an element of self-preservation. Such offending is often found when there is a paranoid aspect to the mental state or personality of the offender.
   For instance, consider the case of a man of 40 with a paranoid personality disorder, who set fire to the upstairs flat as he experienced the occupants' noise as an overwhelming and unbearable intrusion and a deliberate attempt to persecute him. He became preoccupied with the neighbours and hypersensitive to any movement or noise at all. After a series of encounters, escalating in aggression, he set the

fire. The purpose of the violence in this case was to remove a perceived threat. At one level he was uninterested in the victims but just wanted them 'gone'.

2. There are criminal acts, fuelled by sadism, where the gratification comes from the cruelty inflicted on the victim and their subsequent suffering. *An example here is a man of 20, who, in the presence of friends, breaks into a home, ties up the householder and threatens him with a shotgun, not only to obtain money, but also, as he described later, to produce a sense of gratification and excitement.*

Therefore, observing the nature of a patient's interactions with other patients and with staff and elucidating whether the internalized relationships reflect a paranoid or a sadistic attachment can be helpful in understanding behaviour and assessing risk.

In addition, it is important to elucidate affect states (also part of OPB). Maden (2007) summarized research which demonstrates the importance of emotions such as fear, anger or distress as factors in whether or not patients who suffer from schizophrenia act on their delusions or not. Examination of offending needs to analyse not only in detail the actions and behaviour associated with the offence but also the nature of the pivotal role of affect in reoffending.

Psychodynamic theory posits the impossibility of any therapeutic relationship being neutral and takes account of the irrational in behaviour, as much as the rational. As Hinshelwood (2004) has described:

> It is essential to avoid the objectification of a patient, a pseudo-scientific stance which denies the reality of the patients in a ward . . . they . . . are not mice in a laboratory but are people who form relationships with members of staff, creating a dynamic situation in which there will be repetition of attachments and thoughts within the therapeutic relationship itself.

The definition of OPB, to which I have already referred, emphasizes the importance of observing behaviours; indeed, it is implied by the name itself. It also suggests that those observing the patient are in an objective situation from which they see the behaviour. The psychodynamic model expands the notion of behaviour to include, not only observed interactions with other patients, staff members and the institution, but also mechanisms of defence; affect states; unconscious and conscious fantasy; guilt and shame, and remorse and reparation, which are not solely directly demonstrated but inferred from various aspects of a person's functioning.

Such an assertion is not without its problems. The explanatory value of psychodynamic claims about the mind, and its functioning, has been fiercely debated, and psychoanalysts and psychodynamic therapists have, at times, been guilty of indifference to the criticisms. A central issue concerns whether psychoanalysis and its derivatives are a science or a hermeneutic discipline and the elasticity of psychoanalytic concepts. Milton et al. (2004, Chapter 5) describe five main critiques, including truth and knowledge claims, and also summarize the approaches to research (Chapter 6), making a distinction between conceptual and outcome research. Bateman and Holmes (1995) argue for interesting parallels between the findings of cognitive science and developmental psychology and those of psychoanalysis.

Attachment theory emerged from a collaborative approach between ethology, experimental parent–child research and the psychoanalytically derived theories of Bowlby (Fonagy, 2001). Mentalization-based treatment (MBT) was developed by Bateman and Fonagy making use of the attachment model and is an evidence-based treatment for borderline personality disorder (Bateman & Fonagy, 2004). Gabbard et al. (2005) describe the research findings of the various psychotherapies (including psychodynamic) in the treatment of the cluster 'A' and 'B' personality disorders: narcissistic, borderline, histrionic, avoidant, dependent and obsessive–compulsive. Although there is quite good efficacy for the brief dynamic treatments and a growing body of evidence for more medium-term treatments, there is as yet a paucity of 'gold standard' evidence for psychodynamic treatments. However, there is evidence for their use as an adjunct in the treatment of complex conditions.

In Chapter 2, Sturmey describes the various approaches to case formulation, including the psychodynamic, which is criticized for being too reliant on history. This valid criticism is due, in part, to the development of psychoanalysis, based as it was on individual treatment within the consulting room and an overemphasis on Freud's metaphor of analysis being an archaeological dig. When managing a patient, it is more helpful to see the task as examining the 'remains' as they exist in the present. This requires a focus on phenomenology, i.e. how the person is functioning at an inter- and intrapersonal level in the here and now. The psychodynamic perspective cannot stand alone but needs to be embedded within a multidisciplinary approach with its multiple viewpoints.

As McGauley (2009) states, psychodynamic psychotherapy has remained popular within forensic psychiatry settings, because it contributes an added dimension to the understanding of offending, both for patients and staff, even if it is not possible to utilize it as a specific treatment. Sturmey (Chapter 2) suggests that 'aggression is not a property of the person, their diagnosis or personality, but rather is a property primarily of interpersonal situations'. A psychodynamic perspective lends itself to the task of understanding interpersonal situations and I discuss later on how it might be incorporated into the construction of a case formulation which could aid in risk assessment and management.

SOME IMPORTANT PSYCHODYNAMIC MECHANISMS

It is not possible to summarize all the psychodynamic mechanisms that have been associated with offending, but the description of some key ones will demonstrate aspects of the model. Their elucidation can help reveal repetitive patterns of relating, or OPB, to use the paradigm of this volume.

MECHANISMS OF DEFENCE

Defence mechanisms consist of protective psychological devices employed by the psyche, so as to reduce anxiety deriving from unwanted or unbearable thoughts and feelings in order to minimize psychic pain, reduce internal states of conflict, maintain psychic equilibrium and regulate self-esteem. Most are unconsciously employed and making them explicit is an important part of treatment. They are a part of normal life and can be both adaptive and maladaptive. They may be understood in terms of the history of a patient, but their origin is not necessary to observe them. They are habitual so their repetition could be a factor in considering OPB.

The defences employed by those suffering from personality disorder associated with violence and sexual offending are described in the following sections.

Denial

This refers to the denial of an external reality. For example, 40% of a sample of men who had committed a homicide described a partial or total loss of memory for the killing (associated with intoxication and high states of emotional arousal such as a perceived separation (loss) of a partner; Kopelman, 2006). For some this may be due to a failure to register the event, and for others it may be due to telling an untruth so as to avoid unwanted external consequences, but, for a proportion, it operates so as to avoid unwanted psychic consequences, for example, shame or guilt. Distinguishing between instrumental lying and denial is always difficult but is important to attempt. It will only emerge after a period of observation when the denial and its consequences will be seen in context.

Clinical Vignette. A patient who committed a homicide was open to admitting this but very resistant to exploring his conviction for indecent assault on a minor. Similarly, on the ward, he was able to own up to feelings of wanting to hit another patient, but reluctant to complete an assessment to examine his risk of sexual offending. In this he was exhibiting clear denial of a particular aspect of his destructiveness due to the shame associated with being a nonce (sex offender).

Rationalization

This refers to a wish to explain away an action on the grounds that it was a rational response to circumstances.

Clinical Vignette. A man convicted of an assault on his partner justified it in terms of her flirtatiousness with men. On the ward the same patient justified his angry outburst against a member of staff on the grounds that he was not given paracetamol for a headache when he wanted it.

Undoing

This describes a simultaneous acceptance of responsibility for an act quickly followed by a statement which undoes that acceptance.

Clinical Vignette. A man convicted of sexual offences on children states in a therapy group: 'I should not have assaulted those children . . . because I love children'. In reality he does not love children, otherwise he would not have abused them and he has undone his first statement with his second. When challenged about his non-attendance at a later group, he says: 'I know I should have come but . . . I was at the Job Centre looking for a job'. With the second statement, he attempts to avoid challenge regarding his anti-therapeutic acting-out and thus repeats the thinking underlying his offending.

Splitting

This is a primitive defence mechanism where internal objects and external people are experienced either as all good (idealization) or as all bad (denigration), thus avoiding a healthy ambivalence which incorporates both the good and the bad in the internalized representation of the other. This can often be found in borderline pathology where intense attachments are made quickly to someone new – friend, lover or therapist – only to disintegrate rapidly when the person feels failed.

Clinical Vignette. A patient who sabotaged many foster placements as a child by quickly perceiving the foster parents as having failed him, leading to aggressive outbursts, repeats this on the ward where he quickly sabotages his therapeutic relationships with staff when he perceives their failure of him, for example not seeing him as soon as he asked.

Projection and Projective Identification

This is another primitive defence mechanism and describes the way in which unwanted aspects of the self are located in another person, who may then be attacked for being experienced as demonstrating that unwanted aspect.

Clinical Vignette. A man of 40 with a long history of violence describes feelings of humiliation and helplessness when being terrorized by his violent stepfather. This has led to multiple attacks on men, whom he perceives as disrespecting him even in a minor way such as bumping into him by accident. In a therapy group he reacts with anger towards a group member who smiles, accusing him of not listening to what he says.

All the examples above demonstrate that the underlying affects (which can be conscious and unconscious) such as fear of humiliation, avoidance of guilt and shame are common to many of the situations described. Thus, not only is there a repetition of habitual defences, but there is also repetition of affect states.

Examples such as those described above suggest that observing such patterns is simple. However, this is not so when staff are caught up in the often demanding therapeutic environment. Space to think and reflect can disappear in the day-to-day management of a demanding patient group. This leads on to the consideration of how the behaviour and mental functioning of our patients can impact upon us. Although this can affect optimal treatment, the corollary is that it can also be used as a source of information for repetitive patterns of relating and behaviour.

STAFF RESPONSES AND PATTERNS OF RELATING

In his paper 'The Response Aroused by the Psychopath', Symington (1980) helpfully describes the importance of recognizing and understanding the responses both in ourselves and in the system in which we work (the individual and systemic responses) to a patient. Doing so can make explicit the repetition of patterns of relating. As Davies (1996) writes: 'Professionals who deal with offenders are not free agents but potential actors who have been assigned roles in the individual offender's own re-enactment of their internal world dramas'. This metaphor describes the unwitting way that professionals can enact aspects of the internal world; for example, young female staff working with men who suffer from personality disorder can represent the longed for mother/lover or the rejecting mother/lover and sometimes move between these positions. Patients can become possessive, jealous, abusive and cruel – all of which can be triggers for escalating aggression or other acting-out such as withdrawal from treatment. However, if this process can be identified and moved from being hidden to explicit then there is an opportunity to 'stop and think', which can interrupt a potential repetition and become a therapeutic opportunity.

Psychiatry, even forensic psychiatry, with its emphasis on gaining corroborative information, has a tendency to concentrate on the patient's own narrative, often obtained by multiple questions. However important this can be, what becomes clear in working with patients is that they often do not know their own story or have a limited and rehearsed version of their development, relationships, offending, motivation and capacity for destructiveness. The aim of psychodynamic therapy is to help patients not just learn but emotionally 'own' a more reality-based and complex narrative. Psychiatric diagnosis can be a helpful aspect of assessment but has its limitations, based as it is on a categorical model. Offenders with personality disorder have multiple and complex problems alongside a diagnosis of personality disorder, for example, poor family and social support, comorbid substance misuse and other mental disorders such as depressive disorder or post-traumatic stress disorder.

Psychiatry, psychology, occupational therapy, nursing and the other professions involved in the treatment of patients on a ward have as their basis a positivistic model and rational view of the world. There is an assumption that the staff and the institution are not only 'well', but are caring and compassionate, that is, lacking forensic features. In contrast, the psychodynamic model emphasizes the importance of understanding the delinquent, aggressive and destructive aspects of ourselves, and of our units, and of their potential to be mobilized in patient–staff interactions (Van Velsen, 2009). Thus, as carers, we can be directly involved in the repetition of the OPB. This model moves away from a concrete emphasis on what is explicitly observed and stated by a patient, and utilizes unsaid and other forms of (meta-) communication, such as the transference and countertransference.

The transference is defined as the way in which internal object relationships are reflected, both in the feelings aroused in a patient and in their interactions with a therapist, for example, the experience of persecutory, seductive or disinterested feelings on the part of the patient.

The feelings aroused in the therapist or staff member by the patient are described as the countertransference. Illuminating this can provide helpful insight into the patients, as unwanted aspects of the patient's psyche can be located in the therapist. However, the therapist or any staff member is also a person with their own complex emotional makeup and internal working model (as well as working in a complex system, which may be more or less healthy). It is essential to distinguish between what belongs to the patient and what belongs to the staff member, because projecting feelings of rage or disappointment onto a patient can be destructive and persecutory; for example, there can be a fine line between challenging a patient and being cruel or dismissive. This is familiar territory for patients who have often had adverse experiences not only in early life but in prisons and other institutions. A helpful illustration of this derives from the two inquiries into Ashworth, a maximum secure hospital (Blom-Cooper et al., 1992; Fallon et al., 1999). In the first inquiry, it was found that patients had, at times, been bullied and physically abused. This reflects a loss of boundaries and identification, reflected in staff behaviour, with the offending aspects of the mentally disordered offenders. The Fallon inquiry, only seven years later, described a regime where the patients were engaged in delinquent and subversive behaviour, for example, poor monitoring of child visits and the staff had seemingly turned a blind eye, colluded or felt helpless. In this case the staff and the system were identified with the victims of the men who were there. Of note, this was not about isolated incident but a systemic culture that had emerged. The group of patients were similar, and the two systemic responses reflected different aspects of the interpersonal functioning of the men. The ability of the staff to reflect and formulate difficulties was absent in both situations. Elements of OPB were demonstrated by staff as well as patients; that is, it reflected a network of relationships. It is the potential of staff to be part of OPB that a psychodynamic perspective, in particular, can be of assistance in describing.

This repetition, and the ability to observe and describe it, is central to the psychodynamic method and analogous to the internal working model and attachment patterns. This means, of course, that it is not just what a patient says that matters, but all aspects of the communication, for example, tone of voice, bodily stance and affects, both explicit and implicit. Revealing such dynamics in the complex system of an inpatient setting involves a sophisticated and consistent support and supervision structure including individual and group supervision, reflective practice and training.

Clinical Vignette. A young man of 25 with a diagnosis of borderline personality disorder and a history of self-harm and repetitive exploitive relationships with women was receiving weekly psychotherapy from a female trainee. He had violently assaulted two previous girlfriends because he perceived them as not spending time with him, i.e. neglecting him. It emerged during supervision that the sessions had crept up from 50-minute sessions to two-hour sessions reflecting the patient's wish not to be abandoned at the end of the session and the trainee's wish not to neglect him; at some level, the trainee had been seduced by the patient's presentation of his neediness. The risk is that the situation would escalate to a point where the therapist could become the object of an assault, i.e. OPB.

As illustrated above, describing the transference/countertransference can be useful within a whole therapeutic setting, although different responses are aroused in different staff. Making all of these explicit will help in the formulation.

Clinical Vignette. A man of 35 with convictions for fraudulence (pretending to help elderly people with roof repairs but in fact conning them) and domestic violence against females, associated with jealousy, has been in treatment in a prison-based therapeutic community. He has a strong relationship with one of his two small group facilitators (therapist A), who, in turn, believes that the patient has made significant strides in his treatment regarding disclosure and examining underlying problems. Amongst other staff some also have his view, but many do not, including the second group facilitator (therapist B), who believes that the patient is being manipulative and deceptive. The patient's perception is that other staff are not only being unfair to him but attempting to interfere in his relationship with therapist A. Case discussion and supervision allow the staff to identify the OPBs, namely the 'conning' of therapist A and the patient's possessiveness. Therapist A describes her own feelings of having a special relationship with the patient and how she had been drawn into defending him. When raised in the group, it leads to a frightening verbal attack on therapist A because the patient experiences her as leaving him and aligning with the rest of the staff.

This is a complex scenario containing an intermingling of multiple behaviours and cognitions. It also demonstrates the 'risk' of addressing the OPB as patients can be very loath to link their current behaviour with their offending.

Although not the remit of this volume, I would like to note that as well as understanding destructiveness in a patient who has committed an offence, it will also be important to acknowledge resilience factors, as the mobilization of these might provide a way forward therapeutically.

USING A PSYCHODYNAMIC APPROACH

One purpose of this volume is to demonstrate an evidence base for the concept of OPB from a variety of perspectives and disciplines. Although it derives from a forensic psychology perspective, I hope I have demonstrated that a forensic psychodynamic perspective could be useful in expanding its application. It is important to consider how this may be done. There is evidence for the importance of identifying the potential for patients and staff to act out (Adshead, 2002; Norton & Dolan, 1995). This reality, however, also provides an opportunity to utilize such acting-out as part of the observation and assessment of a patient, in particular when viewed through the prism of previous behaviour and repetitive interpersonal interactions.

Capturing the information will necessitate a system where staff can feel safe and contained when divulging and exploring difficult or confusing responses (Ruszczynski, 2008). Constructing a useful and dynamic (in all senses of the word) formulation will require supervision and assessment settings where the following questions can be explored by staff:

How do I experience the patient?
What responses does the patient arouse in me? Are they different to the responses of my colleagues?
What do I 'know' about the patient and what have I forgotten – do I remember his offending?
How does the patient relate to me?

There have been tools such as the operationalized psychodynamic diagnosis (OPD: Gundel, 2008) which can be adapted to help in this task, but such enquiry can also be part of formulation meetings, case discussion and group scoring exercises.

REFERENCES

Adshead, G. (2002). Three degrees of security: attachment and forensic institutions. *Criminal Behaviour and Mental Health*, *12*, 31–45.

American Psychiatric Association (2000). *Diagnostic and Statistical Manual of Mental Disorders: DSM-IV-TR* (fourth edition), text revision. Washington, DC: APA.

Bateman, A. & Fonagy, P. (2004). *Psychotherapy for Borderline Personality Disorder: Mentalizaton-Based Treatment*. Oxford: Open University Press.

Bateman, A. & Holmes, J. (1995). *Introduction to Psychoanalysis: Contemporary Theory and Practice*. London: Routledge.

Blom-Cooper Sir, L., Brown, M., Dolan, R. & Murphy, E. (1992). *Report of the Committee of Inquiry into Complaints about Ashworth Hospital*, Cmnd 2028, Vols 1 and 2 (Chairman: Sir Louis Blom-Cooper). London: Her Majesty's Stationery Office.

Blumenthal, S. (2009). A psychodynamic approach to working with offenders: an alternative to moral orthopaedics. In A. Bartlett & G. McGauley (Eds), *Forensic Mental Health: Concepts, Systems and Practice*. Oxford: Open University Press.

Daffern, M., Jones, L., Howells, K., Shine, J., Mikton, C. & Tunbridge, V. (2007). Editorial. Redefining the definition of offence paralleling behaviour. *Criminal Behaviour and Mental Health*, *17*, 265–73.

Davies, R. (1996). The inter-disciplinary network and the internal world of the offender. In C. Cordess & M. Cox (Eds), *Forensic Psychotherapy: Crime, Psychodynamics and the Offender Patient*. London: Jessica Kingsley.

Fallon, P., Bluglass, R., Edwards, B. & Daniels, G. (1999). *Report of the Committee of Inquiry into the Personality Disorder Unit*. Ashworth Special Hospital, Volume I Cm 4194-II. London: Her Majesty's Stationery Office.

Fonagy, P. (2001). *Attachment Theory and Psychoanalysis*. Other Press: New York.

Fonagy, P. (2003). Genetics, developmental psychopathology and psychoanalytic theory: the case for ending our (not so) splendid isolation. *Psychoanalytic Inquiry*, *23*, 218–47.

Freud, S. (1914). *Remembering, Repeating and Working-Through*. Standard edition, X11. London: Hogarth Press.

Gabbard, G.O., Beck, J.S. & Holmes, J. (2005). *Oxford Textbook of Psychotherapy*. Oxford: Open University Press.

Glasser, M. (1996). The assessment and management of dangerousness: the psychanalytical contribution. *Journal of Forensic Psychiatry*, *7*, 271–83.

Gundel, H. (2008). *Operationalized Psychodynamic Diagnosis OPD-2: Manual of Diagnosis and Treatment Planning*. Gottingen: Hogrefe & Huber.

Hawes, V. (2009). Treating high risk mentally disordered offenders: the dangerous and severe personality disorder initiative. In A. Bartlett & G. McGauley (Eds), *Forensic Mental Health: Concepts, Systems and Practice*. Oxford: Open University Press.

Hinshelwood, R.D. (2004). *Suffering Insanity: Psychoanalytic Essays on Psychosis*. New York: Brunner-Routledge.

Jones, L.F. (2004). Offence paralleling behaviour as a framework for assessment and interventions with offenders. In A. Needs & G. Towl (Eds), *Applying Psychology to Forensic Practice*. Oxford: BPS Blackwell.

Kopelman, M.D. (2006). Crime and amnesia: a review. *Behavioral Sciences and the Law*, *5*(3), 323–42.

Maden, A. (2007). *Treating Violence: A Guide to Risk Management in Mental Health*. Oxford: Oxford University Press.

McGauley, G. (2009). Introduction to the psychotherapies for mentally disordered offenders. In A. Bartlett & G. McGauley (Eds), *Forensic Mental Health: Concepts, Systems and Practice*. Oxford: Open University Press.

Milton, J., Polmear, C. & Fabricius, J. (2004). *A Short Introduction to Psychoanalysis*. London: Sage.

Moffitt, T.E. (2005). Genetic and environmental influences on antisocial behaviours: evidence from behavioural genetic research. *Advances in Genetics*, *55*, 41–104.

Moffitt, T.E., Caspi, A. & Rutter, M. (2006). Measured gene – environment interactions in psychopathology: concepts, research strategies and implications for research, intervention and public understanding of genetics. *Perspectives on Psychological Science*, *1*, 5–27.

Norton, K. & Dolan, B. (1995). Acting out and the institutional response. *Journal of Forensic Psychiatry*, *6*, 317–32.

Ruszczynski, S. (2008). Thoughts from consulting in secure settings. In J. Gordon & G. Kirtchuk (Eds), *Psychic Assaults and Frightened Clinicians: Countertransference in Forensic Settings*. London: Karnac.

Symington, N. (1980). The response aroused by the psychopath. *International Review of Psycho-Analysis*, *7*, 291–98.

Van Velsen, C. (2009). Psychotherapeutic understanding and approach to psychosis in mentally disordered offences. In A. Bartlett & G. McGauley (Eds), *Forensic Mental Health: Concepts, Systems and Practice*. Oxford: Open University Press.

World Health Organization (1992). *The ICD-10 Classification of Mental and Behavioral Disorders: Clinical Descriptions and Diagnostic Guidelines*. Geneva: World Health Organization.

PART III

CONCLUSION

Chapter 20

SUMMARY AND FUTURE DIRECTIONS

LAWRENCE JONES

Consultant Clinical and Forensic Psychologist, Lead Psychologist, Peaks Unit, Rampton Hospital, Nottinghamshire Healthcare NHS Trust, UK.

MICHAEL DAFFERN

School of Psychology and Psychiatry, Monash University, Principal Consultant Psychologist, Forensicare, Australia and Special Lecturer, Institute of Mental Health, University of Nottingham, UK

JOHN SHINE

The Millfields Unit, Centre for Forensic Mental Health, London, UK

This book is the product of a series of meetings between the three editors, which occurred in 2006. Our prior efforts, Lawrence Jones' theoretical conceptualization and recommendations for clinicians interested in working with offence paralleling behaviour (OPB); John Shines' work on developing conceptual frameworks for forensic therapeutic communities based on criminogenic risk factors; and Michael Daffern's research into the functions of problem behaviour in secure psychiatric hospitals – all resulted in a shared interest in OPB and a desire to refine and expand the framework. Early in these discussions, we recognized the paucity of academic writing delineating best practice in forensic case formulation, despite its central role in clinical forensic practice. We also reflected on the focus within forensic psychology on structured risk assessment methods and formal group treatment programmes. Although the merits of these particular assessment methods and treatments should not be underestimated, (1) they rely on the capacity to adequately formulate an individual offender's problem behaviours, and (2) they are occasionally inadequate for clinicians charged with the task of understanding and remediating an offender's problem behaviours. These points may be particularly relevant to patients with severe and complex presentations, such as those based in units for individuals with severe and dangerous personality disorder.

Although the three editors are all psychologists and have spent much of their professional careers working in secure settings, the OPB framework was not intended to be used exclusively by psychologists, nor was it devised specifically for practitioners of a particular theoretical orientation. Readers may feel that there is an abundance of chapters written from a behavioural or

Offence Paralleling Behaviour: A Case Formulation Approach to Offender Assessment and Intervention Edited by Michael Daffern, Lawrence Jones and John Shine

cognitive behavioural orientation. This does not deny the fact that practitioners from divergent theoretical orientations can draw on the framework to assist assessment, treatment and management of offenders (see Chapter 1 by Jones and Chapter 12 by Shine) or that the framework is only relevant to staff of secure facilities. Several authors (e.g. Gresswell and Dawson, Chapter 5) demonstrate the utility of the OPB framework for community care and assessment of offenders and alleged offenders.

An edited book was not the primary purpose of the editors' initial discussions. The most pressing task was to reconsider the definition of OPB offered by Jones (2004) and use of the framework. This purpose arose against a background of concern generated by anecdotal reports and observations by the editors that the original definition (1) may be overinclusive and (2) that the framework may have been misused – not through malice but due to misunderstanding. It came to our attention that the behaviour of some offenders, which had only a spurious relationship with an offender's offending, was being used as evidence that an offender required additional confinement and resulted in a refusal of leave or release from custody. With Kevin Howells, Chris Mikton and Victoria Tunbridge, and helpful comments from Jason Davies, Caroline Logan, Peter Sturmey and Ray St Ledger, an editorial addressing these problems urging caution was prepared (Daffern et al., 2007). Having reviewed the chapters in this book, it is reassuring to see the balance and an acknowledgement of the limitations in the framework's application. The review of case formulation by Sturmey emphasizes the importance of the framework whilst expressing an appropriate degree of caution for staff invoking the OPB framework.

None of the contributors to this book took umbrage at the definition of OPB offered by Daffern and colleagues (2007), though Mann and colleagues have noted that some people find that this definition is difficult to grasp. On reflection, in an attempt to increase the rigour and intensity of OPB analyses, we may have made the definition too cumbersome, and we may also have made an error by suggesting that only those behaviours occurring after an offence should be considered offence paralleling. This is incorrect. Offenders may engage in OPB prior to an offence, a point noted by Jones (2004, p. 38). The stalking of mental health professionals (Daffern, 2010a) following hospitalization is an example of an offence that may have paralleling behaviours that are evident in the psychiatric hospital environment. For instance, many patients who stalk clinicians after discharge appear to do so because they felt misunderstood, wronged or mistreated during hospitalization (Sandberg et al., 2002). These patients may well show behaviour during hospitalization (e.g. vexatious complaints, threats and inappropriate attempts to secure intimate contact) that parallels their behaviour following hospitalization. Gresswell and Dawson also apply the OPB framework to the task of sexual offender risk assessment in an attempt to determine whether past (possibly) OPB may indicate future offending risk.

The aim of this book is to assemble and present various methods that are being used to identify and use OPB. Our intended audience is academics and clinicians who are interested in case formulation within forensic psychology and others who are explicatively researching or using OPB in their clinical practice. We also hope this book will be a stimulus for empirical research and further conceptual and theoretical refinement of this framework. At present, there is an absence of empirical evidence to support any one particular offence paralleling methodology. The varied approaches to the assessment of OPB are offered for readers to consider, scrutinize, evaluate and apply, if appropriate.

In calling for contributions to this book, we were specifically interested in similarities and differences in approaches to OPB conceptualization and use. After reviewing the chapters, it is fair to say that there is more similarity than difference. In the following section, we present the major areas of similarity and comment on some important differences in conceptualization and recommendations for practice. We shall express what we believe are important considerations for practitioners invoking the OPB framework.

SIMILARITIES AND DIFFERENCES

Offence Paralleling Behaviour versus Offence Analogue Behaviours

Several chapters have outlined methods that may be used to conceptualize and delineate OPBs. For example, Daffern drew upon the general aggression model (GAM) to focus assessors on what he understands to be the relevant aspects of an offender's psychological functioning prior to or after a violent offence and which aspects of the behavioural sequence in previous or subsequent (potential) OPBs should be the focus of scrutiny to determine similarity. The GAM encourages a focus on *knowledge structures* such as scripts and schemas and beliefs about violent behaviour. A focus on these knowledge structures dissuades assessors from placing too much weight on behaviours that occur prior to during or after an offence that are irrelevant (e.g. having a cup of tea the morning before a murder and having a cup of tea for breakfast in prison; L. Jones, personal communication, 4 August 2009). The example described above (i.e. a cup of tea) is, of course, trivial. It is offered to highlight the fact that only some emotions, behaviours and thoughts will be important and relevant to OPB analyses. Gresswell and Dawson also highlight this point when they refer to behaviours that co-occur, but which are not functionally related to the offending behaviour.

Chapter 10, by Gordon and Wong, offers not only alternate nomenclature (offence analogue behaviour) but also a conceptualization of behaviour observed during imprisonment that we believe is different from OPB. Offence analogue behaviours are manifest criminogenic needs. These needs are not necessarily offence paralleling in the same way Jones (2004) and Daffern et al. (2007) have defined OPB; the presence of offence analogous behaviours does not indicate that the individual is engaging in a way that is functionally similar to specific past or future criminal behaviour. These manifestations, which may indicate persistent criminogenic needs or unique custodial reactions, are probably important to treatment planning and risk assessment. Unlike Chapter 6, by Daffern, which aims to encourage a focus on important and relevant aspects of a sequence of behaviour (sequence being emphasized by several authors including Jones, and Gresswell and Dawson) to determine similarity, Gordon and Wong's approach is to examine institutional behaviour to search for manifest criminogenic needs indicated by the VRS. The dynamic risk factors assessed by the violence risk scale (VRS) are not offence paralleling in their own right, they are simply (important) manifest criminogenic needs. Of course, it may be that when an offender shows manifest criminogenic needs this manifestation is also a part of an OPB sequence. However, this may not necessarily be the case. For example, consider the case of a violent offender who is imprisoned after killing a female intimate in a drunken argument and who then sexually assaults her. In prison this offender may use violence to obtain tangible goals or to defend against threats by other prisoners. Although the two behaviours may reflect persistent problematic thinking supportive of violence, poor *emotional control* and indications of a *violent lifestyle* (*emotional control* and *violent lifestyle* are dynamic risk items on the VRS) that indicate persistent risk for violence, the two behaviours have different determinants and functions, and as such these are not OPBs. Gordon and Wong's conceptualization of offence analogue behaviour is likely to be a useful adjunct to the VRS.

Reliability and Validity

Several authors acknowledged the unknown reliability and validity of the OPB framework (see, for instance, Chapters 2 and 3). These concerns apply to clinical case formulation generally. Although the OPB framework has face validity amongst staff and offenders (see Chapters 13 and 14), and there is some, albeit limited, evidence that some aggressive behaviours in custody are offence paralleling (Daffern et al., 2009), it is important that future research is undertaken to ensure methods to assess OPB are consistent with an accepted definition, lead to a high level of agreement among raters, are related to criminal recidivism (if used in risk assessments) or are demonstrably similar to past offending behaviours of interest. Jones' *practice algorithm* (Chapter 4) may enhance observer agreement and also improve validity, though this method itself requires empirical scrutiny. Sturmey makes several recommendations to assist exploration of reliability and validity issues, and these include reliability trials on elements of case formulation including 'the reliability of identifying current and historical variables that affect the target behaviours; and on the reliability of translating a formulation into an idiographic treatment' (Chapter 2). Treatment validity may be evaluated 'in randomized controlled trials in which interventions based on case formulation are compared to treatment as usual' (Chapter 2). This would provide a useful test of the relative validity of the OPB approach versus the offence analogous behaviour approach of Gordon and Wong. The offence analogous behaviour approach might specify generic treatments based on the presence of criminogenic need, whereas the OPB approach should yield to specify idiographic treatments based on individualized case formulation. In practice, these idiographic treatments are likely to require supplementation by generic offender rehabilitation programmes (e.g. anger management and problem-solving).

The Utility of the Offence Paralleling Framework for Different Disciplines

The appeal, face validity and potential utility of the OPB framework have been noted by authors from varying disciplines – occupational therapy, psychiatric nursing, psychiatry and psychology. Spearing, Wasteney and Morgan have shown how so-called lifestyle paralleling behaviours, essentially an application of OPB to occupation (linking crime as an occupation to equivalent occupation within the custodial environment) can be used by occupational therapists to assist their treatment planning and assessment of risk. This approach allows for appraisal of subtle changes of relevant activity by offenders that may be taken into account by occupational therapists when they are attempting to identify and understand changes in risk and response to treatment during secure care. Spearing and colleagues' notion of lifestyle paralleling behaviour may bear some semblance to two of Gordon and Wong's VRS dynamic risk factors, namely *criminal lifestyle* and *work ethic*. The rating of these two dynamic items requires assessors to determine whether the offender is showing evidence of a poor work ethic or a persistent criminal lifestyle (perhaps characterized by a preference for criminal behaviour to secure tangibles rather than satisfy these needs through paid employment). Reiterating the points made earlier differentiating the offence paralleling and offence analogue models, the VRS items measure persistent criminogenic needs that may not necessarily be related to the individual's past offending behaviour. A case formulation encompassing comprehensive evaluation and comparison of similarity in occupation at the time of offending with behaviour within the institution is required to ascertain whether the individual is engaging in lifestyle paralleling behaviour.

Martin has revealed the critical role of psychiatric nurses in secure psychiatric settings; similarly, Dowdswell has shown the potential for prison officers to enact change with prisoners through informed and appropriate contingent responding to OPB. These accounts reveal how staff from a range of disciplines are attentive to offenders' paralleling behaviour. The role of custodial staff in the monitoring of offenders in secure environment is also noted by Mann and colleagues and by McDougall and colleagues, both of whom presented methods that relied on accurate and valid assessments of OPB by custodial staff.

Face Validity with Prisoners

The face validity of the OPB framework is evident in the two accounts of prisoner perspectives from 'Lawrence' at HMP Grendon and through the research presented by Natalie Bond and Gail Steptoe-Warren. That some offenders accept that some of their behaviour in custody is similar to their past criminal behaviour represents a complex demand for prisoners. Attempting to engage a prisoner in 'necessary' treatment or supervision because 'evidence' of persistent problem behaviour has been identified is difficult. The prisoner may believe this 'evidence' will result in further treatment (which they may find unpleasant) and/or incapacitation (which they will probably resent). Resistance to intervention and denial of similarity is therefore highly likely in some prisoners exhibiting parallel behaviour; these prisoners may highlight external causes for their institutional behaviour. This is vividly shown in Lawrence's account of OPB in a forensic therapeutic community. Lawrence describes how it is easier to see OPB in others than in oneself and how, once OPB has been identified as a potential area for further therapy, intense resistance can be activated: 'I have found that the emotional weight that supports my belief can be so great that I will fight tooth and nail to justify my actions' (Chapter 14). Lawrence's account offers one of a very few service user perspectives in this field and is a powerful reminder to clinicians of the strong reactions that can be evoked when the OPB construct is invoked.

For staff, these instances of parallel behaviour reflect an immediate opportunity to intervene, to assess change and to attempt engagement. The difficult task for staff is to intervene immediately in a collaborative manner, engaging and motivating the offender rather than confronting them with 'evidence' when the offender is reluctant to engage or accept the need for change. Statements like 'I told you there was still something wrong with you!' or 'I told you that you still needed treatment!' (and the like) are punitive responses, reflecting frustration with offenders' reluctance to participate in treatment. There is a well-established literature on factors that affect treatment effectiveness in psychological therapies, for example, the quality of the therapeutic alliance, the group or ward atmosphere, the capacity of therapists to elicit emotional expression and the capacity of the therapist to link key cognitions, affect and behaviour to events in the past and present. These points are particularly important in working with sensitive constructs such as OPB. There is a challenge for those who work with the OPB construct to develop optimal ways of utilizing therapeutic methods to work with OPB in ways that do not result in increased resistance to treatment or that create a sense of being labelled or harassed by clinicians.

The aforementioned points relate to how staff communicate with offenders in need of treatment and bring us to the issue of language relevant to the OPB framework.

Language

One reason for the spread of the term 'OPB' is that the term is intuitively appealing and apparently meaningful to those professionals who regularly work with offenders. Unfortunately, despite appeal and possible meaningfulness, OPB is another in the long list of abbreviations and acronyms that mental health professionals must remember and appreciate. The additional abbreviations that have been introduced to enhance the OPB framework (prosocial alternative behaviour, PAB; detection evasion skills, DES; unique custodial reactions, UCR) and those introduced by Gordon and Wong (offence analogue behaviour, OAB; offence reduction behaviours, ORBs) may not be as appealing, necessary or meaningful. Although we have introduced additional concepts to generate a more rigorous framework, it is important to understand whether clinicians benefit from these additional abbreviated terms. Mann and colleagues' training needs analysis revealed that practitioners had difficulty understanding the published definitions of OPB. It is possible that the additional terms we have introduced to improve comprehensiveness and prevent misapplication of the framework have added unnecessary complexity and that they are unwieldy. We maintain that prosocial alternative behaviour and the consideration of detection evasion skills and unique custodial reactions are important; whether staff need to remember these additional abbreviations to adequately assess and treat offenders in line with the OPB framework is unclear. We would encourage feedback and debate around the issue of terminology that helps elucidate the OPB framework in ways that avoid unnecessary jargon and are helpful to professionals and service users.

Training

Very few contributors specified training requirements for staff using the OPB framework. Mann and colleagues offer some helpful suggestions. They revealed that training 'is essential, even for professionals who are highly experienced at risk assessment' (Chapter 7) and that 'The main objectives for such training should be to increase understanding of the OPB construct (i.e. a knowledge-based objective), to improve confidence at establishing functional similarity (i.e. a clinical objective) and to improve the way in which risk assessors write about OPB (i.e. a skill objective)' (Chapter 7). In view of these recommendations, Mann and colleagues have developed a training programme for correctional staff. Others, including McDougall and colleagues, Jones, Daffern and Fritzon have all detailed sophisticated methods for assessing and monitoring OPB. The training needs of staff will, of course, depend on the approach that is to be used. For example, those using Daffern's methodology would need to be familiar with OPB generally, as well as the GAM.

Expansion to Drug and Alcohol Misuse and Dependence

A novel application of the OPB framework to substance abuse and dependence has been presented by Thomas and Hodge (Chapter 17). For staff working with offenders and non-offenders who have a history of drug and/or alcohol dependence the evaluation of change in secure settings is a difficult task. It is also a difficult and critical challenge for statutory releasing authorities attempting to determine whether an offender, whose criminal behaviour may co-occur with substance use, is still dependent on alcohol or other drugs and therefore at risk of further criminal behaviour. Thomas and Hodge have invoked the notion of substance paralleling behaviours as a way of encouraging scrutiny of behaviours within secure settings that may reflect dependence. Scrutinizing these indicators of dependence is likely to be beneficial to drug and alcohol clinicians and to release decision-making boards. Although this application has intuitive appeal and face validity, such as OPB and lifestyle paralleling behaviour, 'substance paralleling behaviour' needs to be subjected to empirical scrutiny to determine reliability and validity.

A Developmental Focus

The developmental focus, which highlights the evolving nature of an offender's repertoire of criminal behaviour, was recommended by several authors, most notably Gresswell and Dawson, who recommended multiple sequential functional analysis (MSFA). MSFA encourages the parsing of an offender's case history to clarify the determinants, acquisition, evolution and functions of their problem behaviour over time. This method encourages consideration of the developmental stressors and requirements at different stages of the offender's life. This need for a developmental approach is reinforced by the review by Al-Attar, who highlights the diverse functional needs of youth and how these differ from adult offenders. Al-Attar argues convincingly that the different needs and capacities of young people must be considered when comparing the offending behaviour of a young person with their behaviour in custody as an adult.

The Situationalist Perspective

Numerous contributors (e.g. Jones, Daffern, and Mann and colleagues) argued for recognition of environmental factors peculiar to the custodial environment that may contribute to problem behaviour during incarceration. Jones has labelled these reactions to the secure setting unique custodial reactions. Mann and colleagues argue that underlying propensities must be considered alongside environmental forces, which may both trigger and suppress these propensities. Ignorance of environmental determinants of problem behaviour and normative responses to each environment may result in staff attributing psychopathology to offenders when these behaviours are simply 'normal' responses to environmental demands. It is also critical, when considering whether behaviour is caused by the environment, to determine whether the prisoner/inpatient lives within a comparable subculture or environment in the community. In such cases it is reasonable to conclude that the behaviour observed in prison is paralleling; the problem behaviour is therefore likely to continue following release. This is because the same social and environmental determinants exist in the community and therefore activate and maintain the problem behaviour across settings.

Ethical Issues

Mann and colleagues highlight important ethical issues relevant to the OPB framework. The issues relate to consent, honesty and accuracy, and role conflict. Proper training, adoption of a *practice algorithm*, appreciation of necessary considerations and minimum standards for an OPB assessment (see below), and further refinement and testing of the framework in line with recommendations made by Sturmey, should contribute to greater integrity and ethical practice.

Therapeutic Climate

One of the primary reasons for preparing this book was to highlight the potential of informal interactions occurring outside formal, often structured, psychotherapeutic activities. This aim arises in the context of a strong belief in the potency of the therapeutic climate and informal interactions to enact change. Despite there being a large body of research that shows that the therapeutic climate in prisons and secure psychiatric units impacts on treatment outcome (e.g. Beech & Hamilton-Giachritsis, 2005; Melle et al., 1996, cited by Howells et al., 2009), and evidence that therapeutic communities may be effective in the treatment of offenders (see Chapter 12), the what works literature has paid inadequate attention to the role of the therapeutic climate (Howells et al., 2009; see also Daffern et al., 2007). Some programmes do however offer general guidelines. For example, 'the violence reduction program . . . emphasizes the need for a positive therapeutic environment by establishing a pro-social milieu, supporting pro-social attitudes and behaviours, and substituting positive peer-group pressure for negative peer-group pressure' (Daffern et al., 2007, p. 271). However, rather than simply providing the supportive foundation in which 'more potent' interventions can occur in group or individual sessions, the OPB framework provides a shared clinical formulation for multidisciplinary teams of how present behaviour may be linked to underlying patterns of lapsing and relapsing, which can be used to inform progress on interventions. The framework helps all unit staff know which behaviours are important and should be the focus of attention.

Staff responses to aggressive incidents in secure settings are still focused on containing the harm caused and returning the institution to normal operation as soon as practical so that programming is not disrupted. A central tenet of the OPB framework is that staff respond to emergent OPB in a manner that impacts positively on its developmental course, lessening the likelihood of further paralleling behaviour during institutionalization, and offending behaviour following release. A related requirement, emphasized by several authors, is that the therapeutic environment and intervention provide an opportunity for novel skill development (prosocial alternative behaviour; PAB) that may generalize to the community. As institutions work hard to limit opportunities for aggressive behaviour, they create artificial environments where offenders are not exposed to the prototypical stressors and temptations they need to master without recourse to criminal behaviour. Although some offenders require restrictive intervention, the creation of an extraordinarily secure environment may paradoxically maintain or increase the risk of offending. If the organization does not take risks so that offenders can learn new skills through exposure to prototypical stressors, then opportunity for effective rehabilitation is reduced and the community bears the risk.

NECESSARY CONSIDERATIONS AND MINIMUM STANDARDS FOR AN OPB ASSESSMENT

Numerous methods for identifying and working with OPB have been proposed in this volume. Given the lack of empirical scrutiny, no one method should be considered definitive; delineating the most appropriate method is a challenge for researchers. Nevertheless, despite some differences, there is sufficient consistency amongst experts to justify the creation of a list of important points and minimum standards that should be considered by staff when they invoke the OPB framework. These are listed below and are additional to the issues noted above:

1. Not all topographically similar behaviours observed in custody are offence paralleling. Problem behaviours, including sexual and non-sexual violence, may arise in the context of unique environmental stressors or transient psychological states; they may reflect normative adaptations to the secure setting. Some problem and criminal behaviour occurring in custody that is only tenuously related to past offences may reflect general criminal propensities or criminogenic needs that are indicative of persistent risk of criminal behaviour. The presence of criminogenic need does not indicate that any particular criminal behaviour will manifest;

the nature of the offender's behavioural repertoire and their daily living environments will determine their future criminal behaviour.

Before determining whether an individual is engaging in OPB, it is important to understand 'normal' responses to incarceration and compare the determinants of the specific offender's behaviour at the time of their previous offending with their current behaviour, taking into account a developmental focus and present environmental demands. Importantly, early during imprisonment, OPB may resemble (topographically) offence patterns seen prior to incarceration. Later, the degree of topographical similarity may lessen. This is due to the environmental forces that shape behaviour into 'more effective' or 'appropriate' behaviour for that environment. These changes must be anticipated; they render evaluation of change in long-term institutionalized offenders complicated and show why a reliance on topographically similar behaviour alone cannot be studied to determine change. Further, it may be argued, on the basis that planned or offensive/goal-driven acts show greater consistency over time as compared with reactive acts (as they are not as situationally dependent), that the OPB framework may be more useful for those offenders with entrenched, consistent and idiosyncratic patterns of offending, particularly when these acts are 'more' 'planned'.

As the determination of similarity is complex and there is at present no research that demonstrates adequate predictive validity for a well-documented offence paralleling assessment method, we are of the opinion that the OPB framework should be applied cautiously by release decision-makers. Several authors have explored the potential and judicious application of the framework to risk assessment. In this context it may be used to structure clinical judgements of risk using OPB as an adjunct to structured risk assessment methods, or as an alternative to these methods when there is no valid structured risk assessment method for the particular offender or risk assessment task. Future research must, if OPB is to have any role in the risk assessment process, demonstrate adequate inter-rater reliability and comparable predictive validity (to structured risk assessment methods). Structured risk assessments are presently well placed to support risk assessments. Although many structured risk assessment instruments invite clinical adjustments (the OPB framework may be a useful method to support assessors in this regard), it would be unwise at present to suggest that the OPB framework is a comparable risk assessment strategy unless the offender or their problem behaviour is so unique that the available risk assessment instruments are seriously flawed and as such cannot be used. If the OPB framework is to be used to assess risk, then adherence to Jones' practice algorithim and a structured approach, such as that recommended by Daffern, is recommended.

2. In contrast with the reservation shown towards the application of OPB to risk assessment, the framework may have more immediate application to treatment planning and provision. OPB has high face validity with prisoners. This should encourage collaborative working relationships and intervention based on observation of offence paralleling and prosocial adaptive behaviour. Offenders should be made aware that assessment and intervention occur at all times of the day during their care. This is the more ethical approach. It is also important that offenders understand that staff will respond to OPBs in a way that hopefully alters the course of the offender's problem behaviour. This type of intervention has been referred to by Lillie (2007, p. 159) as 'corrective'; it is designed to disrupt maladaptive patterns, thereby providing an in situ opportunity for new learning (see also Daffern & Day, 2010).
3. The OPB framework promotes comparison of two or more sequences of behaviour to determine similarity. An evaluation of similarity should be conducted by comparing functional analyses. As such, an adequate functional analysis (Sturmey, 1996) of the offender's criminal behaviour is a prerequisite for an OPB assessment. This assessment must include a focus on important causal determinants of the behaviour and adherence to a valid model of

the specific criminal behaviour. The analysis should encompass assessment of the individual's full repertoire of problematic and prosocial behaviour rather than an exclusive focus on an individual criminal act or index offence. It should have a developmental focus, and it should elicit the functions of the problem behaviour over time. Multiple sequential functional analysis (MSFA) may be a useful method for exploring the development of the offender's behaviour. This developmental approach should lead to projections about the individual's expected behavioural trajectory whilst incarcerated (akin to Jones' 'practice algorithm'). Making predictions about the nature of expected OPB may encourage systematic recording and observation that is required to determine whether the offender has changed; this may result in more reliable and valid monitoring that is independent of chance observations that are affected by observer bias.

Regarding MSFA, it should be noted that this method was initially described without any superimposed structure. It was not developed specifically for risk assessment purposes. A cautionary statement is therefore advisable. MSFA allows for the analysis of an individual's problem behaviour to be conducted idiographically, guided by the mental health professional's skills and familiarity with the presenting problem behaviour. This is consistent with the principle of aetiological heterogeneity (that an individual's problem behaviour has unique origins), a cornerstone of behavioural assessment methods. However, the well-known attribution and appraisal errors affecting conventional unaided appraisals of risk have the potential to misguide a clinical assessment paradigm such as MSFA. MSFA may not take into account those characteristics of the person, their history and current functioning, which are known risk factors for aggressive behaviour and which should be considered by risk assessors. To ensure the MSFA approach is comprehensive and systematically inclusive of empirically valid indicators of risk, a structured MSFA (sMSFA) may be helpful (see Daffern, 2010b). The structure that underpins the sMSFA could be drawn from valid structured risk assessment instruments and models relevant to the offender and their specific problem behaviours.

4. Behaviour should be labelled as offence paralleling when there is sufficient similarity in function and when there is consistency in important, idiosyncratic, causal social cognitive variables. Similarity *should not* be determined by considering only high base-rate behaviours that do not reflect persistent habits that are peculiar to the individual or that indicate unique behavioural patterns (see Chapters 5 and 6). Evaluating change requires consideration of OPB, prosocial adaptive behaviour (PAB), detection evasion skills (DES) and recognition of unique custodial reactions (UCR). Improvement, and therefore a reduction in risk, should only be considered when there is evidence of reduced OPB *and* evolving PAB. When there is persistent OPB but no PAB, then stability in the level of risk should be assumed. Emergent DES should be suspected when there is no evidence of PAB but a reduction in OPB. If the individual's problem behaviour repertoire is expanding, which may include persistent or increased OPB, the individual may be showing signs of worsening.

   Ascertaining whether there is sufficient similarity to warrant labelling a behaviour offence paralleling will always be faced with the fact that the two or more behaviours will show some, but not complete similarity. Reflecting on earlier discussion, a more conservative approach should be used when labelling a behaviour 'offence paralleling' when the task is to assess risk. The key question is how similar two behaviours need to be to warrant labelling them as offence paralleling. Davies and colleagues have made several recommendations for evaluating change; they identify the reliable change index as one method that may allow staff to determine whether change has occurred and whether the amount of change is significant. They also identify the need to determine whether change is clinically meaningful and relevant and whether it is stable. They (Chapter 18) provide a useful reference for those interested in evaluating an individual's progress.

5. Finally, it is important to note that the OPB framework may not be a useful or efficient assessment and treatment framework for all offenders. As noted by Daffern (Chapter 6), 'certain patients may not ever show entrenched or consistent aggressive behaviour ... [which] raises the possibility that the OPB framework may only be justified for ... [certain] offenders .... Versatile offenders who are indiscriminate in their aggressive behaviour may not necessarily benefit from the additional resources dedicated to treatments inspired by OPB assessment'. Offenders with uncomplicated needs who can participate in treatment programmes with demonstrated efficacy may not benefit from an idiographic case formulation approach to treatment. However, offenders with multiple disorders or problems, or those offenders who do not benefit from standard treatments or who do not belong to populations for whom there are valid risk assessment instruments, may benefit from an idiographic approach. This point is emphasized by Haynes (1998) in his judicious recommendations for idiographic treatment planning: 'The social and personal significance of behaviours associated with pre-intervention assessment varies across behaviour problems. A 10% failure rate for a standardised intervention programme for nailbiting may not warrant extensive pre-intervention assessment to design individualized intervention programmes that would reduce the rate to 5%. However, more extensive pre-intervention assessment may be warranted by a proportional increase in the effectiveness of interventions for suicidal, self-mutilatory or socially violent behaviours' (p. 393).

CONCLUSION

Editing this volume has provided us with a unique and satisfying opportunity to call upon eminent scholars and interested clinicians to assist in the development of a case formulation approach to offender assessment and intervention. We are grateful for their contribution. This book is offered at an important juncture in the field of forensic practice. Several principles of effective offender rehabilitation have been established, and reliable and valid risk assessment technologies are available to appraise risk. However, these principles, methods of treatment and assessment technologies are also the subject of criticism. We have prepared this book, in part, because we believe that idiographic case formulation, which is *the most important* clinical skill, is a condition of all assessment and treatment work, and that case formulation has received insufficient attention in recent years.

The OPB framework seeks to enhance, rather than act as an alternative to structured interventions and structured risk assessment methods. In saying this, some offenders do not respond to contemporary structured programmes and do not come from groups on whom structured risk assessment technologies have been validated. The OPB framework may prove to be a credible alternative for assessment and treatment of these offenders. We hope that this book will act as a catalyst for improved clinical practice and increased scholarly work on case formulation in forensic psychology. Ignorance of OPB impairs comprehensiveness in risk assessment and reduces opportunities for contingent responding that supports offender treatment. We hope the OPB framework will be useful for staff who need to assess and treat offenders in secure care.

REFERENCES

Beech, A.R. & Hamilton-Giachritsis, C.E. (2005). Relationship between therapeutic climate and treatment outcome in group-based sexual offender treatment programs. *Sexual Abuse: A Journal of Research and Treatment*, *17*, 127–40.

Daffern, M. (2010a). The emergence and persistence of stalking behavior in psychiatric units: application of the offence paralleling behavior framework. *The Journal of Behavior Analysis of Offender and Victim – Treatment and Prevention*, 2, 133–142.

Daffern, M. (2010b). Risk Assessment for Aggressive Behaviour in Personality Disorder. In A. Tenant and K. Howells (Eds.), *Using Time, Not Doing Time: Practitioner Perspectives on Personality Disorder and Risk* (pp. 15–32). Wiley.

Daffern, M. & Day, A. (2010). Implications for the prevention of aggressive behaviour within psychiatric hospitals drawn from interpersonal communication theory. Manuscript under review.

Daffern, M., Jones, L., Howells, K., Shine, J., Mikton, C. & Tunbridge, V.C. (2007). Refining the definition of offence paralleling behaviour. *Criminal Behaviour and Mental Health*, *17*, 265–73.

Daffern, M., Howells, K., Manion, A. & Tonkin, M. (2009). A test of methodology intended to assist detection of aggressive offence paralleling behaviour within secure settings. *Legal and Criminological Psychology*, *14*, 213–26.

Haynes, S. (1998). The changing nature of behavioural assessment. In A. Bellack & M. Hersen (Eds.), *Behavioral Assessment: A Practical Handbook* (pp. 1–21). Boston, MA: Allyn & Bacon.

Howells, K., Tonkin, M., Milburn, C., Lewis, J., Draycot, S., Cordwell, J., Price, M., Davies, S. & Schalast, N. (2009). The EssenCES measure of social climate: a preliminary validation and normative data in UK high secure hospital settings. *Criminal Behaviour and Mental Health*, *19*, 308–20.

Jones, L.F. (2004). Offence paralleling behaviour (OPB) as a framework for assessment and interventions with offenders. In A. Needs & G. Towl (Eds), *Applying Psychology to Forensic Practice*. Oxford: BPS Blackwell.

Kiesler, D.J. (1996). *Contemporary Interpersonal Theory and Research: Personality, Psychopathology, and Psychotherapy*. Toronto: Wiley.

Lillie, R. (2007). Getting clients to hear: applying principles and techniques of Kiesler's interpersonal communication therapy to assessment feedback. *Psychology and Psychotherapy: Theory, Research and Practice*, *80*, 151–63.

Melle, I., Friis, S., Hauff, E., Island, T.K., Lorentzen, S. & Vaglum, P. (1996). The importance of ward atmosphere in inpatient treatment of schizophrenia on short-term units. *Psychiatric Services*, *47*, 721–26.

Sandberg, D.A., McNiel, D.E. & Binder, R.L. (2002). Stalking, threatening, and harassing behaviour by psychiatric patients toward clinicians. *Journal of the American Academy of Psychiatry and Law*, *30*, 221–29.

Sturmey, P. (1996). *Functional Analysis in Clinical Psychology*. Chichester: Wiley.

INDEX

Note: Page numbers in italics refer to tables